Building a
DEMOCRATIC NATION

A

History of the

United States

to

1877

Volume 1

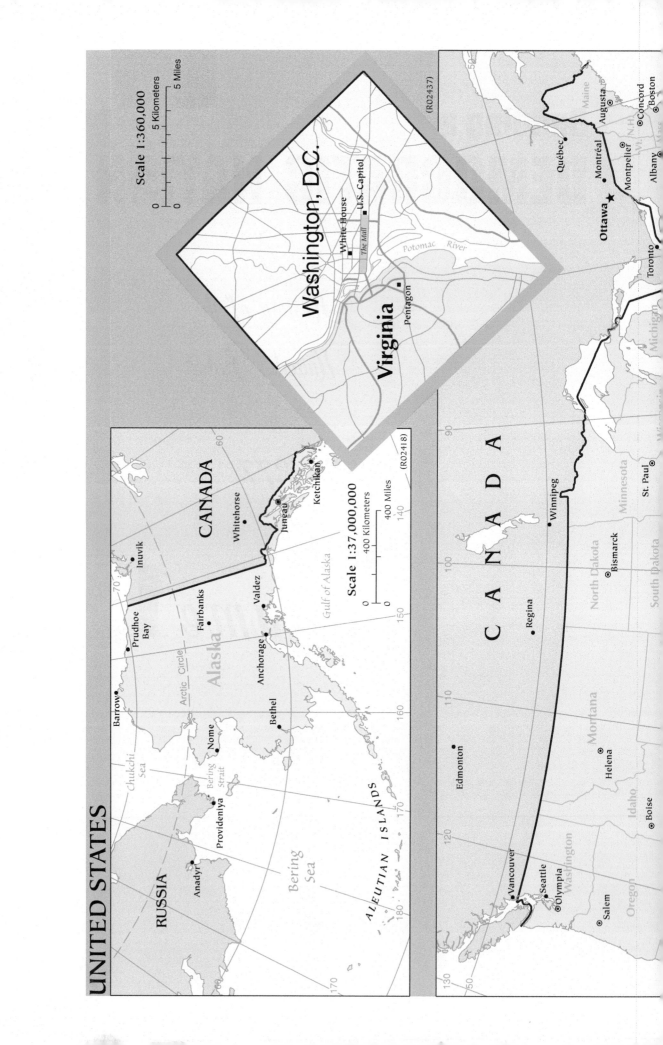

UNITED STATES

RUSSIA

Anadyr

Providentya

Chukchi Sea

Bering Strait

Nome

Barrow

Prudhoe Bay

Inuvik

Arctic Circle

Fairbanks

Alaska

CANADA

Whitehorse

Bethel

Anchorage

Valdez

Juneau

Ketchikan

Bering Sea

ALEUTIAN ISLANDS

Gulf of Alaska

Scale 1:37,000,000

0   400 Kilometers

0   400 Miles

(RO2418)

Washington, D.C.

White House

U.S. Capitol

The Mall

Pentagon

Virginia

Potomac River

(RO2437)

Scale 1:360,000

0   5 Kilometers

0   5 Miles

CANADA

Vancouver

Seattle

Olympia

Washington

Salem

Oregon

Idaho

Boise

Edmonton

Helena

Montana

Regina

Winnipeg

North Dakota

Bismarck

South Dakota

Minnesota

St. Paul

Québec

Maine

Augusta

Montréal

Montpelier

N.H.

Concord

Boston

Albany

Ottawa

Toronto

Michigan

CANADA

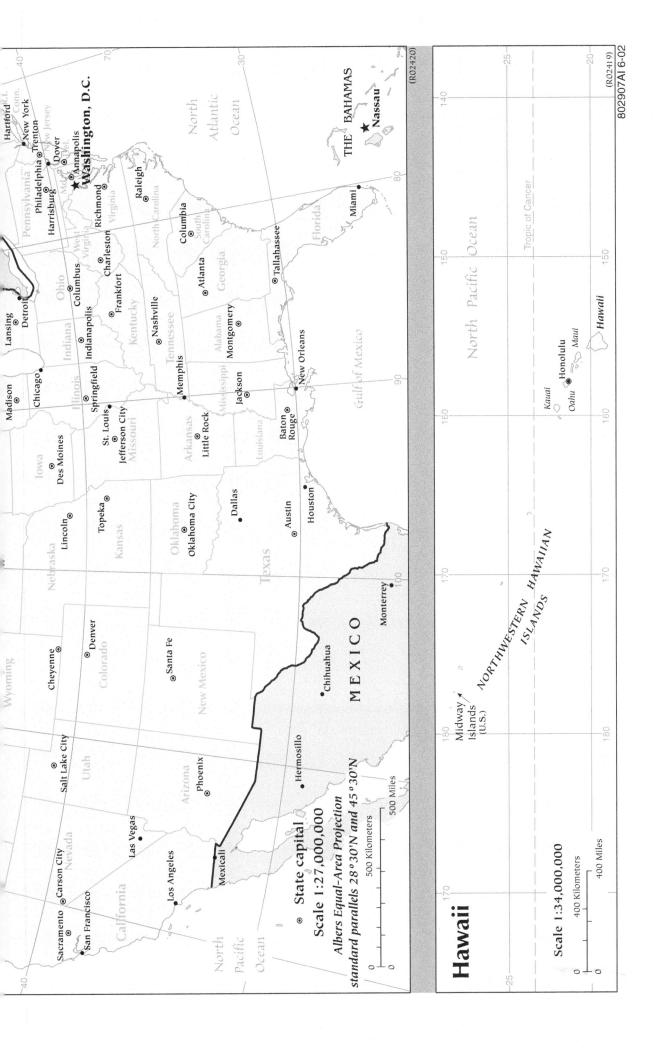

Hartford
Conn.
R.I.

New York
Trenton
New Jersey

Dover
Del.
Annapolis
Md.
Washington, D.C.

Pennsylvania
Philadelphia
Harrisburg

Richmond
Virginia
West
Virginia

Raleigh
North Carolina

Columbia
South
Carolina

Charleston

Georgia

Tallahassee

Florida

Miami

Detroit
Lansing

Ohio
Columbus

Indiana
Indianapolis

Frankfort
Kentucky

Nashville
Tennessee

Memphis

Atlanta

Alabama
Montgomery

Madison
Chicago

Illinois
Springfield

St. Louis
Jefferson City
Missouri

Jackson
Mississippi

Baton
Rouge
Louisiana

New Orleans

Iowa
Des Moines

Topeka
Kansas

Little Rock
Arkansas

Oklahoma
Oklahoma City

Dallas

Austin

Houston

Texas

Lincoln
Nebraska

Denver
Colorado

Santa Fe
New Mexico

Chihuahua

Monterrey

MEXICO

Gulf of Mexico

Wyoming

Cheyenne

Salt Lake City
Utah

Phoenix
Arizona

Hermosillo

Las Vegas
Nevada

Carson City
Sacramento

San Francisco

Los Angeles

Mexicali

California

North
Pacific
Ocean

North
Atlantic
Ocean

THE BAHAMAS

★ **Nassau**

(R02420)

⊙ State capital
Scale 1:27,000,000
Albers Equal-Area Projection
standard parallels 28°30'N and 45°30'N

500 Miles

500 Kilometers

0

0

40

70

30

80

90

100

40

Hawaii

North Pacific Ocean

Tropic of Cancer

NORTHWESTERN HAWAIIAN
ISLANDS

Midway
Islands
(U.S.)

Kauai
Oahu Honolulu
Maui

Hawaii

25

20

140

150

160

170

180

170

160

150

25

Scale 1:34,000,000

400 Miles

400 Kilometers

0

0

(R02419)

802907AI 6-02

Building a
DEMOCRATIC NATION

Fourth Edition

A History of the United States to 1877

Volume 1

William E. Montgomery | Andrés Tijerina

AUSTIN COMMUNITY COLLEGE

Kendall Hunt
publishing company

Maps found at beginning and end of text Courtesy of the Perry-Casteñeda Library Map Collection, University of Texas at Austin

Cover image © Francis G. Mayer/Contributor/Getty

www.kendallhunt.com
Send all inquiries to:
4050 Westmark Drive
Dubuque, IA 52004-1840

Copyright © 2010, 2012, 2014, 2017 by William E. Montgomery and Andrés Tijerina

PAK ISBN: 978-1-5249-7983-6
Text Alone ISBN: 978-1-5249-8024-5

Published in the United States of America

Contents

Preface

Building a Democratic Nation

As we enter the twenty-first century, our eyes naturally focus ahead. It's important, though, that as a nation, as subgroups within the nation, and as individuals we take time to reflect on the past.

Why study history? We often hear that it repeats itself anyway. But it really doesn't. The world changes; situations are not the same as before, even if human nature seems to be. Studying history shows us that, just as it provides us with a valuable perspective for understanding the present. *Building a Democratic Nation* treats "the past as prologue," demonstrating that to a significant extent the decisions and actions of preceding generations continue to influence our lives today. Moreover, understanding the past helps us to know whether we are living up to our founders' dreams and expectations or suffering their worst nightmares. Reading history can lead to rational decisions, ones that might positively shape our future and the future of our children and grandchildren. Studying history can be very personal too, enabling us to answer existential questions like "Who am I?" "How did I get here?" and "Where am I going?"

As it chronicles the history of the United States, *Building a Democratic Nation* emphasizes empowerment, which is what democracy is basically about. This certainly isn't a simple story; nor is it always pretty, although it is in many ways unmatched and profoundly inspiring. We, the authors, trace the complex interactions of people from diverse backgrounds, who had varying interests, and who harbored fundamentally different hopes for the future. At the country's inception, democracy was not a particularly popular concept. Ironically, Native Americans and Africans represented cultures that were in some ways more democratic than European cultures. *Building a Democratic Nation* tells the story of the formation of the United States as a republican experiment that evolved into a more democratic nation. It's the story of multiple and often shifting identities merging unevenly and incompletely and not always willingly into a national consciousness.

Although democracy typically evokes thoughts of philosophy and government, our story never loses track of real people, ordinary and extraordinary, and their personal perspectives on the local, national, and global events that shaped their destinies and the destinies of others around the world.

The audience for *Building a Democratic Nation* is a large and varied one, including the many students who enroll in United States survey history courses each year. A large number of these students attend open-admissions schools, including community colleges, and present profiles markedly different from traditional undergraduates. Many are not history majors and often think of taking history as having to memorize "one damn thing after another."

Although the vast majority of professors who teach United States history survey courses rely on textbooks as the basic source of information, those books often turn students off even though they are based on solid research, are well-written, and are dressed up in lots of color and graphics. We believe that's because students don't know how to read history textbooks, and the books don't show them how to organize the material in order to pass their courses. Consequently, they don't read them. Many don't even buy them. We have written *Building a Democratic Nation* to address those specific issues.

We conceived and wrote *Building a Democratic Nation* with "three P's" in mind. The first "P" stands for **prose**. The dynamic narrative that unfolds in *Building a Democratic Nation* simulates the voice of one teacher-historian speaking engagingly to students. The narrator tells America's story from multiple perspectives: global, national, local, and personal, analyzing the information so that readers can understand not only what happened but also why it happened and with what consequences. Connections between different parts of the past and between the past and the present also teach valuable lessons. Sometimes those lessons are clear and direct, as when the racial intolerance led to slavery and "Jim Crow" and when the concepts of women that produced "separate spheres" recurred later as sexual harassment and glass ceilings. At other times, as with the Boston Tea Party of 1773 and the Tea Party Movement of 2010, what appears to be "history repeating itself" turns out to be way more complicated and ambiguous than that.

The second "P" is for **pedagogy**. *Building a Democratic Nation* is more than historical literature; it is a teaching tool with devices designed to assist student readers to a fuller understanding of the history of the United States. Those devices include queries, a technique that master teachers have utilized ever since Socrates. Questions placed throughout the narrative aid students in digesting the subject matter first in small and then in larger portions and to advance from relatively simple levels of learning to higher, more complex ones. In addition to queries, the text contains a program of drawings, paintings, photographs, charts, and maps that help students visualize the past.

The third "P" represents **price**. Recognizing how daunting the prices of most textbooks are, the authors, together with Kendall Hunt's developmental and executive staffs, are committed to making *Building a Democratic Nation* a full but affordable history of the United States from 1877 to the present. And we're striving toward that objective while providing a book with sufficient readability to serve as the basic source of information in survey courses.

Organizing the Story

Building a Democratic Nation is organized into four parts, each containing four chapters devoted to a major period in early American history. These time periods possess the logical unity that generations of history instructors have appreciated. The groupings also provide convenient divisions for examination purposes. Each part begins with a brief introduction called the **Global Perspective** that brings to the reader's attention the fact that this country has never existed in a vacuum. The United States has always been part of larger, transnational networks. References to the Global Perspective within the chapters bring the reader's attention to relevant global themes in appropriate ways. Within this broader global context, *Building a Democratic Nation*, Volume 1, is divided into these four chapter groupings:

1. Globalization and Early America: Background for Nationhood to 1760

   Chapter 1: From Different Worlds, Beginnings to 1492

   Chapter 2: European Conquest, 1492–1600

   Chapter 3: English Colonization: Profiting Materially and Spiritually, 1607–1675

   Chapter 4: Growth and Conflict, 1675–1760

2. Empire and Revolution: Foundations of Republican Societies, 1760–1815

   Chapter 5: Making a Nation, 1760–1783

   Chapter 6: One Nation or Many, 1783–1789

   Chapter 7: Redefining the Nation, 1789–1800

   Chapter 8: Into a New Century, 1800–1815

3. The Era of Industrialization and Democratic Nationalism, 1815–1860

   Chapter 9: Awakening National Identity, 1815–1830

   Chapter 10: Building a More Democratic Society, 1820–1840

   Chapter 11: Striving for a Better America, 1815–1860

   Chapter 12: Factory and Plantation: Industrialization North and South, 1840–1860

4. Stirrings of Nationalism, 1830–1877

   Chapter 13: Manifest Destiny, 1835–1850

   Chapter 14: The Union in Crisis, 1850–1861

Constructing the Story: The Theme

In constructing the story of the United States, we have organized as much information as possible around a central theme stated clearly in the title: *Building a Democratic Nation*. The book homes in on how national identity has influenced the building of a democratic nation. United States history survey courses are fundamentally studies in national history; yet students often enter and exit those courses with little understanding of what national identity means or what a democratic nation really is. National identity is not synonymous with being subject to the authority of the United States, but we endeavor to show how identity and nationhood were involved in the formation of the United States and how they made the nation simultaneously more and less democratic. Within the theme of identity and democratic nation-building lay several fundamental and personally relevant questions: who is included, who is excluded from nationhood, and how and why the composition of the nation changed over time. The theme of building a democratic nation appears throughout the book, unifying every chapter and uniting all of them.

But the history of the United States is too big and much too complicated to fit neatly within any single theme. *Building a Democratic Nation* tells other stories too. This is not majority or consensus history but rather an inclusive and sometimes conflict-ridden narrative. *Building a Democratic Nation* weaves together many vital social and cultural threads with political, economic, and military ones. But we show the complexity of cultural identity and the historically shifting boundaries of nationhood in ways that students in basic survey courses can comprehend.

The authors also bring out many interesting twists in the nation-building process. For instance, men and women who have historically been excluded from full membership in the American nation—that is, denied complete citizenship in the United States or otherwise discriminated against—have been among the strongest advocates of its ideals. Cherokee Indians used the Constitution of the United States as the pattern for their national government. A convention of women in Seneca Falls, New York, demanded equal rights in terms drawn directly from the Declaration of Independence. African Americans invoked the principles of the American Revolution and the Bill of Rights in calling for their inclusion in the building of a democratic nation. In their espousal of American ideals, oppressed men and women have forced the building of a more democratic nation from the bottom up.

Building a Democratic Nation explores the tension between national, racial, ethnic, class, and gender identities, relationships that have produced painful dilemmas for many Americans. For example, in one dramatic episode in 1800, a revolt by hundreds of slaves in Richmond, Virginia, seeking freedom and equality as written in the Declaration of Independence and endowed by their Creator is betrayed by other slaves. The dilemma confronting enslaved African-Americans involved supporting rebellion against oppression and running a great risk of painful retaliation or acquiescing and thereby safeguarding themselves, their families, and their communities. What a horrible choice, and that was part of what the struggle to build a democratic nation entailed.

Telling the Story: Perspectives

Building a Democratic Nation examines American history from many perspectives. From a Global Perspective, the narrative places American history in an international context. And from the Local Perspective and Personal Perspective it further analyzes America's past from narrower points of view, ones that students can easily relate to and understand.

(1) **The Global Perspective.** As touched on above, four short Global Perspective essays situate the United States in a larger, international context. Without taking sides on the question of America's uniqueness or presenting mini- world histories, The Global Perspective feature identifies significant international developments that call readers' attention to the fact that this country has never existed in a vacuum.

(2) **The Personal Perspective.** Each chapter begins with a personal vignette that offers human interest and personalizes the major threads of the chapter. For example, Chapter 4 begins with a brief story

set in 1704 about John Williams, a Massachusetts minister whose family was taken captive in a raid by French and Indian soldiers. The vignette casts illuminating light on the complex dynamics of national and cultural identity.

(3) **The Local Perspective.** The Local Perspective focuses on developments in particular locales. This accomplishes several purposes. It brings the national story closer to home. The local perspective features are set off from the regular text because sometimes they unfold off the main stage featured in the chapter. For example, the discussion of industrial and agricultural capitalism in Chapter 12 concentrates on the states east of the Mississippi River while The Local Perspective from the Washington Territory relates a different story unfolding concurrently that will come into more prominent play later in the text. In that way, The Local Perspective can help provide a more continental panorama.

Navigating the Story: Teaching and Learning Tools

Building a Democratic Nation employs some time-honored features, such historical timelines, located at the beginning of each chapter to brief students on the events to come. Graphic images—drawings, paintings, photographs, maps, and charts—are included to help readers visualize the past. And the layout has been designed for comfortable reading and to support student learning.

Research shows that queries aid students by teaching them how to process information. Just as teachers employ keys or signals in classroom lectures and discussions, *Building a Democratic Nation* uses questions as signals to readers. Questions are also valuable assessment tools. Three types of questions guide readers up the ladder of thinking skills from basic definitions and identification of information to higher-order cognitive processes.

(1) **Signal Questions.** Placed in the margins at the beginning of each section, Signal Questions announce the central idea of that section so that students know at the outset of each section what to look for as they read. Signal Questions point student readers to information that is the foundation of the section and upon which the remainder of the chapter will build. The authors of *Building a Democratic Nation* and the teachers who use it want to be as clear and direct as possible about what students are reading and why they are reading it. That way history is not just a huge, discouraging mass of information, and it becomes more learnable. Signal Questions typically ask students to identify, define, and list pertinent information located in the section. They are not thinking questions as much as reading aids. They give shape to the "forest" of facts. The answers are normally what instructors look for in their assessments of basic reading comprehension. There is one fairly general signal question for each section; however, detailed learning objectives are available in the ancillary *Student Guide for Building a Democratic Nation.*

(2) **Thinking Back.** *Building a Democratic Nation* also keeps the story alive and holds the reader's attention with section-ending thought questions that encourage students to think back over the material they've just read, encouraging them to link information from several subsections. Thinking Back accomplishes that objective much the way teachers use review questions in their classrooms. In class or in study groups, they invite discussion by asking, for instance, "How democratic was American society at that particular point in time?" Thus, Thinking Back questions simulate the classroom setting, giving the narrator a "teacher" persona. They also strengthen the narrative voice.

(3) **BEFORE WE GO ON.** This section of chapter closing questions complements the Signal Questions and Thinking Back questions that come earlier and draws together the central ideas of individual sections within chapters. These questions range from lower- to higher-level thinking and challenge students to pull all the information together, establish a personal relevance, and create a bridge from the text materials to the present.

- Two questions at the end of each chapter lead students to recapitulate the main ideas. These questions reinforce the Signal Questions in each section.

- Two more questions encourage students to analyze those main chapter ideas in terms of "building a democratic nation."

- "Connections" questions relate chapter threads to the fundamental theme of the book as stated in the title *Building a Democratic Nation*. But Connections also aims to help students relate the past to the present. For example, Chapter 1 ends with two Connections questions.

  - Assume that you could make a new world in North America by choosing the most desirable aspects of both Native American and European worlds, as they existed before they came together. Which ones would you select?

  - As you look at America today, what do you notice that might be traced back to ancient Native Americans? What do you see that might have originated in Europe? And what could have just as easily derived from either one?

Concluding Each Chapter

The differing "perspectives" along with the basic text material within each chapter provide the context for questions that actively engage the learner in multiple-levels of thinking and assist them in successfully navigating this textbook.

(1) **Conclusions.** Chapter conclusions not only summarize the chapter material but also point out the long-term significance of the events just discussed, showing students how past lives touch theirs. For example, on the implications of the Industrial Revolution and slavery, Chapter 12 concludes that while the South's plantation slavery system and the North's industrial factory systems both were dynamic and market oriented, one was rooted in the past while the other was oriented toward the future. This type of conclusion reinforces the text where, whenever appropriate, the narrative point of view looks forward in order to emphasize the continuity between the past and present.

(2) **Suggested Sources for Students.** These are end-of-chapter lists that guide students to the most informative, analytical, and interpretive materials for additional investigation. This feature points students to the most current scholarship and also to seminal work, accessible monographs, and particularly useful Web sites. Brief annotations explain why these books, films, and Web sites are important.

Supplementing the Story

In addition to the text itself, users will find supplemental learning and teaching aids. *A Student Guide for Building a Democratic Nation* contains chapter summaries, glossaries, and detailed learning objectives. A test bank for teachers provides questions drawn from the signal and thinking back questions in the text as well as the learning objectives contained in the *Student Guide*. Together, these components will make *Building a Democratic Nation* a complete teaching and learning system as well as an accessible yet scholarly history of the United States.

Acknowledgments

In keeping with our goal to make this book and its ancillaries relevant, up-to-date, and accurate, we have enlisted reviews, commentary, and other forms of assistance from colleagues. We gratefully acknowledge the helpful suggestions of the following:

Philip Cochran, Austin Community College
David M. Dean, Frostburg State University
Luther Elmore, Austin Community College
Wendy Gamber, Indiana University
David Haney, Austin Community College
Martha Meacham, Austin Community College
Richard Milk, Texas Lutheran University and Austin Community College
Stephen Mings, Austin Community College
Teresa Thomas, Austin Community College
William S. Rose, Austin, TX

William E. Montgomery
Andrés Tijerina

About the Authors

After William Montgomery received his Ph.D. in history from the University of Texas at Austin, he began teaching at Austin Community College, where he was a founding member of the faculty, History Department chair, and recipient of the college's award for teaching excellence. He is now emeritus professor of history.

For the last forty-three years, he has taught the United States survey course along with African-American history. During the 1989–90 academic year, he was a Fulbright Professor at the National University of Lesotho in southern Africa, where he taught United States history, African-American history, and twentieth-century world history.

He is the author of "*Under Their Own Vine and Fig Tree: The African-American Church in the South, 1865–1900*" (1993), nominated for the Bancroft Prize, as well as, scholarly journal articles and essays on the general subject of African-American history.

Andrés Tijerina is a Professor of History at Austin Community College. He received his B.A. from Texas A&M University, his M.A. from Texas Tech University, and his Ph.D. from the University of Texas at Austin. Dr. Tijerina has taught at those institutions and at U.T.S.A. Before teaching, he served as a state agency Executive Director for the State of Texas and as a group manager for Motorola, Inc. in Austin.

Dr. Tijerina has authored and co-authored numerous articles and books, and has received state and national book prizes for his own books *Tejanos and Texas Under the Mexican Flag*, published by Texas A&M University Press as well as *Tejano Empire: Life on the South Texas Ranchos*. His most widely read work is the publication of his Vietnam War combat memoirs in the *Time-Life Books* series *The Vietnam Experience*. As a pilot in the Air Force, Dr. Tijerina flew over 100 combat missions in Vietnam, receiving the Air Medal and the Distinguished Flying Cross, and he retired as a Major of the U.S. Air Force and Liaison Officer for the U.S. Air Force Academy.

He has received Teaching Excellence Awards and was recently appointed by Texas Governor Rick Perry to the Historical Representation Advisory Committee and to the Texas Review Board for the National Register of Historic Places with the Texas Historical Commission. Dr. Tijerina is the General Editor for an endowed Book Series for Texas A&M University Press. He is a member and a Fellow of the Texas State Historical Association, a past member of the Committee on Minority Historians for the A.H.A. and Past Chairman of the Committee on Community Colleges for the Organization of American Historians. He is also Vice President of the Texas Institute of Letters. He is recipient of the 2012 Equity Award of the A.H.A.

The Global Perspective

Globalization and Early America, 1492–1750

We hear a lot about "globalization" these days, especially the internationalization of capital and trade. Many American corporations obtain raw materials from far corners of the globe, shift labor-intensive manufacturing to low-wage countries, and even maintain offshore headquarters and bank accounts. Critics complain that this type of globalization exploits poor people, degrades the environment, and weakens national autonomy. Defenders respond that it improves the quality of human life, sparks economic innovation, and spreads democracy throughout the world. There are different kinds of globalization too. Stateless terrorism and disease pandemics require global responses to counteract them. And technologies like the Internet and satellite television have internationalized politics and culture.

> What does a global perspective reveal about early American history?

Oddly though, as key as the global perspective is to understanding the United States today, it is rarely used in examining early American history. Historians often look through a narrower lens, focusing on what became the United States. For instance, they point out that because Christopher Columbus' daring 1492 voyage failed to reach its Asian objective its only noteworthy outcome was the inadvertent one of setting the stage for New World colonization. But in truth, Columbus' epic journey resulted in nothing less than the transformation of world economic and military power. Indeed, the eighteenth-century British philosopher Adam Smith, in his book *Wealth of Nations* (1776), called Columbus' voyage, along with the Portuguese mariner Vasco da Gama's remarkable 1497–8 circumnavigation of Africa, "the greatest and most important events recorded in the history of mankind."

From a global perspective we can see that Europe's initial encounters with North America had little to do with building a mighty New World civilization but rather with transforming Old World civilizations. From the sixteenth century to the middle of the eighteenth century, European colonies in America were only remote, albeit increasingly valuable, outliers to a world economy directed first from metropolitan capitals situated

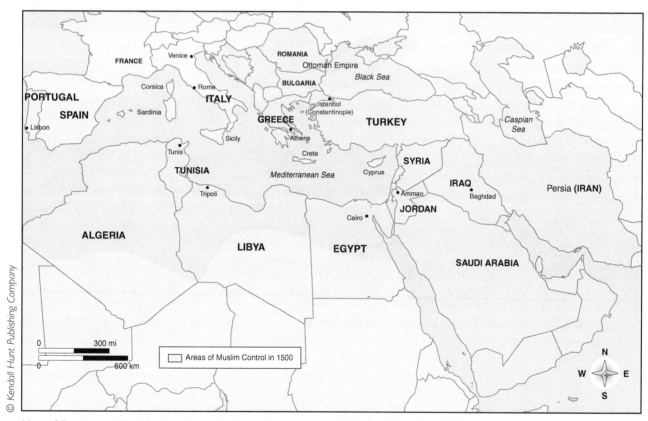

Map of Europe and the Mediterranean Basin showing areas under Muslim Control in 1500.

around the Mediterranean Sea and then from commercial headquarters located along Western Europe's Atlantic coast. At the start of the sixteenth century, Europeans paid more attention to an epic contest between Christian and Muslim civilizations, one with profound global implications, than to America. And therein lay the larger, global significance of Columbus' trans-Atlantic voyage to America.

From its birth on the Arabian Peninsula early in the seventh century, Islam had aggressively expanded its power. Arab Muslims established regimes throughout the Middle East. In the eighth century, North African Muslims invaded the Iberian Peninsula (today's Spain and Portugal). In 1453, Turkish Muslims conquered Constantinople, the ancient Christian city situated at the northeastern end of the Mediterranean, and renamed it Istanbul, the capital of the far-flung Ottoman Turkish Empire. By the end of the sixteenth century, the Ottoman Turks had parlayed trade connections into political hegemony over an area extending from India to Africa to Europe. In the process, the Ottomans enriched themselves with silver from China and gold from Africa and absorbed into their cultural lives the science, technology, and philosophy of ancient India, Persia, Greece, and Rome. By Columbus' time, the Muslim Ottoman Empire comprised a cosmopolitan, effectively governed, and prosperous global civilization, perhaps the most magnificent in the world at that time.

European Christians rallied against expanding Muslim power. As early as the eleventh and twelfth centuries, Christian armies had engaged in a series of bloody but inconclusive Crusades against "Islamic infidels" in the Middle East. In Europe itself by the end of the fifteenth century, Christian forces had re-conquered the Iberian Peninsula, paving the way for the emerging, modern nation-states of Portugal and Spain. These "culture wars" hardened Christian attitudes against "infidels" and "heathens" whether Muslim, Jewish, African, or later Native American. Indeed, the Europeans' rationale for conquering, dispossessing, and even destroying Native Americans and their civilizations derived partly from the earlier Christian battles against Islam.

Capitalism played an equally important role in enhancing Europe's position in the world and shaping the future of North America. Through the fifteenth century, the Ottoman-controlled Mediterranean basin constituted the world's most dynamic economy. Historians and economists disagree over exactly when, where, and how capitalism originated; clearly however, the economy of the sixteenth-century Ottoman Empire was a capitalist one organized around investing in profitable trade. The Ottomans entered into partnerships with rich and powerful merchants in the Italian city-state of Venice who raised capital and utilized instruments of credit to finance overland trading caravans to Asia and Africa. Among the commodities that changed hands were woolen cloth from northern Europe, silk and porcelain products from China, pepper and other spices from India, and gold and ivory from Africa. In addition, the Ottomans acquired human slaves from Africa and Europe.

Handsome profits from these commercial exchanges beckoned enterprising Europeans in Atlantic-facing nation-states who were largely locked out of the Mediterranean-based global economy by Ottoman trade restrictions. But during the second half of the fifteenth century, merchants in Lisbon imagined breaking the Ottomans' commercial monopoly by sailing around the Mediterranean southward through the Atlantic Ocean to the tip of Africa and then into the Indian Ocean to reach the Indies (India and the spice islands of southeast Asia. See the map on p. 4.). Portugal's far-sighted Prince Henry, known to history as "the Navigator," grasped the ramifications of such a maritime venture. "[I]f you are strong in ships," he declared, "the commerce of the Indies is yours." He understood the obstacles too: a lack of information about ocean wind patterns; a dearth of ships big, and fast, and maneuverable enough for long-distance voyages; and limited navigational devices for determining distance and location. Through innovation and by learning from other sea-faring cultures, Portuguese mariners contributed much toward overcoming those obstacles.

By the end of the fifteenth century, all that remained was for adventurers to prove the feasibility of ocean voyages. Vasco da Gama helped Portugal undermine Ottoman global power by sailing around Africa and across the Indian Ocean and then repeating the voyage with heavily armed vessels. The Portuguese employed naval power to establish trading colonies from Africa to Southeast Asia, a key element in a new, European-based trans-Atlantic global economy and one that was central to imperial power through the nineteenth century. Through the sixteenth century, Portuguese merchants dominated the rich spice and silk trade, and Lisbon became one of the world's most important port cities.

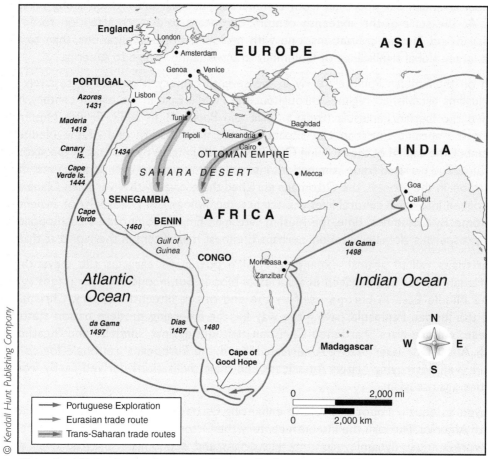

Map of the Globe showing Portuguese Maritime Exploration, 1487-1498.

While the Portuguese looked south around Africa and then east across the Indian Ocean for wealth and power, Spaniards gazed west across the Atlantic, toward the same object: Asia. The world was a sphere; learned people knew that. But how large? Christopher Columbus, a mariner from the Italian city-state of Genoa, calculated it was small enough for ships to sail west directly across the Atlantic from Europe and reach Asia quicker than by navigating around Africa. He persuaded the Spanish Crown to back him. Columbus was wrong, of course, and he compounded his mistake by failing to account for the two Americas. Many accounts of American history turn away from Europe at that point and concentrate on the dramatic and profound consequences of Columbus' "great mistake" on what was to become the United States.

But in an epic round-the-world voyage in 1519-22 that vindicated Columbus, Spanish sea captain Ferdinand Magellan proved that oceans were actually great global passageways that linked continents rather than barriers that divided them. Nations possessing powerful navies could utilize the world's oceans to assemble and maintain global empires. Over the next four centuries, the Atlantic, Pacific, and Indian oceans allowed Europe to project great economic and military power into Asia, Africa, and the Americas. Atlantic-facing nations—Portugal, Spain, France, the Netherlands, and England—became the global powerhouses of the sixteenth, seventeenth, and eighteenth centuries. The centers of global power shifted from the Mediterranean to Western and Northern Europe. In the seventeenth century, Amsterdam supplanted Lisbon as a world trade capital. In the eighteenth century, London took its place as the financial and political nexus of an English trade empire stretching from India to North America. European sea power not only frustrated Muslims but also proved catastrophic for Asians, Native Americans, and Africans.

During the three decades following Columbus', da Gama's, and Magellan's dramatic voyages, expanding Spanish, Portuguese, Dutch, English, and French commercial interests incorporated Asia, the Americas, and Africa, along with their native inhabitants, into great global trade networks. Initially, the Europeans sought to trade for locally produced gold, silver, and other various luxury products, but soon they turned their energies to the cultivation of various agricultural products—sugar especially but also rice, cotton, and American tobacco, relying on native populations for the necessary labor. In the Americas, Europeans laid claim to vast areas of territory that they endeavored to develop into markets for European manufactured goods. They built coastal towns along the Atlantic seaboard that functioned as seaports and merchant centers where exports were sent on their way to European markets and incoming manufactured goods, mail packets, and immigrants kept the New World and the Old World economically and culturally linked. By 1750, hundreds of ships annually sailed back and forth across the Atlantic, and that two-way traffic transformed societies on both sides of the ocean.

For the most part, the utilization of Native Americans as a workforce failed, leading Europeans to tap into other supplies of labor. The flow of Africans to America was part of an international slave trade designed to meet the demand for labor within the expanding global economies. Slaves arrived in coastal ports for work assignments in the interior regions and the beginning of new, grueling, and often tragically shortened lives. These African migrations were forced by the demands of the rapidly expanding European global economies. By 1750, merchants, slave-ship captains and their crews, and American planters had systematically robbed Africa of millions of its strongest and most productive men, women, and children.

Enslaved Africans were not the only inhabitants of the New World with connections to the Old World. Servants, settlers, soldiers, and government and church officials from Spain, France, England, and elsewhere populated North America. Some were Catholic, some Protestant, and some Jewish—even a few Muslims. All left family and friends in the Old World. Few if any initially thought of themselves as Americans, a term that was generally applied to Indians. Multiracial and multicultural colonists frequently clashed, but sometimes they banded together to rebel against imperial authority.

In a world that seemed much larger then than it does now, Americans understood and often appreciated their global connections. Cultural identity then was a complex and evolving phenomenon, as it is today, and by studying early American history from a global perspective we can acquire a deeper and richer understanding of the intricacies of the colonial experience.

THINKING BACK

1. How did Europeans break the Ottoman Empire's global trade monopoly?

2. Although Columbus failed to reach his immediate objective, how did he lay down the basis for future global empires?

Chapter 1

DIFFERENT WORLDS: FROM BEGINNINGS TO 1492

A PERSONAL PERSPECTIVE: KENNEWICK MAN AND ANZICK CHILD TELL THEIR STORIES

> **What do the remains of Kennewick Man and Anzick Child tell us about who the first Americans were and where they came from?**

Some 9,000 years ago, a 40-year-old man's life ended in present-day Washington State, near today's town of Kennewick. He may have died alone. That's impossible to say for sure, but he did not live alone. His friends or kin carefully laid out his body on its back and buried it.

In 1996, the man's skeleton surfaced in front of two college students who were walking along the Columbia River. Something caught their eye in the shallow water. It was a human skull, and nearby they found more bones. The young men notified the police, who summoned the county coroner and a local archaeologist who gathered up a nearly complete human skeleton. The remains were obviously old; however, the results of scientific carbon-dating were stunning. This was one of the most ancient human skeletons ever found in North America, and it offered important clues to a long unsolved mystery: "Who were the first Americans, and where did they come from?" As word of **Kennewick Man** spread, a huge controversy erupted. Local Native Americans associated with the Colville Indian Confederation believed that they already knew the answer and were tired of non-Indian anthropologists desecrating Indian burial sites trying to find out. The Indians were certain that the remains of the man they call **Ancient One** were one of their ancestors and demanded that he be turned over to them for re-reburial. Federal law, specifically the Native American Graves Protection and Repatriation Act, agreed with them. The Army Corps of Engineers, which managed the land on which Ancient One had been found, took temporary possession with the intention of turning the bones over to the Indians.

A group of scientists, however, pleaded for time to run tests to determine if in fact Kennewick Man was ancestral to local Native Americans. Based on old theories about cranial size and shape, the scientists concluded that modern Indians had not descended from Kennewick Man. They theorized that he had migrated from eastern Asia to Alaska across today's Bering Strait, but concluded that subsequent migrations from other places, maybe even Europe, and along other routes brought more people of different types to North America. Over time these relative newcomers produced modern Native Americans.

As the legal contest and the scientific debate raged over the ancestry of modern Indian ancestry, Ancient One silently revealed some details of his life and experiences in one of the great migrations in human history. He died at about 40 years of age, stood 5 ft. 7 in. tall, and weighed a muscular 160 lb. Ancient One hunted large and small mammals, and he probably fought other humans, all with spears thrown with his right hand and hard enough to damage his shoulder socket. A spear point was embedded in his pelvis, perhaps from a fight when he was 15 or 20 years old. He also suffered six broken ribs and a skull injury. Ancient One clearly lived a hard life. He also used spears to jab down at cold-water fish, a staple of his diet. Curiously though, he ate mostly marine fish and animals, even though the Pacific Ocean was 300 miles away from his final resting place. No doubt, Ancient One traveled widely to hunt and, maybe, to trade with other people.

On February 17, 2017, the telling of Ancient One's story ended. His remains were repatriated and the Colville Indians secretly, ceremoniously returned him to the earth. But stunning and intriguing as his tale is, the story of a toddler, born 3,000 years before Ancient One, casts even brighter light on the origins of Native Americans. In 1968, the little boy's remains were accidentally unearthed by a construction crew employed by the Anzick family in central Montana. He had been buried with a large cache of hand-chipped and fluted projectile points and an elk-horn tool of some kind. These projectile points were similar to other artifacts found previously throughout North America and classified as "Clovis" artifacts, from a culture that originated more than 13,000 years ago. This boy is known as **Anzick Child**, after the family who owns his burial land. We don't know why or how he died, but we know that he is a missing link in the chain of understanding of how and when the first human beings appeared in the Americas.

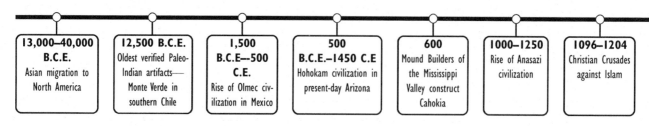

| 13,000–40,000 B.C.E. Asian migration to North America | 12,500 B.C.E. Oldest verified Paleo-Indian artifacts— Monte Verde in southern Chile | 1,500 B.C.E.–500 C.E. Rise of Olmec civilization in Mexico | 500 B.C.E.–1450 C.E Hohokam civilization in present-day Arizona | 600 Mound Builders of the Mississippi Valley construct Cahokia | 1000–1250 Rise of Anasazi civilization | 1096–1204 Christian Crusades against Islam |

In 2014, a team of molecular biologists completed sequencing Anzick Child's genome. In comparing his DNA with that of other Native Americans, they found that Anzick Child is the direct ancestor of 80% of all Native Americans living in North and South America. Furthermore, Anzick Child is genetically related to people in eastern Asia. This evidence confirms that first Americans originated in Asia, not Europe, and that this little boy's relatives created all the remarkable pre-European civilizations of North and South America. Furthermore, genetic trails link Asia, Europe, and Africa as well as the Americas.

These intercontinental and transoceanic linkages mark the starting point for this history of the United States and its many diverse people and cultures. *Building a Democratic Nation* begins here.

THINKING BACK

1. Who were Kennewick Man and Anzick Child?
2. What do Kennewick Man and Anzick Child tell us about the first Americans?

THE LOCAL PERSPECTIVE: FOCUS ON NORTH AMERICAN LANDSCAPES

> **What are some of the most important geographical features of North America?**

Scholars have pointed out that environment influenced how ancient people lived. Even modern societies are blessed and cursed by local weather patterns, geographical terrain, and the availability of water and other natural resources. Understanding history requires a sense of the places where people lived—not just the overall continental landscape but also the smaller regional environments.

Although the ground beneath our feet seems solid and stationary, the earth's continents actually float on seas of molten iron, sulfur, and other minerals. Over millions of years, as the earth's surface slowly cooled after its fiery beginning, hard crusts or plates formed. Eventually these floating plates broke apart, drifted, and crashed into one another. Much of

North and South America split away from Europe and Africa, leaving the great Atlantic Ocean between them. Continental collisions resulted in massive uplifts that we recognize as mountain chains. During the age of dinosaurs, such a collision gave rise to the **Appalachian Mountains** that run parallel to the Atlantic Coast from Georgia through New England. Gradual erosion caused by wind and precipitation wore the Appalachians down. On their eastern flank, rolling hills called the **piedmont** slope toward the fertile coastal plain known as the **tidewater**. The Appalachians and their flanks are the most outstanding topographical feature of the East Coast. Out West, a similar shift of a great Pacific plate pushed up the **Rocky Mountains** from Mexico into Canada. Other collisions produced the **Sierra Nevada** and Coastal ranges from California through British Columbia.

Plate shifts also caused the release of enormous amounts of heat from below the earth's crust, sometimes resulting in powerful explosions of molten rock known as volcanoes. Volcanic mountain cones popped up within the southern Rockies and the **Cascade Mountains** from the California-Oregon boundary into Washington State. Only a few volcanoes in North America remain active today, but in 1980, an earthquake caused the devastating eruption of Washington's Mount St. Helens. Of great importance over the long human history of North America has been the exposure of rocks containing valuable minerals such as gold, silver, copper, and lead caused by mountain uplifts and volcanic eruptions.

Between many of North America's mountain ranges, water collected in inland seas surrounded by lush, tropical vegetation. Sediments laid down over millennia included the remains of an enormous variety of prehistoric plants and animals. Over eons, decomposed trees and other vegetation, buried under layers of soil and rock, produced vast coal and petroleum deposits. Uplifts and climate change ultimately drained the inland seas, leaving sedimentary sandstone and limestone formations in the Great Basin between the Rockies and the Sierra Nevada Mountains. During periods of global warming, ice sheets melted to form the **Great Lakes**.

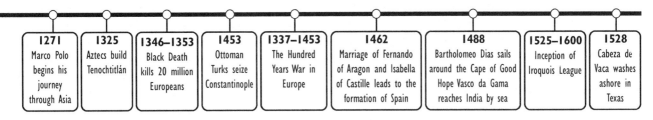

1271	1325	1346–1353	1453	1337–1453	1462	1488	1525–1600	1528
Marco Polo begins his journey through Asia	Aztecs build Tenochtitlán	Black Death kills 20 million Europeans	Ottoman Turks seize Constantinople	The Hundred Years War in Europe	Marriage of Fernando of Aragon and Isabella of Castille leads to the formation of Spain	Bartholomeo Dias sails around the Cape of Good Hope Vasco da Gama reaches India by sea	Inception of Iroquois League	Cabeza de Vaca washes ashore in Texas

Climate change has always played a key role in the evolving ecology of North America. Over long stretches of time, tens of thousands of years, temperatures dropped and then rose in prolonged cycles. The last very cold climate period, called the **Pleistocene** epoch, began 120,000 years ago. By 11,500 years ago, temperatures had climbed significantly again, nearly to today's levels. Wind currents, too, affected climate patterns. Over the eastern half of the continent, surface winds from the Atlantic Ocean and the **Gulf of Mexico** kept the air humid and dropped abundant rainfall. West of the Mississippi River, high-altitude wind currents known as the jet stream carried moisture inland from the Pacific Ocean, providing a very wet climate in today's Pacific Northwest. Among the western mountain ranges, rising air from the surface collided with damp air aloft to generate summer rains and winter snows. In the eastern shadows of the Sierra Nevada and Rocky Mountains, air depleted of moisture kept the land arid or semi-arid.

Climate change coupled with geologic evolution produced other significant regional features. During cold periods, advancing glaciers from the north crept over ancient forests and changed their composition. A cold environment also favored the growth of softwood pine and spruce trees (called coniferous because they have cones and needles). Such forests still cover much of New England today. As the climate warmed and the ice sheets retreated, hardwood deciduous trees (ones that shed their leaves) spread northward from what is now the Southeastern United States. As late as the sixteenth century, roughly 45 percent of the United States was forested, and four-fifths of those forests were located east of the **Mississippi River.**

Melting glaciers and snow-packs formed some of the great rivers that cut through the landscape. Over 3 million years ago the **Colorado River,** flowing westward out of the central Rocky Mountains, began slicing through bedrock at the rate of six feet every thousand years to form the **Grand Canyon** on its way to the Pacific Ocean. From the northern Rockies, the mighty **Columbia River** both slashed and meandered its way to the Pacific. The **Missouri River** and **Arkansas River** drained the eastern slopes of the Rockies, flowing into the Mississippi River, one of the continent's newest rivers, and finally into the Gulf of Mexico, which is connected through the **Caribbean Sea** to the Atlantic Ocean. The **Rio Grande River** flows from the southern Rockies to the Gulf of Mexico and serves as part of the United States' southern boundary. The ironically named **New River,** one

of the oldest rivers on earth, originates in the Appalachian Mountains and flows through the present-day states of Virginia and West Virginia and into the Kanawha River, which in turn joins the **Ohio River,** the largest tributary of the Mississippi.

On this slowly but constantly evolving environmental stage thousands of years ago, dramatic human migrations marked the beginning of American history, producing the first human populations of what eventually became the United States.

THINKING BACK

1. What were the major mountain ranges of North America, and what caused them.
2. How did climate change contribute to the landscape of North America?

THE BEGINNINGS OF NATIVE AMERICAN SOCIETIES

An essential part of a people's identity comes from the fundamental questions "Who am I?" and "Where did I and others like me come from?" But the answers, and the exact origins of human societies in North America, remain unclear. For centuries, Native Americans have based their understanding of ancestral origins on traditions passed down from generation to generation. Known as **creation stories,** these traditional narratives have become part of the cultures of Native American peoples. Native people have not been the only ones whose cultures include creation stories. Numerous European fables tell of original Americans coming from ancient Greece, Ireland, and a mythical land known as Atlantis. Archaeologists also have explanations.

How Native Americans Explain Their Origins

Nobody knows for sure when or how the first people got to North America or from where they came, but we can assume that they emigrated from some other place. Such an explanation appears in many Native American creation stories.

Although Native American creation stories vary from group to group, most include a creator, or **Great Spirit,** and the migration of people from a distant place of origin to

> How do many Native Americans explain their ancestral origins?

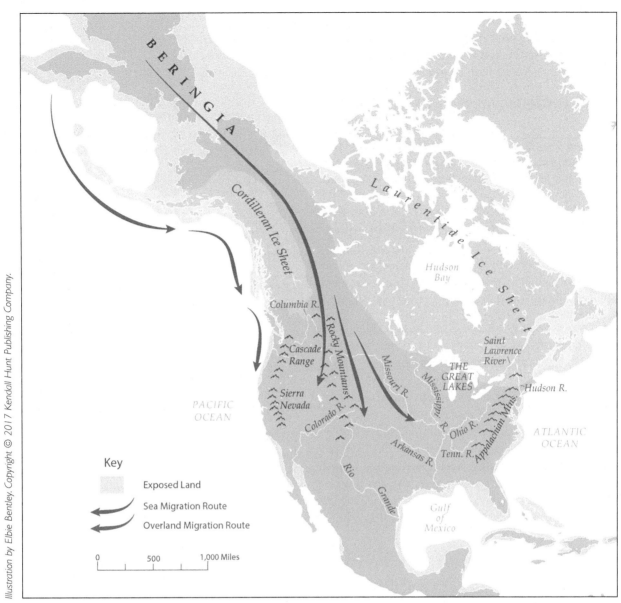

Archaeologists believe Paleo-Indians migrated from Asia to North America during the last Ice Age and then followed the coast or migrated through mountain and glacier passes southward and eastward.

ancestral lands in the Americas. The **Blackfeet** people of Montana, for instance, tell of Old Man, whose father was the Sun and mother was the Moon and who came from the south to create birds, animals, and grass. Old Man fashioned a woman and a child out of clay and declared: "You must be people." Other Native Americans believe that their ancestors emerged from an underworld. According to the **Lakota Sioux** of the northern prairies and plains, spirits representing the sun, moon, five winds (four directional ones plus the whirlwind) led humans to the earth's surface through a cave in the Black Hills of today's South Dakota. **Pueblo** Indians of New Mexico and Arizona tell of two sisters who emerged from the underworld. One became Corn Mother, the

supplier of food; the other, impregnated by the rain, gave birth to sons and daughters who became leaders of clans representing the sky, rain, fire, and corn.

European Americans have often rejected Indian explanations of the peopling of North America in favor of their own, most of which involve the migration of the original Americans from some other place. Some Europeans in Cabeza de Vaca's time believed Native Americans emigrated from Europe or the Middle East. Judeo-Christian scripture tells of the expulsion of Hebrew tribes for breaking God's law and their migration to "a distant land never yet inhabited by man." Certain Bible scholars held that Native Americans were the Lost Tribes of Israel, as did Mormon founder Joseph Smith. Most interestingly, in 1590 a Spanish Catholic priest named Joseph de Acosta theorized that the first Indians had migrated from Asia across a land bridge to North America.

What Archaeologists Have Found

When and how do archaeologists believe the first people came to North America?

Modern archaeologists also seek to explain where the first people to inhabit North America came from. Their method is to examine and interpret human artifacts and draw inferences from their age, composition, and configuration. Clues as to when and how the first people came to North America are scarce and sometimes confusing; indeed, thus far nobody has been able to validate any theory to everyone's satisfaction.

The most widely accepted scholarly explanation, based on archeological and geological data, holds that the first Americans migrated from northeast Asia at the tail end of the Pleistocene ice age, some 15,000 to 38,000 years ago. At that time, advancing glaciers captured moisture from the sea as it evaporated and fell as precipitation. The phenomenon caused sea levels to fall appreciably, exposing portions of an intercontinental plateau, called **Beringia** after the Danish explorer Vitus Bering. Nomadic Asian hunters trekked across Beringia, a windswept tundra perhaps a thousand miles wide, in pursuit of giant mammoths and mastodons, smaller bison, camels, and horses. Gradually the hunters reached North America.

After a few thousand years—a mere tick of the geological clock—global temperatures increased again. Northern ice sheets melted, resulting in rising sea levels that inundated Beringia, created the Bering Strait, and stranded the Asian migrants in North America. Receding glaciers may also have opened routes for people to migrate farther eastward through the Rocky Mountains, across present-day Canada, and southward into what is the United States. Some people may have traveled along the Alaskan/British Columbian coasts and then inland. In any event, migrations eventually reached Central and South America.

Not enough information has yet been gleaned to prove the Asian migration scenario, but scientific and scholarly sleuthing has revealed evidence to support it. In the 1930s, investigators near Clovis, New Mexico, discovered fluted spear points situated near the bones of ancient mammals in a way that strongly suggests human hunters had made the spears and used them to kill the animals. Employing sophisticated carbon-dating technology developed in the 1950s, archaeologists later estimated that the bones, and thus the spear points embedded in them, were at least 11,000 years old. Similar objects from other archaeological sites indicate a continuing migration across a vast area of North America. Furthermore, similarities between **Clovis** spear points and those made by ancient hunters in Russian Siberia, along with common language patterns, suggest cultural links between Native Americans and Asians, while dental analysis and DNA samples establish biological commonalities.

For decades, most archaeologists assumed that because no artifacts older than the Clovis spear points had been found, those objects mark the beginning of human occupation of America. But while the Clovis specimens can point to where the first Americans came from they cannot tell us exactly when they arrived. Ansick Child (see p. 8) has pushed the date further back than the original Clovis findings. Even older objects may still await discovery. In fact, objects including a human footprint recently unearthed at Monte Verde in Chile apparently pre-date Clovis and have led many scholars to push back the date of entry to America to perhaps 30-40,000 years ago, approximately the same time as when modern humans settled in Europe. And the new discoveries have invited speculation about whether sea voyages might have been involved.

At present, uncertainty and disagreement persist among archaeologists. Despite the new findings, staunch defenders of the Clovis timeframe remain unconvinced. Furthermore, one modern Native-American argument asserts that archaeologists are attempting to de-legitimize Indians as no more native to America than Europeans. But curiously, while archaeological methods differ from the allegorical origin stories common in Native American traditions, both use migration theories to explain Native American beginnings.

Image © Brian Brockman, 2010. Used by permission of Shutterstock, Inc.

Clovis hunters attached these fluted stone points to spears for hunting large mammals

Understanding Paleo-Indians

What do we know about Paleo-Indians of North America?

Regardless of where **Paleo-Indians** ("Paleo" = ancient) came from, over the subsequent millennia they left behind specimens of their weapons, tools, dwellings, remnants of their cooking fires, and even scraps of food and clothing, tantalizing details about the lives they lived. As they dispersed in small kinship bands across this New World, Paleo-Indians exploited the resources at hand, spearing and netting fish, hunting mammals, rodents, and birds not only for food but also for skins, sinews, bones, feathers, and antlers, and foraging for editable roots, seeds, berries, and fruits. Where resources were plentiful, as along the Pacific Coast, they probably remained in fairly small areas and in multifamily groups. Where it was less abundant they ranged more widely and in smaller units. Although it is virtually impossible to know what Paleo-Indians thought, in general, they apparently adapted to their environment rather than sought to change it.

Paleo-Indians on the **Great Plains** hunted mammoths, mastodons, and other large mammals with spears, stalking the lumbering beasts a few at a time and occasionally stampeding herds over cliffs in mass slaughters, indicating a high degree of social organization as well as the development of rudimentary technologies for butchering and preserving meat. They fashioned garments from pieces of animal hide sewn together using sinew for thread and bone needles. Their toolkits contained stone and bone scrapers, and pounders that allowed them to skin and butcher their kills and prepare meal from seeds and nuts.

Noting that as many as 80 percent of ancient North America's large mammals disappeared as human populations increased, some researchers have concluded that Paleo-Indians caused, or at least contributed to, mass extinctions. Perhaps so, but this remains a hot topic for debate. After all, other mammals such as bison, elk, and deer, which Paleo-Indians also hunted, survived and some actually increased in number. Climate change certainly figured into animal extinctions and other ecological changes as well. Rising temperatures and diminished rainfall radically altered animal habitats, severely reducing grazing ranges and water supplies. While some animal species succumbed, others withstood the effects of environmental and ecological change though adaptation. Bison, for instance, adjusted to shorter range-grass and drier winter forage, and eventually great herds grazed across the breadth of the Great Plains.

Most Paleo-Indians did not depend solely on big game for their livelihoods. Instead, they developed diverse and resourceful economies. Ancient North American Indians hunted smaller animals like deer and rabbits, fished rivers, lakes, and coastal waters, and foraged for various plant foods, developing appropriate technologies for obtaining, preparing, and storing food. Desert dwellers, for instance, learned to weave the fiber from yucca plants into baskets for carrying and storing seeds, berries, nuts, and tubers. Such regional ways of life lasted for thousands of years.

THINKING BACK

1. Where do most archaeologists believe the first humans in North America came from? When do they think the first people appeared in North America, and how do they believe they got here? What other explanations of human beginnings in North America have been offered?
2. How did environment, including climate change, influence Paleo-Indians' ways of life, and how may humans have altered their environment?

FROM FORAGING TO FARMING

Some 10,000 years ago, amid warming global climates, people in various parts of the world began producing food instead of living from hand-to-mouth as hunters and gatherers. They sowed seeds in gardens and harvested mature food crops while simultaneously domesticating wild animals. Decisions to manipulate plants and animals were probably not part of any visionary plan or ideology. Rather, they were the result of people's slow adaptation to changing circumstances: the diminished availability of wild food, increasing access to varieties of plants and animals suitable for domestication, and the arrival of neighbors and visitors who introduced them to domestic foods and techniques for planting, harvesting, storing, and processing them. Ancient people of the **Fertile Crescent** of modern Iraq launched the **Agricultural Revolution** by domesticating wheat, peas, olives, sheep, and goats. Independently, ancient Chinese did likewise with rice, millet, pigs, and silkworms. Over the next 2,500 years or so, these and other products spread fairly easily across the vast breadth of **Eurasia**.

The shift from foraging to farming represented a crucial milestone in human social evolution. Farmed land yielded up to 100 times more nutrition than forest and grassland. With relatively reliable food supplies close at hand, agricultural people grew healthier, reproduced more rapidly, and became more sedentary. Multiple extended family units clustered in towns where they constructed relatively permanent buildings. They organized social hierarchies of laborers, artisans, priests, and civic leaders, laid out extensive trade networks, and fought to defend their territory against intruders.

Complex social organization along with science, technology, art, and economies capable of sustaining large populations are important aspects of **civilization**, but agriculture was the essential building block. And in many parts of North America, civilizations depended on corn.

Corn: The Basis of Native American Agriculture

> **Where did North American food cultivation originate, and how did it impact people's lives?**

Five thousand years after the initial shift to agriculture in Eurasia, Native Americans independently developed their own agriculture. Indians residing in the Andes and Amazon regions of South America began harvesting potatoes; meanwhile, **Mesoamericans** in southern Mexico did the same with corn. Slowly, agriculture moved toward North America.

Corn (also called maize) probably originated in southwestern Mexico from a wild grass known as **teosinte**. Ancient people gathered teosinte for its kernels, selecting the best ones for eating and inadvertently dropping some on the ground where they germinated and sprouted into new plants. Wild teosinte was not particularly appealing though because of its rock hard kernels, nor did it much resemble modern corn plants. But by carefully selecting and replanting only the most suitable specimens, Indians eventually produced plants that anyone today would recognize as corn, and over the next several thousand years, corn cultivation spread northward into the United States.

Corn possessed greater nutritional value than wheat being richer in carbohydrates and vitamins. Indians fashioned stone mortars and pestles to grind corn into a coarse meal. Adding water to cornmeal produced a pasty *masa* that Indians heated on hot stones to make those tasty thin pancakes Spaniards later called *tortillas*.

Native Americans developed other food plants as well. Beans nicely complemented protein-poor corn by providing important amino acids and preventing pellagra, a deficiency of the vitamin niacin. Moreover, beans and corn could be dried and stored for later consumption. Indians also grew squash, whose vines ran along the ground and helped suppress garden weeds. Native people hollowed out squash gourds, let them dry, and used them as food and water containers. The combination of corn, beans, and squash became the "three sisters" of North American Indian diets.

Despite the advantages of a steadier food supply, early agricultural communities still faced daunting challenges. Dependence on food crops required intense, sustained, and sometimes coerced labor. Agriculture also altered the environment, often with devastating ecological consequences. Clearing and cultivating fields diminished forests, which in turn contributed to drought, flooding, and reduced wild animal populations. Furthermore, urban congestion made people more susceptible to bacterial and viral infections, psychological stress, and mobile attackers.

Agriculture also affected society and culture. Abundant food did not guarantee its equal distribution. Food became a measure of wealth and its accumulation the basis for vertical stratification because some people possessed more food-wealth and thus more power and status than others. Agricultural societies also divided themselves horizontally according to gender and work responsibilities. Women cultivated crops, ground corn, cooked meals, and raised children. Men hunted, waged war, and typically governed civic life. Men and women who were not primarily food producers designed and constructed buildings, made pottery, and crafted tools and weapons. And agriculture redefined Native Americans' relationship with the spirit world. Priests appealed to gods and spirits that seemed to control those vital natural forces, especially rainfall, that determined whether harvests would be abundant or meager.

Gardening was one important facet of agriculture. Tending domesticated animals was another. In Europe and Asia, the two went hand in hand, but not so in North America.

Life Without Domesticated Animals

With the exception of dogs, which were bred from wolves and used for meat, hunting, and carrying light loads, the ancient Indians of North America did not domesticate animals. This fact distinguishes them from their counterparts in Europe and Asia who from 10,000

Why did ancient Indians of North America not domesticate large mammals, and what disadvantages did that ultimately create for them?

to 4,500 years ago domesticated assorted large and small animals. Cattle, sheep, goats, and pigs supplied them with meat, milk, leather, wool, and fertilizer. Horses pulled vehicles and plows and bore riders, including warriors. Cats guarded grain larders from rats and mice, and chickens and turkeys provided eggs and feathers.

North Americans' notable lack of domesticated animals was due mostly to the characteristics of the wild animals they had to work with, not their own shortcomings. The fact that Native Americans domesticated dogs about the same time that other people did suggests that they were inclined to domesticate animals and knew how to do it. But for thousands of years, only a scant few animal species were suited for domestication. As a matter of fact, until the beginning of the twentieth century, only 14 of the 148 large terrestrial mammal species in the world had been domesticated, and only one was native to the Western Hemisphere. Certain biological and behavioral traits in certain mammals make them candidates for domestication. They must be easily and cheaply fed (ideally grazers), mate and reproduce in captivity, grow fairly quickly and have short reproductive cycles. They must also possess calm, predictable, and social behavior patterns (no mountain lions). The absence of just one of those traits makes domestication very unlikely.

The only large mammals of the Western Hemisphere that possessed all those traits were llamas and alpacas, and the Indians of the South American Andes did domesticate both of them. Perhaps due to the great distances and the inhospitable tropical regions that separated North from South America, however, llamas and alpacas were not transferred north of the equator until modern times. There had once been North American mammals that would have been candidates for domestication, such as horses and camels, but they became extinct at about the time of the first human migration to the continent.

The absence of domesticated animals from the Western Hemisphere, particularly five herbivores (sheep, goats, cattle, pigs, and horses), was a critical detriment to Native Americans, and not just because of the food, clothing materials, and work potential they missed out on. The fact that Native Americans did not live in close proximity to herds of domestic animals perhaps minimized their exposure to germs that cause lethal diseases. That might seem like a blessing; however, in light of the Indians' ultimate encounters with Europeans, the consequences were enormous. Among the deadly epidemic diseases caused by germs originating in domesticated animals were measles, tuberculosis, and smallpox, and people residing in Europe and Asia began contracting those diseases thousands of years ago, probably from contact with their livestock. Victims who did not die from the diseases acquired lifetime immunity from recurring infections. But since Native Americans never contracted the diseases, they acquired no immunity. So when Europeans arrived bearing their deadly pathogens, the Indians were susceptible.

Looking back from the vantage point of the twenty-first century, we might think of the transition from hunting and gathering to gardening and herding as inevitable, but people sometimes had good reason to make other choices. Many Native Americans in areas where wild food was abundant or where environments did not support agriculture, continued to hunt and fish and gather plants and seeds for food. In some areas, like California and the Midwest, among today's bread, vegetable, and fruit baskets, agriculture did not take hold until the last two centuries when outside colonizers entered those areas, removed the Indians, and initiated it.

Powerful Civilizations Arise in Ancient Mexico

As far back as 3,500 years ago, some of the world's most sophisticated civilizations developed in Mesoamerica. Villages grew into large cities with complex social organization and sophisticated cultures. Massive stone buildings—temples, palaces, schools, and markets constructed by thousands of workers without the use of wheels—lined broad streets and spacious plazas. In addition to impressive buildings, artisans produced sophisticated tools and weapons like the bow and arrow, cotton textiles, and ceremonial carvings and ceramic ware. Olmec, Maya, Toltec, and Mexica (Aztec) civilizations attained high levels of scientific accomplishment and Mayans developed a written hieroglyphic language. These people also established trade networks throughout Mesoamerica and into North America.

What were the major Mesoamerican civilizations and their most outstanding achievements?

From approximately 1200 **B.C.E.** ("Before the Common Era") to 600 C.E., **Olmec** (a word that means "rubber people," perhaps for the rubber plants in Mesoamerica) culture developed patterns that

Image © Dmitry Rukhlenko, 2010. Used by permission of Shutterstock, Inc.

Pyramid of the Sun, the ancient Toltec temple in Teotihuacán, offers a prime example of the architectural and engineering achievements of Mesoamerican civilizations long before the arrival of Europeans.

other Mesoamericans followed. Olmec astronomers tracked the stars and planets, and mathematicians conceived the number zero. Women cultivated corn, beans, and squash along with avocados, peppers, and tomatoes while mostly male craftsmen created decorative objects of jade and sharp arrowheads of obsidian. Merchants traded these products with outsiders for such goods as dried meat and animal hides.

The development of indigenous Mesoamerican empires, with one powerful society dominating others, began around 500 B.C.E. with the city-state of **Teotihuacán**, located just north of modern Mexico City. With perhaps 200,000 residents, Teotihuacán was one of the world's largest metropolises. Two towering stone pyramids dominated the city, one honoring the sun and the other the moon. A temple honored the powerful feathered-serpent god Quetzalcoatl, and a myriad of other stone buildings, decorated with carvings and paintings, adorned the city. Teotihuacán's imperial history was highlighted by the conquest of **Maya** city-states to the south, on the Yucatan Peninsula, but the city declined after 700 C.E., perhaps unable to feed its large population and falling to attacking enemies. By 950, cultural descendants of Teotihuacán, known as **Toltecs,** established a new empire. Toltec militarism was evident in gigantic warrior statues, but in addition, Toltec language became the civilized tongue of central Mexico, where it survives today and reveals the extent of Toltec cultural dominance.

In the fourteenth century, Toltecs in turn fell victim to invasion by **Mexica** (pronounced "ma-sheeka") conquerors who swept down from northern Mexico. The name **Aztec** (from Aztlán, their mythic homeland) is given to the hundreds of thousands of Mexica and other people who comprised the last indigenous empire in central Mexico. The Mexica built **Tenochtitlán** (today's Mexico City) on an island in Lake Texcoco and connected it by causeways to other towns along the shore and surrounding cornfields. With a population of 300,000 in the fifteenth century, over three times the size of Paris or London, Tenochtitlán was a magnificent city of pyramids, stone palaces, canals, and aqueducts that supplied its inhabitants with fresh water from the surrounding mountains. Atop a central ceremonial pyramid, religious leaders sacrificed the hearts of slaves and captured enemy soldiers, perhaps as many as 3,000 or 4,000 per year, to the gods who made the corn grow. Powerful Mexica leaders also extracted tribute from neighboring towns and cities in the form of food and gold used for decoration by the Mexica elite.

These elaborate civilizations influenced the cultures of neighboring and even far-flung people. A vigorous trade network spread corn, bean, and squash farming and probably ideas about town planning and religious rituals into the distant heartland of North America.

The Anasazi: Ingenious Farmers

Over 2,000 years ago, Native Americans began farming in the difficult, semi-arid lands of the American Southwest. People known as **Hohokam** in southern Arizona and **Anasazi** in the Four Corners of Arizona, New Mexico, Utah, and Colorado invested increasing amounts of time and energy into growing corn, beans, squash, and cotton. They also made clay pots for cooking and storing food and constructed buildings of stone and **adobe** as residences and for ritual ceremonies and storing food.

> **How did farming societies in the Southwest cope with their harsh environment?**

In the early stages of their history, the Hohokam resided in pit houses arranged in small villages scattered across the upper Sonoran Desert. Later they constructed rooms above ground. Culturally, they resembled Mesoamericans. As the number of Hohokam increased, villages grew into towns, some housing several hundred people. Expert stonecutters crafted jewelry from malachite, opal, and turquoise. Artisans made bowls, tools, and other utilitarian items for daily use. Stone figurines carried religious meaning while decorated ceramic pottery replaced woven baskets as food and water containers. Successful farming led to the rapid diffusion of Hohokam society as their trading networks reached from Mexico to the Pacific Coast and the Great Plains. Trading cotton and surplus food, the Hohokam acquired brightly plumed macaws and parrots, onyx bracelets, and copper bells.

Hohokam farmers faced extreme desert conditions, and to cope with their environment they engineered elaborate irrigation canals to channel water from the mountain-fed Salt River. Today, the city of Phoenix relies on a water project built literally on top of Hohokam irrigation canals. In the fourteenth century, though, Hohokam civilization began a steady decline as villages lying beyond the canal system failed to produce sufficient food to sustain the growing population. A prolonged drought caused massive crop failures. And the Hohokam contributed to their woes as water-borne minerals flowing through their irrigation canals layered fields with a salt crust that withered crops. By about 1450 the Hohokam had abandoned their villages and irrigation networks and returned to a life of foraging and non-irrigated farming. Their present-day descendants, the **Akimel O'odham** (Pima) and **Tohono O'odham** (Papago), have lived that way for centuries.

Farther north, on the high plateaus where the four corners of New Mexico, Arizona, Colorado, and Utah meet, the **Anasazi** (meaning "ancient ones") built large communities in and around **Mesa Verde** and **Chaco Canyon**. In this "land of little rain," the Anasazi collected precious runoff from intense summer showers as it cascaded from the mesa tops and directed it to fields of corn, beans, squash, and

Image © Josemaria Toscano, 2010. Used by permission of Shutterstock, Inc.

The Anasazi constructed large towns in an arid and fragile environment, indicating high level architectural and engineering skills as well as political organization.

cotton. This required effective centralized authority to mobilize legions of workers for intensive, short-term labor. To house their burgeoning populations, Anasazi townspeople built multistory stone apartment complexes and dug subterranean ceremonial rooms known as *kivas,* where spiritual leaders conducted ritual ceremonies to appease gods and spirits. Extensive road networks linked scores of Anasazi towns and villages, and mesa-top signal stations utilized bonfires for visual communication.

Like the Hohokam, the Anasazi were a cosmopolitan people who traded local turquoise for exotic sea shells, copper, and colorful feathers from the Pacific Coast and Mesoamerica. They produced pottery for cooking, eating, and storage, and like Mesoamericans, the Anasazi tracked cycles of the sun and moon and devised a very reliable calendar.

The golden age of the Anasazi (750 to 1300) came to an end when the absence of rain caused food supplies to drop below rising levels of demand. Attacks from marauding bands may also have driven the people to other locations to the south and east. When Europeans, including perhaps Cabeza de Vaca, arrived in the Southwest in the early 1500s, scores of villages dotted the upper valley of the Rio Grande and the mesa country westward to northeastern Arizona. The people living there today, whom Spaniards called **Pueblos** from the word meaning "village," bear many cultural similarities to the Anasazi.

Eastern Woodlands Mound Builders

As far back as 3,500 years ago, Indians living in the eastern woodlands of the United States began transitioning from hunting and foraging to agriculture and trade. Large, permanent settlements, social differentiation with unequal distribution of wealth and status, powerful chiefs with centralized authority, and large burial mounds were among the traits that distinguished what archaeologists call the **Woodlands** culture. **Mound Builder** towns were scattered along the Gulf Coast and through the fertile valleys of the Mississippi River and its tributaries.

> **What distinguished the Mound Builders of the eastern woodlands from other North American agriculturalists?**

Around 1500 B.C.E. in the low, marshy Mississippi delta around Poverty Point in present-day Louisiana, a community of perhaps 2,000 Native Americans piled thousands of baskets of earth into eye-catching earthen mounds arranged in concentric ridges around a central plaza 600 feet in diameter. While no artifacts have been found to provide researchers with clues as to the mounds' exact purpose, seven hundred years later, people living north of the Ohio River constructed similar earthen works. Artifacts excavated from those mounds strongly suggest that they were burial sites. And the fine quality of the artifacts—copper bracelets, woven cloth, obsidian tools, seashells, and tobacco pipes—indicate that those buried in the mounds had belonged to a social elite. Furthermore, the copper, probably from the Great Lakes region, along with mica from the Appalachian Mountains and pearls and shells from the Gulf of Mexico imply the existence of a trade network that covered most of the eastern United States. Gradually, population in mound-builder towns dispersed into the interior of the eastern woodlands, and simultaneously people developed bow and arrow technology that improved hunting efficiency and took the first steps toward the cultivation of corn, beans, and squash.

From 800 to 1500 C.E., mound-building ways of life underwent further transformation. **Mississippian** people living in the Mississippi River Valley expanded the cultural patterns laid down in the Woodlands tradition. Many Mississippian societies were organized around complex **chiefdoms** characterized by concentrated authority and social inequality. The largest of the Mississippian mound-builder communities, **Cahokia**, was a city-state located a few miles east of present-day St. Louis. Occupied as early as 600 C.E. and reaching a population of 20,000 in the thirteenth century, Cahokia featured an enormous ceremonial pyramidal mound similar in appearance to those in Mesoamerica, although constructed of earth rather than stone. A solid slab of clay 900 feet long, 650 feet wide, and as tall as a ten-story building, the flat-topped mound was apparently the exclusive domain of civic leaders: priests and Cahokia's superior chief. Other smaller, conical mounds, 120 in all, served as ceremonial and mortuary sites.

Cahokia declined in the fourteenth century, tracking the general downward trajectory of Mississippian culture and corresponding roughly to the abandonment of Anasazi towns in the Southwest and a short-term but potent chilling of North America's climate known as the "little ice age" that ravaged continental cornfields. In addition, when Cahokia's population had been on the upswing, workers had cleared mas-

Serpent Mound, Adams County, Ohio. One of the most intriguing constructions of the Mound Builders of North America, it resembles a snake devouring an egg.

sive amounts of the surrounding woodlands for cornfields, a deforestation that led ultimately to damaging floods. Fortifications surrounding the central ceremonial mound suggest the erosion of the elite's authority and mounting warfare, adding further to the society's woes. By 1500 Cahokia's population had dispersed, organizing other, smaller communities throughout the Mississippi Valley.

Indian burial mounds containing gifts bestowed by the living upon the departed for use in another place have led researchers to deduce the development of common religious beliefs and practices among early Native Americans. And the presence of far-flung trade networks indicates one way by which culture was transferred from one group to another.

A World View Among Native Americans

Although North American Indians on the eve of contact with Europeans comprised a cultural mosaic, they also shared attributes and characteristics. Among these were fundamental ideas about leadership and governance, about social and family life, about ownership of land, and about the universe and their role within it.

In general, Indians maintained **tribal identities** (based on lineage and culture) without the formal government bureaucracies that characterize modern nation-states. Political systems were largely village based, and leadership flowed from respect earned through experience, although lineage was a factor too. About leadership, one early European noted that Indian "leaders do not have absolute authority. They just state what should be done and others do so if they want." Chiefs had proven themselves effective in mediating conflicts and in building alliances through gift-giving gestures of goodwill. War leaders demonstrated their bravery and prowess in combat. And priests attained status through successful appeals to spiritual powers. There were exceptions to decentralized political systems however. For instance, the **Natchez** along the Gulf Coast and the **Powhatan** of Virginia were inherited chiefdoms, and the **Iroquois** in the Northeast organized a formal confederacy.

> What common beliefs and practices did Indians share, and how did they regard their place in the world?

Even without highly centralized authority though, social order prevailed. Custom demanded compensation if one person or family caused damage or loss to another. For serious offenses such as murder or even accidental death, the rule of retributive justice was applied: the offenders themselves, or their relatives, or even their villages were made to suffer comparable loss or provide appropriate compensation. Frequently, families adopted captured enemies as replacements for lost loved ones.

Extended families comprised the fundamental unit of most Indian societies. Households included parents, children, and grandparents with descent often following the female line. Women presided over most domestic chores, took charge of farming, and participated in political decision-making. For instance, women usually issued the call for "mourning wars" against enemies for the purpose of taking captives to replace villagers who had died. Men hunted and fought with competing tribes. Rearing children was a joint parental responsibility, and typically Indian parents did not hustle children into adulthood but rather indulged them with much playtime. At the other end of the lifespan, elders commanded respect and were often consulted in family and tribal matters.

Indians valued balance and harmony. Disorders ranging from disease to war and famine were thought to result from natural imbalances. Most Indians were territorial, with a clear sense of their native territory. Indians often greeted strangers with gifts in order to lay down a basis for friendly relations; however, trespassers were often treated harshly. Courtesy, common in human interactions, was extended to animals as well; indeed, Indians did not draw sharp distinctions between animals and human beings. Likewise, they blended the natural with the supernatural; spirits and deities coexisted with humans. Like the ancient Mesoamericans, North American Indians regarded celestial objects such as the sun, moon, and stars as

deities or governing spirits that controlled their world and tracked their movement in order to determine the most auspicious time to plant crops, hold religious ceremonies, prepare for hunting, and marry.

North American Indians saw themselves as integrated into nature rather than rising above it. According to Alaskan Eskimo tradition, "In the very first times, both people and animals lived on the earth, but there was no difference between them.... A person could become an animal, and an animal could become a human being." In most Native American belief systems, animals—and humans as well—possessed spirits that lived on after death. Anthropologists call this **animism**. Animals made themselves available to be killed by human beings who owed them respect and were obliged not to mangle the body of a slain animal or leave it to rot. Nor were humans to kill more animals than they needed. To violate any of these taboos would make the spirit of the animal angry, and other animals would refuse to sacrifice themselves to humans.

Indians were not passive when it came to the environment. They managed it, not always well, and often changed it profoundly. The Anasazi had harvested hundreds of thousands of trees for the beams in buildings in Chaco Canyon, and in desert areas, Pueblo Indians followed patterns of irrigation laid down by their Anasazi forebears. Woodlands tribes set low-grade

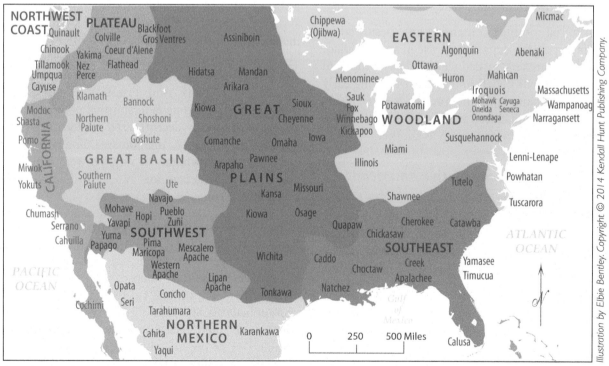

Some of the Native American tribes Who Occupied North America When Europeans Arrived

fires to clear forest land for planting and underbrush to induce the growth of grasses that attracted deer for hunting. Cahokia farmers deliberately reduced bison, deer, and pigeon populations in the vicinity to prevent them from trampling or devouring their crops. Indians were sensitive to and dependent upon the environment, but they could hardly be called environmentalists in the modern sense of trying to keep their physical surroundings exactly the way they found them.

THINKING BACK

1. What advantages and disadvantages did agriculture bring to ancient Native Americans?
2. What similarities and differences existed in the corn-based civilizations of Mesoamerica, the Southwest, and the eastern woodlands?
3. What cultural characteristics did many Native Americans of North America share?

REGIONAL CULTURES IN NATIVE AMERICA

The highly centralized Hohokam, Anasazi, and mound-building civilizations had disappeared by the early sixteenth century, but many other Native American societies flourished at the time of European contact. Although it is impossible to know the exact population size of Native America by 1500, there were perhaps 70 million Native Americans out of 500 million people in the entire world. The vast majority of those Native Americans belonged to the urban societies of South America and Mesoamerica with perhaps 7 million residing north of the Rio Grande River.

Through thousands of years of migration, social interaction, and cultural give and take, the Indians of North America developed many common cultural traits; however, they did not constitute a single, homogeneous people or culture. Instead, Native Americans adjusted their living patterns to the resources and demands of their particular surroundings.

Migratory Indians of the Great Plains and Basin

What kinds of lifestyles characterized the Indians of the Great Plains and Great Basin deserts?

Early in the twentieth century, Hollywood depicted Great Plains Indians as fearsome warriors, mounted on horseback, with feathered headdresses blowing in the wind. These images are mostly caricatures.

Plains Indians actually became riders only after acquiring European horses in the seventeenth and eighteenth centuries.

Sedentary tribes engaged in both hunting and agriculture; nomadic Indians relied more on hunting and foraging. The **Mandan Sioux**, whose circular earthen lodges lined bluffs along the upper Missouri River in present-day North Dakota, were expert corn farmers. They also hunted deer and bison and wild birds. Through rituals and ceremonies, religious leaders appealed to the spirits associated with the sun, the rain, and game animals to provide for their people.

Other hunter-forager groups drifted to the southern Plains. People the Spaniards called **Apaches** migrated from Canada late in the fifteenth century, hunting deer and trapping rabbits and other small animals. They erected temporary brush shelters for protection against rain and cold. The **Navajo**, linguistic relatives of the Apaches, also moved in from Canada, settling in the canyon lands once inhabited by the Anasazi. They established commercial relations with nearby Pueblos and gradually took up farming and Pueblo handcrafts such as weaving and jewelry making. **Comanche** bands relocated from the northern Rockies. They specialized in hunting bison on the southern Plains, carried deer- and antelope-hide teepees for shelter, and traded meat and hides to the Pueblos for corn and beans.

The **Shoshone** and **Paiute** occupied the semi-arid to arid **Great Basin** between the Rocky and Sierra Nevada mountains. Isolated by their rugged environment, they engaged in little if any commercial interaction with outsiders and by the early 1500s had not yet developed agriculture. They designed clothing to protect themselves against severe heat and cold and baskets and shelters for easy portability. Men hunted antelope in teams, running them into corrals constructed of sagebrush and rocks and killing them. Women did the butchering. Boys accompanied adults in the autumn rabbit hunts when the animals' hair was thick. The more people involved in the hunt, the greater the kill and thus the more plentiful was the food and pelt supply.

Native Americans of California and the Pacific Northwest

Numerous and diverse societies dotted the Pacific Northwest. Along the coast, from southern California to Alaska, the climate was relatively mild; the sea and wild plants yielded sufficient food. Inland, however,

What kinds of people inhabited the Pacific Coast, and how did they live?

the environment was harsher and food sources less reliable. Life was more of a struggle.

Most Native Americans of the Northwest coast lived in permanent villages, in homes constructed of heavy timber. There were no unifying governments, but **clans** (families who claimed a common ancestor) united many villages. Marriage within clans was generally forbidden, thus forcing young women and men to take spouses from other villages. Moreover, in many communities matrimony brought men into their wives' families, creating what anthropologists call **matrilineal** families (ones that trace decent through the mother's side).

California's **Chumash** occupied coastal settlements in the vicinity of modern Santa Barbara, including offshore islands. California was one of the most populated regions of ancient North America. From oceangoing plank canoes, Chumash hunters preyed on seals, sea lions, sea otter, swordfish, sardines, halibut, and tuna, supplementing this seafood diet with meat from terrestrial animals like deer and with wild berries and acorns, which they stored in silos made of willow branches. Artisans crafted functional as well as beautiful tools and utensils from local soapstone. Chumash men and women decorated their bodies and garments with shells and mother-of-pearl.

Chinook and **Salish** people living along the forested coastline from Oregon to Alaska also relied heavily on seafood, including whale meat. From seals they took pelts that they sewed into the fur clothing that kept them warm in the damp, chilly climate. They used timber from the woodlands to construct sturdy, flat-roofed plank houses and dugout canoes for whale hunts. They fashioned polished stone into strong, sharp blades used to cut heavy timber and to carve smaller pieces of wood. Elites in most communities conducted highly theatrical "potlatch" ceremonies which featured the feasts and gift-giving that reinforced their high position in society. Chinook and Salish woodworking skills were evident in elaborately carved and painted totem poles that symbolized the people's religious beliefs.

Inland, on the vast plateau of present-day Washington, Idaho, and Oregon, the **Coeur d'Alene**, **Spokane**, and **Yakima** people produced cultures very different from their coastal neighbors. In the summer they hunted deer and elk and gathered berries and roots; in the autumn they set up camps near rivers where they caught spawning salmon and smoked enough of them to last through the snowy winter.

Eastern Hunters and Farmers

How did the various Eastern tribes live?

In the dense woodlands from the Mississippi River to the Atlantic seaboard, the large Native American population was composed of many individual tribal cultures. They spoke at least sixty-eight different languages; competed for territory, food, and captives; and organized themselves in various ways. Like people across ancient North America, tribal lifeways reflected adjustments to the environment and, in many instances, lessons learned from the failure of large-scale agriculture as practiced at ancient Cahokia. For instance, woodlands people typically maintained small gardens of corn, beans, and squash.

Eastern woodlands tribes who lived across the northern rim of the continental forest, from the Great Lakes to Maine and southward along the Atlantic coast to North Carolina, included the **Huron** in Canada and the **Delaware** and **Powhatan** along the east coast of the United States. These tribes spoke related languages that anthropologists classify as **Algonquian**. In present-day Maine, the early autumn frosts and late spring thaws severely limited the growing season; thus, local **Abenaki** people grew only scant quantities of corn and relied largely upon meat from beaver, moose, caribou, mink, squirrels, and rabbits along with salmon, shad, smelt, and sturgeon from the coastal rivers and bays.

To the south, **Wampanoags** occupied villages featuring long, multifamily residences and separate structures for food storage. Residents gathered in central plazas to celebrate feasts and attend ceremonies. Outside the village, Wampanoags managed the landscape for the purpose of hunting and gardening. They cleared thick forest underbrush to induce the growth of grass that attracted deer. Like most agricultural people everywhere, Wampanoags structured their social lives around the rhythm of the changing seasons. During the relatively short summers, women cultivated fields with hoes made from the shoulder blades of deer and fertilized them with fish heads. Like Mesoamericans, they planted mostly corn, beans, and squash. Village men netted fish and lobster. Autumn activities centered on hunting and preserving food to sustain them through the region's very long winters.

Among the **Iroquois,** who occupied the eastern fringe of the Great Lakes and the valleys running through the Appalachian Mountains, women ruled the fields, giving them considerable control of village food supplies and, consequently, political power as well. As heads of family clans, Iroquois women, participated in most important political decisions and presided over the multifamily residences, called **longhouses**, where meetings of representative chiefs, chosen by Iroquois women, took place. Iroquois often call themselves **Haudenosaunee**, or "the people of the longhouses."

Most Iroquois villages erected heavy palisades to protect themselves against enemy attacks, indicating that tension existed among the Iroquois tribes themselves and between them and neighboring Hurons. Conflicts led to the formation of a confederation of five Iroquois tribes—the **Seneca, Cayuga, Onondaga, Oneida**, and **Mohawk**. Iroquois tradition holds that a peacemaker named Deganawida and his disciple Hiawatha founded the **Iroquois League**, probably sometime between 1450 and 1536. Member tribes joined forces to protect each other's interests, and all League decisions required unanimous consent of the tribes in order to preserve the autonomy of each one.

Several Indian societies of the Southeast, descended from the previous mound-builder civilizations, were also present when Europeans arrived. The **Caddos** and **Quapaws** along the Arkansas River and the **Natchez** of the Lower Mississippi Valley flourished as small, limited chiefdoms through the end of the fifteenth century. Other groups lived in communities, raising crops of corn, hunting forest animals, and fishing. **Choctaws** inhabited today's Mississippi and Alabama. Communities of **Creeks** built their houses on earthen mounds, suggesting the lingering influence of the ancient mound-builders. **Cherokees** comprised the region's largest confederacy, incorporating more than sixty towns situated in the southern Appalachian Mountains. Remnants of the Indian societies of the Florida peninsula, among the first to be displaced by European intrusions, later fused into the tribe known as **Seminoles**.

Thus, long before the arrival of Europeans, Native Americans had populated America with many different and complex societies, dynamic communities that constantly adjusted to circumstances and often moved to different locales. Like people in Europe and elsewhere, many Indian societies had made the crucial transition from hunting and gathering to farming. Indian corn enabled Native Americans to build and govern some of the largest cities in the world, albeit sometimes too large to sustain. And like people everywhere throughout time they sought to understand themselves and the world in which they lived. They expressed themselves through artisanship, mathematics, ritual, and music. Over many centuries, the millions of Indians who inhabited ancient North America established and then modified ways of living as circumstances changed. Hardly the inconsequential, almost inanimate, objects that Europeans typically took them to be, they responded to their environment and altered it, not just to survive but to improve their lives.

THINKING BACK

1. What cultural traits characterized the migratory Indians of the Great Plains and Great Basin, the Native Americans of California and the Pacific Northwest, and the inhabitants of the Eastern Woodlands?
2. How do those characteristics show the effect of environment on Native Americans' way of life?

WEST AFRICA

As Indian societies developed in the Americas, major and sometimes corresponding transformations took place in Africa, the world's second largest continent and most likely the birthplace of *homo sapiens*. Conversion to agriculture triggered a population explosion throughout the grassy sub-Saharan prairie known as the Sudan, a vast area of some 3.5 million square miles that divided the African continent into the Muslim and largely Arab north and the mostly black south. Overland trade routes stimulated further growth in the Sudan, linked sub-Saharan Africa through the Mediterranean sea to Europe and Asia, and led to the organization of large kingdoms. In the tropical regions of equatorial West Africa, smaller kingdoms and autonomous villages played a role in the emerging slave trade.

Economic and Social Development of West Africa

Plant cultivation spread from the Middle East to the Nile Valley in Egypt some 7,000 years ago. From there, agriculture expanded across the Sudan, reaching West Africa 2,000 years

How did agriculture, iron, and commerce affect the societies of West Africa?

ago and subsequently advancing southward into tropical forest regions in equatorial Africa. In the Sudan, the principal crops included cereal grains like millet and sorghum. In addition, residents raised cattle. To the south, yams, bananas, rice (from Asia), goats, and fowl were major food sources. Metallurgy, a science probably acquired from North Africa, developed extensively in Benin, which became a center of iron mining, smelting, and manufacturing. Iron tools proved a boon to agricultural production. By the beginning of the fifteenth century, the spread of mixed agriculture—farming and herding—along with ironwork accompanied the migration of Bantu-speaking people from Nigeria to eastern and southern Africa.

As in America, the shift to agriculture profoundly altered African social patterns. People settled in permanent villages with clay and matted-roof dwellings and storage facilities. Villages usually comprised extended families, some patriarchal and others matriarchal, and most communities featured a gender division of labor that made women responsible for the fields and the rearing of small children and put men in charge of hunting, herding, and war. Clans widened kinship networks and knit villages together.

Community well-being was closely tied to traditional West African religion. People typically believed in a supreme creator who invested all things with spirits whose good will had to be ritually solicited. Lesser gods oversaw the sun, moon, and water, and they too had to be honored to keep them favorably disposed toward the community. Rituals that included sacred places, objects, and dances and music were intended to elicit the gods' favor. Kinship networks also reached into the spirit world. Dead ancestors possessed the power to mediate on behalf of the living against evil spirits that might inflict such harm as

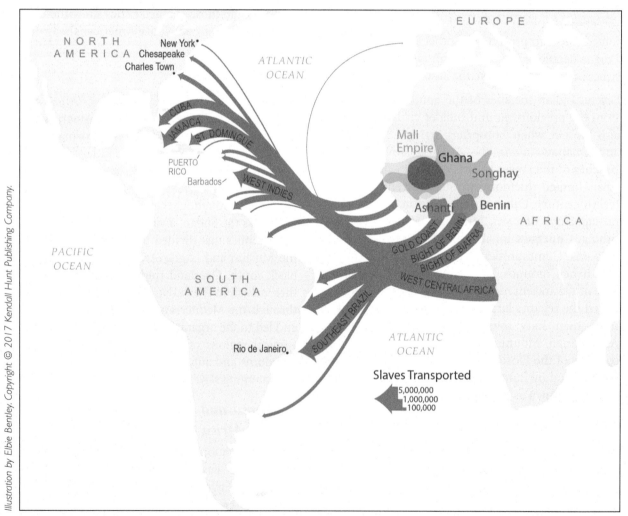

Once powerful sub-Saharan empires had declined substantially by the sixteenth century, and by the eighteenth century West African supplied millions of enslaved laborers to European plantations in the Americas.

illness and ruinous drought. Funeral ceremonies helped the dead on their journey into the spirit world, where they gained the power to protect and to speak directly to their living relatives.

Villages were also politically organized under head-men or chiefs. Affiliated villages formed provinces under the administration of provincial governors. Provinces frequently coalesced into kingdoms. Rulers, from village chiefs to kings, usually possessed some perceived ability to communicate with the spirits that controlled the physical environment. They also wielded military power. Successful rulers, however, were more than mere dictators. They were politicians who built coalitions of village, tribal, and clan leaders by bestowing gifts on them and attending to their people's needs.

Between the eighth and tenth centuries, yet another development helped transform West Africa: commerce with the Muslim-dominated Mediterranean world. Arab merchants in North Africa led camel caravans laden with salt, silk, cotton, and beads south across the Sahara in exchange for gold from the West African **Gold Coast.** Merchant caravans transported tons of gold each year back through North Africa into Europe and Asia. Trans-Saharan commerce stimulated the rise of urban centers and also introduced Islamic culture into the heartland of Africa, including financial record keeping, written language, and building techniques.

Commerce also met a growing demand for slave labor. For centuries, Africans had enslaved lawbreakers and prisoners taken in war. Most slaves worked as servants in the households of elite families; enslaved women often became concubines. But many slaves toiled in gold mines. African slaves maintained their own farms or practiced trades on the side, and typically a slave's status was not passed to other family members. Merchants occasionally transported slaves across the Sahara to Arab, Ottoman, and even European households.

The Rise of African Empires

How were West African empires ruled, and what changes did they trigger?

Commerce certainly fostered the development of large and powerful empires. Starting in the ninth century, strongmen in Ghana, Mali, and Songhai built vast kingdoms in West and Northwest Africa (see map on p. 24). At the

The association of Africans with the degradation of slavery can overshadow the technical skill and creative imagination of African artistry and craftsmanship.

same time, skilled diplomats in much smaller Benin kept more powerful neighbors at bay and preserved their own independence.

West African kings ruled largely through military power. Tenkamenin, who reigned over ancient **Ghana**, commanded an army of 200,000. But imperial rulers also possessed a perceived ability to mediate with powerful spirits, and that mystical power gave them a sort of "divine right" to rule. Ghana's kings sat atop a social hierarchy from which they extracted tax revenues, largely from the gold trade. As one visitor to ancient Ghana observed: "Its king is mighty, and in his lands are gold mines. Under his authority are various other kingdoms—and in all this region there is gold."

Mali was larger, better organized, and even more powerful than Ghana, which it ultimately supplanted. Mali's king, Mansa Musa, who converted to Islam, encouraged the expansion of Muslim culture in West

Africa. **Songhai**, stronger still, reached its zenith early in the sixteenth century. Around 1500, a visiting merchant noted that the Songhay metropolis of Timbuktu contained a "great store of doctors, judges, priests, and other learned men that are bountifully maintained at the king's cost and charges. And hitherto are brought diverse manuscripts or written books out of . . . the north African states, from Egypt to the Atlantic Ocean which are sold for more money than any other merchandise."

By the end of the sixteenth century the great empires of West Africa had fallen. Smaller coastal kingdoms remained, but great change was in store as European explorers and merchants began to penetrate the region at the close of the fifteenth century.

THINKING BACK

1. How did agriculture and the rise of empires transform the people of West Africa?
2. What impact did the trans-Saharan caravan trade have on the people and societies of West Africa?

THE BEGINNINGS OF MODERN EUROPE

Historians call the segment of European history between the collapse of the Roman Empire in 476 and the Renaissance of the late 1400s the **Middle Ages**, and during that time, Europe underwent an extended transformation. The changes resulted in part from powerful invasions that brought destruction and new cultural influences. First, migratory waves of Germanic and Slavic settlers swept from east to west across Europe, followed by Arab and Turkish Muslims (see the Global Perspective, p. 3), **Scandinavian** raiders, and finally **Mongol** hordes from Central Asia. Then between 1346 and 1353, a horrible plague known as the **Black Death** devastated both Europe and Asia. "A third of the world died," reported a contemporary chronicler. He may have exaggerated, but the pandemic did wipe out as many as 20 million Europeans—perhaps as much as half the continent's population. Although many people interpreted the plague as an act of God, the immediate culprit was probably a deadly bacterium or perhaps a virus transmitted by rodent fleas. Reeling from these assaults, Europeans hunkered down in defensive postures. But adjustment and recovery ensued; Europeans gradually rebuilt their

societies, broke out of their protective isolation, and became aggressively expansionist. By 1500, Europe was ready for global extensions of its power.

The Rise and Demise of Feudalism

The upheavals of the Middle Ages put Europe on the defensive, a situation illustrated by the large number of stone castles built by noble lords to protect themselves, their families, and others who lived within their domains. Europeans also improvised various hierarchical social relationships that historians call **feudalism**. Noble lords, who ruled absolutely over their territories, retained armies commanded by lesser warrior **vassals**. Lords rewarded their vassals' loyalty with estates, or fiefs, along with privileged status. Wealthy landowners, whether lords or warrior vassals, in turn held dominion over peasants on their manors. Landlords protected the **peasants** and gave them small strips of land to farm in return for rent payments and, above all, the peasants' allegiance. Some peasants fell into a slave-like condition called **serfdom,** and the least fortunate became outright slaves—Eastern European Slavs for instance, whose ethnic name provided the root for the English word "slave."

> How did the European social system known as feudalism work, and why did it decline?

Few Europeans in feudal times enjoyed control over their lives. Typically, the conditions of their birth determined the kind of life they were destined to live. Being born a peasant meant a bare existence. Prices and wages were pitifully low. Peasant women worked in the fields alongside men and bore the additional burden of oppressive laws and customs that rendered them legally inferior to men. When a woman married, she relinquished to her husband most of her rights and all of her property. And being born a peasant meant, in most cases, dying a peasant. The nobility enjoyed much more opportunity than common folks, but their status was inherited and closed off to commoners. Noble lords controlled the bulk of Europe's forests and farmland, and with land ownership came not only wealth but also high social standing and political power. Lordly families maintained their property intact and their noble titles from one generation to the next through **primogeniture**, laws and customs that allowed eldest sons to inherit their fathers' entire estates. The younger brothers of privileged sons often found careers as priests, bureaucrats, or vassals while their sisters' best chances for comfortable and rewarding lives came by marrying into other landed families. The result of this situation was **aristocracy**— a society dominated by a few wealthy and privileged individuals holding all the valuable lands for centuries.

During the later Middle Ages, Europe's fragmented feudal structures slowly combined into more centralized **nation-states**. Smart, energetic, and resourceful lords employed their armed followers to conquer weaker lords, or they married strategically into other noble families. By whatever means, dominant lords forced inferior ones to acknowledge their sovereignty and to pledge their allegiance. The most triumphant lords became royal **monarchs** (kings and queens) who established some of the most fundamental institutions of modern government: legislatures for enacting laws (England's Parliament for instance), bureaucracies for collecting taxes, law-enforcement officials for extending royal power throughout the nation, and courts for punishing offenders. The monarchs allied themselves with the Catholic Church, thereby acquiring Christian authority, or a **Divine right to rule**. Meanwhile, the peasants and vassals began to shift their allegiance to the state, which the monarchs personified. Nation-states promoted national and ethnic identity as well, including common national languages and cultural pride. But one important feudal principle remained intact, though often more in theory than in practice: if a monarch broke faith with his underlings, they were no longer obligated to him. Frequent peasant revolts and plots against monarchs attest to that reality.

By the end of the fifteenth century, the countries farthest along the road to nationhood were England, France, Portugal, and Spain. In what historians call the **Hundred Years War** (1337–1453), English and French royal families, descended from common French ancestors and supported by rising nationalism, battled for control of France. Despite England's superior military organization and the staggering devastation inflicted on the French people, France proved too much for England to swallow. England mostly relinquished its claim to French territory, but the spirit of nationalism engendered among both the English and the French fueled an intense and persistent rivalry. Meanwhile, Portugal also emerged as a unified nation-state on the Iberian Peninsula, and in 1462, next door, a campaign to expel the Islamic Moors (see the Global Perspective, p. 3), combined with the marriage of Queen Isabella of Castille and King Fernando of Aragon, united Europe's largest Spanish-speaking domains under a dual monarchy.

Suddenly Spain stood at the pinnacle of power on the European continent.

The Spanish Reconquest

Three major events combined to launch Spain into prominence among European nations in the fifteenth century. One was the political marriage of Fernando and Isabella. Another was the successful and profitable voyage of Christopher Columbus under the flag of Spain. The third event was the final victory of the Spanish Christians over the Muslim invaders in 1492. The Muslims, a mixture of Arabs and Berbers from North Africa known as **Moors**, had dominated Spanish Christians since invading the Iberian peninsula in 711 C.E. Indeed, the Spanish unification and the defeat of the Moors explains why Spain was the only nation that could support the expedition of Columbus that year. And the victory of the Spanish Christians had the most lasting influence on European conquest and domination in the Western Hemisphere.

> **What characteristics did the Reconquest imprint on the Spaniards who came to America?**

Spaniards were the first Europeans to conquer and settle in the Western Hemisphere, and they set in motion many of the patterns of conquest and domination for the following waves of European immigrants. Spain's national character was forged by the fire of almost 800 years of fierce warfare to regain the Iberian Peninsula for Christianity. The Spaniards called this struggle *La Reconquista*, or **The Reconquest**. Devotion to their Catholic faith made them among Christianity's most militant defenders. It gave them an intolerant view of Islam and other religions, and it gave them a powerful army that fought fiercely and took no prisoners. Ironically, Moorish domination had cast a strong cultural influence on the Spaniards as well. After 800 years under Moorish overlords, Spaniards had adopted the Arabic diet of mutton, rice, chickpeas, carrots, watermelon, citrus fruits, and sugar. They learned Arabic medical practices, irrigation, and a mathematics called algebra. They adopted not only cavalry tactics from Moorish soldiers, but also the Arabs' love for and loyalty to their monarch. Spanish women learned to dance to Arab musical chords, to ride side saddle, and to wear facial veils as Moorish women had done among them for 800 years. Eventually, Spanish men learned to ride, fight, and conquer better than their Moorish invaders. Spaniards never developed feudalism to the same extent as the French and English had.

Spanish men were more valuable as free soldiers than as serfs; moreover, Spanish commoners did not develop a serf's resentment of aristocrats and monarchs, but instead grew to respect them. By 1492 in Spain, royal authority and military power were combined under a Catholic King, *El Rey Católico*.

The Reconquest unified Spain as a dominant military power, ready to spread its conquest across the oceans. It cast a militant imprint on the Spanish people, their religion, and their monarchy. But its deepest impact would be on the conquered Native American peoples of the Western Hemisphere who would be dominated for centuries by male, intolerant, and Catholic Spanish soldiers who arrogantly called themselves conquerors, *Los Conquistadores*.

The Commercial Revolution

> **What brought on the Commercial Revolution, and how did it impact Europe?**

Feudalism had been based on the land, and most of the emerging nation-states were territorial ones, but by the late Middle Ages many Europeans were moving into towns, stimulating vibrant commercial economies and political power largely independent of monarchical control.

The terrifying Mongol armies under Genghis and the other great khans that swept simultaneously into eastern Europe and China during the thirteenth century actually helped spark Europe's **Commercial Revolution**. Europeans responded to the Mongol invasions with diplomatic initiatives intended not only to restore peace in Europe but also to expand European influence into distant lands. Accompanying European diplomats into the capitals of the Mongol khans, mendicant friars belonging to the Catholic Church's Franciscan and Dominican orders established enclaves of Western Christianity. At roughly the same time, in 1271, the Venetian Marco Polo traveled to China and wrote a fascinating account of his adventures. Polo's descriptions of Asian products caught the attention of European merchants who envisioned enormous profits through trade. By the fifteenth century, merchants in the Mediterranean basin, the Italian cities of Venice and Genoa and the Portuguese port of Lisbon especially, were deeply engaged in Asian commerce. In exchange for cotton textiles from India, spices from Southeast Asia, and silk and porcelain from China, European merchants exported woolens, linen, metals, and animal hides, making up for the lower value of European products with African gold.

The principal arteries of the early Asian trade ran through the Red Sea and the Persian Gulf to the Indian Ocean, or through the Black Sea and overland by caravan across central Asia (see the map on p. 4). Both routes were long and dangerous. Losses to bandits and pirates, natural hazards, and customs duties bit deeply into profits. Portuguese mariners sailed along the west coast of Africa searching for new, shorter, and safer shipping routes between Europe and Asia. In 1488 the Portuguese navigator Bartolomeo Dias rounded the southern tip of Africa, subsequently named the Cape of Good Hope because it led into the Indian Ocean and the rich markets of India. Dias' nervous crew forced him back to Portugal before reaching his goal, but in 1498 Dias' countryman Vasco da Gama, accompanied by an African Muslim navigator, completed the voyage to India.

Expanding commerce and contact with Asia nurtured new attitudes, institutions, and processes that pushed European economies toward modern **capitalism**. The accumulation of cash and credit, a sense of adventure, and the aggressive pursuit of new opportunities developed among merchants in northern European towns as well—Hamburg, Bruges, and Antwerp. These city merchants gained virtual control of trade between the ports of Northern and Western Europe and those in the Mediterranean, Africa, and Asia with innovations like business registers that kept track of debts, contracts, and revenues and facilitated the development of banking and credit. They also constructed "factories," which were not really manufacturing facilities but rather storage buildings used for distribution of commodities. Factories along the west coast of Africa became trade centers and depots for the later transatlantic slave trade.

The success of European merchants resulted in the accumulation of wealth that altered European cultures. Asian imports introduced Europeans not only to spices and fine cloth but also to eating utensils. Table manners improved and a more refined aristocratic culture emerged among the wealthy. Part of this culture was a renewed appreciation for art and learning, particularly among the European elite.

Advances in Technology

Europe's expanding commerce with Asia and eventually the European encounter with America might not have been possible without several

> **What new technologies facilitated European expansion?**

technological inventions and improvements. An efficient printing press with movable type, invented in the 1440s, made it possible to publish and distribute large amounts of information, including geographic and technical data. Many ancient texts, which contained the most current and complete data concerning astronomy and global geography, circulated among educated Europeans. In addition, publication was in vernacular European languages, not just Greek and Latin, which widened public access to printed information. New navigational devices, especially the **compass**, which Europeans acquired from the Chinese, made extended sea voyages safer and more feasible. Most European navigators relied on the magnetized compass needle to indicate direction and charts prepared by experienced mariners to show their location. Previously, mariners had no reliable way of determining direction in open water, particularly under cloud cover; thus most previous maritime navigation had been within sight of land.

Advances in ship design also facilitated the growth of commerce. Mediterranean shippers favored a type of vessel known as the **caravel**, a small, fast, and highly maneuverable sailing craft ideally suited for exploring uncharted coastal areas. The caravel was a marked improvement over bulkier vessels that displaced more water and thus moved more slowly and required greater wind power. Portuguese engineers designed the caravel's sleek hull, while the rigging originated among Arab mariners. Rotating triangular, or lateen, sails allowed the caravel to sail under more varied wind conditions than the fixed "square" rigging of traditional European sailing vessels. The ship's shallow draft meant that it did not sit deep in the water, enabling it to float across treacherous shallows.

Firearms also served Europeans well. **Gunpowder**, developed by the Chinese, and the weapons that utilized it provided Europeans with a tactical advantage over less technologically advanced people they encountered in their global explorations. Even before muskets and cannons became very accurate and capable of inflicting much harm, the explosions they caused struck fear into enemies who had never seen or heard them. This was the expanding European world.

THINKING BACK

1. How did feudalism work, and why did it begin to decline late in the Middle Ages?

2. How did the Commercial Revolution and advances in science and technology prepare Europeans for world exploration?

CONCLUSION

American history did not begin when Europeans "discovered" America. It started long before. What was once thought to be a New World was actually an ancient world inhabited and managed by numbers of diverse peoples. From Alaska to today's Mexican borderlands, the first people to live in what became the United States designed tools, developed crops, built cities, traded widely, and worshipped spiritual forces they believed controlled their world. They were not a single, unified group but a number of diverse groups speaking different languages, living in and adapting to different environments, and following different customs. They derived their personal identities from particular families, clans, tribes, and kingdoms. Still, common traits were apparent, mostly cultural characteristics that resulted from their environment. Their cultural legacy remains visible in contemporary American culture, as in place names like Massachusetts, Mississippi, and Dakota, the widespread cultivation of corn, and irrigated farming in much of the arid West.

Meanwhile, across the Atlantic Ocean, African and European economic, political, and technological development set the stage for the convergence of three different but in some ways similar worlds. Neither Africans nor Europeans constituted a unified people any more than the Native Americans did, but in Europe the beginnings of nationalism and national identity were emerging. The consolidation of political power, the commercial revolution and expanding trade, and advances in learning and technology established important values and institutions that would eventually become part of the culture of the United States. "A man cannot set his hand to more liberal work than making money," proclaimed the fifteenth-century Italian writer Leon Battista Alberti, or, as the account book of a contemporary businessman read: "In the name of God and profit."

European and African values differed strikingly from those of Native Americans half a world away. These different worlds had much to offer each other. The question was, how would they interact and what would be the impact of their encounter? Would they share or try to impose their ways on the other?

SUGGESTED SOURCES FOR STUDENTS

Colin G. Calloway, *One Vast Winter Count: The Native American West before Lewis and Clark* (2003), is a superb, easy-to-read and understand treatment of Native Americans of the Western United States. The book pays close attention to how Western Indians adapted their cultures to regional environments.

Carlo M. Cipolla, *Before the Industrial Revolution: European Society and Economy, 1000-1700* (1996), presents an examination of the important commercial revolution in Europe.

Vine Deloria, Jr., *Red Earth, White Law: Native Americans and the Myth of Scientific Fact* (1995), asserts that white historians have distorted history to make immigrants of American aboriginal Indians.

Thomas D. Dillehay, *The Settling of the Americas: A New Prehistory* (2000), has reset the timetable for the initial settlement of North and South America. The archaeologist who excavated Monte Verde, a Paleo-Indian site in Chile that is now the oldest in the Americas, Dillehay and his findings reopened the question of when and how the first human beings came to North America.

Kathleen Du Val, *The Native Ground: Indians and Colonists in the Heart of the Continent* (2006), discusses the relationships that Native Americans had with the land, including a sense of ownership, as well with neighboring Indians and colonizing Europeans.

Patricia Galloway, *Choctaw Genesis, 1500-1700* (1995), is a remarkable, pioneering study of the origins of one of the major Indian cultures of the Southeast. Drawing an incredible amount of information from three early Spanish accounts from the sixteenth and early seventeen centuries and research in many archaeological sites, she accounts for the formation of Choctaw culture.

Alvin M. Josephy, ed., *America in 1492: The World of the Indian Peoples Before the Arrival of Columbus* (1991), is a valuable collection of essays by specialists in early Native American history that describes various groups of Indian people who occupied North America and the islands of the Caribbean at the time of Christopher Columbus. The first section presents Native American societies by region and the second examines their cultures topically.

Calvin Luther Martin, *The Way of the Human Being* (1999), offers a probing and sensitive treatment of Native American worldviews. Martin puts the reader into the mind of Native Americans and contrasts what the Native American sees with what European-Americans perceive. The book is both historical and contemporary, and the author suggests ways that the two points of view might converge.

William H. McNeil, *The Rise of the West* (1963), remains the standard history of Europe during the late Middle Ages and Renaissance.

John Reader, *Africa: A Biography of a Continent* (1998), offers a broad view of Africa from the appearance of *homo sapiens* to the present. Written in a lively style with a general audience in mind, the book approaches ancient Africa and its people from a historical rather than an archaeological perspective, leading some archaeologists to complain, but for an overview it is solid and highly readable.

David E. Stannard, *American Holocaust: The Conquest of the New World* (1992), estimates that 100 million Native Americans populated the Americas before the arrival of Europeans. The precipitous decline in that number after the arrival of Europeans he characterizes as nothing short of genocide. Early estimates of Indian numbers tended to be much lower than what scholars today accept, perhaps to downplay the staggering losses that Native Americans suffered.

Merlin Stone, *When God Was a Woman* (1978), draws important comparisons and contrasts between women in Europe and in Native America.

Barbara Tuchman, *A Distant Mirror: The Calamitous 14th Century* (1978), describes in vivid style the condition of Europe in the late Middle Ages. The award-winning historian highlights the Black Death and the Hundred Years' War.

Sally Roesch Wagner, *Sisters in Spirit: Haudenosaunee (Iroquois) Influences on Early American Feminists* (2001), examines the importance of women in Native American societies and their later influence on women's roles in the United States, an often-overlooked but key subject

BEFORE WE GO ON

1. What similarities do you see in the civilizations of America, Africa, and Europe at the end of the fifteenth century?

2. How did the civilizations of America, Africa, and Europe differ from each other?

Building a Democratic Nation

3. Democracy, as a concept for social and political organization, did not exist in the centuries before 1500; indeed, certain aspects of American Indian, African, and European civilizations stifled any movement in that direction. What aspects of those cultures would have to change before democracy could take root?

4. Assume that you could make a new world of freedom and democracy by choosing the most important traditions in Native American, West African, and European worlds. Which ones would you select?

Connections

5. What similarities can you identity between the way Indian cultures adapted to local environments and modern regional cultures in the United States?

6. As you look at the United States of today, what do you observe that might be traced back to or be somehow analogous to aspects of ancient Native American civilizations? Similarly, what do you see that might have originated in Africa and Europe? What could have just as easily derived from any of the three?

Chapter 2

EUROPEAN CONQUEST, 1492–1600

A PERSONAL PERSPECTIVE: ALVAR NUÑEZ CABEZA DE VACA, A EUROPEAN ENCOUNTERS A NATIVE AMERICAN WORLD

Cabeza De Vaca and a Handful of Other Survivors Wash Ashore on What Later Would be Known as Galveston Island by Barbara Whitehead. Courtesy of Wittliff Collections, Texas State University, San Marcos.

> **How did Cabeza de Vaca and the Indians of coastal Texas differ from each other?**

In November of 1528, two makeshift barges carrying ninety-six famished and exhausted Spaniards washed ashore on Galveston Island in present-day Texas. Remnants of an army of conquest, these castaways came from the Mediterranean world. For the next eight years they dwelled among various Native Americans (the Spaniards called them Indians) in a very different world. The leader of the band, Alvar Nuñez Cabeza de Vaca, later gave Spanish authorities an account of his experiences, and his personal perspective allows us to see how he and Native Americans perceived each other.

For thousands of years, Europeans and Native Americans had not known of each other's existence. Separated by the Atlantic Ocean, they developed very different ways of life, or **cultures**. For instance, Cabeza de Vaca did not recognize governmental authority among these Karankawa Indians—no kings or princes, courts or judges like in Europe. Also unlike most Europeans, who lived their entire lives as farmers and herders exactly where they were born, the Indians moved from one location to the other with the changing seasons. During the cold winter months, they resided in coastal villages, sleeping in brush shelters and warming themselves by fire. They did not cultivate crops or raise livestock; instead, they gathered shellfish, potato-like roots, pecans, and mesquite beans. In late spring, women loaded their families' belongings on their backs, and everyone moved inland where the women and children harvested wild prickly pear cactus while the men and older boys hunted rabbits, javelinas (mammals that resemble pigs), deer, and occasionally bison. Cabeza de Vaca noted that they made tools and weapons—like scrapers, diggers, bows, and arrows—but out of wood, bone, and stone instead of metal like Europeans.

Having long since adapted to their environment, the Indians of coastal Texas seemed in much better condition than the Spaniards. Like most travelers in foreign lands, Cabeza de Vaca took note of the local residents; he described the Indian men as "tall and handsome" and the women as attractive and graceful. And the Indians must have noticed that these haggard foreigners looked, as Cabeza de Vaca himself put it, "like the very image of death." Indeed, since the Spaniards had lost everything coming ashore, even their clothes, they were literally and metaphorically naked and dependent on the Indians for survival. But adapting to their new situation was not as difficult as it might seem, for the Spaniards found many aspects of the Indians' ways similar to their own. For instance, Cabeza de Vaca, like the Indians, believed that spirits exerted power, for ill and for good, over living people. Once, when villagers asked him to heal a deathly ill man, he waved a Christian cross very much like Native Americans used talismans to drive away harmful spirits. When the patient recovered, Cabeza de Vaca quickly gained a reputation as a healer and thereafter was accorded greater freedom. He also inserted himself into the Indians' trade economy, bartering such products as combs and bows and arrows, which actually resembled items Europeans had used for centuries.

Cabeza de Vaca's narrative offers many important insights, but his personal perspective was limited by

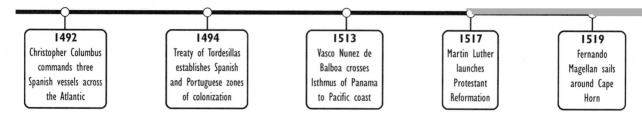

1492	**1494**	**1513**	**1517**	**1519**
Christopher Columbus commands three Spanish vessels across the Atlantic	Treaty of Tordesillas establishes Spanish and Portuguese zones of colonization	Vasco Nunez de Balboa crosses Isthmus of Panama to Pacific coast	Martin Luther launches Protestant Reformation	Fernando Magellan sails around Cape Horn

his own experience and understanding. His account does not tell us everything he saw and thought, nor was he completely objective in his assessments of himself and the Native Americans he encountered. Like most people—Europeans, Africans, Asians, and Native Americans—Cabeza de Vaca believed he and his own people were superior to all others. He was a literate Christian and Spaniard and proud of it; Indians, on the other hand, had no written language, and because they were not Christians he classified them as **heathens**. And while he noted cultural differences from tribe to tribe, he believed they were all uncivilized and thus fundamentally inferior to Europeans. Thus, while Cabeza de Vaca came to respect the Indians in many ways, he could never fully comprehend them, and therefore his account was distinctly biased.

Fortunately, our understanding of early, pre-literate Native-American societies does not depend entirely on the personal perspectives of outsiders. Archaeologists have discovered tools, pottery, textiles, and even foods that have survived through the ages, giving us detailed although incomplete pictures of ancient Indian societies. Excavations in south Texas where Cabeza de Vaca visited have yielded spear and arrow points chipped out of **obsidian**, a type of volcanic glass not naturally present in that area. In all likelihood, local Indians acquired the obsidian by trading seashells with people far to the south in Mexico. Such archaeological information sometimes corroborates and sometimes contradicts the accounts of eyewitnesses like Cabeza de Vaca. Thus in attempting to comprehend the people who lived ages ago, historians look at the past from many different perspectives.

Historians once taught that American history began when Europeans arrived on the scene and turned a wilderness into a civilized and ultimately a democratic nation. But long before their encounters with Europeans, Native Americans had organized complex societies. They were originally immigrants too, probably migrating from Asia as they hunted and gathered food. Most of them eventually took up some form of agriculture, and some built large cities and mighty empires.

Across the Atlantic, similar transformations took place. On the African continent, ancient people converted from hunting and foraging to agriculture and industry, likewise producing prosperous and powerful kingdoms. Overland caravans hauled gold from equatorial regions northward across the vast Sahara Desert into the commercial Mediterranean economy. They returned bearing valuable trade goods and many foreign influences, including Islam.

By the end of the fifteenth century, changes had also begun to reshape Europe. Politically and culturally unified societies merged into complex nation-states. Powerful rulers commanded vast resources for exploration and conquest, demanded the allegiance of large populations, and helped to form national identities. A Commercial Revolution transformed Atlantic-facing economies and set the stage for European intrusions into Asia, Africa, and North America.

Cabeza de Vaca's encounter with Native Americans was not the first episode in the epic story of building a democratic nation, coming as it did almost two generations after Columbus. But it does illustrate some important elements of the story, particularly the disparate people from far-flung parts of the world, very different in many ways yet in others very much alike, who found themselves face-to-face on the same landscape.

THINKING BACK

1. How would you differentiate between the cultures that Cabeza de Vaca observed and his own native culture? How were they similar? How was Cabeza de Vaca's account biased?
2. Ancient Native Americans left no written documents, and Cabeza de Vaca's account is insufficient for reconstructing the complex world of early North American Indians. How can artifacts like obsidian points combine with historical documents to help us understand how Native Americans lived?

1519–21	1521	1524	1526	1528–36
Cortés conquers the Aztecs	Ponce de Leon shows Spaniards that Florida is part of North America	Giovanni da Verrazzano explores upper Atlantic coast	Lucas Vasquez de Ayllon establishes first European colony in what became the United States	Spaniards explore Gulf coast from Florida to Texas and Cabeza de Vaca leads survivors across Southwest to Mexico

THE EUROPEAN ARRIVAL

During the last years of the fifteenth century, Western Europeans dramatically circumvented the centuries-old monopoly that Mediterranean powers had held over global commerce (see the Global Perspective, pp. 2-4). Europe's global expansion had been prepared by decades of crusades against Muslims along with growing commerce within Europe itself and long distance with the Middle East and Asia. Adventure, ambition, and religious zeal drove a handful of daring souls to explore a world still largely unknown to them. Years before Columbus, Italian and Basque fishermen netted cod off the coast of today's Newfoundland. Whether they encountered coastal woodlands people is not certain but likely. What later arrivals found in the Caribbean islands surprised them very much, for they believed they had reached Asia. Ironically, the Native Americans the newcomers encountered were probably descendants of ancient Asian immigrants. The first Spanish explorers and the Native Americans of the Caribbean islands, Florida, and Mexico viewed each other through cultural lenses that distorted what they saw. Spaniards soon resolved to conquer Native Americans and establish permanent colonies in America.

The Age of Exploration

What inspired the early seafaring explorers?

For ages, the sea had charmed and challenged Europeans. In the eleventh century, Viking adventurers led by Leif Ericsson established a settlement in North America called Vinland (today's Newfoundland), which they soon abandoned. Most Europeans of the late fifteenth century knew nothing about the Vikings, and only recently have archeological excavations unearthed the remains of their long wooden houses. Myths about islands of paradise, however, far to the west in the Atlantic Ocean, did circulate through Europe during the Middle Ages. Ancient poets had written of lands of "pure delight" beyond the horizon, about the lost cities of Atlantis and Antilia, and about the voyages of St. Brendan, an Irish mariner who allegedly reached North America in the sixth century. Such tales inspired seafaring Europeans to their own feats of exploration. So did more mundane attractions, like codfish. In all likelihood, English and Spanish fishermen dried their catches on the shores of Nova Scotia and Newfoundland as early as the 1450s.

In addition to achieving personal glory, these European voyagers hoped to get rich and to spread Christianity. Italian merchants had become wealthy from trade between Europe and Asia through the Mediterranean Sea. But merchants in Western Europe considered how to bypass the Mediterranean. European-Asian commerce might yield even greater profits if the losses and expenses involved in the long sea and overland routes could be substantially reduced. And if in the process, non-Christian people could be converted to the Catholic faith, so much the better. For the Catholic Church, exploration became an important means for advancing Christianity.

Such thoughts inspired the seafaring explorer Christopher Columbus. What distinguished Columbus from earlier explorers was that he led a national enterprise, his exploits were published, and he initiated a permanent migration of settlers. It remains uncertain just when and how this son of a Genoese cloth weaver reached the conclusion that he could sail west across the Atlantic to the Indies (as most Europeans referred to India and its neighboring islands), but it was an idea that other mariners had already pondered. Educated Europeans of the time, Columbus included, understood that the earth was round. Ancient scientists, especially the Egyptian-born geographer and Roman citizen named Claudius Ptolemy, had demonstrated that fact, and during the Middle Ages European scholars had recovered and translated Ptolemy's texts, especially his *Geography*. Disagreement about the earth's size and the layout of oceans and continents existed, however, since

1535	1538	1539–42	1540–42	1579
Jacques Cartier explores St. Lawrence River	Fray Marcos de Niza leads expedition to find *Cibola*	Hernando de Soto explores the Southeast	Francisco Vasquez de Coronado explores the Southwest	Francis Drake explores California coast on voyage around the world

there was then no known method of measuring it. In his calculations, based on Ptolemy's *Geography* as well as a plethora of recent maps, charts, and travelers' accounts, Columbus still overestimated the breadth of **Eurasia** and then compounded the error by underestimating the earth's circumference by about one fourth.

Columbus' calculations—erroneous though they were—convinced him that crossing the Atlantic Ocean by ship was feasible. He had courage enough to try, but he needed financial support to buy seaworthy vessels, equip and supply them, and hire crews. What followed, then, was not the heroic achievement of one person but rather a large-scale joint enterprise involving many men and women.

Seeking Royal Backing

> **Where did the financing for Columbus' voyage come from?**

Interest in discovery was widespread and navigators sought financial backing from European monarchs regardless of nationality. Since he resided in Portugal and knew of Portuguese interest in exploring new sea routes to the Indies, Columbus appealed to King Joao II (John II) for support. But the Portuguese monarch turned down the proposition, partly because of Portugal's commitment to establishing a route south and east around Africa (see map p. 4). In addition, Joao II doubted Columbus' calculations, as did a committee of experts who reviewed the plan.

Rejected by the Portuguese, Columbus next appealed to the two Spanish sovereigns Isabella and Fernando. Preoccupied at the moment with conquering Muslim-controlled areas of Spain (see the Global Perspective, p. 3), they initially declined Columbus' solicitation, but in 1492, with the Muslims finally defeated, the Spanish monarchs agreed to supply Columbus with three ships, crews to man them, and the necessary provisions for a trans-Atlantic expedition.

The royal couple's reward would be riches, glory, and God's favor, but Columbus stood to gain handsomely too. Fernando and Isabella bestowed upon him the title "Admiral of the Ocean Sea" (as the Atlantic was then called), and named him Governor-General of any lands he might discover. The monarchs also assented to Columbus' demand for 10 percent of "all gold, silver, pearls, gems, spices, and other merchandise" he might find. A half-hour before dawn on August 3, 1492, the day after the Catholic Church ordered Jews expelled from Christian Spain as part of a program of religious cleansing, Columbus' flotilla put to sea from the tiny port of Palos. Fear and intolerance thus joined hands with soaring aspirations, opposite sides of the human spirit, on this momentous day.

The Momentous Voyage

The three vessels, two caravels known as *Pinta* and *Niña* and the larger, slower flagship called *Santa Maria*, sailed south to pick up trans-Atlantic trade winds. They took on provisions in the Canary Islands, and from there the ships' sails caught the steady breezes that carried them westward. Throughout the trip, Columbus lied to his crew about how far they had gone so they would not become discouraged. After four weeks at sea, he told them they were near the **Indies**. Then in the predawn moonlight of October 12, a spotter caught sight of an island in what is called today the Caribbean Sea, near modern Florida. Full of excitement, the flotilla sailed through the present-day Bahamas, encountering the native people and looking for signs of the gold and great cities they expected to see.

What mixed thoughts must have raced through the minds of the crewmembers? Expecting to find large and prosperous cities, they saw only villages of nearly naked natives. But the reality before them did not dim their

> **To what extent did Christopher Columbus fulfill his promise to the Spanish crown?**

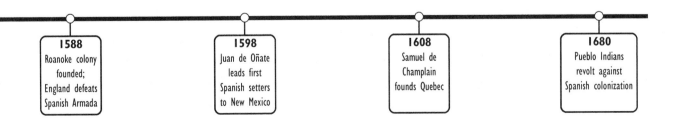

1588	1598	1608	1680
Roanoke colony founded; England defeats Spanish Armada	Juan de Oñate leads first Spanish setters to New Mexico	Samuel de Champlain founds Quebec	Pueblo Indians revolt against Spanish colonization

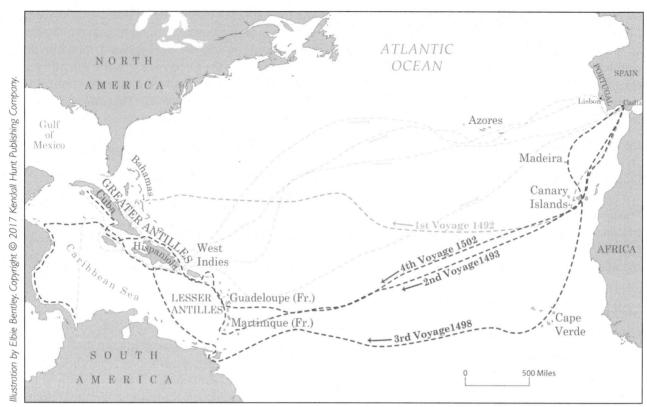

From 1492 to 1502, Christopher led four voyages westward across the Atlantic. On the first voyage, he and his crews encountered what we know today as the Bahama Islands. In subsequent ventures, Columbus and his men explored the coast of Venezuela and the east coast of Central America.

imagination, or diminish their enthusiasm. They listened intently as the natives gestured toward other islands, where they could find gold. Columbus, contemplating how the expedition might fulfill his promises to Fernando and Isabella, confided to his journal that the natives "ought to make very good slaves," adding further, "I believe that they could very easily become Christians." After *Santa Maria* ran aground and sank, Columbus left a contingent on the island of Española (shared today by Haiti and the Dominican Republic). Then, with samples of gold decorations worn by the natives, colorful parrots, and some Indians too, he returned to Spain with *Pinta* and *Niña*.

Their return caused a tremendous stir. Delighted by Columbus' report, Fernando and Isabella authorized a second expedition of seventeen ships, 1,700 men, and horses and other livestock to establish a permanent colony on Española. The Portuguese protested this Spanish incursion into what they had hoped would be their monopoly of the Asian trade (everyone still thought Columbus had reached the Indies). The Catholic Church attempted to resolve the dispute before it grew worse. Pope Alexander VI drew a longitudinal line dividing the world into two hemispheres. All lands to the west of the line were to

be Spain's; all lands to the east would belong to Portugal. In 1494, the two countries signed the **Treaty of Tordesillas** formalizing the demarcation. Other nations of the world ignored the arrangement.

Spain's interest began shifting from trade with China to exploiting the area now called the West Indies. Spanish explorers discovered a little gold on Española, and Columbus, now governor of the Spanish colony, required the local Indians to collect the precious metal and ordered that Indians who failed to produce their quotas would have their ears and noses cut off. To provide the Spanish monarchs and his other financial backers with a satisfactory return on their investments, Columbus allowed the Indians to be sold as slaves. Isabella disapproved, insisting that the colonists treat the Indians "lovingly"; nevertheless, the Spaniards continued to mistreat the Indians. Beaten, enslaved, and subjected to new and deadly diseases introduced by the Spanish intruders, the Native Americans fought to defend themselves but died in staggering numbers.

Columbus eventually completed four voyages to the West Indies, sailing along the coasts of Venezuela and Honduras in a vain search for the Asian mainland. His failure to govern Spain's new possessions effectively led to his arrest by Spanish authorities. He never conceded, as other Spaniards did, that he had not opened the back door to Asia, although he did acknowledge that he had come upon "un otro mundo"—another world. He died in 1506, a wealthy but frustrated and ignored man. One of the ironies of the Columbus drama is that the names "Indian" and "West Indies" that he used to identify the Caribbean islands and their native inhabitants perpetuated the confusion that tormented their "Discoverer." The ultimate insult to Columbus came when the first European map of the world to include the lands Columbus had encountered labeled them "America," after the Italian businessman and minor explorer Amerigo Vespuccci.

Controversy has enveloped Columbus from his own day to the present. He evoked strong responses from contemporaries, both those who admired and supported him and those who condemned him. Modern historians too have aligned themselves more or less into camps of defenders and critics. His defenders describe a daring navigator who introduced European civilization to America. Many admit that Columbus made mistakes, usually attributable to incomplete knowledge or pressure from backers and subordinates eager for riches. This heroic image of Columbus became standard fare in generations of American history textbooks.

Recently, however, a new image of Columbus has emerged in both popular and scholarly historical literature. In 1992, the five-hundredth anniversary of Columbus' first voyage evoked angry protests from many Native Americans. Today's historians are more apt to point out Columbus' role in the ruthless exploitation of the Western Hemisphere and Native Americans. They cite his shortcomings as a colonial governor, and experts in navigation have asserted that Columbus possessed more luck than skill.

The real Christopher Columbus remains obscure despite the monumental role he played in European and American history. Historians will continue to debate his character and his abilities. But fame is, at least partly, a matter of timing, and no one can doubt that Columbus seized his moment.

Spanish Colonies in the West Indies

> **How did Spain treat the West Indian islands that it claimed?**

In the aftermath of Columbus' voyages, hordes of adventurers descended on the West Indies, claiming land, conquering the natives, and establishing European settlements on the islands of Española, Puerto Rico, Cuba, and Jamaica. One of these *conquistadores*, Bernal Diaz, explained their motivation. They came "to serve God and His Majesty, to give light to those who were in darkness, and to grow rich, as all men desire to do." Thus, greed and arrogance as well as idealism and optimism motivated Spanish colonization, which established patterns followed by later European colonizers in North America.

The Spaniards initially hoped to extract precious metals from the islands, but as that dream faded they turned to raising crops and livestock. The Spanish crown bestowed land grants on favored individuals, establishing a landed Spanish elite in the Indies. The grants in effect divorced the native people from the land and made the Indians trespassers on Spanish plantations. The new Spanish landlords adapted to the environment. Most European staples, such as wheat, chickpeas, and grapes, did not grow well in the islands; however, native plants like tobacco and sugar imported from the Canary Islands flourished and provided profitable exports to Europe. The Spaniards also raised hogs and cattle on their *ranchos*. The owners' brands identified the animals, and herders on horseback rounded them up periodically for slaughter.

Spanish landowners needed laborers and quickly began organizing local Indians into an involuntary workforce. The system they developed derived from the feudal practice of requiring peasants to pay tribute to local lords. The Spanish *encomienda* system obligated local Indians in a specific area to pay tribute to a designated Spaniard lord, usually as a reward for the lord's service to the Spanish crown. The tribute was supposed to be in the form of corn, animal skins, or gold, but it often resulted in forced Indian labor. Although not slavery, as that labor system later developed, the *encomienda* was nevertheless brutal and exploitative.

Ecological Consequences of Conquest

Spanish economic transformation of the West Indies set in motion one of the most massive ecological transformations in human history. In less than a century Europeans radically altered not only the Indians' world but also their own. The

> **What were some of the ecological consequences of European conquest of America?**

biological exchanges between Europe and the Western Hemisphere—the transfer of products, plants, animals, and diseases sometimes labeled the "**Columbian exchange**"—permanently changed the ecologies of both areas. Whether the Indians or the Europeans made better use of the land is debatable, but the two groups of people regarded the land very differently. In general, Europeans exploited the land for profit whereas Indians did so more for subsistence. But there were also important similarities. Both lived directly off the land, farming, hunting, and fishing.

The exchange had positive and negative ecological consequences. Europeans introduced new methods of agricultural production, like the use of plows with iron blades, as well as new types of food, including sugar, wheat, and peas. But they also denuded woodlands. Indians altered the landscape too, by clearing forests and cultivating grasslands, but the Europeans attacked forests, for they disliked and even feared them. In European folk culture, forests were the domain of trolls, witches, and wild beasts. Woodland clearing exposed the land to wind and heavy rains that eroded the soil and reduced its fertility. These changes destroyed the habitat of various birds, insects, amphibians, and mammals. They also altered the balance of plant species, causing some to disappear and others to become dominant.

The Europeans also brought many domesticated animals to North America. The Spaniards introduced chickens, hogs, goats, sheep, cattle, and horses to America, and other Europeans brought other species of livestock. Domesticated animals provided settlers with food (meat, milk, and eggs), hides for leather straps, shoes, and harnesses, tallow for candles, and muscle power for tilling the soil and hauling heavy loads. Recognizing the uses to which they could put European animals, Native Americans incorporated many of them into their cultures, changing their diets, economies, and methods of hunting and waging war. As grazing animals, though, domestic livestock ravaged the ecosystems of the Caribbean islands by eating down native grasses. On the mainland of North America, bluegrass and other plants that Europeans carried with them to America became dispersed in their new environment.

Conversely, Europeans shipped American corn, beans, and potatoes (native to South America) across the Atlantic where they became staples of European diets. More nutritious than cereal grains, the American foods improved the overall health of Europeans and contributed to increased longevity and expanded populations. During the sixteenth century, Europe underwent a tremendous population explosion, a demographic phenomenon attributable at least in part to

nutritious foods derived from America. Not all products from the Americas were so beneficial. Europeans quickly became addicted to American coffee and tobacco, stimulants that provided a quick energy boost but had little nutritional value.

One of the most dramatic ecological consequences of contact was the catastrophic depopulation of Indian societies. Indians died in enormous numbers after contact with Europeans and exposure to the infectious diseases that Europeans brought with them (see p. 15). Within just a few years of contact with Europeans, virulent epidemics devastated native populations. Bartolomé de las Casas, a Catholic priest who had participated in the conquest of Cuba in 1511 but later strongly denounced the plunder of Indian societies, estimated that 3 million native people had lived there at the time of the Spaniards' arrival. A census in 1518 showed that scarcely 100,000 remained; by 1548, only 500 were still alive.

Disease, however, is not always correctly understood. For instance, germs could travel both ways across the Atlantic. One disease that might have been transferred from America to Europe was syphilis, perhaps carried by returning seamen from Columbus' first voyage. Furthermore, disease-causing germs do not alone account for the massive depopulation of Indian societies. European colonization led to massive dislocation and break-up of Indian communities, debilitating changes in Indian diets, and brutal, bone-crunching forced labor. Europeans were not merely passive conveyors of smallpox and measles; they were active participants in the violent reduction of Indian societies throughout the Americas.

In taking control of the larger islands in the Caribbean, Spain began building the first of Europe's powerful overseas empires. Even though the small amount of gold extracted disappointed the Spaniards, income from West Indian plantations bolstered Spain's royal treasury and enhanced its ability to expand its power over other parts of the New World.

THINKING BACK

1. Why was Christopher Columbus's first voyage so momentous?
2. Why would Native Americans take a dimmer view of Columbus' voyages than Europeans?
3. What was the "Columbian Exchange."

SPANISH CONQUEST OF THE MAINLAND

America presented Spanish soldiers and other adventurers with an opportunity to acquire the sort of glory, power, and fortune that most persons only dreamed about. Many of them were younger sons of landowners who could expect to receive little from their families since according to the prevailing custom of primogeniture, the right of inheritance belonged solely to the eldest son. Acquiring treasure in America was one alternative way of obtaining wealth and status. As these persons poured into America, they used superior European technology to overpower and make the Indians work for them. They believed that the Indians had no legitimate claim to the land because they were not Christians and did not exploit the land for profit. The plantations the Spaniards built became increasingly profitable, but the lure of gold and silver remained irresistible. For a century after Columbus, Spanish explorers and *conquistadores* sought their fortunes. Meanwhile, the Spanish crown endeavored to establish permanent settlements like New Mexico, which included mixed-race settlers and Catholic missions to convert Native Americans to Christianity and impose European culture upon them.

Establishment of New Spain

> **How did New Spain come into being, and how did it develop in its early years?**

Soon after laying down settlements in the West Indies, Spaniards explored the coastline of the Gulf of Mexico and other points west. They sought contact with the native people in order to Christianize and otherwise "civilize" them as well as to learn about the location of gold. The Spanish crown was eager to expand its domain.

In 1519 Hernán Cortés led several hundred soldiers on an expedition, sailing from Cuba to the western end of the Gulf of Mexico and finally landing at the present-day site of Vera Cruz. Previous reconnaissance had turned up evidence of Aztec gold. Burning his ships to prevent his soldiers from turning back, Cortés marched his troops up to the high plateau of central Mexico, past towering volcanoes, and down into the great central valley. Along the way, the Spaniards recruited local fighters who hated their Mexica rulers. The Aztec emperor Montezuma invited the bearded Spaniards into his capital at Tenochtitlán, and once inside, the Spaniards captured Montezuma and began slaughtering the city's residents. Aztec warriors counterattacked,

driving the Spaniards from the city. Cortés rallied his troops, but it was the smallpox infection that ravaged the Aztecs, and after many days of bloody fighting, the Spaniards completed their conquest of the city.

The collapse of the Aztec empire was an unlikely historical event made possible by several critical factors. The Aztecs' initial uncertainty about the Spaniards probably doomed their chances of winning. Moreover, the Aztecs' definition of military victory involved subjugation and forced tribute along with the taking of prisoners rather than annihilation of the enemy. More than once during the long battle they might have destroyed the Spaniards with a massive assault, but they did not do so. Furthermore, the Spaniards' steel swords, artillery, and horses gave them tactical superiority. They also had many Indian allies who evened the numbers considerably. The conquest of the Aztec empire was not an isolated event; rather, it established a pattern of military subjugation that led to Juan de Oñate's conquest of the Pueblos.

The Spaniards justified their aggression by declaring their intent to "civilize" the Indians. To obliterate Aztec culture and the people's cultural identity, Cortés ordered the destruction of Aztec temples and other ceremonial buildings in Tenochtitlán and erected a new capital on its ruins, **Mexico City**. There, Spaniards established an administrative bureaucracy that, among other things, restructured Native American societies. Cortés became the overlord of a colony the Spaniards called **New Spain**, from Mexico northward to the Great Plains, Rockies, and the Pacific Coast. Ironically, while Spaniards believed themselves superior to Indians, they incorporated many aspects of Indian culture into their colonial societies. Spaniards adopted Indian place names, grew native crops, married Indian women, and produced a mixed-race population they called ***mestizos***.

Roman Catholic missionaries from the monastic and mendicant orders of Europe followed on the heels of Spanish armies and government authorities. Although they introduced the Indians of New Spain to Christianity, they enjoyed only limited success in converting them. Many Indians agreed to baptism, to accept Catholic missions in their communities, and even to work on mission lands, but they did not change their personal religious beliefs and secretly conducted traditional religious ceremonies and rituals. Indians welcomed metal plows, knives, and saws that the missionaries provided and also obtained horses and mules, which they used as work animals, along with cattle and sheep from which they derived food, leather, tallow, and wool. But the cost of these exchanges was control of their labor and autonomy. Moreover, marriage to Spanish settlers diminished the full-blood Indian population. The harshness of the Spanish conquest spawned hatred among native people that erupted violently from time to time.

Officials in Spain desired order and loyalty in the colony, and not just from the Indians. Suspicious of the independent power of the *conquistadors*, the Spanish monarchy restructured the government of New Spain, replacing Cortés as governor with a viceroy who was directly responsible to the crown. Soon Spanish bureaucratic authority, centered in Mexico City, penetrated the remotest areas of settlement. A royal tribunal called the **audiencia** allowed Spanish citizens and Indians alike to file formal complaints of mistreatment by soldiers, civilian officials, or landowners. Thus, the *conquistadores*, whose usefulness ended when areas of settlement were relatively secure, were gradually phased out and government bureaucrats put in place.

A key function of the government of New Spain involved developing a method of using Indians as laborers. Spaniards had come to Mexico for glory, not drudgery. The *encomienda* system that operated in the West Indies was a ready-made solution to New Spain's labor problem. It served both to organize Indian labor and to reward Spaniards for loyal service to the crown. The tribute that the *encomenderos* (the Spaniards who received *encomienda* privileges) demanded of local Indians, together with goods imported from Spain, enabled the Spanish elite to live comfortably if not extravagantly. Soon, however, large numbers of settlers arrived from the islands and from Spain. Wealthy newcomers obtained land grants from Spanish officials and established *ranchos* on which they raised large herds of livestock, primarily cattle and horses; poor people worked fields on communal farms.

Within three-quarters of a century, Spaniards had established a stable and prosperous dominion on the mainland of North America. The subsequent history of New Spain is an integral part of the history of the United States. The societies that grew up along the northern frontiers of New Spain directly shaped the complex identity of people in the Southwest.

Reconnoitering the Mainland

In extending their domain from the Caribbean islands to New Spain during the sixteenth century, Spaniards accumulated considerable information about the western Gulf of Mexico, but they knew little yet about the landscape along the northern Gulf and the Atlantic coasts. Further exploration produced a clearer picture of the lands Spain claimed.

> **For what purpose did Spaniards reconnoiter the North American mainland?**

When the Spanish explorer Juan Ponce de León first arrived in the area that is today's Florida, he believed he had found another island. He sailed from Puerto Rico in 1513, drawn perhaps by legends of a "fountain of youth" that filled medieval mythology, but more likely by the hope of finding gold and Indian slaves to replace the rapidly disappearing native population of the Caribbean islands. Coming ashore near present-day Daytona Beach on Florida's east coast, he claimed the territory for Spain. Indians, aware of the Spanish penchant for plunder, prevented him from remaining on shore, so he sailed south through the keys and up the west coast perhaps as far as Port Charlotte before returning to Spain. He obtained permission from the Spanish crown to establish a settlement in Florida, and in 1521 he set sail. Once again, however, hostile Indians attacked, fatally wounding him and forcing abandonment of the enterprise. In between Ponce de León's expeditions, a voyage by Alonso Alvarez de Peñeda along the Gulf coast from Florida to Mexico proved that Florida was actually part of the North American continent.

Meanwhile Spaniards began mapping the Atlantic coast north of Florida. Slavers came ashore near present-day Charleston, South Carolina, as early as 1514. In 1526 an expedition attempted a permanent settlement on the Georgia coast, but sickness and the lateness of the season forced abandonment of Spain's first colony in what became the United States.

The Spanish explored the Pacific coast as well as the Atlantic. In 1513, Vasco Nuñez de Balboa crossed the **Isthmus of Panama** to become the first European to gaze upon the Pacific Ocean from America, but it was not until the defeat of the Aztecs that Spaniards began exploring the long western edge of the continent. In 1533, a Spanish vessel captained by Fortún Ximénez reached La Paz Bay at the southern end of the Baja (lower) California peninsula. The most remarkable Pacific voyage, even though it failed to reach its objective, was that of Juan Rodriguez Cabrillo. In 1542 Cabrillo anchored in San Diego Bay on the first leg of a planned journey up the coast of California and across the Pacific to China. Although Cabrillo died soon afterward, his three ships continued north as far as the 42nd parallel before stormy seas forced them to return to Mexico. The Pacific expeditions allowed Spaniards to complete the coastal mapping of North America, and on the basis of those explorations Spain laid claim to territory from the Atlantic to the Pacific.

Reconnoitering North American coastlines produced valuable information that helped Spaniards understand the continent's geography. Based on this information, Spanish explorers probed deep into the heartland of America.

The Quest for Cíbola

> **What did the pursuit of fabled cities of gold, called *Cíbola*, yield?**

The products of ranching and planting in New Spain, although profitable, hardly satisfied the Spaniards' hunger for riches. Adventurers continued to obsess about gold. *Conquistadores* demanded tribute from their subjects, but they actually obtained very little gold that way. Some Spaniards turned eagerly from tribute to a quest for seven golden cities, based on both European and Aztec legends. They called these places *Cíbola*.

Early in 1528 a reconnaissance expedition of about 300 men set sail from Cuba under the command of Pánfilo de Narváez. Its objective was to explore the coast from Florida to New Spain. Hostile Indians, disease, and starvation decimated the army as it advanced first on foot and then by makeshift barges. In November about ninety-six shivering survivors staggered ashore on the Texas coast. After six years in captivity, three Spaniards, including Alvar Nuñez Cabeza de Vaca (whose story is told in the Personal Perspective, pp. 36-38) and the African slave named Estevan, finally escaped. The tiny band trudged westward, surviving by convincing the Indians that they were healers. This "so inflated our fame over the region," Cabeza de Vaca recounted, "that we could control whatever the inhabitants cherished." The Spaniards reported "undeniable indications" of gold, copper, and other precious metals and understood from the Indians that large and wealthy towns lay further west. In 1536 they stumbled into a remote Spanish outpost in northwestern Mexico, and their odyssey was finally over.

Two years later Viceroy Antonio de Mendoza, a hardworking bureaucrat also eager for fame, dispatched a party led by missionary Fray Marcos de Niza and Estevan to the far northern frontier to find the fabled golden cities. Reaching the adobe villages of Zuñi in the western part of present-day New Mexico, Estevan entered alone, ahead of the others. The Indians tolerated him for a while, but his arrogance offended them, and finally they killed him. Although Fray Marcos himself never set eyes on Zuñi, he reported to authorities upon his return to Mexico that gold filled the Indian pueblo.

Mendoza ordered out another search party, this one commanded by the thirty-year-old soldier Francisco Vásquez de Coronado. The Spaniards attacked Zuñi to obtain food and to avenge Estevan's death but found no gold. The frustrated Coronado fumed that Fray Marcos "has not told the truth in a single thing he said." But the party did explore and draw valuable maps of the area from the Gulf of California and the Grand Canyon northeastward to the Great Plains, before returning to Mexico despondent and empty-handed. Ironically, Coronado had passed close to rich deposits of gold, silver, and copper that would lure later generations of prospectors and mining companies to the Southwest. Other Spaniards unearthed rich deposits of silver at Zacatecas, Mexico, in 1548, which, added to mines in Peru, ultimately fulfilled Columbus's promise to Isabella and Fernando.

Over the next fifty years, other expeditions explored New Spain's northern frontier. Most were unauthorized by Spanish officials in Mexico City; however, in 1595 the viceroy commissioned Juan de Oñate to establish and govern a colony on the upper Rio Grande River. In 1598, Governor Oñate led a caravan of soldiers, missionaries, and settlers across the Rio Grande to lay the foundation for the frontier province of New Mexico. The colony struggled. Oñate's brutal suppression of Indian resistance did not cow the Pueblo Indians, who attacked and sometimes killed Spaniards when the opportunity arose. When the Spaniards failed to find gold or silver, they turned to raising corn and grazing livestock, extracting a meager subsistence from the arid landscape. Catholic priests fanned out and established missions among the Indians. Some disheartened settlers abandoned New Mexico and returned to New Spain, charging Oñate with mismanagement. In 1606, the viceroy recalled the governor, thus ending Oñate's bid for glory, but in 1610 Oñate's successor founded the capital of Santa Fe, which is today the oldest state capital in the United States.

At the same time that Spanish explorers were reconnoitering the southwest, other Spaniards set out to explore the interior of Florida, the Spanish designation for what is now the entire southeastern United States. In 1539, Hernán de Soto, a veteran Spanish

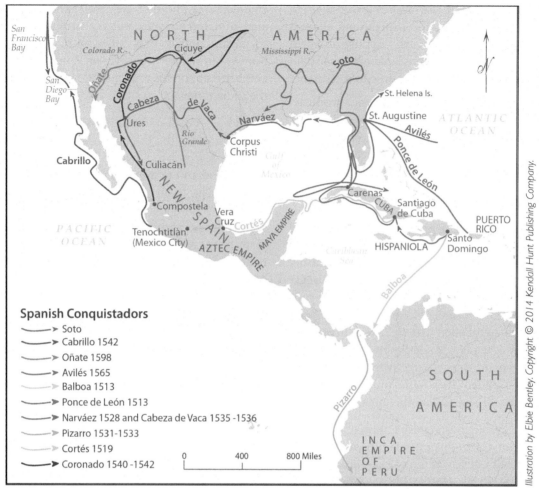

Spanish Exploration and Conquest of the Americas, 1513-1598: During the century following Christopher Columbus' voyages to America, Spaniards reconnoitered the Atlantic, Gulf, and Pacific coasts of North America. Meanwhile, Francisco Pizzaro conquered the Inca Empire of South America.

conquistador, assembled a party of 600 Spaniards, mostly soldiers but including at least two women and some Catholic friars, and landed with them on the west coast of Florida. The Spaniards' arrival was a sad day for the thousands of Native Americans living in the area. Many of them knew enough about Spaniards to fear and hate them, and de Soto was indeed fearsome. An acquaintance claimed he was "much given to the sport of hunting Indians on horseback." The army rampaged through the southeast from Florida to North Carolina, across the Appalachian Mountains, and into areas that are today the states of Tennessee, Alabama, Mississippi, Arkansas, and Louisiana. Along the way, the Spaniards sacked Indian towns and villages, stole supplies of corn and beans, and spread deadly diseases. The Indians fought back as best they could, but by the time the Spaniards' long march ended in 1543, the number of Indians remaining in the region had fallen by half. De Soto sickened and died while on the march. The survivors built boats and drifted from the mouth of the Mississippi River to the coast of northeastern Mexico.

Spanish reconnaissance failed to turn up fabulous treasures, but the expeditions of Spanish explorers, colonizers, and marauders did achieve a few "firsts." They were the first Europeans to cross the Appalachian Mountains, the first to reach the Mississippi River by land, and the first to navigate it. They added substantially to Europeans' knowledge of continental North America. Their impact on Indian societies was profound. In their often-deadly wake, they left many broken Indian communities. Some of the survivors migrated to other locales, sometimes merging with tribes such as the Cherokee, Chickasaw, Choctaw, and Creek. The Spanish presence in New Mexico upset traditional trade relationships between the farming Pueblo peoples and hunting groups like the Apache and Navajo, who were forced to find other ways to obtain food.

Fortifying Florida

What value did Spain see in Florida, and what happened to Spanish plans to expand its boundaries?

Although Spanish reconnaissance in North America had turned up no riches, Spanish conquests in Mexico had paid off in huge amounts of silver and gold. To protect those treasures, the Spanish crown decided to establish military and naval bases on the coast of Florida to defend the eastern flank of its North American empire against European rivals. In 1559, an expedition of 1,500 soldiers and settlers from Vera Cruz crossed the Gulf of Mexico to Pensacola Bay and built a small town and garrison there, the first European settlement in what is now the continental United States. This initial effort to colonize the area failed due to a hurricane and food shortages; within two years the settlers evacuated the area.

French settlements on the east coast represented the first threats to Spain's North American empire. In 1564, a colony of French Protestants (see p. 52), called **Huguenots**, had built a fortification near present-day Charleston, South Carolina, and soon planted a small settlement at the mouth of the St. Johns River at the site of today's Jacksonville, Florida. Spanish treasure ships sailed along the coastline before picking up the westerly winds that would carry them back across the Atlantic to Europe. As one Spaniard reported: "We are compelled to pass in front of their port, and with the greatest ease they can sally out with their armadas to seek us." In 1565, Spain's King Felipe II commissioned a seafaring adventurer named Pedro Menéndez de Avilés to secure Florida and drive the French out. With 1,000 Spaniards, including 300 soldiers, some of whom were African slaves, Menéndez founded a post that he named St. Augustine, and from there, he attacked and defeated the French. Then, following his own dreams of glory, he set out to establish Spanish dominion along the Atlantic seaboard all the way to Newfoundland. He dispatched an expedition to cut an overland road to the silver mines of Mexico. The party reached the Smoky Mountains of Tennessee before turning back when the distance turned out to be much greater than Menéndez had calculated.

To expand the boundaries of Spanish Florida northward, Menéndez sent an expedition of Catholic missionaries to establish an outpost on Chesapeake Bay. Accompanying the missionaries was an Indian youth whom a Spanish sea captain had captured from that location some time earlier. The Spaniards who had educated him called him Luis de Velasco, after the viceroy of New Spain, but his Indian name was Opechancanough, and he was probably the younger brother of Powhatan, the chief of a powerful Indian confederacy in the vicinity of Chesapeake Bay. In 1570, the missionaries settled on the bank of a river that thirty-seven years later would become the site of England's first permanent colony on the North American mainland. But within a year, the local Indians, perhaps angry with the missionaries for attempting to change their culture, killed them. Luis de Velasco returned to his people and resumed his Native American identity.

Pedro Menéndez de Avilés' dreams of a greater Florida faded. The logistical problems were beyond the management and resources available to Spain at that time. Spain's North American empire had reached its farthest extent.

THINKING BACK

1. What did Spanish empire building in North America accomplish?
2. What other courses of action might Spain have taken in North America, and what outcomes might such alternatives have produced?

COLONIZING NEW MEXICO AND FLORIDA

Early in the 1600s, Spain considered abandoning its outposts in New Mexico and Florida because explorers and colonists had found little of value there. Indian resistance to Christianity disappointed and discouraged Catholic missionaries. Nearby French colonies threatened Spanish settlements in Florida. An Indian uprising in Florida in 1597 took the lives of a number of missionaries and destroyed many Spanish outposts. Until the founding of Pensacola in 1698, St. Augustine was the sole Spanish settlement in Florida, and it had all the appeal of a hellhole. Muddy streets and shabby palmetto huts discouraged potential settlers; frequent Indian and pirate attacks frightened them. "It is hard to get anyone to go to St. Augustine," the governor of Cuba reported, "because of the horror with which Florida is painted." New Mexico was hardly better, offering only the adobe hovels of Santa Fe and a few other tiny villages. Through the sixteenth century, no other European country had established mainland colonies that directly threatened Spain's silver mines in northern Mexico or its vital shipping lanes through the Gulf of Mexico. However, that picture changed

Taos Pueblo, New Mexico. Spanish Catholic missionaries sought not only to Christianize Native Americans but also to encourage them to live in villages.

considerably early in the seventeenth century, motivating Spanish officials to renew and expand their commitment to colonizing the northern borderlands as a buffer against European rivals. The impact on Native American societies was profound.

The Work of Spanish Missionaries

| What roles did the Spanish missionaries play in North America? |

Proclaiming that spreading the Christian gospel was "the principal purpose for . . . new discoveries and settlements," in 1573 the Spanish crown announced that Catholic missionaries would function as explorers and pacifiers of its American dominions. A caravan of heavily loaded wagons and thirty Catholic missionaries lumbered into Santa Fe in 1629, bringing to fifty the contingent of Spanish priests in the colony. A similar number labored in Florida. These Franciscan friars (priests belonging to the missionary order of St. Francis of Assisi) had pledged themselves to a life of celibacy and poverty, living off alms and laboring to bring souls to God.

In both New Mexico and Florida, missionaries entered native villages and attempted to convert the inhabitants to Christianity. They then induced the residents to build churches. Most missionaries avoided extreme force, even when the Indians resisted their efforts. "With suavity and mildness," Fray Estevan de Perea of New Mexico explained, "an obstinate spirit can better be reclaimed than with violence and rigor." To punish dissenters, however, some did resort to violence, usually flogging.

Successful missionaries learned local languages well enough to convey the basics of Christianity to the native people. Often, they focused their efforts on children, whom they found easier to sway than adults. Sometimes the foreigners' religious rituals, images, and sacred objects reminded the native people of their own practices and beliefs. The missionaries also brought cattle, sheep, and hogs into the native villages as incentives, providing the people with new and additional sources of food and other products. If all else failed, the missionaries could summon the deadly power of Spanish soldiers, a show of force that usually convinced the Indians at least to listen to the missionaries.

Ultimately, proselytizing worked only if the Indians cooperated, which they usually did if they stood to lose too much by refusing or if they thought they could gain some advantage, such as a powerful ally. Most Indians did not respond with great enthusiasm to the missionaries' appeals, and it is not difficult to understand why. As one priest admitted, "we who are Christians [have] caused so much harm and violence."

Missionaries often exaggerated the number of Indians they converted, casting doubt on the reported figures. One bishop recorded administering confirmation rites to over 13,000 Native Americans during a tour of Florida in 1674–75. In typical European fashion, he registered amazement that the Indians were so "clever and quick to learn." But such reports, even if accurate, do not reveal the depth or sincerity of conversions. In some cases, no doubt, Native Americans converted to Christianity, but often they merely tacked elements of the newcomers' religion onto their core beliefs. Early enthusiastic reports of successful conversions among the Indians often dissolved into pessimism. The friars struggled valiantly, but as one of them admitted: "It has been impossible to correct their [the Indians'] concubinage, the abominable crime of idolatry, their accursed superstitions, idolatrous dances, and other faults."

Spanish missionaries tried to change not only the Indians' religious beliefs but also their identities. They believed the Indians were more likely to become Christians if they thought an behaved like Europeans. They urged them to speak Spanish, use European tools, wear European clothes, and adhere to European standards of sexual modesty, which became a major issue. The priests especially abhorred the Indians' sexuality, which they deemed ungodly, and usually sought to suppress it. The Indians openly celebrated the meeting of a human woman's egg with a man's sperm as the equivalent of corn seed joining with the rain to renew life.

Forced Indian Labor and Other Abuses

How did the Spaniards organize Indian labor, and what abuses ensued?

"No one comes to the Indies to plow and sow," New Spain's Viceroy Luis de Valasco remarked about his countrymen, "but only to eat and loaf." To create such a lifestyle, Spaniards in both New Mexico and Florida attempted to organize native people into a labor force. Although the crown ceased granting new *encomiendas* in the 1500s, the system continued to operate well into the seventeenth century on the remote New Mexico frontier. Although it failed to take root in Florida, compulsory Indian labor on roads, fortifications, and public buildings became an established practice

in both colonies and was written in law as the ***repartimiento***. Different from the *encomienda*, which technically involved tribute rather than labor, Spaniards often misused both systems to force Indians to work on private landholdings.

The government in Spain passed laws ostensibly to protect Native Americans from exploitation, while individual Spaniards in New Spain devised an equal number of ways to circumvent them. *Encomenderos* often demanded more corn, cotton blankets, or animal hides than the Indians were accustomed to producing. These levies were especially burdensome in times of drought or extreme cold. Public officials were legally obligated to pay natives for work, but they generally paid only a pittance—if they compensated them at all. They frequently pressed Indians into personal service under threat of punishment and often sexually abused native women. Alejandro Mora raped his servant woman "to determine if she was a virgin." When she resisted, she told Spanish officials, "he hung me from a roof-beam and beat me."

Due to the efforts of antislavery advocates, Spain officially outlawed Indian slavery in the sixteenth century. In far-away New Mexico, however, slavery flourished despite Spanish laws. Most often, Spaniards victimized the Apache, who fiercely resisted efforts to "civilize" them. Governor Juan Ignacio Flores Mogollon observed that settlers "take them to distant places to sell" as laborers and servants. Local governors as well as an official known as the **Protector of Indians** were supposed to prevent such abuses, but they seldom did. Provincial governors often had no other source of profit than the forced labor of local Indians.

Indian Revolts

Late in the seventeenth century Indian resentment over Spanish abuses, especially the exploitation of Indian labor, erupted into bloody violence. Missionaries professed to be the Indians' protectors, but some took advantage of them too, employing native

What triggered Indian rebellions against Spanish control, and to what extent did they succeed?

villagers to do most of the physical labor around the missions.

In New Mexico the rivalry between government bureaucrats and the missionaries over control of the Indians reached a crucial point, as did the level of Indian bitterness. Such tensions weakened Spanish solidarity throughout the territory and convinced the Indians that the time was right for rebellion. A prolonged drought that parched their crops and pushed them to the edge of starvation intensified the natives' frustration. Apache raids on local Indian storehouses further diminished the Pueblos' dwindling food supply. When prayers to the Christian god failed to bring relief, the Pueblos appealed to their traditional deities.

In 1680, a Pueblo religious leader whom the Spaniards knew as Popé organized villages along the Rio Grande and as far west as the **Hopi** mesas in Arizona in a plot to attack missions and settlements. Officials in Santa Fe had punished Popé and several other Indians for conducting illegal religious ceremonies. That experience hardened his resolve to extract revenge. In the summer, Popé dispatched runners to participating villages, each runner carrying a knotted rope. By untying one knot each day the plotters counted the days until the planned attack. Indian allies of the Spaniards betrayed the plot, allowing some missionaries and ranchers to reach safety in Santa Fe. But the sudden and furious Indian attack resulted in the deaths of nearly 400 of the 2,500 Spaniards in New Mexico, including twenty-one of the thirty-three missionaries. A thousand terrified settlers and officials huddled in the governor's palace in Santa Fe for a week until the besiegers allowed them to flee to El Paso. With the Spaniards gone, the Indians destroyed churches, burned ranch houses, and spurned everything the invaders had brought or taught them. Native people once again ruled the Southwest.

Several times over the next decade Spanish authorities dispatched armed forces to regain control of the province. Although the Spaniards caused much death and destruction among the Pueblos, the Indians did not submit to their authority. Then in 1692 a soldier and mid-level Spanish aristocrat named Diego de Vargas led an army into Pueblo territory vowing that if the Indians resisted he would "destroy them." Vargas found the Pueblos disunited—some of them wanting to ally with the Spaniards against rival Pueblos—and Popé dead. Spreading word that he had not come "to kill them, rob them, or carry off their women and children, but to pardon them so they might again become Christians," Vargas and his force of fifty soldiers and 100 friendly Indians entered Santa Fe without firing a shot. However, Vargas understood that many Pueblos were not yet ready to put on the Spanish yoke, so he went back to El Paso. When he returned to Pueblo territory the next year with a much larger company of soldiers, settlers, and missionaries, the story was different. The Indians put up stiff resistance and submitted only after the Spaniards launched a series of vicious attacks killing hundreds of native people.

All in all, the **Pueblo Revolt** proved more harmful to the Indians than to the Spaniards. In over two decades of upheaval, Spaniards killed as many as 3,000 Indians and destroyed several villages, many of which were never rebuilt. In 1696 the Indians made a last desperate strike against Spanish control in New Mexico. This time the coordinated Pueblo attacks that had been so successful in Popé's rebellion sixteen years earlier failed to materialize, and the Spanish easily put down the revolt. Thereafter, Spaniards and Pueblo Indians settled into a permanent and mostly peaceful though unhappy coexistence.

Native Americans in Florida also took up arms against Spaniards, but the dynamics of rebellion differed from the Pueblo revolt, as did the outcome. The presence of English adventurers was the biggest difference. English raiders destroyed Spanish Catholic missions and offered rum, guns, ammunition, and other goods to Indians to induce them to take up arms against the Spaniards. As a result of English pressure on Florida, missionary activity there virtually ceased. Two Spanish officials declared to the king: "In all these extensive dominions and provinces, the law of God and the preaching of the Holy Gospel have now ceased."

___

THINKING BACK

1. To what extent did Spain succeed in imposing its rule on New Mexico and Florida?
2. Catholic missionaries claimed success in converting Indians to Christianity, but how did the Indians maintain a measure of control over their lives? What other contributions did the missionaries make to Spanish colonization of North America?

___

SPAIN'S EUROPEAN RIVALS

The European countries that entered the expanding trans-Atlantic commercial network of the sixteenth and seventeenth centuries closely guarded the trade that flowed from New World territories. For a century after Columbus, Spain claimed a monopoly over American colonization and commerce. Before long, however, Spain's European competitors discovered how much valuable sugar, tobacco, and bullion Spanish galleons contained. The treasure that the colonies shipped back to Spain included approximately 16,000 tons of silver and another 200 tons of gold. Spain's success in colonizing America attracted other interested Europeans who did not acknowledge the Treaty of Tordesillas. Some came to plunder Spanish shipping while others sought to trade with the Indians. Still others sought a new life as permanent settlers in America.

Smugglers, Pirates, and Slavers

Portuguese Fort Sao Jorge da Mina (Fort St. George's of the Mine). Constructed in 1482 on the coast of today's Ghana, Elmina, as it came to be called, was a shipping point for Africans forced into the Atlantic slave trade. This tunnel led to the slave ships.

> **How did pirates and smugglers threaten Spain's American treasures?**

The quickest and easiest way that rivals could intrude on Spain's domain was by smuggling and stealing. During the late sixteenth and early seventeenth centuries, French, English, and Dutch vessels financed by their governments and by private investors, transported goods from Europe to Spanish settlements in America. Ship captains illegally exchanged wine, tools, fine cloth, and porcelain for gold and silver, which they then returned to their respective countries.

In addition to smuggling, **privateers** (privately owned ships operating under government commissions) plundered Spanish treasure ships. Spain attempted to police trans-Atlantic commerce by arming their transport vessels and sending them in convoys, but ocean sailing in those days entailed many risks. Even if convoys managed to evade pirates and privateers, storms blew into the Gulf of Mexico and the Caribbean threatening the fleets of treasure-laden galleons. Wrecked ships left millions in sunken treasure in the graveyard of the ocean floor.

As the number of Indian laborers dwindled, ships brought cargoes of African slaves to replace them. Because Portugal monopolized commerce along the West African coast, Spain licensed Portuguese shippers to transport slaves to the Americas. This formal agreement, known as an *asiento*, benefited both countries: Spain received the slaves it needed, and Portuguese shippers profited by selling them. Interlopers, including the English pirate John Hawkins, began to force their way into this profitable trade. Hawkins' three voyages carrying slaves from Africa to the West Indies during the 1560s

contributed to growing rancor between Spain and England, even though the slave trade remained in Portuguese hands. Spain destroyed Hawkins's small fleet of slave ships in 1567, but English attacks on Spanish shipping continued, leading to all-out war between the two countries in the 1580s.

Francis Drake was England's most successful pirate. In 1572 he intercepted a shipment of Spanish treasure. Laden with booty, Drake's ship lumbered back across the Atlantic to England. In 1579 his circumnavigation of the globe threatened Spanish settlements along the Pacific coast of Mexico and yielded more stolen Spanish gold to enrich English coffers. The English government did not officially condone piracy but privately encouraged it. In fact, for his exploits, Drake was made a knight. English sea captains frequently attacked Spanish fleets in the Caribbean, which became the scene of an exciting, high-stakes, international competition of piracy to see who could take the biggest prize.

The French in North America

<table>
<tr><td>How successful were the French in contesting Spain's North American dominions?</td></tr>
</table>

France's early involvement in America centered on locating a **Northwest Passage**, an inland waterway that would allow ships to sail through or around the North American continent to Asia. The Spaniard Fernando Magellan actually discovered the only practical sea route across the Atlantic to China when in 1519 his fleet rounded Cape Horn at the tip of South America, an epic voyage completed in 1522 after Magellan's death in the Philippines. Nevertheless the French king Francis I financed an expedition commanded by the Italian mariner Giovanni da Verrazzano, which in 1524 explored the upper Atlantic coast northward from Chesapeake Bay in a vain search for the long-sought Northwest Passage. The French mariner Jacques Cartier explored the coast of Newfoundland in 1534 with the same goal in mind. On a second voyage the following year Cartier sailed up the gaping mouth of the **St. Lawrence River** (see map on p. 103.). The river narrowed considerably, however, as Cartier's ship ascended it, and near the site of present-day Montreal he and his disheartened crew gave up the quest. The explorers endured a harsh Canadian winter before returning home to France.

Some people in France also hoped to establish colonies in unsettled areas of North America to bring it a share of the continent's wealth. As noted earlier, Spain responded to **French Huguenot** settlements in Florida by founding their own fort at St. Augustine. In 1605 another contingent of Huguenots settled in Acadia (Nova Scotia). Their colony of small farms and fishing villages achieved if not prosperity at least stability. In 1608 the scientist and explorer Samuel de Champlain founded the colony of Quebec along the St. Lawrence River.

For several reasons, however, **New France** failed to flourish. The cold climate in the northland was partly to blame. French settlers in inland North America raised a few crops and traded with the Algonquian Indians in the St. Lawrence basin, exchanging iron knives, hatchets, and trinkets for beaver pelts and moose hides. In the early years of the seventeenth century, however, the French government showed scant interest in permanent settlements in North America. The cost of maintaining them was too high and the profits too slim. Moreover, civil war and religious strife at home demanded most of the country's energies and resources.

THINKING BACK

1. Despite Spain's head start in North American colonization, its position steadily weakened throughout the sixteenth century. What signs point to Spain's declining power? How did Spain's rivals take advantage of that situation? How were they successful, or not?
2. What were France's interests in North America, what attempts did France make to colonize North America, and how successful were they?

ENGLAND AND COLONIZATION

Like France, England sought profitable trade with Asia, and that brought English explorers to America. At the same time that Christopher Columbus sought Fernando and Isabella's support, his brother Bartholomew lobbied for backing from England's King Henry VII. Henry declined to support Bartholomew Columbus, but he did agree to sponsor the voyage of the Venetian mariner Giovanni Cabotto (John Cabot). In 1497 Cabot sailed along the coast of Newfoundland in search of a sea route to China. Subsequently, other

© Historical/Contributor/Getty

French explorer Jacques Cartier. Cartier's expedition explored the St. Lawrence River to the present-day site of Montreal, finding an Iroquois village and fields of corn.

English ships probed the North American coast for the Northwest Passage while enterprising English businessmen invested in pirating against Spanish treasure ships. However, English officials showed little interest in establishing permanent settlements in North America. Nearly a century passed before England was ready to undertake a colonial adventure in America. Several issues related to religion and royal authority first required resolution.

The Protestant Reformation

> **What caused the religious turmoil that afflicted Europe early in the sixteenth century?**

Part of the reason for England's lack of interest in colonization lay in the unsettled state of the country's religious affairs. In Europe and in England early in the sixteenth century, resentment over the activities of Roman Catholic clerics reached a critical point. The Catholic Church controlled vast tracts of land, renting them to parishioners for what many regarded as excessive sums. Church members also complained that priests charged exorbitant fees for conducting marriages and funerals. Rumors of sexual misconduct also contributed to mounting anticlerical sentiment.

Doctrinal disputes within the Catholic Church exacerbated the antagonism. Controversies that began on the continent crossed the English Channel to England. The German priest and university lecturer Martin Luther, heeding the admonition of St. Paul that "the just shall live by faith," began criticizing the doctrine of salvation through good works. Arguing that no one could attain heaven by lighting candles, embarking on pilgrimages, or performing good deeds, Luther insisted that salvation could be realized only through God's mercy. He clashed with others in the church over whether the clergy possessed any special spiritual power. Luther believed that God spoke directly to people, not indirectly through the clergy. Priests were merely teachers. The relationship between Luther and the Catholic hierarchy reached a crisis in 1517 when he began publicly criticizing practices such as offering escape from **purgatory** to those who performed such good deeds as contributing monetarily to building cathedrals. Luther, outraged by the idea that a person might buy his or her way into heaven, responded by posting a notice of condemnation, his **95 Theses,** on the door of the church at Wittenberg. Luther attracted a considerable following, especially in Germany where the desire for a national church independent of Rome ran high. Luther did not intend to secede from the Catholic Church, but the

pope excommunicated him anyway. Other dissenters who allied with Luther emerged as the vanguard of a **Protestant Reformation** that permanently divided the Catholic Church, an outcome that Luther himself never intended.

In 1533 John Calvin, a French-born theologian, came to realize that he had been living in a "quagmire of errors" and was covered in "filth and shame." Railing against both Catholicism and **Lutheranism,** he insisted that both misunderstood the nature of salvation. According to Calvin, despite the innate wickedness of all humans, God chose certain persons for salvation. "**Election,**" as the doctrine was known, had little to do with faith and could not be earned by performing good works; it was the will of an all-powerful God. Calvin laid out his theology's central and distinguishing principle: the **doctrine of predestination** in *The Institutes of the Christian Religion* (1536). God determined each person's fate before birth and the individual could do nothing to change it. Calvin did agree with Lutheran reformers that the Catholic Church granted unsubstantiated authority to the clergy, from the pope down to local priests. He went beyond the Lutheran reformers in opposing the church's elaborate ritual, which he claimed drew worshipers' attention away from their sinfulness and consideration of how they might live in closer association with God. In Geneva (Switzerland) he set up a religious community based on his principles; from there, **Calvinism** spread to France, the Low Countries, and Scotland, and then finally to England.

The Royal Divorce

Calvinist belief swept through England, fueling the already smoldering fires of anticlericalism. The religious disputes became high political drama

> **What sparked the English Reformation?**

when King Henry VIII petitioned the pope to annul his marriage to Catherine of Aragon, daughter of the monarchs Isabella and Fernando of Spain. Before Catherine married Henry, she had wed Henry's older brother Arthur in a ceremony that sealed a partnership with Spain. Arthur's sudden death then jeopardized the new alliance. To save it, a marriage was arranged between Catherine and Henry, a maneuver that required papal approval because of a Biblical sanction against a man marrying his brother's widow. The deal was struck, and Henry succeeded to the English throne.

Unfortunately, the royal couple's marriage failed to produce one important thing: a male heir. By 1527 Henry had grown despondent over five children who were stillborn or died in infancy. A daughter, Mary, had survived; however, in that era a female heir invited a disputed succession and perhaps even civil war. Catherine had probably entered menopause, but Henry became convinced that the failure of his marriage to produce a son was God's punishment. By 1529, Henry had resolved to end his marriage to Catherine.

Ordinarily, a monarch who had consistently defended the faith would have encountered little opposition from Rome in dissolving a marriage. But extraordinary circumstances prevailed against Henry. Catherine refused to submit to this humiliation, and she had supportive relatives in high positions, including her nephew King Carlos I of Spain whose armies controlled the Vatican. Under those circumstances, Pope Clement VII opted to withhold a divorce decree. Undeterred, in 1533 Henry secured passage by the English Parliament of "An Act in Restraint of Appeals," which gave the Archbishop of Canterbury the final word on all religious matters in England. Thus, circumventing the pope, Henry divorced Catherine and in the process broke the ecclesiastical bonds with Rome. Subsequent acts completed the **English Reformation** and the creation of the **Church of England**, also known as the **Anglican Church**.

Shortly after Henry's divorce, the king married Anne Boleyn, who soon delivered a child—a girl they named Elizabeth. When a second child, a boy, was stillborn, Henry rejected Anne. Charging her with adultery and treason, he ordered her execution, and then went on to marry a third wife, who finally gave him a son. Henry VIII married three more times before his death in 1547.

The Age of Elizabeth

> **How did Queen Elizabeth I attempt to resolve England's religious disputes and what were its outcomes?**

England's religious upheaval did not end with Henry VIII's divorce. Calvinists hoped that formation of the Church of England signaled the beginning of thoroughgoing reform in church doctrine, liturgy, and organization. But hope dissolved into disillusionment when it became apparent that Henry VIII, a devoted Catholic, had no intention of reforming the church either doctrinally or liturgically. The Church of England remained mostly Catholic except for lacking official ties to Rome and having an English-language service rather than a Latin mass. Throughout the remainder of Henry VIII's reign, Calvinists, increasingly known as **Puritans** because they wanted to purify the church of its Catholic elements, denounced all trappings of "Popery." After Henry's death the conflicts worsened. The government of Edward VI, Henry's Protestant son by his third wife, attacked both Anglicans (members of the Church of England) and practicing Catholics. When the sickly Edward died in 1553, Mary I, the devoutly Catholic but tactless daughter of Henry VIII and Catherine of Aragon, succeeded him. Mary drove the country to the other extreme, exiling many leading Protestants and burning others at the stake. "Be of good comfort," a martyr told his companion as they readied themselves for the flames. "We shall this day light such a candle . . . as I trust shall never be put out." Indeed, it was not.

The reign of Elizabeth I, starting in 1558, marked not only a lessening of religious strife in England but also the beginning of England's ascent to the heights of global power. Rejecting the Protestant theologian John Knox's contention that women were "weak, frail, impatient, feeble, and foolish," the fiery, even bawdy, Elizabeth became England's greatest monarch. Elizabeth I held moderate religious views and hated religious controversy. She admitted faith in Jesus Christ, but "the rest," she scoffed, "is dispute about trifles." Seeking a workable compromise that would end the incessant conflict, she negotiated a settlement that preserved the hierarchical structure and elaborate ceremony of the Church of England while making changes in the prayer book and elsewhere that accommodated Puritan convictions. The easing of religious tensions allowed her to concentrate on other issues of national interest, including colonization.

Henry VIII's divorce from Catherine and England's conversion to Protestantism strained relations with Spain. Attempts to break the Spanish monopoly of American commerce and raids against Spanish settlements in America, coupled with Spanish King Felipe II's campaign to rid Europe of Protestantism, pushed the two countries toward war, which erupted in 1585. The culmination came in 1588, when a mammoth **Spanish Armada** of 130 warships carrying 30,000 soldiers lumbered into the English Channel. In one of the epic battles in naval history, an English fleet, assisted by a terrible storm and heavy seas, repelled the invaders, greatly boosting England's stature as a naval power and English national pride as well.

Elizabeth I and her advisors were not particularly interested in the difficult and expensive commitment required to establish permanent settlements in North America; instead, they favored raids by privateers against Spanish colonies and Spanish shipping. But a group of private investors thought otherwise and began mapping plans for overseas colonies. The group included Martin Frobisher, Humphrey Gilbert, Francis Drake, Walter Raleigh, and Richard Grenville. If their ventures failed to win the Queen's enthusiastic support, they did gain her indulgence. The real question was where to establish a settlement. Several attempts ended in failure. In 1576 Frobisher made the first of several voyages to search for the Northwest Passage and to plant a colony in North America. He accomplished neither goal. In 1583 Gilbert, an experienced Atlantic navigator, laid claim to assorted fishing camps in Newfoundland. Gilbert fully intended to assemble a syndicate to finance a colony further south, but he was lost at sea before the plan materialized.

The Mystery of Roanoke

> **How did the first English colonists and the Algonquian residents of Roanoke and Croatoan relate to each other?**

Following Gilbert's death, Sir Walter Raleigh obtained royal authority to establish a colony in Virginia, so named to honor the virgin Queen Elizabeth I. In 1585, Grenville brought a group of about 100 adventurers to the island of Roanoke, off the coast of North Carolina. Most of the colonists were there primarily to find gold, but the company also included two exceptional men, John White, a trained artist who served as governor, and the Oxford University scholar Thomas Harriot, who showed great interest in learning the language and understanding the culture of the Algonquian villagers who lived on and near the island. White and Harriot believed in the superiority of European over Native American culture. Harriot, for example, expressed "good hope" that the Indians would "honor, obey, fear, and love us." Still, Indian leaders, including Wanchese of Roanoke and Manteo of nearby Croatoan, befriended them, no doubt hoping that trade with the newcomers would benefit them and their communities.

Despite the progress the four individuals made toward mutual understanding, the colonists offended their hosts by demanding food and other supplies. The English attacked Indians who failed to comply, killing several and beheading one of their leaders. The colonists returned to England the following year, leaving behind a seething Indian resentment.

White wanted to try again and persuaded Raleigh to allow him to bring a number of families to settle permanently on Roanoke. The group of settlers who arrived in 1587 included White's pregnant daughter and his son-in-law. White's New granddaughter, Virginia Dare, became the first English child born in America. Understandably, many Indians refused to welcome them; in fact, Wanchese, now an enemy, killed a settler he found fishing along the beach. With supplies running low, White sailed back to England for replenishment; unfortunately, war with Spain and the attack of the Spanish Armada delayed a relief expedition until 1590. From the ships anchored offshore, trumpeters blew "many familiar English tunes," White reported later. No reply came, and members of the relief party who went ashore found nothing. The settlers had vanished. There were no signs of violence, only the words "CROATOAN" carved on a tree, perhaps indicating that they had taken up residence in that village. Stormy seas prevented the ships from reaching Croatoan, and White sadly set sail once again for England.

The fate of the Roanoke settlers remains a mystery. In all likelihood the Indians adopted them, perhaps married them; in other words, the English colonists became Indians. But it is possible that they were killed or even, as some have suggested, that they were lost at sea while attempting to reach some unknown destination. The Roanoke disaster discouraged further English plans to establish permanent overseas settlements. Such enterprise required greater capitalization than a few adventurers could muster and some means of spreading the very great risk.

THE LOCAL PERSPECTIVE: FOCUS ON ROANOKE

> **What insight into the way Europeans and Native Americans perceived each other do we gain by looking closely at England's Roanoke colony?**

England's Roanoke venture lasted only a few years and ended mysteriously and disappointingly; yet, we know much about how the English newcomers and the Native Algonquian residents perceived each other. Unfortunately, most of the insight comes from information provided by the colonists. In several ways, the information they left supports the contention that the English felt a common human bond with the Indians of North America.

Joachim Ganz was a Jewish Czech metallurgist who, with Thomas Harriot, conducted scientific experiments at Roanoke. Technology set the English apart from the local Algonquians, particularly the manufacture and use of metal tools, instruments, and weapons. This was a fact that both the English and the Indians recognized. Recent archaeological excavations at the Roanoke site have unearthed various objects, including fired crucibles, a tiny cup that probably was part of an apothecary's weight set, and charcoal for fueling a small forge. This was doubtless part of the colony's objective of processing copper (if not gold and silver) for export. Harriot's *Brief and True Report of the New Found Land of Virginia*, which he published in 1590, offers a sympathetic representation of Indians.

The first English people to encounter the Roanoke Indians recorded the general impression that external, cultural differences rather than intrinsic ones were all that differentiated Europeans from Native Americans, and that for the most part environment produced those cultural distinctions. Arthur Barlow, a member of a 1584 reconnaissance voyage to Roanoke, described people with distinctly European features, including children with "very fine auburn and chestnut color hair." Barlowe imagined them as living in paradise in a "golden age" of innocence. "We found the people most gentile, loving, and faithful, void of all guile . . . The earth bringeth forth all things in abundance, as in the first creation, without toil and labor."

John White, the London painter who also acted as governor of the final contingent of Roanoke settlers, did not go that far, but he recorded important visual impressions in a portfolio of paintings that were mostly positive insofar as the appearance of the Roanoke Indians was concerned. White's Indians had an Asian appearance with straight dark hair and long, slender arms, legs, and feet. A Flemish engraver named Theodore de Bry later reproduced them, along with Harriot's *Brief and True Report* in a multi-volume collection entitled *The Great Voyages*. Interestingly, though, in his reproductions of White's paintings, de Bry completely changed the physical characteristics of the people—their posture, body proportion, and forehead shape—to conform to contemporary standards of European portraiture. He understood that European curiosity about Native Americans was about their culture not their humanity, and they noticed fundamental similarities as well as more superficial contrasts. Indian talismans, body paint,

and tattoos, evident in White's paintings, stuck English viewers as signs of vain idolatry, but so too did the English use of facial makeup and Christian objects such as the crucifix.

The colonists of Roanoke seem to have been more curious about than repulsed by the Indians. But such an attitude did not last, and in the seventeenth century, English colonists became alarmed about becoming more like Indians and began to formulate racial theories that established immutable differences between them and Native Americans.

THINKING BACK

1. What do the artifacts that archaeologists have unearthed at Roanoke tell us about the intent of the English settlers?
2. What do the written and visual accounts of the English newcomers to Roanoke tell us about how they regarded the Native Americans who were present there?

The Irish Prelude

During the 1560s and 1570s, American colonization was less important to Elizabethan England than the conquest of Ireland. Ireland offered rich land that wealthy investors in England planned to convert into large-scale farms, perhaps alleviating some of England's rising unemployment and producing crops to feed the country's rising population. Above all, England's goal was to transform Ireland into an English society. For Elizabeth I and her courtiers, colonization of Ireland also involved asserting political control in order to establish English culture and values. For instance, Ireland was Catholic and thus a target for conversion for aggressive English Protestants.

> **How does English colonization of Ireland offer a context for understanding English colonization in America?**

The Irish bitterly resented England's takeover of their country and fought fiercely against it. Colonization displaced many local people and turned others into renters of land now owned by English landlords. The English generally regarded the Irish as "wild" and "savage." The Irish, in turn, hated the contemptuous foreigners. Resistance to English colonization led to a brutal campaign of suppression on the part of England. In 1569,

Elizabeth I took steps to stifle Irish opposition. She appointed Sir Humphrey Gilbert governor and put him in charge of a large military force. Gilbert crushed Irish resistance brutally. He ordered massive executions of captured rebels and lined roads with their severed heads to remind the Irish of his determination to prevail.

England's oppression of the Irish preceded American colonization and established a pattern for relationships with native people that English colonists applied to American Indians. Reducing other people to the category of "wild savages" was a technique the English ultimately used in dealing with Native Americans. Brutality was another tactic that the English employed in extending their control over territory in North America.

THINKING BACK

1. Why was England relatively slow in engaging itself in the European competition for North American territory, and what developments prepared England for overseas colonization?
2. What was the nature of England's involvement in North America during the fifteenth and sixteenth centuries, and how did the English respond to the Roanoke disaster?

CONCLUSION

The arrival of Europeans in America set up a clash of cultures. Europeans regarded Native Americans as savage and pagan and therefore without legitimate claim to the land. Their principal objective was to become rich and famous and to honor God by converting the natives to Christianity. Most of the Indians of North America had no personal contact with Europeans, but those who did were willing to negotiate with them. They were not passive pawns in the events that transformed America during the sixteenth century. Before the arrival of Europeans, Native Americans had moved about the country and interacted with each other on sometimes friendly and sometimes not so friendly terms. To the extent that they were able to do so, Indians attempted to establish the basis for interactions with Europeans and to derive what they could from those interactions.

Both Europeans and Indians gained and lost from the contact, but there can be no doubt that Native Americans lost infinitely more. Their societies suffered a catastrophic destruction that forever changed some or eliminated others altogether. The number and percentage of Indians who died as a result of the diseases introduced by the Europeans exceeded the number and percentage of Europeans who fell to the Black Death. It is impossible to know exactly how many Native Americans died, but perhaps as many as 90 percent of the Indian population disappeared within a century of European contact. The destruction of Indian societies was one of the most horrific events in human history.

The clash of cultures also involved Europeans themselves. By the end of the sixteenth century, of the various European nations competing for control of North America, Spain dominated. The Spaniards controlled vast expanses of land, the resources that the land yielded, and a large Native American population—despite their greatly reduced numbers. Over the next two centuries, England and France would change that storyline, as people from those two countries played increasingly dominant roles in the European makeover of North America.

SUGGESTED SOURCES FOR STUDENTS

To examine documents from some of the Spanish explorations of the American West, see Donald A. Barclay, James H. Maguire, and Peter Wild, eds., *Into the Wilderness Dream: Exploration Narratives of the American West, 1500-1805* (1994).

On England and the background of English colonization there are Carl Bridenbaugh's *Vexed and Troubled Englishmen, 1500-1642* (1968) and Wallace MacCaffrey, *Elizabeth I* (1993).

Catherine M. Cameron, Paul Kelton, and Alan C. Swedlund, eds., *Beyond Germs: Native Depopulation in North America* (2015), makes a compelling case for considering European empires as active contributors to the depopulation of Indian America.

Alfred W. Crosby, Jr.'s *The Columbian Exchange: Biological and Cultural Consequences of 1492* (1972) was the first book that fully examined the fascinating subject of the transfer of plants and animals across the Atlantic after European entry into the Americas.

For a description of France's involvement in New World colonization see W. J. Eccles, *France in America* (1972).

For documents pertaining to the Coronado expedition in particular, see Richard Flint and Shirley Cushing Flint, *Documents of the Coronado Expedition, 1539-1542* (2005).

For a superb examination of Spanish Catholic missionaries see Ramon A. Gutiérrez, *When Jesus Came, the Corn Mothers Went Away: Marriage, Sexuality, and Power in New Mexico, 1500-1846* (1991).

Karen Ordahl Kupperman, ed., *America in European Consciousness, 1493-1750* (1995), contains several insightful essays examining European responses to America.

The most recent account of the Roanoke episode can be found in Karen Ordahl Kupperman, *Roanoke: The Abandoned Colony* (1984).

Samuel Eliot Morison's biography, *Admiral of the Ocean Sea: A Life of Christopher Columbus* 2 Vols. (1942), remains the most thorough treatment of the man who opened the Americas to Europe even though it is a prime example of the "great person" emphasis in older historical writing that is not popular among modern historians.

Explaining early American history from the Native American point of view requires special effort because of a dearth of conventional documents. R. C. Padden, *The Hummingbird and the Hawk: Conquest and Sovereignty in the Valley of Mexico 1503-1541* (1967), describes Aztec society before and after the Spanish conquest using a variety of native materials. The book also contains a useful bibliography and an introduction that discusses the use of primary sources.

J. H. Parry, *The Age of Reconnaissance: Discovery, Exploration and Settlement 1450-1650* (1981), examines the technological, motivational, and strategic aspects of European exploration. It focuses on North America and the Caribbean.

Kirkpatrick Sale's *The Conquest of Paradise: Christopher Columbus and the Columbian Legacy* (1990), severely criticizes Columbus and laments his legacy of human and ecological destruction. The book is controversial because of some of the author's extreme views, but it is also provocative.

David J. Weber, *The Spanish Frontier in North America* (1992), is far and away the most thorough and up-to-date study of the exploration and settlement of New Spain's northern frontier from Florida to California.

BEFORE WE GO ON

1. What brought about the European invasion of the Caribbean Basin and the mainland of North America during the fifteenth and sixteenth centuries?

2. According to an old saying, history is written by the winners in the world's great human conflicts. Since most of the documents from which the history of sixteenth-century America has been written come from European sources, it is easy to draw the conclusion that the results of European colonization were triumphal and inevitable. But might the story have gone in different directions? Did European colonization really result in triumph? If so, how, and if not, then why not? Where and how did Native Americans assert themselves and their interests in interactions with Europeans?

Building a Democratic Nation

3. Some time ago, historians tended to emphasize the role of prominent individuals in determining the course of human events. Ordinary people seemed to be nothing but backdrop for the main actors. What evidence do you see that the events of the sixteenth century in America were the result of the actions of a few exceptional people? What evidence suggests that more massive human forces were at work?

4. In the European invasion and conquest of America in the fifteenth and sixteenth centuries, what roles did women play? What determined women's status during those socially formative times?

Connections

5. In the encounters between Europeans and Indians during the fifteenth and sixteenth centuries, both the Europeans and the Indians absorbed certain aspects of the other's culture. What can you see in the cultures of both groups of people that remain a part of American culture today?

6. As we travel from region to region of the United States today, in what parts of the country would you most expect to find remnants of Spanish, French, and English colonization? What would those cultural remnants be?

Chapter 3

ENGLISH COLONIZATION: PROFITING MATERIALLY AND SPIRITUALLY, 1607–1733

A PERSONAL PERSPECTIVE: THE DISORDERLY PINION FAMILY

Scarcely anywhere in seventeenth-century colonial court records does a more dysfunctional family appear than the Pinions of Lynn, Massachusetts. From 1647 to 1665, local magistrates summoned Nicholas and Elizabeth Pinion and three of their children to court twenty-six times and punished them for a wide variety of offenses.

> **Why did colonial authorities regard the Pinion family as a serious threat to society?**

Although their crimes included several assaults, general disorderliness, and even murder, authorities seemed most disturbed by the lack of discipline within the Pinion household. Nicholas, a blacksmith, drew rebuke for public drunkenness, swearing, failing to attend church on Sundays, brawling, and assaulting his wife Elizabeth. Authorities reprimanded Elizabeth for using foul language in public and whipped her publicly for adultery. She also assaulted her husband when he demanded her obedience. After several years, the Pinions moved to New Haven, Connecticut, but the change of scenery did not make

them more orderly. New Haven authorities charged son Robert with profaning the Sabbath and speaking slanderously and daughters Hannah and Ruth with sexual promiscuity, or fornication in the language of the day. Ruth ultimately went to the gallows for murdering her bastard infant.

The Pinions were not a typical New England family, which is precisely why their story is important to consider. Authorities and most residents took great pains to prevent families like the Pinions from settling in their communities. The nuclear family—a mother, a father, and their biological offspring—was the cornerstone of most societies in Europe, Africa, and North America. The seventeenth-century philosopher John Locke declared: "The *first society* was between Man and Wife, which gave beginning to that between Parents and Children." In European-based families, the structure was **patriarchal**, meaning that the father possessed unquestioned authority as the family head, or patriarch. His responsibility was to teach, correct, and protect his wife and children, whose duty was to obey him. The result would be an orderly family. The principle of patriarchy grew out of Christian faith in the Old Testament book of Genesis, where, it is written, God punished Eve for giving Adam forbidden fruit, telling her: "thy desire *shall* be to thy husband, and he shall rule over thee." Civil law in Puritan New England, where the Pinions resided, reflected such Biblical admonitions. As one contemporary legal authority explained: "The common Law here shaketh hand with Divinitie."

By the standard of seventeenth-century Puritan patriarchy, Nicholas Pinion failed miserably to perform his duties as husband and father. In his failure, he offended God, and Elizabeth Pinion affronted God equally by willfully disobeying Nicholas. The Pinion's infidelity to the patriarchal family model, according to Puritan belief, led directly and inevitably to disorderliness, which in turn weakened vital social cohesion. Without discipline imposed by family patriarchs, people would lapse into slothfulness and other sinful behavior that would allow evil in the world to destroy good Christian societies. Thus, since Nicholas could not discipline his family, he posed a serious threat to the community, and civil

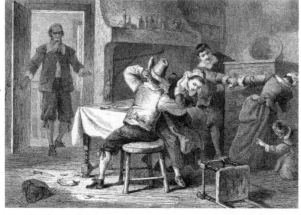

© Bettmann/Contributor/Getty

Stolen Frolic in a Puritan Farmhouse. Puritans feared social disorder, which they believed violated God's wishes. In this engraving, young women and men, probably indentured servants, are behaving inappropriately, as the countenance on the farmer as he walks through the door clearly shows. The Pinion family was just such a disorderly family, and Nicholas Pinion was guilty of failing to impose patriarchal authority.

1607	**1619**	**1620**	**1624**	**1625**	**1630**
English settlers found Jamestown; English Separatists seek asylum in Holland	Virginia House of Burgesses convenes; first documented Africans in Jamestown	Pilgrims draft *Mayflower* Compact before landing at Plymouth	The Dutch establish New Netherland	Virginia becomes first English royal colony	Puritans settle Massachusetts Bay

authorities saw no alternative but to intervene in the management of the Pinion household.

The story of the Pinion family illustrates the constant tension between freedom and authority in early colonial societies. Most colonists, regardless of nationality, came to America in pursuit of personal freedom, but most of them encountered constraints imposed by family patriarchs, government officials, employers, and church authorities committed to maintaining social order. As had been true in Europe during the Middle Ages, elites with property, power, and status, feared the unruly masses because they threatened their possessions. Strong, hierarchical authority was necessary to ensure that the masses, instead of falling into sloth or violence, obeyed the law and engaged in profitable, Godly pursuits.

Families in some areas of English North America were difficult to form and maintain. In the Chesapeake region, for instance, many factors, including a preponderance of males and ghastly mortality rates, hampered family-building. Indentured servitude and slavery also impeded family formation. White fears of servant rebellions led authorities to regulate the freedom of people bound to any form of servitude, including refusing them the right to marry. Yet Africans found ways to establish families despite their enslavement. Africans also succeeded in maintaining Old World identities even as they were acculturated to life in the New World. By contrast, New England settlers usually arrived as families. In the Middle Atlantic colonies, settler demographics, cultures, and social patterns varied widely.

Through most of the seventeenth century, settlers interacted with Native Americans. They incorporated Indians into the expanding Atlantic commercial market, and where and when they could they sought to impose authority over the indigenous people. Initially, the Indians held a strong hand in relations with the newcomers, although disease, settler aggressiveness, and the destruction of their social and economic networks weakened them substantially. It became increasingly difficult for Indians to defend their land when the colonists decided to take it.

THINKING BACK

1. What were Nicholas and Elizabeth Pinion and their children's obligations within patriarchal families, and how did they fail to meet them?
2. How does the Pinion family history illustrate the tension between personal freedom and social order in seventeenth-century colonial America?

THE CHESAPEAKE COLONIES

Even after the Roanoke disaster (see p. 55), the embers of English ambition for North American colonies continued to smolder. From a national standpoint, the overarching reason for colonies was the rivalry that set nations and religious groups against one another. Some Protestant English strategists still conceived of colonies as military bases in the ongoing conflict with Catholic Spain. Others like Sir Walter Raleigh, although representing the English crown, simply could not resist the excitement of conquest. Some historians have said that Spaniards came to America for gold and glory while the English came for religious freedom. In truth, many Chesapeake colonists came for the same reasons as the Spaniards, only, they found no riches in North America. In 1594 and again in 1616, Raleigh led expeditions to find the legendary golden city in South America known as El Dorado. Early in the seventeenth century, however, other ideas began to shape English thinking about colonies. Colonizers imagined American settlements as miniature English societies sustaining themselves by commerce. In the end, however, many ordinary people came to Virginia to improve their lives.

In 1603, Queen Elizabeth I died unmarried and childless, taking with her the fragile balance among Anglicans, Puritans, and Catholics. Elizabeth's successor, her Scottish nephew James I, antagonized Puritans by refusing to reform the Anglican Church. After James I's death in 1625, his son Charles I worsened the situation by deleting predestination from official church doctrine. Puritans turned to **Parliament** for political power. Parliament's elected branch, the **House of**

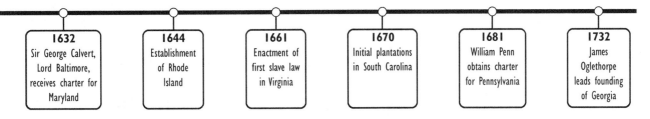

1632	1644	1661	1670	1681	1732
Sir George Calvert, Lord Baltimore, receives charter for Maryland	Establishment of Rhode Island	Enactment of first slave law in Virginia	Initial plantations in South Carolina	William Penn obtains charter for Pennsylvania	James Oglethorpe leads founding of Georgia

Commons, contained many reformers who also wished to curb royal prerogatives. Invoking the ancient "divine right of kings" to rule absolutely, the King dissolved Parliament. In the end, however, Charles I could not sustain his government without Parliamentary taxes and called the lawmakers back in session.

In 1642, religious and political skirmishes erupted into the **English Civil War**: the king and his supporters (Cavaliers) against the Commons (known as Roundheads). By 1649, the Commons' New Model Army, commanded by the ardent Puritan Oliver Cromwell, had defeated the Cavaliers and beheaded Charles I. The Commons proceeded to institute regular and frequent elections, universal manhood suffrage, and measures to protect property rights. Although the new **Commonwealth** discontinued the monarchy, Cromwell became Lord Protector for life. In response to these upheavals, thousands of English men and women left the country, many seeking refuge in America.

During this tumultuous period, the English government paid little attention to overseas colonization. Unlike Spanish colonies, the initial English settlements were private, mostly unsupervised enterprises. The crown granted charters to merchant companies and rich friends and supporters who established the colonies. The merchant companies received wide authority to govern the colonies as best they could.

Promoting the Colonies for Profit and Glory

> **What rewards motivated English colonization, and how did colonizers finance their enterprises?**

The spark that reignited the fires of English colonization was profit. Although colonizers sought to recreate their image of England in America, they always anticipated material rewards. Merchants and investors regarded colonies as moneymaking ventures for raising exotic crops, opening markets for English textiles and metal tools and utensils, and extracting natural resources. But idealism motivated colonizers too. Protestants saw colonial ventures as advancing their religious faith against Spanish and French Catholicism. Protestants did not monopolize colonization, however. In 1621, Catholic statesman George Calvert, the first Lord Baltimore, founded a small, colony called Avalon in Newfoundland partly as an experiment in religious tolerance. And government officials believed colonial settlements could strengthen England in the highly competitive Atlantic world while absorbing some of the country's jobless and homeless.

Neither the king nor wealthy aristocrats wanted to foot the bill for colonial ventures, remembering the financial disaster at Roanoke. So early English colonizers resorted to a type of business organization known as the **joint-stock company**. This prototype of the modern corporation invited investors to purchase stock and receive a share of the profits. Boards of directors managed company operations. **Adventurers**, as commercial capitalists were known, thus generated the cash necessary for overseas colonies. Investors risked only what they invested and hoped for high returns.

Initially, merchant adventurers saw the greatest opportunity for quick profits in the islands of the West Indies. By the middle of the seventeenth century, as many as 30,000 English settlers occupied St. Kitts, Jamaica, and Barbados (see the Local Perspective, pp. 90-92). Island planters produced tobacco, cotton and sugar while also sheltering English pirates who plundered Spanish treasure ships. But the mainland was too vast and rich to be ignored, and during the first half of the 1600s the king authorized colonies in Virginia, along the Atlantic coast between Spanish Florida and Newfoundland.

The Struggle at Jamestown

In 1606, James I granted a charter to the London-based Virginia Company, bestowing on it exclusive authority to do business with Native Americans living along the shores of Chesapeake Bay. In December

> **What was the Jamestown colony's goal, and why was it so difficult to attain?**

1606, the company sent 105 settlers by ship to Virginia. The party included several younger sons of prominent English families, but most came as servants or hired laborers. A number were tradesmen—carpenters and gunsmiths—but few were farmers or soldiers, and there were no women.

In April 1607, the sea-weary voyagers disembarked on the shore of a large river flowing into Chesapeake Bay. They named it the James River in honor of their king and christened their settlement Jamestown. Following instructions, the newcomers searched for a potential passageway through North America to the Pacific and prospected for "all Manner of Gold, Silver, and Copper." They found nothing of the sort, only towering pine trees, some of which they cut for building materials. Meadows, perhaps cleared by local Algonquian-speaking Indians, were blanketed with wild currants, raspberries, and strawberries. Chesapeake Bay teemed with fish, crabs, and oysters, leading one settler to declare: "heaven and earth never agreed better to frame a place for man's habitation." As carpenters erected shelters and a log fort, people began to sicken, for the site was a swampy breeding ground for deadly typhoid fever, dysentery, and malaria. And their drinking water, from the James River, was "full of slime and filth."

Throughout the first summer, the colonists made little effort to feed themselves, relying instead on supplies from England and from the numerous Native American residents. This was partly the result of bad planning by the Virginia Company and partly because the colonists spent too much time searching for gold. But mismanagement alone does not explain the settlers' failure to provide for themselves. Their arrival corresponded with the onset of the severest drought in centuries, one that wiped out the wheat and barley they did plant. Within months, more than half the sick and undernourished colonists died, and only the timely appearance of a supply ship in late December rescued the survivors. To make matters worse, resentful Algonquians ambushed settlers who wandered away from the fort.

In the second year, a twenty-eight-year-old soldier named John Smith was appointed to lead the colony. Smith was a practical-minded veteran of campaigns against Spanish Catholics and Muslim Turks in Europe. Showing little respect for Jamestown's gentlemen, he demanded that the colonists devote more time and effort to supporting themselves. Smith's law was clear and simple: "He that will not worke shall not eate." Many resented his audacity. Colonist George Percy complained that "Smithe wolde rule all and ingrose all authority into his own hands." Nevertheless, his forceful leadership helped Jamestown survive.

Meanwhile, Virginia Company officials solicited additional capital and sent more supplies and settlers, including the colony's first women, to Jamestown. Women, of course, were essential to establishing a traditional, family-based English society. But for Jamestown's beleaguered residents, the hardest times lay ahead. Drought persisted, and with the onset of the fierce winter of 1609–10 colonists and Native Americans alike suffered terribly. Famished settlers gnawed desperately on leather shoes and straps; some even devoured their comrades' corpses. In the spring, the wretched survivors prepared to sail back to England; however, once again, in the nick of time, supply ships arrived with more settlers, food, tools, and livestock.

Everyone grumbled about Jamestown's failure to sustain itself. Colonists carped at company officials for not grasping the difficulties they faced; in London, company directors griped about the colonists' laziness. Governor Sir Thomas Dale (Smith had been severely injured in an accidental gunpowder explosion and returned to England) reported that colonists wasted their time "bowling in the streets." Dale ordered dawn-to-dusk labor and demanded that homes be kept "sweete and cleane." But tough laws alone would not ensure Jamestown's long-term success. That required some exportable commodity.

Reviving the Colony

The Virginia Company eventually shook off its lust for gold and shifted to shipping marketable commodities like furs, sassafras (thought to remedy syphilis), and lumber back to England. James I urged the colony to grow silk, certainly a valuable commodity. But the reversal of Virginia's miserable fortunes came instead from a humbler source—tobacco. Spaniards in the West Indies had observed the native residents smoking tobacco and introduced the practice to Europe. Jamestown colonist John Rolfe bred West Indian tobacco with a local Chesapeake variety and produced a leaf that locals claimed "smoked pleasant, sweete and strong." Here was a source of financial returns and the key to Virginia's future success. In 1614, the first shipload of Jamestown tobacco reached London, and soon a rush to plant tobacco was on. Settlers madly cleared forests, planted tobacco, and established new settlements. Within a decade, Virginia (Jamestown and the other settlements organized together as a colonial unit) was exporting up to 200,000 pounds of tobacco a year.

> What finally turned Jamestown into a relatively stable and successful colony?

The tobacco boom also raised concerns. For one thing, it did not encourage Virginia settlers to grow food. For another, the "stinking weed" grossed out many of the company's officials. James I anticipated modern medical research by condemning smoking as "loathsome to the eye, hateful to the nose, harmful to the brain, [and] dangerous to the lungs." Anxious about the get-rich-quick mentality and continuing cost of supplying the colony with food, the company's directors took steps to make Virginia more stable and self-sufficient by recruiting farm families as settlers. In 1619, the company's chief executive, Sir Edwin Sandys, began distributing fifty-acre allotments, called **headrights**, to individuals who paid their own transportation. Furthermore, a married man received an additional fifty acres for each member of his family. Sandys also sought to diversify the economy by sending specialists in mining, iron manufacturing, glass making, and silk production. These newcomers included Jews and Catholics as well as Protestants from other parts of Europe, giving Virginia a definite multicultural flavor.

Convinced that self-sufficiency would develop better in an atmosphere of self-government rather than under martial law, and being himself a defender of freedom in the House of Commons, Sandys authorized Virginia landowners to elect representatives to meet annually with the governor and a council to enact local laws. Called the **House of Burgesses**, this was the first representative legislative government in English North America. Meeting in the summer of 1619, the burgesses discussed quality standards for tobacco and passed laws against idleness, gambling, and drunkenness.

Sandys' reforms only partially succeeded. Between 1619 and 1622, more than 3,500 newcomers came to Virginia. An iron foundry and a glass factory swung into operation. But while some farmers and tradesmen came with their families, most newcomers were still male servants or tenants. Although reliable data is scarce, a list of colonists in 1625 shows 350 men for every 100 women, and the gender imbalance persisted through the remainder of the century. Mortality remained shockingly high. In the spring of 1622, only 1,200 settlers were still alive. In 1624, James I revoked the company's charter and took over management of Virginia as England's first **royal colony**.

Wry commentators joked that Virginia was built on smoke, and they were right, in more ways than one. The tobacco boom, while making Virginia prosperous, actually disguised its instability. Through the 1630s, people flocked to Virginia not to build lasting communities but to earn money as fast as they could. They did not expect to live there very long. Indeed, men in Virginia could expect to live only half as long as their counterparts in England. Women died even sooner due to the hazards of childbirth. Less than one-quarter of all children born in Virginia grew up in households with both natural parents, and no more than half survived to adulthood. The difficulty of sustaining nuclear families undermined the effort to replicate traditional English society. Consequently, county sheriffs and members of the colonial assembly assumed much of the responsibility for maintaining social order.

Overall, conditions did not improve significantly until after the 1630s when the tobacco boom abated. The high volume of tobacco exports reduced prices in England, making tobacco less profitable to grow and discouraging planters from bringing in large numbers of servants to cultivate it. In addition, wealthier planters in the fertile tidewater areas purchased land from lesser ones and consolidated the rich tobacco land. But Virginia remained an attractive place for immigrant families. Substantial population growth in much of Europe reduced opportunities to acquire farms in the Old World whereas in Virginia's piedmont settlers could obtain cheap land and raise enough wheat, corn, cattle, hogs, and poultry to become self-sustaining and a little tobacco on the side.

Virginia and the Powhatan Confederacy

Most Native Americans residing in the Chesapeake Bay region regarded the English settlers as intruders. Previous encounters with strange-looking and awful-smelling Europeans (who did not believe in bathing) had been unpleasant. Some recalled the arrogant Spanish missionaries and demanding Roanoke colonists of decades before, and encounters with the newcomers were no better. Initially, the English mainly wanted to trade, but soon their intention of settling permanently became clear. The English seemed to the native residents like total incompetents. After all, they could not or would not even feed themselves. Yet they were dangerous and absolutely untrustworthy.

> What type of relationship existed between Virginia colonists and local Indians?

Almost thirty small Algonquian tribes living in the Chesapeake participated in a confederation under the leadership of a venerable chief known as Powhatan. John Smith described him as "a tall, well-proportioned man . . . his head somewhat gray . . . His age near 60." Powhatan ruled through military and diplomatic skill, demanding and receiving tribute from subordinate chiefdoms. Curious about the English, he nevertheless resented their selling merchandise directly to the tributary people and undermining his leverage over them. Furthermore, Powhatan wanted English muskets, cannon, and swords entirely for himself. English weapons would be useful in fighting Iroquois enemies.

At any time during Virginia's early years, an all-out Indian attack could have annihilated the English; Powhatan's people vastly outnumbered them. Furthermore, the Algonquians could shoot arrows faster and more lethally than the settlers could load and fire their heavy, muzzle-loaded guns. Equally important, the Indians were at home and controlled the settlers' food supply. Yet Powhatan never ordered such an attack, probably because he thought the colonists would starve or that he could pick them off one by one. John Smith also kept Powhatan off balance by alternately bullying the Indians for corn and then offering trade goods and alliances. After Smith's departure in 1609, Powhatan encouraged guerilla-like raids against outlying English settlements, but the Indians steadily lost ground as English supplies and reinforcements increased.

A turning point came in 1613 when the English kidnapped Powhatan's favorite daughter Pocahontas, prompting him to accept a truce to ransom her. Pocahontas surprised her father, however, by choosing to remain with the English, one of several Indians and English settlers who crossed the wide cultural divide between the two peoples. She married John Rolfe, accepted the Christian name Rebecca, and in 1617 accompanied her husband to England. Pocahontas sickened and died on the return trip however, and her husband succumbed in Virginia a few years later. The couple's son became a Virginia planter, but Pocahontas' line of descent eventually disappeared from the records. In cultural and political borderlands like seventeenth-century Virginia, Native American and European identities and allegiances occasionally switched. Both Indians and colonists took captives from the other, and people like Pocahontas voluntarily left their native communities and joined others.

Indian-settler hostility actually persisted for many years. With the tobacco boom, hordes of colonists seized prime Algonquian agricultural land. As one Englishman put it, "there is scarce any man amongst us that doth so much as afforde them [the Indians] a good thought in his hart." When Powhatan died in 1618, his brother Opechancanough ascended to power. Opechancanough resolved to rid the area of unwanted interlopers once and for all, and on March 22, 1622, he and his fighters attacked several farms, killing 347 men, women, and children. But some of the subordinate chiefdoms refused to participate in Opechancanough's attack, preferring peace with the English to war. Early warnings kept English casualties lower than they might have been, and because the attack was not totally successful it was a strategic failure. One English survivor declared: "now we have just cause to destroy them by all means possible."

Fighting continued for two more decades, but the balance of power now favored the colonists who killed hundreds of Indians, burned cornfields, and sent captives to the West Indies as slaves. In 1646, Englishmen finally captured and killed Opechancanough. As the number of colonists soared, the Virginia Algonquian population dwindled. Many died while others moved out of the region, joining other Indian communities. By mid-century, scarcely 4,500 Indians remained in the Chesapeake region, and most of them agreed to accept English authority and small allotments of land in what had once been their homeland.

From Virginia's experience, the English concluded that successful colonies should be extensions of traditional English society and culture, and Native Americans had no useful place there. English colonizers adhered to that principle elsewhere as well.

Maryland: A Catholic Haven on the Chesapeake

During the middle decades of the seventeenth century, political turbulence in England played a major role in determining who came to the colonies and why. King Charles I became locked in a bitter and ultimately fatal dispute with Parliament. In a broad sense, the conflict centered on the opposing principles of representative government versus the "divine right" of kings, but a subplot in the story was Charles' tolerance of Catholics.

> How did early Maryland compare to Virginia?

In 1632, Charles I promised a tract of land north of Virginia to George Calvert, Lord Baltimore, a loyal supporter of the monarchy. A converted Catholic and enthusiastic colonizer, Calvert envisioned a baronial society that would also provide a haven for Catholics. When Calvert died, his son Cecilius became lord proprietor of Maryland, the name chosen to honor Charles' wife Henrietta Maria, also a practicing Catholic. Maryland became England's first **proprietary colony**, owned by a single person rather than a company. In 1634 two ships landed the first contingent of 200 settlers on the bank of a tributary of the Potomac River. They called their settlement St. Mary's City. Calvert's brother Leonard took up residence as the colony's governor, ruling in conjunction with an assembly of elected landowners.

Faithful to his father's wishes, Cecilius Calvert tried to distribute vast tracts of land to wealthy Catholics who would bring along able-bodied Catholic workers. Calvert gave the landlords nearly absolute authority over their estates and the men and women who worked the land, reminiscent of Europe's feudal lords. To his disappointment, though, most wealthy Catholics had no desire to settle in Maryland. Thus Calvert resorted

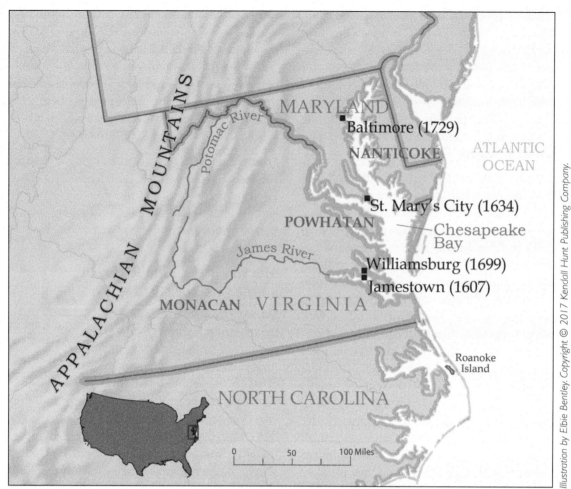

The English settlements of Jamestown and St. Mary's City were situated on the shores of Chesapeake Bay, affording protection from enemy attack and direct, albeit lengthy, connections to Europe. Tensions between the settlers and resident Indians, especially the powerful Powhatan Confederacy, produced many bloody clashes.

to the headright system developed in Virginia to attract yeoman farmers, many of whom were Protestants. Like their Virginia neighbors, Marylanders settled along the navigable rivers that emptied into Chesapeake Bay, wresting the land from the decimated Powhatan Indians and growing tobacco. But Maryland colonists heeded the bitter experiences in early Jamestown and took care to provide themselves with food and to establish permanent communities.

Calvert ultimately failed to make Maryland into a Catholic refuge. Protestants soon comprised the majority of Maryland settlers, and when in the 1640s political strife in England exploded into civil war, they attempted to take over the colony, assaulting St. Mary's City and deposing the governor. Calvert tried to placate the rebels and preserve his authority by appointing a Protestant governor. In 1649, the year that the Puritan army executed Charles I, Calvert acted to protect the rights of Catholics by sending to the Maryland assembly an **Act Concerning Religion**, which it respectfully

passed. The measure established freedom of "conscience in matters of religion" for all who believed in the divinity of Christ. Although excluding Jews and other non-Christians, the act established a degree of religious freedom uncommon in the colonies, but it did not safeguard the Catholic minority's political power. Lord Protector Oliver Cromwell repealed the measure anyway, took the colony away from Calvert, and set up an all-Protestant assembly. Finally, in 1658, Cromwell died and a more moderate English House of Commons restored Calvert's Maryland proprietorship.

Neither did Calvert's manorial vision fully materialize. Some wealthy landowners did establish large tobacco plantations along the Potomac River; however, the relatively low price of tobacco in the 1640s and 1650s suppressed any great economic surge. Instead, Maryland grew steadily, and the colonists dotted the landscape with modest-sized farms. Social order and stability came primarily from institutions like churches and families.

1. What were the principal reasons behind the founding of English colonies in the Chesapeake Bay region of North America, and why was it so hard for the colonists to reach their goals?
2. What comparisons can you draw between Virginia and Maryland in terms of early economic, political, and social development?

BOUND LABOR

Beyond staying alive, the greatest challenge that Chesapeake planters faced was building a reliable workforce. During the tobacco boom, planters could make more money if they had extra hands, and the supply of labor always lagged behind demand, facts that enhanced the value of labor. Impoverished Europeans eager for job opportunities represented a convenient labor pool, but planters in the Chesapeake and other agricultural areas also knew about the shiploads of enslaved Africans being transported to Portuguese and Spanish colonies in Brazil and the Caribbean islands. Was slavery the ultimate answer to their labor problems?

Employing Indentured Servants

> Where did indentured servants come from, and how did the servant system work?

Perhaps three out of four emigrants from England, Scotland, Ireland, and continental Europe who came to English North America during the seventeenth and eighteenth centuries were **indentured servants**. These men, women, and adolescent children could not afford to pay the high price of a ticket to sail across the Atlantic, so they came under contract to work in the homes, shops, farms, or plantations of masters who covered the cost of their passage. Formal contracts spelled out the basic terms of indenture; however, legal documents tell only part of the story of indentured servitude.

The circumstances from which the 75,000 Europeans who immigrated to the Chesapeake colonies between 1607 and 1680 came varied widely. Although younger sons and daughters of farmers and artisans in the Old Country occasionally opted to become indentured servants, most servants were recruited from the legions of unemployed in England, Ireland, Scotland, and continental Europe.

Convicts sometimes received the option of indentured servitude over imprisonment, or judges made that decision for them. And a few unfortunate denizens of London's streets and pubs awoke from a beating or drugging to find themselves on a sailing ship bound for America. Seventy-five percent of indentured servants in the Chesapeake colonies were males, the majority between the ages of fifteen and twenty-four. Half owned no property, possessed no skills, and had few prospects, which explains why most of them risked becoming indentured servants in the colonies. The length of time that most of them remained bound to their masters typically ranged from four to seven years. After satisfying their obligations, servants were free to acquire land or practice a trade. In other words, they could redeem themselves and thus were often called "**redemptioners**."

Indenture contracts and colonial laws specified not only the type of work the servants were to perform but also what employers were obligated to provide—usually food, clothing, and shelter—somewhat like feudal or patriarchal systems. Employers commanded total obedience and were empowered by law to punish disobedient servants, usually by whipping although many servants suffered much more extreme forms of punishment, including torture, rape, and even murder. Although masters and servants occupied grossly unequal positions in these relationships, servants typically possessed enough leverage, because of the supply and demand for their labor, to negotiate work conditions with their masters, and due to the unsteadiness of markets for colonial products and narrow profit margins, many employers cut their maintenance costs by allowing their servants to work independently to earn their upkeep. Furthermore, many indentured servants knew the law well enough to secure legal protection against abuse at the hands of their masters. Colonial court records show that a significant number of servants actually took legal action to force recalcitrant employers to meet their contractual obligations. And of course, servants could, and often did, run away from bullying masters.

Essential though it was to colonial economies, the colonial servant class did not reproduce itself, leading to a constant demand for more immigrants. Indentured servitude was usually a short-term condition, not a lifetime one, and the reproductive years of servant women were relatively short. Indentured servants typically were not allowed to marry until their term of service ended, and law and custom punished unmarried women, regardless of social class, for bearing children, although many certainly did. Most servant women did not marry until age twenty-five. Those who survived their childbearing years could expect to produce six children; however, most died prematurely and gave birth to no more than four. And in those days, half the children of servants died before reaching adulthood. Thus, the numbers did not add up to a naturally stable or increasing servant class.

Resorting to Slaves

How did African slaves live and work in the early colonies?

Another source of plantation labor revealed itself in 1619 in the persons of twenty or so enslaved Africans who stepped off a Dutch ship in Jamestown. Ironically, that was the same year and place where representative government was born in North America.

The African slave trade had begun midway through the fifteenth century when Portuguese merchant mariners exploring Africa's west coast established trading posts (see map p. 24). Initially, the Europeans hawked metal tools, decorative beads, and woolen textiles for African ivory, gold, and pepper. Eventually they began trading for African slaves. When the Spanish conquest of the Caribbean islands led to the extinction of Native Americans there in the sixteenth century, West Indian planters began importing Africans. As the European planters' appetite for slave laborers mounted, Africans themselves became more heavily involved in the traffic, organizing raids against neighboring villages, transporting captives in coffles to coastal ports for loading onto waiting European slave ships in what has been called the "first passage" to slavery.

In the seaports, the crews of slave ships laid their terrified human cargo out on cramped lower decks, tightly chained to minimize movement and to prevent them from escaping or committing suicide by jumping overboard. With as many as 400–500 slaves, each ship began the awful five-week crossing of the tropical mid-Atlantic called the "**Middle Passage**." The miseries slaves suffered during those weeks, both physical and emotional, can scarcely be imagined. Hellish heat, foul air, contaminated food and water, the filth of human excrement created a sewer-like environment. Olaudah Equiano, an Ibo (Nigerian) teenager who endured the voyage, described the "shrieks of the women, and the groaning of the dying," which "rendered the whole a scene of horror almost inconceivable." Death from dis-ease, malnutrition, injury, and suicide carried off one in five from the average shipload, but the captives were so valuable that ship owners would profit even if one out of every three slaves died. Most of the vessels deposited the Africans in the islands of the West Indies. There began the "last passage" into slavery for some of the Africans who were transported to the American mainland colonies.

From the outset, even before actual statutes were written, prejudice led planters in the Chesapeake region to presume that Africans were slaves even though no colonial law specifically said so. Initially, whites treated them about the same way they treated European indentured servants, that is, not very well, but they apparently held Africans in bondage longer, sometimes for life. As the number of Africans increased, authorities enacted slave laws to clarify their status and distinguish Africans from Europeans and Native Americans. The process of constructing legalized slavery began in the 1660s with Virginia and Maryland. In 1665 for example, a Maryland law declared that children born of Africans "shall be Slaves . . . for the Terme of their lives." From its cradle in the Chesapeake, African slavery matured and spread to every corner of England's North American colonies.

Certain features of African slavery in early English North America merit careful note because early colonial slavery was more complex than is often thought. First of all, the initial Africans came through port communities on the African coast and from islands in the West Indies where they had encountered and sometimes converted to Christianity, learned many European languages—like Spanish, Portuguese, French, and English—, and dressed in European clothes. These **Creoles**, that is, men and women born in America but who retained Old World identities, bore names that revealed their complex, international selves: Domingo Mathews, Pedro Negrito, and Simon Congo. Most early African arrivals came to the Chesapeake in lots of ten or twenty—men and women—rather than in boatloads of hundreds and were rather quickly absorbed into colonial societies, often working alongside their owners.

Although enslaved, many Creole Africans refused to be totally subdued. They negotiated the details of their bondage, like indentured servants did. With declining tobacco prices in Virginia during the 1630s and 1640s, planters often operated on the margins of profitability, and in order to save money some allowed slaves to live on their own, grow their own food and hire themselves out to other employers. Although entailing more work, such arrangements provided slaves with a measure of self-control, the opportunity to enter the market economy, and even the opportunity to purchase their freedom.

In 1621, a merchant ship brought a man known to others only as "Antonio a Negro" to Jamestown probably from a Spanish colony. Antonio's story illustrates how some enslaved Africans made the best of a very bad situation in early colonial America. His owner, a small farmer, allowed him to sell a little tobacco and save the proceeds. Antonio married an African woman named Mary. The couple reared children who were baptized in the local Protestant Christian church. Antonio eventually purchased his and his family's freedom, acquired 250 acres, and purchased slaves of his own. In the process, he became Anthony Johnson, a respected member of Virginia society. Indeed, by the end of the seventeenth century, as many as one-third of all Africans in some parts of Virginia were legally free.

Historians once taught that the "middle passage" destroyed African culture. However, African traditions survived, and African Americans built strong families and stable communities despite the destructive power of slave masters.

English colonists also attempted to enslave Indians as the Spanish had done in New Mexico and Florida. Colonist Ralph Hamor wrote that Native Americans "are easily taught" and may, by lenient and "faire usage," be brought into the bound labor force. But the colonists mostly failed in that endeavor, for Indians had equal or greater power than the settlers in their ancestral territory and could easily escape. Moreover, their numbers declined sharply in settled areas. Most slaves on the mainland of English North America were Africans, and thus slavery became associated with blackness.

Although they became increasingly comfortable with strict racial distinctions, colonial Europeans did encourage slaves to acculturate themselves, to speak English rather than their native languages, to dress in European-style clothes, and to rid themselves of body decorations and other forms of African culture. In such an environment, it was difficult, but not impossible, for Africans to maintain their native cultures. Considerable evidence suggests Africans in America blended elements of African and European traditions into African-American cultures. Early Creoles began the process, and later arrivals assimilated local Creole cultures. Recent archeological discoveries along the Atlantic seaboard reveal that Africans built homes using distinctly African designs and techniques. Earthenware, tools, and clothes found in the slave quarters also show traces of African culture. In addition, African-American music, religious beliefs, and marriage and burial customs contained African retentions.

African slaves toiled in every colony from New Hampshire to Georgia. Until late in the seventeenth century, however, the importance of slavery as a labor system and the number of African slaves remained small in most areas outside of plantation regions. Although the exact number of Africans who fell victim to the trans-Atlantic slave trade is unknown, as many as 12 million African men and women may have been transported as slaves to all the Americas from the sixteenth through the nineteenth centuries (see map on p. 24). About 5 percent of the total number of slaves transported to the New World came to England's North American colonies. This means approximately 10,000 during the seventeenth century and 350,000 in the eighteenth. The number of African slaves imported into the English colonies exceeded the number of European immigrants over that same period by a margin greater than two to one.

1. Where did indentured servants come from, how were they able to influence the conditions of their indenture, and why was there no self-sustaining servant class?
2. Why and how did Africans come to be slaves in America, how did early colonial slavery compare with indentured servitude, and how did enslavement affect Africans?

FREEDOM AND AUTHORITY IN NEW ENGLAND

Several hundred miles north of Chesapeake Bay, Puritan emigrants settled the rocky and heavily wooded coast of New England. Like the colonists in early Virginia, New England's first settlers suffered from disease, famine, and exposure. Likewise, they established contentious though co-dependent relationships with local Indians. And their communities were organized along patriarchal lines. Yet various patterns set colonial New England apart from the Chesapeake. Not primarily fortune seekers, Puritan settlers left England and "the falseness of the church of England" to follow their own deep and complex religious convictions. They established idealistic communities in strict obedience to God. Puritans' sense of mission did not rule out material or unequal prosperity so long as "unlimited and insatiable lusts" were held in check. Sin was a constant temptation, and Puritans followed "Divine Wisdom" backed by vigorous authority to keep individuals on the straight and narrow path. As one Puritan minister explained: "Were it not for Government, the World would soon run into all manner of disorders and confusions." The Pinion family exemplified his point. Although New England's political processes involved a large measure of popular participation, Puritan communities were a long way from the democratic societies that are often imagined.

Puritan Migrations

> **Why did Puritans migrate to New England, and what happened when they arrived?**

Circumstances in England drove Puritans to America. Early in his reign, King James I had encouraged hope for purification of the Church of England. He convened a conference to consider eliminating "unholy" ritual, adding more congregational autonomy, and committing the Church to the doctrine of "Salvation by God's Grace," otherwise known as **predestination**. In the end, though, James refused to make any such concessions; in fact he came to view Puritans as dangerous extremists who challenged his authority. His son Charles I went even further, tolerating Catholics (his wife was French Catholic) and appointing as Archbishop of Canterbury—the highest-ranking post in the Church of England—William Laud, who persecuted Puritans.

Most Puritans feared this would provoke God's wrath. A small number resolved to withdraw from the Church of England, which meant emigrating, since to remain in England required paying taxes to support an ungodly church. In 1607, a congregation of **Separatist** Puritans sought asylum in Holland, one of the seven Dutch-speaking Netherlands. Holland was a tolerant country that also enjoyed Europe's highest standard of living. But after a decade, some of the exiles worried that their children were succumbing to "the manifold temptations of the place." They arranged another move, this time to Virginia. In September of 1620, after obtaining financial backing from a company of English merchants, 102 **Pilgrims**, as they have come to be known, and assorted workers hired by the company set sail from Plymouth, England, aboard the ship *Mayflower*. Unlike the initial Jamestown colonists, however, the Pilgrims intended to remain in America permanently.

As stormy seas tossed the tiny vessel, bickering and "mutinous speeches" threatened what the Pilgrims wanted most, a unified and orderly community. As the ship approached Cape Cod, blown far north of Virginia by contrary winds, male leaders of the group drew up the *Mayflower* **Compact**. By this **covenant**, the passengers bound themselves into a "Civil Body Politic" and agreed to obey laws "most meet and convenient for the general good." While part of the foundation for democracy in America, the compact also established an authority from which a permanent colonial government grew. The Pilgrims elected a tradesman named William Bradford as their first governor.

For several days the *Mayflower* sailed along the coast of Cape Cod as the Pilgrims looked for a site with fresh water, a good harbor, and friendly natives (see map on p. 79). Early in December, they disembarked near the deserted Indian village of Patuxet, until recently part of the Wampanoag confederacy that dominated that area. Two decades before, the Wampanoags had comprised 21,000 of the 135,000 Algonquian-speaking Indians of southern New England, but deadly diseases, especially smallpox, introduced by European fishermen and traders had reduced their numbers and destroyed Patuxet. But the Pilgrims saw God's benevolence in the Indians' misfortune. As Bradford wrote, the colonists "fell upon their knees and blessed the God of Heaven" for bringing them safely to their new home. On Christmas day, the Pilgrims began erecting homes in the town they renamed Plymouth.

Suffering from scurvy (a disease caused by acute vitamin C deficiency), half the colony perished during the winter. Then in the spring, an Indian man named Massasoit, a Wampanoag chief, visited Plymouth, accompanied by a translator named Squanto, a Patuxet survivor. Massasoit offered the Pilgrims corn and other provisions in return for English trade goods and help in fighting his Narragansett enemies.

Squanto remained among the Pilgrims, instructing them on growing Indian corn. In the fall of 1621, they celebrated their first harvest with a **Thanksgiving** feast. By the 1630s, Plymouth's 1,000 settlers had established a stable if not profitable colony. The Pilgrims largely failed to break into the Indian fur-trade network with other European traders, particularly the Dutch (see pp. 82-83), but they did purchase additional land from the Indians, and sold corn, wheat, cattle, hogs, and horses to the English immigrants. The Wampanoags soon had reason for concern about their new neighbors and allies, however, especially Miles Standish and the Pilgrim militia who waged war against the Narragansetts so ferociously that even the Wampanoags referred to them as "Cutthroats."

Back in England, mounting political and economic strife roiled the country. Charles I's diplomatic overtures to Catholic Spain offended Puritans. He levied taxes without Parliament's authorization, and when members protested he dissolved Parliament. To tighten England's military defenses, Charles placed regular army officers in charge of local militia units, another unpopular move. An economic depression compounded England's woes, especially in the woolen textile manufacturing area of East Anglia, home to many Puritans who took the hard times as a sign of God's displeasure. John Winthrop, a respected lawyer and country squire, confided to his wife, "I am verily persuaded God will bring some heavy Affliction upon this land."

Amid mounting fear of Divine retribution, some Puritans contemplated emigration. This was no easy decision considering not only the dangers of an ocean crossing but also the heartache of leaving kinfolk and friends. Furthermore, separating from England and its official church went against an important Puritan tenet—God expected them to live *in* the world and not to withdraw from it. Indeed, most Puritans remained in England, agitating for a purer church. But a significant number, including Winthrop, resolved to relocate where they might establish an exemplary society—a "city on a hill"—for England and its church to follow.

To finance the enterprise and govern the colony, Puritans formed the Massachusetts Bay Company, a trading firm with a royal charter permitting it to establish a colony between Cape Cod and Newfoundland. Most importantly, the charter did not specify where the company's directors should hold their meetings. The Puritan emigrants exploited that loophole with a plan to locate the company headquarters in Massachusetts, essentially free from direct interference from the English crown.

John Winthrop. A respected Puritan attorney and landowner, Winthrop despaired if the Church of England did not reform. He led followers to Massachusetts to establish a model church and society, a beacon of light to show English men and women God's way.

In April 1630, after carefully selecting colonists who met the dual criteria of deep Puritan faith and practical skills, the company's leaders signaled the start of the **Great Puritan Migration**. Winthrop, elected the first governor, sailed with the initial contingent of about 400 men, women, and children; 600 more prepared to follow. Two months later, they reached New England. Before going ashore, Winthrop reminded them of their covenant with God, imploring them to "do justly, to love mercy, to walk humbly with our God." He also laid down the ideals for Puritan communities: men, women, and children "knit together . . . as one man," to "abridge ourselves of our superfluities for the supply of others' necessities" and to "delight in each other, make others' conditions our own, rejoice together, mourn together, [and] labor and suffer together." These Puritan visionaries disembarked at Salem, a dingy fishing village. Doubtful that the town could accommodate them and others to follow, they moved to a spot between the Mystic and Charles rivers, founding there the village they called Boston.

The season was too advanced for planting, but in anticipation of their needs the settlers had packed food for winter. Their provisions ran out, however, and starvation and scurvy claimed 200 lives. An equal number returned to England. Thus the Puritan mission seemed like a replay of early Jamestown.

The Puritan Way

> **What was the "Puritan Way," and how did it shape Puritan society?**

Puritan colonists attempted to live according to covenants, or agreements, with each other and with God. Covenants were like contracts; all parties accepted responsibilities and hoped for rewards. Communities pledged to live, as Governor Winthrop had implored, in harmony with one another and in obedience to God. This was the **Covenant of Good Works**. The church and civil government, separate but overlapping entities, maintained the covenants and thus the piety of Puritan communities. Ministers instructed their parishioners on God's will as revealed in Biblical scripture. The General Court of Massachusetts Bay, composed of the governor, Massachusetts Company directors, and representatives chosen by church members from each town, enacted laws against misbehavior and local magistrates enforced the laws and punished wrong-doers. In return for pious behavior, Puritans believed, God would protect them. The covenant with God, however, set up a profoundly troubling dilemma. The Covenant of Good Works collided head-on with the fundamental Calvinist doctrine of **election**, the very basis of Puritan theology, which held that salvation and eternal life resulted from God's grace—given freely and wholly unearned. Furthermore, how could one be absolutely sure of election? Could a heathen who knew nothing of Christianity be one of God's elect?

The founding generation of Puritans idealized their respective communities and the church as coinciding. Such was the **Puritan Way**. Town founders typically signed a covenant "to practice one truth" and "to keep off from us all such as are contrary minded." Puritans limited church membership to **Visible Saints**—those who could show under close public examination that they had undergone the deep spiritual conversion that most of them believed signified election. Only church members were qualified to serve as voters, town selectmen, or representatives to the General Court. Among the initial settlers, whose passion for a pure Christian faith had led them to emigrate from England and endure the great hardships of sailing to an unknown land, sainthood was relatively easy to demonstrate, so virtually all of them became church members.

Puritan zeal led to a reputation for extremism. Even today, the adjective "puritanical" describes people who are joyless or insufferably moralistic. Puritans held themselves to high moral standards and worried about their unworthiness (whether they really were elected), but they were also fully engaged in life, including pleasures of the flesh, which they regarded as God's blessing. But moderation and self-control, except in loving God, were absolute requirements, and excess, with the same exception, was a sin.

Eventually early Puritan idealism gave way to more pragmatic thinking, and many colonial church leaders adopted more tolerant attitudes. Second-generation Puritans, born in America, never experienced the intensity and cohesion that had been forged earlier in the crucible of English persecution. They often felt less passionate about tightly regulated church communities. Moreover, many young colonists found it difficult to prove to their zealous parents the genuineness of their spiritual conversion. Gradually, the proportion of church members in Puritan towns declined, and church leaders worried that their Godly communities would crumble if only a scant few residents qualified for church membership.

In response, church leaders relaxed the standards for church membership. In 1662, the General Court adopted the **Half-Way Covenant**, which extended partial church membership without voting rights to the unconverted children of saints, and two years later gave votes to adult "half-way" members despite protests from hard-liners. Defenders maintained that the measure would allow the church to "nurse up" a new generation of saints.

Growth and Tensions Lead to Fractures

What kinds of strains fractured the solidarity of Puritan Massachusetts?

As things turned out, the story of early Massachusetts Bay differed remarkably from Jamestown. The survival rate in the Bay Colony exceeded that for the Chesapeake region by more than 30 percent. A cooler climate in Massachusetts helped, nurturing fewer deadly microbes. Settlers spent more time and energy on food crops, for their goal was to become self-sustaining rather than instantly wealthy. In addition, many Puritans arrived in family units. With men and women present in nearly equal proportion, populations quickly reproduced. Puritans emigrated from England as political and economic conditions deteriorated. Between 1630 and 1650, some 20,000 English Puritans crossed the Atlantic, but that number was small compared to the flood of servants and slaves pouring into the Chesapeake colonies. In all, largely due to natural increase, by 1680, the settler population of New England topped 60,000.

Although Puritan founders planned permanent communities, not all settlers were permanent residents. Only two out of five settlers remained in their initial destinations. Older towns like Plymouth, Boston, and Salem could not accommodate the steady infusion of newcomers who soon looked elsewhere for land to occupy. Many headed west to the Connecticut River Valley, others northeast along the coast, and still others south to Narragansett Bay. Settlers acquired land from Indians in exchange for trade goods and promises of alliance. Many of them occupied Indian villages devastated by smallpox, leading Governor Win-throp to declare: "the Lord hath cleared our title to what we possess." Some Indians reacted to their misfortune with equanimity; a few even surrendered to the Christians' God who they figured to be responsible. But others grew angry.

The Puritans developed an orderly process for land distribution. The General Court granted all new township tracts. Leading men among a township's founders became custodians of the lands, distributing individual parcels among themselves and any prominent newcomers they admitted to their proprietary group. This system accorded town leaders considerable power to control the growth and economic development of Puritan communities. The best and largest tracts went to heads of families (patriarchs) who were also the most respected Puritan saints. Unmarried drifters and servants stood little chance of acquiring land and gaining full membership in the community because they were not family people. Not at all egalitarian, the system was indicative of the Puritan Way and reflected Puritans' understanding of "Divine Order."

To keep the towns compact and manageable, proprietors assigned individual house lots to residents in town with additional strips of land for them to farm on the town's outskirts—a feudal leftover from the Middle Ages in Europe. Most of the townships' land was either cleared for common pasturage or kept as woodlands to supply villagers with lumber and fuel. Town officials, called **selectmen**, levied taxes for building and maintaining roads and bridges and erecting church meetinghouses. Between 1634 and 1641, forty new towns were founded in Massachusetts Bay in accordance with this well-ordered process.

Despite the founders' emphasis on order and solidarity, dissension fractured many Puritan communities and fueled further colonial expansion. Some residents wanted to live on their outlying farms instead of in town. Those who did move nearer their fields often resented having to travel back into town for church meetings—particularly in bad weather. Newcomers often held unorthodox religious views, a troubling thing indeed for those who believed that the Puritan Way was the only way. "The Scripture saith . . . there is no Truth but one." Many Puritans believed that Satan used dissenters to undermine godly communities. As disagreements increased, colonial government became more oppressive.

Two of Massachusetts Bay's most notable dissenters were Roger Williams and Anne Hutchinson. In 1631, Williams, an amiable graduate of Cambridge University, arrived in Boston with his wife Mary. He was a separatist, however, and his non-conformity quickly got him into trouble. As a friend of the Indians, he complained about the colonists pushing them off their land. As minister of the Salem Massachusetts church, Williams preached freedom of

Anne Hutchinson on Trial. As a woman and a layperson, Hutchinson led religious discussions in her home and criticized the Massachusetts Bay clergy. For those offenses, an all-male tribunal banished her from the colony. The episode exemplified Puritan intolerance of dissent.

religious conscience and the strict separation of church and state. Such unorthodox views struck at the heart of Puritan authority, and in 1635 the General Court banished him. Williams and several followers purchased land from the Narragansett Indians and founded the colony called Providence Plantations.

Anne Hutchinson also challenged Puritan authority. An extraordinary woman with "a ready wit and bold spirit," she arrived in Boston in 1634 with her husband, a wealthy merchant, and their eleven children. Hutchinson was highly skilled in assisting women through the physical and emotional travails of childbirth. In many instances, these prenatal conversations drifted into questions of spiritual salvation, natural enough considering the dangers of having babies. Eventually, Hutchinson gathered groups of fifty or more women in her home for distinctly religious discussions. Puritan authorities had no problem with women meeting privately for Bible study, but they reacted strongly to reports that Hutchinson had disparaged some of the colony's leading clergymen by accusing them of preaching the Covenant of Good Works. When the colony's authorities attempted to silence her, she defied them, laying down the gauntlet.

Those officials, including Governor Winthrop, feared that a woman of Anne Hutchinson's stature and abil-

ities might wreck the colony's patriarchal authority. They had little evidence with which to build a criminal case; nevertheless, they ordered her to defend herself before the General Court. Winthrop opened the prosecution by accusing Hutchinson of sedition, which she deftly parried. Winthrop then asserted that her private meetings had been inappropriate public lectures attended by men and women. She denied that men ever participated and pointed to Scriptures that instructed "elder women to instruct the younger." Winthrop again redirected his questioning, this time to a particular meeting Hutchinson had attended at the behest of Boston's ministers. She admitted to having spoken freely on that occasion, and presumably critically of the ministers, and when some of them agreed to testify under oath that she had brought reproach upon them, Hutchinson was doomed. The judges banished her "as being a woman not fit for our society." Anne Hutchinson, her family, and several supporters moved to Providence Plantations and then Long Island Sound near present-day New York City, where in 1643 she and all but one of her children were killed in a Siwanoy Indian attack.

Social and theological strains in Massachusetts spawned new Puritan colonies. In 1635, a group that included Winthrop's son joined previous migrants in settling the Connecticut River valley. A year later, Thomas Hooker, a charismatic minister who opposed the standards by which Massachusetts authorities admitted persons to church membership, led his congregation to the Connecticut River valley town of Hartford. Two other ministers, John Davenport and Theophilus Eaton, left Massachusetts during the Hutchinson controversy and established a settlement at New Haven on Long Island Sound. In 1639, the Connecticut River towns adopted the Fundamental Orders of Connecticut, a common set of laws that allowed non-church members to vote for government officials. In 1662, Hartford, New Haven, and surrounding towns coalesced into the Connecticut colony. In 1644, a settlement at Newport and Williams' Providence Plantations merged under a royal charter to form Rhode Island. Although the separate colonies produced their own distinctive societies, all of them to some degree shared Puritan characteristics.

Puritan churches remained a potent force in the life of New England colonies. But they failed to fulfill all the hope of Winthrop and the other Puritan founders. Instead of unifying and anchoring Puritan communities, they contributed to growing divisiveness and became less potent shapers of Puritan society.

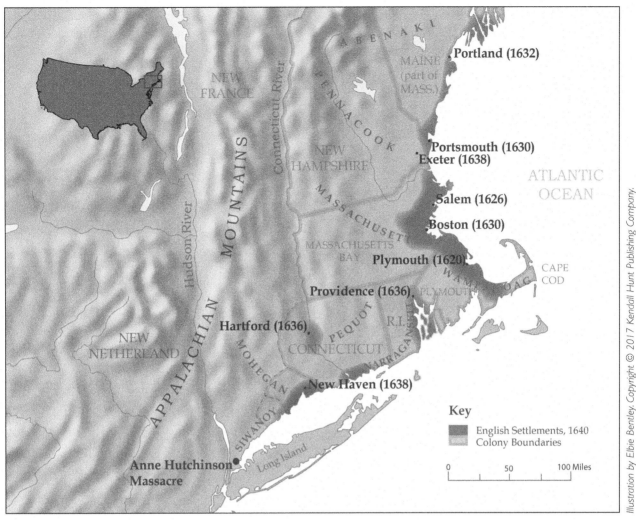

English Puritan settlements along the northern coast of what became known as New England embedded themselves in a region populated by Algonquian and Iroquoian communities.

The Puritan Economy

How did Puritan settlers attempt to make their communities economically viable?

Idealistic Puritan founders imagined prosperous agrarian societies with farmers and artisans residing in self-sufficient towns. But Puritan immigrants knew little about farming in North America. They naturally tried to raise familiar English crops—wheat, barley, rye, and peas, but Indian corn turned out to be the staple food crop, which the settlers supplemented with eggs and milk from cattle along with meat from hogs, sheep, and poultry. A local fungus blighted the wheat, and people soon realized that New England's climate was too cold and the soil too rocky for substantial surpluses—for which there was no huge market anyway, especially when the immigrant flow dried up. Cash crops were out of the question at that latitude, leaving New England economies in more of a subsistence- than a profit-oriented capitalist condition.

Puritan resourcefulness paid huge dividends under those challenging circumstances. Too cash-poor to buy English or European shoes, clothes, leather harnesses, or metal tools, skilled crafters learned to manufacture such products themselves. Women sat at simple spinning wheels making yarn and thread while men operated handlooms to weave wool and linen cloth for clothes, blankets, and tablecloths. Tanners, cobblers, and ironsmiths in every town supplied the local market, bartering for food. Harvesting timber from the region's extensive soft- and hardwood forests was relatively easy and remunerative. Lumber provided building material for houses, barns, and fences, fuel for heating and cooking, and potash for soap. Ship builders cut and shaped tall pines for masts and spars and joined oak planks for hulls and decks. Harnessing power from the region's many rivers, entrepreneurs built sawmills. Sap from maple trees, boiled down, yielded sweet syrup, a process that early settlers learned from the Iroquois.

Codfish was the region's greatest natural resource. The cold Atlantic Ocean teemed with cod. European fishermen had fished off the North American coast for decades, returning their catch to meet the insatiable demand for cod in the British Isles, France, Portugal, and Spain. The English Civil War interrupted English fishing voyages, allowing New England fishermen from coastal towns like Salem, Marblehead, and Gloucester to take over the industry. By 1700, cod was New England's most important export, not only for European tables but also for slaves on plantations in the West Indies. Fortunately, the Massachusetts fishery was warmed by the **Gulf Stream**, which made it fishable during the winter. Farmers often hired on as part-time fishermen during cold weather.

Fishing also spurred other economic enterprises. Shipbuilding was one, motivated by government edict and by individual enterprise. As early as 1641, the Massachusetts General Court declared shipbuilding "a business of great importance to the public good." The town of Salem had already taken steps in that direction, offering land to a London shipbuilder named William Stevens "for the building of ships." Soon, shipyards operated in Gloucester, Portsmouth, and Boston. The raw materials were readily available—timber, pitch and tar for sealing vessels against water, and hemp fiber for canvas sails and rigging. Soon, nearly one out of every three ships flying the English flag originated in colonial shipyards.

Puritan Families and Communities

How did religion and gender shape Puritan families and communities?

The patriarchal family was the fundamental unit of Puritan society. Families read the Bible together, attended church services, and kept abreast of "the good lawes of the Colony." In the relatively healthy environment of New England, families remained intact longer than in other colonies. Although most immigrants arrived as families, roughly one-third of the new arrivals were unmarried, and colonial authorities demanded that they submit to the authority of a family. In the interest of proper social order, colonial leaders encouraged families to cluster in towns.

In addition to ties of blood and affection, relationships of authority and obedience held the Puritan family together. Family identity extended beyond kinship to include servants and even houseguests. Singles, without family attachments, fell under suspicion, and authorities placed unmarried men and women with no families into households. The General Court found one man living "by himself contrary to the law of the country, whereby he is subject to much sin and iniquity," and ordered him to find an "orderly" family to live with or be confined in jail.

The Puritan family was a covenant family, bound by mutual responsibility and relied upon for social order. The ideal family reflected Puritan theology. Just as God held ultimate authority over humanity, husbands and fathers prevailed over dependent women, children, and servants. By those standards, Nicholas Pinion fell far short of what was expected of him. The ideal patriarch ruled through both love, or "filial affection," and fear. Obedience was supposed to be lovingly given too, but backed by the fear of punishment. Most Puritans regarded children as naturally willful and slothful and in constant need of parental discipline. Although rarely enforced, Massachusetts made it a capital offense for children to curse or strike their parents. "Temper therefore your family government," the Puritan minister John Barnard counseled, "with a suitable degree of mildness." Abuse of one's spouse broke the family covenant and constituted grounds for divorce.

Puritanism is not often associated with romantic love, but in fact Puritans did not shy away from either romance or sexuality. They used the phrase "falling in love" and idealized it as the prelude to marriage based on free choice. The custom of "bundling," in which a young couple went to bed wrapped in a blanket (though separated by a board to discourage sexual intercourse), was designed to allow potential spouses to discover physical love. Nearly all New Englanders— 94 percent of the women and 98 percent of the men— married, though they did not rush into matrimony. The average age for brides was twenty-three and for grooms twenty-six, higher than most of England's North American colonies, and one in five women was pregnant at the time of marriage. Defined in terms of respect, affection, and physical attraction, love played a very important part in Puritan spousal relationships.

Women almost everywhere in the seventeenth century world were decidedly inferior to men in terms of status. Most Puritan women, though certainly not Elizabeth Pinion, accepted that station. New England poet Anne Bradstreet wrote that: "Men can do best, and women know it well." But she added: "Preeminence in each and all is yours," regarding men's positions in public and private life. "Yet grant some small acknowledgement of ours." Because women were thought to be weaker and less worldly than men, they possessed fewer rights. They were expected to marry and move under the protection of their husbands. Their basic responsibility was, in the words of one Boston minister, "to guide the house and not guide the Husband." But most housewives had outside duties as well, including gardening, milking cows, slaughtering smaller livestock, churning butter, drawing water from the well, and even brewing beer. Women's status was not uniformly lowly however. Anne Hutchinson, for instance, enjoyed relatively high status, and while generally not permitted to enter trades or professions, many women assisted their husbands, and as widows often operated their late husbands' businesses.

Galvanized by a common purpose, Puritan settlers felt a strong sense of community. Every villager bore responsibility for the entire community's welfare, and citizens gathered to discuss issues of interest and importance in meetinghouses built in the center of every town. Within their means, Puritans sought to care for needy neighbors. They were also committed to the public education of their children. Literacy was essential in a society that believed the Bible must be read and followed. The General Court founded Harvard College in 1636 for the training of ministers, and in 1647 the General Court required all towns of at least fifty families to support a teacher and larger towns of at least 100 families to maintain a school. But the central purpose of Puritan communities was to control and protect their citizenry. As one Connecticut man explained, "it is safest for me to be here . . . where my brethren are about me to observe my behavior and direct me."

Popular participation characterized community governance but only insofar as it promoted and defended Puritanism. The original Massachusetts Bay Company charter allowed stockholders to vote, and that became the pattern for Puritan colonial government. In 1631, all church members who owned land, excluding women, were designated "freemen" and could vote for governor and other colony-wide offices. Puritans regarded unconverted residents who had no propertied stake in the colony as unqualified to make decisions that affected God's chosen people. Elected magistrates oversaw day-to-day government in the village, levying taxes, enacting local ordinances, and resolving political disputes. At annual town meetings, citizens discussed the issues of the day. An admiring Thomas Jefferson later called them the "wisest invention ever devised by the wit of man for the perfect exercise of self-government."

Many misconceptions about Puritan societies have endured through the generations. One is that they were theocracies, that is, governments run by the church. Another is that the town meetings represented the ideal in simple participatory democracy. In fact, the church, although it exerted considerable influence on the civil government, did not enjoy absolute authority. Ministers often commented on political issues and favored certain candidates for office over others; however, they were not permitted to hold civil office themselves, and even the most prominent ministers often watched regretfully as their recommendations went unheeded. No more than four out of ten adult white males met voting requirements in early New England; the number actually declined due to a reduction in church membership. After 1684 in Massachusetts, voting laws no longer required church membership. Being qualified to vote, however, did not always lead to participation in town meetings. Probably no more than a quarter of those who were qualified were politically active.

Yet, these were important elements in a tradition of participatory government that strengthened with the passage of time. Certainly many basic elements for building a democratic nation were present in New England, along with many cultural values that eventually provided the basis for a national identity. But we must remember that indentured servitude and even slavery were also parts of the Puritan Way.

THINKING BACK

1. How did the Puritan societies of New England differ from the colonies of the Chesapeake region?
2. In what way was religious freedom a basis for establishing colonies in New England, and to what degree was freedom of any sort tolerated there?

THE PROPRIETARY COLONIES

By the mid-seventeenth century English colonists had established settlements along Chesapeake Bay and in coastal New England. Corporate merchant companies had been the preferred mode for organizing and financing most of the early colonies. After 1660, however, proprietary grants, like the one that Lord Baltimore received for Maryland, became more common. At least two factors account for this shift. First, in 1660, England restored the monarchy, and the new king, Charles II, rewarded many of his noble supporters with grants of land in America. Historians often refer to them as the **Restoration Colonies**. Second, colonies had never been very lucrative investments for joint-stock companies, and merchant-capitalists now looked elsewhere to invest their money in more profitable ventures. Some of these land grants were located along the Middle Atlantic coast while others were located farther south. Those who received the grants became the proprietors of new American colonies.

From New Netherland to New York and New Jersey

> How was New Netherland different from English colonies, and how did it become New York and New Jersey?

Even before the restoration of the English monarchy, Parliament revved up for competition with the Netherlands for commercial supremacy in the Atlantic. Since winning its independence from Spain, the Netherlands had become a giant in trans-Atlantic shipping and a financial force behind American colonization.

Wampum, made of seashells drilled and strung together in belts usually three to four feet long, were beautiful aesthetically. Because of their great value among most Indian communities of the Atlantic coast, they served as a medium of exchange, used by both Indians and Europeans in the purchase of furs, hides, and manufactured products.

The beginning of Dutch colonization in North America came in 1609 when Henry Hudson, an English ship captain sailing under the auspices of the Dutch East India Company, explored the river that now bears his name, hoping, like many others at the time, to locate the Northwest Passage. Instead he found friendly Algonquian-speaking **Lenni-Lanape** Indians eager to trade oysters, beans, and beaver pelts for beads, metal knives, and hatchets that he carried onboard. In 1614, another Dutch mariner, Adriaen Block, laid claim to the area between the Connecticut and Delaware rivers, naming it New Netherland. These voyages inspired Dutch business interests that sought profits in trade with the Indians. Like the English, the Dutch utilized corporate entities to organize and finance their colonial enterprises, and in 1621 the **Dutch West India Company** received from the government in the Netherlands a monopoly on Dutch Atlantic commerce. The company built a trading post on

the upper Hudson River, called Fort Orange. The company established another settlement at the southern tip of Manhattan Island, called New Amsterdam (after the Dutch commercial and financial center). The West India Company paid scant attention to the western area along the Delaware River, which in the late 1630s drew a few hundred Swedish fur trappers and traders who constructed a fort at the site of present-day Wilmington, Delaware, then christened New Sweden.

Sometime in May or June 1626, Peter Minuit, the West India Company's local governor negotiated with local Lenape to purchase all of Manhattan for a trifling assortment of trade goods. In August of the same year, the company acquired Staten Island in exchange for some "Diffies [duffle cloth], Kittles [kettles], Axes, Hoes, Wampum, Drilling Awls, Jews Harps, and diverse other wares." These were probably the greatest steals in the history of real estate. For years New Amsterdam functioned primarily as a trade center and port. In 1638, its population of 400

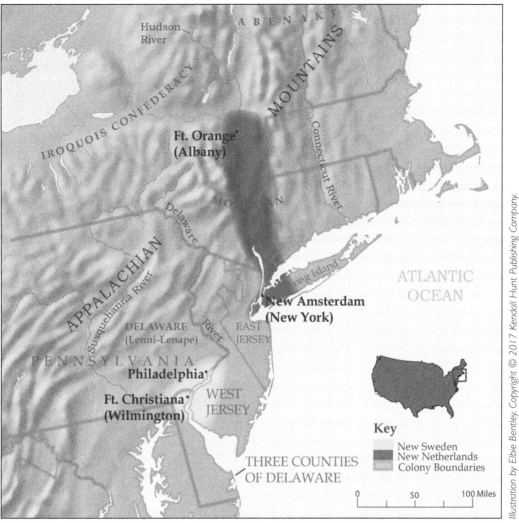

The multi-ethnic and multi-racial populations of these Atlantic coast colonies represented the most culturally diverse of England's North American colonies.

was less than half of Boston's, and one Company official described it as "totally and wholly in a ruinous condition." Not all of the town's residents were Dutch; most were **Walloons** (French-speaking Calvinists from today's Belgium), French, English, Swedish, German, and African.

In 1637, Dutch raiders sponsored by the West India Company captured the Portuguese African slave factory at Elmina and then seized the Portuguese port of Luanda in Angola on the west coast of Africa. Soon the Dutch had gained dominance in the trans-Atlantic slave trade. In the 1630s, the West India Company also gained control of nearly half of Portugal's valuable sugar-producing colony of Brazil as well as several islands in the Caribbean. The company intended most of the African slaves it transported to America for Brazil and the Caribbean islands, but it brought a few to New Amsterdam as well. Company officials envisioned New Amsterdam as a slave distribution point for North America.

But the West India Company concentrated its activities in New Netherland on trade with the Indians. From Ft. Orange, company employees bartered with the Algonquian-speaking **Mahicans** in the Hudson River valley and Iroquois farther west for beaver, otter, and other animal pelts. The pelts then went to markets in Europe where they were in high demand for hats and coats. The company granted some large tracts of land to proprietors called **patroons**, who in turn brought farmers, shopkeepers, craftsmen, and a few more African slaves. The patroons resembled medieval European feudal lords, and the most powerful was Kiliaen Rensselaer, whose estate adjoined Fort Orange.

The commercial nature of New Netherland dictated the colony's relationship with the Indians. Because the colony did not pressure the Indians for land, fewer strains developed than in the areas of English settlement. But New Netherland did not escape Indian conflict altogether, and, typically, the strife intensified as the numbers of settlers increased and the beaver population declined. Epidemics of smallpox, typhus, and measles ravaged the neighboring Lenape, for which they blamed the Europeans; furthermore, the newcomers' livestock trampled Lenape cornfields, causing some angry Indians to kill the offending animals, and occasionally the Europeans who owned them. Hostility flared when the West India Company appointed Willem Kieft governor. Kieft levied taxes on the Indians, ostensibly to pay for their protection, and then used company soldiers to attack their villages. A horrible war ensued, lasting from 1641 until 1645. Approximately 1,600 Indians died in the lower Hudson River valley, on Manhattan, and Long Island, along with scores of whites. Massachusetts Bay exile Anne Hutchinson was one of the fatalities.

Gradually the West India Company lost control of New Netherland as colonists and settlements multiplied. Many of the newcomers were not company employees but independent merchants, artisans, and farmers with families. Puritans from New England settled on eastern Long Island and along the lower Hudson River, tolerated by the West India Company because they, like many company officials, were hard working Calvinists.

In New Amsterdam a stratified society took shape. A merchant class of families like the Philipses and Schuylers occupied the top rung, living in large brick and stone homes with fine imported furnishings. A middle class of carpenters, bakers, brewers, and metal smiths carved out a humbler but still comfortable existence. The balance of the free inhabitants were laborers, wagon drivers, sailors, and soldiers employed by the West India Company and independent merchants. A large number of indentured servants—nearly half the town's populace—toiled in homes, shops, and on surrounding farms. Hundreds of African slaves constructed and repaired buildings, ships, piers, and military defenses. The Company sold other slaves to individuals who employed them in domestic and agricultural work. Some slaves were manumitted and lived as free persons.

In the end, though, the Dutch failed to hold New Netherland against determined English expansion. In 1650, England's Parliament began challenging Dutch Atlantic trade, authorizing privateers to seize Dutch commercial vessels. A year later, it passed a **Navigation Act** that prohibited Dutch ships from commerce between England and its colonies and ignited the first and indecisive Anglo-Dutch war (1652–54). English merchants also hoped to wrest control of the African slave trade from the Dutch, and in 1660 a group calling itself the Company of Royal Adventurers Trading to Africa obtained exclusive rights to the delivery of African slaves to English colonies. Charles II asserted a prior claim to the area occupied by New Netherland and in 1664 granted the territory to his brother James, Duke of York.

In the summer of that year, a flotilla of English ships carrying 400 soldiers swept down on New Amsterdam and forced the feisty governor Peter Stuyvesant to surrender the colony. The Duke renamed the area, including Maine to the northeast, New York. Following the second Anglo-Dutch War (1665–67), the Netherlands formally recognized New York. A Dutch force retook the former New Amsterdam, eventually known as New York City, during the third Anglo-Dutch War (1672–74) and held it for more than a year before giving it back to England.

New York did not change suddenly or radically after the English takeover, but it slowly evolved into a new and distinctive society. Dutch and English cultures merged, both languages contributing to a local vocabulary. The Dutch word for farms, *bouwhuys*, for instance, evolved into "bowery." Jonas Bronck's farm above New Amsterdam became "the bronx." The number of Europeans increased as the Indian population dwindled. A cosmopolitan mixture of Dutch, French, Swedish, German, English, and African differentiated the colony from the more homogeneous Chesapeake and New England settlements.

New York's two population centers followed divergent paths. New York City, the largest and most culturally diverse community in the colony, remained a noisy place of busy shops, horse-drawn wagons and sleds, and town criers shouting out news and proclamations. It also reeked. Garbage and human and animal waste dumped in the streets produced an overwhelming stench and a breeding ground for disease. Albany, formerly Fort Orange, on the other hand, retained its strong Dutch flavor, continuing to function as a fur trading center with the Iroquois and the center of a growing farming community. As the beaver died out and the fur trade declined along the upper Hudson, artisans and farmers shifted from trading with the Indians to providing for the needs of the growing number of colonists in the area.

In 1664, the Duke of York gave away part of his proprietorship, a particularly fertile area west of the Hudson River, to two loyal friends, Sir George Carteret and Sir John Berkeley, who named it New Jersey after Carteret's home Isle of Jersey. The person the Duke appointed as governor of New York, Richard Nicholls, issued another set of grants to the same tracts of land to different groups of settlers, creating overlapping claims. Nicholls promised his grantees an elected legislative assembly in return for small annual tax payments, called **quitrents**, causing them to refuse to recognize the authority of the proprietors. Chaos ensued, and in 1672 Berkeley threw up his hands in frustration and sold his share of New Jersey (East Jersey) to a group of Quaker merchants. Puritan migration into the colony added a number of small Puritan communities in East Jersey, around present-day Princeton, but the absence of a good harbor hampered the area's economic development. Meanwhile, a sizable group of Quakers settled in the western region, and in 1681 when Carteret died, they acquired his West Jersey in an auction sale. Finally, in 1702 the English Crown took over all of New Jersey as it had New York in 1685.

The Quakers and Penn's "Holy Experiment"

Quakers were Protestants known for their intense piety and ridiculed for their tendency to quiver or "quake" with religious fervor. They shared with Calvinists several beliefs about people's association with God: the relationship was individual, salvation did not require the intervention of church officials, and the faithful must crusade constantly against wickedness. What set Quakers apart was their egalitarianism and their belief in direct communication from God, which they characterized as an **Inner Light**. Acknowledging neither churches nor ministers, they came together in meetings to speak and do what God commanded. **Friends**, as they preferred to call themselves, disdained social

> What was the Quakers' vision for a colonial society, and how successful were they in realizing it?

Image © Chrislofoto, 2010. Used by permission of Shutterstock, Inc.

Quaker Meeting House in Jordans, England, with grave of William Penn. No ministers presided over Quaker meetings. Worshippers sat quietly and contemplated God's spirit, the "Inner Light," and no one spoke unless the spirit moved them. One of the other interesting features of Quaker meetings was that women were as free to speak as men.

distinctions. As one Quaker put it, "we are not for names, nor men, nor titles of Government, but we are for justice, and mercy and truth and peace." They also opposed war and other forms of violence.

The Friends' foremost apostle in England was George Fox, a semiliterate tradesman who yearned for the true meaning of life. Fox attracted many followers from England, Ireland, and Germany in his quest for truth. Missionary Friends traveled to the colonies, where they sought converts among the Christian settlers. Their presence became a major irritant to Puritans, who were equally zealous and strong-willed.

A young English aristocrat, William Penn, was one of Fox's converts. At age twelve, Penn said, "the Lord first appeared unto me." Penn's father, an admiral in the navy, supported the monarchy during the English Civil War and after the Restoration. Charles II rewarded him with a knighthood and a vast estate in Ireland. Young Penn attended Oxford, where he was expelled for nonconformity. He also attended one of the inns-of-court—England's law schools—where he learned political philosophy and the workings of government, knowledge that combined effectively with his powerful intellect and fierce will. After failing to complete his formal education, Penn cast his gaze toward America, envisioning there an exemplary religious society, similar to John Winthrop's "city on a hill."

With the help of his family's connections, his friendship with the Duke of York, and the support he and his father had given to Charles II, Penn in 1681 persuaded the king to grant him a large tract of fertile and heavily wooded land west of the Delaware River and between New York and Maryland. He called it Pennsylvania, or "Penn's woods." A second grant of a tract along the lower Delaware River, which mostly non-Quakers inhabited, gave Pennsylvania access to the open Atlantic Ocean.

Before he departed England for his new colony, Penn formulated an elaborate plan of government that he conceived as "a Holy Experiment" in godly and tolerant government, although he struggled to balance the ideal of maximum popular participation with the practical need for support from wealthy and not always so democratic backers who insisted on control of land and commerce. Penn's **Frame of Government** provided for a Council of "lords" chosen by Penn who debated and initiated legislation and whose seats were hereditary and an elected Assembly that could act only on measures submitted to it by the Council. A resident governor chosen by Penn worked with the Council to originate legislation and executed the laws.

The system turned out to be impractical as well as unpopular. Willing to compromise for the sake of harmony, Penn deleted the concept of "lords," allowed members of the council to be elected, and reduced the overall size of the government. Furthermore, in 1701 the **Charter of Privileges** served as a kind of bill of rights and established voting qualifications that enfranchised approximately half the adult white males. Restrictions on taxation, trial by jury, and application of the death penalty only for treason and murder protected civil rights and established Pennsylvania as one of the most progressive of England's colonies.

Penn was steadfast in his devotion to Quaker religious principles. In addition to providing a haven for Quakers, Pennsylvania guaranteed religious tolerance of all Christians. Before long, the number of Anglicans and representatives of other religious groups had become a major presence in the Quaker refuge. Penn insisted that residents of his colony observe the Sabbath so that they "may better dispose themselves to worship God according to their understanding." Quaker worship was highly informal and strikingly egalitarian. Women enjoyed total equality within the religious realm, with the right to speak freely with men during Quaker meetings, as long as the divine spirit moved them.

Eager for Pennsylvania to succeed, Penn recruited new colonists, targeting other Quakers. Even before he had laid eyes on the colony he wrote promotional literature touting it—"600 miles closer to the Sun than England" and filled with "Fowl, Fish, and Wild-Deer." He offered fifty acres of land to each immigrant, including to indentured servants when their term of service expired. His efforts succeeded, and some 8,000 people arrived between 1681 and 1685. Most came from England, Wales, and Ireland; however, in 1683 a small group of Germans founded Germantown, which established a link that drew more German immigrants to the colony. The following year slave traders brought about 150 African slaves to the colony. Subsequently more Africans entered the colony, brought by individual Quaker merchants over the official objection of many other Friends. In the early years, about half of the European immigrants came as indentured servants, and 80 to 90 percent of the others became farmers who owned small tracts of some of the most fertile land along the Atlantic seaboard. A few wealthy settlers bought large parcels of land, purchases that Penn counted on to balance his colony's accounts. Together, Pennsylvania farms worked by families, servants, and slaves produced an abundance of wheat that fed not only themselves but also the slave workforces of the Caribbean islands.

Farm settlements came at the expense of the Indians. Quaker beliefs about fairness governed their dealings with them, especially the Algonquians who resided along the Delaware River, the Susquehanna River valley, and near the Great Lakes. In the end, however, it did not make much difference insofar as control of the land was concerned. The Europeans who came to Pennsylvania wanted property, and Quakers offered to purchase Indian land rather than simply take it. In a letter to the Indians, Penn wrote that he was "very sensible of the unkindness and injustice that hath been too much exercised toward you by the people of these parts of the world." He told them that he intended "to win . . . your love and friendship by a kind, just and peaceable life." Despite these overtures, though, Pennsylvania Indians were losers in the competition for land.

Although most of Pennsylvania's newcomers scattered out over the countryside, Penn immediately developed a plan for the town of Philadelphia, the "city of brotherly love," as a seaport and center of commerce. Having experienced the horror of devastating fires that destroyed much of London in the 1660s, Penn insisted that houses be built of stone and brick and placed in the center of large lots amid gardens and orchards so "that it may be a green country town, which will never be burnt, and always be wholesome." His agents purchased a tract of land from a group of Swedes who had earlier settled between the Delaware and Schuylkill rivers and laid out streets and building sites on a gridiron pattern. To accommodate the large number of immigrants, Philadelphia's home sites had to be considerably smaller than originally planned, but the city's layout still reflected a sense of order and discipline.

Pennsylvania did not turn out exactly the way Penn had planned. He expected harmony and tolerance and was dismayed when colonists complained about the low level of popular participation in government. In 1696, the Assembly won the right to initiate legislation, and in 1701 it became the sole house of the legislature, the only **unicameral** legislature in English North America. Also in 1701, Penn granted autonomy to three counties along the lower Delaware River. At the time of the American Revolution, the informal colony of Delaware became a state.

The Carolinas: Roots of Plantation Slavery

In 1663 Charles II issued a charter to eight aristocratic supporters eager to establish settlements between Virginia and Spanish Florida. They named the area Carolina in the king's honor. Foremost among them were prosperous planters from the West Indies and English nobles. Unlike other idealistic and visionary proprietors, the Carolina proprietors were practical men with considerable experience in colonial activities. They encouraged experimentation in raising olives, hemp, wheat, silk, wine grapes, indigo, cotton, and rice, of which the latter three ultimately proved very successful. Instead of recruiting inexperienced settlers from England, they sought to draw seasoned planters from surrounding areas, principally Virginia and the West Indies. In their initial plans for organizing Carolina, however, the proprietors were unrealistic.

> **What form did the Carolina colonies take?**

In its conception, Carolina looked like a harmonious feudal society. At the top, the proprietors envisioned a small class of noble landowners providing both wealth and wise leadership for the colony. Below them would be a larger number of hard-working freehold farmers, a substantial middle class followed by a servant class to perform the heavy labor necessary for clearing land and producing plantation crops. The plan attempted to balance aristocracy and democracy, thus blending the supposed practical wisdom of wealthy men with the ideal of popular government. One of the proprietors, Anthony Ashley Cooper, Earl of Shaftesbury, and his secretary John Locke, a political philosopher whose writings would provide a rationale for the American Revolution, drafted the **Fundamental Constitutions of Carolina,** which laid down property rights as well as the principle of representative government. The plan was flawed, though, for few English aristocrats were interested in settling in frontier Carolina. Nor did English laborers flock to Carolina without some promise of land. Instead, the settlement of Carolina took place more haphazardly.

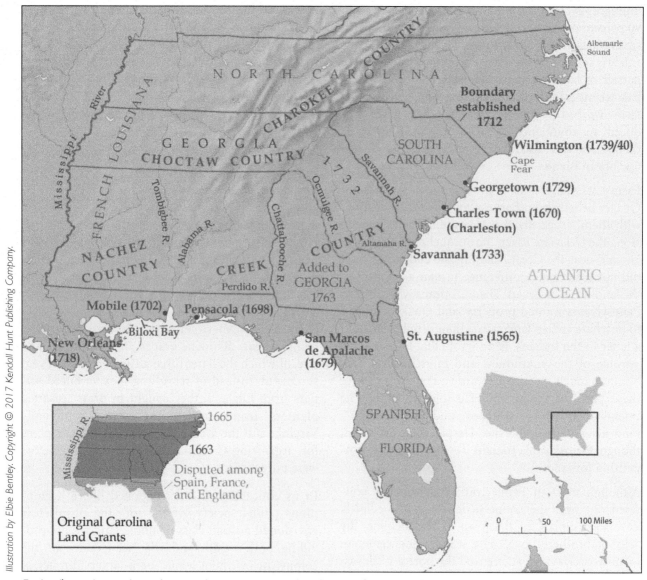

England's southern colonies became the most committed to the use of enslaved African labor.

As early as the 1650s, drifters from Virginia had begun settling in the northern region of Carolina, along Albemarle Sound and south to Cape Fear, an area that came to be North Carolina. Because it was isolated, this colony did not thrive, and the Carolina proprietors paid little attention to it, although by 1665 they had authorized a colonial government with a governor and assembly and acknowledged the principle of taxation only with the people's consent. Some 5,000 newcomers settled in North Carolina by the mid-1670s, producing tobacco, livestock, and naval stores (pitch, tar, and timber for ship building), but the sandy outer banks provided few serviceable harbors.

A far more promising situation existed in the southern part of the colony, in what eventually became South Carolina. There, the landscape and climate seemed suitable for the profitable cultivation of tropical crops. For planters to populate this area, the proprietors looked to the West Indies, especially Barbados where fertile land was becoming increasingly scarce (see the Local Perspective: Barbados on pp. 90-92). In 1770, the first settlement in South Carolina, named Charles Town (later shortened to Charleston), took hold between the Ashley and Cooper rivers. Within two years nearly 400 settlers had established homesteads in South Carolina. Most were English and many came via Barbados, but others included Scots, French Huguenots, and European Jews of several nationalities. The Fundamental Constitutions provided religious freedom for Jews as well as Catholic and Protestant Christians. Indeed, the level of religious tolerance in South Carolina was higher than in most of English North America.

Like English settlers in other regions of the Atlantic seaboard, South Carolinians established relationships with local Indians. In addition to the principal Indian tribes, which included **Catawbas, Cherokees, Creeks**, and **Tuscaroras**, many smaller groups lived and competed in the area for land and power. Most initially welcomed the English as potential allies against their enemies and offered to trade deerskins for English tools, textiles, and trinkets. Soft deerskins proved quite valuable in European markets, where they were used for gloves and other articles of clothing. A few Indians worked in exchange for English trade goods, but English traders soon recognized the value of captive Indians as slaves. Enslaving Indians in South Carolina was not feasible because they easily fled into the backcountry, but the English raided Indian villages or paid Indians to capture other Indians for shipment to the West Indies. Thus, slaves along with deerskins became the first important export commodities for South Carolina.

Many of the immigrants from Barbados began raising cattle, the hides and meat from which supplied the slave plantations in the West Indies. Those who tended the cattle herds that grazed on open meadows called "**cowpens**" were African slaves. In 1683 the South Carolina legislative assembly defined them as slaves by law, but these men and women formed families, experienced a considerable measure of freedom in the remote cowpens, and developed their own economy, marketing surplus poultry and corn and even hiring out their own labor. Indeed, in 1712 the legislative assembly complained that "slaves . . . do what and go wither they will and work where they please."

The measure of control that slaves in early South Carolina exercised over their lives did not mean they enjoyed or even accepted their condition. Many ran away, forming small runaway or **maroon** communities on the frontier, where it was difficult for white authorities to recover them. Others made their way to Charles Town where some managed to sail away on merchant or pirate ships. And Spanish officials in Florida beckoned to fugitive slaves from South Carolina. In San Augustine, they granted freedom to African slaves who agreed to serve in the local militia and made the same offer to slaves who converted to Catholicism.

By the end of the seventeenth century, South Carolina's non-Indian population reached 6,000, of which 2,500 were black. By the early 1700s, South Carolina planters had turned to rice and indigo as primary export crops, and with that transition the colony became proportionally even more black. In 1719, the planter elite rebelled against proprietary control of South Carolina, which reverted to the English crown, and ten years later the same thing happened in North Carolina.

Georgia: England's Last Mainland Colony

Georgia became the last of England's North American mainland colonies. Many of the features that characterized the major regions of English North America—the Chesapeake, New England, and the Middle Colonies—were visible in Georgia. Origins in idealism, the pursuit of commercial profit, the presence of cultural diversity, opposition to and then the evolution of a slave-based socio-economic system, and the belief in a hierarchical system of maintaining order figured in the formation of Georgia, which also served the unique function of a buffer between Spanish Florida and South Carolina.

> For what purposes was the colony of Georgia founded?

In 1732, a group of philanthropists, including the humorless but idealistic James Edward Oglethorpe, became trustees of the Georgia Corporation, which obtained a tract of land south of the Savannah River between Carolina and Florida. Carolina planters had been agitating for fortifications in that strategic borderland to protect their plantations against Spanish and Indian enemies. But an additional interest also motivated Oglethorpe and his colleagues, namely a compelling desire to assist England's poor, many of whom could not find work and wound up in debtor's prison.

Early eighteenth-century English social reformers attributed poverty to deficiencies in character which they believed could be remedied through stern discipline and hard work. Oglethorpe suggested relocating "a hundred miserable wretches" to Georgia where they would be taught to be industrious and responsible citizens. He would take no drunkards "or other notoriously vicious persons." The trustees also prohibited slavery. Oglethorpe insisted that without slaves "the idle will leave the province and the industrious will fall to work."

Of the original trustees, only Oglethorpe ever resided in the colony. He accompanied the initial settlers, established the town of Savannah, and laid out its streets in a symmetrical pattern similar to London's squares and gardens. In 1736, Oglethorpe brought to the colony a second contingent of settlers, including Austrians, Germans, Swiss, Scots Highlanders, and Portuguese Jewish refugees, making the fledgling colony remarkably cosmopolitan.

Ultimately the proprietors' charitable goals gave way to the settlers' economic interests. As Charles Town merchant Samuel Eveleigh observed: "Georgia can never be a place of any great consequence without Negroes." Although the trustees continued to prohibit slavery for several years, residents acquired slaves anyway, and Georgia eventually developed a slave-based economic system in which enslaved Africans provided the labor on the colony's large rice plantations. Profits to be made from the trade in rum led to the repeal of restrictions against alcohol.

Georgia did not fail totally in fulfilling its initial purposes. Negotiations with the Creek, Choctaw, and Cherokee produced alliances against England's Spanish rivals. Fortifications did help protect both Georgia and Carolina from a Spanish attack. In 1752, Georgia's charter expired and the proprietors allowed it to revert to the crown.

THINKING BACK

1. What made the Middle Colonies—New York, New Jersey, Pennsylvania, and Delaware— different from both the Chesapeake and New England?
2. Why and how did the Carolinas and Georgia evolve into societies that relied heavily upon slavery?

THE LOCAL PERSPECTIVE: FOCUS ON BARBADOS

How did Barbados rise and fall as the jewel of England's American colonies? The eastern-most of the Caribbean islands, tiny Barbados, just 166 square miles of land area, was often described as the "richest spot" in England's American empire. That was because Barbados was one of the most successful sugar islands in the West Indies. Beyond its value to England, it supplied sugar-cane molasses as a raw ingredient for colonial rum and served as a market for fish, wheat, and lumber from the mainland North America colonies.

In some ways, Barbados resembled England's mainland colonies. A landed elite dominated society. Its elected legislative assembly was the third oldest in English America (behind Virginia and Maryland). And its labor force was a combination of indentured servants and African slaves. There were striking differences though. For one, by the end of the sixteenth century, Africans outnumbered whites by better than three to one. For another, English settlers did not have to conquer the island, for when the first colonists arrived, Barbados was uninhabited.

In 1625, John Powell, laid claim to Barbados on behalf of King James I, thinking it ideal for an agricultural colony, and two years later his younger brother Henry brought four ships with eighty settlers. Financing came from two London merchant brothers, Sir Peter and Sir William Courteen. Whether the Courteen brothers had bothered to obtain official permission from the Crown to establish the colony is unclear, but what is known is that in 1627 Charles I granted to another English nobleman, the Earl of Carlisle, the sole proprietorship of Barbados with authority to set up political and religious institutions, distribute land to planters, and grant titles of nobility to the colony's inhabitants. By 1632, Carlisle had succeeded, through his chosen governor Henry Hawley, in rallying the landowners to his support and erecting an effective government apparatus to overcome Courteen opposition.

The first English colonists hoped to set up a self-sufficient island economy based on the production of food plus exportable tropical crops. Spanish West Indies plantations raised cotton and tobacco profitably, and the Barbadians turned to those commodities first, along with dye plants like indigo (for blue), logwood (for brown), fustic (for yellow), and brazilwood (for red). Those plants could be grown easily on small plots of land. Furthermore, they did not require a huge workforce; white indentured servants did nicely. Carlisle allocated land to other wealthy and respected Englishmen who constituted an elite class of landowners who controlled the vast bulk of arable land.

The planters built effective relationships with Dutch merchants and ship owners that assisted them in developing their plantations and transporting crops to European markets. They capitalized on the tobacco boom and during the first year delivered several shiploads of tobacco to London. When the

Sugar mills such as this one that operated in the West Indies utilized animals for power. Skilled African slaves operated the machinery. The Dutch brought sugar producing technology to Barbados in the 1640s and 1650s. Because it added considerably to the cost of running a sugar plantation, only the largest and wealthiest Barbadian landowners could afford it.

tobacco market fell apart in the early 1630s, the English government issued a ban on Barbados tobacco to protect Virginia planters, whom London officials favored. The Barbadians shifted to cotton production. Another boom followed by another market bust, and by the 1640s planters were searching for yet another exportable staple.

Barbados planters had been aware of sugar in the Spanish islands and the tremendous demand for it in European households and the English rum-making industry, but growing it was exceedingly labor intensive. In addition, processing raw sugar required expensive machinery and skilled operators.

The Dutch helped out on two fronts after their attempts in the 1640s and 1650s to take over the Portuguese sugar colony of Brazil failed. Dutch merchants sold processing machinery to Barbados planters and Dutch ship owners transported African slaves to the island. Coastal towns like Bridgetown bustled with sugar exports and slave imports. Planters grew fabulously rich. And the boom was felt on the North American mainland too. Supplying Barbados with food became a major economic stimulus in New England and the Middle Colonies. They also shipped wood to the island for fuel, fences, and barrels for shipping sugar and livestock for powering processing mills.

The shift to sugar triggered dramatic demographic changes. The great rush to convert arable land to cane fields boosted land values ten-fold; only the richest residents could afford it—and the other costs of large-scale sugar production. Seven percent of the landowners possessed half the land and labor on the island. By the end of the seventeenth century, their personal wealth was four times that of the Chesapeake's richest tobacco barons. Many of Barbados' landed elite returned to England, leaving overseers to manage their plantations. During the 1660s and 1670s, most of the smaller landowners and freed indentured servants— as many as 8,000—emigrated; many of them ended up in South Carolina.

The sugar boom brought in scores of thousands of additional Africans. Supplies increased as the Atlantic slave trade expanded and prices for slaves declined. Simultaneously, English indentured servants began choosing to settle in Jamaica, a larger island that England captured from the Spanish in 1655. Soon slaves on Barbados outnumbered whites. Plantations often brutally exploited African slaves and produced an appalling mortality—up to one-third of all new arrivals within three years. Yet despite such harsh conditions, Africans established families and a sense of community. Unlike on most Caribbean islands, the gender ratio of incoming Africans slightly favored females, partly because planters believed that slave families would be more stable and less rebellious than unattached males. But the preponderance of females also resulted from the fact that women could and did work in the fields; indeed, in most West African societies women were the principal agricultural producers.

For a while the jewel of England's American empire, Barbados declined in economic importance during the eighteenth century as large islands like Jamaica and the expanding mainland colonies supplanted it. But its long-term significance includes its impact on the settlement of the lower South of mainland North America, especially South Carolina.

THINKING BACK

1. How did the economy of the English colony of Barbados come to rest on sugar?
2. What demographic changes did sugar plantations bring to Barbados?

CONCLUSION

Motives that propelled the founding of England's North American colonies included—economic advancement, religious freedom, and secular idealism. In each of the colonies, differing opinions about establishing and maintaining order, instituting hierarchical authority, and using unfree labor produced tensions that profoundly affected the cultural identities of the colonies and the colonists.

England's early colonial enterprises entailed risks, disappointments, and rewards. Investors in the Virginia Company, as well as the English Crown, hoped to compete with Spain for New World riches and minimize their financial risks by promoting trade with the Indians. The colonists sent to Jamestown suffered horribly, but profits eventually flowed from tobacco, and both the crown and settlers ultimately felt that the rewards justified the disappointments. In neighboring Maryland, proprietor Cecilius Calvert hoped to provide a haven for persecuted Catholics, but he and the English king also intended the colony to prosper, which it did, to the advantage of the colony and England.

The more religiously oriented undertakings, especially those in Massachusetts Bay and Pennsylvania, measured success not by economic gain alone but by the extent to which people lived in harmony with God and themselves. Yet they too came up short of their full expectations. The godly and orderly societies that the first Puritans aimed to build were undermined not by the likes of Nicholas and Elizabeth Pinion, although they and others like them gave cause for great concern, but by rapidly growing communities and differences in values and beliefs that naturally followed. The authorities' ultimate inability to force conformity across gender, generational, and geographical boundaries testified to the great diversity that characterized colonial America and to the complexity of cultural identity, as did the conquest of New Netherland by the English.

England's colonial founders made several fateful decisions, including perhaps the most far-reaching of all—importation of African slave laborers. In associating Africans with slavery, European colonists were also providing the basis for race conflict that would continue for generations. By the first decades of the eighteenth century, societies in every region of English North America had adopted slavery. Africans did not docilely accept their condition; rather, they actively shaped it to minimize its oppressiveness and to provide opportunities for escape. Similarly, Indians made the best of a bad situation. Those who survived the devastating European diseases traded with the colonists to obtain products that they needed or simply desired while using the leverage of their knowledge of the environment and skill in trapping and hunting to obtain alliances with the English that might help them in conflicts with their enemies.

One of the earliest and most significant contributions of the early English colonies was the institution of representative government. Beginning with the House of Burgesses in Jamestown, every colony eventually established a representative assembly chosen by voters. Although limited in scope and participation, the assemblies were the seedlings of democratic government.

SUGGESTED SOURCES
FOR STUDENTS

Ira Berlin, *Many Thousands More: The First Two Centuries of Slavery in North America* (1998), explains the shift from the utilization of just a few slaves to constructing societies whose core values and institutions were founded on slavery.

On New Amsterdam and early New York City see Edwin G. Burrows and Mike Wallace, *Gotham: A History of New York City to 1898* (1999)—a Pulitzer Prize winner.

For a broadly interpretive and comparative study of regional colonial culture read David Hackett Fischer, *Albion's Seed: Four British Folkways in America* (1989). Fischer not only describes regional cultures in colonial America, he traces their European origins.

Kenneth Lockridge, *A New England Town: Dedham Massachusetts, 1636–1736* (1985), shows how settlers established villages and how those towns functioned.

On the relationships between Indians and Europeans consult James H. Merrill, *The Indians' New World: Catawbas and Their Neighbors from European Contact Through the Era of Removal* (1989).

The best overall treatment of Virginia during its early years is Edmund S. Morgan, *American Slavery American Freedom: The Ordeal of Colonial Virginia* (1975). Morgan focuses on the paradox that freedom for Europeans depended on the expropriation of Indian land and the enslavement of Africans.

Mary Beth Norton tells the Pinion family anecdote and provides a careful and insightful examination of women's roles in early American society in *Founding Mothers & Fathers: Gendered Power and the Forming of American Society* (1996).

The awful experiences of enslaved Africans in the Middle Passage is graphically and passionately presented in Marcus Rediker, *The Slave Ship: A Human History* (2007).

For an understanding of how Africans participated in development of the Atlantic world see John Thornton, *Africa and Africans in the Making of the Atlantic World, 1400–1680* (1992).

Camilla Townsend, in *Pocahontas and the Powhatan Dilemma* (2004), rips the long-standing myths about the relationship of Powhatan's young daughter and John Smith. And in a larger sense, Townsend offers a long-needed corrective to the past male and European perspective on the interactions between Jamestown settlers and local Indians.

Lorena S. Walsh, *Motives of Honor, Pleasure, and Profit: Plantation Management in the Colonial Chesapeake* (2010), concluded her research in hundreds of plantation records that successful planters were rational, profit-driven managers ruthlessly bent on extracting maximum labor from enslaved African workers.

A marvelous study of the origins of slavery and African-American culture in South Carolina is Peter H. Wood, *Black Majority: Negroes in Colonial South Carolina from 1690 through the Stono Rebellion* (1974).

BEFORE WE GO ON

1. Why did English people establish colonies on the mainland of North America?

2. How did the European colonists along the Atlantic seaboard interact with Indians and Africans? What power did each of the three groups of people possess, and how did they exercise it?

Building a Democratic Nation

3. In building a democratic nation, Americans have wrestled with the issue of order versus freedom. Some have contended that without order chaos flourishes, as in early Jamestown. Others have noted that order often requires limits on freedom. What sources of freedom, if any, do you see in seventeenth-century America? What examples of social control can you identify?

4. What institutions of self-government appeared in seventeenth-century English North America? How did they function? Who was empowered by them, and why? Who was left out, and why?

Connections

5. Regional cultures were quite pronounced in seventeenth-century America. What elements of those early regional cultures do you recognize in America today? What constitutes American culture to you, and what roots do you notice in the seventeenth century?

6. What issues of race, gender, and class in seventeenth-century America do you recognize today?

Chapter 4

GROWTH AND CONFLICT, 1675–1760

A PERSONAL PERSPECTIVE: JOHN WILLIAMS

Image © Jeffrey M. Frank, 2010. Used by permission of Shutterstock, Inc.

One of the remaining houses in Historic Deerfield, Massachusetts, the site of a devastating attack by French and Indian enemies and the nightmare of John Williams and his family

> **Why did the French and Indians attack Deerfield, and what happened to young Eunice Williams?**

Before dawn on February 29, 1704, the 300 residents of Deerfield, Massachusetts, awakened to the horror of war. A party of fifty Frenchmen and over 200 Huron, Mohawk, and Abenaki Indian warriors attacked their village, slaying thirty-nine residents, burning several houses, slaughtering hogs and cattle, and taking 112 captives. England and France were at war, and although Deerfield's citizens had taken precautions, the suddenness and power of the assault overwhelmed them. The horror lasted only a few moments for those who managed to escape and those who died, including many of the town's youngest children and one of its two African-American residents, a woman named Parthena, enslaved by Rev. John Williams, the town's minister and most prominent citizen. But for the captives, the ordeal continued much longer. Among them were Williams, his wife, and five of their children.

The raiders handed Williams over to French authorities in Montreal and several other captives, including two of Williams' children, to Catholic missionaries.

Over the next three years, Massachusetts' governor Joseph Dudley and businessmen with connections to the French and Indians through the fur trade attempted to secure the hostages' release. Finally, more than three years later, exchanges of French prisoners for the English captives began. Williams was among those initially freed, followed by four of his children. The *Boston News-Letter* rejoiced: "The people of this country are fill'd with joy."

Relief maybe but not joy filled John Williams' heart, for the Indians had killed two of his sons in the initial attack and his wife on the long march. And ten-year-old daughter Eunice remained with a Mohawk family who adopted her. The Mohawks, who according to a contemporary "do not so much as know what it is to correct" children, treated Eunice with extreme kindness. She became attached to them and to Mohawk ways. She adopted the Catholic faith, which she learned from French missionaries. After finally locating Eunice, Reverend Williams pleaded with her to return with him to New England. He discovered, however, that his once-captive daughter had taken a Mohawk identity. Eunice replied tersely, and in Mohawk, "Jaghte oghte," or simply "No."

Williams' account of the Deerfield raid, published as *The Redeemed Captive Returning to Zion*, brings out the Puritan view of New England as "God's sanctuary" in contrast to New France, which he characterizes as an evil wilderness populated by heathens and Catholics. He and other ministers used the experiences of English hostages allegorically to illustrate human sin, punishment by God, followed by redemption. However, Eunice Williams' story also shows that the people and cultures located in adjacent frontier societies often blended together. Eunice's descendents maintained their English family name for generations along with their Mohawk identity. Today, the town that adopted Eunice Williams contains a diverse population with diverse cultural backgrounds, and much the same is true on the New England side of today's United States-Canada border.

The assault on Deerfield was a very personal drama played out in one little corner of a complex global stage. France and England declared war on each other

1675	**1676**	**1682**	**1686**	**1688–89**	**1692–93**
King Philip's War devastates New England	Bacon's Rebellion upends colonial Virginia	La Salle explores Mississippi River and claims Louisiana	Dominion of New England ignites a colonial rebellion against English authority	Glorious Revolution shifts English political power to Parliament	Salem witch scare reveals deep-seeded fear in colonial Massachusetts

in Europe in 1702, and the hostilities spilled onto the North American frontier. Deerfield was situated in a corridor through which valuable beaver furs moved from Iroquois hunters in Canada through ports in New England and across the Atlantic to markets in Europe. This tiny village and its residents were a military target in a great imperial struggle. The relatively small French colonial army often employed Indian auxillaries to boost its power, but the Indians who attacked Deerfield did so for their own personal reasons. English settlers had taken their lands. Indeed, Deerfield was built on the site of the Abenaki village of Pocumtuck, whose residents had been dispossessed. Revenge clearly motivated some of the Indians.

There were other personal perspectives on the Deerfield raid that reveal more about the individual, collective, and often clashing identities in colonial North America. The French troops were not just automatons; they included young, ambitious officers seeking recognition, fur traders protecting their livelihood against English competition, and teenage boys seeking adventure or trying to make a living. Perhaps some of the Mohawks from the Canadian village that adopted Eunice Williams went to Deerfield for captives to replace kinfolk. Although Eunice's father could comprehend her becoming a Mohawk only as the work of the devil, some of the Indians who seized her were Catholic Christians defending their faith against English Protestants.

The Indians who resided on the periphery of all European colonies suffered as a result of colonial expansion. In New Spain, officials sought to buttress frontier defenses to protect valuable Mexican silver mines. French imperial expansion drove deep into the heartland of North America. English colonies showed the clearest signs of growth, economic diversification, and vibrant intellectual and scientific activity. From the 1670s to the 1760s, England's colonies grew from tenuous footholds into anchors of a dynamic continental empire. Likewise, African slaves formed distinctive African-American identities. Diplomacy sometimes kept the peace but other times failed. Change, uncertainty, and insecurity exacerbated social tensions within colonies, proving that growth could be painful.

THINKING BACK

1. Why did Eunice Williams choose to remain with her Mohawk captors instead of returning to her English family in Massachusetts?
2. Looking at the Deerfield raid from a personal perspective, what possible reasons can you see for the attack apart from broad national interest?

THE SPANISH FRONTIER

The rapid expansion of imperial rivals in North America, especially England and France, caused Spanish officials to worry. In enemy hands, Florida could provide bases for attacking Spanish shipping. Mexican silver mines also required protection. Authorities in Mexico City regarded New Spain's northern perimeter as a strategic buffer and sought to fortify it.

Expanding Spanish Borderlands

Like Spain's initial colonization, frontier expansion followed official policy rather than private initiative. To protect against the English in

> **Why and how did Spain develop its colonial frontiers?**

South Carolina, the Spanish fortified St. Augustine, constructing a massive stone fortress, or *presidio*, named Castillo de San Marcos. Nervousness about French exploration and settlement along the lower Mississippi River in the 1680s and 1690s called for military installations on Pensacola Bay. In 1721 the Spanish established a settlement at Los Adaes, the first capital of Texas. The Catholic Church established missions among the local Indians. These included San Antonio de Valero, known as the Alamo. The *presidio* of San Antonio de Bexar preceded the founding the town of San Antonio in 1731.

In the remote Southwest, attack by other Europeans was less likely. The viceroy in Mexico City encouraged civilian settlements there. After the Pueblo Revolt in 1680 (see p. 50), farmers and stock-raisers settled in protected valleys along the Rio Grande from El Paso

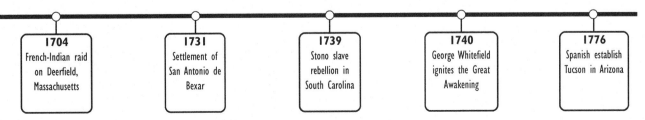

1704	**1731**	**1739**	**1740**	**1776**
French-Indian raid on Deerfield, Massachusetts	Settlement of San Antonio de Bexar	Stono slave rebellion in South Carolina	George Whitefield ignites the Great Awakening	Spanish establish Tucson in Arizona

to near present-day Colorado. Few colonists risked attack by Apache Indians to venture into present-day Arizona, which acquired its name from the Tohono O'odham (Papago) Indian word *Arizonac*, meaning "a place of little springs." But between 1687 and 1711, the Jesuit missionary Eusebio Francisco Kino founded missions below the Gila River and mapped the region as well. Traces of silver lured a few intrepid prospectors, and in the summer of 1776, Spaniards located a military garrison at Tucson to protect them.

Spanish Frontier Society

> **What was the nature of societies on New Spain's frontier?**

Throughout the colonial period, most Spanish frontier citizens lived in New Mexico. Late in the eighteenth century, that province's official population reached 30,000, ten times the number in Florida and Texas respectively. Spanish officials counted all Spanish-speakers in its census enumerations, including baptized Pueblo and mission Indians. In 1764, Spanish census officials in Florida also counted 420 Africans, 80 percent of whom were slaves.

Although record-keepers distinguished between Europeans and Indians, frontier life blurred the distinction. Catholic missionaries endeavored to integrate Indians into Spanish society, and many Christian Indians joined Spanish communities as servants and wage-earning masons, carpenters, and blacksmiths. By the end of the eighteenth century, mission Indians constituted one-tenth of the population of San Antonio, and the governor of New Mexico described the Christianized Pueblo Indians as being "Spaniards in all things." Across the frontier, where Spanish women were scarce, soldiers and laborers married or otherwise mated with Indian women. By the late eighteenth century, nine out of ten Hispanic men and women residing on the frontier contained mixed blood. Africans occupied an ambiguous position. In Florida, Spanish officials allowed black Catholics—slave and free—into the military as soldiers, which provided them with power, status, and some wealth. Blacks frequently married Indians and Spaniards.

Ethnicity, service to the crown, and property all determined where people stood on the social ladder. Pureblood Europeans, whether born in Spain or America, constituted the frontier elite along with military officers, *rancheros* (ranchers), and their families. Clothes symbolized high status—the men's stiff-brimmed hats and leather leggings, and the women's long, pleated dresses with lace and silver embroidery. One foreign visitor noted: "Many will go up to their ears in debt simply to satisfy their pride in putting on a grand appearance." They acquired fancy clothes from Mexico. Women could own property and status. Juana Luján, who died in New Mexico in 1762, bequeathed to her three children a huge ranch with a home containing two-dozen rooms, furniture and paintings, silverware and china, and jewelry and fine clothing.

Most ordinary Hispanic settlers farmed for subsistence and to supply military garrisons with food. They grew native food plants, although the cool, dry Southwest provided an abundance of wine grapes. Some farmers raised tobacco, which both men and women smoked. Settlers everywhere on the frontier maintained herds of cattle for hides, milk, and meat, and horses for riding and pulling wagons. In Florida and along the Gulf coast, hogs, introduced by early Spanish explorers, ran wild. Sheep thrived in New Mexico, supplying mutton for meat and wool for blankets and clothing. But not all frontier Hispanics were agriculturalists. Weavers, carpenters, masons, and blacksmiths also contributed to the subsistence frontier economy.

For plain men, women, and children, daily life was characterized by simplicity, deprivation, and danger. Most people made their own coarse cotton and wool clothing and furnished their small rock and adobe houses with usually no more than a crude bed, a rough-hewn wooden table, and benches. A crucifix or

© Bettmann/Interim Archives/Contributor/Getty

Music and dancing were among the ways Spanish frontier settlers amused themselves. These frontier men and women, according to the original caption of this undated illustration, are "Going to a fandango."

a painting of a Christian saint symbolized their Catholic faith. Smallpox was the biggest killer and threatened soldiers and villagers more than families isolated on large ranches. During a two-month period in 1781, the infection killed 142 Santa Fe residents.

At the bottom of the social ladder were what St. Augustine's governor labeled "dastardly persons": Africans (slave and free), mulattos, and Indians. Laws favored Europeans and discriminated against mixed-bloods, Indians, and Africans. Non-Spaniard criminals could be flogged, but Spaniards could not. Most communities were racially segregated with blacks and Indians relegated to outlying areas.

Spanish settlers often disrupted Native-American trade networks. Missionaries and merchants offered clothing, combs, and beads to Pueblo people in exchange for labor and corn, breaking long-standing relationships between the Pueblos and nomadic Indians, who now resorted to raiding ranches and farms. The Comanche were the most feared due largely to the horses they stole from Spanish settlements and guns they acquired from French traders in exchange for bison meat and hides.

_____

THINKING BACK

1. What prompted officials to step up the level of settlement on New Spain's northern frontier?
2. What type of economic and social systems developed on New Spain's frontier?

_____

THE DYNAMIC FRENCH EMPIRE

The French had initially shown little interest in settling North America. By the 1680s, New France counted only 10,500 residents, mostly Catholics in Canada and Protestant Huguenots in Acadia (today's New Brunswick and Nova Scotia). But afterward, French authorities expanded New France from the St. Lawrence River valley to the Great Lakes and down the Mississippi River to the Gulf of Mexico. As with New Spain, the Catholic Church worked in conjunction with the state to stretch France's North American empire. While commerce with the Indians remained central to the economy, French settlers along the lower Mississippi attempted to develop a staple-crop export trade, utilizing African slaves. As a result, the population of New France reached 70,000 by the middle of the eighteenth century.

The Expansion of New France

The economy of New France depended heavily on the beaver trade. French Canadians enlisted Indians who knew how and where to hunt the animals. The Algonquian-speaking Huron served as middlemen, acquiring

> What kind of relationship did the French and Huron Indians develop?

pelts from Ottawa hunters in the far-north country in exchange for metal hatchets and knives along with muskets, bullets, and gunpowder they obtained by passing the pelts on to French merchants in Montreal and Quebec. The Huron used firearms to great advantage in wars with their bitter foes from the Iroquois League. French authorities pressured the Indians to allow Catholic missionaries to proselytize in their villages. Both the French and the Indians realized the potential for mutually beneficial military alliances, a co-dependency that underlay the raid on Deerfield. (see pp. 98-99)

In the 1640s, the relationship between the French and Hurons began to change. Many Hurons grew to resent the French impact on their communities. French missionaries divided Hurons into Christians and non-Christians, creating dissension and alienation. In addition, the French introduced deadly smallpox. At the same time, the Iroquois launched devastating attacks against Huron towns, dispersing the people. Some relocated in villages close to French towns in the St. Lawrence Valley, but many others migrated to the western Great Lakes where they mingled with various other Native American people.

Pushing Canada to the Great Lakes

Frenchmen followed the Huron migration. Traders called *coureurs de bois* ("runners of the woods") moved in among the Indians, adopting Native ways and often marrying Native American women. Their ability to supply trade goods added to

> What drew the French onto the western frontier, and how did they interact with local Indian societies?

the power these Indian wives of French traders exercised in their communities, enabling them to influence decisions like going to war and making peace. With their mixed-race, *métis*, offspring, they laid the basis for many creole communities. The French traders shipped beaver pelts by canoe to Quebec. Catholic Jesuit missionaries also followed the refugee Hurons.

As they had done previously with Indians in the St. Lawrence Valley, the French established symbiotic relationships with the Indians of the Great Lakes region. The relationships worked because Europeans and Native Americans needed each other and accepted each other's terms. Indians accepted the metaphor of the indulgent "white father" serving his obedient Indian children, but primarily the implied benevolence and mutuality and not the subordination and dependency. Negotiations over the beaver trade or about whether to allow French military outposts followed Indian protocol, in particular the traditional Indian **calumet ceremony**. French representatives smoked a feathered calumet peace pipe and offered gifts—trinkets, shirts, blankets, and even muskets—out of respect. Successful "forest diplomacy" built partnerships based on mutual needs.

Authorities in New France supported commercial and missionary ventures even though some officials worried that instead of making the Indians more "French" the traders were turning into Indians themselves. Officials also approved military outposts along the Mississippi River to curb English colonial expansion in North America. Laying claim to the Mississippi and its vast drainage would give France control of half the continent. In the 1670s, Louis de Buade de Frontenac, the governor of New France, ordered the building of forts along the eastern Great Lakes, and Montreal-based fur traders erected a trading post at Michilimackinac, on the strait between lakes Huron and Michigan, and at Detroit.

Founding Louisiana

<table>
<tr><td>

What led to the founding of Louisiana, and what kind of relationship did the French establish with Indians and Africans?

</td><td>

Late in the seventeenth century, French explorers pushed to the Mississippi River and beyond. In 1673, fur trader Louis Jolliet and Jesuit missionary Jacques Marquette explored the upper Mississippi River. In 1682, an expedition under Robert Cavelier, Sieur de La Salle, floated down the

</td></tr>
</table>

Mississippi River, claiming Louisiana for King Louis XIV. Three years later, La Salle commanded a second expedition across the Gulf of Mexico to establish a base at the mouth of the Mississippi. Locating the river's channels in the swampy delta proved difficult, however, and the party sailed beyond it to Texas, where La Salle's men mutinied and killed him.

In late 1698, foul weather miraculously blew another French naval squadron under Pierre LeMoyne, Sieur d'Iberville, into the Mississippi. The Frenchmen

French success in building relationships with Indians was partly the result of honoring Indian traditions. Smoking the calumet, or "peace pipe," paved the way for many French-Indian agreements.

erected forts on Biloxi Bay and Mobile Bay that the Spanish government called a "thorn which has been thrust into the heart of America." The French now had river trade routes into Indian territory. In 1718, Iberville's brother, the Sieur de Bienville, founded the trading center of New Orleans, which in 1723 became the administrative capital of French Louisiana.

The Indians whom the French encountered were numerous but less centrally organized than they had once been. Smallpox epidemics had diminished the once powerful chiefdoms. Many small villages survived, and some of them reconstituted themselves into new tribes like the Creek, Chickasaw, and Choctaw. By the opening of the eighteenth century, some 70,000 Indians inhabited the territory between the southern Appalachian Mountains and the Mississippi River. Many relatively small Indian communities suffered raids from relatively powerful Creeks and Chickasaws who took captives and sold them as slaves to English traders in Charles Town for muskets, bullets, gunpowder, hatchets, knives, looking glasses, ribbon, needles, cloth, and rum. Thus, many Louisiana Indians welcomed the French newcomers who could supply them with arms.

French colonization of Louisiana followed both common and uncommon patterns. Through the early years of the eighteenth century, Louisiana languished because the French crown was interested only in strategic military outposts. A census of the Gulf Coast outposts in 1708 reported only 122 French soldiers and 77 workers and settlers (24 men, 28 women, and 25 children). A handful of *coureurs de bois* plied the

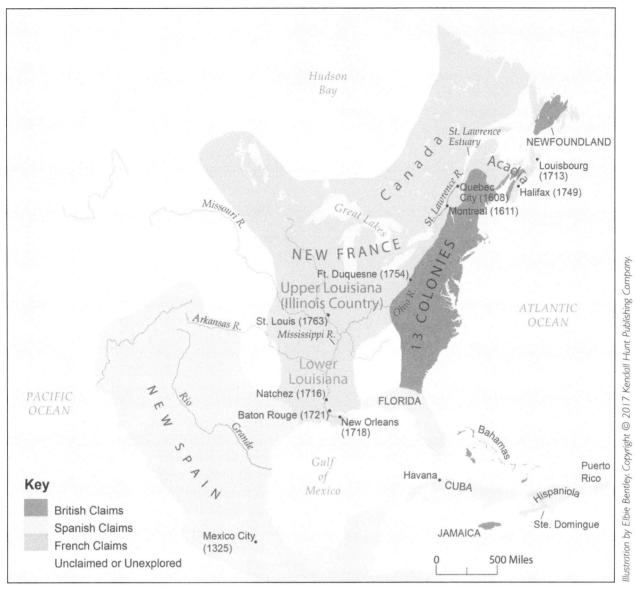

This map shows the extent of European colonization of North America by the 1750s.

Alabama, Tombigbee, Mississippi, and Red rivers, smoking the calumet and trading supplies to Indians for deerskins and bear hides. But the fur trade alone did not make Louisiana profitable.

Economic conditions began to improve between 1717 and 1719 when corporate enterprise took over the colony. Licensed by the king, the **Company of the Indies** brought 7,000 French and German settlers, laborers, and soldiers and sold tracts of land to those who could afford it for tobacco, rice, and indigo plantations along the lower Mississippi River. Finding labor to clear the forest and cultivate and process crops was no easy task. The notoriously independent *coureurs de bois* disdained farming, and even indentured servants, called *engagés,* resisted hard labor in the swampy, unhealthy environment. Attempts to enslave Indians

generally failed. In the European mind, this situation called for African slaves.

The Company of the Indies began transporting shiploads of slaves to Louisiana. Between 1719 and 1731, some 6,000 Africans entered the colony. In 1724, a set of slave laws called the *Code Noir* defined and regulated slavery. The laws required owners to expose slaves to Catholicism but were harsh and restrictive, allowing severe physical punishment for recalcitrance, prohibiting sexual relations with whites, and discouraging slaves from purchasing their freedom. Death rates were appalling. The *sickle-cell trait*, a condition in red blood cells, protected many Africans against malaria but not yellow fever, pneumonia, or dysentery. During the first decade of slave importation, over half the Africans perished. Gradually, however, Africans adjusted to the environment and their population stabilized. Despite the *Code Noir*, a few skilled slaves managed to hire themselves out and purchase their freedom.

Firearms gave the white minority inordinate power, yet, Africans and Indians possessed sufficient strength to undermine the French colonial plantation system. Slaves stole guns and escaped into the woods and with Indian fugitives established armed "maroon" communities. French authorities sought to head off such alliances by rewarding Indians with muskets and powder if they returned African runaways. While this tactic solidified French friendship with Choctaws, it did nothing to placate the Natchez, whose towns occupied the bluffs along the eastern bank of the Mississippi River. "Before the French came amongst us," a Natchez chief declared, "we were men, content with what we had . . . But now . . . we walk like slaves . . . which we shall soon be, since the French already treat us as if we were such." On the morning of November 28, 1729, Indians and Africans attacked a French settlement killing over 200 men, women, and children. French authorities put down the rebellion, but in its aftermath, with rumors of additional African slave revolts rampant, the French government stripped the Company of the Indies of its monopoly. Plans for a slave-based plantation economy in Louisiana went on the shelf.

French explorers, traders, and missionaries continued to probe into the western interior of the continent. They mapped the upper Mississippi and lower Arkansas and Missouri rivers, made contact with Quapaw and Osage Indian villages, and carried on a lively commodity exchange. But the expansion of English colonies from the Atlantic seaboard was far more dynamic.

THINKING BACK

1. How did the French and Indians interact in eastern Canada and in the Great Lakes region?
2. What shape did colonial Louisiana take, and how did Indians and African slaves affect it?

ENGLISH NORTH AMERICA SURGES AHEAD

By the middle of the eighteenth century, England's mainland colonies had surged ahead of New Spain and New France. In the seventy years up to 1750, the number of English colonists grew from 150,000 to 1.5 million, triple the growth rate of Europe. Virginia was the most populous colony, but Pennsylvania was quickly catching up. Improved health accounted for much of the growth, and by the middle of the eighteenth century most colonists were American born. But immigration still contributed significant numbers. A largely unregulated economy and much good land attracted immigrants like a powerful magnet. When Europe was peaceful and prosperous, Europeans stayed at home; when war and pestilence raged, they came to America. But the expansion of agriculture in the colonies also increased the flow of involuntary slave immigrants.

Population Growth and Evolving Health Care

Eighteenth-century colonists lived longer than their forebearers. Infant mortality remained high; one newborn in six died before reaching its second birthday, and smallpox killed more children than any other infection. Benjamin and Deborah Franklin were among the many parents who lost youngsters to the scourge. But most mothers had six to eight babies during their fertile years, more than enough to offset the overall mortality rate, which for North Americans was as much as 20 percent lower than in Europe. The land yielded sufficient food for good nutrition, leaving communicable disease as the greatest threat to human life.

Medical treatments of the time relied heavily on traditional remedies. Physicians knew nothing of bacteria and viruses. They assumed that out-of-balance body

> **What was the primary source of increased longevity?**

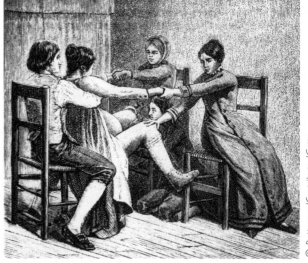

Eighteenth-century childbirth was difficult and dangerous for both mothers and their newborns. During their reproductive years, women stood a 1 in 8 chance of dying of complications, and mortality among infants was ten percent.

© Bettmann/Contributor/Getty

fluids caused most diseases. Standard practice involved draining bad or excessive fluids by induced vomiting and bleeding. Barbers and butchers performed most surgeries, and apothecaries, forerunners of modern pharmacists, prepared medicines, often by borrowing from Indian and African traditions. Tobacco, advised one doctor, "helps digestion, the Gout, and Tooth-ach." In 1729, a Virginia slave named James Papaw gained his freedom by revealing "many wonderful cures." Narcotics, especially the opium derivative laudanum, deadened painful symptoms. Inoculation against smallpox represented a major breakthrough in disease prevention. Doctors rubbed material from a smallpox pustule into a skin scratch, which induced a mild case of the disease that usually resulted in lifetime immunity. In 1721, Boston minister Cotton Mather learned about smallpox inoculation from an African and became a strong advocate for the procedure.

Colonial women assumed a large measure of responsibility for healing. Wives and mothers applied various folk remedies and comforted ailing husbands and children. Midwives typically facilitated childbirth and treated female disorders. Many slave women on southern plantations practiced medicine, a customary role of African women, and learned the medicinal qualities of North American plants as well as European and Indian medical procedures. One South Carolina slave woman was described as "a good midwife and nurse" who "can weigh out medicines and let blood."

Complexity and Diversity Through Immigration

> **Where did the new immigrants come from and how did they fit into American colonial communities?**

Spanish and French colonies experienced similar fertility and longevity but nothing like the rate of immigration as the English provinces. The Spanish crown did not successfully promote immigration. Similarly, France prohibited Protestant Huguenot immigration out of fear of undermining the position of the official Catholic Church. Conversely, the British actively promoted immigration, and the colonies extended voting rights to immigrants with the general exception of Catholics and Jews.

African slaves were the most numerous immigrants. Prior to the 1730s, enslaved immigrants averaged fewer than 1,000 per year, but with the expansion of plantation agriculture, the number increased dramatically. People of African background constituted one fifth of the colonial population at mid-century. More Africans resided in the Chesapeake region than anywhere else in British North America, and they comprised 57 percent of the populations of South Carolina and Georgia.

Approximately 150,000 immigrants came from the British Isles—northern England, Scotland, and Ireland primarily. Some were Catholic but most were Protestants, including descendants of Scottish Presbyterians who had colonized northern parts of Ireland late in the sixteenth century. Called **Scots-Irish**, they arrived in large numbers in labor-short Pennsylvania, but their clannishness, aggressive pursuit of land, and defiance of authority led to conflicts with Quakers. Many of the Scots-Irish drifted southward through the eastern foothills of the Appalachian Mountains into western Virginia and North Carolina. Others traveled further west along the Great Western Road into the upper Ohio Valley.

Despite the fact that most British immigrants came to America to improve their lives, there was a darker side to the story for some. Beginning in 1717, British judges sentenced convicts to colonial servitude, typically for periods of seven to fourteen years. By 1775, some 50,000 convicts had arrived in America. Upwards of 80 percent were unskilled males in their twenties and thirties. Their crimes were mostly against property, among the 200 capital offenses under the British penal code. Transportation to the colonies offered an escape from the hangman; however, in most cases the convicts' lives as manual laborers were hard, unrewarding, and short.

Germans comprised the next largest group, totaling as many as 90,000. They settled mostly in Pennsylvania, New York, and Maryland. Incorrectly called "Dutch" because in German *Deutsch* means "German," these immigrants were mostly poor farmers fleeing European war and starvation. German immigrants typically pulled up stakes and made their way in family units to Rotterdam and other Atlantic or North Sea ports. There they bought tickets or, more commonly, borrowed the cost of the passage to America from willing ship captains who knew that plenty of work and good wages to repay the loans awaited the immigrant redemptioners. Most found wage employment; those who did not signed contracts to become indentured servants. After working out their obligations, some purchased land while others rented property or sold their labor.

The typical eighteenth-century American, noted the French writer Hector St. Jean de Crevecoeur, was a man "whose grandfather was an Englishman, whose wife was Dutch, whose son married a French woman, and whose present four sons have now four wives of different nations." Crevecoeur aptly if not precisely described of the residents of the Middle Atlantic colonies. Anglicized names—Smith from Schmidt and Elizabeth from Elisabetta—signified the immigrants' assimilation, as did integrated residential patterns, but living in the British colonies did not erase all traces of ethnic identity and chauvinism. Pennsylvania Germans shunned the Scots-Irish. They supported their own Catholic or Protestant Lutheran, Moravian, or Mennonite churches. Likewise, Irish Catholics, Scottish Presbyterians, and French Huguenots maintained their religious traditions.

In the 1680s, a small but steady stream of Jewish immigrants arrived in New York City. Many were Portuguese-speaking Sephardic Jews from Brazil via the West Indies. Their experience in the West Indian sugar trade drew them to New York's commercial district. Jewish merchants prospered and on occasion intermarried with Christian families. But they encountered ethnic prejudice and English policies that limited participation in international trade to Christians. Furthermore, anti-Semitism occasionally turned riotous, as in 1755 when a mob attacked the home of a recent Jewish immigrant merchant. Oliver De Lancey, a prominent Christian, organized the mob even though his wife, Phila Franks, was the daughter of one of New York's most wealthy and respected Jewish families.

About half the immigrants to the British colonies in the eighteenth century were not free; they were indentured servants, slaves, or convicts. Nevertheless, immigration during the eighteenth century brought a large number of families to the colonies, helping to bring the gender ratio closer into balance and providing an additional measure of social stability and order.

THINKING BACK

1. What allowed the population of Britain's North American colonies to increase to the extent that it did through the first half of the eighteenth century?
2. Where did immigrants to America come from, why did they immigrate, where did they settle, and how did they contribute to growth in the British colonies?

TRANSFORMING THE SOUTHERN COLONIES

By 1750, about half the population of British North America lived in the Chesapeake colonies, the Carolinas, and Georgia. Virginia was the most populous of the southern colonies, with 231,000 residents, both black and white. Over the eighteenth century, the southern colonies turned into plantation-based slave societies. Plantations were self-sufficient enterprises; slaves not only produced food but also made such necessities as barrels, bricks, and harnesses. Thus, there were few towns and little need for white artisans or even indentured servants. Slavery defined social life for whites as well as blacks and determined the fate of many Native Americans. The elite members of southern colonial societies were slave owners who lived in large, elegantly furnished houses, and dressed in fine, fashionable clothes. But most southern whites were **yeoman** farmers and artisans who owned few if any slaves. And throughout the period, ships brought more immigrants who pushed into the backcountry.

From Servants to Slaves

In 1650, about 500 Africans resided in Virginia. Most planters owned just a few slaves and worked alongside them in the tobacco fields. By the mid-1700s, however, slave ships had transported nearly half a million Africans to the colonies. This pointed to an important socioeconomic transformation in the southern colonies—a shift from servant to slave labor.

> Why did planters shift from indentured servants to enslaved Africans?

The greater availability of slaves was certainly one reason for the shift. Early in the seventeenth century, the Netherlands broke the near monopoly that Spain and Portugal once held over the Atlantic slave trade. The Dutch kept the cost of slaves high, but in the Anglo-Dutch war of the 1670s, the English Royal African Company took command of the slave trade. As the price of slaves dropped, the number of enslaved Africans in the colonies rose. During the first half of the eighteenth century, South Carolina's slave population ballooned from 4,000 to 90,000 with most of the increase owing to imported Africans. In the Chesapeake area, the slave population swelled to 185,000.

In Virginia, social unrest prompted the shift to slave labor. Indentured servants who completed their terms of service expected land of their own, but the planter elites controlled the fertile coastal **tidewater** land and Indians occupied much of the upland **piedmont**. Angry and unruly, former indentured servants roamed the countryside and occasionally joined bands of runaway slaves. Falling tobacco prices combined with the rising cost of English manufactured goods and annoying taxes to pinch small farmers. Governor Sir William Berkeley worried about rebellion on the part of a colonial populace "wher six parts in seaven . . . are Poore Endebted Discontented and Armed."

Friction among colonists merged with a settler-Indian conflict to spark **Bacon's Rebellion**. As former servants and would-be planters migrated into the piedmont in search for land, they clashed with resident Indians. In the summer of 1675, a couple of local Doeg people stole a farmer's hogs. Whites reacted by killing the first Indians they found—a half-dozen Susquehannocks, a large and powerful tribe. Nathaniel Bacon, a recent arrival from England, took command of a militia composed mostly of farmers and servants along with a few enslaved African Americans to rid the colony of "all the Indians." While Bacon was wealthy, he scorned the entrenched and self-serving tidewater planters "whose tottering fortunes," he said, "have been . . . supported at the public charge" and who now refused to pay for the militia. Governor Berkeley regarded Bacon's army apprehensively and feared an all-out Indian war. He declined to help Bacon, infuriating him and his followers. During the summer and autumn of 1676, Bacon's band not only massacred Indians but also marched to Jamestown, set the capital aflame, and sent Berkeley scurrying for safety. The governor returned, however, with an army of English seamen who routed Bacon's rebels and restored order. Bacon died of dysentery before he could be captured, but almost two dozen of his followers ended up hanging from the gallows.

Bacon's Rebellion exposed the racial and class tensions that existed in virtually every colony. From the start, Chesapeake settlers had competed with Indians for land, but the rebellion essentially ended it. Indian populations of the region were never as strong again. The Susquehannocks migrated northward and joined the Iroquois League just as some Iroquois drifted south along the Appalachian Mountains seeking access to trade in furs and hides. Virginia authorities established several small reservations, and many individual Indians settled onto farms in white communities. Bacon's Rebellion failed to produce a revolution against the planter elite, who retained complete dominance not only in Virginia but also in North Carolina, where a similar uprising collapsed in 1677. Indeed, more fearful than ever of rebellious servants, planters began replacing indentured servants with slave laborers.

Constructing Slave Societies

Slave societies did not just have slaves; they depended on them. To organize, control, and motivate legions of unfree workers, slave owners adopted coercive measures. They put slaves to work under the supervision of hired managers called **overseers** who typically possessed authority to determine what work would be performed and to punish recalcitrant slaves. Strict plantation management provided little time for slaves to tend gardens or work after hours for cash; consequently, slaves found few open avenues to freedom. To strip Africans of their previous identities and to emphasize their dependent status, masters assigned them new names, usually a first name only and one intended to ridicule or demean them—like Hercules, Sukey, or Bossy. Slave owners also forbade African customs like braiding hair and ceremonial dancing and drumming.

> What were slave societies like in the Chesapeake and Carolina low country?

Slaves possessed no legal rights; they were property—slaves for life—and that status descended from mother to child regardless of the father's status. Yet as property, slaves had value to their owners who hated to subject them to corporal punishment that might damage their value. Thus, South Carolina slave owner Robert Raper hid his slave man Abraham because he had committed multiple crimes and "was very near being hanged." But the master-slave relationship was severely unbalanced; planters were often the law unto themselves, able to inflict any punishment they wanted to "correct" a slave. Rarely were white persons punished for abusing or even killing slaves.

Laws curtailed the rights of free blacks as well, virtually equating blackness with slavery and whiteness with freedom. As Virginia's governor put it, this would "make the free-Negroes sensible that a distinction ought to be made between their offspring and the Descendants of an Englishman, with whom they never were to be Accounted Equal." Free blacks could no longer employ white indentured servants, bear arms, or hold public office. In

1691, the Virginia assembly discouraged manumission by requiring that planters send all freed slaves out of the colony.

Early in the eighteenth century, conditions experienced by Chesapeake slaves improved somewhat. When tobacco prices declined, many planters began growing wheat, a less profitable and less labor-intensive crop. Once again, owners allowed slaves to maintain vegetable gardens, raise poultry, and hire out their skills because it reduced the planters' "overhead" expenses. Slaves could also move more freely from place to place. The health of native-born slaves improved as they acquired natural immunities to local diseases. As slaves lived longer, they married and produced children. Many persuaded their owners to purchase their spouses and children, for masters often believed that slaves in stable families were less likely to rebel.

Conditions for slaves remained hard in the Carolina-Georgia low country however. Rice cultivation at the end of the seventeenth century provided the basis for North America's most fully developed slave society. The region was well suited to rice production because low-lying fields could be irrigated from rivers and coastal estuaries. Furthermore, many African slaves already knew how to grow and process rice. By 1720, rice accounted for half the colony's exports. Indigo also flourished. Cloth makers in England converted the plant's juices into a blue dye, and as England's textile industry expanded, the market price of indigo soared. Planters discovered that the indigo plant's growth cycle dovetailed with rice, allowing enslaved men and women to remain productive the year round raising one crop followed by the other. Rice, indigo, and livestock, tended by slaves known as **cowboys**, produced an extraordinarily prosperous economy.

With their profits, planters acquired more land, purchased more African slaves, and squeezed out small-scale farmers. Slaves outnumbered whites in the region by a margin of three-to-one, causing one visitor to note that South Carolina "look[ed] more like a negro country than like a country settled by white people." The new Africans were predominantly "unseasoned" males who toiled in the oppressive heat in flooded rice fields and snake-infested irrigation canals. They perished in fearsome numbers. Relatively few and much overworked and malnourished women often failed to conceive, suffered miscarriages, or died before producing enough children to replace the dead. But rich planters could always import more Africans.

Nevertheless, even South Carolina slaves acquired some control over their working conditions. Planters who did not fully trust their overseers often designated slave foremen known as "**drivers**" to manage the fieldwork, occasionally with direct authority to determine job assignments and to punish (or not punish) field hands. The carpenters and mechanics who built, operated, and maintained the floodgates and processing and storage facilities avoided the most onerous labor. With few skilled whites in the area, slave craftsmen occasionally parlayed their skills into opportunities to work for wages. Even field hands had leverage; they undermined plantation efficiency by feigning illness, breaking tools and equipment, stealing food and whatever else they could, and running away. One planter conceded the need to be more indulgent since runaways "cost me much Trouble and Expense."

Urban slaves constituted a distinct slave subset. Most low country planters built residences in Charles Town and Savannah, where they lived with their wives and children attended by staffs of domestic slaves. Wealthy merchants did the same. Slave women cooked, washed clothes, and cleaned house while men handled home repairs, the gardens, and the horses. Domestic slaves lived in close, sometimes intimate, proximity to whites in tiny add-on rooms and closets in the masters' houses. They dressed like whites, usually in hand-me-down clothes. Other urban slaves labored as seamstresses, weavers, boatmen, messengers, teamsters, and dock and shipyard workers. Many took advantage of unsupervised time to earn incomes, like women who purchased food for their masters' families' meals in local markets and also sold handmade baskets and garden produce.

Africans always found ways to resist their enslavement, which usually took passive-aggressive form, understandable considering the severe punishment meted out for rebellion—from amputation of toes or feet to execution by hanging, burning, or beheading. But resistance also took more active forms, like flight and occasionally even assault and murder of overseers and planters. In 1739, slaves in South Carolina overwhelmed local whites, stole some weapons, and headed for Florida. Along the Stono River, fifteen miles from the border, white militiamen caught and slaughtered them, afterwards lining the roads with their severed heads to remind others of the consequences of rebellion. Yet a few participants in the **Stono Rebellion** did make it to Florida, part of a small but steady stream of fugitives flowing across the British-Spanish frontier.

Although slavery was a racial institution, race was not simply a black and white issue. Slave women often entered sexual relationships with white men—a common form of white male exploitation of slave women—and gave birth to mulatto children. Just how many such relationships there were cannot be precisely determined; however, Johann Bolzius, a visitor to Virginia, noted that mulattos existed "in large numbers." Furthermore, very light-skinned mulattos sometimes passed into white society. But not all such relationships involved black women and white men, as the members of a church in Virginia discovered when one of its white female members "brought public scandal" on herself and the congregation by "committing fornication by cohabiting with a Negro."

Plantation slavery sharply defined slaves as African rather than English in order to diminish, demoralize, and control the slaves. Slaves, however, turned that designation around in developing a distinct African-American identity.

Becoming African American

> How did African-American communities and African-American cultures develop?

By the middle of the eighteenth century, black majorities existed in the low country of the Carolinas and Georgia, and the ratio of blacks to whites stood close to fifty-fifty in the Chesapeake Bay region. Ships continued to unload slaves from Africa, but the number born in the colonies also increased. By mid-century, second-generation slaves constituted four-fifths of the total slave population. Native-born creoles developed an **African-American** culture and identity that set them apart from Africans.

The organization of the black population and the nature of African-American culture varied from one region to another. In the Chesapeake, most slaves lived on small plantations in groups of fewer than twenty. This resulted in extensive contact with Europeans and the absorption of European cultural patterns—a process called **acculturation**. By contrast, in the low country of South Carolina and Georgia, most slaves resided on large plantations in groups of a hundred or more with minimal contact with whites. Furthermore, Africans kept pouring in. African cultural carryovers—filed teeth, plaited hair, and ritual scars—were quite visible. African

names (like Cudjo, Cuffe, and Moosa), ways of speaking, praying, and burying the dead lingered for generations. African traditions fused with European customs to produce a distinct African-American culture. One Anglican Church missionary in South Carolina referred to slaves who spoke "a language peculiar to themselves, a wild confused medley of Negro [African languages] and corrupt English." Slaves who converted to Christianity often blended traditional African spiritual practices and beliefs. Within the slave quarters, Africa remained a strong presence.

The Evolution of a Planter Aristocracy

At the top of the southern social pyramid stood wealthy planters, like those who prevailed in Bacon's Rebellion. They commanded enormous wealth, measured in land and

> What were the sources and features of the planter aristocracy?

slaves. By the 1770s, per capita wealth in the plantation colonies was twice the colonial average. An English visitor noted that planters "live more like country gentlemen of fortune than any other settlers in America." It was a pleasing comparison, for they aped the styles and ways of the English nobility. Tidewater Virginians like Robert "King" Carter and William Byrd II built spacious brick houses in the popular English **Georgian** style furnished with English imports of the highest quality and most current fashion. Rice planters of the Carolina and Georgia low country loomed even larger, ruling their domains with almost absolute authority.

Southern planters engaged in commercial agriculture to make money, but by the cultural standards of the day, it was a masculine and noble calling. They did not work with their hands at the manual tasks of clearing, sowing, and reaping, which they regarded as demeaning. They had slaves for that. Men busied themselves inspecting fields, measuring crop size, shopping for the best commodity prices and credit terms for purchasing imports. Sluggish tobacco prices led planters in Maryland and Virginia into debt to English merchants from whom they purchased luxurious imports. In coastal Carolina and Georgia, however, rice prices remained high and planters were among the wealthiest colonists in North America.

Planters also dominated what civic life there was. Charles Town was the plantation colonies' most vital port town and fourth largest in British North was the established church throughout the southern plantation colonies, although fewer than 10 percent of the colonists regularly attended.

The primary duties of eighteenth-century elite women involved maintaining households and raising children. Women typically married in their late teens and, as mortality declined, lived through a growing number of childbearing years. Planter families, however, did not require children to supplement the work force, so planter women by the eighteenth century generally bore fewer children than their grandmothers had. Inside the "big house," women commanded staffs of domestic slaves who cleaned, cooked, and made slave clothes. But regardless of rank or race, women occupied inferior positions relative to their husbands. Women possessed no political rights. Any property an unmarried woman owned she relinquished to her husband upon marriage. Some women refused to accept their subordinate status. Sarah Harrison of Virginia, for example, shocked those gathered for her wedding. When asked if she would love, cherish, and obey her husband, she declared: "No obey," and she repeated her answer several times before the groom finally said: "I do"—on her terms.

The Southern Back Country

Image © Carolyn M Carpenter, 2010. Used by permission of Shutterstock, Inc.

Shirley Plantation on the bank of the James River in Virginia. The main house was plundered by rebels during Bacon's Rebellion. The current one was completed in 1738. It was designed in the balanced and symmetrical Georgian style and has been in the hands of the Hill and Carter families since the seventeenth century.

America, and its wealthy merchants rivaled the planters' exalted status. However, planters controlled the colonial assembly and in 1722 blocked an attempt to allow the town to govern itself. Community life was more developed in the Chesapeake colonies, even though capitol towns like Annapolis and Williamsburg (after the sack of Jamestown) remained tiny even by North American standards. In Maryland and Virginia, Tidewater gentlemen firmly held the reins of governmental and religious power. By virtue of their status as wealthy males, they held seats in provincial assemblies and on governors' councils. They presided over county courts, and they selected others of their class to constitute grand juries. County courthouses not only housed local government but also, along with taverns, functioned as social gathering places. The planters also served as Anglican Church vestrymen, laypersons who controlled the congregation's business affairs. The Anglican Church

During the first half of the eighteenth century, new settlers sought land in the remote valleys of the Appalachian Mountains from Pennsylvania to Georgia and westward toward French Louisiana. This was an area of oak, hickory, and pine forests dotted with clearings and drained by rivers flowing into the Gulf of Mexico and the Atlantic Ocean. Indian villages and towns still filled the area; some of the Native Americans were refugees displaced from coastal areas by Europeans, but others experienced their first contact with whites. **Backcountry** settlers founded communities with distinctive cultures and identities.

> How did the culture of the backcountry differ from the culture in other parts of English colonial America?

The main flow of backcountry settlers originated along the English-Scottish borderlands and in the northern counties of Ireland with smaller streams of Germans and French Huguenots joining it. These men and women left regions plagued by generations of disputes over national sovereignty, religion, and family pride. Many were accustomed to poverty, taking the law into their own hands, and fighting for their religious beliefs and the honor of their extended families.

Image © KennStilger47, 2010. Used by permission of Shutterstock, Inc.

Pioneer log cabin in Tennessee. Backcountry dwellings were rough and impermanent, reflecting the poor, migratory characteristics of backcountry people. Architecture also revealed European construction techniques as well as a weak sense of personal privacy. One visitor noted about a backcountry family: "They sleep altogether in common in one room, and shift and dress openly without ceremony."

Backcountry communities had limited access to burgeoning coastal markets. Settlers raised a little tobacco but concentrated on wheat, corn, and livestock for food and bartered any surpluses among themselves and the large Indian population of the region—Shawnee, Catawba, Cherokee, and Creek—or marketed them in French and Spanish settlements along the Ohio and Mississippi river networks. Although some of the larger landowners owned slaves, most backcountry families planted, tended, and harvested their own crops. The men built and maintained houses, barns, and fences while women milked the cows, butchered stock for food, cooked, made and mended clothes, and cared for their children. Some African Americans resided in the backcountry, mostly free Creole blacks and runaway maroon slaves living among the Indians.

The backcountry was not egalitarian. Differences in landholdings created a hierarchical social order. Relatively wealthy landowners controlled large tracts of land. They belonged to families who had enjoyed prominence in the Old Country, including the Polks, Calhouns, Jacksons, and Henrys. This backcountry aristocracy, like eastern planters, governed as sheriffs and judges. Below them were yeoman farmers, and at the bottom were the one in every three settlers who owned no land at all. They rented property or worked as wage laborers. Virtually all backcountry settlers lived in crude, sparsely furnished log cabins, both because logs were plentiful and because they intended to move on to more and better land. When William Holte of western Maryland died in 1710, his estate

apart from a house and some land amounted to a few pots, some old furniture, two cows, and two hogs.

Backcountry settlers' blunt manners, culture of retributive justice, and disdain for the tidewater planter aristocrats would later energize a movement for popular democracy.

THINKING BACK

1. How and why did the southern colonies develop into plantation societies, and what cultural characteristics stand out most about them?
2. What social and cultural characteristics differentiated the backcountry?

EXPANDING NORTHERN COLONIES

As in the coastal lowlands and backcountry of the South, northern colonies grew and matured economically and socially, albeit in different ways. During the first half of the eighteenth century, the number of men, women, and children residing in the northern colonies grew six fold. Continued immigration accentuated the distinctive regional cultures while Africans added additional texture, particularly in coastal cities, foreshadowing the rise of urban black cultures. Growth triggered economic changes as well as New England and the Middle Colonies turned increasingly to trans-Atlantic commerce. Colonial expansion strained settler-Indian relationships, and periodically the stresses resulting from growth and change caused upheavals.

The Texture of New England Society

By 1750, tides of change had swept over New England. The close-knit towns of yesteryear gave way to a freer society. But with immigration no more than a trickle since the English

> **What new features gave added texture to New England societies?**

Civil War, New England remained the most culturally homogeneous region of mainland North America. Puritans still ruled the religious realm, pulling in the welcome mat with the approach of Anglicans, Catholics, and especially Quakers whose religious views undermined the role and status of the ministry. But the profit-minded Yankee replaced the pious Puritan as New England's most identifiable type.

Out of necessity more than religious conviction, New Englanders lived more modestly than colonists in other regions—except for settlers in the backcountry. In the 1770s, per capita net worth stood at 33 pounds sterling (Britain's currency), or $3,060 in today's money. That was only a third of the per capita wealth of southern colonists. At a time when a person with 500 pounds worth of property was considered wealthy, not even the wealthiest New Englanders measured up to the standards of southern planters.

Land was New England's most valuable asset, and because population increased while available land did not, real estate values zoomed upward, so much in fact that neither town selectmen nor colonial authorities could afford to reserve public land for the children of faithful Puritans. After distributing all of its original land, Dedham, Massachusetts, received 8,000 additional acres in the upper Connecticut River Valley for the new town of Deerfield. No Dedhamites settled in Deerfield; rather, the proprietors sold the land in the booming real estate market. One of the first big-time New England land developers was John Winthrop's son, John, Jr., who owned property in four colonies.

By the early eighteenth century, the original Puritan goal of self-sufficiency seemed farther away than ever. As parents divided their farms among their adult children, individual holdings and productive capacity shrank. Seventeenth-century New England farms had averaged 200 acres; by 1750 they were scarcely a third of that. To make matters worse, merchant ships unloaded tempting cargoes of tools, household furnishings, tableware, clothing, books, coffee, tea, chocolate, sugar, and wine; such items made life more pleasant and productive, but they were expensive for colonies with little cash money. As the Massachusetts General Court lamented: "So long as our ingate [imports] exceeds our outgate [exports]," the colony would be left "with little mony."

Although the vast majority of New Englanders still farmed, a growing number turned to other endeavors. Their outlook became more commercial and their activities more complex and specialized. Many opened inns and taverns. They served locally made rum, an acceptable substitute for imported wine, although making it required molasses from West Indies sugar islands. Many young adults turned to trades like carpentry, metal work, and watch making. They began as apprentices, training under master craftsmen. After four to seven years, young tradesmen, known as **journeymen**, could market their skills to other master craftsmen looking for permanent employees. If things worked out, they opened their own shops.

Other young operated stores, buying local wheat, corn, cider, cheese, and animals and selling sugar, wine, tobacco, and nails acquired from Boston importers. In the 1740s, young Roger Sherman, later a signer of the Declaration of Independence and delegate to the Constitutional Convention, opened the first store in New Milford, Connecticut. Profitable commerce depended on two essentials: family connections, for townsfolk were reluctant to do business with outsiders, and credit, since gold and silver money was scarce. Invaluable too were roads linking interior towns with coastal market towns like Boston, Portsmouth, Providence, and New Haven.

In the seventeenth century, personal wealth had counted for no more than education and moral character in determining social status. Early Puritans tried very hard to curb greed. Farmers, ministers, and lawyers of modest means occupied leadership positions in New England society. But by the mid-eighteenth century, wealthy merchants had gained prominence. As a consequence of economic expansion, New England society became more stratified, and the gap between rich and poor grew wider. The bulk of the colonists remained simple farmers, living slightly more comfortably than their parents and grandparents. In Dedham in the 1730s, for instance, the richest 5 percent of the residents were mostly farmers who owned only 15 percent of the town's property. But 10 percent of Bostonians—mostly merchants—owned over half the city's wealth.

Social and Economic Development in the Middle Atlantic Colonies

The Middle Colonies maintained the appearance of a cultural patchwork, very different from the biracial South and homogenous New England. In Pennsylvania, New Jersey, Delaware, and New York, adherents to various religious faiths mingled together—Anglicans, Catholics, Quakers, Puritans, Presbyterians, Baptists, French Huguenots, German Mennonites, and Dutch Reformed. Social organization and ways of life were equally diverse. These colonies foreshadowed the cultural pluralism that characterizes that area today.

> **What were the key social and economic characteristics of the Middle Colonies?**

By the mid-eighteenth century, Quakers comprised the third largest religious denomination in the British colonies, surpassed only by Puritans and Anglicans. The influx of Scots-Irish and German immigrants rendered the Quakers a numerical minority in Penn's colony; however, due to their entrenched position in the colony's eastern counties Quakers retained political clout. In 1745, they held 83 percent of the seats in Pennsylvania's legislative assembly. Pennsylvania politics were notably contentious, partisan, and marked by uncommonly frequent elections. Quaker farmers and artisans argued with the Penn family over whether the elected assembly or the proprietor should govern the colony. They also contended with Scots-Irish immigrants for seats in the colonial assembly and to elect the many county officials who levied taxes and enforced laws.

Rejecting New England style conformity as well as the South's rigid hierarchy as models of social order, Friends placed great value on individual freedom. In 1751, to mark the fiftieth anniversary of Penn's Charter of Privileges, the assembly ordered a huge bell placed in the Pennsylvania State House in Philadelphia. Known as the **Liberty Bell**, it symbolized the colony's political ideology. Quakers also favored limited government. Indeed, Pennsylvania was the only colony without an official militia.

New York held less promise than the Delaware Valley for immigrants hoping to get ahead for it contained a landed elite who possessed most of the fertile land. Stately mansions owned by descendants of early Dutch settlers and people with English surnames stood along the Hudson River as far north as Albany. One large landowner, Robert Livingston, married Alida Schuyler van Rensselaer, daughter of one of the most prominent Dutch fur-trading families of Albany and widow of the son of the founder of Rensselaerswyck. Most landowners chose to rent land rather than sell it; thus, immigrants with hopes of purchasing property elected to enter the colonies through the port of Philadelphia rather than New York City.

The Middle Colonies stood slightly above New England in average per capita wealth. Farms yielded abundant supplies of grain, corn, beef, and pork; millers turned the wheat into flour that kept residents well fed. Farms in the Delaware Valley averaged twice the acreage of farms in Massachusetts but were less than half as large as Virginia plantations. Farmers hauled surpluses by wagon or sent them by boat to markets in Philadelphia for shipment to other colonies. The Middle Colonies became the "breadbasket" for communities from Newfoundland to Georgia.

African Americans in the Northern Colonies

Prior to the eighteenth century, African Americans had made up only a small minority of the northern colonial population. The relatively small slave population did not indicate moral opposition to slavery as much as the limited need for additional help where families, indentured servants, and free laborers shouldered most of the workload. Even Puritans' strong religious principles did not stand in the way of slave ownership. John Winthrop had declared: "God Almightie in his most holy and wise providence" ordered mankind so that "some must be rich, some poore, some highe and eminent in power and dignitie and others meane and in subjection." The Massachusetts General Court approved making slaves of "lawful captives taken in just wars [Indians], and such strangers [Africans] as willingly sell themselves, or are sold to us."

> How did northern slavery compare to slavery in the South?

Eighteenth-century economic expansion boosted the need for labor beyond the available supply of free and indentured workers, although not on the same scale as in the South. Operators of large farms in the Connecticut, Hudson, and Delaware valleys, on Long Island and around Narragansett Bay purchased slaves. By the middle of the eighteenth century, 2,000 enslaved blacks toiled in Pennsylvania fields and in farmhouse kitchens. Slavery also took root in the bustling port towns. By mid-century, Newport (Rhode Island) contained 1,000 slaves, Philadelphia 1,400, and New York City 2,000. Wealthy merchants employed slave women to wash, cook, and sew. Artisans put men to work lifting and hauling, and ship-owners used slaves as longshoremen and seamen. While the number of Africans was small compared to the thousands disembarking in South Carolina each year, they accounted for a third of all the immigrants who entered New York between 1732 and 1754.

Many northern slaves bore tribal markings and spoke languages that indicated their African birth. They suffered horribly from contagious diseases that spread like wildfire in close urban living. Because of poorer food, clothing, and shelter, urban slaves perished at a rate one and a half times that of whites. Youth and male-skewed gender ratios also typified direct African imports. One New York merchant declared: "For this market they must be young, the Younger the better." And "Males are best." Under those conditions, it was difficult for slaves to form families, which northern slave owners did not encourage since they desired only small numbers of slaves.

Nevertheless, urban slaves built and maintained communication networks. They talked as they passed one another on the streets. Whites feared unsupervised slave interaction, believing they might spark rebellion. In 1712, a slave revolt shook New York City, and in 1741 fear of another uprising caused white city authorities to burn thirteen black male suspects at the stake and hang seventeen others. More subtly, Africans asserted their freedom by rejecting missionaries' attempts to Christianize them, keeping their African names, and talking among themselves about Africa. In celebrations such as Election Day in New England and Pinkster Day in New York City, they elected honorary leaders. A witness to such a celebration in Newport wrote: "All the various languages of Africa, mixed with broken and ludicrous English, filled the air, accompanied with the music of the fiddle, tambourine, the banjo, [and] drum." Whites tolerated such topsy-turviness, perhaps thinking that make-believe freedom for a day would placate slaves. But blacks occasionally filed formal petitions to public officials asking for real freedom, showing a keen understanding of colonial government, the ideology of freedom subscribed to by colonial officials, and the irony of their plight. In the words of one petition: "We have no Property! We have no Wives! No children!" But "in common with all other men we have a natural right to our freedoms."

Entering the Transatlantic Trade Network

How did international trade affect northern economies?

African slaves were but one commodity in a growing colonial involvement in trans-Atlantic commerce. Southern planters already shipped tobacco, rice, and indigo to England and imported English cloth, silverware, furniture, and various tools. But further colonial participation in the Atlantic economy involved the northern colonies. Dutch founders of New York City left a legacy of commercialism, including a vast trans-Atlantic network of European bankers, Mediterranean and West African merchants with whom to do business, and West Indies markets. By the late seventeenth century, New Englanders had entered the Atlantic commercial network. Northern merchants could not rely on staple exports; instead, they offered an assortment of products that they sold in various European, African, and West Indies markets. They enhanced their profits using their own ships rather than paying for English or Dutch vessels.

Yankee merchants (the word "**yankee**" came from the Dutch, who applied it to New Englanders) sold salted (preserved) cod to England for bills of credit (the source of the later term "dollar bill") with which they purchased manufactured goods that sailed back to New England. These transactions helped offset New England's **trade deficit** (where the value of imports exceeds exports). After the Restoration, the English government tried to protect its own economic interests against colonial competition. Trade laws discouraged colonial fish while allowing timber, furs, whale oil, tobacco, rice, and indigo. (For a fuller discussion see pp. 142-43.) Resourceful merchants turned to other Atlantic markets, carrying fish, rum, grain, and livestock to southern European and Mediterranean ports and returning with citrus fruits and wines. Newport ship captains unloaded fish and rum on the west coast of Africa and loaded gold and African slaves destined for the West Indies.

Philadelphia and New York merchants also got in on the act, shipping flour, cornmeal, beef, bacon, and occasionally Indian slaves to the West Indies and hauling back sugar and molasses. Merchants in the Middle Colonies worked in tandem with those in New England to build a thriving coastal trade, operating fleets of relatively small vessels to gather foodstuffs for trans-Atlantic commerce and to distribute imported products from Newfoundland to Savannah.

This multi-stop Atlantic commerce, sometimes called the **triangular trade**, had economic and social consequences. By the middle of the eighteenth century, exports nearly equaled imports. Great personal wealth accrued to merchants and ship owners who not only prospered directly from trade but also invested profitably in colonial economies. Merchants financed manufacturing and artisanship, especially shipbuilding, sail making, and rope spinning. Shopkeepers, farmers, fishermen, millers, and rum distillers also prospered from expanding markets. The coastal trade promoted colonial interdependence.

But Atlantic commerce made colonial culture more similar to England's. Imported silverware—knives and forks as well as spoons—chinaware, and dresses and suits became common among middle-class households. Thus in their taste and consuming habits, colonial culture began to look more English.

King Philip's War

> **What was the cause and the outcome of King Philip's War?**

The expansion of northern colonial societies placed mounting pressure on Native Americans. In 1675, tension erupted into a bloody struggle known as **King Philip's War**. Abenaki, Narragansett, and Wampanoag Indians living along the north Atlantic coast had put up with settlers' cattle trampling their cornfields, traders cheating them, and colonists pressuring them to sell their land. In 1637, the Pequot in Connecticut had attempted to resist white encroachment by armed revolt. They were annihilated, however. Tensions in Massachusetts escalated throughout the 1670s before reaching a crisis point.

A Wampanoag leader named Metacomet (or Metacom), whom the English called King Philip, coordinated attacks by several tribes against white settlements from Rhode Island to Maine, including a devastating assault on Deerfield. Over two years, some 2,500 whites perished and fifteen towns were destroyed. But the Indians' losses—as many as 6,000 including Philip—ultimately led to their defeat.

Indians attacked Deerfield during King Philip's War. Due to its frontier location, Deerfield suffered repeatedly during the ongoing struggle between England, France, and their respective Indian allies. The French and Indian raid that cost John Williams part of his family was merely the latest.

Altogether one in every ten inhabitants of New England became casualties, a higher percentage than in any other North American war.

King Philip's War signaled the end of autonomy for New England's native people. Approximately 1,000 of the survivors were sold into slavery. Others moved west to reestablish themselves among other Indian communities. Several thousand Mohegans, Pequots, Nipmucks, and Wampanoags had seen their best interests served by aiding the English or remaining neutral, and they did not simply vanish. A 1756 census showed several thousand of them residing in Connecticut, living among whites but maintaining their Indian identities as indicated in probate and child-custody records.

Reorganization and Rebellion

King Philip's War occurred some fifteen years after the restoration of the English monarchy in 1660. King Charles II tightened royal control over the colonies by appointing governors rather than allowing the colonists to continue choosing them. In 1684, the king revoked Massachusetts' charter and placed the colony under a royal governor. The king's brother James II, who ascended the throne upon Charles' death a year later, went further, consolidating the New England colonies into the Dominion of New England, later adding New York and New Jersey. He also abolished the individual colonial assemblies. Edmund Andros, the Dominion's governor, stirred up animosity by enforcing unpopular trade restrictions, imposing taxes without the colonists' consent, and openly promoting the Anglican Church.

> **How did England's attempt to reorganize colonial administration reverberate through the colonies?**

Meanwhile, in England a simmering political crisis involving politics and religion came to a boil. Since the English Civil War, Parliament had gained considerable power at the monarchy's expense. Parliament's supporters called **Whigs** and backers of the monarchy called **Tories** argued bitterly over the proper balance between the two. James II precipitated a crisis by converting to Catholicism and then fathering a son whom he intended to raise as a Catholic. According to English custom, the boy moved to the head of his older Protestant sisters in line to succeed his father, which alarmed Protestants both Whig and Tory. In 1688, Parliament launched a revolution by inviting

James' Protestant daughter Mary and her husband William of Orange, the Protestant ruler of the Netherlands, to take the English crown. In November, William landed with his army on the English coast. When nobody rallied on James' behalf, the king fled to France. This bloodless **Glorious Revolution** further enhanced Parliament's power and advanced the cause of individual liberty, for through a series of laws enacted mostly in 1689, known as the **Revolutionary Settlement**, Parliament declared its commitment to the Whig principle that citizens held inherent **natural rights** that legitimate government was bound to respect.

Learning of the Glorious Revolution, Bostonians staged one their own. In 1689 they grabbed Andros, "the great enemy of the country," threw him in jail, and then packed him off to England. They hoped that William and Mary would restore the Massachusetts assembly and elected governor, but instead, in 1691 the monarchs merged Massachusetts and Plymouth and put the colony under a royal governor. The crown also declared religious tolerance, meaning that membership in the Puritan church was no longer a requirement for voting. Thus, the Glorious Revolution brought mixed results as far as colonial autonomy was concerned.

In New York, the Glorious Revolution exposed festering ethnic, religious, and class resentments. The Dominion of New England's demise created a power vacuum, into which stepped a German immigrant named Jacob Leisler, who declared himself interim governor. Leisler detested the city's Anglican and Catholic "grandees," and for thirteen months he held power with the support of mostly Dutch bakers, brewers, and other tradesmen. In 1691, the man William and Mary appointed governor finally arrived in New York City. The new governor brought treason charges against Leisler, who was hanged following a quick trial. **Leisler's Rebellion** never developed into a full-blown revolution, but afterward the governor and assembly implemented a new judicial system that replaced remaining Dutch laws with English ones.

The Glorious Revolution also reverberated through Maryland. Protestants took advantage of England's turmoil and revolted against the government of the Catholic proprietor, Lord Baltimore. Their leader, John Coode, held power until 1692 when William and Mary dispatched a new royal governor. Baltimore lost his proprietorship, although he regained it by converting to Protestantism. Ironically, Catholics were prevented from holding public office in the colony that originated as a haven for persecuted Catholics.

Although not apparent on the surface, the Glorious Revolution enhanced the status of legislative assemblies in the colonies. An emerging group of pragmatic Whig politicians in England, who controlled Parliament and gained the support of the monarchy as well, chose to work with colonial assemblies to manage the colonies rather than solely through royal governors. Furthermore, England's tacit acceptance of colonial self-government encouraged colonial independence.

"Under an Evil Hand": The Witches of Salem

In the aftermath of the upheavals of the 1670s and 1680s came one of the most intriguing episodes in American colonial history. In 1689 the Reverend Samuel Parris, his wife, 9-year-old daughter Betty, 11-year-old niece Abigail, and the family's West Indian slave Tituba settled in Salem Village, a relatively poor spin-off from the prosperous Massachusetts seaport of Salem Town. Betty and Abigail suddenly fell into fits of grotesque gestures and bizarre utterances, which the girls claimed were caused by witches. Most Puritan townsfolk believed in witches, thought to be Satan's agents for doing harm to others. The village doctor diagnosed the girls as having fallen "under an Evil Hand." Soon two other adolescent girls experienced torments. The question was: who were the witches? The girls first accused Tituba, who confessed to being a witch but in turn pointed to two women as the ones whose apparitions afflicted the girls. Local magistrates accused all three of "entertaining Satan."

> **What might have prompted the witch hysteria in Salem?**

The girls accused others of being witches, and hysteria swept the colony. Local jails bulged with suspects. Nobody was above accusation, but middle-aged, quarrelsome women with enemies fell under the heaviest suspicion. Newly appointed governor Sir William Phips convened a special court that tried 150 accused witches. The most sensational and damning evidence came from the girls, who testified that witches' ghostly specters "did oftentimes very grievously pinch them, choke them, bite them, and afflict them." On the basis of this uncorroborated **"spectral evidence,"** the judges convicted twenty-eight of the accused. Nineteen went to the gallows and one, an eighty-year-old man, was crushed to death under heavy stones. Before the remaining eight could be executed, the fever broke. Phips suspended the trials, and the citizens of Massachusetts acknowledged the wrong that had been committed and prayed for atonement.

Why did the Salem witch scare happen? It was not the only such episode, for belief in witchcraft was common in the seventeenth-century, among Europeans, Native Americans, and Africans. Most people credited supernatural forces with controlling worldly events. Not surprisingly, the vast majority of legal proceedings against accused witches in colonial America took place in Puritan communities, where people were constantly alert for evil spirits. But the hysteria that gripped Salem was uncommonly intense. Perhaps the tension between the stagnant village and the prosperous town was behind it. Most of the accusers came from the village and most of the accused were associated with the town. Perhaps the tormented girls had eaten rye flour contaminated with the argot bacteria that can cause hallucinations. Or maybe devastating Indian attacks caused worried citizens to see other signs of God's displeasure, namely witches. We may never know for certain. What is especially interesting, though, is that in a time of prejudice, intolerance, and apprehension, Puritans looked for the sources of devilment within themselves.

THINKING BACK

1. What were the men and women like who populated the northern colonies, and how did their ways of life differ from people in the South?
2. What changes took place in the northern colonies, what tensions did they produce, and how were the major conflicts resolved?

THE LOCAL PERSPECTIVE: FOCUS ON CONNECTICUT

| What does the history of colonial Connecticut show about the difficulty of maintaining unity of purpose? |

The history of colonial Connecticut typified New England's experiences. (See map on p. 80.) From the time of the colony's settlement, the Puritan church had maintained firm control over ecclesiastical and civil matters. Indian wars temporarily shattered the colony's peace, but the social fabric did not begin to fray until

after the formation of the Dominion of New England.

The first sign of change came when towns lost the power to allocate land. Further damage to the towns' integrity occurred when farmers, unwilling to travel each day from their homes in town to the outer boundaries of their farm plots, began to build secondary homes away from town, and eventually converted them into permanent residences. These new residences were beyond the reach of town government, schools, and churches. Ministers feared that people living outside of town would "degenerate to heathenish ignorance and barbarism."

As the cohesion of Connecticut's towns weakened, contention increased. Issues such as support of schools, control of militia units, and the location of meeting houses divided townsfolk from those in surrounding villages—not unlike suburbanites and city residents today. The villagers resented paying taxes to support institutions from which they received little benefit; town folk resented having to pay more because fewer people lived in town and more lived in outlying areas. One minister complained that so much contention existed in towns "as to threaten their ruin."

Private ownership of land eroded original communal values and triggered substantial economic expansion. Farmers began to raise and sell crops for profit, which in turn encouraged more merchants to distribute commodities. New businesses in Norwich, Hartford, New Haven, and other communities, required capital, and wealthy businessmen turned to lending money. In an economy that was short on gold for money, farmers, merchants, and manufacturers also looked to government for assistance; in the 1730s the colonial assembly began offering credit and issuing paper currency. Farmers understood that plenty of paper money drove prices up, much to their benefit. Conversely, lenders realized that as prices rose, the value of money used to repay loans declined.

Connecticut's economic expansion had both positive and negative consequences. It contributed in no small way to a population that multiplied nearly three times between 1700 and 1730, mostly east of the Connecticut River. Jared Eliot, one of the colony's foremost citizens, noted that in general people enjoyed "better houses, public and private, richer furniture, better food and clothing; better bridges and highways, fatter cattle and finer horses, and lands bear an higher price." But Ezra Stiles, another prominent resident, fretted about the consequences. "How far the principle of righteousness and moral virtue was affected in the mixt scenes of commerce, God only knows." Without question, the number of debt cases in Connecticut courts, which multiplied nineteen times in the first three decades of the eighteenth century, supported Eliot's assertion that "we have over lived."

Connecticut's economic progress caused rifts in the Puritan churches, especially the ministry. Ministers' attempts to expand their authority over congregations provoked resentment and accusations of "ambitious and designing clergy." Rapid economic growth inevitably ignited disputes, and as one clergyman observed, most personal disputes "end in a quarrel and contention in the church," and regardless of how the minister resolved it "he must unavoidably get the ill-will of one party, and very frequently of both."

Many ministers lamented the woeful spiritual state of Connecticut's once pious Puritan society. Feelings of guilt from forsaking the founders' ideals helped feed the religious revivals that sprang up mainly in the eastern part of the colony in the 1730s. They were attempts to heal society's wounds as well as to save individual souls. The Great Awakening (see pp. 121-23) in Connecticut, though intense, was short-lived. Leaders in Hartford hoped that the revivals would "promote religion and the saving conversion of souls." Revivalist preacher George Whitefield visited the colony for the first time in the autumn of 1740. But many ministers opposed the "screachings, cryings out, faintings and convulsions" that accompanied the revivals. The ministers exerted their considerable influence on the colonial assembly, which outlawed itinerant revivalists. When Whitefield returned to the colony in 1744, he found most pulpits closed to him.

Changes tore away the tight social order that the colony's founders had carefully put into place. The Puritan church, founded as an agency of rebellion against authority in England, ironically found itself in the position of trying to maintain authority at a time when prosperity, science, and religious revivalism challenged the established social order.

THINKING BACK

1. What caused the cohesion of Connecticut's towns to weaken.
2. What effects did Connecticut's economic expansion have on the colony?

REDEFINING COLONIAL SOCIETIES

By 1750, colonial America had fully integrated itself into the Atlantic world. Coastal cities served as the nexus between North America and societies of Europe, West Africa, and the West Indies. Although no more than 7 to 8 percent of Americans lived in urban areas, cities exerted inordinate influence on colonial societies—economically, politically, and culturally. The appearance of sophisticated and cosmopolitan cities signified the transformation of frontier outposts into mature societies. One visitor remarked that Boston possessed "much the same air of some of our best country towns in England." But if colonists followed English cultural patterns, they also developed their own, setting them apart from their forbears and forging American identities.

Urban Cultures

Although colonial cultures had always resembled their Old World roots, the most self-conscious efforts to mimic fashionable English lifestyles took

> What type of culture developed in the cities?

place in the cities. In the late seventeenth century, approximately two dozen colonial communities boasted populations of 3,000 or more. The five largest cities—Boston, Philadelphia, New York, Charles Town, and Newport—were all Atlantic seaports. They prospered from the colonies' expanding involvement in trans-Atlantic commerce, and their residents experienced the greatest contact with the outside world.

At mid-century, Boston, with 16,000 inhabitants, was the most populous, but it soon gave way to Philadelphia with 30,000 residents, 300 houses, and stately public buildings. New York was also growing faster than Boston and was far more diverse. The shouts of town criers and street hawkers, the rumble of iron wagon wheels on cobblestones, and the din of saws and hammers added to the bustle of those multi-ethnic communities. Along with its 12,000 residents, Charles Town featured beautiful mansions, theaters, and churches along its waterfront. Newport, Rhode Island offered summer respite to South Carolina planters and sheltered a motley collection of citizens that included slave traders and privateers.

Cities were both seats of colonial government and commercial centers. Roads and waterways radiated from them to remote towns and villages. Without

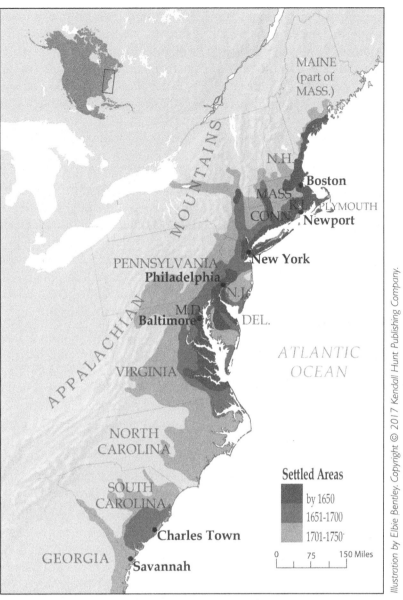

This map shows that the population of Great Britain's North American colonies was largely concentrated between the crest of the Appalachian Mountains and the Atlantic seaboard.

city markets, residents of the countryside would have been unable to purchase imported housewares, tools, and clothes. Cities were information hubs, supporting newspapers (two dozen by the 1760s), debating societies, and libraries. A postal system, instituted by Parliament in 1701, operated from city to city and from the cities to surrounding hinterlands.

Outside of the southern plantation communities, the greatest social and economic inequities existed in the cities. Merchants and their families accumulated substantial fortunes. They built large houses, furnished them with upholstered chairs, tables, and cabinets in the latest English style, dressed in the finest clothes, rode around in fancy horse-drawn carriages. Colonial America's finest artist, John Singleton Copley, earned a comfortable living painting portraits of the elite citizens of New York, Philadelphia, and Boston.

Hard-working artisans, however, made the cities work. Skilled craftsmen in leather aprons tanned animal hides, built everything from wagons to barrels, manufactured shoes and apparel, crafted pewter- and silverware, constructed furniture as elegant as that made by the best English furniture makers, butchered meat, and baked bread and delicious pastries. Two of every three adult males in colonial towns and cities earned their livelihood in industrial trades, as did a few unmarried or widowed women. Wives often assisted their tradesmen husbands in the shop or hawked wares in the streets. Tradesmen set their sons to work at 6 or 7 years of age sweeping floors, unloading and loading material and products, or running errands. Apprentices usually began learning trades as teenagers. The work was hard but often sociable with craftsmen, journeymen, and apprentices enjoying frequent food breaks, singing and chatting during the day, and staying "mildly glad with liquor."

Many artisans earned respectable incomes. About one quarter of Philadelphia's tradesmen left substantial estates. Elias Boudinot, a silversmith, lived in a large home near Benjamin Franklin's residence and maintained contacts with him and other wealthy businessmen. His son, also Elias, attended the College of New Jersey (Princeton), earned a law degree, and settled comfortably in Burlington, New Jersey. But were it not for their network of acquaintances, it would have been easy for the Boudinots to end up like one unemployed bricklayer and his family, in Philadelphia's poorhouse "in a state of starvation and nakedness."

An underclass of slaves, indentured servants, day laborers, and seamen dwelled at the bottom of urban society. With little if any property and hardly a chance of achieving respectability, unbound laborers struggled to make ends meet. When trade was lively, dockside workers pocketed a few cents a day loading and unloading ships. But during hard times they suffered. In 1757, a thousand citizens crowded into Boston's almshouse for shelter and food. But even in the worst of times, poverty in colonial America was less severe than in England. One in ten colonists received public relief of some sort; in England the proportion was one in three. Land was the key difference, for its availability in America provided an opportunity for self-reliance.

Enlightenment Influences

How did the Enlightenment influence the way some Americans thought about themselves?

Through the cities, European ideas flowed into the colonies, carried by immigrants, travelers, and books and newspapers. The seventeenth-century discoveries of Polish astronomer Nicolaus Copernicus, showing the earth revolving about the sun rather than the other way around as long believed, sparked a revolution in ideas known as the **Enlightenment**. English physicist Sir Isaac Newton's mathematical explanation of gravity in *Principia Mathematica* (1687) unlocked another great mystery of the universe and marked a new level of understanding of the physical world. Scientists employed careful and rational methods of experimentation using inductive reasoning, thus another name for the period: the **Age of Reason**. The Enlightenment was not anti-religious, for the exquisite perfection of natural laws could easily be interpreted as evidence of God's infinite wisdom. Nonetheless, Enlightenment thinkers challenged the prevailing belief that all wisdom came directly from Scripture or revelation, and some rational philosophers, known as **Deists**, believed in a God-created universe that functioned according to physical laws.

The philosopher John Locke drew upon Enlightenment reasoning to explain human behavior. In his *Essay on Human Understanding* (1690), Locke argued that infants began life with no predetermined tendencies and lived according to a lifetime of accumulated decisions. In other words, natural laws governed not only the universe but human behavior as well. Understanding natural laws could lead to rational socioeconomic policy and the proper balance between government and individual liberty.

The optimism and pragmatism inherent in the Enlightenment resonated in many American minds, for many colonists appreciated the practical over the theoretical from their own personal experiences and knew a thing or two about progress. Even the utopian Puritans had reconciled themselves pragmatically to the adaptations that dynamic societies dictated. Colonial societies produced notable scientists whose careful study of nature led to a deeper understanding of the American environment. Naturalists like John Bartram of Philadelphia and Alexander Garden of Charles Town described and classified North American plants. John Winthrop, Jr., studied chemistry in order to promote mining in New England, and for his work was admitted to the Royal Society of London, one of the leading scientific academies in Europe.

Benjamin Franklin epitomized the Enlightenment in America. Born in 1706 the son of a Boston candle- and soap-maker, young Franklin was interested in almost everything but failed math in school. After a brief apprenticeship under his brother, a printer,

Image © Lev Kropotov, 2010. Used by permission of Shutterstock, Inc.

"Remember that time is money," some of the practical advice Benjamin Franklin bestowed on tradesmen like himself who aspired to prosperity.

Franklin opened a print shop Philadelphia, where he published the *Pennsylvania Gazette*. In his spare time he developed such practical applications of Enlightenment science as the lightning rod, the Franklin stove, and bifocal spectacles. As a prominent citizen, he sought to improve city life for the bulk of its citizens. "Man," he observed, "is a social being," and the "good men may do separately is small compared with what they may do collectively." He founded America's first lending library, a fire brigade, a police watch force, and an academy that became the University of Pennsylvania. Franklin's *Poor Richard's Almanac* offered practical tips on day-to-day living.

Americans came to believe that societies that followed enlightened leaders possessed infinite potential for progress. That lesson contributed to a growing colonial self-awareness. It was a lesson learned mostly by educated and cosmopolitan people, and one that disturbed some religious leaders.

The Great Awakening

> **How did Great Awakening revivals affect Americans, and whom did they affect the most?**

The transformation of colonial societies together with Enlightenment rationalism left many Calvinists fearful that their communities had lost touch with God. Science, prosperity, and materialistic values eroded religious zeal. Even the Puritan ministry had lost some of its moral authority. By the beginning of the eighteenth century half the white population and most slaves were unaffiliated with any formal church.

Then in the 1720s, a series of religious revivals shook the Middle Colonies, awakening heathens and complacent Christians to their sinfulness and its dreadful consequences. The Dutch Reformed minister Theodore Frelinghuysen preached to his New Jersey congregation that only repentance and heavenly salvation mattered in a world where death struck suddenly and often and where the comforts of nice homes and fine clothes were fleeting compared to an eternity of damnation. Irish-born Presbyterian William Tennent attempted to revive the spirit of God by training ministers from his "Log College" in Neshaminy, Pennsylvania.

Within a decade, highly emotional revivals had spread to New England, ignited there by the Congregationalist Jonathan Edwards. Becoming minister of the church in Northampton, Massachusetts, following his graduation from Yale, Edwards launched his revivals in 1734–35, using emotional rather than intellectual appeals to raise the prosperous town from its religious torpor. "Our people do not so much need to have their heads stored as to have their hearts

Evangelist George Whitefield preaching. Whitefield's power to inspire large audiences made him one of the most notable evangelists in the history of Protestant Christianity.

© Francis G. Mayer/Contributor/Getty

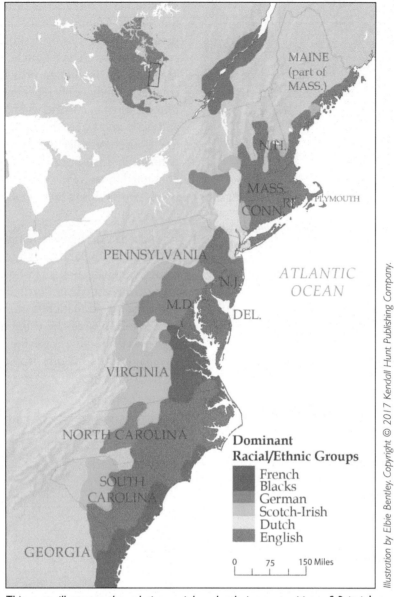

This map illustrates the relative racial and ethnic composition of Britain's mainland North American colonies by the middle of the eighteenth century.

touched," he declared. In 1739 an Anglican minister named George Whitefield, a graduate of Oxford with a useful talent for acting, arrived in the colonies and fanned the local revivals into a wildfire known as the **Great Awakening**. The televangelist of his day, Whitefield publicized each of his seven evangelical tours of the colonies, drawing crowds of thousands. Even Benjamin Franklin fell under his spell. Franklin attended a revival as an observer, but Whitefield "finish'd so admirably, that I empty'd my pocket wholly into the collector's dish." In 1741, Edwards delivered the climactic sermon of the Great Awakening, "Sinners in the Hands of an Angry God." Drawing frightful word pictures, he admonished prideful listeners about

thinking they could escape the wrath of the "God that holds you over the pit of hell, much as one holds a spider, or some loathsome insect." He pushed his listeners into such a state of agitation that they could not sing the closing hymn.

The Great Awakening cut across denominational boundaries. "Don't tell me you are a Baptist, an Independent, a Presbyterian, a dissenter," intoned Whitefield, "tell me you are a Christian, that is all I want." "**New Lights**," as the evangelists called themselves, caused deep rifts within Protestant denominations. Gilbert Tennent, William Tennent's son, warned against the "Danger of an Unconverted

Ministry," a reference to established Congregational and Anglican ministers. Contemptuous "Old Lights" ridiculed the revivalists, scoffing at the "screechings, cryings out, faintings and convulsions."

The revivals also caused deep social rifts, for both the theology and the structure of the Great Awakening contained threads of egalitarianism. The evangelicals described a God who judged everyone equally and preached that salvation was available to all. By inviting vocal interaction between the pulpit and the pew, the New Lights blurred the lines of ecclesiastical authority and at the same time eliminated some of the prevailing gender inequality. Encouraged to express themselves openly in revivals, women felt freer to do so elsewhere. Similarly, the Great Awakening ignored racial distinctions. Revivalists preached to slave as well as white congregations and even welcomed African Americans into the pulpit.

More than a momentary phenomenon, the Great Awakening produced lasting effects. Before the Great Awakening, the only colleges in the colonies trained orthodox ministers. Harvard (1636) educated Puritan sons. William and Mary (1696) catered to Virginia Anglicans. Connecticut Puritans founded Yale (1701) to counteract Harvard's perceived liberalization. But Presbyterian New Lights founded the College of New Jersey (later Princeton University) in 1746 and Dutch Reformed revivalists founded Rutgers two decades later. Where New Lights failed to capture the established denominations they became leading forces in the emerging Baptist and Methodist denominations.

Changing Identities in White, Red, and Black

| What forces shaped an emerging American identity? |

Over time the cultural bonds that tied Americans with Europe, Africa, and pre-Columbian America weakened and new identities took hold. Distinctively American cultures took shape, textured by regional, ethnic, and class characteristics, but nevertheless distinctively American.

The arrival of Europeans changed Native Americans' way of life forever. Displaced by the newcomers, killed or enslaved by Europeans and their adjuncts, and victimized by smallpox and other diseases, Indian people lost control of their native lands and significant components of their cultures. Although a few communities, like those of the Pueblo people in Spanish New Mexico and Arizona, remained relatively intact, most Indian societies east of the Mississippi River disappeared or reconfigured themselves. Unlike Spanish and French Catholic missionaries who sought to convert Indians to Christianity as part of their countries' colonization program, English colonists made less effort to do so. Puritans had been far more interested in building communities of Saints than in proselytizing Indians. In the mid-seventeenth century, Puritan minister John Eliot did undertake an Indian mission, partly to facilitate alliances, and a few converts settled in one of the two-dozen "praying towns" in Massachusetts and Connecticut. That did not protect them, however, for during King Philip's War the English destroyed most of the towns.

Many Native Americans replaced traditional tools and materials with European ones. They hunted with firearms rather than bows and arrows, wore clothing made of cloth instead of animal skins, and began using iron tools in place of stone ones. Contact with Europeans also changed the Indians' methods of hunting. Whether through the erosion of religious taboos or a deepening dependence on European trade goods, the eastern woodland Indians altered their relationship with wild animals, becoming commercial trappers and virtually destroying beaver and deer populations. The French explorer and fur trader Nicholas Perrot noted of the Great Lakes Chippewa that they "have degenerated from the valor of their ancestors, and devote themselves solely to the destruction of wild animals."

Contact with Native Americans also changed Europeans. Hector St. Jean de Crèvecoeur claimed: "thousands of Europeans are Indians." Some whites did adopt Indian culture: French trappers and traders and, like Eunice Williams, some captives who forsook English society. Crevecoeur mostly referred to backwoods settlers who found the Indians' way of life better suited to their circumstances than European manners and customs. But he exaggerated. Those Europeans did not really become Indians. Rather, they remained white frontier types who borrowed piecemeal from the Indians or, according to George Washington, chose to live "as ignorant as the Indians." Some Indian words became common in English vocabulary: moose, raccoon, skunk, pecans, succotash, and hominy. But they facilitated commerce and the acquisition of Indian land and did not fundamentally alter English language patterns. Still, the colonists adopted some aspects of Indian culture and thus became more American than their European cousins. Corn and beans for example, remained a staple in colonial diets instead of wheat and green peas.

Africans, too, contributed to emerging colonial cultures. Words like "banjo," "yam," and "canoe" worked their way into the English vocabulary. Frying food, especially in the southern colonies, rather than boiling or baking it in the European fashion, moved from the African-American to the European-American realm as they merged with cultural remnants from Europe.

In all, the interactions of various racial and ethnic groups, while never functioning like a melting pot to produce a uniform new product, did create ways of thinking and behaving that were not exactly like European or Indian or African ways. Rather, a new and distinctly American culture, blending aspects from all three traditions, was beginning to emerge.

THINKING BACK

1. What did modernization mean to colonial America?
2. What tensions did changes produce and how were the resulting conflicts resolved?

THE STRUGGLE FOR EMPIRE

From the start, Spanish, French, and English global empires had clashed in North America. From Louisiana, a wedge driven provocatively between Florida and Texas, Frenchmen sold muskets to Indians for animal furs and hides, while English South Carolinians plundered Spanish Florida for Indian slaves. English and French colonists wrestled for access to the North American fur trade, occasionally raiding interior shipping and exchange centers. But the need for goods also tempted frontier colonists to trade with their adversaries.

Late in the seventeenth century, European conflicts spread to North America, merging with ongoing colonial strife. European nations competed for power and wealth. Louis XIV of France, a member of the dynastic Bourbon family that bore many European royal crowns, built the continent's mightiest army largely to enhance his personal glory, and weaker countries sought to balance Louis' singular power with collective strength. Spain, whose Bourbon rulers had failed to utilize American gold and silver effectively to expand the country's economy, struggled to hold its far-flung imperial possessions while England angled for commercial opportunities. One important difference between the European and colonial wars was that European armies were professional, national, and well equipped, whereas the colonial forces were largely undisciplined and poorly armed militia whose tactics differed markedly from those of their European counterparts.

Early Colonial Wars

In a series of wars commencing in the 1680s and continuing for seventy-five years, England fought alongside various allies but consistently against France. William III took England into the League of Augsburg to prevent France from absorbing neighbors. The War of the League of Augsburg (1689–1697) ended indecisively as far as Europe was concerned. But in America, where English colonists called it **King William's War**, the conflict had important consequences. The Iroquois League, allied with England, suffered the loss of one quarter of its people in attacks by the French and their Huron allies. As a result, the Iroquois declared neutrality in future European conflicts. That approach allowed them to trade with both England and France without, they hoped, risking embroilment in the foreigners' wars but deprived the English of potent allies.

> What issues brought on the early colonial wars, and what impact did they have on the American colonies?

In 1700, the death of Spain's childless King Carlos II touched off the next European war as France and Austria pressed rival claims to the Spanish throne and Spain's American colonies. England, objecting to a united French and Spanish Catholic monarchy, joined with Austria and Holland in the War of the Spanish Succession (1702–1713). The conflict, called in the colonies **Queen Anne's War** after the reigning English monarch, ended with the Treaty of Utrecht (1713), which separated the French and Spanish monarchies, granted England a monopoly of the trans-Atlantic African slave trade, and awarded England a portion of of France's North American colonies, including Acadia. The English renamed it Nova Scotia. And the political union of England and Scotland in 1707 produced the United Kingdom of Great Britain.

There followed a generation of peace in Europe, helped along by Louis XIV's death, but colonial tensions persisted. Commercial competition in the Caribbean led to another outbreak of war. Spaniards, enforcing a trade agreement with Great Britain, boarded a British ship and sliced off the ear of its captain, Robert Jenkins. Subsequent outrage in England precipitated the **War of Jenkins' Ear** (1739), which merged with the War of the Austrian Succession (1740-48). In that war's associated colonial fracas, known as **King George's War,** France again allied itself with Spain. South Carolinians tried but failed to capture the Spanish fortress at St. Augustine; however, New England troops supported by the British navy took the strategic French fortress of Louisbourg on Cape Breton Island. News of the victory triggered patriotic celebrations in the colonies, but the Treaty of Aix-la-Chapelle, negotiated by European diplomats, returned all conquered territories.

The cost of these indecisive wars proved staggering and led to increased taxes on the subjects of the countries involved. The wars also exacted a heavy human toll in the colonies, including the Deerfield massacre (see pp. 98-99). Through them, however, colonists pursued their own interests independent of Great Britain's. Merchants in Albany carried on a brisk trade with the French in Canada as well as the Susquehannock and Shawnee towns in the Ohio Valley.

The French and Indian War

What were the causes and outcome of the French and Indian War?

In the early 1750s, the pattern reversed and a North American quarrel triggered a European imperial war. The Seven Years' War (1756–1763), or the **French and Indian War** as British colonists called it, grew out of the British-French struggle for control of the Ohio River valley. The Ohio River provided a vital link between French Canada and Louisiana, and based on long-standing relations with the Indians, officials claimed that these lands "unquestionably belong to France." The British saw things differently. In French hands, said a British official, the Ohio territory "would further strengthen them and weaken us." Neither view considered the claims of Delaware, Susquehannock, and Shawnee people who lived in the region.

In 1749, the Iroquois who asserted their own dominance over the eastern fringe of the Ohio Valley sold to a group of Virginia developers called the Ohio Company a large tract of land near the headwaters of the Ohio. Canadian officials immediately reacted by constructing a string of forts to discourage "any notions they [the British] may have of making settlements there." In 1753 Virginia dispatched George Washington, a twenty-one-year-old major in the Virginia militia and a member of the Ohio Company, to demand that the French withdraw from the region. They ignored him, and Washington returned to Virginia.

The following year, Washington returned with a regiment of Virginia militia and instructions to seize Fort Duquesne, at the site of present-day Pittsburgh. Along the way, the Virginians skirmished with a French patrol. Recognizing their peril, deep in a wilderness and facing a superior force from Ft. Duquesne, they threw together a makeshift fortification aptly named Fort Necessity. French and Indian fighters soon encircled it, and after a bloody shootout in which the Virginians lost a third of their number, Washington surrendered. The French allowed the English survivors to return to Virginia. Despite the disaster, Washington felt exhilarated. "I heard the bullets whistle," he wrote his brother, "and, believe me there is something charming in the sound."

During the same year, delegates from several English colonies met in Albany to consider a confederation of the colonies to provide for their common defense. Benjamin Franklin submitted a plan calling for a council of delegates elected by the colonial assemblies and a governor appointed by the king. But Franklin's **Albany Plan** failed to win the support of independent-minded colonists.

In February 1755, British army general Edward Braddock arrived in Virginia with a regiment of British regular soldiers and orders to capture Fort Duquesne. Though battle-hardened, Braddock lacked experience in North American warfare. Washington and a contingent of Virginia militia accompanied Braddock and his British Redcoats (thusly known because of their red uniform jackets). Hacking a road through the mountain forests, the British came to within a few miles of Fort Duquesne when, on July 9, a small army of French and Indian fighters ambushed them. In the hail of bullets and arrows, the British lost 900 of 1,400 men including sixty-three of eighty-six officers, Braddock among them. Following this shocking disaster, the British suffered defeats at Crown Point on Lake Champlain and Fort Niagara on Lake Ontario.

In 1756, Britain and France formally declared war, and Prime Minister William Pitt took charge of Britain's military strategy. Pitt boasted: "I know that I can save this country and that no one else can." To do so, he increased the regular army forces in the colonies and appointed Jeffery Amherst and James Wolfe to lead them. On the European front, Pitt forged an alliance with Frederick II of Prussia and subsidized him to fight against the French on the continent.

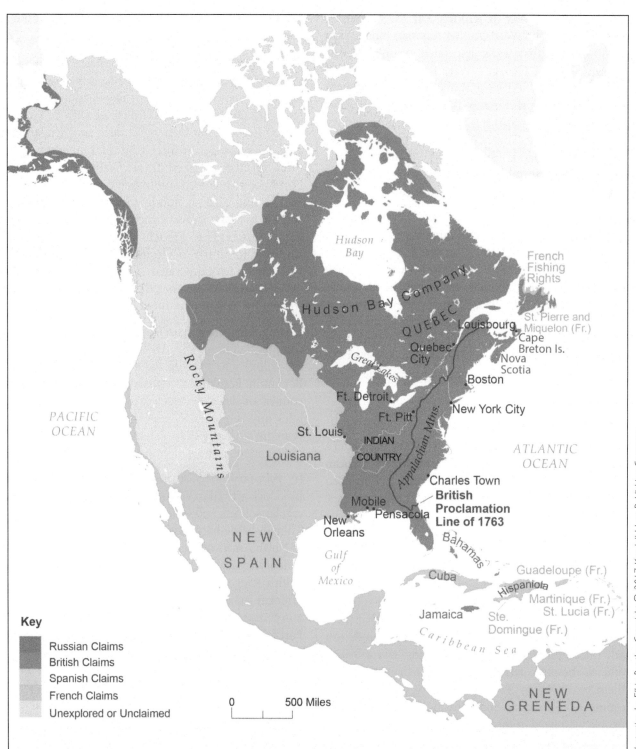

The French and Indian (Seven Years') War substantially altered the Europeans' imperial map of North America. France lost all of its continental territory while Great Britain was the big winner.

Pitt's strategy paid big dividends. Retaking Louisbourg and finally conquering Fort Duquesne in 1758, British and colonial troops along with fighters from the Iroquois League which abandoned neutrality and allied with the Anglo-Americans, went on to win sev-eral more pivotal battles. Finally, in September of 1759, Wolfe directed a British assault on the city of Quebec. Opposing British and French armies fought European style, firing from formation on the adjacent Plains of Abraham. When the smoke cleared, both

Wolfe and the French commander the Marquis de Montcalm lay dead, but the British had triumphed. The Battle of Quebec marked a turning point in the French and Indian War. As one exuberant colonist exclaimed: "The country is all in ecstasy upon the surprising news." By 1760, the war in North America was virtually over although fighting in the Caribbean continued. A peace treaty in 1763 formally ended the war.

Redefining North American Empires and National Identities

What impact did the French and Indian War have on the political boundaries of North America and colonial identity?

In the Treaty of Paris of 1763, France relinquished to Britain virtually all of Canada and Louisiana east of the Mississippi River. French settlers now became British subjects. Cuba, which Spain had lost to Britain during the fighting, went back to Spain in a trade that handed Florida over to the British in return. In a separate arrangement, France ceded New Orleans and Louisiana west of the Mississippi to Spain, bringing a new cultural influence as well as a new national association to that territory. Britain now controlled virtually all of North America east of the Mississippi while Spain maintained its colonial empire in the West.

Of the European countries involved in the war, France lost the most, but the Enlightenment philosopher Voltaire expressed the feelings of most war-weary French citizens: "I like peace better than Canada and I think that France can be happy without Quebec." French men and women in America were not always so philosophical, and French culture continued to influence the trans-Mississippi West. During the war, British officials had arrested many French Acadian men and women, and between 1765 and 1767 nearly 800 of the internees where resettled in Louisiana, becoming the ancestors of people known today as **Cajuns**. The plight of the Acadians later helped inspire Henry Wadsworth Longfellow to compose his famous romantic poem *Evangeline*.

The French and Indian War also altered the perceptions that many British colonists had of themselves. The victory seemed as much theirs as Britain's. Colonists began to see themselves not as British dependents—the little "children" of the "mother" country—but as self-governing societies, capable of managing their own affairs. Though far from united by a common identity, the residents of Britain's North American colonies nevertheless were developing an awareness of themselves as a distinct people.

War and Indian Identity

What provoked Indian wars like Pontiac's Rebellion and what were their consequences?

France's former Indian allies lost some of their political autonomy in the war. British military commander Jeffery Amherst rejected the French practice of gift giving as a prelude to negotiations. "They must be punished" for wrongdoing, he declared, "not bribed." Settlers from the British colonies caused the Indians even greater anxiety. To one Delaware leader, these settlers were "too strong for God himself." The Cherokees also felt the sting of defeat even though they were initially British allies. Wooed by the British because of their location between the Carolina settlements and the powerful French-backed Choctaws in Louisiana, the Cherokees failed to commit themselves militarily to the Anglo-American war effort. For their reluctance, British troops and Carolina and Virginia militia inflicted heavy damage to many of their towns. In 1761 Cherokee leaders signed a treaty acknowledging British sovereignty.

For some time, Indian leaders had condemned the drunkenness, quarrelsomeness, and commercial game hunting they observed among their people as evils associated with Europeans. The Delaware prophet Neolin envisioned Indians driving white people away, and in the spring of 1763, the Ottawa war chief Pontiac organized a multi-tribal campaign to expel the British. Pontiac led a siege of the British garrison at Detroit and directed allies to attack Pittsburgh (formerly Fort Duquesne) and Fort Niagara. Although the British successfully defended all three, the Indians did capture a number of smaller outposts.

By the end of 1763 both the Indians and the British were ready for peace. Liberal-minded General Thomas Gage replaced Amherst as British military commander, and William Johnson, Britain's principal negotiator, committed the British to a policy of gift giving to conclude alliances. In response to **Pontiac's Rebellion** the British government issued the **Proclamation of 1763** forbidding new settlements west of the Appalachian Mountains. Its purpose was to regulate western settlement to placate the powerful Delaware and Shawnee, thus preventing further costly frontier fighting.

Pontiac's Rebellion also brought out class and sectional divisions within colonial societies. Indian attacks led white settlers in western Pennsylvania to call for militia protection. When the provincial assembly, dominated by Philadelphia's Quaker elite, failed to support them, westerners took matters into their own hands. In January 1764 angry farmers from Paxton and other towns set upon two peaceful Conestoga Indian communities and massacred men, women, and children before marching toward Philadelphia intent on seizing control of the colonial government. When the assembly voted more funds for frontier defense and Pontiac's Rebellion ended, the **"Paxton Boys"** dissolved, but the tension between whites and Indians on the frontier and back-country whites and the eastern elite remained.

To many colonists, British officials appeared more sympathetic to the Indians' troubles than to theirs. The Proclamation of 1763 seemed like an attempt to block them from the territory jointly won in the French and Indian War. Many simply ignored the proclamation and moved into Tennessee and Kentucky. The British government's decision to station 10,000 regular troops in the colonies, presumably to preserve the peace, alarmed some colonists. They had proved their mettle in the French and Indian and other colonial wars. They could defend themselves. Why were so many British troops now necessary?

CONCLUSION

From the 1680s until the middle of the eighteenth century, Europe's American colonies expanded in many ways, and inevitably that expansion produced tension, such as what produced the attack on Deerfield. Spain fortified its interior provinces from Florida to Arizona to protect its rich silver mines but did little to encourage New Spain's economic development. The French did more to promote commerce in New France, including forging valuable Indian alliances and attempting to erect a slave-based plantation society in Louisiana. But ultimately, both Spain and France were obsessed with checking the expansion of England's colonies rather than nurturing their own colonial societies.

English colonies grew at a startling rate, pushing Indians out of the way and laying down lasting economic and cultural patterns. The development of plantation agriculture in the Chesapeake and Carolina-Georgia low country led to bi-racial slave societies integrated into a trans-Atlantic economy. Even while enduring brutal slave regimes, tens of thousands of Africans asserted surprising power in shaping those societies and in creating a distinct African-American culture. To the north, Puritan societies transformed themselves into Yankee commercial communities. Immigration from Europe and some from Africa reinforced the cultural patchwork of the Middle Colonies and a backcountry milieu that would blossom later into popular democracy.

Change brought strains that erupted in bloody clashes with Indians, slave resistance, and class strife. Prosperity and the development of seaboard cities yielded a mid-century crisis of identity in British North America. On the one hand, through trans-Atlantic commerce colonists became increasingly tied to England. But on the other hand, experiences like the Great Awakening bred distinctiveness and a positive self-consciousness. By the end of the Seven Years War, the British had established their dominance over the eastern fringe of North America. But whether management would be in the hands of colonists or officials in London remained a crucial question.

SUGGESTED SOURCES FOR STUDENTS

Books

James Axtell, *The European and the Indian: Essays in the Ethnohistory of Colonial North America* (1981), uses the techniques of history and anthropology to explain how Europeans and Indians thought about themselves and each other.

Carol Berkin, *First Generations: Women in Colonial America* (1996) treats European, African, and Indian women in all of England's colonies.

The best explanation of the process of colonies with slaves becoming slave societies is Ira Berlin, *Many Thousands Gone: The First Two Centuries of Slavery in North America* (1998). By extension, Margaret Ellen Newell, *Bretheren by Nature: New England Indians, Colonists, and the Origins of American Slavery* (2015) explains how New England Indians became enslaved.

Richard L. Bushman, *From Puritan to Yankee: Character and the Social Order in Connecticut, 1690-1765* (1967), studies the transformation of Connecticut from a colony based on discipline and religious values to a commercial society.

Colin Calloway presents an excellent overview of Indian history, including relations with Spanish and French colonists west of the Appalachian Mountains, in *One Vast Winter Count: The Native American West before Lewis and Clark* (2003).

For a full explanation of the Deerfield raid see John Demos, *The Unredeemed Captive: A Family Story From Early America* (1994).

Gregory Evans Dowd, *Groundless: Rumors, Legends, and Hoaxes on the Early American Frontier* (2015), examines the prevalence of rumors and lies where validation of information swirling through isolated communities was difficult if not impossible.

Paul Kelton, *Cherokee Medicine, Colonial Germs: An Indigenous Nation's Fight Against Smallpox, 1518-1824* (2015), combats the established assumption that germs were almost exclusively responsible for the demise of North American Indian populations with the argument that Anglo-American colonialism was the principal culprit.

Jill LePore, *New York Burning: Liberty, Slavery, and Conspiracy in Eighteenth Century Manhattan* (2005), offers not only an insightful look into the shadowy lives of African slaves in New York City but also a brilliant example of how to draw understanding from original sources.

James Merrill, *Into the American Woods: Negotiators On the Pennsylvania Frontier* (1999) brings to light the shadowy go-betweens, Indian and European, who made negotiations and coexistence possible.

For a full examination of the development of African-American cultures, Philip D. Morgan, *Slave Counterpoint: Black Culture in the Eighteenth-Century Chesapeake & Low Country* (1998), is a must-read.

Daniel Richter opens the window into Native American societies in *Facing East from Indian Country* (2001).

BEFORE WE GO ON

1. How does a global context of dynamic, trans-Atlantic European empires help us understand North America in the late seventeenth and early eighteenth centuries?

2. How did the imperial struggles of the eighteenth century affect the national identities of North Americans?

Building a Democratic Nation

3. Measuring success by (a) the number of settlers, (b) the freedom enjoyed by settlers, and (c) the staying power of settler societies, which of the European colonial powers in North America was the most successful? Explain why.

4. Citing specific examples of European colonists' relationships with Native Americans and African Americans, describe the balance of power among them. What specific factors gave each group power over the others and what factors limited their power.

Connections

5. Those who study human behavior often argue whether innate traits or environmental factors are more influential. Considering that debate, how would you show that environment influenced the development of societies in North America during the late seventeenth and early eighteenth centuries? How would you demonstrate that the cultures that emerged in North America resulted from attitudes, behaviors, and institutions that people brought with them to their new environment? What can you say about differences and similarities between regional environments and behaviors in the United States today compared to the late seventeenth and early eighteenth centuries?

6. What developments during the late seventeenth and early eighteenth centuries indicate that England's North American colonies were on the road to democracy? What evidence might you cite to indicate that a democratic America was still a long way off?

The Global Perspective

Empire And Revolution: Foundations of Republican Societies, 1750–1815

How did identity and nationhood figure in global empires and revolutions?

Two epic storylines ran through the late eighteenth and early nineteenth centuries: empire and revolution. In 1450, for example, Muslim empires from the Mediterranean to South Asia controlled most of the channels of global commerce, but by 1750 they had lost most of that power as Dutch, British, and French empires supplanted them. Then revolutions shook many of the European empires. Although different in fundamental ways, these revolutions drew inspiration from common sources and experimented with various forms of democratic government. Themes of cultural identity and nationhood also stand out in the stories of empire and revolution.

One of the wealthiest and most heavily populated of the seventeenth and eighteenth century empires encompassed India. Muslim invaders entered India from Afghanistan and spread their hegemony over most of the Asian subcontinent. This Mughal Empire reached its zenith early in the seventeenth century in part by adopting policies of cultural tolerance and assimilation. The Mughal emperor Akbar married a Hindu princesses, appointed a Spanish Catholic missionary to tutor his son, and allowed as many as 30 percent of the office-holders in his government to be non-Muslims. Agriculture, industry, and commerce flourished. In addition to foodstuffs, men and women grew pepper, sugar, silk, cotton, and tea. Artisans manufactured printed cotton cloth in a contract system whereby merchants supplied them with materials and cash. Textiles soon attracted Portuguese, Dutch, French, and English merchants who sold them along with other Indian products in the rapidly expanding markets of Europe.

Rising European commercial empires ultimately brought about the disintegration of the Mughal Empire as the foreign powers bargained for control of India's commerce and territory. The Portuguese established trading colonies in Goa and Bombay; the French acquired Pondicherry; and England, through its East India Company, built fortress-like trading centers in Madras and Calcutta. These were not settler colonies; instead, foreigners managed and exploited native human and natural resources. The English East India Company not only profited enormously by exporting tea but also served as Great Britain's surrogate in India. During the European imperial wars of the eighteenth century, Britain grew stronger, beating France decisively both in India and in North America, and in both areas British officials turned from the "benign neglect" of previous years, especially toward North America, toward a tighter imperial grip.

The stakes in Europe's eighteenth-century imperial wars were high, and so was the financial cost. As the European monarchies endeavored to reduce their crippling debts, they ignited revolutions that rocked North America and Europe and eventually spread to the Caribbean and most of Central and South America. The American Revolution, which originated in a quarrel over taxes but turned into a struggle for independence, heralded the onset of what historian Robert R. Palmer called "the age of the democratic revolution." The American Revolution's **liberal revolutionary ideology** sprang from roots in ancient Greece and the modern European Enlightenment. It rested on the dual principles of transcendent natural rights and representative government. These constituted the essence of **republican** societies and made them far more democratic than traditional monarchies. To rally popular support for a new republican body politic, leaders of the American Revolution sought to forge a **national identity** out of disparate colonies. Thomas Jefferson argued eloquently for a new **nation** united by English liberties while Thomas Paine stirred national passions by identifying America with the more universal "rights of man." But many Americans wished only for political independence from Great Britain and not an end to class privilege and slavery, and certainly not the inclusion of Native Americans in the new nation.

The idealism of the American Revolution helped spark the French Revolution. Unlike the American Revolution, however, the French Revolution was not anti-colonial. A faltering economy and mounting royal taxes blamed on imperial wars combined with feudal political and social systems to move France toward a more representative government. The French Revolution adopted many of the icons of the American Revolution and subsequent mechanisms of nation-building, like constitutional conventions. In May of 1789,

King Louis XVI convened the Estates General, a three-part legislature representing nobles, Catholic clergy, and everyone else to devise a legitimate way to impose taxes. Later that year, masses of working-class Parisians rioted against food shortages, high prices, and unemployment. They stormed the prison fortress called the Bastille and liberated political captives, creating a symbol of a new French national identity, like the American Revolution's "Boston Tea Party." A National Assembly dominated by the wealthy *bourgeoisie* issued a Declaration of the Rights of Man stating: "Men are born and remain free and equal." The National Assembly also modernized French laws and institutions and in 1791 produced a constitution that limited monarchical power.

Reaction outside France was swift and strong. In Britain, political leader Edmund Burke condemned the French Revolution, maintaining that only with a privileged aristocracy could nations avoid chaos. Mary Wollstonecraft not only defended the French Revolution but also extended the concepts of liberty and equality to women. Jefferson, United States minister to France, allowed his Paris home to be used as a revolutionary meeting place while in the United States, Alexander Hamilton wrote to the French Marquis de Lafayette, a hero who had served on General George Washington's staff, of his "apprehension" that success might breed excess. Several European monarchies threatened to intervene, and as they did the French Revolution grew more radical. In 1792, a popularly elected National Convention abolished the monarchy and proclaimed a French Republic. A radical faction within the National Convention called Jacobins arrested King Louis XVI and in January of 1793 sent him to the guillotine.

Regicide marked the beginning of what historians call a "second revolution." The National Convention declared war on much of monarchical Europe, and patriotic workingmen and women mobilized behind the Republic as "citizens" rather than "subjects." The Convention disestablished the Catholic Church, abolished hereditary titles, dismantled capitalism, and gave birth to a prototype socialist economy, with prices fixed by the government and businesses nationalized. Hamilton had proved prophetic. The National Convention confiscated landed estates, and Jacobin party leader Maximilian Robespierre launched a savage Reign of Terror that sent thousands of aristocrats to the guillotine. Even Lafayette narrowly escaped with his life. Ever more radical groups succeeded each other as the revolution careened out of control.

With the Reign of Terror, the French Revolution burned itself out. In 1794, Robespierre's rivals in the National Convention arrested and executed him. Soon a coalition of moderate middle-class Frenchmen and rural peasants in the Convention reversed the economic reforms, drafted a new constitution that diluted democracy, and set up a five-man ruling Directory. And in 1799, one of the directors, the extraordinary general Napoleon Bonaparte, took control of the country. To achieve his main objective, a rebuilt French Empire, Napoleon reorganized the legal and administrative systems in France and its possessions. In the process he extinguished most of the liberty and equality that the Revolution had achieved, but most French citizens appreciated the relative order and stability he provided.

Both revolutionary idealism and Napoleon's empire building triggered other revolutions. In the French Caribbean island of St. Domingue, African slaves invoked "liberty and equality" in rebelling against their masters and creating the black republic of Haiti. The Haitian Revolution fostered two transnational identities: one among enslaved Africans and another among fearful slave owners throughout the Western Hemisphere. Among the *creole* settler populations of Spanish and Portuguese colonies in Central and South America, documents like Paine's *Common Sense* and the Declaration of Independence fueled smoldering resentment against imperial taxes and regulations, the powerful Catholic Church, and the ruling elite born in Portugal and Spain. In Venezuela, Francisco de Miranda, who led a revolution against Spain, noted: "Two great examples lie before our eyes, the American and the French Revolutions." And Napoleon's wars against European monarchies, including Spain and Portugal, destabilized those imperial regimes sufficiently to encourage colonial revolts. Like the American Revolution, revolutions elsewhere in the Americas were primarily concerned with independence and not social engineering.

If the American Revolution opened the age of democratic revolution, the French Revolution took it to extreme, even frightening, lengths. Miranda, the Venezuelan revolutionary, looked at both for a model but concluded: "Let us discreetly imitate the first; let us carefully avoid the disastrous effects of the second." The American Revolution, regarded by many historians as the more conservative of the two, endured, partly because its leaders, unlike French revolutionaries, had long experience in governing through their colonial assemblies. In addition, the Americans were committed to individual liberty whereas French Jacobins aimed for social equality. Albeit gradually, the American Revolution led to a more democratic nation while the French Revolution went into reaction, and Latin American revolutions seldom moved beyond shifting power from one elite to another. But the rhetoric of the French Revolution found reincarnation in many Marxist movements of the twentieth century.

A Global Perspective provides us with a better understanding the American Revolution and the process of building a democratic nation that followed. By placing these events in a global context we can more easily evaluate their importance, for the Revolution not only affected Americans but it also influenced others, who in turn influenced the United States.

THINKING BACK

1. What similarities and differences can you see in the eighteenth and early nineteenth-century revolutions in North America, France, the Caribbean, and Central and South America?
2. From a Global Perspective, how would you assess the importance of the American Revolution?

Chapter 5

BECOMING A NATION, 1750–1783

A PERSONAL PERSPECTIVE: SARAH AND JOSEPH HODGKINS

> **How did Joseph and Sarah Hodgkins experience the Revolutionary War?**

On the morning of April 19, 1775, several hundred British Redcoats marched from Boston toward nearby Concord. Their mission was to seize muskets and gunpowder stockpiled by colonists under authorization of the Massachusetts provincial assembly. Meanwhile, three members of an organization called the Sons of Liberty galloped ahead to alert sleeping citizens. The drama signaled the start of a war in which Americans from Massachusetts united with those from New York, Virginia, and other colonies to fight for independence. Sarah and Joseph Hodgkins of Ipswich, along with scores of thousands of other men and women, including African Americans and Native Americans, joined the struggle.

The American Revolution turned the Hodgkins' lives upside down. Both believed in "the Cause," but they felt the acute strain of war. Joseph was a thirty-one-year-old shoemaker who, like most able-bodied men his age, served in his town's militia company, known as Minutemen because they were prepared at a minute's notice. After the battle of Bunker Hill in 1775, his unit was incorporated into the Continental Army of what became the United States, and Hodgkins eventually attained the rank of captain. In 1776, he and other New Englanders made up two-thirds of the Continental Army. While Joseph was at war, twenty-two-year-old Sarah cared for their four children and her aging father-in-law. She also took charge of the family's farm. Like her husband, Sarah believed in the redemptive power of sacrifice. When, in late 1776 as the British chased the Continental Army through New Jersey, she wrote to Joseph: "I think things Look very dark on our side but it has been observed that mans extremity was Gods opportunity and . . . I hope God will appear for us & send Salvation and deliverance to us in due time."

The hardships that Joseph Hodgkins endured in his four years of service are difficult to imagine today. Soldiers walked from one battlefield to another carrying their equipment on their backs. They often had no shoes or clothing sufficient for the cold winters. Filthy camps bred dysentery, typhoid fever, and smallpox. Amazingly, Joseph fell ill only twice, once with "camp fever" (dysentery) and a second time with smallpox, which he contracted by inoculation. "This may inform you that I am in good health," he assured Sarah by letter. "We had a very hot engagement [at Bunker Hill] yesterday." Good fortune saved him from wounds, but one musket ball "went under my arm and cut a large hole in my coat." Joseph also survived the miserable winter of 1777-78 at Valley Forge. "If not for winter clothes," which Sarah made for him, "I must go naked."

Sarah Hodgkins faced dangers herself. With armies nearby, the threat of plunder and rape was ever present. Sarah escaped that type of misfortune but not severe privation. She seldom complained about shortages of sugar, molasses, coffee, and salt, of preparing meals, slaughtering and putting up meat, sewing shirts and knitting stockings for her husband, or stretching what little cash she had. By 1778 it took four months of a soldier's pay to buy a bushel of wheat. Joseph sent money to help, but army pay was pitifully small.

Revolutionary fervor inspired self-sacrifice, but patriotic duty often clashed with personal attachments and longings. "I would not Be understood that I should Chuse to March," Joseph confided to Sarah, and she shared her loneliness: "I have got a Sweet Babe almost six months old but have got no father for it." Sarah opposed Joseph's re-enlistment after his Ipswich unit disbanded. He was one of only seven Ipswich men who remained in service, and by then, the Continental Army had changed from one-year to three-year commitments. Remaining in the army, she wrote, would be "inconsistent with your duty to come home to your family." Sarah's appeals did not bring Joseph back, except for furloughs, but they did elicit reassurances. "[Y]ou think I Dont Care much about you. But my Dear you are allways near my hart & in my thoughts."

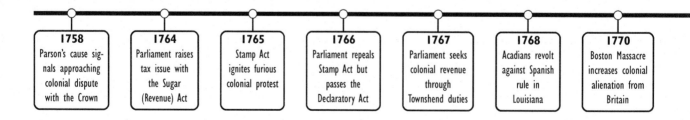

1758	1764	1765	1766	1767	1768	1770
Parson's cause signals approaching colonial dispute with the Crown	Parliament raises tax issue with the Sugar (Revenue) Act	Stamp Act ignites furious colonial protest	Parliament repeals Stamp Act but passes the Declaratory Act	Parliament seeks colonial revenue through Townshend duties	Acadians revolt against Spanish rule in Louisiana	Boston Massacre increases colonial alienation from Britain

The war clearly strained the Hodgkins's marriage. Early in the war, Joseph and Sarah wrote each other frequently, although not often enough to satisfy either one. "My Dear," Sarah pleaded, ". . . I wish you would write oftener." When the intervals between Joseph's letters grew longer, Sarah's tone became more negative. "It seems you are tired of writing. I am sorry you count it trouble to write to me." But despite the frustration and hurt feelings, Sarah and Joseph communicated love and even passion for each other. "[G]ive regards to Capt Wade [Joseph's tent mate]," Sarah wrote, "and tell [him] I have wanted his bed fellow pret[t]y much these cold nights," prompting Joseph to reply: "I gave your Regards to Capt Wade[.] But he Did not wish that you had his Bed fellow but I wish you had with all my heart." Through the trials of war and afterward Joseph and Sarah remained, as they signed their letters: "Your most af[f]ectionate and loving companion till Death. . . ."

Learned and respected Americans articulated the ideals of the American Revolution eloquently and persuasively, but winning independence from Great Britain came from the sacrifices of ordinary men and women like Joseph and Sarah Hodgkins. And for many ordinary Americans, the results were irreversible losses of property, health, limbs, and life. In June 1779, Joseph Hodgkins resigned from the army, disheartened and uncertain of the country's future.

As the Hodgkinses struggled with their conflicting loyalties and duties, so did many other Americans. The American Revolution dissolved many old attachments and forged new ones. Until then, most Americans regarded themselves as loyal British citizens. New identities were often weak, and at some point in the war, many soldiers doubted that independence would or should be the outcome. One in every five Americans, including large numbers of enslaved African Americans, remained loyal to Britain. By war's end, thousands of Loyalists had left for Canada, the West Indies, and England. Most Indians tried to remain detached from this "English fight," but the Revolution sucked in several tribes.

The war for independence gave birth to a new American nation. The freedom that came with independence, however, meant different things to different people. For New Englanders like the Hodgkinses, freedom implied largely autonomous communities. Aristocratic southern planters regarded freedom as the right to own slaves. For enslaved people, freedom meant release from bondage. Backcountry people, whose notion of freedom included freedom from taxes and government meddling in their affairs, impinged on the freedom of Native Americans. The Declaration of Independence had proclaimed that "all men" were equal, but what about women? The ideals, symbols, and institutions of the American Revolution set the stage for democratic nationhood, but it was just the beginning.

THINKING BACK

1. What sacrifices did Joseph and Sarah Hodgkins make for the Revolutionary Cause?
2. How did the war affect their personal relationship?

GOVERNING THE COLONIES

Until the restoration of the monarchy in 1660, the English government had paid scant attention to the mainland North American colonies. Afterward, it attempted to form a closer attachment, as in the Dominion of New England, although the later Stuarts (Charles II and James II) centered their attention on colonial trade. The analogy that Britons liked to use in defining the relationship between England and the colonies was the "mother country" and her dependent "children." But through the first half of the eighteenth century the maturing colonial "children" built political institutions that allowed them to govern themselves and to develop independent identities.

Patterns of Government

In theory, government in England (Great Britain after 1707 when England and Scotland united) gave voice to

1773	1774	1775	1776	1777	1778	1781	1783
Tea Act invites Boston Tea Party	Coercive (Intolerable) Acts and First Continental Congress	War begins at Lexington, Concord, and Bunker Hill	Declaration of Independence forms the United States	American victory at Saratoga	French alliance boosts American cause	American triumph at Yorktown and British defeat at Pensacola	Treaty of Paris acknowledges American independence

What were the
roots of colonial
government?

society's three recognized components: royalty, nobility, and the common people. The Crown (monarchy) belonged to the royal family. Parliament's **House of Lords** included all nobles who inherited both their titles and their seats. The **House of Commons,** whose members were elected by adult male property owners, represented all the others and was, again in theory, the most democratic part of the British government. Many people in the British Empire regarded British government as the most representative one in the world.

The monarchy and the two houses of Parliament each had primary responsibility in particular governmental areas, although the relationship between the Crown and Parliament changed significantly during the seventeenth century when the Civil War and the Glorious Revolution boosted Parliament's power. Parliament exercised legislative or lawmaking authority. The Bill of Rights to the English Constitution, enacted in 1689, specifically forbade the monarchy from imposing taxes or taking the country to war without Parliament's consent. Both the Commons and Lords had to agree for legislation to become law, but the important power to initiate tax legislation resided in the House of Commons alone. The monarchy became the executive or law enforcement branch of government. For that big job, the Crown had for centuries relied on a group of roughly three dozen

advisers known as the **Privy Council**. But after 1714, with the ascendance of King George I and his successor George II, both German by birth and largely unfamiliar with British politics, the monarch fell under the growing influence of politicians in Parliament who formed a cabinet of ministers. This further enhanced Parliament's power over the king. The first cabinet ministry included a group of Whigs led by Robert Walpole, England's first prime minister (although that title was not used until much later).

The Enlightenment theorist John Locke, who had supported the Glorious Revolution, had laid out basic Whig principles in *Two Treatises of Government* published in 1690. Locke invoked the concept of a "**social contract**" whereby societies formed governments for the purpose of protecting the people's "**natural rights**" to life, liberty, and property. In other words, Whigs believed that government originated with the people, and if government failed to secure their rights or threatened them, thus violating the social contract, it forfeited its legitimacy. Under such circumstances, citizens had the right to change the government and ultimately to overthrow it. Although Locke wrote in purely hypothetical terms, Americans had actually engaged in such contracting with the Mayflower Compact (see p. 74). Locke did not advocate **democratic** government though, for he, like most Whigs, believed that direct popular rule bred chaos. Instead, Locke argued for government by the people's chosen representatives, enlightened and extraordinary

Image © Mikio Oba, 2010. Used by permission of Shutterstock, Inc.

Both houses of Parliament are located here, Westminster Palace, in London

persons who would protect and promote the common people's interests. This was the essence of **republican** government, which Whigs believed balanced popular participation in government with sound aristocratic reasonableness.

Representation in government begged the question of legitimacy from the colonists' point of view because they elected no members of Parliament. So, did Parliament have a legitimate right to govern them? For the most part, British officials answered "yes," contending that each member of the House of Commons represented all subjects (citizens) and not just those who elected them. But political leaders in the American colonies rejected the idea of **virtual representation** and regarded their own colonial governments as the only guarantors of their rights.

In many ways, colonial governments resembled that of the mother country, although as with most offspring, the resemblance was not identical. Although the colonies had neither royalty nor nobility of their own, their governments contained executive and legislative branches similar to the Crown and Parliament. But no single pattern of government existed throughout the colonies. Although most colonies had originated either as corporate or proprietary enterprises based on charters issued by the Crown, by the 1760s all but eight had lost their original charters and had become royal colonies. Maryland, Pennsylvania, and Delaware continued as proprietorships, and Connecticut and Rhode Island were the only corporate colonies.

Colonial governors served the interests of those who selected them: the Crown in the case of royal colonies, the proprietors in the propriety colonies, or the voters in Connecticut and Rhode Island. In some ways the governors emulated the British monarch. For instance, colonial governors possessed broad executive power, including command of the militia in order to enforce law and order; however, their power to appoint persons to government office (called "patronage") was limited. But they wielded more power than the Crown in other areas. They could veto measures passed by the colonial legislatures, whereas the Crown had lost that power after the Glorious Revolution. Governors also could call legislative sessions and dissolve them at their pleasure while the British monarch was bound to convene Parliament every three years and call for elections at least every seven. Governors often initiated legislation, usually in consultation with a council of advisers that also served as the upper house of the colonial legislature and as the highest appeals court in the colony. In royal colonies, the Crown appointed members of the governor's council. Governors lacked the prestige of the Crown, and in most colonies they gradually lost effective power to the colonial legislatures.

© 2010 JupiterImages Corp.

The governor's mansion in Williamsburg, Virginia, was built in the eighteenth-century's popular "Georgian" style. It combined elegance and simple grace.

Colonial legislatures mirrored Parliament, but again with some important differences. The lower house, whether called the Burgesses in Virginia, the Representatives in Massachusetts, or just the assembly as in most colonies, embodied the principle of representative government. Legislatures gained most of their strength from the "power of the purse," meaning control of taxing and spending, which extended to the governors' salaries. In that respect, the legislatures had more power than Parliament.

Legislative assemblies were representative but not democratic, for only a minority of the colonists could vote. As Thomas Jefferson explained to a friend: "A choice by the people themselves is not generally distinguished for its wisdom." By the mid-eighteenth century, the colonies no longer imposed a religious requirement for voting (nor did England), but they did set property qualifications. According to a prevailing assumption held by ruling elites in both Britain and the colonies, people who owned no property possessed no independent political will. Their employers, landlords, or masters could easily manipulate them, or worse, they might use political power to dispossess property owners. Since women, Indians, and blacks seldom owned property, they generally could not vote. Property requirements in England excluded nine out of ten adult males, but in the colonies, where land was more abundant, three out of four adult white males qualified. In eastern regions, though, where large landowners possessed most of the property and large numbers of urban laborers owned no none, as few as 40 percent of the white males met the property qualification. In any event, voters typically elected planters, lawyers, and wealthy merchants to the assemblies and, after election day, the people's representatives paid little attention to them.

Yet in allowing the social elite to lead, the masses did not relinquish the right to resist officials who displeased them. Yeoman farmers, town artisans, laborers, seamen, indentured servants, and even slaves challenged governors and their elected representatives. In the 1740s in New Jersey, armed farmers rioted against attempts by aristocratic landowners, backed by colonial officials, to confiscate their property and turn them into tenants. They declared that "when property is made uncertain and precarious, this bond [the social contract] is broken." In the 1750s, similar tenant uprisings broke out in the Hudson Valley of New York, and expressions of popular resentment over the rule of the elite frequently took the form of street riots in seaport towns.

Harassment of obnoxious officials and occasional riots and insurrections exemplified a common if not universally approved exercise of direct political action. Indeed, popular anti-elitist, anti-authoritarian eruptions were as important in the impending struggle between Britain and the colonies as the political theories of John Locke.

Controlling Colonial Trade

Throughout the colonial period, England saw its colonies as economic resources. Colonial agriculture and commerce carried enormous profit- and revenue-generating potential for English businesses and a government indebted by frequent costly wars. English merchants sought to bar foreign rivals, especially the Dutch, from the profitable colonial trade, and both the government and commercial men wanted to boost English shipbuilding to meet the needs of the growing merchant marine and the royal navy. But from the colonial perspective, trade was not about enriching English merchants and shippers; rather, it produced profits and wages for colonists themselves. Through the late seventeenth and early eighteenth centuries, officials in England sought to regulate colonial commerce and to define the colonies as dependents subordinate to the mother country.

> Why and how did England tighten its grip on the colonies?

English policy makers—both the king and Parliament—believed, as did the Dutch, that nations grew richer or poorer through trade. Since exports brought cash into a country and imports reversed the money flow, England endeavored to establish favorable trading relationships with other nations. Colonies could help by supplying valuable raw goods that England would otherwise have to import. They were also markets for English manufactured products. Adam Smith, the Scottish economist whose *Wealth of Nations* (1776) later became a classic in free-market economic theory, was the first to refer to such state-managed commercial systems as "**mercantilism**," a term that stuck.

Efforts at systematic trade regulation began during the time of the Commonwealth. In 1651 Parliament passed a Navigation Act banning Dutch ships from English and colonial ports. Parliamentary regulation continued after the Restoration. The **Navigation Act of 1660** required that goods transported to or from the colonies be carried in ships made either in England or America and that three-fourths of the crews be English or colonial English. The act also

enumerated or identified colonial products, including sugar, tobacco, dyewoods, cotton, and indigo, that could be shipped only to England or to another colonial English market. The legislation was intended to ensure that all of these American products were available to English consumers, while also generating customs revenues for the English Crown. Parliament later added rice and molasses, pitch, tar, and turpentine (the latter three being products used in shipbuilding) to the list. The **Navigation Act of 1663** required that colonial imports first pass through England where they were unloaded, taxed, and re-exported. This gave English merchants a share of the profit from the colonial import trade while adding significantly to the cost of colonial imports.

While some aspects of the mercantilist system benefited the colonies, many colonists resented it because mercantilism served English economic interests first and sometimes at the colonists' expense. Tobacco planters in the Chesapeake complained about lower prices for their crops in England than they could get in other markets. New England merchants simply ignored the laws. Smuggling developed into a thriving business, as Yankee ship captains picked up enumerated goods in one colonial port, transported them to another colonial port—thereby meeting the letter of the law—, and then carried them directly to lucrative continental European markets. Authorities in Massachusetts refused to prosecute the violators, as most of them were well known. When a special English agent, Edward Randolph, demanded that the colony obey Parliamentary law, Massachusetts responded by declaring that according to its charter "legislative power is and abides" in its citizens alone.

England tried to crack down on violations with both Parliament and the Crown asserting authority. Parliament passed the **Navigation Act of 1673** requiring ship captains to post bond guaranteeing that enumerated goods went to England as required. In 1675, King Charles II began erecting a bureaucratic structure for law enforcement through a committee of the Privy Council, called the **Lords of Trade**. They oversaw colonial matters in general, picking royal governors, writing detailed instructions that defined their power and responsibility, and demanding thorough and regular reports regarding the status of the colonies. Customs officials in the colonies monitored compliance with trade regulations. To tighten controls further, Charles II and James II sought to convert private colonies into royal colonies, separating New Hampshire from Massachusetts in 1676, annulling Massachusetts' charter eight years later, and setting up the Dominion of New England. Finally, in 1696 William III scrapped the Lords of Trade for a new agency called the **Board of Trade** to supervise imperial trade policy. That same year, another Navigation Act ordered that accused customs violators be tried in juryless vice-admiralty courts in which an appointed judge, presumably immune to local prejudices, would rule on the case.

Parliament also sought to rationalize the imperial economy by eliminating colonial competition with important parent industries in England. The **Woolens Act (1699)** prohibited the manufacture of textiles in the colonies. The **Hat Act (1732)** restricted the making of beaver hats, and the Iron Act (1750) outlawed the production of finished iron products. The **Molasses Act (1733)** placed heavy duties on molasses imported by New England rum distillers. The New Englanders purchased molasses from French, Spanish, and Dutch sugar planters in the West Indies as well as from the English Caribbean colonies of Barbados or Jamaica. When English sugar planters complained of having to share markets with American colonists, Parliament stepped in and helped them out.

Despite all the measures to regulate the colonial trade, strict control was impossible. London could not maintain enough customs agents to catch smugglers or pay them sufficiently to make them invulnerable to bribes. Nor could Parliament prevent artisans and shopkeepers from manufacturing and retailing woolens, hats, or iron products. The colonists discovered ways around laws they found unacceptable. Remarkably, however, most of the time they obeyed the laws because they were loyal to the British Empire.

THINKING BACK

1. What were the roots of colonial government? How did colonial government resemble that of the mother country, and in what ways was it different?
2. How did England attempt to use its North American colonies to its benefit, and how did the colonies respond?

COLONIAL GRIEVANCES AND AMERICAN IDENTITY

Discord between the British imperial government in London and the North American colonies deepened after the French and Indian War. Colonial pride in being part of the British Empire began dissolving into resentment and suspicion as the London government tightened regulations and, by attitude as well as action, underscored the colonies' subordinate status. Perhaps Parliament felt more intensely than did Americans the stresses of global imperial competition; many colonists put colonial freedom above all else and increasingly focused on British violations of their rights. As British political commentator Edmund Burke remarked, the colonists "augur misgovernment at a distance and sniff the approach of tyranny in every tainted breeze." Indeed, most colonists subscribed to republican principles of freedom. In Britain's diverse colonies, though, not everyone agreed on what freedom meant.

A turning point in colonial relations with Britain came in 1760 with the death of George II and the ascendance of his twenty-two-year-old grandson as King George III. Unlike his immediate Hanoverian predecessors, George III was English through and through and determined to rule and not just reign as a figurehead monarch dominated by Whig politicians whom he distrusted. Unfortunately, the immature king chose for key ministerial positions men like George Grenville who exhibited little political adeptness and stumbled from one botched policy to another. Also unlike previous regimes, George III and his ministers were less interested in promoting trade with the colonies than in forcing them to submit to imperial authority.

American Political Cultures

Some American concepts of freedom or liberty grew out of British Whig theory. Whigs valued both liberty and social order and acknowledged the difficulty of having both since maximizing one naturally minimized the other. Popular government was good, but not democratic government in the hands of the landless masses who threatened social order and thus the liberty of propertied citizens. Representative, republican government best ensured liberty. Representative government "does not *infringe* liberty" like autocratic government, explained English theorist Richard Price, "but establish[es] it."

> **What signs suggested that colonial views of government differed from those prevailing in England?**

Whig theory also valued elevating the common good above self-interest. The Whig term for this was **republican virtue**. Whigs regarded it as the key to good government, and American political leaders generally agreed. John Adams, soon-to-be a prominent revolutionary patriot, referred to ordinary farmers and tradesmen as the "common Herd of Mankind," certainly not a flattering description for the majority of his countrymen.

Although they shared the same political philosophy, British and American Whigs looked at the British Empire differently. Most British Whigs, especially those in Parliament and in the king's ministry, placed an ordered empire, one based on the acceptance of central governing authority, above the interests of the colonies—for the common good. Many Americans disagreed, insisting that such a priority inevitably led to tyranny for they believed that most British politicians were corrupt. "We are still the same people with them in every respect," noted Virginia planter George Mason, "only not yet debauched by wealth, luxury, venality & corruption." Mason overstated the colonists' republican virtue, but his "we" and "them" language suggests an emerging American self-consciousness—an American national identity.

Through the seventeenth and early eighteenth centuries, British officials largely indulged local government in the colonies either because they did not have time for the colonies or because they valued colonial trade and did not want to upset the relationship. Colonial reaction to the Dominion of New England provided a valuable lesson. During the imperial wars of the mid-eighteenth century, though, illicit American trade with the enemy led Parliament to assert its legislative supremacy as British merchants and naval officials, who exerted great influence on Whig representatives, urged tighter control over America's revenues and its vast resources. Some colonists complained of Parliamentary tyranny.

Two early episodes brought out the clash between British and American perspectives. In 1748, Virginia's House of Burgesses set the salary of Anglican clergymen at 17,280 pounds of tobacco (tobacco served the colony's cash-starved economy as currency). In 1758, however, a drought damaged the tobacco crop and prices rose three times higher than normal, meaning that the purchasing power of each pound of tobacco increased threefold. To head off a windfall profit to the clergy, the Burgesses—most of whom were large property owners loath to pay more taxes to pay the clergymen, authorized cash payments equivalent to tobacco at two pennies a pound. When the parsons challenged the measure, the Privy Council vetoed it, declaring that any colonial legislation reversing previously enacted statutes was unenforceable until approved by the Privy Council.

Patrick Henry protested London's intrusion into Virginia's affairs. An eloquent landowner and lawyer, Henry argued: "a king by disallowing acts of this salutary nature . . . degenerates into a tyrant, and forfeits all rights to his subjects' obedience." By talking about the king forfeiting the obedience of his subjects, Henry foretold of the Declaration of Independence.

The second incident occurred in 1761 when the British Crown and Parliament sought to put an end to illegal colonial trading during the French and Indian War through **writs of assistance**. These general search warrants allowed British officials to rummage through colonial shops and warehouses for illegal merchandise. Young Boston attorney James Otis, Jr., representing the city's merchants, called the writs "instruments of slavery" and asserted that such an act of the British government "against the constitution is void." Otis, like Henry, challenged the legitimacy of Britain's rule over the colonies, charging that king and Parliament had violated the rights of Americans as loyal British subjects. "Then and there," John Adams later recalled, "independence was born."

In these early controversies, Americans like Otis and Henry who voiced opposition to Parliament insisted on the colonists' freedom to manage their own affairs since they were not represented in Parliament. But it is important to note that while they demanded freedom for themselves, they did not extend the idea of liberty to others who felt oppressed and politically disfranchised.

Emerging Democratic Impulses

Apart from defining the colonies' relationship to Great Britain, American political cultures nurtured some very democratic ideas. To many colonists, the rhetoric of freedom and tyranny described their attitudes toward local ruling elites, in particular, the wealthy merchants and aristocratic landowners who had the attention of colonial governors, held most of the seats in the colonial assemblies, and hand picked county sheriffs.

> What kinds of democratic impulses surfaced in the colonies?

One of the wellsprings of radical thought was a group of British Whigs who had grown disillusioned by the selfishness and corruption they observed in the Whig ministries. Among the radical Whigs were essayists John Trenchard and Thomas Gordon who from 1720 to 1723 collaborated on *Cato's Letters*, political tracts that condemned tyranny and touted limited government, representative government, and government that respected personal liberty. An estimated one half of private libraries in colonial America at the time of the Revolution contained copies of some or all of the essays.

Another source of what the Anglican minister Charles Woodmason termed "democratical and common wealth principles" was the Great Awakening (see pp. 121-22). New Light Presbyterian preachers along with Baptists and Moravians delivered a distinctly anti-authoritarian, anti-elitist message. They were especially effective in arousing backcountry farmers against the official Anglican Church. This not only helped launch the revolt against Great Britain but also, in North and South Carolina especially, an insurgency against wealthy planters and corrupt governors, assemblymen, and sheriffs (see p. 149). Indeed, one revivalist urged his followers "to question and judge all and refuse subjection to every proper judicature."

And for many colonists, freedom was not a rhetorical abstraction but a driving aspiration for their literal existence. For indentured men and women, slaves, free African Americans, and Native Americans, motivation did not spring solely from philosophical tracts or newspaper essays—although many knew full well what was going on around them—but rather from the yearning to be free from masters or from poachers and land speculators. Such was the impulse in the 1750s that drove African-born slave Venture Smith to make the first of many determined but unsuccessful breaks for freedom from his master in Connecticut, accompanied by three white indentured servants. Smith ultimately succeeded, and while most enslaved Americans did not, the goal of many was nothing short of revolution against a system maintained or acquiesced in by the same persons complaining metaphorically about colonial enslavement by British masters. As Benjamin Franklin noted: "Every slave may be reckoned a domestic enemy."

Addressing Imperial Problems

At the conclusion of the French and Indian War, the British government grappled with problems stemming from the acquisition of France's former territories. Eager to take

> Why and how did Parliament seek to raise tax revenue in the colonies?

advantage of French evacuation of the rich Ohio Valley, colonists scrambled for possession. Clashes between settlers and Shawnee, Mingo, Delaware, and other Indian nations of the region had prompted George III to issue the **Proclamation of 1763** barring settlement west of the crest of the Appalachian Mountains (see p. 127). While improving relations between Native Americans and British authorities, the Proclamation fed resentment among colonists, for not only did it close the door to land-hungry immigrants from Europe and the sons of daughters of New England and Chesapeake yeoman farmers but it also canceled the speculative ventures of a number of prominent Virginians, including George Mason and George Washington.

The British government ran up a huge debt during the French and Indian War. Garrisoning British troops in America to enforce the Proclamation of 1763 added to the government's expenses. Paring down the debt and paying the expenses meant raising taxes. With British taxpayers already groaning under a backbreaking tax burden, George Grenville, the king's treasury minister and Parliament's majority leader, looked for new revenue sources. Parliament had never taxed the colonies for the purpose of taking money from them, although the colonial assemblies had taxed their citizens for money to build roads, and Parliament had levied taxes on colonial trade in order to make imports too expensive to buy, in which case no money would actually be collected. Grenville looked to tap into North America's money supply.

In 1764 Parliament passed the **Revenue Act**, also called the **Sugar Act**, which targeted American molasses imports—a lively but illegal commerce under the Molasses Act. Grenville intended to legitimize the molasses trade by paring the molasses duty in half, scarcely more than smugglers customarily paid to buy off officials. The Revenue Act also added various European wines to the list of "enumerated" products the colonists had to purchase from English merchants. Another of Grenville's measures, the **Currency Act** of 1764, prohibited the use of paper money in the colonies, which labored under chronic shortages of gold and silver coins. The ban on paper currency threatened to depress colonial economies. Some colonial merchants and dockside laborers objected to these measures because they expected they would dampen trade and affect their livelihoods. But members of the North Carolina and Virginia assemblies raised a vital principle, insisting that their

constituents possessed an "exemption from the burden of all taxes not granted by themselves"—in other words "no taxation without representation."

In the spring of 1765, Parliament passed the **Stamp Act**, which taxed legal documents, newspapers, diplomas, playing cards, and similar items, requiring that they bear a stamp showing that the tax had been paid. Authorities designated special tax collectors to distribute the stamps. Benjamin Franklin, in London at the time as the agent for Pennsylvania, suggested to Grenville an alternative approach, requisitioning money from the colonial assemblies, a tactic that would respect the right of loyal British subjects to give their consent through elected representatives. But Grenville refused, doubting that the colonies would tax themselves and determined to assert Parliament's sovereignty. Grenville's refusal made it clear that Americans did not possess the same constitutional rights as the men and women residing in Britain. Thus diminished by British government officials, some Americans began to reinvent themselves.

For most Americans, this was a difficult time, as Franklin's experience showed. He urged a close friend in Philadelphia to accept appointment as a tax collector, but he also expected a strong reaction to the Stamp Act in the colonies, advising his friend that "coolness and steadiness" would eventually reconcile the people to the measure. "In the meantime, a firm loyalty to the Crown and faithful adherence to the government of this nation will always be the wisest course for you and I to take, whatever may be the madness of the populace." But Franklin, one of America's most astute political observers, failed to anticipate the storm of colonial protest that blew up.

Colonial Resistance to the Stamp Act

News of the Stamp Act reached the colonies within weeks of its passage, and the reaction was swift and strong. Journalists and pamphleteers,

> How did Americans react to the Stamp Act?

themselves directly affected by the new tax, condemned Parliamentary taxation for the purpose of raising revenue. Taxes were gifts by the people's representatives to their government, they said. Taxation without representation amounted to confiscation and an assault on their liberty. Grenville's measures, wrote Stephen Johnson of Connecticut, were the first step in a nefarious scheme "to rivet the chains of slavery upon us forever."

Citizens, male, female, black, and white, took to the streets of colonial cities to protest the Stamp Act.

In May, Patrick Henry presented to Virginia's House of Burgesses six resolutions variously denouncing the Stamp Act. Henry's oratory reflected radical colonists' determination to revive the "country's dying liberty." He asserted Virginia's "*exclusive*" right to tax its inhabitants, thus rejecting the concept of virtual representation in Parliament. Thomas Jefferson, a young law student and gentleman planter at the time, listened raptly to Henry's "splendid display," while more conservative burgesses responded with shouts of "treason." The assembly passed four of Henry's resolutions, and copies of these **Virginia Resolves**, along with the two more radical ones that were not passed, circulated among the other colonies.

The most violent response to the Stamp Act occurred in economically distressed Boston, where opposition to parliamentary taxation mixed with resentment of increasing social and economic inequality. A small group of artisans and shopkeepers, calling themselves the **Sons of Liberty**, directed their anger at tax collector Andrew Oliver and Lieutenant Governor Thomas Hutchinson, a descendant of the colony's famous dissenter Anne Hutchinson. Hutchinson believed in personal liberty but more so in social order and Parliamentary

authority. He and Oliver represented Boston's elite, and many common citizens focused their fury on them and their property. On the night of August 14, Ebenezer Mackintosh, a poor cobbler and veteran of the French and Indian War, led an angry mob that destroyed Oliver's house. Twelve nights later, Mackintosh's mob descended on Hutchinson's house and tore it to pieces. Later they danced and cheered around a pole erected in the working-class part of Boston, calling it a **Liberty Tree.**

The "damned rebellious spirit" in Virginia and Massachusetts inspired colonial resistance elsewhere. Angry colonists threatened stamp collectors in New York and Newport if they dared to distribute the hated revenue stamps. Responding to a circular letter issued by the Massachusetts House of Representatives, twenty-seven delegates from nine colonies gathered in New York during October of 1765 to consider tactics for securing the act's repeal. The other colonies, Virginia, New Hampshire, North Carolina, and Georgia, voted to support the **Stamp Act Congress**, which issued a **Declaration of the Rights and Grievances of the Colonies** acknowledging Parliament's right to regulate trade but not to levy taxes on the colonies. It also organized a boycott of English trade goods. Grenville's ministry did not survive the Stamp Act crisis, not because of the colonial unrest but because George III did not like him. The King replaced Grenville with the Earl of Rockingham, a moderate who favored repeal of the Stamp Act. English merchants who felt the bite of American boycotts also urged the government to relent. Former Prime Minister William Pitt supported the colonists, declaring that Parliament was "entirely wrong." In 1766, Parliament repealed the Stamp Act, but not the principle of sovereignty. The **Declaratory Act** reasserted Parliament's right to legislate for the colonies "in all cases whatsoever." In other words, Parliament demanded nothing less than total submission. Parliament's words did not offend the colonists as much as its acts, and within a matter of months new measures came forth.

The Townshend Act Leads to Bloody Confrontation

The next crisis did not arise until George III scrapped the weak Rockingham government and asked the aging and ailing Pitt, now the Earl of

> **How did the Townshend Acts deal with the tax issue, and how did colonists react?**

Chatham, to form a new one. Chatham's lieutenant, Charles Townshend, took charge of financial policies and touched off a new controversy. Townshend remembered some by Benjamin Franklin that while Americans objected to direct (internal) taxes they did not oppose external taxes on foreign trade. In 1767 Townshend proposed taxes on glass, lead, paint, paper, and tea imported into the colonies, and Parliament enacted them. He also set up an American Board of Customs Commissioners, headquartered in Boston, to supervise tax collection and utilized the juryless vice-admiralty courts to try smugglers. Townshend hoped not only to raise substantial sums but also to use it to pay royal governors, freeing them from dependence on colonial assemblies.

Colonists saw right through the **Townshend Acts**. "Is it possible to form an idea of Slavery more compleat, more miserable, more disgraceful," exclaimed Boston's fiery radical and former brewer Samuel Adams. Franklin and Townshend had grossly erred; Americans objected to all Parliamentary levies, internal or external. John Dickinson, a respected landowner and lawyer, hoped that protests against the Townshend Acts would be peaceful, unlike the Stamp Act riots. Between December 1767 and February 1768, he addressed a series of *Letters from a Farmer in Pennsylvania* to London officials in which he painstakingly explained that since Americans had no representation in Parliament they could not consent to taxes. In February 1768, Adams and James Otis persuaded the Massachusetts House of Representatives to issue a **Circular Letter** to every other colony calling for a joint petition to Parliament to repeal the Townshend Acts.

Non-violent protest took other forms too. Another colonial boycott of British goods aimed to pressure British merchants. American men and women showed their support by wearing shirts, pants, dresses, shoes, stockings, a hat, gloves, and even wigs manufactured in the colonies. Women of Lancaster, Pennsylvania, produced over 35,000 yards of woven cloth in one year to replace the loss of boycotted British fabrics. Colonists eschewed English tea. One Philadelphia resident supported the boycott in verse.

For the sake of Freedom's name

(Since British Wisdom scorns repealing)

Come, sacrifice to Patriot fame

And give up Tea, by way of healing

This done, within ourselves retreat.

The Industrious arts of life to follow

Let proud Nabobs storm and fret

They cannot force our lips to swallow.

Keeping the protests peaceful was virtually impossible, however, and again, the stormiest clouds gathered over Boston. Authorities in London instructed Massachusetts' governor Francis Bernard to force the colonial assembly to rescind the Circular Letter. When the representatives refused, Bernard suspended representative government. When the customs commissioners learned that in the previous two and a half years officers had arrested only six suspected smugglers and successfully prosecuted just one, they resolved to clamp down on illicit commerce. In April 1768, customs officials attempted to seize merchant John Hancock's sloop *Liberty*, sparking an ugly riot. The violence caused British authorities to order Redcoats into the city and added to the provocation by invoking the **Quartering Act** that required the colony to accommodate the soldiers. Scuffles between gangs of citizens and off-duty soldiers in Boston were a common occurrence.

The bloodiest confrontation took place on the frigid evening of March 5, 1770. A crowd of protesters collected outside the customs house on King Street and began taunting a British sentry. They shouted angry insults, calling him a "damned rascally scoundrel son-of-a-bitch." Captain Thomas Preston brought in reinforcements who lined up in front of the customs house with their muskets loaded and their bayonets pointed at the crowd. When someone in the street hurled a chunk of ice that struck a soldier and caused him to slip, the troops fired, hitting eleven of the civilians. Three died instantly, including Crispus Attucks, a seaman and perhaps a fugitive slave who had been one of the leaders of the Boston crowd. Two others succumbed later in what the colonists immediately condemned as the **Boston Massacre**.

A court acquitted Captain Preston and all but two of his men of wrongdoing, which further eroded colonial respect for British authority. Lawyer John Adams, as fiercely resistant to British tyranny as any colonist but fearful of radical mobs taking to the streets, defended the British officer, blaming the crowd for the incident. The Boston Massacre played into the hands of colonial radicals who cited the killings as further evidence that the London government had gone mad with power and was determined to reduce all Americans to slavery. Colonial resistance was becoming more determined.

Insurgency Against Colonial Elites

> **What ignited insurgencies against colonial elites, and how did they impact the growing colonial conflict with Britain?**

While the crises over the Stamp Act and Townshend Acts drew colonial men and women in colonial seaports into concerted protests against what they regarded as illegal British authority, other insurgencies targeted oppression perpetrated by colonists themselves.

In the backcountry of North Carolina, yeoman farmers groaned under burdensome taxes levied on them by their assembly representatives—wealthy planters for the most part and the Anglican Church from the colony's eastern regions. When the cash-starved farmers could not pay the taxes, local sheriffs and judges evicted them and sold their property to land speculators. Anger grew into fury when the assembly voted a huge appropriation from tax revenue to build a mansion for Governor William Tryon. Led by a spirited settler named Herman Husband, who had left the Anglican Church to join the Society of Friends, the farmers organized the **Regulator Movement** with the goal of regulating or, more properly ending, "the unequal chances the poor and the weak have in contention with the rich and powerful." Governor Tryon refused to address the farmers' grievances, declaring he would try, condemn, and hang "all those who bear the title of regulators." Among Tryon's supporters were planters who at the time were active in the colonial protest against British tyranny. In May of 1771, the governor mobilized the colonial militia and crushed an armed force of Regulators near the Alamance River. Husband, whose Quaker pacifism forbade his participation in violent conflict, did not join in the battle, but Tryon did execute six other Regulators.

In New York's Hudson Valley, angry renters staged a revolt when their aristocratic landlords began canceling all long-term leases and replacing them with short-term ones. At first, the protests were

acts of individual defiance, such as when tenant Joseph Paine girdled and felled 1,200 trees on Livingston Manor and reportedly told another that Robert Livingston, the owner of the sprawling estate who joined the rebellion against British tyranny, could "kiss his a-s." Through the Stamp Act and Townshend Act crises, tensions mounted, and joining the tenants' revolt were Wappinger Indians who had never been paid for the land that had been taken from them and doled out to the landlords in the seventeenth century. In July of 1766, tenants armed with clubs and pitchforks marched on New York City, where of some of the landlords, active in the Sons of Liberty, maintained mansions that the rioters planned to tear down and where the tenants hoped to find allies among urban working people. But Governor Henry Moore called out the militia along with British regular troops stationed in the city and put the rioters to flight.

The tenants' rebellion did not produce a poor-people's coalition against the elite; nor did the Wappingers receive compensation for their lost land or the Regulators obtain redress of their grievances. But when the American Revolution compelled Americans take a stand for independence or loyalty to the Crown, the bitter taste of these defeats influenced their decisions.

THINKING BACK

1. How did the perspectives of American colonists and British government officials differ on the importance of freedom within the empire? Accordingly, which colonists opposed British regulations and taxes and why?
2. What specific situations developed in the 1760s that contributed to the formation of a distinctive American identity?
3. By the end of the 1760s, how democratic were colonial American societies, and how did colonial elites and poor Americans differ in their understanding of freedom?

UNTYING THE IMPERIAL KNOT: FROM COLONIES TO NATIONHOOD

Tensions eased later in 1770 when George III asked the amiable Frederick Lord North to form a new ministry. Under North's direction, Parliament repealed most of the Townshend duties but kept the tax on tea as a matter of principle. During this "pause in politics," life returned to a more normal footing. The colonists dropped the non-importation campaign and imports from Britain nearly doubled. Sporadic clashes occurred, such as in June 1772 when radicals in Rhode Island burned the British patrol boat *Gaspée* that had run aground in Narragansett Bay while chasing an American ship suspected of smuggling. The British admiralty set up a commission of inquiry, separate from colonial courts, to identify and hold suspects. The commission could find no witnesses to the incident; nevertheless, as word spread, colonists became alarmed that British authorities would bypass colonial judicial systems. In Virginia, Thomas Jefferson, Richard Henry Lee, and Patrick Henry persuaded the House of Burgesses to appoint a committee of correspondence to conduct regular exchanges with similar groups in other colonial legislatures (only Pennsylvania refused to participate). The committees signified a growing colonial unity and stiffening resistance to the actions of the government in London. But then the issue shifted from Parliament's right to tax to whether the British government had any authority over the colonies at all. Resistance thus turned into revolution.

Tea Act Trickery Backfires

<table>
<tr><td>What was the motive for the Tea Act, and how did colonists receive it?</td></tr>
</table>

In addition to concerns about the growing colonial defiance, Lord North worried about the woeful financial condition of the East India Company, one of the major players in the British imperial economy (see the Global Perspective pp. 134-36). The firm traded in tea purchased in India and distributed throughout the British Empire; unfortunately, an enormous tax burden cut deeply into the company's profits. Boycotts and smuggling had virtually eliminated the American market. Lord North conceived of a clever plan.

The **Tea Act**, which Parliament passed in 1773, rebated some of the taxes the company paid in England. Furthermore, the act granted the company a monopoly on the distribution of tea in America; thus, it reduced the price of East India Company tea while cutting colonial merchants out of the profitable retail tea business. Thus Lord North might bail the East India Company out of trouble and at the same time seduce the Americans into buying relatively cheap English tea and paying the hated Townshend duty.

If the prime minister believed he could outsmart the colonists, however, he was greatly mistaken. As news of the Tea Act spread through the colonies, protesters prepared to prevent the unloading of tea. In New York and Philadelphia, angry crowds turned away ships carrying the tea. Authorities in Charleston managed to unload the cargo and store it in a warehouse, but it was never sold and eventually rotted. In Boston, where radical colonists and royal officials remained at one another's throats, the arrival of East India Company tea on board the *Dartmouth* on November 28 set up a dramatic showdown. On the evening of December 16, Ebenezer Mackintosh and the Sons of Liberty made their move. Curiously disguised as Indians, they marched to the wharf, boarded the ship, and tossed 90,000 pounds of tea into Boston harbor. This audacious act of defiance came to be known as the **Boston Tea Party**.

Parliament and Colonists Dig In

The Boston Tea Party enraged the King George III and his advisors. The mob's actions, they asserted, showed an utter disregard for law and authority. Even the sympathetic Chatham characterized the episode as

<table>
<tr><td>Why did Parliament pass the Coercive Acts, and how did the colonists respond?</td></tr>
</table>

"criminal." In January of 1774, members of the Privy Council vented their anger on colonial agent Benjamin Franklin in an episode that illustrated the hardening of positions on both sides of the imperial dispute. Franklin had hoped for reconciliation, so with the intent of blaming a lower official for offensive British policies, he had sent documents to Massachusetts purporting to show that Governor Thomas Hutchinson had been reporting falsely about the colonists' intentions. But his dispatch touched off an angry reaction in Boston, and the Privy Council in London assailed him publicly, accusing him of fomenting rebellion. Franklin remained in London for several months then returned to Philadelphia disillusioned about those who were running the empire and prepared to join the resistance.

The conflict between Britain and the colonies had hardened into a constitutional issue over authority. Lord North correctly summed matters up: it was no longer "a dispute between internal and external taxes . . . but we are now to dispute whether we have, or have not any authority in that country." In the spring of 1774, Parliament reacted to the Boston Tea Party by passing a series of **Coercive Acts** that severely punished Bostonians. The Boston Port Act halted maritime commerce, except for shipments of food and fuel, until the town paid for the tea. The Massachusetts Government Act forbade town meetings without royal permission. The Impartial Administration of Justice Act moved the trials of royal officials accused of crimes in the colonies to courts in England. A new Quartering Act once again required colonial citizens to accommodate British soldiers in their homes. To the colonists, the Coercive Acts were **Intolerable Acts**. Although not included in the Coercive Acts, the **Quebec Act** established French civil law and the Roman Catholic Church in Quebec and extended that province's boundary south to the Ohio River, a conciliatory gesture intended to bond the predominantly French population more tightly to Britain. Rebellious American colonists, however, who were overwhelmingly Protestant, resented the measure because it promoted the Catholic Church in the coveted Ohio Valley. Moreover, by placing the Ohio country into Quebec, the Quebec Act jeopardized the massive grants previously made by Virginia, which claimed the territory, to speculators that now included Patrick Henry and Thomas Jefferson as well as George Washington and George Mason. They and many other colonists put the Quebec Act together with the other "Intolerable Acts."

Requiring Boston to pay for the Tea Party was one thing, but striking at cherished local government was quite another. The Coercive Acts reinforced the growing perception that Parliament intended to destroy colonial liberties. That, George Washington wrote to a friend, was "as clear as the sun in its meridian brightness." King George III's assent to the acts signaled the Crown complicity with Parliament. Still, a number of colonists, perhaps most, agreed with Pennsylvania's John Dickinson that "everything may yet be attributed to . . . half a dozen . . . fools or knaves" and not to Great Britain as a whole. Furthermore, Dickinson hoped, the colonists would continue to petition the Crown to redress their legitimate grievances rather than resort to violence.

To consider their options, every colony except Georgia commissioned delegates to attend a **Continental Congress** that convened in Philadelphia on September 5, 1774. The fifty-six representatives gathered in Carpenters' Hall, a meeting place for tradesmen, and included many men who now were becoming recognized as colonial leaders: Samuel and John Adams, Patrick Henry, and John Dickinson. "More sensible and fine fellows you would never wish to see," one colonist said. Despite the presence of a few firebrands, however, Congress proceeded cautiously.

The delegates debated a wide range of options, from attacking British Redcoats in Boston to creating an inter-colonial legislature that would cooperate with Parliament in governing the colonies. They finally adopted a **Declaration of Rights**, which reiterated their objection to parliamentary taxation while declaring that they would "cheerfully consent" to regulation of their trade. They also agreed that until the oppression of Boston ended and the broader issue of sovereignty was resolved, a **Continental Association** would organize another boycott of British commerce. Congress encouraged the formation of local vigilante committees to enforce the boycott. The delegates adjourned on October 26 with a call for a Second Continental Congress to meet the following May.

Many citizens applauded the delegates as they returned home. Among the general colonial population, hope ran high that firmness would induce Parliament to back down. But several delegates were less optimistic; they sensed trouble ahead. The conservative-minded detected a readiness to embrace what Joseph Galloway of Pennsylvania called the "ill-shapen, diminutive brat, INDEPENDENCY." They believed independence was neither legal nor practical. Radicals worried about defections that could derail the resistance. Most colonial assemblies endorsed the Congress's action. Consequently, under orders from officials in London, royal governors dissolved those colonial legislatures. Committees of safety and unofficial elected assemblies for all practical purposes took over the operation of colonial government. Governors in royal colonies continued to hold their positions but without support they were powerless.

Not every American fell into line behind the Continental Congress, the Continental Association, or the local committees of safety, which created tension and led to abuses. "Damn them all," snorted one Virginian. Opposition to the Association resounded in areas such as Georgia where whites feared the loss of British arms at a time of frequent Indian attacks. Quakers, who refused to swear oaths, also withheld support from the boycott. Many colonists remained indifferent. The committees of safety and patriot mobs tried to intimidate those who refused to rally to the cause. They harassed non-supporters by branding them "enemies of the country." Incidents of tarring and feathering and other mistreatment occurred frequently. Because Samuel Jarvis of Fairfield County, Connecticut, opposed the resistance, vigilantes broke into his house, stripped Jarvis, his wife, and his four children completely naked, and rowed them into Long Island Sound. They then forced the Jarvises to wade ashore totally exposed to heckling onlookers.

Such measures did little to inspire confidence in the virtue of rebellion. But a chain of dramatic events did a lot more.

The Shots "Heard 'Round the World"

What led to the outbreak of fighting, and what did the early skirmishing produce?

During the winter of 1774-75, rumors flew that Britain was preparing to crush the spreading rebellion. In November 1774, George III declared to Lord North that the colonies "are in a state of rebellion" and "blows must decide whether they are to be subject to this country or independent." North preferred conciliation but would not compromise Parliament's fundamental authority over the colonies. He offered to refrain from taxing them if they paid their share of imperial expenses but was ready to use force. The Continental Congress rejected North's **Conciliatory Proposition** as an insufficient concession. In the meantime, Lord Dartmouth, the minister for American affairs, ordered General Thomas Gage, who had replaced Hutchinson as Massachusetts' governor, to seize weapons and ammunition that the colonists had stockpiled in Concord, a few miles west of Boston. Dartmouth was confident that such a show of force would put an end to the resistance of a "rude rabble without plan."

During the evening of April 18, 1775, in response to Dartmouth's orders, Gage sent a regiment of 900 troops on a march from Boston to Concord. Gage hoped to avoid detection, but colonial sentinels, perhaps alerted by Gage's American-born wife, spotted troop movements and used a system of lantern signals from the steeple of Boston's Old North Church to alert residents. Outside of town, Paul Revere, a Boston silversmith, and William Dawes set out on their famous midnight ride to warn Sarah and Joseph Hodgkins and their fellow citizens that the Redcoats were coming. At dawn on April 19, the British soldiers reached Lexington, where about seventy militiamen had gathered on the grassy area known as the "green." The British commander ordered them to disperse,

but as they did so, someone fired a shot followed by a volley from the British muskets that ripped through the militiamen, killing eight and wounding ten more. This was the opening skirmish of the Revolutionary War.

The British continued on their mission, reaching Concord later that morning. There another force of Minutemen deployed to meet them. The Minutemen held their fire as the British gathered up a few weapons and five hundred musket balls (the colonists had removed the rest of the arms). Then, at midday at the North Bridge just outside of town as the Redcoats began their return march to Boston, the Minutemen attacked. Concealed behind the trees and rock fences that lined the road, they picked off the British a few at a time. Retreat turned into rout, and by day's end the British had lost 73 dead and 174 wounded, almost three times as many casualties as the colonists suffered.

News of the fighting spread rapidly through the colonies and to England and the European continent as well. The shots "Heard 'Round the World" signaled the first in a sequence of revolutions that occurred during the late eighteenth century (see the Global Perspective, pp. 134-36). Massachusetts was aflame with excitement, and militia units converged outside of Boston, where they laid siege to the town. Many citizens who had managed up until then to sustain some loyalty to England now felt alienated. Abigail Adams, John Adams' wife, wrote to friends that when British soldiers "secretly fell upon our people" it signified that "tyranny, oppression, and murder" were the "reward of all the affection, the veneration and the loyalty which has heretofore distinguished Americans."

The Final Steps to Revolution

Although most Americans still hoped for reconciliation, perhaps autonomous status within the empire, the dispute over taxes had escalated into a war. On May 10, 1775, the Second Continental Congress, now acting as a national government, convened in Philadelphia to deal with the crisis. Its task was to wage war without dashing any last chance for peace. That same day Benedict Arnold, a former New Haven, Connecticut, pharmacist and now the colonel of a militia regiment, along with Ethan Allen and his regiment of Vermont volunteers known as the Green

How did the conflict with Great Britain change after Lexington and Concord?

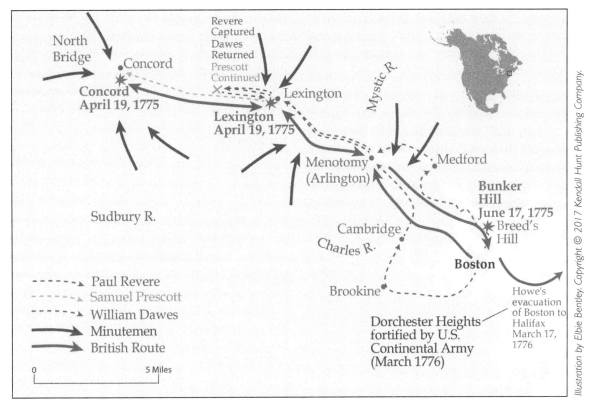

North
Bridge

Concord
Concord
April 19, 1775

Revere
Captured
Dawes
Returned
Prescott
Continued

Lexington
Lexington
April 19, 1775

Mystic R.

Menotomy
(Arlington)

Medford

Bunker
Hill
June 17, 1775
Breed's
Hill

Sudbury R.

Cambridge
Charles R.

Boston

Brookine

Dorchester Heights
fortified by U.S.
Continental Army
(March 1776)

Howe's
evacuation
of Boston to
Halifax
March 17,
1776

- - - - → Paul Revere
- - - - → Samuel Prescott
- - - - → William Dawes
━━━━→ Minutemen
━━━━→ British Route

0   5 Miles

Illustration by Elbie Bentley. Copyright © 2017 Kendall Hunt Publishing Company.

Lexington, Concord, and Bunker (Breed's) Hill were the opening engagements of the American Revolutionary War, fought even before the signing of the Declaration of Independence.

Mountain Boys assaulted Fort Ticonderoga, a British garrison on Lake Champlain that contained over 200 cannon. The Americans entered the dilapidated outpost at night, taking the slumbering soldiers by surprise. Allen shouted to the astonished British commander, who was trying to put on his pants, "Come out of there, you damned old rat." The British surrendered without a shot being fired.

In preparing for full-scale war, Congress used money contributed by the colonies to raise a Continental Army, the recruits coming mostly from New England, and asked George Washington, one of Virginia's representatives, to command it. Washington wore his officer's uniform to the Congress, indicating how much he wanted the command. But an army of New Englanders would not be easy for him to manage for some of the troops resented the idea of a slave owner from Virginia lording it over them. Indeed, some New England delegates had favored Massachusetts' Charles Lee, a veteran British army officer, to lead the army. Washington told fellow Virginian Patrick Henry: "Remember, Mr. Henry . . . from the day I enter upon the command of the American armies, I date my fall, and the ruin of my reputation." Then leaving his wife Martha at Mount Vernon, their Virginia plantation overlooking

the Potomac River, Washington drew up his last will and testament and set out for Boston.

Outside the city, Massachusetts militia units had fortified several positions on nearby heights. British General Gage resolved to drive the colonists off. On June 17, about 1,500 Redcoats stormed the American position. The leader of the assault, General William Howe, did not expect the Americans to fight. In fact, he brought along a servant bearing a wine decanter on a silver tray for his relaxation. From behind breastworks, the militiamen fired on the British troops, leaving bodies strewn "as thick as sheep in a fold." Only when they ran out of ammunition did the Americans withdraw. The **Battle of Bunker Hill**, misnamed since the fighting occurred on adjacent Breed's Hill, hardly qualified as a British triumph. They took the ground, but at the frightful cost of 226 dead and 828 wounded. American casualties totaled 411. With more victories like that, one British officer later remarked, there would be nobody left to send the news back to London.

Two weeks afterward, General Washington arrived in nearby Cambridge with the daunting task of training new recruits and forming the ragtag militiamen into a unified Continental Army. He believed, as

European commanders did, that order, discipline, and authority were the keys to military success, but trained or not, the Americans were ready to fight, and Washington appreciated that.

At the same time that it was preparing for war, Congress sent conciliatory signals to the British Crown. In July, after Bunker Hill, John Dickinson drafted an **Olive Branch Petition** stating in the most respectful terms Congress's hope for reconciliation. "**The Declaration of the Causes and Necessities of Taking Up Arms**," drafted largely by Thomas Jefferson, pointed out that while Americans felt justified in resisting enslavement, "we mean not to dissolve the Union which has so long and so happily subsisted between us." However, George III refused even to acknowledge the petitions. In October, he told Parliament that the Americans were engaged in a "desperate conspiracy" that, he said, was "manifestly carried on for the purpose of establishing an independent empire." In December, the British government outlawed all colonial commerce and in effect declared war on American shipping by allowing for the confiscation of ships and forcing or impressing their crews into the British Navy.

Meanwhile, the war swung back and forth for the Continental Army. A two-pronged offensive into Canada, aimed at winning French Canadian support, turned into disaster. In November, one force under General Richard Montgomery took Montreal. A month later, a second one commanded by now General Benedict Arnold, joined by Montgomery, laid siege to Quebec. With winter setting in and enlistments about to expire, the two commanders decided to attack. But in the fighting, Montgomery was killed, Arnold was severely wounded, and the troops suffered heavy casualties. The Americans withdrew from Canada, which remained outside of the Revolution. However, during the winter, troops from Fort Ticonderoga dragged 100 cannons across 300 miles of snow and ice to Boston, where Washington deployed them on Dorchester Heights overlooking the city. The British position inside Boston was now untenable, and in March, 1776, the Redcoats withdrew to Nova Scotia. The British evacuation of Boston served as an antidote to the distressing failure of the Canada offensive.

The Difficult Decision for Independence

A "frenzy of revenge seems to have seized all ranks of people," Jefferson had reported after the first blood had spilled at Lexington and Concord. Still, most colonists imagined somehow patching up the quarrel with Britain. Even John Adams confessed to being "as fond of reconciliation . . . as any man." But stronger than his fondness was his conviction that liberty depended on independence. "The cancer [of corruption] is too deeply rooted and too far spread to be cured by anything short of cutting it out entire."

> **When and why did a majority of the colonial citizenry conclude that independence was the proper course of action?**

During the winter of 1775–76, many moderates joined the independence camp. Thomas Paine, a failed businessman, radical English Whig, recent immigrant, and talented political writer, aroused popular passions with his pamphlet *Common Sense*. Paine called for independence and used many devices of persuasion to induce the undecided to choose revolution. One was to point out the apparent illogic of an island governing a continent. Shortly after *Common Sense* appeared, George III hired several regiments of German soldiers to help crush the rebellion, news of which many colonists received with deep foreboding.

Even so, in 1775 about 20 percent of all the colonists remained loyal to Britain. Their choices were often personal rather than ideological. Jonathan Sewell of Massachusetts had formed a network of friendships among royal officials when he entered the legal profession and remained attached to them throughout the crisis. In 1775 he departed America for England and never regretted his decision. However, Sewell's wife Esther longed for her American friends and family. Philadelphia Quaker merchant Henry Drinker's conscience would not permit him to support armed rebellion. Loyalists were most numerous in New York and Pennsylvania and fewest in Massachusetts, but identification with Great Britain was evident everywhere. Members of the colonial elite, especially those with government appointments or merchants tied closely to England, often remained loyal to Britain. Numerous laborers and small farmers of the Chesapeake region, long resentful of the merchant and planter aristocracy, declared allegiance to the Crown when their wealthy neighbors opted for independence.

African-American slaves made choices too, as did Indians whose communities were situated along the edges of the United States. Men and women heard the rhetoric about freedom from the slavery of Parliamentary laws, but for them slavery was not rhetorical. Freedom meant escape from their masters, and many slaves took advantage of spreading disorder to abscond. Others revolted. In June 1775, South Carolina authorities tried and executed ex-slave Thomas Jeremiah, known as Jerry, for inciting a slave revolt. A New Jersey escapee who called himself Colonel Tye led a band of fifty runaway slaves and servants who fought in conjunction with the British but primarily for their own freedom. In November 1775, Virginia's governor, Lord Dunmore, proclaimed freedom for any slave who joined British military forces. During the Revolution, at least one out of every five slaves took shelter under British protection, sometimes bearing arms, often performing manual labor, and sometimes winding up back in the hands of their rebellions masters.

Iroquois, Shawnee, Creek, and Chickasaw nations had established peaceful and advantageous commercial relationships with English merchants since the end of the French and Indian War. It was the American colonists that threatened them the most. Loyalty to Britain was an easy choice for many Indians.

Loyalists suffered severely for their decisions. One patriot minister exhorted his congregation to "curse those cowardly, selfish, cringing, lukewarm, half-way, two-faced people, and . . . treat them as out-casts." **Patriots** seized Loyalists' property and sold it at public auction. Approximately 80,000 Loyalists fled into exile during the Revolution. A large number, including 5,000 black men and women, settled in Canada. Many Loyalists migrated to the West Indies. Others, like Thomas Hutchinson, took up residence in England. Few of them found either acceptance or contentment. Racial prejudice against African Americans among whites in Nova Scotia motivated 1,190 black refugees to sail on to West Africa where in 1792 they founded the colony of Sierra Leone.

Loyalists were not only innocent victims. Loyalist battalions augmented British forces and attacked supporters of the Revolution, often brutally. In the South and out in the western territories, they played major roles in the war. In the Ohio territory, they murdered white settlers and Indians thought to be supporting the Revolution. In addition to serving as combatants, both men and women, black and white, served the Crown as saboteurs, spies, and informants.

About one-fourth of the colonial population, including many backcountry and newly arrived residents, remained uncommitted to either side. Some saw little difference for themselves between Patriots and

Image © Victorian Traditions, 2010. Used by permission of Shutterstock, Inc.

Benjamin Franklin, John Adams, and Thomas Jefferson review a draft of the Declaration of Independence. Although Adams was more out front in the independence movement, Jefferson possessed superior literary talent and was the Declaration's principal author, prompting Adams later to complain that the Virginian made off with "all the glory."

Loyalists. One New Jersey man observed: Let who will be king, I will know that I shall be the subject." Others remained emotionally attached to the countries of their birth. A young Lutheran minister named Nicholas Collin refused to swear allegiance to either the revolutionary cause or George III. "Being a Swedish subject, I could not give my oath . . . to any but my own government."

By spring of 1776, radicals who favored independence had gained control of the resistance movement. Communities everywhere proclaimed that since George III and his party in Parliament had violated the covenant with his subjects, they could rightfully dissolve their allegiance to his tyrannical government. Colonies declared themselves independent states. In June, the Virginia assembly instructed its delegate to the Continental Congress, Richard Henry Lee, to offer a resolution that "these United Colonies are, and of right ought to be, free and independent States, that they are absolved from all allegiance to the British Crown, and that all political connection between them and the State of Great Britain is, and ought to be, totally dissolved."

As Congress debated Lee's resolution, it appointed a committee consisting of John Adams, Benjamin Franklin, Roger Sherman, Robert R. Livingston, and Thomas Jefferson to draft an explanation of the decision for independence. The other four deferred to Jefferson, a radical and a brilliant writer. On July 2, 1776, Congress passed Lee's resolution unanimously, and on July 4, after heavy editing of Jefferson's draft to improve its style and temper its tone, Congress approved the **Declaration of Independence**. All the delegates except John Dickinson and three others eventually signed the document. Congress printed copies and distributed it throughout the country. The die was cast.

The British Crown did not acknowledge the Declaration of Independence. Thus, an independent United States was still hypothetical. Not until other countries, including Great Britain, recognized American independence would it be a fact.

THINKING BACK

1. How did colonial protest against British government policy and the goal of protecting liberties under the British constitution evolve into a movement for independence?
2. What choices did the colonists have to make as the crisis deepened? What influenced their decisions?
3. How democratic was the resistance movement as it built toward the goal of independence? What democratic ideals emerged? For what reasons did some choose not to support independence?

THE LOCAL PERSPECTIVE: FOCUS ON IDENTITY AND REVOLUTION IN *LUISIANA*

Although half a continent away from the center of the American Revolution, residents of Louisiana could understand rebellious British colonists' frustration with distant rule and oppressive regulations. Spain had acquired French Louisiana west of the

> How did the French citizens of Louisiana respond to Spain's takeover in 1763?

Mississippi River in 1763 following the French and Indian War to buffer the riches of New Spain against aggressive settlers from the British colonies. Conflicts over identity and nationhood in their newly acquired territory gave Spanish officials many headaches. Furthermore, paying for the administration of a vast territory strained Spain's royal coffers. Former citizens of French *La Louisiane* chafed under the authority of Spanish *Luisiana*. The Spanish Crown utilized the existing French civil and military structures rather than instituting new ones, but a Spanish legal system significantly altered the lives of Louisiana's predominantly French and African-American Creole residents.

Luisiana's first governor, Don Antonio de Ulloa, was a scientist and scholar but unfortunately also a tactless administrator. Ulloa refused to consult with the local residents who were used to running their own affairs, and his arrogance undermined Spanish authority among the colony's French residents. But the problems were political as well as cultural and personal. For budgetary reasons, Ulloa reduced customary gifting to Quapaw and other Indians and imposed trade restrictions on French merchants who had been accustomed to trading with whomever came calling: French, English, Dutch, or Indian. Independent-minded French Acadians (exiles from Nova Scotia and the forebears of today's Louisiana Cajuns) were frustrated too. They wanted to settle where they pleased, but since Ulloa's priority was defense against the British and their Indian allies, he ordered the Acadians to settle around established forts along the northeastern frontier to provide additional manpower in case of attack by enemies. Their rejected petitions to be allowed to choose their own home sites heightened tensions.

On October 28, 1768, several hundred Acadians descended on New Orleans. After fortifying themselves with wine, they joined French insurrectionists and deposed Ulloa. Spanish authorities appointed the Irish-born Alejandro O'Reilly to succeed Ulloa, and O'Reilly, a soldier, restored order and executed the rebellion's ringleaders. But he did allow the Acadians to relocate. Most chose to live along the lower Mississippi River or in the bayou country of southwestern Louisiana. O'Reilly also relaxed the trade restraints and resumed the French custom of providing generous gifts to Indians. As a result, Spanish administration of Louisiana showed substantial improvement.

Spain's grip on the province steadily weakened, however. More French immigrants entered Luisiana during the Spanish period than during the years of

French sovereignty. Refugees from the Canadian frontier settled in and around St. Louis (then still part of the Luisiana territory). These French émigrés preferred Spanish Catholic rule to British Protestantism, but they retained their French identity and Creole French language. English and Scots-Irish settlers from South Carolina and Georgia also migrated into the territory, some traveling as far as Texas where they founded Gálveztown (Galveston), the first Anglo settlement in the Spanish borderlands and named for Bernardo de Gálvez who served for a time as governor of Luisiana and as Spanish viceroy of New Spain.

Relationships between Africans and Europeans in colonial Louisiana differed strikingly from those in other areas of North America. French colonists had accepted mixed-race children as white; however, Spanish law established a hierarchy of race categories based on skin color. The Spanish slave code required slave owners to establish a price for their slaves and allowed slaves to buy their freedom. Consequently, the number of free African Americans in Spanish Luisiana was exceptionally high—one in four of all African Americans in New Orleans by the 1880s. Although Luisiana's free blacks included many prosperous individuals, like Santiago Durom, the first licensed African-American physician, most held menial and low-paying jobs as seamstresses, laundresses, carpenters, and shoemakers.

The switch from *La Louisiane* to *Luisiana* permanently affected the province, particularly the southern part known as the district of Orleans. Even today evidence abounds of the Spanish presence. Two fires, one in 1788 and the other in 1794, destroyed much of the French Quarter. Rebuilt, it included many Spanish-style wrought-iron balconies and central courtyards. The Cabildo in downtown New Orleans stands as a reminder of the Spanish government that designed and constructed the city's first levees and drainage canals. Racial intermingling within the French Quarter and elaborate funerals and carnaval traditions of the African-American population further accent Spain's influence.

THINKING BACK

1. What caused the revolt against Spanish authority in October of 1768?
2. What signs of Spanish influence in Louisiana are visible today?

FIGHTING FOR INDEPENDENCE

Since the British Crown intended to use force to put down the American rebellion, independence would have to be won on the battlefield. At the outset, the United States faced great odds but also some encouraging prospects. Although Britain possessed enormous military might, many British men and women opposed the war, including a third of the members of Parliament and the author of a pamphlet who dreaded a war "against an enemy we now find united, active, able, and resolute." Still, George III and his ministers could draw on a comparatively large population for soldiers and workers and a superior industrial capacity for weapons, ammunition, and other military hardware. Britain possessed a highly trained and disciplined army, supplemented by regiments from the German principality of Hesse-Cassel, and an impressive navy. The challenge was figuring out how to divert sufficient resources to America to suppress the colonial rebellion while still maintaining an adequate force at home to fight European foes.

The Americans fought on their own ground, which gave them certain advantages. Local women provided food and clothing, nursed sick and wounded troops, and gathered intelligence regarding British forces. Skilled gunsmiths manufactured long-barreled rifles that, in the hands of expert marksmen, were deadly over a range of 200 yards. Militia units formed spontaneously to harass British armies and supplement the Continental Army before impending battles. While not always trained and disciplined, the Americans possessed a zeal that came from devotion to a cause. Furthermore, the Americans could win simply by avoiding being destroyed and exhausting Britain's will, whereas the British had to crush the rebellion. And finally, the American Revolution became a global war as the United States obtained help from France and Spain.

Bearing Arms

Raising and maintaining an effective fighting force challenged Revolutionary leaders almost as much as the Redcoats did. At the outset, the country relied on volunteer soldiers.

> **What problems did the Continental Congress encounter, and how did it solve them?**

The patriots' fear of tyrannical authority made them suspicious of a trained professional army. At first, after Lexington, Concord, and Bunker Hill, it seemed like an army might be necessary for only a short time.

In this illustration, the African-American soldier Peter Salem is shown shooting British Major Pitcairn at the Battle of Bunker Hill.

Most adult male citizens, like Joseph Hodgkins, were enrolled in local militia units and stood ready to defend their homes and communities. According to a writer in Philadelphia: "The Rage Militaire, as the French call a passion for arms, has taken possession of the whole Continent." After the first year, however, the privations of army life, uncertain pay, homesickness, discouraging defeats, and the looming prospect of a prolonged war dampened enthusiasm. Desertions multiplied in the second year of the war and enlistments fell sharply.

Although exact figures are difficult to determine, approximately 250,000 Americans served in the military. The Continental Army remained small, never exceeding 11,000 soldiers, and typically only about 5,000 stood fit for duty at any one time. Congress placed the responsibility for raising troops on the states, giving them annual quotas. Most men preferred to serve in the militia because they could remain closer to home to be with their families and continue to work on their farms and in their shops. The Continental Army also had to compete for recruits with the small American navy and much larger fleet of **privateers**. Serving on a privateer (a privately owned vessel) offered the prospect of a share of any captured vessel and cargo.

Army recruiters had to overcome another obstacle to enlistment. Military discipline dictated the sacrifice of personal freedom. Citizens were willing to make such sacrifices for a short-term enlistment, but commanders needed commitments of three years or more. To boost long-term recruitment, Congress late in 1776 authorized incentives—bonuses of $20 and 100 acres of land—for enlisting for the duration of the war. The next year, as incentives failed, it resorted to drafting soldiers.

The soldiers' sloppiness and unruliness perturbed their officers. "They are an exceedingly dirty and nasty people," George Washington complained. They refused to bathe and ignored latrines, causing rampant health problems. Undisciplined soldiers discharged their muskets into the air for the fun of it or shot at rabbits and birds, endangering their comrades' lives. Their resistance to drills made them difficult to command under enemy fire. It was impossible, remarked one officer, "to advance or retire in the presence of an enemy without . . . falling into confusion." More than once during the initial months of the war, Washington confessed to a "want of confidence."

Gradually, the Continental Army became more professional. Troops kept their camps cleaner, although they never matched British tidiness. They also became more disciplined. Part of the reason for this change was the appointment of the Prussian Friedrich von Steuben (who claimed to be a baron) to shape up the army. Steuben was one of a few Europeans—another was the dashing young French Marquis de Lafayette—who served on Washington's staff. The blustery Steuben succeeded marvelously as a drillmaster. His training exercises improved the army's appearance, performance, and morale.

The Revolution ultimately came to depend on the professional Continental Army. The poor and the unfree, including indentured servants and slaves, filled its ranks. Financially strapped young men (ranging in age from early teens to early twenties) snapped up enlistment bonuses. If financial gain motivated them to enlist, however, they also developed an *esprit de corps*. The public distrusted a professional army because of its association with tyranny, and an unwillingness to support the Army adequately probably reflected that attitude. Americans preferred a citizens' army, like the militia. Competition raged in numerous pamphlets and letters during the war as to who was truest to the republican principles of the Revolution—the Continental Army professionals who suffered extreme privation to secure the victory or the militia's citizen soldiers.

African Americans volunteered their services from the beginning of the war. The names they gave to enlistment officers indicate why—Jeffery Liberty and Peter Freedom for example. Connecticut officials promised a slave named Caesar that he would be free "on condition of Enlistment and faithfully serving out the time of Enlistment." Most slave soldiers probably became free, but certainly not all of them. James Robinson of Maryland was sold back into slavery after the war. Two considerations caused the states to accept slaves and free blacks: the slowing pace of white enlistment and the British policy of freeing slaves who joined their forces. Northern states enlisted slaves and free blacks; however, only Maryland in the South did so.

Women also played a critical role in the army. Eliza Wilkinson told a friend that if she had a husband who shirked his duty she would "despise him from my soul." Women like Sarah Hodgkins supplied their husbands and sons with clothes, and they often defended themselves and their homes from British and Loyalist bands. Nancy Hart of Georgia was known as the "war woman" for reportedly grabbing a musket and holding at bay a group of Loyalist soldiers who had swept down on her log cabin and demanded food and drink. Women were paid by the army to nurse the sick and wounded, prepare food, and do the laundry. The army also included assorted "camp followers"—the wives of officers and men, women looking for work, and prostitutes. Regulations actually allowed women in the ranks. Mostly they carried water, but sometimes they took up arms. The famous Molly Pitcher (Mary Ludwig) watched her husband die in battle and then took his place in a field battery.

American military forces were seldom outnumbered during the Revolutionary War. Their weapons were usually of equal or superior quality to those carried by British and **Hessian** troops. The biggest weakness was their lack of experience and discipline, but as the war continued, they became more experienced and better disciplined.

Trying Times

Both British and American planners considered various strategic options. British naval officials proposed blockading American ports; however, that

> **How did the fighting go during the 1776 campaign?**

was impractical given the lengthy coastline and the other tasks required of the navy. Secretary of state Lord George Germaine favored a campaign of terror against the populace, but in general the British command disapproved of such measures. Key military officers recommended destroying American armies, no easy task considering that the war was largely an insurgency carried on by citizen militias, or capturing major towns even though 95 percent of Americans lived in small towns or on farms. The best option was to establish enclaves and recruit Loyalists, whose numbers the British grossly overestimated, to restore royal authority.

American options were equally problematic. Representatives in the Continental Congress urged simultaneous defense of each state despite limited resources. Having allies would help; however, both France and Spain held back because of doubts about American perseverance and fears that the ideals of freedom and equality might undermine their own imperial regimes. One strategy that worked involved using privateers to strike at British shipping. Washington and most of his generals thought the Continental Army should avoid showdown battles and engage the British only where they were vulnerable; some American officers advised a guerrilla war. During the Revolution, Washington employed elements of all those strategies, starting with the decision to defend New York from an anticipated British assault in the summer of 1776. After the British evacuated Boston in the spring, Washington redeployed his 20,000 Continentals and local militia units to Long Island to await the Redcoats.

General Sir William Howe and his brother Admiral Lord Richard Howe were in charge of the British campaign. They planned to take New York City, which they believed harbored many Loyalists. Success would give the British control of the Hudson River, enabling them to isolate New England, the nerve center of the rebellion. During the summer, in the most massive land-sea operation ever seen before, some 400 transports ferried 42,000 British and German Hessian troops directly from England and Nova Scotia to Staten Island. The Howe brothers' personal feelings about the war were complex; they believed that Parliament had violated Americans' liberties and privately hoped for a peaceful resolution of the conflict. But it was their duty to crush the revolt.

Late in August, General Howe moved his army to Long Island, where, after an amphibious landing, the troops assaulted the Continental Army's defensive positions. The Americans were no match for the disciplined Redcoats and Hessians. With Washington and his officers committing several tactical blunders, the British easily drove the Americans from Long Island through Brooklyn and had them on the verge of annihilation. But Howe did not follow up, perhaps assuming the Americans were finished. In a dense fog, the Americans crossed to Manhattan; then Howe resumed the offensive. Unable to defend New York City, however, Washington retreated northward through Harlem to White Plains where the Americans tried to defend Fort Washington on the eastern shore of the Hudson River. It was another poor decision, as British and Hessian regiments stormed the garrison, inflicted heavy casualties, and took many prisoners. Once again Howe failed to follow up, and most of the Continental Army managed to slip across the Hudson River into New Jersey.

With New York City in British hands, troops under General Charles Lord Cornwallis pursued the Continental Army into New Jersey. Meanwhile, Admiral Howe took the fleet along with a detachment of British troops to Newport, Rhode Island. Leaving many pieces of artillery behind, Washington's Continental Army retreated southwestward across New Jersey. In December, the Americans confiscated every boat they could find and crossed the Delaware River into Pennsylvania. To avoid capture by the approaching British forces, members of the Continental Congress fled nearby Philadelphia, reconvening in Baltimore. Unable to find more boats to pursue the Americans across the river, Cornwallis deployed his regiments in scattered forward positions on the eastern side of the Delaware, in New Jersey.

Suspending military campaigns during the winter months was common practice among European style armies. But Washington recognized the fragile psyche of his demoralized army, as did Thomas Paine, one of America's first war correspondents. Paine heard the murmuring of the troops, some of whom believed they should have won on Long Island and felt betrayed. "We are sold," they whispered. They hated retreating, and desertions multiplied as the Continental troops reached the end of their enlistment with no intention of reenlisting. Washington could muster a scant 5,000 men, and Paine feared the collapse of public morale as well. Putting his pen to work again, as he had in calling for independence, Paine composed a pamphlet entitled *The American Crisis*. "These are the times that try men's souls," it began. "The summer soldier and the sunshine patriot will, in this crisis shrink from the service of his country; but he that stands it now deserves the love and thanks of man and woman."

If the Continental Army made winter camp, the soldiers would likely drift away. So Washington resorted to an unorthodox mid-winter campaign. Re-crossing the icy Delaware River on the night of December 25, the Americans surprised a garrison of Hessians in Trenton and handed them a stinging defeat. Cornwallis rushed in reinforcements and seemed to have the Americans trapped, but they slipped away and struck another British garrison at Princeton. After a fierce battle, the Redcoats and Hessians fell back to New Brunswick, near New York City. The Americans were exhausted but exuberant. Washington persuaded many of them to reenlist and finally allowed the men to rest in nearby Morristown, New Jersey.

In the span of nine days, the Americans had triumphed in two small but very important battles. The full significance of **Trenton and Princeton** cannot be measured in terms of the number of men engaged. These were small-scale engagements, but they had freed most of New Jersey from enemy control. More importantly, the victories revived the patriots' sagging spirits. After Captain John Chester arrived at his

Connecticut home on furlough in January, he wrote to a fellow officer: "You cannot conceive the joy and raptures the people were universally in as we passed the road." Finally, Washington had redeemed himself after the defeats at New York.

The British were unperturbed by the Americans' successes, but they noticed a surging morale among soldiers and civilians. British troops did not understand why the Americans did not see that they were beaten. The reason for American optimism, of course, was that the British had mounted their maximum effort, and yet, at year's end they controlled only New York City and Newport, Rhode Island. Furthermore, the Americans had more citizens under arms than the British had, and the Continental Congress was busily recruiting European allies.

Lining Up Allies

> **Who did Revolutionary leaders look to as allies?**

France, itching to avenge its loss to Britain in the French and Indian War, was America's most likely ally. The French foreign minister, the Comte de Vergennes, calculated how much France might gain from a British loss. Vergennes was a cautious man, however, and wondered if the Americans would surrender, or agree to a reconciliation with Great Britain that would give them autonomy. For the time being, France refused to offer open support, but it did supply covert aid to the Revolutionaries. To impress upon the French government the mutual advantage of supporting the United States more fully, the Continental Congress in December of 1776 dispatched Benjamin Franklin to Paris as United States commissioner to France.

Spain also monitored the war. The Spanish Crown looked unfavorably upon colonial rebellions but relished the prospect of a British defeat. Spanish authorities diverted resources away from military campaigns against the Apache in New Mexico to shore up defenses along the Mississippi River. The viceroy in Mexico City placed California on alert as British maritime explorer James Cook sailed along the Pacific coast. *Californios* contributed a tax to their own defense, as did residents of Sonora and New Mexico. Texas *rancheros* supplied beef to Spanish troops defending Louisiana. Spanish traders shipped muskets and gunpowder to American patriots through Texas and Louisiana, and negotiators built alliances with Indians along the upper and lower Mississippi River to offset British partnerships with Indians in Florida.

Most of the Indian nations east of the Mississippi River supported the British because of previous treaty agreements. Some Iroquois leaders hoped to preserve autonomy through neutrality, a position the American patriots encouraged. The Continental Congress actually sent a delegation to the Iroquois Confederacy to explain to them that the war was a "family quarrel." One Oneida chief agreed: "We are unwilling to join on either side of such a contest." But British officials urged an Iroquois partnership, and most of the Indians feared an American triumph would lead to aggressive white encroachment onto their land.

Neutrality proved a hopeless dream though. The Oneida and Tuscarora supported the Americans while most of the other Iroquois followed the powerful Mohawk leader Thayendanegea (known to the British

Thayendanegea, known to the British and Americans as Joseph Brant, was a Mohawk chief who had supported the British in the French and Indian War and continued to do so during the American Revolutionary War. Thayendanegea was also a Christian missionary among the Mohawks and helped translate the Bible into the Mohawk language.

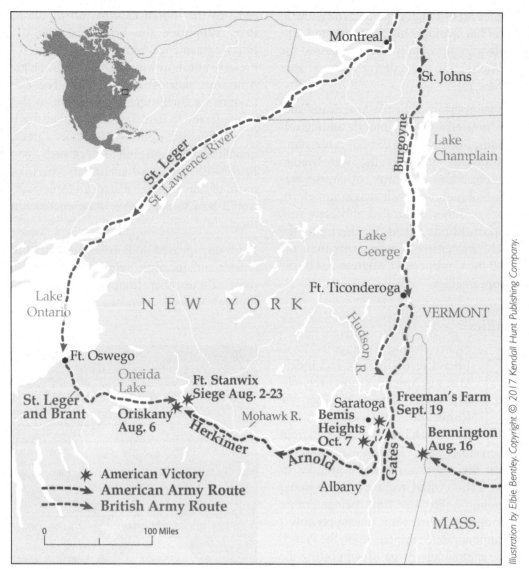

The campaign leading to the British surrender at Saratoga in upstate New York was a critical turning point in the Revolutionary War.

and Americans as Joseph Brant) who fought with the British. The Iroquois Confederacy was shattered. During the summer of 1779, General John Sullivan led a Continental Army in a sweep through western New York that devastated the Iroquois villages. The hapless survivors either fled to Canada and the Ohio country or settled on reservations.

The Cherokees also provided British and Loyalist forces with powerful allies in the southern backcountry. In the summer of 1776, large numbers of Cherokee warriors attacked settlements, and although South Carolina militia units retaliated furiously and Cherokee chiefs signed an agreement the following year ceding their remaining lands in the state, many warriors continued fierce attacks throughout the area.

A Turning Point: The 1777 Campaign

In 1777, the British resumed their plan to isolate New England. General John Burgoyne would bring his army down from Canada to Albany, New York, by way of Lake Champlain and the Hudson River, linking up there with General Howe's army advancing northward from New York City. Additional regiments of British Regulars, Hessians, American loyalists, and Mohawk and Seneca Indians commanded by General Barry St. Leger and Joseph Brant marched east from Oswego on Lake Ontario to reinforce Burgoyne. The convergence of these forces would achieve the British objective.

> **How did the 1777 campaign turn out?**

Burgoyne was a pleasure-seeking aristocrat who loved the theater as much as the army. He played the part of conqueror on the American stage as he prepared to move against the "hardened enemies of Great Britain." His entourage included officers' wives and servants, his mistress (the wife of his commissary officer), wagonloads of champagne and finery, and the regular assortment of camp followers. "We had conceived the idea," said one British officer, "of our being irresistible."

Burgoyne was also a gambler. He risked his army by extending its fragile supply lines through a rugged and hostile countryside. American General Horatio Gates, a popular Virginian, led the northern wing of the Continental Army. The British campaign began late and proceeded as planned, but by September the Redcoats had bogged down. St. Leger's column laid siege to American forces at Ft. Stanwix, but after Americans under General Nicholas Herkimer engaged the British at nearby Oriskany in a bloody battle that resulted in particularly heavy Indian casualties, the British retreated. Meanwhile, Benedict Arnold and a detachment of Americans chased the retreating British back into Canada. Then in mid-October in two engagements near the village of Saratoga and known as the **Battle of Saratoga**, Burgoyne's men suffered frightful casualties. Running out of supplies and with no sign of Howe's army, Burgoyne surrendered his entire force, a total of 5,800 officers and men, twenty-seven pieces of field artillery, and over 5,000 small arms.

What had happened to General Howe? In July 1777 he loaded 18,000 men on transports in New York City, but instead of sailing up the Hudson to rendezvous with Burgoyne, Howe steered his ships southward into Chesapeake Bay in a move against Philadelphia. Washington positioned his 11,000 Continentals and militia to defend the city. In September Howe's army struck the Americans along Brandywine creek. The Redcoats dislodged the Patriots in bloody fighting and then streamed into Philadelphia. The city could not accommodate the entire British army for the winter, so Howe garrisoned many of his troops in nearby towns. The largest contingent was located in nearby Germantown. On October 4, the Americans stormed Germantown in a daring predawn attack, but a thick fog brought confusion and retreat. The Americans lost nearly 1,000 men, and Philadelphia remained in British hands. The dispirited, half-starved Americans spent the winter miserably bivouacked at Valley Forge.

The suffering at Valley Forge was legendary. Congress could not supply the men with food or blankets because the states refused to contribute funds, and 2,500 died. But the army had fought well, even in defeat, and it remained intact. As spring approached,

the mood of the troops was confident, and that, coupled with Burgoyne's surrender at Saratoga, kept the Revolutionary cause alive.

Meanwhile in Paris, Franklin helped convince Vergennes that the time had come to enter the war. Not only had American determination and fighting ability during the Battle of Saratoga impressed the French, but so also had a British offer of reconciliation. In February 1778, France agreed to a **treaty of friendship and commerce** with the United States, which opened French ports to American ships, and a military alliance that promised French military support. The Franco-American alliance put an entirely new face on the war.

Fighting in the West

Beyond the Appalachian Mountains, in territory that, until the Treaty of Paris of 1763, had been French Louisiana, western settlers from Britain's Atlantic coast colonies divided over the Revolution, with a substantial amount of Loyalist sentiment competing against Patriot fervor. The trans-Appalachian area was the scene of some of the war's most savage fighting.

> **How did the trans-Appalachian West figure in the war?**

During the 1760s, conflicts between Shawnee and Cherokee Indians and incoming whites grew increasingly bloody. Despite the Proclamation of 1763, land-hungry whites had crossed the Appalachians and settled on Indian hunting grounds, provoking violent attacks by Shawnee and Cherokee war parties. Most of the newcomers settled below the Ohio River in an area known as Kentucky, territory over which both Virginia and Pennsylvania had asserted jurisdiction but exercised little control. General Thomas Gage described backcountry settlers as "too numerous, too lawless and licentious ever to be restrained."

The British government sought to mediate frontier conflicts. In the **Treaty of Fort Stanwix** in 1768, the British induced the Iroquois to relinquish Kentucky to the white settlers. The Shawnee and Delaware nations retained the area north of the Ohio River. The Shawnee and Cherokee, both ancient enemies of the Iroquois and long-time inhabitants of Kentucky, disregarded the treaty since they had had no hand in making it. By 1774, Indians threatened to drive settlers back across the Appalachian Mountains, leading Virginia's governor, Lord Dunmore, to commence a war that culminated in a victory of sorts over the Indians. A number of their leaders acknowledged British sovereignty but others refused.

The infusion of American colonists into Kentucky continued as developers and speculators, like Richard Henderson of North Carolina, sold more Indian land to homesteaders. Henderson named his colony Transylvania. In 1775, Daniel Boone blazed a trail through the Cumberland Gap, and subsequently hundreds of men, women, children, and enslaved African Americans migrated to the "blue grass" country. (For more on Boone, see pp. 174-75). Fierce fighting occurred frequently as Indians sought to expel the white "poachers" and Indian-hating white settlers took revenge with equal or greater savagery.

With the outbreak of the Revolutionary War, the British enlisted Indians against the Americans. The Indians' response was not usually based on support for or rejection of either the idea of monarchy or the Patriots' republican principles. Most Indians acted in their own interests, believing that the British were less likely to take their territory away from them than were the aggressive American Patriots. From Detroit, Canada's lieutenant governor Henry Hamilton armed war parties and paid bounties for American scalps, for which the Americans nicknamed him "hair-buyer." Outrages committed by settlers, like the murder of the respected Shawnee peace leader Cornstalk and the slaughter of 150 Christian Delaware Indians in Pennsylvania, drove many western Indian communities into the British camp. In February 1779, George Rogers Clark led an army of Virginians against British garrisons. At Vincennes, in present-day Indiana, the Americans defeated Hamilton's battalion of British and Indian troops. The Americans sent Hamilton in shackles to Virginia and tomahawked captured Indians.

In 1779, Spain's King Carlos III declared war against Britain as an ally of France, though not of the United States. The British hoped to gain control of the Mississippi River to lock up the fur trade in upper Louisiana and to encircle the rebellious colonies. However, Spanish forces seized British garrisons at Natchez and Baton Rouge along the lower Mississippi River. The British, with Sioux and Sac and Fox auxiliaries, attacked St. Louis but failed to take it. Then in March 1780, a Spanish fleet and army commanded by Bernardo de Gálvez a forced the British to surrender Mobile, a key Gulf port, and a year later took Pensacola, the capital of Britain's loyal colony of West Florida.

Thus Spain maintained nominal control of the lower Mississippi Valley and Florida after regaining it from

the British, protecting its valuable New Spain asset and the gold and silver shipping lanes through the Gulf of Mexico, The British in Canada, however, continued to hold a strong position among the upper Mississippi Valley tribes due to their ability to supply them with trade goods. The Indians skillfully parlayed the European rivalry into agreements with both Great Britain and Spain to secure their own freedom—at least temporarily. And the United States benefited from Great Britain having to fight both Spain and France, both powerful enemies, in theaters like the Caribbean and Europe. The global aspect of the American Revolutionary War was wearing Great Britain down.

Turning Everything Upside Down

British defeats along the Gulf Coast foreshadowed the climax of the Revolutionary War in the East. After Saratoga and the Franco-American alliance, France became Britain's primary enemy; consequently, Britain diverted much of its military force to the Caribbean for clashes with the French. As part of its revamped strategy, the British command designed a major southern campaign, hoping to enlist Loyalists to augment its reduced military and naval forces. British officials also wooed Cherokee, Creek, Choctaw, and Chickasaw Indian allies in Florida. But North Carolina and Virginia militia inflicted severe punishment on Cherokee villages on both sides of the Appalachians, and Creeks, Choctaws, and Chickasaws did not help much along the Gulf Coast.

> **What finally caused the British to give up?**

Implementation of Britain's new strategy against the Patriots began in the spring of 1778 when General Sir Henry Clinton replaced Howe and moved his army from Philadelphia to New York, barely escaping from Washington's Continental Army at the Battle of Monmouth, New Jersey. In the fall, Clinton dispatched 3,500 troops from New York to Georgia. On December 29 they took Savannah. A year later Clinton himself departed New York with fourteen warships, ninety transports, and 7,600 troops and sailed through stormy waters to Charleston. In May 1780, after an exhausting siege, the American defenders surrendered. This was the only occasion during the war when the Americans lost an entire army.

Clinton returned to New York and turned the southern army over to Lord Cornwallis, who proceeded northward through the Carolinas with instructions to leave Loyalists in control behind him. In August, the

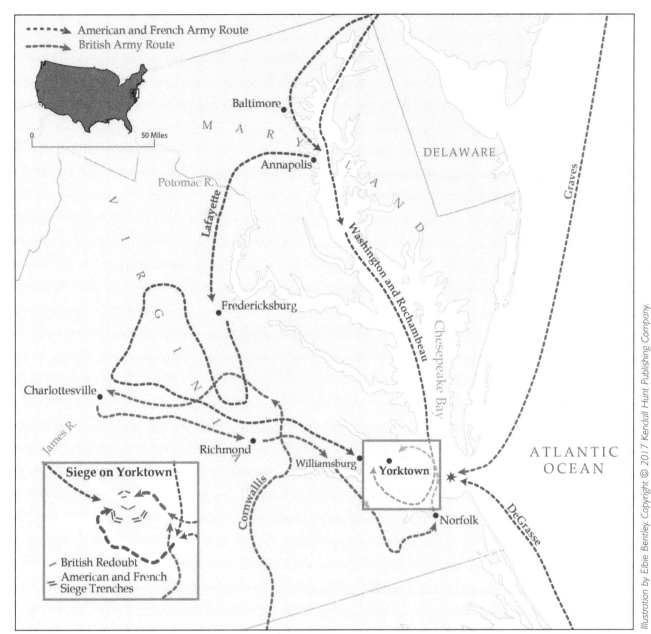

British general Cornwallis' surrender at Yorktown signaled the beginning of negotiations leading to the Treaty of Paris of 1783 and the formal end of the Revolutionary War.

southern wing of the Continental Army, which Congress had placed under the command of Horatio Gates, surprised the British near Camden, South Carolina. Gates dishonored himself though by fleeing the battlefield, and once again the British prevailed.

By 1780, the Revolutionary cause looked dismal. The Continental Congress still could not pay or adequately supply its troops, nor were the states supporting the military effort. Some soldiers threatened to mutiny; others, like Joseph Hodgkins, declined to reenlist. The Continental Army shrank to fewer than 6,000 effective troops. In September 1780, Benedict Arnold, resentful

at having been consistently passed over for promotion despite his important contribution to the American victory at Saratoga, where he received another serious wound, and opposed to the French alliance, offered to turn over the fort at West Point on the Hudson River to the British. He made the offer in writing to a British officer named John André, who was captured with the incriminating documents. André was hanged as a spy and Arnold deserted to the British, who made him a brigadier general.

Britain's southern campaign ignited savage fighting between Patriots and Loyalists. In October 1780, a

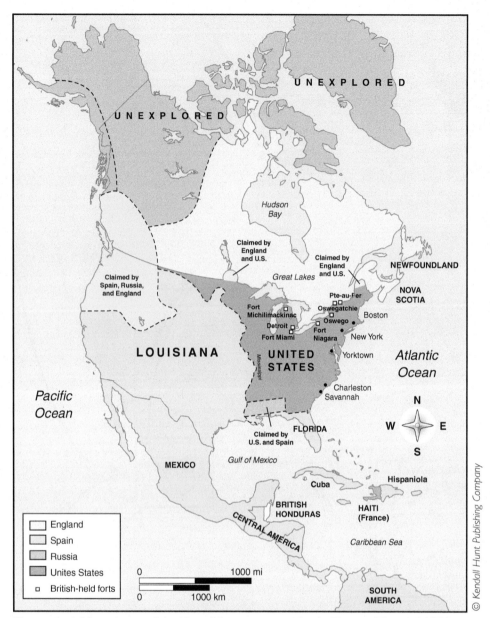

The territorial boundaries of the United States were set by the Treaty of Paris of 1783.

Loyalist band led by a daring and impetuous Scot named Patrick Ferguson fought a ferocious battle with Patriot partisans at King's Mountain, South Carolina. The rampaging Patriots shot Ferguson dead from his white charger and avenged earlier murders of Patriots by slaughtering scores of Loyalist troops who tried to surrender. Overall, though, the British overestimated Loyalist strength, and Cornwallis grew frustrated by his inability to muster their support. His army mainly brought out the curious "to stare at us."

In December of 1780, American prospects brightened when Nathaniel Greene replaced Gates as commander of the Continental Army in the South. Greene defied conventional tactics by dividing his force in the face of the enemy, sending a detachment to forage for food. He got away with it though. In January 1781, Greene's troops annihilated a British cavalry unit at **Cowpens,** in South Carolina. Unable to corner the elusive Greene, Cornwallis abandoned the Carolinas in favor of a campaign in the Chesapeake region. Raiding through Virginia in the spring of 1781, British forces routed the Americans from Richmond, ran the Virginia assembly out of its temporary headquarters in Charlottesville, and nearly captured Governor Thomas Jefferson, who fled to Monticello, his plantation, a scant ten minutes ahead of the oncoming Redcoats. Afterward, Jefferson had to defend himself against charges of cowardice and neglect of duty in the defense of the state.

Cornwallis and Clinton, however, could not agree on a decisive campaign. Cornwallis fortified a position at Yorktown, on the Virginia peninsula between the James and York rivers. He felt secure with the British navy patrolling the seaboard. Clinton remained in New York, where Washington and the French general Comte de Rochambeau stood watch with a 16,000-man Franco-American army. During the summer a French fleet sailed into Chesapeake Bay, setting the scene for the Revolutionary War's climactic battle.

Washington and Rochambeau decided to attack Cornwallis. Leaving a detachment behind to hold Clinton in New York, they deployed their forces around the British position at Yorktown. When the French warships blasted Admiral Thomas Graves' British fleet in September and forced it to withdraw to New York for repairs, Cornwallis was trapped. From their positions, Washington and Rochambeau directed a heavy and steady artillery bombardment at the British entrenchments. On October 19, with the band playing the tune "The World Turned Upside Down," he hoisted the white flag.

Lord North likened the British defeat at the **Battle of Yorktown** to a bullet through the heart. The fighting was over. The revolutionary drama now shifted to the peace table.

At the Peace Table

> Who were the winners and losers in the intricate negotiations that led to peace?

In 1779, Congress had named a commission comprising Benjamin Franklin, John Adams, Henry Laurens, and John Jay to negotiate a peace treaty. After Cornwallis' surrender the British were ready to talk, but it was not Yorktown by itself that brought London officials to the peace table. America's allies inflicted other crippling injuries. French warships won engagements in the West Indies and even attacked vessels in the English Channel. The British public had tired of the war. Besides, England's most valuable overseas possessions were not the thirteen mainland colonies. They were not worth the continued cost of defending them.

The Americans met with a British representative in Paris. Congress insisted on consulting France before agreeing to peace terms, but its main concern was a favorable treaty, and Britain was more agreeable to what the Americans wanted than France was likely to be. In addition to independence, Congress wanted permission for American fishermen to fish the coastal waters off Newfoundland, to set the western boundary for the new nation at the Mississippi River, and Britain to cede Canada and Nova Scotia to the United States. Franklin also suggested that Britain allow American imports as before and that England compensate Americans for losses suffered during the war.

The British remained reluctant to recognize American independence, the French hoped to limit American territorial acquisitions, and the Spanish Crown focused on its concerns. Not until November 1781 did the British accept American independence. The Americans did not inform France of the terms of the agreement until after it had been reached; however, the treaty would not take effect until France and Britain made their own peace. A crucial French naval defeat in the West Indies and the failure of an all-out Spanish assault on Gibraltar at the entrance to the Mediterranean Sea brought on a general European accord in 1782.

Most of the participants in the American Revolutionary War signed the **Treaty of Paris** in September 1783. The agreement acknowledged American independence and redrew the political boundaries of North America (see the map on p. 166). American territory extended from the Great Lakes to Florida, which Spain reclaimed from Britain. The treaty established the Mississippi River down to the 31st parallel as the western boundary. Britain retained Canada and granted fishing rights to Americans along the Newfoundland banks. The United States agreed to ask the states to restore confiscated Loyalist property.

The Treaty of Paris totally ignored the interests of the many Indians who inhabited western lands and who had participated in the war on one side or the other. The Shawnee were dismayed that the British had given away their territory. One Indian expressed the tribes' sense of betrayal: "In endeavoring to assist you," he said to a British official, "it seems we have wrought our own ruin." They would certainly have a battle on their hands protecting their land from the Americans. Farther south, the Cherokee, Creek, Choctaw, and Chickasaw nations faced a certain onslaught of American settlers that jeopardized their native lands between the Appalachians and the Mississippi River. Indeed, some Creeks gave up and migrated into Spanish Florida, where they blended with Seminoles. Beyond the Mississippi River in the Louisiana territory, the Indians' position was much better. Both the Spanish and the British vied for their friendship offering gifts and trade goods for Indian pelts and furs.

1. What were the key moments in the Revolutionary War, and why were they so?
2. Why might it be said that the skirmishing at Lexington and Concord were "shots heard 'round the world," and what difference did it make that other countries heard them?
3. In considering the way the Revolutionary War was fought, how democratic was the United States?

CONCLUSION

From the 1760s to 1776, Americans moved from resisting Parliamentary taxes to complete rejection of all British government authority. From demonstrations in the streets, the movement evolved into a reasoned and philosophical assertion of the fundamental human right to liberty. Could the violence and bloodshed of the Revolution have been avoided? Probably, but ultimately, independence for the North American colonies was very likely only a matter of time. The length of time it took for Americans to commit to a complete separation from Great Britain suggests a willingness to accept autonomous status within the empire. In the short term, British policy precipitated a crisis that could not be resolved, and Americans were forced to make choices of allegiance and ultimately of nationhood before many were ready to do so. The United States came into being before a collective national identity did. Could the Americans have prevailed alone over one of Europe's superpowers? It is hard to imagine an American victory without foreign assistance. How fortunate it was for the Revolutionary cause that the crisis with Great Britain came at a time of intense European rivalry. In other circumstances the imperial governments of France and Spain might not have assisted a colonial revolt. The colonies did their part too, joining together in a remarkably unified effort. The question that arose after the Revolution was whether this was one united country or thirteen separate and sovereign ones.

SUGGESTED SOURCES FOR STUDENTS

The book that has most influenced recent generations of historians in their thinking about the nature of the Revolution is Bernard Bailyn, *The Ideological Origins of the American Revolution* (Rev. ed., 1992).

For how Indians responded to the Revolution, and how it affected them, see Colin Calloway, *The American Revolution in Indian Country* (1995).

Kathleen DuVal, *Independence Lost: Lives on the Edge of the American Revolution* (2015) describes and explains the meaning of war and independence for Europeans, Africans, and Indians living in the lower Mississippi Valley and Gulf Coast at the time of the American Revolution.

David Hackett Fischer, *Washington's Crossing* (2004), offers a fresh, engaging treatment of the battles at Trenton and Princeton, showing that they came not amid despair but rather soaring optimism.

To learn about the African-American experience, see Sylvia Frey, *Water from the Rock: Black Resistance in a Revolutionary Age* (1991). She argues that black liberation was important to the revolutionary movement.

Pauline Maier, *American Scripture: Making the Declaration of Independence* (1997), elaborates on the drafting of scores of declarations of independence by various colonies and local communities as well as the significant role that the Continental Congress played in the final draft of the Declaration of Independence.

An excellent overview of the Revolution with description and balanced analysis is Robert Middlekauf, *The Glorious Cause, 1763-1789* (1982).

Gary Nash, *The Unknown American Revolution: The Unruly Birth of Democracy and the Struggle to Create America* (2005), presents the revolution through the aspirations of the poor, the enslaved, and the Native American. Nash contends that the Revolution was based on more than abstract principle.

Charles Royster, *A Revolutionary People at War: The Continental Army and American Character* (1975), considers how American ideas of war affected the Continental Army. It is excellent cultural and military history.

Herbert T. Wade and Robert A. Lively, eds, *This Glorious Cause: The Adventures of Two Company Officers in Washington's Army* (1958), contains the letters of Joseph and Sarah Hodgkins.

BEFORE WE GO ON

1. What brought on the dispute between Britain and its North American colonies?

2. How did the United States win the Revolutionary War, considering all the disadvantages it faced?

Building a Democratic Nation

3. When and why did Americans come to feel that they were not British, and did democracy have anything to do with it?

4. Some historians have seen the American Revolution as a movement to preserve self-government. Others have described it as the beginning of a truly democratic nation. How do you see it, and what leads you to that conclusion?

Connections

5. What principles emerged from the American Revolution, and how do they continue to inspire us today?

6. How democratic was the American Revolution, and what impediments to building a democratic nation were present during the Revolution that still exist today?

Chapter 6

ONE NATION OR MANY, 1781–1789

A PERSONAL PERSPECTIVE: DANIEL BOONE, A NATIONAL SYMBOL

Daniel Boone was both a real person and an archetypal American hero.

How did Daniel Boone become the archetypal American hero?

By the 1780s Daniel Boone's exploits as a woodsman and Kentucky pioneer had become legendary. In 1769, he and five companions followed the Great Warrior's path through the Cumberland Gap into the mostly unsettled territory known as Kentucky, still then part of Virginia. Four years later Boone returned as guide for an emigrant party. They turned back after an attack by Cherokee Indians in which Daniel's eldest son was tortured and killed, but Boone later settled with his family and others at a site along the Kentucky River that came to be called Boonesborough. While Daniel Boone was a real person, the truth about his life has for generations been swirled together with legend.

The man who created the mythical Daniel Boone was John Filson, a schoolteacher and surveyor. Intrigued by local tales, Filson tracked down the famous hunter and interviewed him at length. Filson's biography, *The Adventures of Col. Daniel Boon*, appeared in 1784. Boone was fifty years old by then. Most of the country had heard of him; indeed, voters had elected him to the Virginia state assembly. Filson's book was an instant bestseller in America, and an even greater hit in Europe. It made Daniel Boone an international celebrity, a person who embodied the ideals of courage, self-reliance, and devotion that Americans and their admirers abroad associated with the new republic. Filson's Boone was a "natural man" who lived simply, unselfishly, and mostly in solitude, very much like the "noble savage" Indians imagined by English philosophers.

Societies become nations when they develop a keen sense of their common background and interests. In other words, nationhood involves sharing particular ways of life and strong attachments to one another—cultural unity. Nations also create legendary heroes who personify cultural values. One powerful influence on the emerging American nation was the trans-Appalachian frontier. Although at the end of the eighteenth century most Americans had never seen the frontier and did not understand it very well, they thought of it as something important, the opportunity to be free, which in those times meant owning land, bettering themselves, and becoming self-reliant. To a considerable extent, land in the interior of the continent determined how they thought of themselves, and it dominated the images of America that Europeans held.

For a long time, Americans had negative impressions of the forested lands beyond the Appalachian Mountains. They imagined a wilderness inhabited by brutish Indians. During the Revolutionary War, the

1769	1777	1780	1781	1782	1783
Daniel Boone blazes the Wilderness Trail into Kentucky	Congress accepts the Articles of Confederation and submits them to the states for ratification	Pennsylvania enacts the first emancipation law	Maryland is last state to ratify the Articles of Confederation	Rhode Island rejects the Nationalists' Impost Plan	Newburgh military conspiracy dissolves

Shawnee Indian people in the Ohio country had allied with the British to oppose the United States, often brutally. But in victory, post-Revolutionary Americans looked differently at the West, not as wilderness to be conquered and tamed but as something more positive, a cleansing agent against the corruption of civilized society. The archetypal American hero was transformed too, from the "civilized" European to Daniel Boone, the "natural man" whose skill and self-reliance allowed him to prosper within the wilderness.

The real Daniel Boone grew up in southeastern Pennsylvania, and he loved the wilderness. By the time he was a teenager he had become a skilled hunter. Boone and his family watched an endless parade of covered wagons carrying pioneers along the Great Wagon Road into western Virginia and North Carolina. In 1750 the Boone family joined the cavalcade, settling along the Yadkin River in the backcountry of North Carolina.

Boone married Rebecca Bryan there in 1756. They raised their family in a log cabin near several of their relatives. A domestic crisis threatened the marriage when Daniel returned from a two-year hunting and Indian fighting trip to find that Rebecca was pregnant. She had naturally presumed him dead—obviously grounds for terminating a marriage and establishing new relationships. According to stories whispered among the Boone's neighbors, Daniel's brother Ned was the child's father. Daniel and Rebecca struggled to rebuild their marriage, an effort made even more difficult by Daniel's selfish and prolonged absences. Two and a half years passed before Rebecca conceived again. Eventually, the Boones succeeded. Seven of their ten children married and produced seventy grandchildren. In those days, backcountry households often included twenty or more family members. Moving his family to Kentucky, Boone, along with other settlers, battled the Shawnee for control of the fertile bluegrass region.

The mythical Daniel Boone helped Americans of the post-Revolution era define their national values. During the Revolution, Americans of diverse backgrounds had embraced the principles of a republic—namely freedom, the supreme authority of the people, and limited government. Property was the key to realizing those republican principles. The mythical Daniel Boone was a noble man of action who also sought solitude and a true understanding of life in nature. He combined the natural law of the wilderness with the Enlightenment belief in the supremacy of reason. Boone personified traits that Americans believed would make their nation successful: selflessness and freedom. Ironically, the real Daniel Boone guided settlers from the East into the wilderness of Kentucky, and with them they brought civilization that eventually destroyed the wilderness and transformed the "natural man" into a farmer, salt-miner, merchant, and real-estate agent.

During and after the Revolution, Americans called upon those qualities to deal with the enormous task of building social and political institutions that reflected their republican principles. Through individual choices and collective decisions, they addressed such contradictions to republican ideals as gender discrimination and slavery—not always honorably perhaps but as well as they could. Diversity was as much a defining characteristic of the people of the United States as was a commitment to republican values. Indeed, diversity in race, gender, class, and ethnicity led to strikingly different approaches to nation building. So great were those differences that conspiracies and rebellions threatened to wreck the new nation or—as many thought of it—to hijack the Revolution. First with the Articles of Confederation and then with the Constitution, Americans sought to build a viable republic that stretched across half a continent—a radical if not yet truly democratic experiment.

THINKING BACK

1. How were the real and the legendary Daniel Boone similar and different?
2. What was it about Daniel Boone that captured the imagination of the Revolutionary generation of Americans?

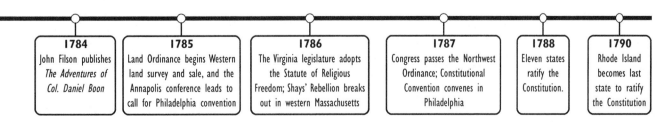

1784	**1785**	**1786**	**1787**	**1788**	**1790**
John Filson publishes *The Adventures of Col. Daniel Boon*	Land Ordinance begins Western land survey and sale, and the Annapolis conference leads to call for Philadelphia convention	The Virginia legislature adopts the Statute of Religious Freedom; Shays' Rebellion breaks out in western Massachusetts	Congress passes the Northwest Ordinance; Constitutional Convention convenes in Philadelphia	Eleven states ratify the Constitution.	Rhode Island becomes last state to ratify the Constitution

SHAPING REPUBLICAN SOCIETIES

A zest for remodeling old colonial societies into new republican ones ran high in the aftermath of independence. John Adams noted that a "radical change in the principles, opinions, sentiments and affections of the people" had overwhelmed old attachments. But thinking of the Revolution as just a struggle for independence does not adequately convey the full scope of those changes. Patriotic slogans like "Freedom and no Stamp Act" not only revealed anti-colonialism, they also expressed a new vision for America's future, a new **republican** scheme for organizing society, one that acknowledged the ultimate authority of the people. Realizing that republican vision required implementing those Enlightenment principles embedded in the Declaration of Independence—universal rights to "life, liberty, and the pursuit of happiness."

Alongside egalitarian ideals that maximized the people, however, remained deeply rooted and opposing traditions and prejudices that minimized them. For instance, Revolutionary rhetoric reinforced the importance of owning property, heretofore the primary basis for hierarchy and inequality in a largely agrarian society. Economic developments also influenced the growth of institutions, and not always in the same ways as Revolutionary republicanism. The Revolution did not represent a sharp break with the past; rather, it culminated a century of steady change. Bursting with self-confidence, citizens of the new republic pushed their national boundaries to their legal limits and beyond, heightening tensions with Native Americans as well as Spaniards and Canadians. Independence and contact with different cultures on America's frontiers helped form a national identity.

The Republican Agenda

> In what ways did changes in American society reveal the establishment of republican values?

The tremendous idealism of the Patriots' cause is impossible to ignore. As Thomas Paine wrote: "We have it in our power to begin the world again." That was neither a modest nor a selfish proposal. In resolving various issues that surfaced during and after the Revolutionary War, the country's leaders remodeled their communities. Pamphleteers had written passionately about freedom

The Declaration of Independence's most elegant phrase, that "all men are created equal" with the "unalienable rights" to "life, liberty, and the pursuit of happiness" has been hard to live up to.

and equality, referring often to the ancient Greek republics. Common citizens, African Americans, and women of all classes embraced those Revolutionary republican values, as did predominant white males. They anticipated a more egalitarian society than their mothers and fathers had known. In several areas their dreams became reality, but in others they did not.

For instance, the Revolution undermined patriarchal authority, at least as far as monarchy was concerned. "Where is the king in America?" Paine asked. "In America," he answered, "the law is king." The personal authority of kings and royal governors yielded to the impersonal and more objective sovereignty of law, written by the people through their elected representatives—the essence of republicanism. The people were no longer subject to the whims of rulers. Now they governed through their elected representatives. This was indeed a liberal—even radical—idea in the eighteenth century.

For many Americans, an aristocratic elite with inherited privileges had no place in a republican society. John Adams typified his generation's distaste for such aristocracy, with its "Scorn and Contempt and turning up of the nose." Formal designations such as "esquire" after a man's name fell from general use. Even the republican—but notably dignified—George Washington came under criticism when he and other former Continental Army officers organized the Society of the Cincinnati, a fraternity whose exclusive and hereditary membership was not sufficiently republican. Egalitarian republicans like Samuel Adams charged that the Society of the Cincinnati represented "as rapid a Stride towards an hereditary Military Nobility as was ever made in so short a time." They associated aristocracy with self-indulgence and moral weakness. When a group of wealthy young Bostonians formed the Sans Souci Club for pleasant evenings of fine food, good wine, and cards, Sam Adams again exploded in indignation: "Say my country, why do you suffer all the intemperances of Great Britain to be fostered in our bosom, in all their vile luxuriance?"

Republican reformers also condemned special privilege in the form of established religion. At the time of the Revolution, nine states privileged certain churches with official status, including tax support—the Congregational (Puritan) Church in Massachusetts, Connecticut, and New Hampshire and the Anglican Church in New York and the South. Dissenters in those states could not hold public office, risked fines and were even imprisoned for their religious beliefs. Some suffered having their property taken (for that was what a tax amounted to) to support a church and a religion to which they did not belong. This distinctly un-republican set-up led to efforts to **separate church and state**.

In 1776, Virginia's **Declaration of Rights** included "the free exercise of religion," and three years later, Thomas Jefferson, a Deist who maintained membership in the Anglican Church, authored the Virginia **Statute for Religious Freedom**. Citizens possessed a "natural right," Jefferson wrote, to hold and express any opinion on religion. Patrick Henry sidetracked the measure out of concern that weakening churches would undermine society's moral foundation. Henry introduced an alternative bill that provided state support for all Christian churches. James Madison, Jefferson's neighbor and political ally, argued against Henry, observing that "bigotry" and "persecution" often accompanied the fusion of church and state. Madison persuaded the legislature to pass Jefferson's statute in 1786. The other southern states followed suit.

In most of New England, the Congregational Church had enjoyed official status since early colonial times. Only Rhode Island had established genuine religious tolerance. But in the aftermath of the Revolution, dissenters, including the **New Lights** of the Great Awakening, demanded the right to support whatever local church they preferred without having their taxes go to the Congregational Church. But change came slowly to New England, and not until 1833 did Massachusetts become the last state to separate church and state.

The Revolutionary republican tide also washed away many archaic forms from the states' legal systems. Reformers updated and liberalized state penal codes, attempting to make punishments proportional to offenses. In revising Virginia's criminal statutes, Jefferson followed two principles. The first, foreshadowing modern criminology, held that society should reform criminals rather than merely punish them. Fewer crimes carried the death penalty. However, the other principle was the Biblical retribution: "an eye for an eye." Thus, punishments remained harsh. As Edmund Pendleton of Virginia observed, "if you mean to relax all punishments and rely on virtue and the public good as sufficient to prompt obedience to laws, you must find a new race of men to be the subjects of it."

Revolutionary reforms swept aside traditional inheritance laws too. For generations English aristocrats had utilized the mechanisms of **primogeniture** and **entail** to keep their vast estates intact, and many colonies had incorporated them into their statutes. Primogeniture meant that in the absence of a will the eldest son inherited all of his father's property. Entail prevented estates from being divided. Even though people with property could designate any, or as many, inheritors as they wished in their wills, state legislatures erased the old laws as a matter of principle.

These legal changes sought to realize the republican ideals of freedom and greater equality, both of which depended on property. However, women's property rights remained severely restricted, and for African-American slaves, the problem was that in the eyes of the law they *were* property—somebody else's.

Gender, Slavery, and Revolutionary Republicanism

The Declaration of Independence proclaimed "all men are created equal," but it did not say explicitly women were equal to men. A few Revolutionary-era women, white and black, pointed out

> How did the revolutionary generation deal with the contradiction between republican principles and the condition of women, slaves, and indentured servants?

that, after having done their share to achieve independence from British tyranny, they were entitled to more equal treatment. Abigail Adams admonished her husband John, a member of the Continental Congress, to "remember the ladies, and be more generous and favorable to them than your ancestors."

However, the male-dominated early republic continued to restrict women's rights under the guise of protecting them, and only a few women openly dissented. The principle followed was called *femme couvert*, meaning that women's supposedly physical and intellectual weaknesses dictated that they should be subordinated to or "covered" by their fathers and husbands, who made legal and political decisions for them. The British jurist William Blackstone, whose *Commentaries on the Common Law* was widely followed in post-Revolutionary America, explained that "the disabilities, which the wife lies under, are for the most part intended for her protection and benefit." Thus a woman's property automatically passed to her husband when she married. Without property, men claimed, women had no political responsibility. Thus, voting remained an exclusively male right, except in New Jersey, which until 1807 allowed female property owners (essentially widows and unmarried women) to vote.

Within the domestic realm, women remained covered by their husbands in more ways than one. Benjamin Trumbull, representing Connecticut's Congregational ministers, wrote in 1788: "The wife hath not the power of her own body, but the husband." Divorce remained very difficult for women trapped in unhappy, exploitative marriages despite Revolutionary rhetoric that made "the pursuit of happiness" a natural right. Lawmakers continued to strive to maintain the family as the primary buttress of social order. In 1785, Pennsylvania enacted the republic's first divorce law providing that where one spouse deserts the other or commits adultery, "the laws of every well-regulated society ought to give relief to the innocent and injured person." But the case of sixteen-year-old Nancy Shippen Livingston illustrates the difficulty women faced in trying to escape domestic abuse. The daughter of rich Philadelphia parents, she was courted by a dashing young Frenchman who had little money but bright prospects. Her father disapproved, noting: "A bird in hand is worth 2 in the bush." He married Nancy off to Henry Beekman Livingston, a member of two aristocratic New York families. Livingston turned abusive and tried to

abscond with the couple's young daughter. In New York, where the Livingstons resided, divorce required special enactment by the legislature, not to mention expensive and effective lobbying. And even if she succeeded in divorcing him, Henry would gain sole custody of their child. Nancy Livingston was thus locked in a miserable marriage, living separately, until her husband finally decided to divorce her.

Despite the continued confinement of females in Revolution-era America to the domestic realm, many women assumed one decidedly civic activity: promoting public virtue through **Republican Motherhood**. Through most of the eighteenth century, republican virtues such as honesty, fidelity, and disinterestedness had been seen as male qualities. But Republican Mothers took charge of teaching them to their children to preserve and foster a republican society. Women were also supposed to chastise wayward husbands. Thus women became society's shining models of republican virtue.

But to instruct her children properly in republican principles, many women contended, a Revolutionary Mother must be educated. The question was: What type of education? Judith Sargent Murray of Gloucester, Massachusetts, a powerful and articulate spokeswoman for gender equality, insisted that if women had the same opportunities as men to learn history, geography, and astronomy they would show comparable intellectual achievement because the female mind had the same capacity as the male one. Her book *On the Equality of Sexes* (1792) was a landmark in American feminism but more extreme than most women of the time felt comfortable with. Benjamin Rush, a Philadelphia physician, advocated women's education according to a curriculum designed to train women to be Republican Mothers and manage their financial affairs should their husbands die. But males generally held misgivings about intellectual education for females. John Trumbull held a typical man's view of educated women. He inquired lyrically:

And why should girls be learned or wise,

Books only serve to spoil their eyes

The studious eye but faintly twinkles

And reading paves the way to wrinkles.

A few women took it upon themselves to obtain an education. Sarah Pierce opened **Litchfield**

Academy for girls in 1792, teaching seven young women in her Connecticut home. Several similar academies appeared, especially in the Middle Atlantic and Northeastern states. Although confined to the domestic sphere, some women slowly gained new opportunities for intellectual growth and self-fulfillment. They were, moreover, now identifiable by their first names and not just the last names that they shared with their husbands, and, at least as revealed in the family portraits of the period, they were seen more as partners in marriage than as dependents.

Portraits were mainly of elite women and their families, though, the women who could afford to fill the role of Republican Motherhood. Lower class white women remained burdened with household chores: washing, sewing, cooking, milking cows, tending gardens, delivering and tending to the physical needs of their children. Free black women, as the Pennsylvania Abolition Society reported in 1795, "both married and single, wash clothes for a living." Most women found it difficult to muster the resources required for ideal Republican Motherhood.

Slavery flatly contradicted the Declaration of Independence's noble assertion that "all men are created equal." Many white people acknowledged that fact. Abigail Adams observed: "It always appeared a most iniquitous scheme to me, to fight ourselves for what we are daily robbing and plundering from those who have as good a right to freedom as we have."

Thomas Jefferson, author of the Declaration of Independence, recognized the discrepancy between lofty republican principles and the harsh reality of slavery. He had denounced slavery in his initial draft of the Declaration, only to watch other delegates from the South strike anti-slavery passages from the final document. Most planters, including Jefferson, tried to reconcile slavery with republican ideology. Jefferson, who owned nearly 200 slaves, reasoned that immediate emancipation would strain the economy, leave the freed people helpless, or lead to the "extermination of the one race or the other." In the Chesapeake, no comprehensive emancipation plan emerged; however, because the tobacco-based economy did not recover from the damage caused by fighting armies and the loss of British markets, many planters turned more and more to less labor-intensive crops like wheat. George Washington noted: "I have more working Negroes ... than can be employed to advantage in the farming system." This

weakened individual planters' commitment to slavery. During the 1780s, slave owners in Virginia freed some 10,000 slaves. In 1791, Robert Carter of Virginia liberated his 500 slaves, and in his will George Washington manumitted his slaves after the death of his wife Martha.

Blacks felt the republican paradox more painfully since they were the victims of slavery. Primed by Great Awakening evangelists who preached spiritual equality, African Americans read or heard the Patriots' calls for liberty and equality, and they did not simply wait for republican-minded whites to liberate them. Many slaves took the initiative to purchase their freedom, and that of their spouses and children as well. Those black men and women who remained in bondage gained leverage in negotiating with their masters for better living and working conditions.

Manumission in the Chesapeake led to an increase in the number of free blacks. Virginia and Maryland legislatures made it easier for masters to manumit (free) their slaves. By 1810, there were more than 108,000 free African Americans in Virginia and Maryland, or 10 percent of the region's black population. Many of those free blacks resided in such newly burgeoning towns as Baltimore, Richmond, and Norfolk where they interacted freely with slaves who themselves enjoyed considerable freedom of movement.

In coastal North Carolina, South Carolina, and Georgia, social and economic conditions were quite different. Slave owners had little incentive to free their slaves (though some did), for although the war had reduced plantation production and foreign markets, rice cultivation recovered after the war (indigo did not), and planters began to grow cotton. Indeed, with cotton, the plantation system expanded from the low country into upland interior districts, and as the demand for slaves increased, the African slave trade continued to bring thousands of new African slaves into the region.

In the North, slavery was weaker than anywhere in the South and more vulnerable to abolitionist pressure based on republican principles. During the Revolution, many slaves took advantage of British occupation of seaports to escape and melt into the urban population. During and after the war, slaves petitioned state officials to free them, citing the "Natural and Unalienable Right to that freedom which the Great Parent of the [Universe] hath bestowed equally on all mankind." In 1777, Vermont outlawed slavery in its constitution, although few slaves resided there. More lived in Massachusetts, where public opinion generally condemned human bondage. The state's new constitution, adopted in 1780, stated that "all men are born free and equal"—without exception. When a man named Quok Walker sued for his freedom in 1783, the Massachusetts superior court ruled in his favor. In Pennsylvania, the Philadelphia Quaker merchants John Woolman and Anthony Benezet had denounced slavery for years, and in March 1780, Pennsylvania enacted the United States' first emancipation law freeing slaves.

Slave owners in Pennsylvania as well as New York and New Jersey put aside republican principles and obstructed legislative efforts to abolish slavery. Large farmers continued to profit from slave labor and turned the Declaration of Independence upside-down by arguing that emancipation violated slave owners' natural right to their slave property. Pennsylvania's emancipation law did not free any slave on the spot; it freed only slaves born after 1780 and only when they reached twenty-eight years of age—well past their prime productive years. New York and New Jersey lawmakers passed similar halfway emancipation laws while simultaneously strengthening their states' slave codes as large farmers imported more young Africans. During the 1790s in New York, where an emancipation law was not enacted until 1799, the number of slaves actually increased by 25 percent and the number of slave owners by over 30 percent.

Revolutionary republicanism also weakened and eventually destroyed indentured servitude. With all the talk of freedom, many in the United States regarded all forms of bound servitude as "contrary ... to the idea of liberty this country has so happily established." Some citizens mounted campaigns to raise money to release servants from indenture. Many employers either voluntarily or under pressure hired paid "trainees" rather than apprentices. Fewer individuals were willing to work as servants, and those who did were less controllable than before. In the prevailing atmosphere of republicanism they could demand and get the respect they desired. White domestic workers insisted that their employers refer to them as "help" instead of the more demeaning term "servant," and many refused to address their employers as "master" or "mistress." Even as early as 1775 in Philadelphia, the proportion of unfree workers (slaves and servants) had

dropped to 13 percent of the workforce from nearly half at mid-century. By 1800, only 2 percent of the city's workers were not free.

African Americans and the Pursuit of Happiness

Despite Revolutionary rhetoric, ostensibly free black men, women, and children did not possess anything approximating the same freedom and opportunity for the "pursuit of happiness" that whites enjoyed. African Americans who were free generally could not vote, serve on juries, or give testimony in court against white people. However, free blacks did not merely settle for what whites gave them. Growth in the free black population testified to African-American women and men's determination to share in the promise of a republican society.

> **How did African Americans assert their freedom?**

The population of free blacks increased as slaves in all parts of the country gained their freedom through manumission or running away from their masters. Natural increase, as African Americans formed strong families, also contributed to the increasing numbers of free blacks. Nationwide, the number of free African Americans reached 59,000 in 1790 and almost doubled over the next decade. Over half of the free people of color resided in the South, mostly in or near towns. In the North, by 1790 four out of every ten African Americans were free and tended to collect in port cities such as Philadelphia, New York, and Boston. One white New Yorker complained: "Whole hosts of Africans now deluge our city."

Migration to urban areas was deliberate. Jobs for men and women were more plentiful there, providing them with greater opportunities for economic advancement and forming and maintaining families than existed in the countryside. In addition to domestic labor such as cooking, washing, and cleaning, black women manufactured baskets, sewed items of clothing, and sold fish, crabs, and other food products in street markets. Black men typically found work in other types of menial labor: driving wagons and carriages, cleaning and performing building and grounds maintenance, and on the wharves making rope, caulking ships, and loading and unloading cargo. But a few African Americans became butchers, hatters, or brewers, usually catering to other blacks because of white domination of larger artisan markets. A very few blacks, like sail-maker James Forten of Philadelphia, became wealthy. Economic opportunities were also limited in the towns of the Upper South, but in Charleston and Savannah, free blacks took advantage of the presence of relatively few white artisans. However, a greater commitment to slavery and fear of free blacks igniting slave revolts in the Lower South created an extremely precarious situation for free African Americans there.

Free African Americans exercised their freedom every way they could. They dropped the slave names their masters had assigned to them and assumed new names of their own choosing. Sometimes they used the family names of whites like Jackson and sometimes physically descriptive ones like Brown, but they often registered last names such as Freeman or Liberty that reflected their free status. Community spirit soared, manifested in frequent picnics, parades, and the continuation of Pinkster and Election Day celebrations; however, free blacks' isolation from the mainstream revealed some of the boundaries of their freedom. Revolutionary ideology established the right to freedom, albeit vaguely, but not the right to live anywhere, to a job, or to a living wage. For example, formal and informal restrictions confined free blacks to certain neighborhoods, prevented them from entering high-status professions like medicine and the law, and, because they limited their earning capacity, curtailed their self-reliance.

Turned away from mainstream American social life, African Americans established self-help social institutions, including schools. Whites sometimes assisted black initiatives. New Jersey, for instance, provided segregated schools for the education of African-American pupils. In New York City, the **Society for the Promotion of Manumission** helped blacks found the African Free School. But whiles also resisted black initiatives. For example, stiff opposition from whites kept enrollment at black schools small. Some African Americans sought freedom in independent Native American towns whose male populations had been depleted by war casualties. African-American men married Indian women and acquired access to property. This altered both the composition of the communities and the nature of their cultures. The father of the famous merchant and sea captain Paul Cuffee was a formerly enslaved African and his mother was a Wampanoag with property and status.

African Americans took great pride in their social organizations, evident in the use of the word "African" in the names they selected for their institutions. Before the Revolution, a congregation of slaves and free blacks met regularly in Savannah, Georgia. Their preacher was a slave, George Leile. In 1788 the congregation became recognized as the First African Baptist Church of Savannah. In Philadelphia in the 1790s, Richard Allen organized the **African Methodist Episcopal Church**. In 1816, he also helped organize African Methodist churches in Philadelphia, New York, and Baltimore into the African Methodist Episcopal denomination. In 1821, other African Methodists founded the **African Methodist Episcopal Zion Church**. Churches were valuable assets to African-American communities. In addition to religious experiences, they provided opportunities for socializing and gaining skills in managing organizations. African Methodist churches also played active parts in anti-slavery activities.

African Americans in towns of the North and South also formed mutual aid, charity, and fraternal societies. These organizations assisted members who suffered from injury or disease; they provided burial insurance to help African Americans maintain that important end-of-life ritual. In Philadelphia, Richard Allen and Absalom Jones organized the **Free African Society**. It promoted self-help and self-esteem by holding regular meetings to discuss common issues and solutions. In Boston in 1787, a Methodist minister, Prince Hall, founded the first African-American Masonic lodge.

Several African Americans won personal acclaim for extraordinary talent. A young slave named Phillis, who belonged to Susannah Wheatley of Boston, became one of the most famous poets in American history. Among Phillis Wheatley's poems was a tribute to George Washington, who cited it as "striking proof of your great poetical talents." Although her poetry seldom referred directly to slavery, Wheatley nevertheless spoke out directly against human bondage. The scientist, mathematician, and engineer Benjamin Banneker achieved international renown. In 1791 Banneker began publishing an almanac that impressed learned persons on both sides of the Atlantic. His calculations of the positions of celestial bodies caused Thomas Jefferson to

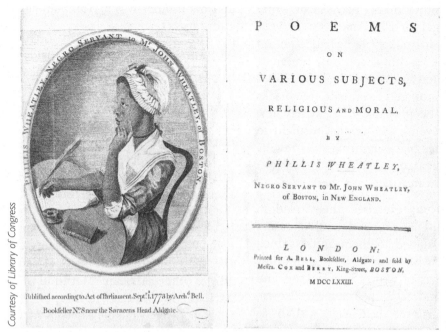

Phillis Wheatley and her book Poems on Various Subjects, Religious and Moral, *published in London in 1773, represented great personal achievement. They were also sources of pride for many African Americans.*

Courtesy of Library of Congress

remark: "Nobody wishes more than I do to see such proofs as you exhibit that nature has given to our black brethren talents equal to those of other colors of men."

As women and African Americans pushed to extend the boundaries of their freedom, people of both genders and various cultures moved onto the nation's geographic frontiers. There, settlers from the United States and Native Americans inhabitants struggled for different types of freedom.

Expanding the Nation's Frontiers

> **How did Revolutionary ideals influence expansion into the trans-Appalachian region?**

As the ink dried on the Treaty of Paris, hardy, freedom-seeking men and women from the eastern seaboard settlers streamed into the trans-Appalachian West carrying their axes, hoes, and spinning wheels. From a few pioneers living in fear of their lives in fortified stations, Kentucky's settler population, including slaves, grew to 73,000 by 1790. Approximately 36,000 newcomers had pushed into Tennessee, as far West as the Cumberland Valley around Nashville. As the settlers' numbers multiplied and they formed militia companies, the Indians became less of a threat. But travel remained dangerous, and settlers generally traveled in armed groups. Bloody Shawnee-led resistance north of the Ohio River kept all but the most intrepid pioneers out of that area for the time being.

During the Revolutionary War, which looked to many Indians like an English civil war, the Iroquois, Shawnee, and Cherokee aimed to defend their towns, fields, and hunting grounds. Some sided with the British, and Continental forces and groups of armed partisans like Daniel Boone's Kentucky neighbors punished them severely. As Boone wrote, the whites "spread desolation throughout their [Shawnee] country." A delegation of Iroquois, Shawnee, and Cherokee Indians told a Spanish official in St. Louis that the American Revolution was "the greatest blow that could have been dealt us, unless it had been our total destruction." To avoid that outcome, some Indians relinquished their land to the United States and moved elsewhere, amalgamating with other Indian people. In the 1784 **Treaty of Ft. Stanwix,** the Iroquois opened their land to white settlement, and many Indians resettled in Canada. In the **Hopewell Treaties** of 1785 and 1786, Choctaw, Chickasaw, and Cherokee leaders conceded land in the lower Mississippi River valley. But the Indians had a card to play—trade—and they promised to trade with both American and Spanish agents in exchange for protection. However, Shawnee Indians played another hand, maintaining relations with British Canada and obtaining arms to fight against settlers from the United States.

182 Chapter 6—One Nation or Many, 1781–1789

The settlers came from various backgrounds. They included Continental Army veterans cashing in land bounties, German, Scots-Irish, and English immigrants, and speculators, merchants, and lawyers from the East who comprised the new western gentry. Most settlers, like William Clinkenbeard, who arrived in Kentucky in 1780, were intent on rising from the lower rungs of the economic ladder. Clinkenbeard and the other men built lean-tos and then log cabins near their cornfields set in forest clearings. The settlers raised corn for food for themselves and their livestock. If things went well, after a year or two they planted tobacco and wheat for sale. In addition to raising livestock they trapped beaver and hunted deer, buffalo, and turkey. John Hedge ate turkey-pot-pie "till I got so tired I never wanted to eat any more as long as I lived."

By the early 1790s a measure of stability had come to Kentucky and Tennessee. Industries appeared: salt works, blacksmith shops, gristmills, and tanneries. Merchants shipped flour, beef and pork, and tobacco down the Ohio and Mississippi rivers to markets. Possessing little cash, farmers bartered with merchants or drew credit from them. Surpluses soon grew. Robert McAfee's father, like others, "raised an abundant crop which he sold to new settlers which poured into Kentucky every year." Informal governments evolved into county administrations, which maintained the militia, kept records of land claims, built roads, and punished lawbreakers. For horse stealing, Elias Pybourn had both ears cut off, thirty-nine lashes laid on his back, and the letter "H" branded on his cheek.

Americans pushing the frontier southwestward threatened Spain's tenuous hold on Louisiana and West Florida (essentially the southern edges of present-day Alabama and Mississippi). The border between Florida and the United States was unclear. The Treaty of Paris (1783) set it at the 31st parallel, but Britain's separate cession of Florida to Spain drew the line above the 32nd parallel from Georgia to Natchez on the Mississippi River. Numerous Americans settled in that disputed area. They were hundreds of miles away from the silver mines of Mexico, and the American frontier settlers were more interested in farming than claim-jumping; nevertheless, the riches of New Spain had never seemed so vulnerable. Sonora's governor looked with apprehension upon the "new and independent power" on the North American continent.

In the face of onrushing Americans, Spanish officials geared up several protective mechanisms.

They pieced together alliances with the Creek, Choctaw, and Chickasaw Indians. In 1784 Spain closed the Mississippi River to the United States, thus depriving Westerners of access to outside markets. Unable to induce Spaniards to settle in the borderlands, Spain enticed foreigners with land grants and access to the port of New Orleans. For their part, the settlers had only to swear a loyalty oath to Spain. Although they were not the settlers that Spain preferred, Americans took advantage of the offer and moved into Florida and Louisiana. Louisiana's governor, Baron de Carondelet, warned that the United States might take over the frontier "without unsheathing the sword."

Spanish policy was not as hare-brained as it might seem. Many Kentuckians and Tennesseans were ready to renounce their own national government, which could not protect them against Indian attacks. They were disgusted by its inability to guarantee access to New Orleans. By becoming Spanish subjects they could obtain the right to use the Mississippi. Settlers also directed their resentment at Virginia and North Carolina, which insisted on maintaining authority in the territories. Many westerners warmed to suggestions that they should join Spain rather than remain part of the United States.

In 1784 John Jay, representing the United States, opened talks with Don Diego de Gardoqui, Spain's minister to the United States. Their discussions focused on the New Orleans issue. The Spanish crown was predisposed to keep the door to New Orleans tightly shut, and the United States had nothing with which to pry it open. Gardoqui did offer a commercial treaty to which Jay responded favorably. But trading navigation rights for an agreement beneficial only to northeastern commercial interests fanned the flames of western anger. Southern congressmen, sympathetic to the western cause, blocked further negotiations on the Gardoqui proposal.

The trans-Appalachian West was not the only expanding Anglo-American frontier. The push into western New York absorbed land abandoned with the destruction of the Iroquois Confederacy during the Revolutionary War. In 1786, William Cooper purchased 29,000 acres of forested land adjacent to Lake Otsego, at the headwaters of the Susquehannah River. An impoverished wheelwright who married the daughter of Richard Fenimore, a prosperous Quaker farmer, Cooper merged the cash he acquired from his wife with that of several rich investment partners to buy the land.

Offering generous credit, Cooper sold off his land in small parcels to settlers. Many buyers moved in from western Massachusetts. New England's diminished farms and depleted soil combined with the magnetic attraction of commercial agriculture in New York to spur Yankee emigration. Industrious and independent-minded, the newcomers were well suited to Cooper's rugged domain, but even they struggled to clear enough land to feed themselves. Cooper helped as much as he could, arranging markets for potash (wood ash used to make soap) and maple sugar.

By the 1790s, economic conditions had improved. Otsego County contained over 21,000 residents. Cooperstown, the county seat and in the twentieth century the location of Major League Baseball's Hall of Fame, was a prosperous town with seventy-eight houses (one-half of which were two-story homes), five stores, and three taverns. Residents included a druggist, a baker, a saddler, and a house painter. In the center of town stood stately Otsego Hall, Cooper's two-story brick mansion and the home in which his son, the novelist James Fenimore Cooper, grew up.

As much as he wanted to be treated like a patriarch and an aristocrat, however, William Cooper was not accorded such high esteem. Wealthy but not of a prominent family with a college education and genteel upbringing, he received a cold shoulder from the aristocratic Hudson Valley land barons he admired—Robert R. Livingston and Philip Schuyler among them. He represented the western gentry of self-made individuals, as good with their fists as with their wits.

Busy and aggressive in their aspiration to get ahead, settlers on the frontiers of the United States felt little sense of nationhood. But back east, efforts were underway to forge an American identity.

Forging an American Identity

| How did writers and painters contribute to the formation of an American identity? |

Nations typically celebrate defining moments in their histories. Although the history of the United States was very new, post-Revolutionary scholars interpreted its highlights, especially Revolutionary episodes as defining moments. David Ramsay, a Charleston physician, did so in *A History of the Revolution of South Carolina* (1785) and *A History of the American Revolution* (1789). Mercy Otis Warren—the sister of James Otis—did so as well in her *History of the Rise, Progress and Termination of the American Revolution* (1805), the first such history written by a woman.

Philadelphia's Benjamin Rush urged Americans to teach their children distinctively American (republican) values. Thomas Jefferson believed that education "engrafts a new man on the native stock." Proponents of a national education system advocated a national university, "where the youth of all the states may be melted (as it were) into one mass of citizens." The country declined to establish a national system of schools, but education became a mechanism for cultivating patriotism and civic pride. "Foreign education is directly opposite to our political interests," Noah Webster said. Webster hoped that the American vocabulary would evolve into an American English language. "Provincial accents," he said, "are disagreeable." He compiled a dictionary that formalized American dialect and spelling.

The Revolutionary era spawned a number of legends of the new nation like the mythical Daniel Boone. An Episcopal minister turned itinerant book salesman, Mason Weems, wrote the immensely popular *The Life and Memorable Actions of George Washington* (1800). "Parson" Weems introduced the "little hatchet and cherry-tree" story through which generations of school children learned about the mythical George Washington, the republican hero who could not tell a lie.

At least among the elite, artists helped greatly in defining the nation by immortalizing its heroes and their feats. Painters, most notably John Trumbull, Gilbert Stuart, and Charles Willson Peale, depicted scenes of the Revolutionary War and painted portraits of the young nation's leaders. "The greatest motive I . . . have for engaging in . . . my pursuit of painting," Trumbull explained, "has been the wish of commemorating the great events of our country's Revolution." Stuart immortalized George Washington in over 100 likenesses. Poets Philip Freneau and the African-American Phillis Wheatley expressed the meaning of the Revolution in verse.

THINKING BACK

1. What did "republican" mean, and how did the ideals of Revolutionary republicanism change the fabric of American society?
2. How did republican America treat women, African Americans, and Native Americans?

FREEDOM *VERSUS* ORDER

Revolutionary-era Americans did not believe in direct participation in government by all races, genders, and classes—what we call **democracy** today. They presumed the existence of innate differences in the quality and capabilities of people, what they understood as the "natural distinctions of rank." John Jay, like many aristocrats, believed that the masses of people "are neither wise nor good." If allowed the freedom to take up places in government, they would turn that freedom into chaos. Therefore, some measure of structured order and restraint on direct, participatory democracy was thought absolutely essential to the future of the republic. The question that Americans faced was how much freedom and how much structured order was ideal. Hardly anyone wanted a monarchy, or a return to the old patriarchal system; nevertheless it seemed crucial that men of true virtue should become the country's leaders. A second important question to consider concerned how much autonomy to extend to the separate states and how much authority to invest in a national government. It is easy today, after more than 200 years of successful nationhood, to minimize the founders' profound anxiety about the republic's survival. But the possibility of failure was real to them. "The new Governments we are assuming," John Adams confided to Abigail, "will require a Purification from our Vices, and an Augmentation of our Virtues or they will be no Blessings."

Erecting New State Governments

In July of 1776, the colonies had declared themselves "free and independent states." Accordingly, the states adopted new constitutions that eliminated all references to the British crown. They took steps to insure that power derived from the people and experimented with various forms of republican government.

> Why did people feel the need to write new state constitutions, and what forms did the new state governments take?

Republicans believed that constitutions, the most fundamental allocation of power to government, should originate with the people. During the Revolution, several state legislatures had drafted provisional constitutions for the individual states. But that practice gave the constitutions no higher authority than ordinary statutory law. Thus, in subsequent years, special conventions of popularly chosen representatives convened to draw up new state constitutions, beginning in 1780 with Massachusetts. Most states eventually convened such conventions. Connecticut and Rhode Island were the only states that did not. They retained and merely updated their colonial charters.

Revolutionary leaders based their designs for new governments on a set of widely held republican assumptions. Government, John Adams said, should "be in miniature an exact portrait of the people at large." Its powers must be defined by "higher law," that is, a constitution drafted by the people's elected representatives. Those representatives should be persons of civic virtue, "natural aristocrats" wealthy enough not to be distracted by affairs of the market place, learned enough to understand theories of government, and experienced enough to shoulder the responsibilities of leadership. Finally, government should be dominated by a legislature composed of the people's elected representatives rather than by a governor as in colonial days. The long and unpleasant experience with royal governors left people with a distaste for executive authority.

A number of difficult questions arose about who constituted "the people." Should everyone have the right to vote, or just certain people? On which criteria should that decision rest—property, gender, race, or aptitude? Adams thought any discussion of who should be included in the "body politic" was bound to produce only frustration or endless debate. "There will be no end of it," for "women will demand a vote, lads from twelve to twenty-one will think their rights are not enough attended to, and every man who has not a farthing will demand equal voice with any other in all acts of state." In general, women, children, and African Americans were eliminated from the electorate. Property qualifications differed from state to state. Pennsylvania abolished all property requirements, Maryland maintained high property qualifications, or a "stake in society," and the other states ranged in between.

Another important question involved the distribution of power within state governments. Pennsylvania adopted the most democratic system with a constitution that provided for a single, unicameral (one-house), legislature in which all constituencies were represented. Its constitution eliminated the office of governor because it was "too monarchical" and created instead an executive committee that reported to the legislature. The Maryland constitution was the most conservative; it called for a strong governor and a bicameral, or two-house legislature, consisting of a legislative assembly (the lower house) and an upper house elected by free adult males (black as well as white) with property. Members of both houses met high property qualifications and represented the state's propertied elite. The convention did not submit the constitution to the people for ratification. Most state constitutions created such bicameral legislatures, following the English example, along with an executive officer usually called the governor. The framers reasoned that one house would empower the virtuous but somewhat unpredictable common people while the other brought into government the "wisdom and foresight" of the "better sort." The young political leader from New York, Alexander Hamilton, explained about his state: "the senate [the upper house] was to the commonwealth what ballast is to a ship." Because of many negative experiences with royal governors during colonial times, the framers of most state governments did not do as Maryland did and instead generally avoided awarding very much power to the new executive offices.

Skepticism of all government officials prevailed in the climate of Revolutionary America. Common wisdom held that frequent elections would keep legislators honest. "Where annual election ends," went a saying of the day, "slavery begins." Democratic state leaders wanted to ensure that the people themselves, not the politicians they elected, actually ruled.

A Confederation of Sovereign States

> **How did the country settle the debate over a strong national government versus independent states?**

In 1776, the nation's leaders had felt the need for some sort of central government to keep the thirteen states united. There was a war to win, and as Benjamin Franklin put it, "we must all hang together. Otherwise we shall most assuredly hang separately." But few people yet accepted the idea of a sovereign or supreme national government. In the summer of 1776, the Continental Congress appointed a committee to draw up a plan for a new government. Its chairman, the conservative lawyer John Dickinson now of Delaware, proposed a strong central one. Opponents thoroughly revised Dickinson's plan, however, and the finished document, called the **Articles of Confederation and Perpetual Union**, was submitted to Congress in November of 1777. It stated that each state "retains its sovereignty, freedom and independence."

The states retained "every power . . . which is not . . . expressly delegated to the United States." Not many powers were delegated to the new central government. The Confederation government could declare war and negotiate treaties, but it could not impose taxes or regulate commerce. Nor did it possess exclusive power to create coins and currency. These powers remained with the states.

The concept of government under the Articles of Confederation was a "league of friendship" which reflected the views of the most liberal-thinking, democratic-minded republicans. There would be no independent executive, only a one-house Congress. Large states (with large populations) preferred proportional representation in Congress, giving them more votes than less-populous states. But smaller states demanded equal representation, and they prevailed. Although states could send from two to seven delegates to Congress, each state would have only one vote. A majority vote of the states was required to pass ordinary legislation; more important matters demanded the assent of nine states. Reinforcing the principle of state sovereignty, the Articles stipulated that any amendments must have the assent of all the states. The principle became known as **majority rule**.

Congress also required that all thirteen states ratify the Articles of Confederation. Several issues and the circumstances of the Revolutionary War caused delays, but by early 1779 twelve states had approved the Articles. Only Maryland's objections stood in the way of adoption. The problem for Maryland was how to manage or distribute western land. Dickinson's original draft had proposed that states relinquish all land claims west of the Appalachian Mountains and that management of the "public domain" be placed in the hands of the Confederation government. The Articles, however, allowed states like Virginia, whose colonial charter extended its western boundary all the way to the Pacific Ocean, to retain their western lands.

Marylanders were outraged. Why should they be cut off from land opportunities in the West while Virginians were allowed to take advantage of them? Why should they have to pay taxes to support their state government while Virginia raised revenue by selling its vast public lands? Behind the fairness issue stood a second consideration: wealthy and powerful Maryland speculators hungered for valuable western land and the profits they could make by obtaining the land cheaply from their state government and selling it to settlers.

Virginia finally broke the deadlock in January 1781 when its assembly voted to cede its western claims to the national government. The British inadvertently nudged matters along with its devastating military campaign in the Chesapeake toward the end of the Revolutionary War. The Continental Congress promised to defend Maryland in return for the state's ratification. So in 1781 the Articles of Confederation received the endorsement of the thirteenth and final state even though Virginia and North Carolina did not actually relinquish their western land until years later.

A "Critical Period" for the Republic

In his commencement address to Harvard's 1787 graduating class, John Adams described to the students a nation under the Articles of Confederation that groaned "under the intolerable burden of . . . accumulated evils." Immediately after the Revolution, he said, the country had entered a "critical period." Independence from Britain seemed secure, yet perils abounded. In Adams' estimation, and that of others whose backgrounds convinced them that social order was essential to protect freedom from the destruction of democratic chaos, the absence of discipline and control under the Articles threatened the survival of the new nation. Without restraints to hold selfish inclinations in check and without coercive authority at the national level to force the states to act in the common interest rather than their own, the United States would not be able to deal with the challenges that lay ahead.

> **What problems confronted the country after the Revolution?**

Many Americans deplored the erosion of social order that accompanied the Revolution. They recalled the various restraints that had once caused them to hate Parliament and British imperial regulations. "This revolution," wrote David Ramsay, "has introduced so much anarchy that it will take half a century to eradicate the licentiousness of the people." Some state legislatures, representing working people (especially indebted farmers) more than people with property, enacted a multitude of debtor-relief measures, including laws that authorized the printing of paper currency without gold backing and laws that postponed the payment of loans. Rhode Island was notorious for such enactments. In aristocratic societies, the interests of the masses are subordinated to those of the privileged few, but the young Virginia congressman James Madison feared the opposite in the United States. "It is much more to be dreaded that the [elite] few will be unnecessarily sacrificed to the many."

Other citizens felt differently. They were quite comfortable with decentralized government and railed against the "monarchists" who wanted to curb liberty in the name of order. They complained about aristocrats who lacked the "virtue that is necessary to support a republican government" because they refused to subordinate their personal interests to the common good. Opposing factions quarreled bitterly.

Several of the evils that Adams described in his commencement address stemmed from weaknesses in the Confederation government. The lack of taxing authority handcuffed Congress, as did its inability to compel the states to help meet the cost of government. "New Hampshire," one citizen groused, "has not paid a shilling . . . and does not ever mean to pay one to all eternity." Financing the war had been a constant struggle. Congress could neither meet its own expenses (including soldiers' pay) nor repay its domestic and foreign investors.

Continental-minded **nationalists** advised amending the Articles to provide Congress with the authority to tax, and thus to raise revenue needed to meet operating expenses. Robert Morris, a wealthy Philadelphia banker and the Superintendent of Finance, led the nationalists, along with a man named Gouverneur Morris of Pennsylvania (no relation) and Alexander Hamilton. In 1781, they proposed an **impost** plan authorizing a tax of 5 percent on imports.

The impost required an amendment, since it would add to the power that the Articles of Confederation allotted to Congress. All of the states saw the advantage of the impost, except Rhode Island, and without its approval the amendment failed. The episode pointed out not only the government's weakness but also the Articles' inflexibility. One state could stymie the other twelve.

The failure of the impost led to another serious crisis that unfolded late in 1782, before the Revolutionary War was officially over, and involved disgruntled

Continental Army officers. Following the British surrender at Yorktown, Washington had repositioned 11,000 Continental troops at Newburgh, New York, to keep a wary eye on British troops still in New York City. As they awaited the outcome of peace negotiations, without back pay or promised pensions, word came of the impost failure. Angry because this meant a further delay in receiving their pay, officers sent a petition asking Congress to make paying them a top priority. Nationalists, including Hamilton, hoped the crisis would strengthen their argument for enhancing Congress' power. Meanwhile, some of the officers conspired with General Horatio Gates to take over the army from Washington's command and perhaps even the country.

At a grievance meeting in Newburgh on March 15, 1783, Washington addressed the officers. As he lifted his spectacles, the general seemed more human and vulnerable than they had ever seen him. "Gentlemen, you must pardon me. I have grown gray in your service and now find myself growing blind." His words drew tears from the men and defused the potential rebellion, and in doing so helped subordinate military power to civilian authority.

But the nation's economic woes worsened. Bad weather in 1784 and 1785 caused crop failures, and the massive loss of slaves to the British during the war crippled the South's economy. Independence from Great Britain placed the United States outside of the British mercantilist network. While Americans had rebelled against that mercantilist system, they now realized that the British Empire had also guaranteed markets. British **Orders in Council**, which were policy declarations from crown officials rather than Parliamentary laws, closed English and West Indian markets to American commodities, a severe blow to New England commercial and ship-building interests as well as to farmers everywhere. Despite the 1778 treaty with France, American merchant ships carried few cargoes to French ports. Thomas Jefferson, the United States' minister to France, tried but failed to negotiate trade deals. American commerce and agriculture plunged into depression.

The free flow of expensive British merchandise into the United States added to the economic problems. Merchants in Philadelphia, New York, and Boston purchased goods, often on credit, in anticipation of rising local demand after the privations of war. A resulting trade deficit siphoned off the country's limited cash and crippled its commerce. The appropriate response would have been to limit British imports; however, Congress was powerless to regulate trade.

Diplomatic failures accentuated Congress' impotence. Stipulations in the Treaty of Paris regarding the recovery of prewar debts and the restoration of confiscated Loyalist property required compliance by the states, but Congress could not force such compliance. In retaliation, Britain kept its troops in frontier military forts at Oswego, Niagara, and Detroit. The national government could neither persuade them nor force them to withdraw. The continued presence of British redcoats on American soil rose to the level of national humiliation.

John Jay's controversial negotiations with Spain over the Mississippi River and New Orleans fueled speculation that the Confederation would disintegrate. This was the most ominous situation that the young republic faced during the mid-1780s. In 1787 a rogue by the name of James Wilkinson, who had been a Revolutionary War general, sold his allegiance to Spain and extended to Spanish authorities the hope that Kentucky and Tennessee might desert the United States.

Thus nationalists insisted that on many fronts freedom from strong government threatened social order and the future of the republic. In their zest for liberty, Americans had created chaos. They had not given their leaders the ability to solve problems that might destroy their new nation.

Success in the West

Although the Confederation government had failed to deal successfully with several important postwar issues, it did succeed in implementing policies for settling the **Northwest Territory** (comprising today's states of Ohio, Indiana, Michigan, Wisconsin, and Illinois). In anticipation of heavy settlement as soon as Indian resistance was broken, Congress adopted the **Land Ordinance of 1785** authorizing the surveying of land and the organization of townships. The pattern was a grid, with each township a thirty-six-square-mile block of land, divided into 36 sections. Each section consisted of 640 acres (1 square mile). One section was reserved for public education, and the rest were sold at public auction with a minimum bid of $1 per acre. The minimum purchase

> **What policies did the United States adopt for settling the West?**

was one section, or 640 acres. These terms were cheap by modern standards but favored speculators since few poor farmers had that kind of money. Speculators then sold the land to settlers in smaller parcels and on credit.

Surveys began later that year. The newly appointed government geographer, a former British career soldier named Thomas Hutchins, led a team into the Ohio country carrying survey instruments and muskets in case of Indian attacks. Due to the presence of menacing Shawnee and Delaware fighters, the work progressed very slowly, but Congress had established the important principle that public land would be distributed in small parcels and at fairly inexpensive prices. Jefferson had suggested making the territory available free to settlers; however, the nation's debts made such a policy impractical. The early development of western territories came from thousands of ordinary citizens establishing small commercial farms, a process very different from the initial English colonization of North America.

Two years later Congress passed another important western land law, the **Northwest Ordinance of 1787**. Pressure from land-development syndicates like the Ohio Company encouraged congressmen to prepare for the staged admission of the Northwest Territory to the Union as full-fledged states. From three to five territories were authorized, each one initially administered by a governor appointed by Congress. When the adult population of a territory reached 5,000 it could elect its own legislature, and when it achieved 60,000 it could petition Congress for admission as a state.

The ordinance was noteworthy for two reasons. First, it set precedents that, with few exceptions, governed the political organization of western territory through the next century. All new states would enjoy equal standing in the Union with the original thirteen. Second, the ordinance banned slavery in the Northwest Territories. The antislavery proviso won the unanimous consent of the states. Southern slave owners were willing to support it because the ban did not jeopardize slavery in the South.

Arthur St. Clair became the first governor of the Northwest Territory. He established his administration in Marietta, Ohio, in 1788, settled just months before by New Englanders under the auspices of the Ohio Company. St. Clair proceeded to appoint judges, create county governments, and proclaim a series of laws "conducive to civilization as well as morality and piety."

THINKING BACK

1. How did the question of order versus freedom pertain to the structure of governments in the United States?
2. How did the Articles of Confederation represent a victory for the advocates of freedom, and how did the problems the nation faced under the Articles of Confederation strengthen the argument for more order?

FORGING "A MORE PERFECT UNION"

By 1786, concern about the Republic's future had reached the level of urgency. People all over the country admitted that something had to be done about the economic problems and social disorder. Nationalists, of course, had been saying so all along. The "vile State governments," dominated by special interest and parochialism, had forsaken the general good. "I do not conceive," George Washington professed, "we can exist long as a nation without having lodged somewhere a power which will pervade the whole Union in as energetic a manner as the authority of the state governments extends over the several states." Following several unsuccessful efforts to modify the Articles of Confederation, nationalists changed their strategy from offering amendments to drafting a new constitution. A crisis during the winter of 1786–87 staggered the nation and set the stage for a constitutional convention that redefined the nation.

Shays' Rebellion

For two years farmers in western Massachusetts had struggled through economic depression. Unable to earn enough money to pay their bills, they risked being thrown into debtors' prison and losing their farms. Petitions demanding debtor-relief laws flooded the state legislature in Boston. These laws would have delayed the payment of debts and authorized the state to print paper currency, putting more money into people's pockets and therefore pushing up the prices of commodities that debt-ridden farmers produced. But the eastern merchant-financiers who controlled the legislature would have no part of it because such measures would have delayed the recovery of the money

> **What ignited Shays' Rebellion, and what was the outcome?**

they had lent and caused price inflation that allowed debtors to pay back loans with money worth less in terms of its purchasing power than what they borrowed. Instead, lawmakers raised property taxes more than 60 percent between 1783 and 1786. Angry farmers finally took matters into their own hands.

Many villages organized militia units, very much as they had during the Revolution. These bands of armed and desperate men closed several local courts and threatened judges who conducted legal proceedings against debtors. In August 1786, a thousand such citizens swarmed into Northampton. The leader of the citizen militias was a Revolutionary War officer named Daniel Shays.

Conservatives in Massachusetts and elsewhere decried this "internal insurrection." Edward Rutledge of South Carolina warned that the mobs intended to abolish all legitimate debts and redistribute property. Conservatives demanded a strong response before the rebellion got totally out of hand. It was high time "to clip the wings of a mad democracy." Fearful Boston

Proclamation by the State of Pennsylvania offering a reward for the capture of Daniel Shays, revealing the fear of rebellion throughout the country. Shays and his followers believed they were acting in the spirit of the Revolution, and from his diplomatic post in France, Thomas Jefferson agreed, writing that "a little rebellion now and then is a good thing." Sam Adams, however, contended that there was no place for rebellion in a republic.

citizens raised money for an army, which faced off against the rebels in Springfield on January 25, 1787. The farmers' rage had chilled in the bitter winter cold, and after suffering two dozen casualties, including four fatalities, in a brief battle, the rebels scattered. Two weeks later the government army cornered more Shaysites in the town of Petersham and routed them. Shays escaped and fled to Vermont. Convicted *in absentia* of leading an armed rebellion, he was sentenced to death but later pardoned by Massachusetts governor John Hancock.

Shays' Rebellion shook the country and awakened citizens around the country to the weaknesses of the Confederation government. It strengthened the argument of nationalists that the central government needed more power if the republic was to survive. The chaos that nationalists predicted had arrived, and more people now favored boosting Congress' authority. Indeed, a movement to do so had already begun. In September 1786, at Virginia's initiative, representatives of five states had met in Annapolis, Maryland, ostensibly to discuss issues of trade. But at least some of the participants, Madison and Hamilton in particular, urged a national conference in Philadelphia the next year to discuss specific problems and perhaps offer amendments to the Articles of Confederation. Then came Shays' Rebellion.

From Paris, where he was serving as America's envoy to France, Jefferson expressed another view of Shays' Rebellion. In January 1787, he wrote to Madison: "A little rebellion now and then is a good thing, and as necessary in the political world as storms in the physical." Madison disagreed and concluded that more than a few amendments to the Articles of Confederation were necessary to save the republic.

Inventors of a New Nation

In the spring of 1787 Congress authorized a national convention in Philadelphia. Its "sole and express" purpose was to revise the Articles of Confederation. On May 25 a quorum representing nine states gathered in the Pennsylvania state house, known today as Independence Hall. Eventually fifty-five representatives attended. The delegates quickly selected George Washington to preside. They were eager to get down to business, although it was unclear exactly what that was.

> **What were the delegates to the Constitutional Convention like, and what did they hope to accomplish?**

The early arrivals waited for their colleagues who drifted in over the country's still primitive roads. Heavy rains in some areas bogged them down. Those who arrived early entertained themselves by strolling along the city's crowded, elm-lined streets. Some stopped to chat with old Ben Franklin, now "a short, fat, trunched old man, . . . bald pate and short white locks," in his house on Market Street. Rooming houses did a booming business, as did taverns. Artist Charles Willson Peale's natural history museum, with its fossils, stuffed animals, paintings, and life-sized wax figures, was one of the most popular attractions in town.

The delegates to the **Constitutional Convention** were among the country's "best and brightest," although they were certainly not "an assembly of demigods," as Jefferson later described them. Mostly lawyers, merchants, and planters, they seem remarkably young to us today. Many were in their thirties, but they were experienced men, brilliant and learned, with quirks and peculiarities that made them fascinatingly human.

Their comparative youth helps explain why most of the delegates were nationalists. With a few exceptions they had come to adulthood with America, itself a young nation. Twenty-one had fought in the Revolutionary War, usually as junior-grade officers. Three out of four had sat in the Confederation Congress where they viewed events from a national rather than a state perspective. Many were too young to have formed their identities at an earlier time when people thought of themselves as primarily Virginians or New Yorkers.

Except for Franklin and Washington, the delegates were not the best known of the Revolutionary generation. One of the most notable intellects belonged to James Madison, a prim, scholarly graduate of Princeton who often fussed about his health. Madison's careful notes remain our clearest look at the debates, which took place under strict rules of secrecy to protect the delegates from outside pressures. Even the windows and doors of the meeting room were tightly shut. Other participants who contributed importantly to the deliberations included the stately George Mason of Virginia, the piercingly logical Scotsman James Wilson of Pennsylvania, the wooden-legged and gregarious New Yorker Gouverneur Morris, and the quiet but shrewd Roger Sherman, a merchant from New Haven, Connecticut.

Many of the Revolution's celebrities were conspicuously absent. Jefferson, who opposed a strong central government, was in Paris as ambassador to France. John Adams, a nationalist, represented the United States in Great Britain. Thomas Paine, still the aspiring entrepreneur, was in Europe peddling a new design for an iron bridge. Revolutionary firebrands Samuel Adams and Patrick Henry refused to participate in the convention. They suspected that despite its mandate the convention intended to scrap the Articles of Confederation. The agrarian interests that controlled Rhode Island's legislature declined to send a delegation out of their fear of a strong central government made up of merchant-creditors who would stamp out paper currency.

The major challenge facing the delegates was the need to strengthen the central government while preserving liberty. Their bitterest disagreement was whether the United States should remain a confederation of sovereign states or become a consolidated nation-state. Sherman, Elbridge Gerry of Massachusetts, and Virginia's Mason were states' righters, although that term did not exist in those days. They agreed with the French philosopher Baron de Montesquieu that republican governments work only in small territories, where the people share a common culture and interest and are not rent by faction. On the other side of the issue, Hamilton and James Wilson advocated an extremely nationalist point of view. They would have just as soon do away with the states altogether. "Will a citizen of *Delaware* be degraded by becoming a citizen of the *United States*?" Wilson asked. Madison stood between the extremes but decidedly in favor of a stronger national government.

Nationalism or Confederation?

Madison guided the deliberations from the opening gavel. Convinced that the states possessed excessive power and used it badly, he had studied political theories for alternative systems of government. He disagreed with Montesquieu and the states' righters. Small states, he argued, can easily be dominated by a special interest, which may ignore everybody else's rights. Large societies are likely to contain multiple, competing interests that must build coalitions. Building on the principles of constantly shifting majorities, along with internal **checks and balances** to prevent the abuse of power, Madison formulated a plan for a new central government, sharing it first

What were the Virginia and New Jersey plans?

with other members of the Virginia delegation. When Washington brought the convention to order, Madison seized the initiative. Rather than suggesting amendments to the Articles of Confederation, he called for an entirely new framework of government.

Madison's **Virginia Plan** proposed a sovereign national government representing people, not the states, and a mechanism to ensure against legislative excess and "mobocracy." It authorized the national government to tax, regulate commerce, and veto state legislation. It proposed a bicameral legislature with representation proportional to each state's population. Voters in each state would elect representatives to one house, and that house would choose members to the second. An executive branch with a veto over the legislature and an independent judiciary to resolve disputes completed the outline.

After two weeks of debate, William Paterson of New Jersey, who disapproved of national sovereignty, submitted an alternative plan. Paterson conceded the need for stronger national authority but denounced the Virginia Plan for going too far. His **New Jersey Plan** essentially amended the Articles of Confederation to enhance Congress's authority. People did not complain about the framework of decentralized, legislative government, Paterson insisted. "[W]hat they wish is that Congress may have more power."

The wrangling continued into the summer. Wilson refuted Paterson by pointing out that the delegates were free to "propose any thing" they wished because they had the power "to conclude nothing." The convention was only recommending changes that the people could accept or reject. Hamilton proposed an extreme concentration of power in a central government with an elected monarchy, a plan he modeled after the British system. The Virginia Plan seemed tame by comparison. The delegates ignored Hamilton's proposition, and by a better than two-to-one margin they approved the outline of the Virginia Plan.

Working Out the Details

| How did the delegates resolve the deadlock over representation? |

Approving the outline of the Virginia Plan did not end debate. The going actually got tougher, not easier. The deputies still had to resolve significant differences over representation. The small states favored equal representation regardless of population; Virginia argued that

equal representation choked the voice of citizens in the larger states and violated the hallowed republican principle of majority rule.

In July a committee offered a solution suggested by Connecticut's Roger Sherman. The **Great Compromise**, sometimes called the Connecticut Compromise, provided that representation in the House of Representatives would be apportioned according to population while in the Senate each state would have equal representation. Madison and Wilson protested against "departing from justice in order to conciliate the smaller states, and the minority of the people," but the convention adopted the compromise.

As the temperature and humidity inched upward in the meeting hall, the sweltering delegates plodded on. On August 6 a special committee submitted a draft constitution reflecting the points on which a majority of the delegates seemed to agree. In debating the draft clause by clause, several major issues regarding the executive office surfaced. One, a presidential veto over acts of the legislature, went straight to the heart of the widespread fear of tyranny. "Can one man be trusted more than all the others?" Sherman asked. Wilson countered that where a strong executive did not restrain the legislature, chaos or tyranny always ensued. The delegates voted for the executive veto. Another debate occurred over the method of selecting the president, and another reconciliation committee came up with the plan for the Electoral College with its system of election by electors rather than directly by the people.

Slavery and the Constitution

| How did the delegates address the matter of slavery? |

Slavery became, in the words of Madison's secretary, a "distracting question" for the delegates, not because it raised a moral dilemma but because it touched vital economic interests. Apportioning representation according to population raised the question of how slaves would count in determining a state's population. With the South's large proportion of slaves, to count them would enhance those states' voting strength in the House of Representatives while also increasing the slave states' liability insofar as direct taxes levied by the national government was concerned. The South's delegates wanted to count slaves for representation but not for per capita taxation. Northern delegates argued that slaves should be counted for both or neither. The convention decided on the **three-fifths rule** that the Congress under the Articles of Confederation had previously devised: five slaves would count as three free persons. This decision was not based on logic, for how could three of very five slaves be people while the other two were not? But it was the stuff of political deal-making. Maryland's Luther Martin reacted angrily. Slavery in the fundamental law of the country "is inconsistent with the principles of the revolution and dishonorable to the American character." But there slavery stood, not in explicit terms—the Constitution did not contain the word *slave*—but by intimation in the fundamental law of the nation.

The delegates then turned to a related and also highly emotional issue—the African slave trade. Martin proposed the prohibition of further imports of slaves. South Carolina and Georgia representatives heatedly argued against such restrictions and threatened to reject the constitution if it were included. The issue was resolved when it became linked to a concurrent discussion about requiring a two-thirds vote of the legislature to approve commercial regulations. New Englanders opposed such a measure and struck a deal with the southerners. They would not vote to prohibit the slave trade if the southerners voted against the commercial provision. Done.

The Outcome: A Federal Republic

What kind of government did the Constitutional Convention finally propose?

By early September all of the issues were resolved, although to no one's total satisfaction. A few of the delegates had thrown up their hands and gone home. Three who stayed to the end, Elbridge Gerry, Edmund Randolph, and George Mason, refused to sign the final document. But on September 17, thirty-nine delegates who had accepted the many compromises affixed their signatures to *The Constitution of the United States of America*. "I consent . . . to this Constitution," Franklin said, "because I expect no better, and because I am not sure that it is not the best." The delegates then adjourned to the City Tavern to celebrate.

The Constitution established a balance between "democratical" and "aristocratical" elements within three distinct branches of the national government—the legislature (Congress), the executive (the president), and the judicial (the Supreme Court). The most democratic part of the new government was the House of Representatives. Its members

would serve two-year terms. Senators would serve six-year terms, the president four, and Supreme Court judges for life (or as long as they behaved themselves). Because its members were less responsible to the voting public than the House of Representatives, the Senate was generally regarded as less democratic and more aristocratic.

The principle of **separation of powers** reflected the delegates' collective decision to restrain democracy. Each of the three branches would possess specific powers. Congress' powers were primarily legislative, to make laws. The president's responsibilities were executive, to enforce the law. The Constitution provided for a Supreme Court and allowed Congress to establish other courts. The judicial power of the courts involved resolving disputes under the laws and treaties of the United States.

A second principle, that of **checks and balances**, further limited democracy. The Constitution gave the president (a less democratic office) the power to veto acts of Congress (a more democratic branch). But Congress could override the president's veto by re-passing the vetoed bill by a two-thirds vote. The president would appoint Supreme Court judges "by and with the Advice and Consent of the Senate." The Constitution even built checks and balances into the Congress. Both houses had to agree to a bill before it could become law; thus, either house could effectively negate the other.

The delegates compromised on the most fundamental question: confederation or nationalism. The new system was a **federal** one, meaning that sovereignty was shared between the national and state governments. The Virginia Plan had proposed giving Congress power "to negative all laws passed by the several States." That would have established a sovereign national government and greatly reduced the power of the states, but a majority of the delegates rejected that proposal. Instead, they limited Congress' power. It could borrow money, regulate commerce, coin money, declare war, levy taxes (except export duties), and perform other functions that were clearly defined. The states retained certain powers upon which the national government could not encroach, including defining and recognizing marriage, supervising public education, and regulating commerce and industry within individual states.

Unquestionably, however, the national government was supreme. The Constitution stated unequivocally that the laws and treaties of the United States "shall be the supreme Law of the Land." Furthermore, the document gave broad discretionary power to Congress, stating that it may "make all Laws which shall be necessary and proper" in carrying out its duties. That ambiguity has served the country well in the centuries since by giving the government authority to deal with issues that the framers of the Constitution could never have imagined.

Some have questioned the framers' wisdom in leaving so many interpretive doors open and have argued that the powers of government should be limited to precisely those that the framers' intended. But **original intent** is probably impossible to determine since the Convention's debates were held in secret. James Madison took detailed notes, but he did not prepare them for publication until years later, after his and the other delegates' memories had certainly faded. Furthermore, the Constitution was largely a collection of compromises, reflecting what its drafters regarded as political possible rather than what they originally intended.

Ratification: Federalists and Anti-Federalists

> **Why did the Federalists prevail over the Anti-Federalists?**

In drafting the Constitution, the convention delegates clearly exceeded their charge. They were not amending the Articles of Confederation but destroying them. They did not follow the Articles' amendment provision that required the unanimous consent of the states. That would have doomed the Constitution because Rhode Island would surely have opposed it, and other states might have also. Instead, the delegates decided that ratification of the Constitution would need the approval of only nine states. Support from all the states was desirable, however, because it would grace the new government with more legitimacy.

According to republican principles, only the people could promulgate a new government. Thus, the vote on the Constitution required specially elected ratifying conventions rather than state legislatures. If approved by state legislatures, the Constitution could claim no higher authority than ordinary statutes and could logically be amended by subsequent legislatures. Furthermore, as Edmund Randolph pointed out, the stiffest opposition would come from "the local demagogues who will be degraded by it from the importance they now hold."

Immediately after the Constitutional Convention adjourned, supporters and opponents prepared for the ratification battle. Proponents called themselves **Federalists**, sticking their opponents with the label **Anti-Federalists**, to emphasize their negativity. For the most part, the Federalists were better organized for the fight and had more effective leaders than the Anti-Federalists. Anti-Federalists feared the concentration of power and demanded amendments to the Constitution safeguarding individual liberty before they would support it. Federalists promised to add a bill of rights after the Constitution was approved.

Ratification looked easy when six states quickly endorsed the Constitution. The votes in Delaware, New Jersey, and Georgia were unanimous. Pennsylvania, one of the largest states, ratified by a two-thirds margin. Maryland and South Carolina climbed on board early in 1788. Anti-Federalists in Massachusetts had two powerful voices, John Hancock and Sam Adams. But Hancock was won over by the possibility of becoming vice president in the new government and Adams, despite hating concentrated power, favored a national union. By again conciliating Anti-Federalists with promises of amendments, the Federalists prevailed. The same tactic worked in Virginia, whose convention debated the Constitution in June. Patrick Henry was wild and erratic in his opposition. He attempted to scare the delegates into voting against the Constitution, warning that slavery would come under certain attack from the central government. But the Federalists carried the day with reasoned arguments. The Constitution went into effect when New Hampshire became the ninth and decisive state to ratify in June of 1788; however, Virginia was such an important state that a union without it was inconceivable. Virginia ratified a week later with a call for adding a bill of rights.

New York's participation was also crucial to a successful union, but Governor George Clinton commanded a strong Anti-Federalist opposition there. The Anti-Federalists pulled out all the stops, and so did the Federalists. Alexander Hamilton, John Jay, and James Madison collaborated on the *Federalist Papers*, brilliant essays on government that countered the Anti-Federalists' objections. More important in turning the tide, however, was news that Virginia and New Hampshire had ratified.

North Carolina and Rhode Island were the last of the thirteen states to approve the Constitution. North Carolina initially rejected it, but a second convention in November 1789 reversed the decision. Rhode Island finally approved the

Constitution in May 1790.

THINKING BACK

1. In what ways could the Constitution be seen as a triumph for the advocates of order?
2. How did the ratification campaign turn on the issue of order versus freedom?

THE LOCAL PERSPECTIVE: FOCUS ON "ROGUE ISLAND"

What caused Rhode Island to delay ratifying the Constitution?

Tiny Rhode Island had a long-standing reputation of going its own way. Radical ideology had rooted itself deeply there, even back in Roger Williams' day in the seventeenth century. The state showed its intransigence with its rejection of Robert Morris' impost plan in 1781. Public opinion in the state ran strongly in favor of keeping the power to tax imports at home—not giving it to Congress. Most Rhode Islanders believed that after Virginia ceded its western land to the United States in 1781, Congress had the ability to raise all the revenue it needed through land sales. Besides, relinquishing power over its own commerce violated Rhode Island's constitution.

Favoring the loose confederation of states under the Articles of Confederation, Rhode Islanders refused to send delegates to the Constitutional Convention in Philadelphia in 1787. They were loath to give Congress taxing authority that would make the national government independent of the states. The Rhode Island commitment to state sovereignty largely explains the enormously popular legislative decision in 1786 to issue £100,000 in paper currency. It was, after all, the state's right and responsibility to address its own economic problems. Designed primarily to relieve indebted farmers and business people, the law required creditors to accept the currency in payment of all debts.

For two years after enough states had ratified the Constitution to establish a new union, Rhode Island voted down repeated attempts to convene a special ratification convention. Since the Constitution gave the national government exclusive power to coin money, the new regime stood against the state's interests. In February 1788 the state legislature referred the Constitution to town meetings, and the vote against ratification was 2,708 to 237. The results were somewhat misleading, however. Providence and Newport, where Federalists were strong, protested the referendum, and only twelve persons in those cities voted.

Although after the requisite nine states had ratified the Constitution Rhode Island's approval was not needed, Federalists wanted very much for all thirteen states to participate in the republic. One of the strategies that Federalists employed in dealing with "Rogue Island" was to discredit its political leadership. Tactics included claims that a self-serving radical party of "dishonest debtors" who favored depreciated paper money thwarted more virtuous Federalists in towns like Newport and Providence who recognized the chaotic financial condition of the country.

Finally, in 1790, the situation changed. Providence and Newport threatened to secede from the state. Independence for Rhode Island under those circumstances did not seem practical. In January the legislature finally voted to call a ratification convention. In May the delegates approved the Constitution, but only by a margin of two votes.

THINKING BACK

1. Why was the government of Rhode Island committed to paper currency?
2. Why did Rhode Island finally come around to ratifying the Constitution?

And Who Shall Lead?

From our vantage point more than two centuries later, ratification of the Constitution seems like the beginning of a smooth transition from one government to another, but for Americans of the Revolutionary generation it was far from that. The secrecy of the Constitutional Convention had left a bad taste in many mouths. Anti-Federalists had lost the ratification contest, but most of their objections remained, or even seemed validated. The Federalists' campaign had been successful, but it had not succeeded without chicanery—like the charade of "revising" the Articles of Confederation when the real intent was to scrap them. If the Federalists would so easily resort to trickery and deceit to create a new Constitution, what would they do once they held the reins of power? Who could be trusted to lead? There was, after all, no bill of rights. Throughout 1788, such questions swirled through the country, aired out in newspapers and in taverns and coffeehouses everywhere.

Answers did not come right away because the states moved slowly to enact new election laws. Until they did, the new national government remained more abstract than concrete. Indeed, some states did not conduct elections until February and March of 1789, but when they did it became clear that Federalists had been chosen to fill most seats in the House of Representatives and the Senate.

The greatest anxiety about the new government centered on the presidential office. After all, in the wrong hands the presidency could turn into a monarchy. Interestingly however, there was virtually no doubt about who should and would fill the office of President of the United States. That man would be George Washington, the only person who could bring instant legitimacy to the new government. Washington had successfully led the country during the crises of the Revolution, not just as commander of the Continental Army but also as the *ex officio* administrative leader of the government. More importantly, he had turned power back to the people once independence had been obtained.

The Constitution provided that the president would be chosen not by the people directly but by an **Electoral College**. Each state was allotted one elector for each congressman and senator it sent to Congress, and each elector had two ballots, undifferentiated but presumably one for president and one for vice-president. Individual state election laws, in turn, determined who chose the electors. Congress under the Articles of Confederation, in one of its final acts, had determined that electors should be chosen by January 7, 1789. This was not much time in an era when it took days or weeks for information and people to move even a few hundred miles. Meeting in their respective state capitols on February 4, each one of the electors cast one ballot for Washington,

who was thus elected unanimously. The other electoral ballots went to other respected leaders. John Adams received half the number of votes given to Washington but more than any other candidate and thus became vice president. The stage was set for the next act in building a democratic nation.

CONCLUSION

The Revolution established basic principles around which Americans began building a nation. They remodeled their societies to conform to Revolutionary republicanism—subordinating personal interest to the common good, ending aristocracy and special privilege, and ensuring that power derived from the consent of the people. But the Revolutionary generation retained many aspects of colonial life, like slavery, and what they were not equipped to change they bequeathed as a challenge to posterity. For three-quarters of a century, millions of African Americans remained unfree. It took 130 years for women to gain legal voting rights. In many ways we are still striving today to fulfill the Declaration of Independence's promise of the right to "the pursuit of happiness" against economic, social, and political inequities.

After struggling for a decade with a loose confederation of sovereign states, Americans redefined themselves. Under the Constitution, a federal system of government emerged, with power shared between the states and the federal government and an attempt to strike a balance between aristocracy and democracy. Questions remained. Would the Anti-Federalists' predictions of tyranny come true? Would the Federalists' assurances prove correct that the new government would solve problems that the old one could not?

SUGGESTED SOURCES FOR STUDENTS

Debate about the Constitution began with Charles A. Beard's *An Economic Interpretation of the Constitution of the United States* (1913).

For insights into African American life, see Ira Berlin and Ronald Hoffman, eds., *Slavery and Freedom in the Age of the American Revolution* (1983).

Issues of manners and taste receive authoritative coverage in Richard Bushman, *The Refinement of America: Persons, Houses, Cities* (1992).

Philip Freneau, *The Poems of Philip Freneau Written Chiefly During the Late War* (1786), represents some of the earliest expressions of a national identity.

A very readable treatment of gender issues in the new republic is Linda K. Kerber, *Women of the Republic: Intellect & Ideology in Revolutionary America* (1980).

Jackson Turner Main, *The Antifederalists: Critics of the Constitution, 1781-1788* (1961), offers support for the economic interpretation of the Constitution.

Forrest McDonald, *We the People: The Economic Origins of the Constitution* (1958), is an intense refutation of Beard's thesis.

Jack N. Rakove, *The Beginnings of National Politics: An Interpretive History of the Continental Congress* (1979), examines the problems of establishing a national government.

Jack. N. Rakove, *Original Meanings: Politics and Ideas in the Making of the Constitution* (1996), answers the perennial question, "What did the founders intend"?

Class antagonism figured prominently in the settlement of the frontier. Alan Taylor describes it brilliantly in his prize-winning *William Cooper's Town: Power and Persuasion on the Frontier of the Early American Republic* (1995).

Gordon S. Wood, *The Creation of the American Republic, 1776-1787* (1969), scrupulously explores the philosophical bases for the making of state and national governments.

The most important re-examination of the Revolution's impact on American society to appear in many years is Gordon S. Wood, *The Radicalism of the American Revolution* (1991), which portrays the Revolution as pivotal in the dismantling of privilege and patriarchy on the way to a republican and ultimately a democratic society.

BEFORE WE GO ON

1. How did the question of freedom *versus* order take form as Americans sought to build a new nation?

2. What were the successes and failures of the Articles of Confederation, and how did the delegates to the Constitutional Convention in 1787 hope the new Constitution would provide a more effective government?

Building a Democratic Nation

3. What signs do you see of growing budding democracy in the new nation? What types of people were most likely to be democratic? Who were the most likely to oppose democracy and favor social and political systems that favored the elite?

4. What were the sources of an emerging American identity?

Connections

5. What aspects of life and society in the United States today can you attribute to efforts by Americans in the 1780s to live up to the promise of the American Revolution?

6. Compare today's political debates over the role of the national government to those that led to the drafting of the federal Constitution?

Chapter 7

REDEFINING THE NATION, 1789–1800

A PERSONAL PERSPECTIVE: JOHN ADAMS AND WILLIAM MACLAY

On left: Vice-President John Adams. On right: Senator William Maclay.

For three weeks in the spring of 1789, during the first session of the new Congress, Vice-President John Adams and Senator William Maclay of Pennsylvania squared off in a series of personal exchanges over matters of protocol and etiquette. Today their debate seems like a silly tiff—lectures from the fussbudget Adams (whose Constitutional duties included presiding over the Senate) and Maclay's incessant objections. After all, there was important work for Congress to do. But their debate provides a personal perspective on some of the burning public issues of the day—the definition of a republic and how to preserve republican principles.

> **How do John Adams and William Maclay illustrate the ideological divide between Americans?**

Adams, the patriarch of a notable Massachusetts family, believed, as many New Englanders did, in authority, collective freedom more than individual liberty, and "dignified and respectable" government. Citizens would not respect and obey their government otherwise. As the first presidential inauguration approached,

Adams became agitated: "How shall I behave?" he asked the senators. Should they stand or sit while President George Washington delivered his inaugural address? Symbols and gestures conveyed important meaning: standing implied deference to the speaker while being seated connoted equality. The senators decided to stand. Maclay, a Scots-Irish Presbyterian from western Pennsylvania, reacted strongly against such symbolism. "I was up [only] as often as I believe was necessary," he recorded in his journal, ridiculing Adams and ranting against the people's representatives kowtowing to the chief executive.

On the day after Washington's inauguration, Adams and Maclay tangled over the wording of the Senate's response to the president's address, followed by a debate over "what style or titles . . . to annex to the office of President and Vice-President." Adams asked that the Senate's minutes refer to Washington's "most gracious speech." Maclay was outraged. "I cannot agree to this," he recorded in his diary, and again took the floor. He pointed out that those were the very words that Britain's Parliament used to describe King George III's proclamations. "I consider them improper." The "minds of men are still heated" from the Revolution, and anything that suggested royalty would certainly give offense. Adams could not imagine anyone taking offense from such innocuous language; however, most senators agreed with Maclay that the simple word "speech" without any adjectives was sufficient.

From there, the discussion shifted to presidential titles. How should the Senate address the president? Adams liked "His Highness the President of the United States of America, and Protector of their Liberties." Such designations were commonplace in the Old World and helped establish the dignity of and respect for government. But Maclay insisted that exalted titles and other forms of excessive deference might encourage closet monarchists. Calling him simply "The President of the United States" was fine with Maclay, although Adams grumbled that the

1769	1789	1790	1791	1793	1794
Gaspar de Portolá and Junípero Serra found the first Christian mission in California	George Washington inaugurated as first president. Congress passes a tariff law and the Judiciary Act and recommends the Bill of Rights to the states. Convening of Estates General launches French Revolution.	Hamilton delivers *Report on Public Credit.*	Hamilton delivers *Report on Manufactures.* Bill of Rights ratified. Vermont joins the Union. Washington signs charter of Bank of the United States. Philip Freneau begins *National Gazette.* Arthur St. Clair and his army defeated by Indians in Ohio.	Eli Whitney invents cotton gin. Louis XVI beheaded. Citizen Genêt stirs up controversy.	Whiskey Rebellion suppressed. John Jay signs controversial treaty with Britain. Anthony Wayne's army defeats Native Americans at Fallen Timbers in Ohio.

word "president" brought to his mind the humble leader of a fire company or cricket club. In the end, Congress decided that nothing more than "President" was necessary.

Both Adams and Maclay were patriots who supported the federal government and the Constitution; they agreed that in a republic, government derived its just powers from the people. However, they held strikingly different ideas about how best to secure the republic. Adams thought that common people had to be guided by individuals better than they, that is, by public officials esteemed for their virtue, independence, and high social standing. In the ruling circles of Europe, which were familiar to Adams through his distinguished diplomatic service to the United States during and after the Revolution, titles went hand-in-hand with noble status. For Maclay, whose background was more provincial, the trappings of royal government struck him as "quite the reverse of republican respectability."

In the 1790s, many ideological issues having to do with nationhood and identity divided the country, pitting adversaries like Adams and Maclay. Federalists had ratified the Constitution, and while not a numerical majority in the country, they controlled the new government. Mostly of English background, they sought to promote nationhood as the only way to preserve the republic from economic chaos and foreign enemies. Others, often Scots-Irish and German in origin and culture and formerly Anti-Federalists who had opposed the Constitution, worried that the Federalists actually intended to convert the republic into a British-style constitutional monarchy. Beyond the Appalachian Mountains, threats came more from Indians and the British in Canada who armed them, and many settlers identified as much with Spain as with the United States. In the absence of established political processes, Americans improvised new ways of dealing with public controversies like Secretary of State Alexander Hamilton's economic policies and how to respond to the French Revolution. Political parties attempted to persuade voters to support their cause. Unfortunately, the deep anxiety that many people felt provoked ferocious personal attacks and even an attempt to destroy political opposition. The absence of party discipline turned Federalists against themselves and contributed to the Republican victory in the extraordinary election of 1800. Launching the new nation proved difficult indeed.

THINKING BACK

1. What particular issues did Adams and Maclay debate during the first session of Congress?
2. How did those debates reflect the basic ideological differences that divided Americans?

TO FORM "A MORE PERFECT UNION"

In 1789, the United States had a new Constitution but not yet a fully operational republican government. Details about structure and power still had to be worked out, and that raised troublesome questions as both William Maclay and John Adams discovered. Many former Anti-Federalists could not reconcile an energetic central government with their republican ideals. Might the government not seize power from the states or the watchful eyes of local citizens and create a monarchy? Former Federalists wanted to work the levers of the new government to forge a unified and prosperous nation. They contended that if voters chose virtuous representatives the government could be trusted.

> How did different regional and class perspectives produce contrasting views about government?

To some extent, these contrasting views reflected different regional and class perspectives among Americans at that time. Farmers and artisans living in upstate New York and along the eastern foothills of

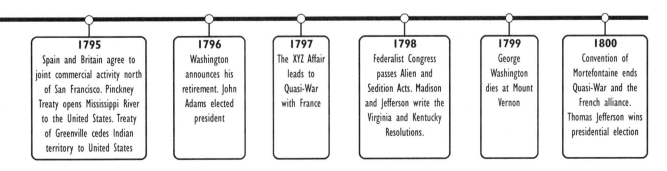

1795	1796	1797	1798	1799	1800
Spain and Britain agree to joint commercial activity north of San Francisco. Pinckney Treaty opens Mississippi River to the United States. Treaty of Greenville cedes Indian territory to United States	Washington announces his retirement. John Adams elected president	The XYZ Affair leads to Quasi-War with France	Federalist Congress passes Alien and Sedition Acts. Madison and Jefferson write the Virginia and Kentucky Resolutions.	George Washington dies at Mount Vernon	Convention of Mortefontaine ends Quasi-War and the French alliance. Thomas Jefferson wins presidential election

Settlers in the backcountry feared the new national government more than they trusted it.

the Allegheny and Appalachian mountains from Virginia southward to the Carolinas and Georgia perceived little need for a centralized government. Many of them were independent-minded German Lutherans or Scots-Irish Presbyterians like Maclay. One traveler described them as "extremely tenacious of the rights and liberties of republicanism." They supplied most of their basic needs, living modestly in relatively egalitarian circumstances. They had only limited access to newspapers and did not feel threatened by Native Americans or other enemies in ways they could not handle themselves. Thomas Jefferson, although a wealthy Virginia planter, idealized these self-sufficient **yeoman** farmers, hailing them as "the chosen people of God." Like them, Jefferson and other great planters in the South hated overbearing government and the taxes that inevitably came with it. But the agrarian alliance was not perfect, for farmers sniffed an air of haughtiness around the planters and resented their speculative land deals that gobbled up huge tracts of public land.

Agrarians not only distrusted centralized government, they disliked cities. From the agrarian perspective, which generally overlooked the brutal dehumanization of black slaves, cities bred evils that corrupted republics. Urban merchants accumulated excessive wealth not from their own labor but by charging interest on loans. Impoverished artisans and laborers toiled for others instead of themselves, breeding

an unrepublican subservience. But the influential Scottish philosopher David Hume had a different view on such inequality. In a commercial economy as opposed to a subsistence, agrarian economy, Hume explained, merchants invested in profitable industries and overseas trade that not only enriched them but also eventually created new markets, jobs, and greater wealth and living standards throughout the country. Drawing from Hume and his observations of early British industrialization, Alexander Hamilton envisioned an urban merchant class in the United States investing in a diversified and commercialized economy. Hamilton was certain that if the agrarians had their way, the country would "sink into a fatal atrophy, and, in a short time, perish." Moreover, the new national government could and should play a crucial role in promoting economic development.

Contrasting views of human nature and the respective roles of leaders and citizens in a republic also came under consideration in setting up the new government. Elitist republicans like Connecticut's Roger Sherman contended that common citizens "should have as little to do" with governing as possible because they "[lack] information and are constantly liable to be deceived." After electing trustworthy rulers, the masses should obey the government. But a more democratic, optimistic view held that common citizens could learn to be effective participants in the governing process. Jefferson became the most recognizable symbol of this form of republicanism, and his Virginia neighbor James Madison built a political organization around it.

But Americans from most backgrounds agreed that George Washington could be trusted to head the new government. A Federalist who often acted like a "patriot king," Washington nevertheless embodied true republican principles. Even the ultra-democrat Thomas Paine declared that his moral authority was "sufficient to put all those men called kings to shame." In the end, however, raging political battles engulfed even Washington and jeopardized what the Constitution's framers hailed as "a more perfect union."

Number One Among His Countrymen

> **How did George Washington attempt to legitimize the new government?**

Legitimizing the new government and making it the operational center of the world's largest and most diverse republic topped President Washington's list of priorities. Success depended on his reputation for dignity, public virtue, and sound judgment as well as on his ability to mediate between supporters of the new government and those who distrusted it.

Washington was well equipped for the task, for while his experiences as a military commander and slave owner taught him to value power and discipline, he believed in government by the people's consent.

Those who planned the first presidential inauguration also aimed at legitimizing the government. On April 16, 1789, president-elect Washington set off by coach from his Mount Vernon estate on the Potomac River for New York City, the republic's temporary capital. Along the way, town leaders bestowed honors on him and women cast flowers in his path. On April 30, Washington donned a plain suit and his military dress sword and walked onto the portico of Federal Hall where he pledged to uphold the Constitution. Afterward, New York's chief judge Robert R. Livingston cried out: "Long live George Washington, President of the United States." Both Adams and Maclay seemed satisfied.

Washington's friend and fellow army officer Henry "Lighthorse Harry" Lee later described him as "first in war, first in peace, and first in the hearts of his countrymen." But Washington would not have appealed to today's democratic tastes. Stern and erect, he embodied his era's ideal of aristocratic refinement. Liverymen chauffeured him through New York's crowded streets in an elegant coach and six white horses. He wore a powdered wig, preferred

Courtesy of Library of Congress

George Washington delivers his inaugural address, April, 1789, in the old city hall in New York City.

Martha and George Washington, from an unfinished portrait by Gilbert Stuart

formal bows to egalitarian handshakes, and enjoyed elegant "levees," but he only tolerated the weekly receptions.

"I walk on untrodden ground. There is scarcely any part of my conduct which may not hereafter be drawn into precedent." Washington set many precedents that have defined republicanism in the United States. His retirement after two terms fixed a term limit that eventually found its way into the Constitution as the Twenty-Second Amendment. After Congress created the first three executive departments (Treasury, State, and War), Washington consulted the department heads individually and convened them as an advisory group. As such, the president's **Cabinet** has remained an important arm of the executive branch of government.

Washington selected his Cabinet with an eye on cultivating "the good will of the People" and avoiding the impression of rotten **patronage** that had discredited royal government in colonial times (see Chapter 4). Cabinet officials represented the most populous states and had been actively involved in the Revolution and subsequently in national affairs; therefore, they stood generally high in public esteem. Hamilton and Jefferson were the stars. The brilliant, energetic, and urbane Hamilton from New York became the first secretary of the treasury. Jefferson, Washington's fellow Virginian and drafter of the Declaration of Independence, served as secretary of state. Lesser lights included Henry Knox of Massachusetts, one of Washington's Revolutionary War officers, as head of the War Department and Edmund Randolph, another Virginian as attorney general. Washington did not include Vice President John Adams in Cabinet

meetings, a precedent that lasted until early in the twentieth century. Thus marginalized, Adams complained that the vice presidency was "the most insignificant office that ever the invention of man contrived." More than to his Cabinet members, Washington looked to James Madison, a member of the House of Representatives for counsel. The disadvantage of a representative Cabinet was that the philosophical fissures in the country also divided the administration.

Gaps in the Constitution also led to disagreements and the setting of other precedents. For instance, the Constitution made the president responsible for making treaties, but only with the Senate's "Advice and Consent." However, what exactly was the Senate's role supposed to be? The problem appeared when Washington brought a proposed treaty with western Indians to the Senate expecting its prompt and perfunctory approval. Maclay felt hurried and asked for a committee to study the treaty draft and make recommendations. Obviously frustrated, Washington huffed: "This defeats every purpose of my coming here." Washington regained his composure, and the Senate ratified the treaty, but it was the last time he or any president sought the Senate's advice in drafting treaties. From then on, the Senate's role in treaty making has been limited to "consent."

In the fall of 1789, Washington toured New England so the public could see him as the personification of the new government. But while throngs cheered, Massachusetts' Anti-Federalist governor John Hancock tried to maneuver Washington into calling on him at his official residence. The symbolism reflected a pecking order, placing a state governor above the president of the United States. Washington refused, and finally Hancock agreed to call on the president, bowing to Washington's towering authority and the supremacy and legitimacy of the national government.

First Order of Business

Instead of running roughshod over Anti-Federalists, the Federalists who dominated both houses of Congress initially reached out to them. During the ratification debates, Anti-Federalists had criticized the lack of a bill of rights protecting individual liberties and states' rights. Indeed, two states, North Carolina and Rhode Island, had refused to ratify the Constitution because it had no

> What pressing issues did the first Congress address?

bill of rights, and seven states ratified contingent upon the quick enactment of amendments. Many Federalists suspected the Anti-Federalists of planning to hijack the amendment process to strip away Congress' taxing authority, but Madison suggested approximately twenty amendments to the House of Representatives, which sent seventeen to the Senate, which in turn passed twelve of them on to the states for ratification. By December 1791, the necessary three-quarters of the states had ratified ten of the amendments, dropping one relating to how representation in the House should be calculated and another restricting Congress in setting its own pay.

These first ten amendments to the Constitution made up the **Bill of Rights**. The first eight protected individual liberty from infringement by the federal government. The First Amendment guaranteed freedom of religion and speech and since its adoption has been one of the most controversial. It declared, "Congress shall make no law respecting the establishment of religion" or prohibiting "the free exercise thereof." Jefferson saw it as "a wall of separation between church and state," but over the years the First Amendment has sparked rather than resolved bitter disputes over prayer in public schools, religious symbols in public places, and the toleration of some religious expressions but not others. Similarly, government and citizens have argued over the practical meaning of free speech and press. In recent times, the Second Amendment has also provoked controversy. The amendment provided, "A well-regulated militia being necessary to the security of a free state, the right of the people to keep and bear arms shall not be infringed." Some have contended that this guarantees a citizen's right to carry any kind of gun while others see it as an anachronism framed at a time when the country relied on citizen soldiers for national defense.

Enacting the Bill of Rights had short-term and long run benefits. Because of it, North Carolina and Rhode Island ratified the Constitution. Both Madison and Washington keenly felt the necessity of establishing the government's legitimacy, and the Bill of Rights helped accomplish that. And over time, the values it incorporated into the Constitution set benchmarks for republican freedom.

Federalists focused even more attention on filling out the judiciary. The Constitution provided for a supreme court of unspecified size and "such inferior Courts as the Congress may from time to time ordain and establish." **The Judiciary Act of 1789** set the

number of Supreme Court justices at six (later increased to nine), created thirteen federal district courts, and organized the districts into three appellate circuits. Two Supreme Court justices and one district judge presided over each circuit court session. There were not enough federal courts and was not sufficient access to them over the country's primitive roads for the federal judiciary to supplant state courts altogether; furthermore, the Judiciary Act placed most original jurisdiction (where cases are heard for the first time) with state courts. But rulings from state courts could be appealed to the national Supreme Court, so, like the Constitution itself and the Bill of Rights, the Judiciary Act of 1789 was a political compromise between Anti-Federalists who wished to preserve as much state authority as possible and Federalists who wanted to strengthen the federal government wherever possible.

Nearly everyone in Congress agreed that the government urgently needed revenue to meet its expenses. The preferred source was an **impost**, or tariff, on imports. According to the Constitution, revenue measures had to originate in the House of Representatives, where Madison proposed a bill calling for a 5 percent tax on all imports. He added an enumerated list of mostly manufactured goods to be taxed at slightly higher rates. This would add to the price when those items were sold in American markets, making similar but more expensive American-made products more competitive. Such **protective tariffs** led to lobbying efforts by various producers to add their products to the favored list. It also gave the tariff the dual purpose of raising revenue and promoting certain segments of the economy. Naturally, representatives from areas that did not produce protected goods charged that the government favored special interests. The debate was not particularly heated for the level of protection was moderate and almost everyone who wanted protection from the tariff of 1789 got some.

Madison did raise a storm, however, by adding "a clause or two on the subject of tonnage." He proposed taxing all ships entering American ports by weight, or tonnage, using three different rates: the lowest for American-built and owned vessels, higher rates for ships of countries with which the United States had commercial treaties, and the highest for the ships of all "other powers." Since the United States had commercial arrangements with France that dated from the Revolution, the tonnage provision discriminated against Great Britain in favor of

James Madison, a painting by Charles Willson Peale

France. But this was not merely coincidental; Madison was intensely **Anglophobic** and without question wanted to discriminate against Great Britain. Representatives from South Carolina and Georgia complained, fearing British retaliation against rice and cotton shipped to British ports. Merchants in New England and New York also wanted to avoid a trade war with Britain, hoping instead to improve Anglo-American commercial relations. Congress finally voted for the import tax but against the tonnage discrimination.

In September 1789, Congress completed its first productive session and adjourned. Washington assessed the first few months optimistically, though perhaps naively. "So far as we have gone with the new Government we have had greater reason than the most sanguine could expect to be satisfied with its success." The shiny new government was not the only reason for optimism. Following years of economic frustration, the 1790s brought growth and prosperity.

Expanding the Market Economy

What factors contributed to the expansion of a market economy?

At the time of the Declaration of Independence, not everyone thought of the "pursuit of happiness" as the aggressive pursuit of profit. Most Americans still produced only to meet basic needs in local markets. A French journalist described the typical "give and take" (barter) economy in western Massachusetts: "Instead of money incessantly going backwards and forwards . . . , they supply their needs reciprocally in the countryside by direct exchanges. The tailor and the bootmaker go and do the work of their calling at the house of the farmer who requires it and who, most often, provides the raw material for it and pays for the work in goods. These sorts of exchanges cover many objects; they write down what they give and receive on both sides and at the end of the year they settle, with a very small amount of coin."

During the 1790s, however, increasing numbers of Americans began to produce and sell surplus commodities in distant marketplaces where profit, not merely subsistence, was the end game. Although **market capitalism** seemed to some republicans to contradict the ideal of self-sacrifice, others saw it as enhancing people's living standards and promoting national interests. Benjamin Franklin's "Poor Richard" had touted a commercial economy in one of his famous adages: "The way to wealth is as plain as the way to market." In the final decade of the eighteenth century, farmers and tradesmen joined commercial planters and merchants in traveling down the road to expanding markets.

Thomas Paine remarked that America would prosper as long as "eating is the custom of Europe." During the 1790s, growing European demand for American foodstuffs sparked a surge in commercial activity. Between 1750 and 1800, a time of war and crop failures, Europe's population doubled and exceeded its ability to feed itself. Americans capitalized on Europe's misfortune by supplying wheat, rye, and barley. Farmers in New York and Pennsylvania stepped up grain production, and many Chesapeake planters switched from tobacco to wheat. Between 1790 and 1800, exports jumped from $20 million to $71 million. In addition, new cloth-making machines, especially in Great Britain, stepped up the demand for American cotton.

Another technological breakthrough helped southern planters meet that demand. Cotton grown in coastal South Carolina and Georgia required particular soil and weather conditions, which limited crop size. An alternative variety had the potential of much greater yields because it flourished in a wider range of conditions; however, each cotton flower (or boll) contained dozens of hard, embedded seeds that had to be pulled out by hand before the fibers could be

THE FIRST COTTON-GIN.—Drawn by William L. Sheppard.—[See Page 814.]

Courtesy of Library of Congress

Slaves operating Eli Whitney's cotton gin. A remarkably simple technology, the cotton gin significantly increased cotton production and made slavery more profitable.

spun into thread, an exceedingly slow process. In 1793, a young Yale graduate named Eli Whitney devised a simple engine (or "gin") for extracting the seeds, allowing workers to clean cotton much faster than before. Unfortunately for Whitney, others quickly pirated his **cotton gin**, but as a result, in two years southern cotton production jumped from 140,000 to more than 1.5 million pounds.

Access to markets determined who could take advantage of them. To facilitate marketing and augment natural river ways, states and private entities laid out new

Image © Alexey Stiop, 2010. Used by permission of Shutterstock, Inc.

The Wilderness Road, blazed by Daniel Boone in 1775, carried thousands of settlers and other travelers through the Cumberland Gap in the Appalachian Mountains into Kentucky and Tennessee. A mere footpath in the beginning, the Wilderness Road became an all-weather although still rough road in 1796 when the Kentucky legislature voted funds for its improvement.

roads. One of the first reached from the port city of Philadelphia to Lancaster in Pennsylvania's breadbasket. The road later continued to Pittsburgh. Others stretched into Vermont and western Massachusetts from Boston and from Richmond on the James River into Virginia's Appalachian foothills. Private companies surveyed routes, cleared roadways, and laid down gravel or wooden planks for roadbeds. The farther west the roads went, the rougher the roads became. In fact, many roads were no more than paths, and regulations allowed road-builders to leave tree stumps twelve inches high, causing many wagons to become "stumped" trying to pass over them. Tax revenue financed construction while user fees helped defray maintenance costs, like today's tolls. During the 1790s, the country's road mileage jumped from 1,875 to 21,000. In the Carolinas and Georgia, commercial transport continued to rely on the numerous rivers that flowed into the Atlantic. Even settlers west of the Appalachian Mountains took advantage of expanding markets by floating shipments of hides, wheat, and corn down the Ohio and Mississippi River networks to the Spanish-controlled port of New Orleans.

The expansion of banking further spurred the market-oriented economy. Investing in new land, purchasing tools, livestock, and wagons, and building ships required amounts of capital beyond the resources of most farmers, tradesmen, or merchants. Colonial Americans had not known commercial banks, looking instead to merchants for credit. In 1790, only three banks operated in the country—in Boston, Philadelphia, and New York City. By the end of the decade, twenty-nine state-chartered banks and the Bank of the United States (see p. 212 below) offered credit to borrowers in the form of loan certificates that circulated as currency. Real estate developer William Cooper relied heavily on bank credit to attract settlers from worn-out land in New England to his vast tracts in western New York.

Beginning in the early 1790s, as America's commercial markets began to expand, economic policy rose to the center of public discourse. Many farmers and artisans subscribed to the principles of profit, increased productivity, and expanding markets, giving weight to the arguments made by proponents of a commercialized economy. At the same time, the advocates of agrarianism mobilized against economic transformation.

Hamilton's Vision

The key architect of the Washington administration's economic policy was thirty-four-year-old treasury secretary Alexander Hamilton. Hamilton envisioned a republic with sound credit, a national banking system, a market economy balanced between manufacturing and agriculture, and a strong bond between the national government and the country's wealthy commercial class. The primary influences on Hamilton's vision were British. Brilliant, energetic, and self-confident, he dived into work as soon as the Senate confirmed his appointment. He also enjoyed the backing of a majority in Congress. But Abigail Adams, the Vice President's savvy wife, recoiled from his un-republican "thirst for Fame." William Maclay thought he acted too much like Britain's first lord of the treasury. And both James Madison and Thomas Jefferson disapproved of transforming an agrarian country into a manufacturing one.

> **How did Alexander Hamilton propose to restore the nation's economic health?**

Prospects had not been bright for young Hamilton growing up in the West Indies. His father, a ne'er-do-well Scottish merchant, deserted him and his unwed mother, who died when he was still a boy. But he persevered, becoming a clerk in a merchant office on St. Croix and impressing his employers with a profound understanding of finance. After migrating to Britain's mainland colonies, Hamilton attended King's College (now Columbia) and with the outbreak of the Revolution joined General Washington's staff. After independence, he practiced law and married Elizabeth Schuyler, the daughter of a New York aristocrat. Hamilton looked at the United States under the Articles of Confederation as powerless to manage its economic affairs. Despite the Scottish economist Adam Smith's claim that in unregulated markets the "hidden hand" of supply and demand provided sufficient incentives for economic diversification, Hamilton believed that government should manage economic growth.

Hamilton's first order of business was to use the new government's powers to clean up its credit mess. Approximately $54 million in debts remained from the Revolution and from the Confederation government, mostly in the form of **bonds** (the type of instrument that governments typically used to borrow money). Bonds were promises to repay creditors at some future date, plus interest. Failure to do either

Alexander Hamilton. Dashingly handsome, extraordinarily intelligent, and explosively energetic, Hamilton never lacked confidence, whether leading a charge against British Redcoats at Yorktown, condemning slavery, or pushing his program for rescuing the nation from financial disaster.

had caused the market value of existing United States government bonds to sink to a small percentage of their face value. Creditors at home and abroad had little confidence in them. And what if the country needed money, for national defense perhaps? It could not afford to pay the staggering costs of war. Who would lend it more money? In January 1790 Hamilton sent Congress a detailed *Report on Public Credit* with recommendations on how to remedy the situation.

First, he proposed **funding** the debt, which meant levying taxes and committing the revenues necessary to satisfy its financial obligations. The owners of old government bonds would exchange their old certificates for new ones at full face value. Hamilton intended to show not only the government's good faith but also its ability to raise enough to pay what it owed. But he did not want to eliminate the debt entirely. "A national debt, if it is not excessive, will be to us a national blessing." Borrowing expanded the financial resources available for important projects without requiring oppressive taxes. Furthermore, a funded debt would encourage investors, Hamilton's favorite class, to purchase more government bonds and encourage them to take an active interest in the government.

Most congressmen agreed that the country's future depended on good credit. Said one: "We have . . . a public debt . . . that we must pay." But James Madison objected to Hamilton's way of going about it. He regarded indebtedness as a ruinous "curse," but he focused his concern on the fact that many original recipients of government bonds, including Continental Army soldiers who had received them as pay for military service, had long since sold them off to rich speculators from places like Philadelphia and New York who gambled on a windfall if their value should rise. And that was exactly what Hamilton's funding plan would do. Such a situation was "morally & politically wrong," said Madison, who suggested compensating the original holders. But the House of Representatives rejected that as impractical.

Because some of the states also had unpaid debts, Hamilton recommended that the federal government assume those as well, even though doing so would add $25 million to the national government's overall debt obligation. **Assumption** would minimize the need for state taxes and cause bondholders to look to the national government for interest. Assumption stirred up a hornet's nest, with Virginia's Patrick Henry denouncing the intrusion of federal power into the states' finances. Virginia had already paid off its debt, and assumption would force Virginians to pay additional federal taxes in order to help states like Massachusetts and South Carolina liquidate their debts. Madison persuaded the House to vote against assumption; however, the indefatigable Hamilton turned to Jefferson, his new Cabinet colleague, for help.

Jefferson brought Madison and Hamilton together for dinner, and over food and wine Madison agreed to assumption in return for Hamilton's promise to deliver congressional votes for relocating the nation's capital to a more geographically central site on the Potomac River, where many Virginians had land investments. Congress voted again and this time approved the assumption measure. Government offices moved to Philadelphia until the new capital city could be built. The deal disappointed William Maclay who, along with other Pennsylvanians, had been politicking for the permanent capital.

Through funding and assumption, Hamilton committed the country to a substantial and apparently permanent national debt, very much as Britain had done throughout the eighteenth century with positive results for its economy. Congress completed the funding and assumption program by enacting an excise tax on whiskey to pay the interest on the debt, and in the process, Hamilton lifted the market value of government bonds and created $30 million in liquid capital for public and private uses.

The next question Hamilton faced was how to put this new wealth to maximum use. His answer was to concentrate it in a national bank that would make it available as credit for investment. In December of 1790, he sent Congress a proposal to incorporate a bank similar to the Bank of England. The **Bank of the United States** would achieve its initial capitalization of $10 million by selling shares in the institution—one-fifth to the government and the other four-fifths to private investors. Investors could pay in specie (gold and silver) or in government bonds, which circulated just like money. The Bank would also hold government deposits that would become the basis for loans for public and private enterprises. And the loan certificates would also circulate as currency.

Madison again led opposition to Hamilton's proposal. He based his objection on the recently adopted **Tenth Amendment**, arguing that the Constitution did not explicitly grant Congress authority to create a bank. But this time he had very little support from his congressional colleagues, most of whom recognized the Bank's utility. By a two-to-one vote, Congress chartered the Bank of the United States for twenty-years and sent the measure to the president. Washington trusted Madison, but he was hesitant to exercise the veto power for what would have been the first time. So he requested opinions from key members of the Cabinet. Jefferson argued from the "strict constructionist" point of view that to "take a single step beyond the boundaries . . . specifically drawn around the powers of Congress is to take possession of a boundless field of power." Hamilton countered by insisting that the government's responsibilities in the economic realm, as specified in the Constitution, implied the power necessary to accomplish them. In this case the **implied power** was authority to charter a bank. Hamilton's argument persuaded Washington, and in February 1791 he signed the bill chartering the Bank of the United States with headquarters in Philadelphia and branches in other cities.

Clearly on a roll, Hamilton followed his victories with a sweeping vision statement. His **Report on Manufactures**, delivered to Congress in December 1791, argued skillfully for a commercial economy balanced between manufacturing and agriculture.

He showed how an efficient division of labor would allow farmers to produce significant surpluses in crops and livestock that could sustain artisans who would specialize in manufacturing clothing, tools, furnishings, and luxury items. Moreover, textile machines like those already revolutionizing European industry would provide gainful employment for women and children. Furthermore, the new machines could be used to manufacture corduroys, jeans, and velvets in addition to plain cotton and wool fabrics. Although forward-looking, the report offered no specific recommendations for jump starting factory industry beyond protective tariffs and subsidies to manufacturers.

By seizing the initiative, Hamilton gained critical momentum that helped him to sell his economic program. The effects of restored credit appeared immediately. As the market value of its bonds increased, the government found it much easier to negotiate new loans both in Europe and at home. Infusions of money into the economy pushed commodity prices up, and bank credit contributed to the formation of over thirty new navigation companies and the construction of more than forty new bridges and sixteen turnpikes. And even though many of these enterprises struggled and some failed, Hamilton's financial program laid down the basis for a national market economy.

The personal ideological disputes involving Hamilton, Madison, and Jefferson would have been less significant had they only involved those individuals. But they became key figures in mobilizing thousands of other Americans who shared their views about how best to fulfill the republican promise of the Revolution.

Rising Political Factions: Federalists and Republicans

Even though Hamilton envisioned all classes and sections of the country benefiting equally from his program, his policies pleased some groups more than others. Seaboard commercial interests and speculators certainly profited from expanded credit, and South Carolina and Massachusetts appreciated having their debt burden lifted. But Virginia's patrician planters worried that Hamilton's initiatives would lure otherwise happy farmers into crowded towns and factories and leave them dependent, unhealthy, and demoralized.

> **What concerns lay behind the early rise of political factions?**

James Madison, once Hamilton's collaborator on *The Federalist* papers, saw the potential for tyranny in Hamilton's concept of implied powers, while Jefferson had always been dubious of a strong national government. And many farmers and urban mechanics loathed rich merchants, bankers and industrialists who, as one New York City tradesman put it, "assume the airs of 'the well born.'"

Responses to Hamilton's policies hardened the already divided political culture of the United States. As early as the first session of Congress in 1789, John Adams and William Maclay in the Senate consulted with their respective allies to line up votes for or against proposed legislation. Subsequently, Hamilton and those who supported him, including Adams, called themselves **Federalists** to identify with the Constitution. Critics of Hamilton's measures, such as William Maclay, called themselves **Republicans**, implying that they were genuine republicans while their opponents were closet monarchists. Although Americans today take political parties for granted, in the 1790s parties smacked of conspiracy and even treason against legitimate government. People barely understood the concept of a "loyal opposition." So Federalists and Republicans both disavowed the problematic "party" label while pinning it on the other.

Hypersensitive nerve endings lay beneath partisan philosophical differences, and opponents and supporters of Hamilton's measures fought each other with desperate ferocity and overblown rhetoric. Republicans accused Federalists of conspiring to corrupt the government, just like King George III and his ministers had done. By building a party of bondholders, bankers, and merchants that controlled a majority of the seats in Congress, Rebublicans said, Hamilton was making himself into the American equivalent of a prime minister in George Washington's court. Federalists charged Republicans with trying to preserve a backward, feudal way of life. Hamilton claimed that the "republican interest" was bent on "National disunion, National insignificance, Public disorder and discredit." Anti-slavery himself, Hamilton often denounced plantation Republicans for spouting platitudes about liberty while holding African Americans in slavery.

Leaders of both Federalist and Republican factions were prominent within the government. Washington enjoyed unequaled respect and largely shared Hamilton's vision, but he remained above crass partisanship. Hamilton utilized his connections among bankers, his close association with President

Thomas Jefferson as Secretary of State. Scholarly, scientific, and reticent, Jefferson left his post as minister to France to join the Washington administration. Partisan critics disliked his openmindedness about religion, as when he declared that "it does me no injury for my neighbor to say there are twenty gods or no gods. It neither picks my pocket nor breaks my leg."

Washington, and his command over scores of revenue agents employed by the Treasury Department to build up political support. Vice President John Adams backed administration policies in the Senate. On the other side of the fight, Jefferson most embodied Republican principles. Madison, along with John Beckley, clerk of the House of Representatives, used an extensive correspondence to organize and mobilize opposition members of Congress. In the spring of 1791, Jefferson and Madison traveled through the Hudson River Valley on what they called a botanical tour, but while they recorded plant sightings they also met with New York's opposition leaders Governor George Clinton and Aaron Burr and laid the foundation for a Virginia-New York Republican coalition.

Alongside the Republican elites in the national government, more than thirty Republican political clubs representing the masses sprang up in states from Vermont to South Carolina. Members came mostly from rural, farming backgrounds as well as the urban working classes, and the clubs often expressed their opposition to Hamilton's policies and Federalist elitism in protests and passionate declarations. Many of them attached the word "democratic" to their names. "Let us keep in mind," declared the Democratic Society of Pennsylvania, "that supineness with regard to public concerns is the direct road to slavery, while vigilance and jealousy are the safeguards of Liberty."

Partisan propaganda filled the newspapers. The *Gazette of the United States*, the semi-official organ of the administration and edited by John Fenno, regularly defended Hamilton and his policies. Hamilton defended himself in a number of pseudonymous articles. In 1791, Madison enlisted his college roommate and democratic poet Philip Freneau to edit a new Republican paper called the *National Gazette*. Supported by a State Department clerk job that Jefferson arranged, Freneau blasted away at Hamilton with a barrage of personal insults. "Your liberties are in danger," warned one Republican editor.

Washington detested divisive partisanship and attempted, unsuccessfully, to persuade Hamilton and Jefferson to cease their public feuding. In 1792, as the end of his term approached, he and Martha considered retiring to Mount Vernon. But both Hamilton and Jefferson put their differences aside long enough to persuade Washington to accept a second term. Both of them understood that only Washington's immense prestige could prevent the republic from breaking apart. Her husband's decision to stand for re-election disappointed Martha, but she could not "blame him for acting according to his ideas of duty in obeying the voice of his country." In 1792 Washington won unanimous re-election in the Electoral College.

The theory that political parties promoted free expression and thus representative government gained traction slowly, but the reality of emerging political parties was inescapable. If anything, Washington's second term was even more troubled by partisan conflict than his first, with the added problem of unruly settlers of the trans-Appalachian West, where geographic isolation and radical ideas about personal liberty undermined their attachment to the national government.

THINKING BACK

1. What did George Washington do to establish the new national government's credibility, and how successful was he?

2. In the 1790s, what social and ideological differences divided Americans?

3. What was Hamilton's vision for the United States, to what extent did he succeed in achieving it, and why did his economic program lead to political parties?

TURBULENCE OUT WEST

Despite Federalists' efforts to achieve national supremacy, in the borderlands west of the Appalachian Mountains settlers felt less attachment to federal authority—and to American nationhood. By the mid-1790s, a half-million settlers, white and black, many of them Virginians and New Englanders who had received land grants for their military service during the Revolutionary War, had occupied fertile valleys mostly below the Ohio River. Kentucky became a state in 1792, and in 1796 Tennessee followed. Initially subsistence farmers, they increasingly shipped surplus grains and hides down the Ohio and Mississippi rivers, through the Spanish port at New Orleans, and on to Atlantic markets. North of the Ohio River, the Northwest Ordinance of 1787 declared that Indian lands "shall never be taken from them without their consent"; however, that did not deter land-hungry settlers. Native Americans attempted desperately to hold off.

Rebellion Against Government Authority

To fund Hamilton's debt and assumption programs, Congress in 1791 slapped a seven-cent-per-gallon tax on distilled spirits—one-third the market price of whiskey. Since liquor flowed copiously in eighteenth-century America, the tax was expected to raise substantial revenue. It was also a direct tax, so citizens personally felt the national government's bite. Further, the measure required whiskey distillers to register by June of each year and authorized a squad of government inspectors and tax collectors.

> What does the Whiskey Rebellion illustrate about the use of force in a republic?

Ordinary citizens in many parts of the country objected to the whiskey tax, but backcountry farmers reacted with extra passion because liquor was more than a beverage to them. Corn and rye grains were easier to market as whiskey, and nearly every farm had a distillery. What stayed at home was a medium

Tarring and feathering a government inspector during the Whiskey Rebellion in western Pennsylvania

of barter exchange. Moreover, westerners hated agents from a national government that squeezed them with an exorbitant tax while catering to rich eastern moneymen and land speculators.

In western Pennsylvania, farmers and local merchants campaigned hard against the whiskey tax. Local democratic-republican societies held indignation meetings and flooded Congress with petitions demanding repeal. William Maclay had voted against the tax and now predicted "war and bloodshed," a radical form of **popular sovereignty** such as was occurring in France at the time (see the Global Perspective, pp. 134-36). In 1794, violence did erupt. Many distillers refused to register, and local vigilantes shot holes in the stills of those who did. Angry citizens tarred and feathered tax collectors. In July, hundreds of armed protesters surrounded the house of a government agent, and the ensuing gunfire left two men dead. A month later some 6,000 tax-resisters gathered near Pittsburgh, a developing urban commercial center in the region.

The **Whiskey Rebellion** alarmed President Washington. Hamilton recommended that he send federal troops to crush this conspiracy of "malcontent persons" wishing to "inflame and systematize the spirit of opposition." With Hamilton at his side, Washington led 13,000 state militia and volunteers to the site of the revolt, preceded by an offer of amnesty. The insurrection evaporated even before the soldiers arrived, and although the government arrested the ringleaders, Washington pardoned them.

On the surface, the episode seemed like the triumph of military power over the people. However, as government amnesty agent William Bradford put it,

Washington meant "to convince these people & the World at once of the *moderation & the firmness* of the government." At the same time, virtually every democratic-republican society outside of the region disavowed rebellion against republican government.

The Dark and Bloody Ground

Another factor contributing to unrest beyond the Appalachian Mountains was the continuing failure of the government to crush Indian resistance to white settlement. While acknowledging

> What issue did whites and Indians face on the frontier?

Indian claims to the Northwest Territory, the Ordinance of 1787 anticipated the future by providing for its eventual incorporation into the Union. Indians kept up a determined resistance to encroaching white settlers who descended, in the words of one Native American, "like a plague of locusts." Another declared: "Our lands are our life and our breath. If we part with them, we part with our blood." And they caused many whites to part with their blood also.

In Ohio, Shawnee communities possessed many resources with which to resist the oncoming white tide. One was the British, still spiteful after losing the American Revolutionary War, who supplied them with guns, powder, and bullets from military posts along the Great Lakes. The Shawnee also enjoyed superior numbers, augmented by Miami and other pro-British tribes such as the Seneca, Mohawk, Huron, and Delaware. In 1786, the Mohawk leader Thayendanegea (Joseph Brant) had helped forge a confederation that massed thousands of well-armed warriors. In a message to Congress, a delegation of Ohio Indians called for peace but demanded that all transfers of tribal lands to whites "should be made . . . by the united voice of the confederacy."

The Native Americans' strength no doubt figured into United States government policy, which aimed at conciliating them while establishing national supremacy. Washington conceded that nobody but the Indians had the right to transfer Indian territory and warned settlers that their "rage" for fertile Indian real estate would inevitably lead to bloodshed. In 1790, Congress passed the **Indian Trade and Intercourse Act** that allowed only licensed traders to conduct business with the Indians—an attempt to regulate the flow of liquor into Indian country. However, the government's effort to bring order and national sovereignty to the Ohio territory largely failed, as states continued to make their own treaties with Native Americans while white traders, settlers, and land speculators disregarded government regulations and plied Indians with liquor to obtain their property. Nor could Indian leaders prevent militant warriors from attacking white settlements. Because Washington would not tolerate the murder of settlers, he finally authorized military operations against the Indians.

Early strikes turned into disasters for the whites. The worst came in autumn of 1791 when Ohio's territorial governor General Arthur St. Clair led 1,300 militiamen to the headwaters of the Wabash River where Miami and Shawnee warriors ambushed them, killing 600. Unfortunately for the Indians, their confederacy soon collapsed due to differences over strategy. Thayendanegea thought that only by negotiating the transfer of some territory could the Native Americans salvage enough to live on, but militants refused to give up anything. "Look back and view the lands from whence we have been driven," one Indian leader lamented. "We can retreat no further." But Britain's support ebbed as war threatened in Europe. By the time the United States mounted another military campaign led by General Anthony Wayne in August 1794, the Indians' power had been much reduced. Wayne's troops engaged Huron, Ottawa, Wyandot, and Shawnee fighters in the **Battle of Fallen Timbers**, and with cannon and cavalry they defeated them. The British commander at nearby Ft. Miami refused to open the gates for the retreating Indians, who had no choice but to surrender. The resulting **Treaty of Greenville** (1795) between the United States and leaders of several Indian tribes transferred two-thirds of Ohio to the United States.

The loss of most of their ancestral land shattered Shawnee morale, although the United States agreed to pay an annuity to them and other tribes. Whites established the town of Cincinnati on the Ohio River, and settler families began pushing their way into the interior. Some Shawnee, Delaware, and other Native Americans settled on reserves, and under the tutelage of government agents and Christian missionaries they attempted to adjust to white culture. They modified gender roles so that men tended fields and women took up cloth making. Native Americans dressed in white people's clothes and some converted to Christianity. In despair, many turned to whiskey. However, significant numbers of refugees migrated farther west, crossing the Mississippi River into Spanish Louisiana.

The migrating Indians entered an area where Native people were still largely in control. Spanish authorities welcomed them as a buffer against the expanding United States; however, resident Osage and Pawnee Indians were less hospitable. Osages pounded their neighbors in all directions, Indian and Spanish, leading a Spanish official in St. Louis to report: "For this reason it is necessary to temporize with them to some extent, handle them as tactfully as possible in order to restrain their excesses." In the 1790s, Spain sought to regulate commerce with trans-Mississippi tribes through monopolies granted first to the St. Louis-based Creole French trader Auguste Choteau and his younger half-brother Pierre and subsequently to the Spanish merchant Manuel Lisa. A fragile peace ensued, but the Osage remained, as Jefferson later observed, "the great nation" between the Missouri and Red rivers.

Even farther west, Comanche and Apache raiders caused havoc in Texas and New Mexico. In 1776, the Spanish crown bolstered those two **"Internal Provinces"** and gave them more authority to deal with Indian problems. In the 1780s, New Mexico's governor Juan Bautista de Anza offered the Comanche the choice of peace or war. Although they initially chose war, a military campaign against them eventually persuaded most Comanche bands to choose peace and unrestricted trade with Spanish and Pueblo Indian towns. Throughout the 1790s, Apache bands kept the perimeters of Texas and New Mexico in turmoil.

At best, Native Americans in the borderlands of the trans-Appalachian West could only buy time, whether through armed resistance or negotiations. Clearly, whites would eventually become the dominant population and the United States the sovereign authority, but the Indians applied what power they had to help them negotiate the best possible arrangements.

THINKING BACK

1. How does the Whiskey Rebellion illustrate the tension between freedom and authority in the United States?
2. How did the government of the United States address the conflict between whites and Native Americans in the trans-Appalachian West, how did Native Americans respond, and what was the outcome?
3. How did white expansion into the Ohio country impact residents and authorities in the Far West?

THE LOCAL PERSPECTIVE: FOCUS ON CALIFORNIA

| How did Spanish colonization change California? |

A continent away from the clashes between Federalists and Republicans, California experienced its own transformations. Cultural contact between Spaniards and Native Americans prompted many of these changes. And already, some in the United States envisioned the Pacific Ocean as the western boundary of a republic that stretched from coast to coast.

Its remoteness from Mexico City delayed California's colonization, but during the late eighteenth century, Spain's King Carlos III, eager to expand the frontiers of knowledge, authorized scientific expeditions along the coast. Eventually, rumors of Russian sea otter hunters and British explorers caused concern about the security of New Spain's rich silver mines. Viceroy Antonio de Bucareli voiced that concern: the presence of foreigners "ought to be guarded against."

The process of doing that began in 1769. An expedition under California's new governor Gaspar de Portolá and Father Junípero Serra founded the first colonial outpost at San Diego. The Spaniards marched on to Monterey where they erected a *presidio* and a Catholic mission among the Indians at nearby Carmel. Supplying these remote outposts challenged Spanish officials. They hoped to establish an overland supply route from Sonora, and in January 1774, Juan Bautista de Anza, Sonora's military commander, and Father Francisco Garcés set out with 30 men, 165 horses, and 65 cattle for California. Three months later they reached the coast, and the following year Anza brought some farmers and artisans along with more soldiers, clerics, and livestock. The Spaniards put up another *presidio* at San Francisco and laid out a civilian settler town (*pueblo*) at San José. The overland trail proved unreliable, however, and in 1781, additional colonizers with provisions sailed up the Pacific coast from Mexico and founded Los Angeles and a year after that a *presidio* at Santa Barbara.

During the eighteenth century, the highly regulated Spanish Empire became a financial burden rather than a source of wealth for the crown, which sought to minimize the cost of maintaining overseas possessions. California slowly grew into a self-sustaining but never an export-producing province through the interdependence of the *presidios*, missions, and nearby Indian communities. Troops in the *presidios* defended the coastline while the missions and the few civilian towns sold them food and other basics such as soap, boots, and harnesses. The missionaries used credits from the sales to purchase religious books and paraphernalia, fine cloth, and chocolate from Mexico.

The missions occupied the center of California's economy, incorporating the best coastal lands for grazing and farming. By the mid-1780s, nine missions employing 4,500 baptized Indians produced more than enough wheat, barley, corn, vegetables, and meat to keep everyone adequately fed. The missionaries also supplied Indian labor to the *presidios*. The *encomienda* had been formally abolished in the Spanish Empire, but not all forms of coerced labor. As part of the mandate to Christianize and teach the Indians, mission fathers imposed a rigid labor discipline. Many baptized Indians accepted the regime as a trade-off, for despite severe physical and psychological hardship they acquired Spanish tools, livestock, and skills in masonry and metallurgy that benefited them and their communities. Others rejected the mission labor system. But even many non-baptized Indians worked in the *presidios* and *pueblos* as contract or convict labor (those convicted of breaking Spanish laws).

Whether intentionally or not, the Spanish colonists inflicted tremendous suffering on California's native population. Even before the first missionaries and soldiers arrived, foreign visitors had introduced contagious diseases that depopulated native societies, and the colonists brought more infections. "They live well free," reported one friar, "but as soon as we reduce them to a Christian and community life . . . they fatten, sicken, and die." He was no doubt noticing the consequences of extreme psychological and physical stress. Between 1769 and 1800, the Indian population of coastal California plummeted from 60,000 to 35,000 as the number of missions increased to eighteen.

Civilian settlements in California languished as well. Not until after 1800 did California's Hispanic population approach 2,000. The distance from Mexico to California and government regulations discouraged settlement, and the missions preempted the best land. Military posts constituted the only markets for local produce, since the government prohibited foreign trade, and government price regulations further hamstrung the economy. California possessed tremendous resources, including fertile land and a temperate climate, but bureaucratic red tape retarded economic development. Alexander Hamilton might well have used California to support his case for a diversified market economy.

California remained a lonely outpost at the close of the eighteenth century, but soon the flames of revolution would rage across the Spanish empire. Reforms would make California more attractive to settlers, and as a result the lives of Native Americans would change even more drastically, as would the physical environment. In 1827, settlers introduced goats to California's Santa Catalina Island. Grazing on the island's lush native grass, the animals quickly multiplied, devouring native grasses and depriving native animals of food. Santa Catalina Island illustrates in microcosm the changes resulting from colonization.

THINKING BACK

1. In what ways did colonial California in the 1790s differ from the United States, and how was it similar?
2. What recommendations for California's economic growth might a Hamiltonian Federalist have made, and what recommendations might a Jeffersonian Republican have offered?

PROTECTING THE COUNTRY'S INTERESTS

In the 1790s, the United States faced many challenges in the turbulent Atlantic world. Britain treated the country with utter contempt, continuing to garrison military posts on American soil and supporting Native American resistance to settlement in Ohio. A nervous Spain also attempted to curb United States expansion by barring Americans from navigating the Mississippi River. Although France harbored no malice toward the United States, neither French businessmen nor the French government sought closer ties with the fledgling nation. But the greatest problem the Washington administration confronted grew out of the war that followed the French Revolution (see the Global Perspective, pp. 134-36). As an ally since 1778, France demanded American support while Great Britain was prepared to strangle the American economy to prevent the United States from aiding revolutionary France through trade. Washington's declaration of neutrality won appreciative responses at home, as did a treaty with Spain concerning navigation of the Mississippi River; however, Jay's Treaty with Great Britain ignited bitter controversy. Foreign-policy issues deepened the pre-existing political divisions in the country.

British Aggravations

Anglo-American relations had not yet recovered from the Revolutionary War. Unfulfilled commitments from the Treaty of Paris irritated both the British and the Americans. Americans still owed British creditors $14 million, a significant amount of money in those days equivalent to $240 million in today's dollars, and British Redcoats continued to maintain garrisons on United States territory around the Great Lakes. If George III could not completely accept losing the colonies, many Americans could not let go of their Anglophobia either.

> **How did Great Britain aggravate the strains in Anglo-American relations?**

Opinion about Great Britain roughly divided along lines previously drawn by Treasury Secretary Hamilton's economic policies. On the one hand, democratic-minded Republicans hated Britain's aristocratic society and feared that commercial and financial connections to Britain might lead to reattachment to the British Empire. Hamilton had in fact linked his economic program to British trade. Ninety percent of American imports came from Britain, and import duties on British goods comprised a major part of the treasury's revenue. But on the other hand, northern merchants and fishermen along with South Carolina planters stood to profit from access to British West Indies markets, which Britain had denied them since independence. Thus, Federalists had reason to resolve Anglo-American disputes and draw closer to their former rulers. Indeed, Hamilton confided to a British representative that he "preferred a connexion with you, to that of any other country."

In 1791, Britain finally sent a minister to the United States. George Hammond, a young bachelor eager for reconciliation, cut an attractive figure in Philadelphia society. He married an American, Margaret Allen, but nothing could diminish anti-British prejudices in the United States. Moreover, Jefferson was not interested in improving Anglo-American relations as long as Britain continued to violate the Treaty of Paris. Nor did Hammond's superiors in London show much desire for reconciliation, authorizing him to discuss issues but instructing him to agree to nothing.

The Washington administration, unable to speak with a single, coherent voice because it contained sharply differing points of view, sputtered and stalled in its early ventures into foreign affairs. While Jefferson vented his hatred of Britain, Hamilton conducted his own decidedly pro-British diplomacy.

The French Revolution and American Politics

| What impact did the French Revolution have on American politics? |

In its initial stages, Americans applauded the French Revolution, proud to see France following in their path. Even the Federalist *Gazette of the United States* cooed its approval. But the growing chaos in France, the rising violence, and the abolition of religion, which Thomas Paine lauded in his book *The Age of Reason*, shocked many Americans. William Short, recently the American *charge d'affaires* in France, exclaimed, "those mad and corrupted people . . . under the name of liberty have destroyed their own government." That happens, Federalists said, when the masses gain unrestrained power. Republicans adjusted to each radical turn in the French Revolution. Jefferson deplored the bloodletting but asked: "Was ever such a prize won with so little innocent blood?"

Revolutionary France waged war against monarchy across Europe, first against Prussia and Austria and then against Spain and Britain. The European war put the Washington administration in a difficult situation. The Franco-American treaties of 1778 committed the United States to defend French interests in the West Indies, an obligation that could lead to war. Neither Federalist nor Republican leaders believed that entering the conflict would serve American interests. Hamilton argued that the treaties had been signed with the former French government and that when French revolutionaries had executed the king, Louis XVI, and abolished the monarchy they had terminated all Franco-American agreements. Even Jefferson advised against involvement—"a disagreeable pill to our friends, tho' necessary to keep out of the calamities of a war." This was one issue on which the two agreed. On April 22, 1793, Washington issued a **Neutrality Proclamation** declaring the United States to be "friendly and impartial" toward all belligerents and threatening to prosecute any citizen giving aid to either side.

Earlier that month, 30-year-old Edmond Charles Genêt arrived in Charleston, South Carolina, as French minister to the United States. The charming but arrogant Genêt represented the then-ruling Gironde party, who instructed him to obtain American aid for French military strikes against Spanish Florida and Louisiana and the British West Indies. The people of Charleston gave Genêt an enthusiastic public welcome, as did other Republicans as he journeyed to Philadelphia. Capitalizing on rampant anti-British and growing anti-Spanish sentiment in the West, he began immediately to raise an army and convert captured British ships into privateers, all in blatant disregard of Washington's Neutrality Proclamation.

Citizen Genêt (in revolutionary France, the egalitarian term *citizen* replaced *Monsieur*, the equivalent of *Mister*) knew little and cared nothing about American politics. In Philadelphia, Americans toasted him. "I live here in the midst of perpetual fetes, I receive addresses from all parts of the continent," Genêt said. But he misunderstood and counted on Jefferson and the American public to override the Neutrality Proclamation. Jefferson even told him explicitly that the United States could never permit France to use American ports to attack Britain. When Genêt said he would make his case directly to the American public and arranged for the fitting out of another captured British ship as a privateer right under the government's nose, Washington demanded his recall.

Only Genêt's poor timing equaled his audacity. As Genêt was embarrassing Jefferson and offending

Washington, his Gironde party fell from power in France. Maximilien Robespierre and the even more radical Jacobins began marching Girondists to the guillotine. Genêt asked for asylum in the United States, which Washington graciously granted. But his contempt had seriously hurt the Republican party and pushed the Washington administration closer to Britain.

"Damn John Jay"

What issues between Britain and the United States was John Jay supposed to resolve, and why did his treaty stir up such a controversy?

In 1794 the tide of war in Europe shifted in France's favor. A sense of urgency gripped London. The British government ordered a blockade of French ports. By blocking needed supplies and income from valuable West Indian trade goods, the English hoped to strangle France and turn ordinary French men and women against the Revolution. France also waged economic warfare and attempted to blockade the British Isles.

These developments directly affected the United States. American vessels transported cargoes from the French West Indies, traffic that France ordinarily limited to its own merchant fleet. By international understanding, ships of neutral nations were permitted to carry non-military supplies to belligerents, but Britain declared that ships excluded from trade with France in peacetime could not participate in wartime. British warships seized American vessels and confiscated cargoes destined for French ports. Within months the British navy had captured 250 American ships. France violated American neutral maritime rights too by seizing ships going to British ports, though on a lesser scale.

To help meet the Royal Navy's mounting manpower needs, British ship captains resorted to drafting seamen from confiscated American merchant ships—a practice known as **impressment**. Royal officials defended the practice by insisting that they took only British-born subjects with obligations to the British crown and deserters from His Majesty's service. But impressment denied the right of a British subject to become a naturalized foreign citizen. Furthermore, the British navy took not only British-born subjects but many native-born American citizens as well. These actions offended American national pride.

British maritime outrages added to the lengthy list of American grievances. To resolve them, President Washington sent Chief Justice John Jay to negotiate a treaty. Arriving in London in June 1794, Jay immediately pressed the American case against British affronts. He demanded evacuation of the northwestern forts, compensation for slaves taken during the Revolutionary War, the cessation of ship seizures, and access to British markets in the West Indies.

British officials' view of the United States differed somewhat from their earlier position. They could see that America contained a richer market for British manufactures than the Indian villages, which were dwindling rapidly. This disposed them to concede on the issue of abandoning the frontier forts. Opening the West Indies trade might benefit Britain by removing a cause for retaliatory American tariffs. However Britain's desperate military situation dictated an unyielding stance on American ships trading with France. Thus in the treaty that Jay negotiated, the British agreed to allow limited access to the West Indies. They also agreed to vacate the forts. In return, the United States promised not to impose discriminatory tariffs on British goods. **Jay's Treaty** (1794) also confirmed the right of Native Americans to move across the U.S.-Canada border without impediment. But Jay's Treaty contained no mention of neutral rights.

Knowing that Republicans were bound to complain about that omission, Washington kept the treaty under wraps before submitting it to the Senate in June 1795. As expected, Republicans denounced Jay's Treaty as a betrayal of France, republican ideals, and neutral rights. "Damn John Jay," they declared. "*Kick this damn treaty to hell,*" added Republican congressman Blair McClenachan. Federalists vigorously defended Jay's Treaty. The alternative, they claimed, would be a ruinous war with Britain. By a strict party vote, the Federalist majority ratified the treaty twenty to ten—barely meeting the two-thirds vote required to approve. Republicans in the House tried to block the appropriations necessary to implement the treaty, but opposition finally gave way.

Jay's Treaty was as good an agreement as the United States was likely to get. Great Britain simply would not hamstring its own war effort. In some respects, it was even a good treaty for the United States. Westerners, for instance, cheered the removal of British troops. Farmers and merchants equated prosperity with uninterrupted British commerce.

Even shippers were satisfied because they profited enough on cargoes that reached European markets to cover the cost of those that did not. By accommodating British concerns, the treaty helped avoid what could have been a disastrous war with England. But its effect on partisan politics was deeply divisive, widening the rift caused by Hamilton's economic program.

Pinckney's Treaty: A Western Triumph

> How did Thomas Pinckney's negotiations with Spain exemplify adroit diplomacy?

As Washington's second term drew to a close, the American public felt satisfied with his administration's increasingly adroit diplomacy. And why not? Jay's Treaty was more positive than negative, and special United States envoy Thomas Pinckney of South Carolina bagged several plums in negotiations with Spain's Foreign Minister Manuel de Godoy over frontier issues.

Spanish possession of Florida and Louisiana hindered the United States' westward expansion. Spain had sought to keep the aggressive Americans at arm's length from its silver mines in New Spain, partly by denying the United States access to the Mississippi River and the port of New Orleans; however, topsy-turvy European affairs caused the crown to adjust and then readjust its position. The execution of the French king led to a Spanish alliance with Britain. But in 1795, as French armies poured into Spain, Spanish officials double-crossed Britain and made peace with France. Spain anticipated British retaliation. In fact, Godoy believed that Jay and the British were collaborating on a plan to attack Spanish Louisiana. Pinckney capitalized on Spanish edginess to strike a diplomatic *coup*. Meeting in the Spanish town of San Lorenzo in October 1795, Pinckney and Godoy signed an accord giving Americans permission to navigate the Mississippi and to deposit their goods on wharves in New Orleans while awaiting trans-shipment to markets abroad. In addition, Godoy agreed to recognize the 31st parallel as Florida's northern boundary, which favored the United States.

The **Treaty of San Lorenzo**, or **Pinckney's Treaty**, unclogged western commerce along the Mississippi River. It contributed substantially to American economic prosperity. Certainly from westerners' standpoint, administration foreign policy—Jay's Treaty, the Treaty of Greenville, and now Pinckney's Treaty—was a huge success.

Republicans and Federalists: The Election of 1796

> How did foreign policy considerations contribute to the development of political parties?

By election time in 1796, any hope of avoiding political parties had vanished. Republicans even criticized President Washington for harboring monarchists and "anglomen" in his Cabinet. "Curse on his virtues," Jefferson complained of Washington's vaunted fair-mindedness, "they've undone his country." No one roasted Washington over a hotter fire than Benjamin Franklin Bache, old Ben Franklin's grandson (known as "Lightning Rod Junior") and publisher of the Philadelphia *Aurora*. "If ever a nation was debauched by a man," claimed Bache, "the American nation has been debauched by Washington." Sixty-four years old and disgusted with public life, Washington announced his retirement. His **Farewell Address**, published in September, warned "against the baneful effects of the spirit of party," advice that few political activists in the country heeded.

The emerging political parties embodied conflicting ideologies and appealed to different interests. Republicans resisted the trends that seemed to them like threats to individual liberty: an encroaching national government, industrial manufacturing, a mounting public debt, and alignment with Great Britain. The Republicans' leadership, mostly Virginians and New Yorkers, advocated commercial agrarianism, artisanship, and empowered state governments. In 1796, Jefferson, who had resigned from Washington's Cabinet three years earlier, led the party. He enjoyed the support of small farmers, especially in western locales, as well as urban artisans and Irish and German immigrants.

Federalists pointed the country toward a modern, diversified economy and a unified nation, but they feared revolutionary tides. They valued the stability and order of an aristocratic society against the turmoil of rising democracy. Federalists adhered to the theory that ordinary people's ungoverned passions rendered them untrustworthy. Support for Great Britain exemplified their conservative social philosophy and commitment to Anglo-American trade. Their commercial policies established them solidly in the shipping and mercantile regions of the Northeast and coastal South Carolina.

When President Washington announced his retirement, Fisher Ames, a Massachusetts Federalist, compared the announcement to "a signal, like dropping a hat, for party racers to start"—although neither party looked much like the super-charged competitors of today's parties. As confederations of state organizations loosely tacked together by immediate issues, parties lacked the national organizations, internal discipline, and nominating processes that define modern political parties. Candidates did not openly campaign for votes; self-promotion conflicted with prevailing notions of proper decorum. Signs of modern parties were evident, however, in the declining frequency of independent voting in Congress and also in the growth of grass-roots organizations.

The Republican **congressional caucus** (a meeting of party leaders to nominate candidates) endorsed Thomas Jefferson for president and New York's Aaron Burr for vice president. Federalists selected John Adams and Thomas Pinckney. Alexander Hamilton, who also had resigned from Washington's Cabinet, attempted to sabotage Adams, whom he intensely disliked, and push Pinckney into the presidency. Recall that at that time, electors cast two unspecified ballots; the candidate receiving the most votes became president and the runner-up became vice president. Hamilton convinced some South Carolina electors to write Pinckney's name on one ballot and waste the other one. However, several Adams electors got wind of the scam and threw away their Pinckney votes. Consequently, Adams wound up with 71 electoral votes and Jefferson 68. Not only had Hamilton's scheme failed, but the country now had a president from one party and a vice president from the opposition. Congress remained firmly in Federalist hands.

The 1796 election demonstrated Americans' ambivalence about political parties. Party line balloting in the Electoral College had never occurred to the drafters of the Constitution. As political parties coalesced, presidential and vice presidential candidates would regularly receive the same number of votes and ties would become routine. The Twelfth Amendment, adopted in 1804, overcame that problem by requiring separate ballots for president and vice president.

THINKING BACK

1. How did foreign policy issues blend with previous political divisions to deepen party divisions in the country?
2. Despite stirring controversy, Jay's Treaty contributed positively to America's national interests. How did it do that?

3. How did the election of 1796 show that the framers of the Constitution had failed to account for the appearance of the two party political system?

INTO THE WHIRLWIND OF PARTY POLITICS

For the next four years, leaders with extreme Federalist leanings ran roughshod over the country's politics. While Vice President Thomas Jefferson spent most of his time at home at Monticello experimenting with new crops and an innovative nail factory, President John Adams braced for "the storm which is gathering over us," with domestic politics growing increasingly furious and the European war that followed the French Revolution threatening to embroil the United States. Adams seldom enjoyed soaring popularity. He talked too much and spoke intemperately. His Puritan forebears would have approved his modest lifestyle but not his personal vanity. Faultfinders ridiculed him as "His Rotundity." A second-rate Cabinet loyal to Hamilton drove Adams into tantrums. One argument ended with the President "dashing and tramping his wig on the floor." Adams acquitted himself well under trying circumstances, but even in triumph, he failed to achieve the acclaim from American citizens that he believed was his due from long service in founding and guiding the nation.

The Divisive XYZ Affair

An angry French official condemned Jay's Treaty as "the equivalent of an alliance with their [the United States'] former oppressor [Great Britain] . . . against a faithful ally, and a generous liberator [France]." If Americans allowed Britain to interfere with their shipping, as the French believed, then France would do the same. French cruisers seized over 300 American merchant vessels in the Caribbean, boosting insurance rates fivefold. France expelled the United States' minister, Charles Cotesworth Pinckney (Thomas Pinckney's brother). Anxiety mounted in the United States over the possibility of a French invasion.

> What was the issue in the XYZ Affair, and how did the episode affect American politics?

Adams administration officials disagreed about a response. The president hoped to avoid hostilities;

however, hawkish Federalists demanded war, notably Secretary of State Timothy Pickering. Adams decided to send John Marshall, Elbridge Gerry, and Pinckney to Paris to negotiate a settlement. France's foreign minister, the wily Charles-Maurice de Talleyrand, who represented the new French government called the Directory, did not want war either, but he decided to let the Americans fret. When the envoys arrived in Paris in October of 1797, three of Talleyrand's agents demanded "something for the pocket"—meaning a $250,000 bribe. Such transactions were customary in European diplomacy, but the Americans were outraged. "No, no, not a six-pence" Pinckney allegedly replied. He and Marshall indignantly returned to the United States, leaving Gerry to keep diplomatic channels open.

Republicans flew into their own rage when they learned of the mission's failure. They suspected Adams of duplicity. When Republican congressmen demanded a full disclosure of the mission's records, Adams obliged, substituting the letters X, Y, and Z for the names of the French agents. The revelations exposed the French bribery attempt. "Millions for defense," went the outraged cry, "but not one cent for tribute." The **XYZ Affair** embarrassed Jefferson and hurt the Republican party because of their close ties with the French government, but it brought acclaim to Adams. One observer noted that "since man was created and government was formed no public officer has stood higher in the confidence and affection of his countrymen than our present President now does." Support for the administration spilled over to other Federalists, who swept the congressional elections of 1798.

Quasi-War with France

The XYZ Affair and French plunder of U.S. merchant vessels in the Caribbean called for revenge. In 1798, anti-French mobs wearing Federalist emblems demonstrated in favor of war. With Hamilton pulling the strings, Congress rescinded the Franco-American treaties and authorized attacks on French vessels. It expanded the standing army by 10,000 men and authorized a 50,000-man reserve force. The nation solicited George Washington to lead the armed forces, which he agreed to do only if Hamilton were second in command. Adams strongly objected to giving Hamilton military authority but acquiesced in preparations for war. Congress also stepped up naval construction, commissioning over forty new warships (including the frigates *Constitution*, *United States*, and *Constellation*) and created the Navy Department and Marine Corps. To pay for the build-up Congress levied a tax on land, houses, and slaves.

> What kind of conflict was the Quasi-War with France?

Courtesy of Library of Congress

XYZ Affair. In this British cartoon, unprincipled French government agents plunder the vulnerable United States while European leaders in the background laugh at the spectacle.

By the end of 1798, the United States and France had thrown themselves into an undeclared naval war in the Caribbean. It has been called the **Quasi-War** because it remained undeclared and limited to naval operations. Although Hamilton and his Federalist backers discussed grandiose plans for war, Adams' more moderate objective was to defend American ships and seamen and to repel any French invasion of the United States. Abigail Adams expressed frustration with the Quasi-War. "Why, when we have the thing, should we boggle at the name?" But the United States could not gain much from an all-out war. Besides, war fever began to subside as soon as fighting commenced. Fisher Ames, the Massachusetts Federalist, sagely advised: "Wage war and call it self-defence."

American naval vessels and privateers fared well in the Quasi-War. They defeated two French frigates, captured about 100 French privateers, and recovered more than seventy American ships that had fallen into French hands. With the security of American commerce restored, insurance rates for American shipping declined drastically and the volume of trade rebounded to prewar levels. It was a pleasing little war from the Federalists' standpoint, but Republicans regarded it as part of a Federalist plot to unite the United States with Great Britain and crush political opposition.

Silencing the Opposition

> What was the intent of the Alien and Sedition Acts, and what specifically did they do?

In an effort to cast opposition to the Quasi-War as treason and to weaken the Republicans' base of support, Congress in 1798 passed four acts, known as the **Alien and Sedition Acts**. The chief instigator was Hamilton, riding the crest of political power.

One of the measures, actually called the **Naturalization Act**, extended from five to fourteen years the residency requirement for citizenship. It slowed the entry into the electorate of immigrants, especially Irish, who were arriving in growing numbers and—bitter over continued British oppression of their homeland—tended to support the Republicans. Two **Alien Acts** allowed the government to deport foreign citizens as threats to national security. The most notorious of all was the **Sedition Act**, which outlawed "malicious writing or writings against the Government of the United States . . . with intent to defame or bring . . . [it] into contempt or disrepute." Violations were punishable by fines and imprisonment.

The Sedition Act sought to stifle dissent. The prime targets were Republican newspapers, which had increased in number and virulence. But even plain citizens might be dragged into court for venting personal feelings. In all, the government prosecuted fourteen Republicans under the Sedition Act. The most celebrated case involved Vermont Congressman Matthew Lyon. He had earlier attained notoriety when, on the floor of the House of Representatives, he spit in the face of Federalist congressman Roger Griswold and provoked an ugly brawl. A year later "Spitting Matt" suggested that President Adams should be committed to a madhouse. A grand jury promptly indicted and a court convicted him of sedition. The judge sentenced Lyon to four months in jail and a $1,000 fine.

Although the Sedition Act seems like a violation of the First Amendment, it was consistent with eighteenth-century understanding of free press and by extension free speech. Common law had defined free press as the absence of "prior restraint." In other words, the government could not prevent a person from speaking but could punish him afterward. The Sedition Act did not impose prior restraint; moreover, it allowed truth as a defense. If a statement was factually correct it was not seditious. The law also allowed juries to render verdicts in sedition cases instead of judges. Thus, in a technical sense, the Sedition Act expanded free speech, although its intent was clearly oppressive. But constitutional or not, the Alien and Sedition Acts damaged the Federalist party's popularity.

Some Republicans struck back. Meeting in July 1798, Jefferson and Madison secretly composed two sets of resolutions denouncing the Sedition Act as unconstitutional. Both sets declared that the Constitution was a compact between the states, which reserved all power except those explicitly enumerated in the Constitution and given to the national government. Jefferson's resolutions, presented to the Kentucky legislature, went on to propose that states possessed the right "to nullify . . . all assumptions of power by others within their limits" and ultimately to secede from the Union if they so decided. This issue of whether states possessed the right to disregard unconstitutional federal law later became known as **nullification**. That, along with the view that the Union was a voluntary compact among the states would later support southern secessionists leading up to the Civil War. Madison's more temperate argument, submitted to the

This political cartoon illustrates the fight between Vermont representative and Republican Matthew Lyon and Connecticut congressman and Federalist Roger Griswold on the floor of the House of Representatives in 1798. Onlookers seem either bemused or eager to encourage their champion to defeat his opponent. Partisanship during the 1790s was often intense and sometimes led to violent affairs of personal honor.

Virginia legislature for its approval, avoided nullification and secession, declaring instead that the Alien and Sedition Acts were "alarming infractions" of constitutional guarantees of free speech. The **Virginia and Kentucky Resolutions**, as passed by those two states, signified the continuing struggle between nationalists (Federalists) and the proponents of states' rights (Republicans). No other state adopted them and ten flatly rejected them. The prevailing view was that the federal judiciary, not the states, should determine the constitutionality of federal law. Far from being disheartened, though, Jefferson was more confident than ever of the rightness of Republican ideology.

Peace with France

On what terms did the Quasi-War finally end?

After safeguarding American shipping through successful prosecution of the Quasi-War, President Adams sought to restore peace. France, facing military reverses in the European war, wanted peace also. War had only pushed the United States closer to Great Britain. Talleyrand, embarrassed by the XYZ Affair, now moved to "put an end to differences that should never have arisen." In February 1799, Adams shocked Hamiltonian Federalists by dispatching a team of envoys to negotiate

an end to the conflict with France. Hamilton and his supporters, of course, still hoped for all-out war with France. This was no impulsive decision on Adams's part, for reliable sources indicated that French foreign minister Talleyrand was ready to settle the dispute. It was also a courageous decision made above politics and in a supercharged political environment. A thunderstruck Secretary of State Pickering publicly denounced the decision; Adams replaced him with John Marshall of Virginia, and in doing so broke completely with Hamilton and the extremists of the Federalist party.

The political climate in both France and the United States had changed radically in a year. As the American peace team crossed the Atlantic, Napoleon Bonaparte seized control of the French government. The Revolution now over, Bonaparte promised order and stability. When Washington died in December 1799, Bonaparte ordered gestures of mourning throughout France. In the United States, all but the most extreme Federalists welcomed an end to the war. Burdened by taxes and fearful of the army, the public demanded peace.

The negotiations proceeded swiftly after Bonaparte and the Americans broke an impasse over the status of the Franco-American treaties of 1778 and indemnities for lost American shipping. The **Convention of**

Mortefontaine, signed in October 1800, essentially disposed of both the treaties and the indemnities. France received trade privileges on terms equally favorable with those extended to Great Britain in Jay's Treaty. The agreement received a cool reception in Congress, but neither Republicans nor Federalists raised serious objections.

With the end of the Quasi-War, American merchants resumed their profitable trade with the French West Indies. The United States had freed itself from an entangling alliance with France, one that would only spell trouble as long as France was locked in its struggle with Great Britain. Adams had acted courageously in initiating the peace process against the wishes of powerful members of the Federalist party, but he had jeopardized his chances of reelection.

The Election of 1800

> How did the election of 1800 show the rising tide of democracy in the United States?

Partisan bitterness raged as the 1800 elections approached. Excoriations and epithets filled the newspapers, broadsides, and personal correspondence. Republicans branded Federalists as "monarchists," and Federalists warned of a "Jacobin" reign of terror. "Should the infidel Jefferson be elected to the Presidency," wrote one Federalist journalist in the style of the blustery personal attacks that characterized the politics of the day, "the *seal of death* is that moment set on our holy religion, our churches will be prostrated, and some famous prostitute, under the title of Goddess of Reason, will preside in the Sanctuaries now devoted to the Most High." Mobs scuffled in the streets. Republican newspapers played up an earlier sex scandal involving Alexander Hamilton. Republicans warned German-Americans in Pennsylvania that Federalist-imposed taxes and the Provisional Army were intended to oppress them. John Fries, a local farmer, led frightened and angry citizens in obstructing tax collections. Adams immediately dispatched troops to stop the demonstrations, "which, I am convinced," the president declared, "amount to treason." A court convicted Fries of treason and Supreme Court justice Samuel Chase sentenced him to hang, although Adams eventually pardoned him. Consequently, Pennsylvania's German-Americans became confirmed Republicans.

Instead of riding the rising tide of democracy that had reduced or eliminated property qualifications for voting in several states, the Federalists tried to stem it. They continued to use the Alien Act to prevent newcomers from gaining citizenship and joining the electorate and the Sedition Act to muzzle the Republican press. When Federalists lost the legislative election in New York, one of the eleven states where legislatures chose the state's presidential electors, Hamilton tried unsuccessfully to persuade Governor John Jay to allow the outgoing Federalist legislators to choose the electors rather than the incoming Republicans. Utilizing Jefferson's and Madison's extensive correspondence with southern agrarians, Pennsylvania's city and rural democrats, and Aaron Burr's organization of workingmen in New York City, Republicans brimmed with confidence.

Despite the growth of national political parties, regional identities and personal ambition remained stronger than devotion to national party organizations. Northern Federalists supported Adams for president at a time when nomination amounted to party leaders in the various states coming to some decision about whom to support. For geographic balance to the ticket they selected Charles Cotesworth Pinckney of South Carolina for vice president. The Republicans backed Jefferson for president because of his prestige and Aaron Burr because of the prospect of his delivering New York. Hamilton reopened Federalist divisions by attempting to thwart Adams, who had infuriated him by his determined independence and who, he declared publicly, was unqualified to be president because of serious "defects in his character." Behind the scenes, Hamilton once again persuaded South Carolina electors to discard their Adams votes in order to bring Pinckney in first. But as far as the returns were concerned, Hamilton's machinations did not matter, for Jefferson and Burr both received 73 electoral votes to Adams' 65. The Republicans also won majorities in both houses of Congress. It was a total and decisive victory for the Republican party.

Adams and the Federalists were clearly the losers, but the winner had yet to be determined. In the electoral vote, still not differentiated into presidential and vice-presidential ballots, Jefferson and Burr received equal numbers, tossing the election into the "lame-duck" Federalist-controlled House of Representatives. The balloting was by state, each casting one vote. Burr's political organization in New York City (later known as Tammany Hall) had been crucial to the Republican victory, and he refused to step aside. For a week the election remained deadlocked. Federalists finally decided that Burr was more dangerous than Jefferson. "For heaven's sake," Hamilton pleaded, "let not the Federal Party be responsible for the elevation of this Man." On the thirty-sixth ballot, the House elected Jefferson—a new president and a new party for a new century.

THINKING BACK

1. What evidence can you cite that the political system in the United States was still evolving, and how did politicians manipulate it during the late 1790s?

2. What did the election of 1800 reveal about Americans' evolving perceptions about the nature of the republic?

CONCLUSION

An expanding economy, reliable tax revenue, good credit, and an army and navy made the United States stronger in 1800 than it had been in 1789. Hamilton's economic program laid the foundation for the kind of diverse economy, specialized workforce, and urbanized society that eventually characterized the United States. The country avoided potentially disastrous international conflicts and reached pragmatic agreements with Britain, Spain, and France. As the republic expanded westward, incessant pressure from settlements pushed Native Americans out of Ohio, a mixed legacy but one that clarified the definition of the republic so as to exclude Native Americans. Many displaced Indians moved further west, into territories claimed by other Indian nations and by Spain, thus putting additional pressure on Spain's empire in North America. Along the Pacific coast, Spanish garrisons and Catholic missions were signs of the Spanish crown's attempt to tighten its grip on California, but it was not a firm one, partly because of restrictive imperial economic policies.

The stability and strength of the United States at the close of the eighteenth century are probably more evident today than they were at the time. Philosophical differences turned into angry partisan confrontations that challenged the vision of a harmonious republic of virtuous leaders and trusting, obedient citizens. Political parties formalized and intensified the debates over the national government's power, who should rule, and where the United States should look for friends in the world. Although we take hard-fought election campaigns for granted today, partisan rancor troubled many Americans who experienced it for the first time. In the end, Republicans proved to be better organizers than the Federalists, who despite their many successes stood on the edge of disintegration at the close of the eighteenth century. The shortest-lived of all major parties in American history, the Federalist party could not adjust to the reality that the United States continued to grow into a more democratic nation.

SUGGESTED SOURCES FOR STUDENTS

Essays in Douglas Ambrose and Robert W. T. Martin, eds., *The Many Faces of Alexander Hamilton: The Life and Legacy of America's Most Elusive Founding Father* (2006), offer fresh insights into Hamilton's goals, policies, and legacy.

For the Republican viewpoint on redefining the nation, see Lance Banning, *The Jefferson Persuasion: Evolution of a Party Ideology* (1978).

Susan Branson, *These Fiery Frenchified Dames: Women and Political Culture in Early National Philadelphia* (2001), explains that women's roles in the public sphere were often political, such as in holding French-style and distinctly Republican salons attended by many of the country's political leaders.

Ron Chernow, *Alexander Hamilton* (2004), has written a brilliantly insightful portrayal of Washington's controversial secretary of the treasury in all of his brilliance and vulnerabilities.

William C. Davis describes the opening of the lower Mississippi Valley to settlement in *A Way Through the Wilderness: The Natchez Trace and the Civilization of the Southern Frontier* (1995).

The diplomatic history of the period has not achieved better coverage than provided by the eminent scholar Alexander De Conde. His *Entangling Alliance: Politics and Diplomacy Under George Washington* (1958) and *The Quasi-War: Politics and Diplomacy of the Undeclared War with France, 1797-1801* (1966) cover the entire period.

The most authoritative and comprehensive discussion of the period appears in Stanley M. Elkins and Eric McKitrick's superb *The Age of Federalism* (1993). Biographical vignettes introduce the major figures.

Joseph J. Ellis, *Founding Brothers: The Revolutionary Generation* (2001), offers the personal perspectives of a small group of the period's leading figures, cutting through the harsh rhetoric of the time to clarify issues that troubled Americans.

Joanne Freeman, *Affairs of Honor: National Politics in the New Republic* (2001), describes the rise of political parties in the 1790s and the high-voltage political discourse in a deeply divided nation.

An enlightening analysis of the lives of African Americans in Spanish Louisiana is Kimberly S. Hanger, *Bounded Lives, Bounded Places: Free Black Society in Colonial New Orleans, 1769-1803* (1997).

The best survey of the settlement of the trans-Appalachian West in the 1790s is Malcolm J. Rohrbaugh, *The Trans-Appalachian Frontier: People, Societies, and Institutions, 1775-1850* (1978).

Thomas P. Slaughter, *The Whiskey Rebellion: Frontier Epilogue to the American Revolution* (1986), brings out the broad implications of the brief insurrection in western Pennsylvania.

BEFORE WE GO ON

1. How did the Federalists contribute to the creation of a more stable national government?

2. What foreign policy challenges confronted the United States during the 1790s, how did the Washington and Adams administrations deal with them, and why did many Americans react negatively to administration foreign policies?

Building a Democratic Nation

3. Why were political parties regarded with such suspicion in the 1790s, and what purpose(s) did Federalists and Republicans fill during the 1790s, especially with respect to increasing democracy?

4. How did economic developments in the 1790s make American society more democratic? How did they make the United States less democratic?

Connections

5. What aspects of politics in the 1790s are evident in the political discourse, partisan identities, and election campaigning in the United States today?

6. What aspects of today's economy in the United States are traceable to Federalist programs in the 1790s?

Chapter 8

New Challenges for the Democratic Republic, 1800–1815

A PERSONAL PERSPECTIVE: HAMILTON AND BURR, AN AFFAIR OF HONOR

The Hamilton-Burr duel at Weekawken, New Jersey, July 11, 1804

> **How did the Burr-Hamilton duel come about, and what does this personal experience reveal about the culture of the time?**

At dawn on July 11, 1804, two small rowboats crossed the Hudson River from New York City to the bluffs near Weehawken, New Jersey. One boat carried forty-eight-year-old Vice-President Aaron Burr, grandson of Great Awakening revivalist Jonathan Edwards and Republican tactician who in 1800 had nearly become president. In the other sat Alexander Hamilton, a year younger than Burr and the architect of Federalist domestic and foreign policies. The two men were heading for an "interview," the day's euphemism for a pistol duel. Each man brought along his "second," a representative who made all the arrangements. A physician was also present. Burr had challenged Hamilton, and according to the unwritten *code duello*, Hamilton accepted.

This was one of the most famous shoot-outs in American history, mainly because of the prominence of the two men. Hamilton fired quickly, missing by a wide margin. Burr then took careful aim and pulled the trigger, his bullet striking Hamilton just above the hip, glancing off a rib, penetrating his liver, and lodging in his spine. Mortally wounded and in agonizing pain, Hamilton was taken to the New York City home of his friend and wealthy banker William Bayard where he died the next day, watched over by his devoted wife Elizabeth. Hundreds of mourners attended his funeral, among them bankers, merchants, former Revolutionary War officers, and foreign dignitaries. Burr's defenders contended that he had acted honorably and rid the country of a dangerous monarchist; however, authorities in New Jersey charged him with murder. Burr took refuge among friends in Georgia, but when state officials seemed disinterested in pressing their charges, he returned to Washington, D.C. and resumed his responsibilities, including presiding over sessions of the United States Senate.

We wonder why such brilliant and successful men risked their lives so rashly. Even though duels seldom produced fatalities, they were still potentially lethal, as Hamilton well knew because two years earlier his son had been killed in a duel. Was it simply hotheadedness? Burr had felt deeply insulted when, during the recent New York gubernatorial election campaign, Hamilton called him "despicable," "despotic," and "dangerous"—mild-sounding language today but fighting words back then. This was Burr's second duel. Hamilton had an explosive nature too; during the debates over Jay's Treaty (see pp. 220-21), he had challenged two political opponents to duels, though nothing came of it. Was Hamilton suicidal, despondent over his son's death and the rise to power of Jeffersonian Republicans who might undo all he had put together to strengthen the young nation? "Every day," he lamented after the Republican party's victory in 1800, "proves to me more and more that this American world was not made for me." Probably not, for more than temper tantrums or inner demons lay behind the Hamilton-Burr confrontation.

During this time of emerging democracy, American voters relied heavily on the character of public

---

1800	1801	1801-04	1802
Gabriel Prosser's slave revolt conspiracy discovered. Spain returns Louisiana to France in Treaty of San Ildefonso	Outgoing Federalist Congress passes Judiciary Act of 1801. John Adams makes "midnight appointments" to federal judiciary	United States fights war with Tripoli to halt pirate attacks on American ships in the Mediterranean	James Callender breaks Jefferson-Hemings scandal. Government establishes West Point military academy. Yazoo land scandal uncovered

officials—their selflessness, honesty, and courage. Political leaders who failed the honor test lost their personal and public reputations, which is one reason why political discourse often shifted from ideological or policy disagreements to negative campaigning and sometimes ended in duels. Hamilton had wounded Burr's reputation and thus jeopardized his political career. Burr demanded either an apology or the opportunity to rescue his reputation on the field of honor. Hamilton felt he had no choice but to participate, since he believed that Burr was an unprincipled man. He could not make himself apologize, and if he declined Burr's challenge, he would dishonor himself and jeopardize his own public renown. But on the night before the duel, he wrote that he would either hold his fire or waste his shot.

Hamilton regarded Burr as a much more dangerous character than Thomas Jefferson as far as the country's future was concerned. "If he [Burr] can [,] he will certainly disturb our institutions to secure himself *permanent power* and with it *wealth*." Burr probably did participate in schemes to dismember the United States, one of them ironically a conspiracy with disaffected Federalists and others with foreign agents; however, he was never convicted of treason. Hamilton had dabbled in political intrigue too and did so with arrogance and recklessness, as in the Alien and Sedition Acts. But Hamilton never sought to destroy or even weaken the United States. He distrusted democracy and decried the Republicans' election victory; nevertheless, he had given the country effective fiscal policies, a national bank, and incentives for economic diversification. He identified strongly with the young nation and its future.

Early in the nineteenth century, questions about nationhood continued to arise, and the Hamilton-Burr duel showed the strength and weakness of American national identity. Clashing ideas about the nature of republican government continued to divide the country. Hamilton's nationalist vision even seeped into the Republican party after his death causing great consternation among orthodox Republicans while remnants of the Federalist party recruited Burr, the Republican vice president, to help them lead New England and New York out of the union.

Aaron Burr was not an ideological politician. His position in the Jefferson administration resulted from his ability to rally New York City's workingmen for the Republican ticket in 1800. Jefferson distrusted Burr as much as Hamilton did, suspicions that Burr amply confirmed. Despite the label his Federalist opponents had attached to him during the election, like the "Parisian revolutionary monster," Jefferson was no radical democrat, as his ambivalence toward slavery and the Bank of the United States attested; nevertheless, he and fellow Republicans broke sharply with their Federalist predecessors on many fronts. The Jefferson administration and Republicans in Congress cut taxes and spending without jeopardizing economic prosperity. Indeed, the nation prospered economically. The Republicans failed to purge the judiciary of all Federalist judges, but Jefferson greatly enhanced his and his party's political stature by purchasing Louisiana, applying a broad interpretation of Constitutional power to accomplish the acquisition. The country remained largely dependent on foreign manufactures and markets and was militarily weak; thus, the outbreak of war between Great Britain and France once again threatened disaster. Jefferson utilized economic sanctions like those that had worked during the lead-up to the Revolutionary War, but the embargo failed abysmally, giving Federalists new political life. Jefferson's successor, James Madison, fared little better, and in 1812, Congress declared war on Great Britain, what some people at the time, and since, have regarded as a second war for American independence.

THINKING BACK

1. Why did Aaron Burr and Alexander Hamilton, prominent men with so much to lose, risk their lives and reputations in a duel?
2. From their personal perspectives, what do we learn about the strength of American identity at the beginning of the nineteenth century?

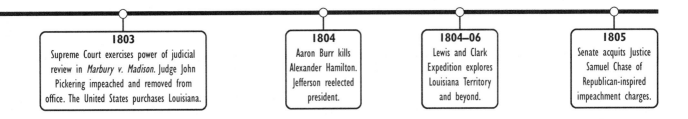

1803	1804	1804–06	1805
Supreme Court exercises power of judicial review in *Marbury v. Madison*. Judge John Pickering impeached and removed from office. The United States purchases Louisiana.	Aaron Burr kills Alexander Hamilton. Jefferson reelected president.	Lewis and Clark Expedition explores Louisiana Territory and beyond.	Senate acquits Justice Samuel Chase of Republican-inspired impeachment charges.

THE "REVOLUTION OF 1800"

The Republican election triumph in 1800 brought the curtain down on the Federalist era. Later in life, Thomas Jefferson, the Republican party's leader and winner of that year's presidential contest, characterized his election as the "**Revolution of 1800**" despite the razor-thin margin of victory. He went on to explain that the election was "as real a revolution in the principles of our government as that of 1776." Democratic Republicans had thwarted elitist Federalist attempts to expand federal government power in ways that seemed to endanger personal liberty. Trust in the natural talent and virtue of ordinary citizens triumphed over the belief that only a few people of wealth and education possessed the capacity to govern. The defeated Federalists handed over the reins of power to the triumphant Republicans, a remarkable event in itself, for as Margaret Bayard Smith, a prominent commentator noted: "The changes of administration, which in every government and in every age have most generally been epochs of confusion, villainy and bloodshed, in our happy country take place without any species of distraction, or disorder." But while much did change as a result of the "Revolution of 1800," the Republican party's ascendancy did not bring the universal freedom and equality as the Declaration of Independence had grandly promised.

"We Are All Republicans"

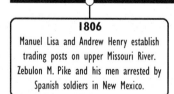

To what extent did Thomas Jefferson's inauguration suggest revolutionary change in America?

Jefferson's simple inauguration ceremony on March 4, 1801, the first held in the tiny national capital of Washington, District of Columbia (D.C.), brimmed with symbolism. The lanky, fifty-seven-year-old widower donned a plain suit and walked from his boarding house along the rutted dirt street leading to the still-unfinished Capitol building to be sworn into office. By eschewing a fancy carriage, this first Republican president rejected the excesses and haughtiness of his Federalist predecessors. As outgoing president John Adams' son, John Quincy Adams, noted

afterward: "Whatever the merits or the demerits of the former administrations may have been, there never was a system of measures more completely and irrevocably abandoned and rejected by the popular voice. It never can and never will be revived."

Yet, to the Federalists Jefferson offered reconciliation, for he was not the demon his opponents had feared. His inaugural address, read in a voice so soft that his audience could barely hear, contained two primary aims. The first was to forge a national political consensus. Jefferson disapproved of political parties despite their being an established fact of the country's political life. He hated divisiveness, much preferring harmony. Besides, he assumed that all but the most stalwart Federalists would endorse his vision for an expanding but peaceful America. He had not opposed the Constitution during the ratification process thirteen years earlier, only the subsequent machinations of Alexander Hamilton and those whom Jefferson regarded as monarchists. "We are all Republicans, we are all Federalists," he told his listeners. As for the diehards who thought of him as a "Parisian revolutionary monster," Jefferson proposed tolerance—a very different attitude from that embodied in the Federalists' Sedition Act. "Let us . . . unite with one heart and one mind. Let us restore to social intercourse that harmony and affection without which liberty and even life itself are but dreary things."

Secondly, and more importantly, Jefferson's inaugural address provided an opportunity to define republican principles. "Wise and frugal" republican government, he said, stayed out of people's lives. It did not employ taxes to "take from the mouth of labor the bread it has earned." It treated its citizens fairly, providing "equal and exact justice" to all its citizens. It ensured freedom of religion and the press, paid its debts, and respected "the decisions of the majority" as expressed in free elections. The absence of peaceful remedies for grievances caused revolution or other resorts to force. As for the proper distribution of power in a multi-layered federal system, Jefferson stated that state governments were "the most competent ... for our domestic concerns and the surest

---

1806
Manuel Lisa and Andrew Henry establish trading posts on upper Missouri River. Zebulon M. Pike and his men arrested by Spanish soldiers in New Mexico.

1806-7
Napoleon implements Continental System. Aaron Burr accused and tried but finally acquitted of treason.

1807
British frigate *Leopard* attacks the *Chesapeake*. Congress passes Embargo Act.

1808
Congress outlaws the African slave trade. James Madison elected president.

bulwarks against anti-republican tendencies." The main purpose of the national government was to maintain order at home and safety abroad, and it should be kept under civilian rather than military control. "This," he declared, "is the sum of good government."

Although the inaugural address set forth a political strategy of capturing the middle of the political spectrum, it also revealed Jefferson's naturally moderate tendencies. While he envisioned the continuation of an agrarian nation, rather than an industrial one, he also saw commerce serving as the "handmaid" of agriculture. The Republican triumph in 1800 did not signal a dramatic revolution, but it did portend many significant changes.

Jefferson as a National Leader: The Mettle of the Man

How did Jefferson exemplify the ambiguities of moral character?

Thomas Jefferson was a man of perplexing contradictions and an enigmatic persona. With a highly developed sense of honor, he nevertheless suffered moral failings. Although Jefferson denounced the licentiousness of Europe's aristocracy, as a young man he once "offered love to a handsome lady" who happened to be the wife of his Virginia neighbor, and as United States envoy in Paris after his wife Martha had died, he fell in love with another married woman. Serene and sunny by disposition, Jefferson drew hate mail from his political opponents. One letter-writer addressed him as "you red-headed son-of-a-bitch." Jefferson believed that goodness and reason resided in human nature, but he loathed people's ignorance and incivility. And despite possessing sophisticated tastes developed during extended stays in Paris, New York, and Philadelphia, he dreamed of a country of independent yeoman farmers living happily on the land. Furthermore, he seemed not to distinguish between large landowners and slaveholders like himself and simple yeoman farmers.

Jefferson's tastes redefined the presidency. Preferring simplicity to regality, Jefferson often wore a tattered red jacket and ragged slippers when he received callers at the new presidential mansion. He also dispensed with formal and elaborate presidential receptions, favoring more intimate dinner parties. At state banquets, dignitaries seated themselves willy-nilly around a circular table. Britain's notably aristocratic minister to the United States, Anthony Merry, boycotted these "democratic" functions. As president, Jefferson gave only two public speeches—his first and second inaugural addresses—partly because of his oratorical deficiencies but also because he wished to avoid pretentiousness. Not until the twentieth century did presidents again address Congress in person.

Courtesy of Library of Congress

THOMAS JEFFERSON
President of the United States

President Thomas Jefferson. This engraving shows Jefferson to be a man of science, a scholar, the embodiment of classical Greek republicanism, and the author of the Declaration of Independence.

1809
John Jacob Astor employees establish trading outpost on the Pacific Coast. American soldiers defeat Indians in Battle of Tippecanoe.

1812
The United States declares war against Britain. Louisiana admitted to the Union.

1814
Treaty of Ghent formally ends War of 1812.

1815
Americans defeat British in the Battle of New Orleans.

As an accomplished lawyer, scholar, scientist, and inventor, Jefferson assembled hundreds of books that became the core of the Library of Congress. Much later, President John F. Kennedy joked to a gathering of Nobel laureates that they constituted the greatest collection of talent in the White House since Jefferson dined there—alone. Jefferson ordered written on his tombstone the achievements of which he was most proud: author of the **Declaration of Independence**, founder of the University of Virginia, and composer of the **Virginia Statute of Religious Freedom**. Although he never traveled west of the Appalachian Mountains,

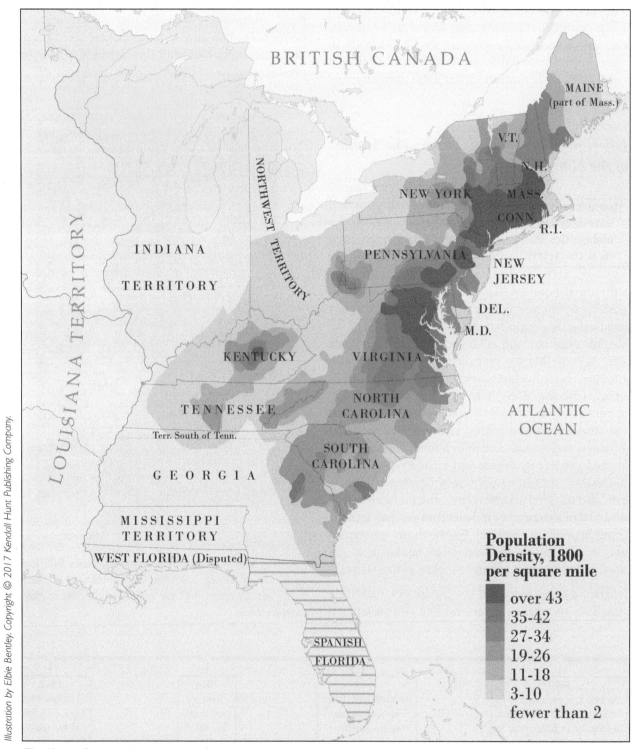

Illustration by Elbie Bentley. Copyright © 2017 Kendall Hunt Publishing Company.

Population Density, 1800 per square mile

- over 43
- 35-42
- 27-34
- 19-26
- 11-18
- 3-10
- fewer than 2

The United States at the beginning of the nineteenth century.

he avidly read explorers' accounts of North America. Part of his interest stemmed from his tremendous scientific curiosity, but he was also convinced that an expanding democratic republic, whose population in 1800 had reached 5.3 million, depended on opening western lands to settlement.

Native Americans possessed the vast bulk of North America's fertile land; thus Jefferson had to take them into account as he sought to realize his vision. In general, Jefferson viewed the Indians as "in body and mind equal to the white man." As he told a visiting delegation of Indians: "In time you will . . . become one people with us; your blood will mix with ours" and you "will spread with ours over this great [land]." For that to happen, though, Indians would have to forsake hunting and transform themselves into farmers. In this, Jefferson overlooked the reality that most Indian communities had depended on farming for centuries. He also wanted them to learn how to spin and weave thread into cloth and to exchange tribal claims to land for individual ownership. To a considerable extent, Cherokees and Creeks of North Carolina, Tennessee, Georgia, and today's Alabama and Mississippi did so. Jefferson's idealism mixed with self-interest, for he reasoned that Indian farmers would require less land than Indian hunters and their loss would be white settlers' gain. As he told one government Indian agent, " a coincidence of interests will be produced between those who have lands to spare . . . and those who . . . want lands." Thus, Jefferson declaimed to Native American people: "We will never do an unjust act towards you."

Jefferson's vision of an expanding democracy did not include African Americans. Jefferson did not emancipate most of the enslaved people at Monticello, let alone press other slave owners of the South to do so. In addition to the striking contradiction between Jefferson as the author of the Declaration of Independence's powerful statement about universal freedom and Jefferson as the owner of over two hundred slaves, there was the matter of his relationship with Sally Hemings, an enslaved woman twenty-five years younger than he. Jefferson acquired Hemings as part of his wife Martha Wayles' inheritance. Sally was actually Martha's half-sister, sharing the same father. But Martha's mother was a prominent white woman while Sally's mother was an enslaved African-American woman. In the 1780s, after Martha Jefferson's death, the fourteen-year-old Hemings joined Jefferson in Paris, where they entered a lasting, sexual relationship. After returning

with him to Monticello in 1790, she gave birth to the first of seven children, all of them light skinned and resembling Jefferson. Hemings could have remained in Paris and become free, since France did not then acknowledge slavery, but instead, she trusted Jefferson to free their children once they reached adulthood.

In 1802, a vitriolic journalist and disappointed office-seeker named James Callender revealed to the public the Jefferson-Hemings relationship. Federalists taunted Jefferson, an extremely private man, and demeaned "Black Sally" as the president's concubine. Jefferson maintained total silence on the matter, and his white children and grandchildren did the same.

The importance of the Jefferson-Hemings story reaches beyond their private lives, for it illustrates a much-ignored fact about race in America: black and white worlds often intersected in intimate ways. In his **Notes on the State of Virginia**, Jefferson carefully separated black people from white people by physical, emotional, and intellectual characteristics, even though four of his children were in all likelihood neither white nor black—they were both. The probability that Jefferson co-produced two families instead of one brings the identity of Hemings' descendants under a different light. For generations, whites had denied the Hemings family its legacy—descent from one of the great founders and defining icons of the American nation. Their story also gives new meaning to who was an American in Jeffersonian America.

Democratic Revolution: Gabriel Prosser's Conspiracy

Slavery created many painful dilemmas for otherwise democratic-minded Republicans. Jefferson had once said that rebellion against tyranny was a good thing; however, despite admitting that slavery was morally wrong and slaves had the right to be free, he never said that slaves possessed the right to rebel. During the 1790s, he had kept abreast of the slave-led revolution in St. Domingue, a French colony on the island of Española in the Caribbean (see the Global Perspective, p. 135), and was disturbed by it.

> How did Jefferson respond to the aspirations of slaves for freedom?

In the 1790s, thousands of African and mixed-race islanders, free as well as slave, caught the fever of revolution. Their long struggle for liberty finally culminated in 1804 with the founding of the black republic of Haiti. News of the **Haitian Revolution**, carried by French refugees to the United States, excited hopes and fears. African Americans celebrated it and made one of the revolution's leaders, Francoise-Dominique Toussaint L'Ouverture, a hero while slaveholders, Republican as well as Federalist, in Virginia and elsewhere braced for their own slave rebellion. In Virginia, Governor James Monroe, a neighbor of Jefferson's and an ardent Republican who had championed the French Revolution, warned that "the scenes which are acted out in St. Doming[ue] must produce an effect on . . . our slaves, and it is our duty to be on our guard to prevent any mischief resulting from it." Massachusetts Republican Abraham Bishop observed the contradiction: "We have firmly asserted, *that all men are free.* Yet, as soon as poor blacks ... cried out, *It is enough,. . .* we have been the first to assist in riveting their chains."

In August of 1800 near Richmond, Virginia's new capital city, a slave known as Gabriel had learned about the rebellion in St. Domingue and planned to duplicate it with an insurrection of his fellow Virginia slaves. Gabriel was a blacksmith who had negotiated with his owner, Thomas Prosser, to live and work in Richmond. A large number of slaves and free blacks resided in the rapidly growing city, and they formed an African-American community that maintained links to the slave quarters on outlying plantations. As they met in the streets, markets, and churches, they talked about freedom.

The time was right to revolt. The threat of war with France had evaporated, and the state had stored away its weapons and ammunition in the Richmond armory. Gabriel Prosser saw an opportunity for arming large numbers of slaves. He recruited a thousand or more to launch an attack, set for the night of August 30. One group would ignite tobacco warehouses as a diversion while others seized the armory. They planned to kill every white person they found except those they regarded as friends, particularly anti-slavery Methodists and Quakers and Governor Monroe. Prosser intended to hold Monroe hostage until the state emancipated all slaves.

Although the rebels had laid their plans carefully, fate did not reward them. On the designated evening, a torrential thunderstorm washed out the bridge leading into town, preventing participants from surrounding farms and plantations from joining the revolt. Moreover, two of the conspirators, Pharoah and Tom Sheppard, had alerted the authorities, who

acted quickly, arresting scores of suspects. Officials executed nearly thirty. Prosser hid out for several days, but other slaves betrayed him to authorities. He was arrested, tried, and sentenced to hang.

From the gallows, Prosser compared himself to George Washington. "I have adventured my life in endeavoring to obtain the liberty of my countrymen, and am a willing sacrifice to their cause." The rebels identified with the American republic and its Revolutionary creed, from which they drew inspiration for their rebellion against tyranny. But most slave owners, many of whom were Republicans, refused to permit the precedents of the American Revolution to be appropriated for the purpose of destroying the cornerstone of their own society.

Gabriel Prosser's Conspiracy raised issues of identity for African Americans. Why did some slaves betray others who were willing to fight and die for freedom? Were not all slaves in the same boat? The answer is complicated. No doubt, some enslaved men and women did not believe the plot would succeed, and they feared reprisals. Pharaoh and Tom Sheppard counted on rewards for sounding the alarm, and both were indeed freed. Pharaoh actually became an overseer, a position of trust and responsibility on slave plantations. No record exists of rebels retaliating against those who had not supported the conspiracy. Freedom was a common goal among Richmond's slaves. The question was how to achieve it, by collective action to destroy the system or individual acquiescence to advance within it.

The scare also raised questions for Virginia slave owners who, like one who wrote a letter to the *Virginia Gazette*, winced at "the existence of slavery in one of the freest republics on earth." While a few planters emancipated their slaves (more Virginia slaves were freed between 1776 and 1812 than at any other time prior to the Civil War), the vast majority thought emancipation was financially impractical. White slave owners also declined to share their state and their identity with black people. Moreover, they concluded that if a slave rebellion should actually arise, they possessed sufficient power to crush it.

The fear that African slaves might ignite slave uprisings led to support in Virginia and elsewhere for outlawing the African slave trade. The Constitutional Convention in 1787 had agreed to keep the slave trade open for at least twenty years, but abhorrence of the traffic was widespread. Every state except

South Carolina had forbidden the importation of African slaves. Most northern states had abolished slavery or never allowed it. Slave owners in Virginia and Maryland had all the slaves they needed as the continuation of sluggish world tobacco markets drove more Chesapeake planters toward less labor-intensive wheat production. Only South Carolina and Georgia demanded more slaves since planters in upland regions of those states were developing cotton as an alternative to rice. Eli Whitney's **cotton gin** triggered the rapid expansion of cotton production.

The only obstacle to a federal ban on the importation of African slaves concerned enforcement, for banning the trade without meaningful sanctions would accomplish little. Early in 1807, after much debate over penalties, Congress finally passed and Jefferson signed a measure outlawing the importation of African slaves. Violators would forfeit their illegal slave cargoes but the law required that confiscated African slaves be turned over to state authorities and sold at public auction, which meant that Africans would enter slavery through the domestic marketing system. On New Year's Day of 1808, the law took effect.

The election of 1800 that Jefferson proclaimed a revolution represented a milestone for the young republic, but not insofar as African Americans were concerned. Jefferson believed slavery would ultimately destroy everyone's freedom, but he also convinced himself that ending it suddenly would lead to economic ruin and race war. He put the dilemma this way: "[W]e have the wolf by the ear, and we can neither hold him, nor safely let him go."

THINKING BACK

1. What did Thomas Jefferson mean by the phrase "Revolution of 1800"? What evidence do you see to justify it?
2. What indications do you see that suggest the extent of Jefferson's commitment to making the United States a more inclusive and tolerant society?
3. How do the stories of Sally Hemings and Gabriel Prosser illustrate the dilemma of slavery in a republican society?

REPUBLICANS IN POWER

In the aftermath of Jefferson's inauguration, Federalists sulked and waited to see what the Republicans were going to do. Yale president Timothy Dwight spoke for many Federalists when he denounced the "blockheads and knaves" who were now running things. Throughout the 1790s, the Republicans had resisted the consolidation of power in the national government. Not surprisingly, most Federalists now thought Jefferson intended to strip power away from the government. But that was not his goal, and the Federalists' sharpest mind, Alexander Hamilton, voiced guarded optimism about that. While he and Jefferson had taken opposite positions on the great issues of the 1790s, Hamilton respected Jefferson's "solid pretensions to character" and figured he was more moderate than he seemed.

Implementing Republican Government

The Republican party that Jefferson led incorporated a wide range of political views, ones that were not always compatible with each other. Southern planters, like

> How did Jefferson implement his plan for republican government?

Virginia's John Randolph, subscribed to the Republican agrarian ideology that Jefferson had once espoused, but as slave owners they could hardly be called democrats. Many had been Anti-Federalists

Swiss-born Albert Gallatin was Jefferson's Treasury secretary.

during the debates over the Constitution and now labored to redirect power from the national to the state level. In contrast, Republicans in the new trans-Appalachian states of Kentucky, Tennessee, and Ohio (the latter admitted to the Union in 1803), and in the Middle Atlantic and New England states, were remarkably democratic for their time, having no use for property requirements that limited the number of adult white males who could vote and hold public office. In many states they managed to establish universal white manhood suffrage. They changed several state constitutions to provide for the election of judges, and by 1804 eight of the seventeen states in the country chose their presidential electors by direct popular election. As a result of these reforms, popular participation in government, particularly at the state level, increased substantially over what it had been during the Federalist years. In Pennsylvania, for example, the number of adult white males voting for governor increased from roughly one-quarter during the 1790s to nearly three-fourths by 1808.

At the national level, the Jefferson administration and Republicans in Congress formulated public policy with little input from the grassroots. They focused on what they regarded as the Federalists' most damnable legacy: a mammoth $83 million debt and internal taxes like the whiskey excise that went with it. Soaking ordinary working people through taxes and using the revenues to pay interest to rich speculators who held the public debt was unconscionable to them. The Federalists had also used taxes to build a menacing standing army and to pay hundreds of revenue agents to harass the citizenry.

Secretary of the Treasury Albert Gallatin of Pennsylvania, a Swiss immigrant who spoke with a heavy accent, shared Jefferson's views on fiscal matters. Together they drew up a strict budget that severely slashed government spending. The federal bureaucracy was a prime target for cuts. The bigger the government, the more it cost to operate and the more tax revenue it required, thus less money was available for liquidating the debt. In those days, government engaged in few activities—primarily distributing the mail, collecting taxes and tariff duties, selling public land, and patrolling the country's borders. The Treasury Department, the largest in the executive branch, contained only 1,285 employees. Nevertheless, Jefferson sought to curb bureaucratic growth. Along with his frugal personal habits, the president employed only a single personal secretary despite his massive official correspondence. Republicans in Congress funded few new government positions, mainly a handful of postal clerks and postmasters.

The budget ax also fell heavily on the military. With the Whiskey Rebellion still fresh on their minds, Republicans feared a standing professional army that could be used to suppress citizen freedom. State militia units composed of citizen soldiers, they believed, were entirely adequate for defending the nation's borders. Accordingly, Congress reduced the army by one third, to 3,000 men. But simultaneously, in 1802, they sought to improve the quality of army officers by founding the United States military academy at West Point, New York. The navy underwent major modification as well. Construction of new frigates (heavily armed naval vessels and the mainstay of warship fleets of the day) ceased; Jefferson kept only six frigates and ordered the building of a fleet of much smaller, inexpensive gunboats for patrolling rivers and coastlines. Although military and naval cost savings were substantial, the inadequacies of the country's armed forces in the War of 1812 (see pp. 252-54) showed that this course of action carried its own risks.

In addition to budget cuts, the Republican-controlled Congress repealed all internal taxes, relying exclusively on import duties and the sale of western land for necessary revenue. "What farmer, what mechanic, what laborer ever sees a tax-gatherer in the United States?" Jefferson proudly asked. Altogether, Republican budget management succeeded in substantially reducing the debt. By the end of Jefferson's second term, the debt stood at $57 million.

Republicans slashed and burned other hated remains of Federalist policies as well. Congress simply allowed the Alien and Sedition Acts to expire and then restored the shorter five-year residency requirement for citizenship. Jefferson pardoned Republican editors who had been convicted under the Sedition Act and ordered their fines refunded. But Jefferson showed his pragmatic side with respect to the Bank of the United States. What "is practical," he declared in a letter to a friend, "must often control what is pure theory." Jefferson still harbored doubts about the Bank's constitutionality, but Gallatin convinced him of its necessity for economic growth. "It mortifies me," Jefferson said, "to be strengthening principles which I deem radically vicious," but "we can never completely get rid of his [Hamilton's] financial system." The Bank supplied credit that helped stimulate commercial activity (transportation primarily) and prosperity, a link that Jefferson recognized as essential to the nation's overall health.

The commerce that Jefferson envisioned involved agricultural produce transported to Europe and exchanged for manufactured products. He was certain that as the western territories came under the plow, the volume of American exports would increase, allowing for more imports without unbalancing American trade or stimulating the growth of the industrial cities that he so despised. Numbers did not bear him out, for between 1800 and 1810, the per capita gross national product increased by only .7 percent, substantially less than the previous decade when Hamilton's policies lifted the country out of the deep depression of the 1780s.

The Big Sweep

In addition to shrinking the size of the government, Jefferson faced the question of who should fill available offices. Loyal Republicans expected him to reward them with government posts known as **patronage**. Washington and Adams had appointed mostly Federalists, and Jefferson claimed that fairness demanded the appointment of more Republicans. This **spoils system** (a term drawn from the "spoils" or the treasures captured in war) smacked of corruption, though, and Jefferson resisted more radical Republicans' calls for a wholesale sweep of Federalists from office and their replacement by Republicans. Jefferson kept 132 Federalists in their posts, but he removed bureaucrats he deemed unqualified and filled their positions and vacancies created by death and retirement with Republicans—a total of 158 by the end of his presidency.

The judges whom Adams had appointed after the 1800 election particularly annoyed Republicans. Jefferson called these **midnight appointments** an "outrage on decency." Between the 1800 election and Jefferson's 1801 inauguration, before newly-elected congressmen took their seats, the **lame-duck** Federalists had passed the Judiciary Act of 1801, which Adams signed three weeks before leaving office himself. The measure created nine new circuit court judgeships, relieving Supreme Court justices of the burden of traveling considerable distances over bad roads to preside over those mid-level appellate courts, and ten new district courts. It also allowed Adams to pack more Federalists into the judiciary against the voters' clear preference for Republicans in government. Literally by lamplight on the evening before he departed, Adams prepared court appointments, including one for his wife's nephew. To top it off, the Judiciary Act reduced the number of Supreme Court justices from six to five, so Jefferson would be unable to replace the next justice who died or retired.

Republicans were furious. In January 1802, the new Republican-controlled Congress debated a motion to repeal the Judiciary Act. But that raised the constitutional question of whether Congress possessed the power to destroy federal courts. On a strictly party-line vote that belied Jefferson's assertion that "we are all Republicans, we are all Federalists," Congress repealed the Judiciary Act of 1801 and passed the Judiciary Act of 1802 that took away the new judgeships created by the Federalists and thus restored the necessity for Supreme Court justices to continue riding circuit, which they did until 1869. Stopping the Federalists' court-packing was clearly a political triumph for the Republicans, but their victory was less than complete.

Marbury v. Madison

Adams' last-minute appointments included John Marshall as chief justice of the Supreme Court and William Marbury as justice of the peace for the

> **How did Marbury v. Madison influence constitutional history?**

District of Columbia. Both soon made history. Marshall got into office under the wire, but Marbury's credentials lay on the secretary of state's desk, undelivered, when the Jefferson administration took office. Jefferson instructed his new secretary of state, James Madison, not to deliver Marbury's papers. The frustrated Marbury then went directly to the Supreme Court and asked for a **writ of mandamus**, an order compelling Madison to hand over the appointment. Marbury based his request on the Judiciary Act of 1789 that authorized the court to issue writs of mandamus. This confrontation set up one of the most famous cases in Supreme Court history—*Marbury v. Madison* (1803).

As a Federalist, Chief Justice Marshall sympathized with Marbury, but his keen political instincts told him to consider the consequences of issuing the writ. The judiciary was the weak reed of the national government because it did not possess the power to enforce its decisions. Responsibility for enforcement belonged to the executive branch, and Marshall understood very well that if the court granted Marbury's petition, Jefferson and Madison would ignore it. Such an outcome would not only fail to satisfy Marbury but it would also underscore the court's weakness. In the decision, which Marshall wrote on behalf of a unanimous bench, the court scolded Jefferson and Madison for disregarding Marbury's "vested legal right" to the appointment and then pronounced the Judiciary Act of 1789 unconstitutional because it gave the Supreme Court a power unauthorized by the Constitution. By not stipulating that a party seeking a writ of mandamus must go first to a lower court, the Judiciary Act had unconstitutionally added to the Supreme Court's **original jurisdiction** (the types of cases heard originally by the Supreme Court rather than on appeal from a lower court).

Thus the Supreme Court exercised the power to determine the constitutionality of congressional legislation. Republicans had insisted that the states held that power. Jefferson angrily declared that judicial arbitration of what is constitutional was "a very dangerous doctrine indeed, and one that would place us under the despotism of an oligarchy." Additionally, Marshall's ruling reinforced the principle of checks and balances, a doctrine that at the time was meant to bridle democracy. Marshall cleverly enhanced the judiciary's stature among the branches of the federal government without the executive's endorsement. But the Republicans won something too, for they had prevented Marbury from taking his seat on the federal bench. In the long run, the Supreme Court has kept the Congress in check even though it has rarely invalidated federal legislation.

The Impeachment Caper

Why and how did Republicans attempt to remove Federalist judges?

Federalists still held control of the federal court system, and Republicans knew that it would take years before they could install a new majority on the bench. Few Federalists died in office, Jefferson complained, and none resigned, but impeachment proceedings might provide a way to get rid of them. The necessary grounds were unclear; impeachable behavior included treason, bribery, and other "high crimes and misdemeanors." But many Republicans contended that being a Federalist constituted an impeachable offense against the people's liberty, a doubtful principle that certainly was not in keeping with Jefferson's early conciliatory tone and seemed to imply that only Republicans could be true Americans.

Republican leaders carefully picked cases to test the feasibility of impeachment. At Jefferson's suggestion, the effort began with District Judge John Pickering of New Hampshire. A troubled alcoholic, Pickering embarrassed himself during a trial in 1803. Rumors flew that he had gone mad. A year later the Republican majority in the House of Representatives charged him with various offenses and the Senate voted to remove him from office.

Thus encouraged, the Republicans set their sights on Associate Justice Samuel Chase of the United States Supreme Court. Chase was a signer of the Declaration of Independence, but as a federal judge, he had thrown the book at Republicans accused under the Sedition Act. Jefferson's son-in-law characterized Chase's frequent tirades against Republicans as "*indecent and tyrannical.*" His case, more than Pickering's, would determine whether impeachment could become a useful political device. While presiding over a Baltimore grand jury, Chase unleashed a bitter harangue against a Republican-backed proposal in the state legislature to abolish property qualifications for voting. Universal suffrage, he shouted, "will . . . destroy all protection of property; and our republican constitution will sink into a mobocracy."

After Chase's outburst, an angry Jefferson asked Republican Congressman Joseph Nicholson: "Ought this Seditious and official attack on the principles of our Constitution and on the proceedings of a State to go unpunished?" The House drew up articles of impeachment. The Federalist press called it a Republican power play, which it clearly was. The *New York Evening Post* reported: "The simple truth is, Mr. Jefferson has been determined from the first to have a judiciary, as well as a legislature, that would second the views of the executive."

Chase's Senate trial, which commenced in January of 1805, was a dramatic spectacle. Spectators jammed the gallery. Presiding was Vice President Aaron Burr, under indictment himself in the dueling death of Alexander Hamilton. A reporter caught the irony, noting that in the past "it was the practice . . . to arraign the *murderer* before the *Judge*, but now we behold the *Judge* arraigned before the *murderer*." John Randolph of Virginia presented the case against Chase. Impeachment, he insisted, was a political proceeding that did not require an indictable offense. Chase and his lawyers asserted the judge had merely exercised his right to free speech. Removal from office, they claimed, required corrupt or criminal behavior. The prosecution failed to convince two-thirds of the senators that Chase was guilty of more than rudeness.

Both Federalists and Republicans often invoked the principle of free speech for themselves while denying it to others. Had Chase been convicted, the Republicans probably would have impeached more Federalist judges, including Chief Justice Marshall. The result would have been a new judiciary every time the elected branches of government changed hands. The federal courts have never been impervious to political influences, but the failure of the impeachment maneuver shielded the bench from constantly changing political winds and maintained separation of powers.

The Quids Strike Back

> **Who were the Quids, and why were they important?**

Jefferson was a pragmatic politician, which partly explains his paradoxical stand on slavery as well as his grudging support for the Bank of the United States and his acquiescence in the Louisiana Purchase treaty (see p. 244). From his inauguration, Jefferson sought to make room for moderate Federalists in the Republican party. A small group of southern planter Republicans, however, accused Jefferson of trading party principles for expanded federal government power. They sought to restore purity to Republican ideology. They called themselves Old Republicans, but journalists tagged them the "Tertium Quids," a dismissive phrase meaning "third something"—neither Republican nor Federalist. Their most vocal spokesman was Jefferson's bad-tempered cousin John Randolph of Virginia.

The Quids broke openly with Jefferson in 1802 after exposure of a fraudulent land deal. A group of speculators received 35 million acres of public land from the Georgia legislature in a western district known as the Yazoo territory, in present-day Mississippi. Virtually every one of the legislators who voted for the sale had been bribed. The legislature subsequently canceled the transaction, but not before third parties had purchased parcels from the speculators. Jefferson proposed untangling the mess by giving other public land to the third-party buyers. The Quids praised his honest intentions but attacked the proposal as totally improper. Randolph and the Quids thus fractured the heretofore-solid ranks of the Republican party.

The United States Supreme Court finally resolved the Yazoo dispute when the hapless purchasers challenged Georgia's invalidation of the original grants. In **Fletcher v. Peck** (1810), the court ruled that the original fraud did not affect the validity of the ensuing purchases. Even more importantly, the Supreme Court expanded its power of judicial review

to cover state laws. Chief Justice John Marshall had once again skillfully strengthened the Federalists' bastion of power.

In many ways, the Quids remained purer insofar as their commitment to republican principles were concerned than the mainstream of the Republican party. From the beginning of his administration, Jefferson had tried to lure moderate Federalists into the Republican camp, which he largely managed to do. But in the process, he lost some of the Old Republicans. It did not matter, however, because the Republicans party became the majority party, and Jefferson ensured growing support for the Republican party by his policies pertaining to the trans-Appalachian West.

Demands for Indian Land

Despite Jefferson's repeated promises that Indians would not be forced to relinquish land, actual government policy followed his rather aggressive statement

> **Why and how did Republicans take Indian lands?**

that they must "either incorporate with us as citizens of the United States or remove beyond the Mississippi." In either case, they would lose. Growing states like Georgia, Tennessee, and Ohio set out to extinguish Indian land claims. Settlers ignored the boundaries set in the Treaty of Greenville (see p. 216) and other agreements between tribes and the government of the United States. Jefferson supported the whites' demands for the Indians' land, sending special commissioners to negotiate new boundaries and permission for the United States to construct roads through Indian territory and to establish way stations along the roads to accommodate travelers. He justified the relentless pressure on the Indians by declaring that they would be much better off by giving up their "waste & useless" lands and using payments from the government to develop what remained. The **Indian Intercourse Act of 1790** stipulated that the government could acquire Indian land only through treaties, but as Jefferson pointed out to a delegation of Creek chiefs, whenever "you wish to sell, we shall be ready to buy."

Indians generally resisted further cessions; thus, the Jefferson administration proceeded slowly, eschewing military force. But the Creeks, Cherokees, Chocktaws, and Chickasaws of the Southwest and the Shawnees, Delawares, Miamis, Potawatomies, and Shawnees of the Northwest had little chance of holding their own, particularly after Spain ceded the Mississippi River to France. Secretary of War Henry Dearborn dispatched

Tenkswatawa: spiritual leader of the Shawnee who attempted to revitalize traditional Native American culture

agents to negotiate new treaties with the Indians, openly bribing and tricking Indian leaders, encouraging them to run up debts to merchants that could be paid only by selling land. By 1809, the government had acquired millions of acres both south and north of the Ohio River—most of Ohio and significant portions of today's Indiana and Illinois—as well as rights to build and maintain roads across remaining Indian land. Typically, the budget-minded government paid no more than two cents per acre for land it resold to settlers for two dollars. Often not waiting for the transactions to be completed, settlers, both white and black, spread like "oil on a blanket" through Indian country while Indian people disappeared "like snow before the sun," many moving west beyond the Mississippi River.

Those who remained watched the land change. Settlers deforested large areas, cutting trees for their houses, fences, and fuel, and clearing land for cultivation. As they destroyed wildlife habitat, they drove off game animals. County governments paid bounties for wolf and other predator hides. Hunters killed the last bison in Kentucky in the 1790s and decimated beaver populations. "Stop your people from killing our game," one Indian pleaded. "They [the settlers] would be angry if we were to kill a cow or hog of theirs."

Numbers of Indians who remained absorbed various European ways into their culture. They turned to raising livestock. More and more, men and women dressed in woven cloth, some of which they made and some purchased from white merchants, instead of buckskin. Shawnee men stuck feathers, an Indian style, into turbans made of European-style cotton brocade. Indian farmers took up iron tools, plowed the land in furrows like white farmers did, and cooked their meals in metal pots. Christian denominations such as the Moravians, Quakers, Congregationalists, and Baptists sent missionaries to convert Shawnees in Ohio, Cherokees in Tennessee, and Creeks, Choctaws, and Chickasaws in Alabama and Mississippi. In addition to teaching Christian faith and literacy, the missionaries urged the converts to forsake traditional Indian cultures. Indian women frequently married whites and occasionally African Americans. Seminole societies in Florida adopted many runaway slaves, while Cherokees actually adopted the institution of slavery from white southerners, using slaves in a variety of agricultural and commercial jobs. Indians bought liquor from white traders, fueling violence that tore apart families and communities. One missionary observed that among Indians "drinking never passes without the shedding of blood."

Some Indians refused either to relocate or to become assimilated into white society as Jefferson envisioned. Beginning in 1805, a Shawnee spiritual leader named Tenkswatawa—meaning Open Door—urged his people to purify themselves of corrupt and divisive white influences. Fat, alcoholic, and disfigured from a childhood accident, Tenkswatawa (known by whites as the Prophet) had previously lived as an outcast until he experienced a transforming vision. From Christian and native religious teachings, he composed a message of salvation to Indian men, women, and children. He urged them to spurn whiskey, live upright lives, destroy cattle and other things obtained from whites, and return to traditional ways of hunting and farming. If they did, the spirits would look favorably upon them. Tenkswatawa's prophesy ignited a wildfire of religious fervor.

The Prophet's cultural revitalization provided the ideology for a new political confederation. His older brother Tecumseh—the Shooting Star—designed it. William Henry Harrison, Indiana's territorial governor, described Tecumseh as "one of those uncommon geniuses that spring up occasionally to produce revolutions and overturn the established order of things." He inspired the people to defend themselves against the white intruders. "The Great Spirit gave this great island to his red children. He placed the whites on the other side of the water. They were not content with their own, but came to take ours from us. They have driven us from the sea to the lakes—we can go no further."

THINKING BACK

1. How did Republican economic policy differ from policies generated during the 1790s by the Federalists, and what, if anything from those Hamiltonian measures did the Republicans continue?

2. What motivated Jefferson's determination to rid the national government of Federalists, and in the outcome of those efforts, what long term precedents were set for future changes in party control of the executive branch of the national government?

VYING FOR THE WEST

President Jefferson displayed exceptional political skill during his first term, enacting every legislative initiative he brought forward, but his most notable triumph, the Louisiana Purchase, came through good luck. By election time in 1804, the United States had doubled its size, controlled the Mississippi River, and gained possession of most Indian lands between the Appalachian Mountains and the Mississippi. Confident Republican congressmen and senators convened a caucus (or meeting) to select the party's presidential and vice presidential candidates: Jefferson for president and George Clinton of New York for vice president to replace Aaron Burr who had disgraced himself by his duel with Hamilton. Federalists chose South Carolinian Charles Cotesworth Pinckney and Rufus King of New York. In the final tally, Jefferson and Clinton won by a landslide (162 electoral votes to 14 for their opponents), and Republicans increased their majorities in Congress.

Most Americans, including Jefferson, believed the United States was destined to dominate North America—what Jefferson called an "empire of liberty." But Great Britain, France, Spain, and various western Indian tribes still hoped to preserve their territory or recover some of what they had already lost. Furthermore, as Republicans basked in glory, disheartened Federalists brooded in their New England stronghold and contemplated secession.

The Louisiana Purchase

The Mississippi River carried the vital commerce of the trans-Appalachian West. During the first half of 1801, nearly 500 boats drifted downriver to Natchez and New Orleans, hauling substantial quantities of whiskey, tobacco, apples, animal skins, iron, and lead from Kentucky, Tennessee, and Ohio. Under the terms of Pinckney's Treaty of 1795, black dockworkers unloaded these boats and deposited the cargoes on wharves in New Orleans from where they were hoisted on seagoing vessels for transport to markets along the east coast and West Indies. The boatmen and other travelers then followed the Natchez Trace, a narrow footpath through Indian country, back to shipping points like Cincinnati on the Ohio River. Crude inns along the way provided food and shelter to wayfarers. Western commerce seemed secure and destined to grow as more settler-farmers moved in, all pleasing to President Jefferson.

> Why and how did the United States acquire Louisiana?

But in May 1801 came the stunning news that Spain had returned Louisiana, including New Orleans and the vast stretch of plains west to the Rocky Mountains, to France in the secret Treaty of San Ildefonso (1800). In return, Spain received assurances of French protection of Spanish Texas and Florida against the rising tide of land-hungry Americans. Although Spain had never profited greatly from Louisiana, it fit neatly into Napoleon Bonaparte's dream of a reconstructed French empire in North America. Napoleon had emerged from the debris of the French Revolution as France's ruler (initially calling himself "first consul" and then "emperor") and the most dynamic French ruler since Louis XIV (see the Global Perspective, p. 135). He took advantage of a truce in France's prolonged war with Great Britain to advance his imperial plan. The sugar islands of the Caribbean, especially St. Domingue, occupied center stage in Napoleon's scenario, with slaves once again producing sugar and coffee to enrich planters and France's imperial coffers. Louisiana, especially its bustling port of New Orleans, would serve as the island's breadbasket, and possibly as a launching pad for military operations against Canada. To make all this happen, Napoleon had to reclaim St. Domingue from the black revolutionaries who had turned it into the independent republic of Haiti. In December of 1801, Napoleon dispatched a 30,000-man French army to Haiti to reestablish imperial control while another force laid plans for striking Louisiana and then Canada. In Haiti, the French tricked Haitian leader Toussaint L'Ouverture by proposing a truce then arresting him and packing him off to France in chains where he soon died.

Many Americans, including Jefferson and especially those living in the West, found these developments disturbing, for while Spain, a much-reduced military force, seemed like little more than a caretaker of Louisiana, France was quite a different matter. Nothing guaranteed that Napoleon would keep New Orleans open to American river traffic. Indeed, even before the French officially took possession of the city, Napoleon ordered Spain to close it to American shipping. An alarmed Jefferson pointed to "one single spot" on the globe and exclaimed that its possessor "is our natural and habitual enemy." That spot was New Orleans, and the man who once sang France's praises now declared that "the day that France takes possession of New Orleans ... we must marry ourselves to the British fleet and nation." After calming down, Jefferson directed Robert R. Livingston, the American minister to France, and James Monroe, a special minister, to explore the possibility of buying New Orleans and West Florida. The latter was a strip along the Gulf Coast that offered access to the Gulf of Mexico and that Americans assumed Spain had also relinquished along with Louisiana.

Napoleon then stunned the American representatives by offering to sell not only New Orleans but also the entire Louisiana Territory. The Haitian enterprise had collapsed under the ravages of yellow fever and bullets from Haitian forces now led by Jean-Jacque Dessalines and Henri Christophe who received the French surrender in 1803. Without St. Domingue, Napoleon had little use for Louisiana. "Damn sugar, damn coffee, damn colonies," Napoleon fumed. Moreover, he had already shifted his focus to the resumption of war with Great Britain, and in that event, Louisiana would be a liability, especially if

Britain and the United States became allies. These considerations dictated a quick fire sale. Livingston and Monroe leaped at the offer, even without instructions from Jefferson. On April 30, 1803, they and French Foreign Minister Talleyrand signed a treaty transferring the territory.

On the 4th of July the Republican *National Intelligencer* heralded the **Louisiana Purchase**. "We have secured our rights by pacific means. Truth and reason have been more powerful than the sword." For $15 million the United States acquired 830,000 square miles of real estate—just over three cents per acre, truly one of the greatest real estate deals of all time. The treaty did not specify Louisiana's boundaries (see map on p. 234). Jefferson claimed the Perdido River on the east, which would give the United States West Florida, and the Rio Grande River on the west, which included Texas. Spain objected on both counts. When the Americans asked Talleyrand for a precise definition, he quipped: "I can give you no direction; you have made a noble bargain for yourselves, and I suppose you will make the most of it." For the time being, both West Florida and Texas remained officially in Spanish hands, although Spain's hold on those territories was weak. Most significantly, the purchase of Louisiana would provide a staging point to launch an American thrust into Spanish Texas. Indeed, American frontier families began immediately to mass on the Texas border.

The Louisiana Purchase raised not only geographical questions but a few constitutional issues too. Ironically, Federalists known for their loose interpretations of the Constitution pointed out that the Constitution did not specifically authorize the acquisition of new territory. Furthermore, the treaty granted United States citizenship to Louisiana's citizens. The Constitution recognized citizenship only by birth or naturalization. Jefferson suggested amendments, but his advisors pointed out that a delay in ratification might cause Napoleon to change his mind. The administration concluded that the purchase contained too many benefits to fret about minor details. Jefferson rationalized his concerns: "A strict observance of the written laws is doubtless *one* of the high duties of a good citizen, but it is not *the highest*. The laws of necessity, of self-preservation, of saving our country when in danger, are of higher obligation." Thus, the one-time strict constructionist looked broadly upon the Constitution's delegation of power when he believed it was in the national interest to do so. The Senate easily ratified the treaty, with only some New Englanders objecting, and late in 1803, General James Wilkinson took formal possession of Louisiana on behalf of the United States.

Jefferson touched off a controversy when he installed a provisional government with very limited popular participation. He appointed William Claiborne governor, who in turn selected a thirteen-member Assembly of Notables. Louisiana's ordinary residents seemed to Claiborne to be "illy fitted to be useful citizens of the republic," like Jean Lafitte and his band of pirates nesting at Barataria. Many Americans were eager to eradicate Louisiana's *creole* culture—Spanish, French, and African-American—and replace it with customs, language, and laws more typical of the United States. Resistance from French citizens who were culturally dominant, however, forced the administration to agree to the election of a territorial legislature, affirm Louisiana's French civil law, and refer to Louisiana's counties as parishes, as they are known today. In 1812 the lower part of the Louisiana Purchase became the state of Louisiana, the first to join the Union from west of the Mississippi River. The remainder of the Louisiana Purchase continued as a territory for the time being.

By doubling its size, the United States grew instantly into the world's second largest nation in land area. Jefferson and the Republican party collected the political dividends. David Campbell of Tennessee thanked the president for securing "to us the free navigation of the Mississippi. You have procured an immense and fertile country." The Louisiana Purchase contributed greatly to Jefferson's 1804 re-election and enhanced Republican majorities in Congress. The purchase also ensured the Federalist party's minority status. Federalists enjoyed little popularity outside New England.

Mapping the Far West

> What was Lewis and Clark's mission, and what did it accomplish?

In late 1802, even before the Louisiana Purchase had been completed, Jefferson prepared an expedition to explore the upper Missouri River. Officially, the mission's purpose was scientific discovery. Jefferson wanted to know if the Missouri was part of the storied Northwest Passage to China. His books told him that only a short distance separated it from the headwaters of the Columbia River, which flowed into the Pacific Ocean. Twenty years earlier the American sea captain Robert Gray had located the Columbia's estuary on the Pacific coast. Jefferson hoped that a Missouri-Columbia link "may offer the most direct & practicable water communication across this continent for the purposes of commerce" with Asia. He was also interested in building defenses against potential enemy invasions from the Pacific Coast, prompted by British exploration of western Canada.

That prospect excited many east-coast merchants. It would boost the small but potentially lucrative Asian fur trade. Expanding Asian commerce also motivated the North West Company, a Canadian fur trading firm. In 1793 it sent Alexander Mackenzie on a reconnaissance to find a navigable river route to the Pacific. He reached the coast just north of present-day Vancouver, and, like countless other travelers, inscribed his name on a rock: "Alexander Mackenzie, from Canada, by land." Thus the intrepid Canadian reinforced Great Britain's claim to sovereignty in the Great Northwest. But Mackenzie's route over the Canadian Rockies was impossible for animal-drawn wagons to follow. So Mackenzie's feat had no practical commercial value. The British continued their explorations farther south, and Jefferson aimed to cut them off.

Jefferson had political objectives as well. He intended for the expedition to reconnoiter Spanish strength since military confrontation between Spain and an expanding United States was not out of the question. Spanish officials knew about the expedition. Nervous about their silver mining operations, those officials sent troops to patrol the frontier. One official warned authorities in Mexico City that Americans "are already calculating the profit they will obtain from the mines" in northern Mexico.

It was not until after the Louisiana Purchase had been completed that what was called the **Corps of Discovery** took shape. To lead it, Jefferson chose his personal secretary, thirty-year-old Captain Meriwether Lewis. Lewis' army buddy, William Clark, shared the command. In May 1804 their forty-eight-man company left St. Louis and entered the Missouri River in several canoes and a keelboat (a shallow draft vessel usually rowed or poled on rivers and used for transporting freight) loaded with supplies for themselves and gifts for Indians (see map on p. 250). After reaching its headwaters and traversing the continental divide, the party found the Columbia River, following it to the Pacific. The "men appear much Satisfied with their trip," Clark recorded in his journal, "beholding with

Illustration by Elbie Bentley. Copyright © 2017 Kendall Hunt Publishing Company.

President Jefferson was eager to explore and map the Louisiana Purchase, and he authorized the Lewis and Clark Expedition and the Zebulon M. Pike Expedition to accomplish those objectives.

astonishment the high waves dashing against the rocks & the emence Ocian." Clark carved his own inscription on the trunk of a pine tree: "William Clark December 3rd 1805. By Land from the U.States." This strengthened the United States' claim to the Pacific Northwest and made the United States and Great Britain the primary contenders for it. The **Lewis and Clark Expedition** returned safely to St. Louis the next year.

Two unpaid members of the party aided the enterprise in important ways. Clark's slave York helped establish good relations with the Indians, who "wer[e] much astonished" by his appearance, at first thinking his skin was painted black. Indian alliances would be crucial in clashes with Spaniards. The Shoshone woman Sacajawea, the

wife of the French expedition-member Toussaint Charbonneau, served as an intermediary with her people and on more than one occasion kept the Americans out of harm's way by assuring apprehensive Indians of the white men's peaceful intentions.

Lewis and Clark's party followed in the footsteps of many notable explorers of the Far West. Several of the men filled journals with detailed descriptions of Indians, bison, and the breathtaking landscape. They gathered specimens of plants and animals and offered greetings to curious natives from their new "white father." The expedition fulfilled all of its objectives except one—locating the Northwest Passage. The Missouri River was not part of a commercially valuable river network spanning North America.

Commercial interest in the Far West and trade links with China remained keen however, as did competition with the British. Six months after Lewis and Clark, Manuel Lisa and Andrew Henry, successful St. Louis merchants, established fur-trading posts on the upper Missouri. They bought furs from Indians and shipped them back East. John Colter, a Lewis and Clark veteran, became the first white man to behold the boiling waters and spectacular geysers of Yellowstone. In 1811, businessman John Jacob Astor financed two expeditions, one by sea around Cape Horn to establish a trading post on the Pacific Coast and the other overland to establish an overland supply and communication link. Astor's men erected a fort they named Astoria at the mouth of the Columbia River. When the British explorer David Thompson trekked down the Columbia later that year he found the Astorians already trading with local Indians. The Astorians founded a number of auxiliary trading posts in the interior of the Pacific Northwest and negotiated a cooperative arrangement with Russian sea otter hunters based at New Archangel (Sitka, Alaska). Astor, however, sold his whole Northwest operation to the British in 1813 rather than face a possible British military force during the War of 1812.

Although the Lewis and Clark Expedition has been much celebrated in recent years, its importance at the time was overshadowed by explorations further South. Spain remained very concerned about the expanding United States, and with good reason. In July 1806, Jefferson authorized Lieutenant Zebulon M. Pike and a company of men from St. Louis to explore the southwestern frontier of the Louisiana territory and to spy on Spanish military strength in that area (see map on p. 250). Following the Arkansas River, Pike spotted the Colorado peak that now bears his name. During the bitter high-country winter, a Spanish patrol intercepted the Americans and took them as prisoners to Chihuahua. Pike denied spying and authorities in Santa Fe eventually released them. Pike's official report became a bestseller and gave Americans vivid though not always accurate images of the Spanish southwest.

Conspiracy and Intrigue

What were the consequences of Burr's intrigues in the West?

The sprawling, ungoverned Louisiana Territory invited mischief, as did the territories of Alabama and Mississippi and Spanish Florida. And the ambitious Aaron Burr could not resist temptation. Burr's story of intrigue began in New York.

When the Republican leadership dumped Burr as the vice presidential candidate in 1804, he joined a Federalist plot. In Massachusetts, Timothy Pickering and a small group of extreme Federalist dissidents known as the **Essex Junto** hatched a scheme for Federalist-dominated New England to secede from the Union. Believing their prospects for success would be enhanced if New York joined the budding **Northern Confederacy**, they backed Burr in New York's gubernatorial contest in the hope that, if elected, he would lead New York out of the Union. When Burr lost the governor's race he blamed Hamilton and challenged him to the fatal duel. Nothing ever came of the Northern Confederacy, but Burr turned his attention westward.

Burr's movements are fairly easy to track, but not his intentions. By 1806, rumors had begun to surface that he planned to detach some portion of the West—perhaps West Florida, Mexico, or part of Louisiana—from its owner and set himself up as a ruler. Evidence is sketchy; however, Burr assembled an army on an island in the Ohio River. Before he could commit any treasonous act against the United States, General James Wilkinson, the highest ranking general of the army and a Spanish secret agent, informed the Jefferson administration that Burr was engaged in a dangerous conspiracy. Wilkinson himself may have been a co-conspirator. In any event, Jefferson authorized Federal officials to arrest Burr, who was apprehended in Mississippi, and charge him with treason.

Chief Justice John Marshall presided over the trial. Imagine the conflicted feelings of the major figures. Marshall hated Burr, who had "blown the brains" out of the Federalist party. He also intensely disliked Jefferson, who pushed the prosecution out of contempt for Burr. Passions aside, however, the Constitution predetermined the outcome. "No person shall be convicted of Treason," it says, "unless on the testimony of two Witnesses to the same overt Act, or on Confession in open Court." The government had only Wilkinson's letter. Burr confessed to nothing. Marshall had no choice but to instruct the jury to return a verdict of not guilty.

In Europe and elsewhere, rulers had historically used treason to eliminate political opposition. In the Burr trial, Marshall followed the Founders' intention of protecting rather than punishing political opposition by requiring corroborating evidence of a specific act, not just hearsay. Burr was finished as a public figure though, despite his acquittal. He lived abroad for several years before returning permanently to New York.

Aaron Burr was not the only intriguer of his day. President Jefferson plotted against Spain to back his extravagant claims to West Florida and Texas. Soon after the Louisiana Purchase he ordered troops to the border of West Florida to bully Spain and perhaps provoke a rebellion against Spanish rule. He backed down only when his cabinet advised that it looked bad. He did the same thing along the Texas-Louisiana border. When the Spanish commander mobilized Spanish forces to defend Texas, the American military officer in charge, Wilkinson again, negotiated a truce and averted hostilities. The question was whose interest was Wilkinson serving? He sent a bill for his services to the viceroy in Mexico City. Texas had once again become the vital buffer protecting New Spain from foreign aggression, but against all preventive measures, individual Americans penetrated the border and infiltrated the eastern portion of the territory.

THINKING BACK

1. How did American Indians respond to the influx of settlers into their lands?
2. What dreams did Thomas Jefferson have for the West, and how were they fulfilled?

DEFENDING AMERICA'S HONOR AND INDEPENDENCE

Domestic politics and westward expansion challenged Republican leadership, but the real test for the still-fledgling United States involved protecting its interests from foreign threats. After a warm-up against the **Barbary pirates** in the Mediterranean, the United States became entangled once again in the epic contest between Great Britain and France. In waging all-out war, the European powerhouses ran roughshod over American economic interests, disregarded the rights of private American citizens, and offended national honor. The result has been called a second war for American independence. Simultaneous to the European war and in important ways tied to it, the conflict between Native Americans of the trans-Appalachian West and the United States

reached a climax as Tecumseh's armed confederation of Shawnees, Delawares, Creeks, and other tribes allied with Great Britain. The outcome of the War of 1812 was a shattering defeat for the Indians and an escape from potential disaster as well as a boost to Republican principles.

"To the Shores of Tripoli"

For centuries, pirates based in the North African states of Tripoli, Morocco, Algiers, and Tunis had plundered merchant vessels in the Mediterranean Sea. They

> **Why did the Barbary states extract tribute from foreign governments, and how did the United States respond?**

stole valuable cargoes and enslaved captured crews and passengers. The Muslim rulers of those states demanded protection money from foreign countries whose vessels were subject to pirate attack. Because of their reputation for brutality, these North African domains were known in Europe and America as the Barbary, or "barbarian," states. European and American governments grumbled but usually paid the extortion money because the commerce was worth it. American trade in the Mediterranean equaled $10 million, 15 percent of all the country's foreign commerce. George Washington and Congress had pushed naval expansion in part to defend American trade, but the Adams administration had agreed to pay for protection; indeed, Adams sent the pasha (ruler) of Tunis a gift of jeweled firearms as a gesture of friendship.

In 1801, the United States fell behind in its payments to Tripoli, located in modern-day Libya. Pasha Yusef Karamanli angrily chopped down the American consulate's flagpole—a dramatic declaration of war. Jefferson suspended his plan to downsize the navy and dispatched a squadron of warships to blockade Tripoli. His action gave Americans cause for toasts, public rallies, and blustery patriotic speeches. It also produced a new national hero, Captain Stephen Decatur. In February of 1804, Decatur led a daring raid into Tripoli Bay to scuttle the frigate *Philadelphia*, which had run aground and fallen into enemy hands. The pasha threw the ship's crew into a dungeon. To force the release of the American prisoners, Decatur also helped Commodore Edward Preble's flotilla blast the city. A dramatic march across the desert by a United States Marine platoon took the port town of Derna and inspired the famous phrase in the "Marine's Hymn"—"to the shores of Tripoli."

A treaty in 1805 brought the war to a close and ransomed some 300 American hostages. Even though the treaty called for the United States to make payments to Tripoli, the **Barbary War** was a limited victory, since the pasha had demanded $3 million in redemption but accepted a paltry $60,000. One politician boasted: "the Barbary States have been taught their first lessons of humiliation." After the War of 1812 the United States stopped all tribute payments.

The United States and the Napoleonic Wars

How did the resumption of war in Europe affect the United States?

A bigger challenge for the United States arose when Napoleon abruptly ended the truce with Great Britain barely two weeks after the Louisiana Purchase. Once again the two giants dragged most of Europe into war. The armies of Napoleon and his allies swept across the continent. A triumph at Austerlitz on December 2, 1805, gave Napoleon military dominance on land. At sea, however, the British navy had gained a distinct edge two months earlier when Admiral Horatio Nelson crushed the French fleet at **Trafalgar**.

Initially, the war had a positive effect on the United States, buoying the American economy. As neutrals, American merchants traded with both sides, and accordingly the value of American foreign trade doubled. But with neither Britain nor France able to gain the upper hand militarily against its enemy, both waged economic warfare. To deny their opponents needed supplies, though, both France and Britain had to control American commerce. In 1806 and 1807, Napoleon issued a set of decrees that established his **Continental System**. By these measures, Napoleon endeavored to exclude Britain from all European trade. Napoleon directed the French navy to intercept neutral ships, American ones in particular, heading to or leaving from British ports. London responded with **Orders-in-Council** (1807) that blockaded French-controlled Europe. The British navy was ordered to seize all neutral vessels—again especially American ships—carrying goods to French ports. These policies caught American shippers in a vice, as both France and Britain attempted to clamp down on America's valuable trans-Atlantic trade. Between the start of the war and 1808, the British captured over 500 American merchant ships and the French 300 more.

Maintaining Britain's naval superiority hinged on keeping ship crews at full strength. As casualties and desertions mounted, naval authorities turned to pressing into service British subjects, including those who had emigrated and acquired foreign citizenship. They also sought to recover deserters from the navy, a significant number of whom served on American merchant ships. Armed press gangs felt free to board American ships and take away crewmen. Indeed, they impressed as many as 10,000 sailors between 1805 and 1815 and did not bother to distinguish between native-born Americans and British subjects. This contemptuous disregard for citizenship rights not only inflicted great personal pain on individuals who were illegally impressed but also wounded American national pride.

On June 22, 1807, the British frigate *Leopard*, cruising off the Virginia coast, intercepted the American warship *Chesapeake*, a newly constructed frigate suspected of having four British deserters among its crew, as it emerged from the port of Norfolk. When the American captain refused to heed the *Leopard's* warning to stop, the British ship opened fire, killing three American crewmen and wounding eighteen. A British boarding party then removed the four British deserters. This direct attack on the United States, which was at peace with Britain, outraged many Americans who called for war. President Jefferson, hoping to avoid hostilities, appealed to Britain for an apology. London did in fact reprimand the *Leopard's* commander and offered to compensate the American victims and their families, but the British government declined to renounce its wartime policies. As a result of the *Chesapeake* Affair, anti-British feeling grew.

Although no pacifist, Jefferson urged measures of "peaceful coercion" rather than military action to resolve the United States' conflicts with Britain and France. In December of 1807, Congress responded to Jefferson's recommendation by passing the **Embargo Act**, prohibiting all foreign trade. Jefferson reasoned that holding American ships in port would keep them safe from attack while both Britain and France were denied the American products their economies depended upons. Under this pressure, Jefferson believed, the belligerents would eventually return to "some sense of moral duty" and respect America's neutral rights. But the Embargo did not pan out has Jefferson had hoped, for while the British and French tightened their belts and went on with their war, American ship owners watched their empty vessels rock idly at dockside and their revenues evaporate. In only one year, the value of American exports fell from $108 million to $22 million and imports dropped 40 percent. People in many walks of life felt the embargo's bite—tobacco, cotton, and wheat farmers who could no longer market their crops; craftsmen and laborers in port towns with no work; and merchants who had nothing to buy or sell. The embargo was not a total disaster though, as smuggling continued at a brisk pace and the shortage of manufactured imports gave a boost to incipient American manufacturers. But the embargo was hugely unpopular. Critics ridiculed the "damnbargo." Meanwhile, customs officials in maritime New England looked away when ships illegally left or entered port, and Jefferson's hate mail multiplied, leading him to call for enhanced power to force compliance with the law, which Congress provided, including the use of federal troops.

The Embargo controversy cost Jefferson precious political capital. Many New England and Middle Atlantic Republicans raised their voices in protest. The Embargo also breathed a little life into the almost-moribund Federalist party. In the 1808 elections, James Madison succeeded Jefferson as the Republican party's presidential candidate. Although Madison defeated the Federalist Charles Cotesworth Pinckney 122 electoral votes to 47, the Federalists gained twenty-four seats in the Congress (mainly in New England) and threatened a comeback on a national scale. Feeling the sting of this backlash, Congress in early 1809 repealed the Embargo.

Nevertheless, the government continued to employ the tactic of "peaceful coercion," albeit in a weaker form. In 1809, Congress passed the **Non-Intercourse Act**, which reopened trade with everyone except Britain and France and provided for the resumption of trade with whichever belligerent repealed its obnoxious rules first. But this measure did not succeed either. In fact, the Non-Intercourse Act worked to Britain's advantage since its navy seized more shipping going to France than vice versa. Congress allowed Non-Intercourse to expire in 1810 and passed yet another measure, **Macon's Bill No. 2**, that resumed trade with Britain and France and stipulated that if Britain repealed its Orders-in-Council the United States would suspend trade with Napoleon. The same incentive applied to France. Napoleon announced that he would no longer intercept American ships, leading Madison to suspend trade with Britain. But Britain still refused to repeal its Orders-in-Council.

The War Hawks

Across much of the country, the clamor for war against Britain rose sharply. In the 1810 congressional elections, voters sent to Washington over two-dozen young, first-term Republicans who urged tough action against America's enemies. These breast-beaters came to be known as **War Hawks**. One of them, Henry Clay of Kentucky, quickly showed such extraordinary talent as a legislative leader that Republicans in the House of Representatives elected him speaker. Another War Hawk, John C. Calhoun of South Carolina, declared that it was impossible to end the difficulties with Great Britain "by a sort of political management," referring to the Jefferson-Madison tactic of economic pressure. Only the aggressive protection of America's rights, in the spirit of 1776, could lead the United States to greatness, Calhoun argued. Clay appointed Calhoun to the influential House Foreign Affairs Committee.

Many of the War Hawks hailed from the West, where bloody clashes with Native Americans were common. Whites, whose numbers in the trans-Appalachian West had reached 1 million by 1810, blamed the Indian raids on the British in Canada. Such allegations had some basis, for Tecumseh, who continued to build his **pan-Indian** confederation, received weapons, ammunition, and other supplies from Canada. Canadian officials regarded American westward expansion as threatening and sought Indian alliances. But, the Indians had their own grievances against the United States—unfair purchases of their lands—and did not have to be stirred up by the British. Without specific orders from Madison, Indiana Territory's governor William Henry Harrison moved against the Indian confederacy's headquarters at Prophetstown, near Tippecanoe Creek in northwestern Indiana. On November 7, 1811, while Tecumseh was recruiting allies among the Creek Indians in the Mississippi Territory, Harrison led 1,000 militiamen to Prophetstown, provoking an Indian attack. After fierce and bloody fighting, the Indians withdrew and Harrison ordered his troops to burn Prophetstown. The **Battle of Tippecanoe**, praised by most western whites, raised concerns in Washington for it pushed Tecumseh even further into the arms of the British. As bloodshed along the frontier continued and evidence of British collusion with the Indians multiplied, the War Hawks demanded war against Great Britain.

The rage for war in the South and the Middle Atlantic states, areas crippled by economic depression, focused on Great Britain rather than France even though Napoleon failed to fulfill his promise to suspend the Continental System. There was always the chance he would; furthermore, British officials refused any concessions on American maritime

Who were the War Hawks and why did they want war with Great Britain?

Battle of Tippecanoe, November 7, 1811. American troops commanded by Indiana Territory's Governor William Henry Harrison defeated Shawnee and other fighters of Tecumseh's Indian confederacy while suffering heavy losses themselves. Harrison became a hero among Republicans, many of whom shouted complaints that the British were behind the Indian attacks. And while devastating to Indian morale, the battle pushed Tecumseh toward an alliance with Great Britain.

rights, and the Royal Navy continued to intercept American vessels and impress seamen. Ironically, the most vigorous resistance to the building war momentum came from the people most directly affected by damaging European policies—New England shippers and merchants. Commercial ties with Great Britain made them indulgent of British policies. The hottest passion for war came from a sense of bruised national pride, and New Englanders, feeling alienated from the rest of the nation, exhibited little of it. Most Americans, however, craved respect, and many were prepared to fight for it.

By the summer of 1812, President Madison had convinced himself that war was unavoidable. Although clearly he preferred a peaceful solution to the conflict, Madison could not reverse the oncoming tide of war. In June, he recommended war against Britain, and on the 18th Congress declared it. The vote—seventy-nine to forty-nine in the House and fifteen to thirteen in the Senate—revealed a substantial opposition. Most of it came from the Federalist Northeast. Not one Federalist representative or senator voted for the war declaration. A Congregational minister from Massachusetts urged New England to follow the path of "honourable neutrality," and many Boston merchants carried on an illicit trade with the British throughout the war.

In one of the twists of fate, Britain withdrew its Orders-in-Council two days before Congress declared war. This was the result of pressure from British merchants who were finally feeling the pinch of the American boycott. But the action was too little and too late to avoid war.

The War That Should Not Have Been

Neither Great Britain nor the United States was prepared for the **War of 1812**. Engaged by French armies in Europe, the British military could

> **What were the high points and low points of the War of 1812?**

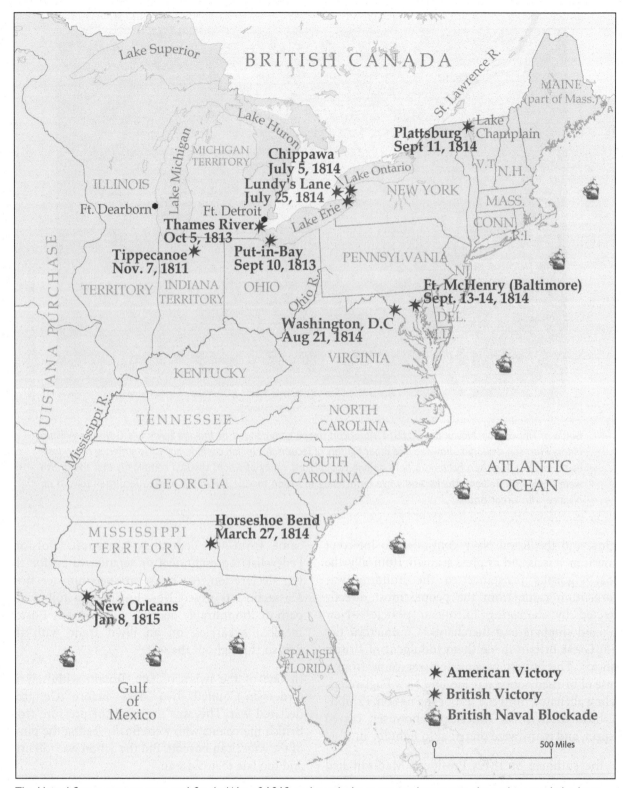

The United States was not prepared for the War of 1812 and was lucky to survive; however, in the end it provided a huge boost to national pride and solidarity.

ill-afford to divert significant resources to North America. The United States had only a skeleton army after Jefferson's retrenchment, and frequently state militias refused to serve beyond their own boundaries. Party leaders rewarded loyalty with military appointments; consequently, as General Winfield Scott observed, "imbeciles and ignoramuses" commanded the army. Henry Dearborn's men called him "granny" because he was old and fat. Able-bodied men declined to enlist when army pay—five dollars a month—was less than skilled wages. By the end of the war, however, enlistments had increased, largely because of bounties of up to 320 acres of land plus cash (more than most civilian workers earned in two years). Nonetheless, the tiny American navy never matched the massive royal fleet, although British naval strength on the Great Lakes was not as overwhelming.

Reluctant New Englanders contended that a war to defend American maritime rights should be fought at sea, but the early action took place along the Canadian border. The Madison administration decided to exploit a sixteen-to-one population advantage over Canada, and almost twice as many regular soldiers. General William Hull, governor of the Michigan territory and a Revolutionary War veteran, with 2,000 troops under banners proclaiming "CONQUOR OR DIE," took Detroit in July of 1812. But the victory was short-lived. A British and Indian force commanded by General Isaac Brock frightened Hull into surrendering. A military court martial condemned Hull to death for cowardice, a sentence later commuted because of his previous record. Ft. Dearborn, at present-day Chicago, also fell into British hands. To the east, an American assault on Fort Niagara in October failed when American militia refused to enter Canada. A halfhearted attack against Montreal in November likewise ended in disaster.

The war began more favorably for American ships at sea. The frigate *Constitution*, commanded by Captain Isaac Hull, became a legend in naval lore during a triumphant battle with the British *Guerriere*. As enemy cannon balls bounced harmlessly off the *Constitution*'s wooden hull, a crewman shouted: "her sides are made of iron." "Old Ironsides" became celebrated in American naval history and is docked in Boston today. In all, the navy defeated six British warships and captured fifty merchant vessels. American privateers swarmed the Atlantic, preying on British shipping. A Halifax newspaper reported in the summer of 1812 that it was "very imprudent for any vessel to sail from this port unless under convoy." These victories boosted American morale and stunned British authorities. As one British official lamented, "It is a cruel mortification to be beat by these second-hand Englishmen upon our own element."

Control of the Great Lakes was key to victory for both sides. It would open invasion routes into Canada and allow the British to supply their forces in the Northwest. An American army succeeded in capturing and burning York (Toronto) on April 27, 1813. The cost was heavy, however, including the life of General Zebulon M. Pike, and the battle was not decisive. But on September 10, 1813, an American naval squadron commanded by Oliver Hazard Perry squared off against a British flotilla at **Put-in-Bay**, on the southern shore of Lake Erie. "We have met the enemy," the victorious Perry exclaimed afterward, "and they are ours." This triumph gave the United States a firm grip on the western lakes.

The British counted on Indian allies for additional military strength. Tecumseh considered the war a great opportunity to bolster his crippled Indian confederacy. He urged Cherokees, Choctaws, Chickasaws, and Creeks to join the alliance with the British. "Let the white race perish," Tecumseh declared. Some Creeks, known as Red Sticks, responded, but the others concluded that peace with the United States offered their best hope for the future. Tecumseh joined the British northeast of Detroit attempting to repel an invading American army. At the **Battle of the Thames River**, October 5, 1813, the Americans prevailed, killing Tecumseh in the process. Meanwhile, the Red Stick Creeks ravaged white settlements in the Mississippi Territory. On March 27, 1814, Andrew Jackson of Tennessee, commanding a militia army, attacked and defeated them in a ferocious slaughter of 800 men, women, and children at **Horseshoe Bend**. The War of 1812 not only removed the Indian leader most capable of forging a unified opposition to white expansion but also for all practical purposes ended Indian resistance to settlement of the trans-Appalachian West.

The war changed unexpectedly with Napoleon's defeat at Leipzig late in 1813 and his subsequent abdication. Peace in Europe released British troops for the American war. The British plan called for campaigns against New England, the Chesapeake, and New Orleans. In August 1814, Sir George Prevost, governor-general of Canada, led 10,000 troops into upstate New York. Prevost was forced to scuttle the campaign, however, when an American fleet under Lieutenant Thomas Macdonough defeated British ships near Plattsburgh on Lake Champlain on September 11. More than blunting the British offensive, the **Battle of Plattsburgh** pushed British officials into a negotiation mode. To his delight, Macdonough received a gold medal from Congress and 1,000 acres of land from a grateful New York legislature. "In one month from a poor lieutenant I became a rich man," he quipped.

Dolley Madison, often called "Lady Presidentress," exerted far more influence on the position of "First Lady" and on the presidency itself than any of her predecessors and successors until well into the twentieth century. Vivacious, witty, and charming, Dolley loved to party but also consulted seriously with her husband on matters of governance and politics. In this painting, portrait artist Gilbert Stuart shows Dolley in one of the French style dresses she favored. French military attaché Colonel André de Bronne described her as "one of America's most valuable assets."

Before the end, though, came America's greatest humiliation of the war. A British force attacked Washington, D.C. in August. President Madison had been slow in providing defenses, and he and the rest of the government evacuated in great haste. Indeed, when British troops entered the president's house they found the dinner table set for forty. The British torched most of Washington—public buildings as well as private ones. Thanks to First Lady Dolley Madison, who supervised the removal of government files, most official records survived. The Library of Congress, however, was not so fortunate.

The invaders then sailed up the Chesapeake to Baltimore, a more important objective because of its commercial and privateering activities. Unable to breach the city's defenses, the British unleashed a bombardment of nearby Fort McHenry. British ships launched 1,500 rounds of mortars and rockets at the fort on September 13 and 14. The attack did little damage, but during the dramatic explosions Francis

Scott Key, an American on board one of the British ships to negotiate the release of an American held prisoner, wrote the lyrics to *The Star Spangled Banner*. Set to the tune of an old English drinking song, it eventually became the national anthem.

By the end of 1814 American fighting forces equaled the British. A crop of courageous young generals asserted themselves. Growing American military strength demonstrated itself along the Gulf coast. A British force under General Edward Pakenham landed below New Orleans in late December. Andrew Jackson took charge of defending the city and the vital lower Mississippi valley with a motley assortment of regulars, frontiersmen, a regiment of free African-American militia, and some pirates. The climactic battle occurred on the morning of January 8. The British redcoats marched across an open field against the heavily fortified American position. American cannon and musket fire raked the oncoming soldiers, their scarlet tunics and white cross-belts making easy targets. British losses were staggering—over 2,000, including Pakenham, compared to only seventy Americans. In the meantime, news of a peace treaty reached the United States.

Making Peace

By the end of 1814 both sides were ready to end the war. The British were exhausted by two decades of war and burdened by debt. War-weariness showed in the United States

> **What were the terms of the Treaty of Ghent, and what did they signify?**

as well. The army remained below authorized levels. Even with bounties and higher pay, Thomas Jefferson observed, "it is nonsense to talk of regulars. [W]e might as well rely on calling down an army of angels from heaven." Mounting desertions further signaled waning enthusiasm. The country's economy was a wreck. The South and New England, both dependent on overseas commerce, suffered enormous hardships.

"The sword was scarcely out of the scabbard," Madison said afterward, "before the enemy was apprised of the reasonable terms on which it could be resheathed." Through diplomatic exchanges, the United States offered to stop employing British deserters on American ships if the British would abandon impressment. The British refused, and countered with demands for territory in Maine, access to the Mississippi River, and a guaranteed Indian territory around the Great Lakes. British and American representatives sat down together in Ghent, Belgium, in August 1814. The American team, Albert Gallatin, John Quincy Adams, Henry Clay, and

Jonathan Russell, dropped demands for an end to impressment. With the war in Europe ended, the issue seemed moot. Recent British defeats led London officials to the conclusion that they could not expect additional concessions from the United States.

The basic terms of the Treaty of Ghent, signed on December 14, restored the *status quo ante bellum* (the situation as it was before the war). The accord contained no statements about maritime rights and restored to both sides any occupied territory, including Indian lands. Special commissions would address boundary disputes later. Both nations promised to help end the Atlantic slave trade. Henry Carroll, Clay's personal secretary, landed in New York on February 11, 1815, with a copy of the treaty. Madison promptly submitted it to the Senate, which ratified it on February 16. Relief found expression on both sides of the Atlantic. The Madison administration, ignoring the many failures, hailed the war as "an event highly honorable to the nation."

Federalists were especially relieved the war was over, but they had already taken steps to protect New England's sectional interests against what one declaration called the Republican administration's "Absolute tyranny over these States." Launching sharp criticism of the Virginia Republican planter aristocracy (first Jefferson and now Madison), Federalists sought to eliminate the Constitution's "three-fifths rule," which enhanced the South's representation in Congress by counting three-fifths of the slaves in determining a state's population. In December, as negotiations continued in Ghent, delegates from five New England states gathered in Hartford, Connecticut, to express several grievances. The **Hartford Convention** drafted several amendments to the federal Constitution. They proposed requiring a two-thirds vote of Congress to declare war, the elimination of the three-fifths rule in counting slaves, a sixty-day limit on embargoes, and restricting presidents to a single term in office. As a team of messengers made their way to Washington to present the amendments to Congress, however, word of the Treaty of Ghent arrived. The successful conclusion of the war undercut the Hartford Convention. Its proposals had no chance of adoption in the atmosphere of celebration that engulfed the nation. In fact, many Americans perceived the Federalists as unpatriotic, a factor in their rapid disappearance after the War of 1812.

THINKING BACK

1. What successes and what failures did Congress and the Jefferson administration experience in defending United States interests?
2. What did the people of the United States gain and lose in the War of 1812?

Image © Heather Lewis, 2010. Used by permission of Shutterstock, Inc.

Spanish Frontier Hacienda Belonging to the Martinez Family Near Taos, New Mexico. Spanish settlers in New Mexico protected themselves from raiding Comanche Indians by enclosing their homes with thick adobe walls with few doors and no windows.

THE LOCAL PERSPECTIVE: FOCUS ON NEW MEXICO

What were conditions like for the residents of Spanish New Mexico at the dawn of the nineteenth century?

By the beginning of the nineteenth century, life for the residents of New Mexico was safer and more comfortable than ever. Many of the terrible Indian conflicts that earlier had kept the territory in turmoil and discouraged settlers had been resolved. In 1817, the population reached 36,000, one-fourth of whom were Indians who had become civilized by European definitions and enjoyed citizenship. Those were mostly the Pueblo people of the Rio Grande Valley whose numbers had increased significantly after decades of decline. Trade, including annual fairs in Taos, provided Indians and settlers alike with commodities and the basis for a peaceful relationship.

Clashes between nomadic Comanche and Apache Indians and *nuevomexicanos* had intensified after the Indians acquired horses and firearms. Horses came from the Spaniards; French traders supplied the guns. Ironically, mounted and armed Comanche warriors terrified peaceful residents the way Spanish *conquistadores* once had terrified Indians. Now outlying Hispanic farms and ranches, flanking protected settlements in the Rio Grande Valley, bore the brunt of attacks. Farmers along the upper Rio Santa Cruz River, northeast of Santa Fe, built new homes around a defensible central plaza in the village of Chimayó. Likewise did the residents of other remote towns like Taos, Ojo Caliente, and Abiquiu.

Spanish authorities in Mexico City, already saddled with expensive defenses against Britain and the United States, could ill-afford ongoing frontier Indian wars. Officials instituted several reforms aimed at reversing the deterioration. New taxes on silver tripled revenues from New Spain. A cordon of presidios from California to Texas bolstered frontier defenses. But only one presidio in Santa Fe was responsible for protecting the entire province. New military regulations boosted the morale of New Mexico's soldiers, called "leather jackets" because of their heavy, protective cowhide coats. And in 1776 the crown created a commander general to administer the defense of all the borderlands, officially called the **Internal Provinces**. These administrative changes were only partially successful, however. The new system reduced some costs, but constant modification of the structure generated a bureaucratic nightmare.

Spaniards confronted Indian hostility with military action and astute diplomacy. They enlisted Pueblos in raids against Comanches. Juan Bautista de Anza, governor of New Mexico from 1778 to 1788, defeated powerful Comanche bands in 1779. Afterward he negotiated a general peace with virtually the entire tribe. He also forged an accord between Comanches and their traditional Navajo enemies. Anza succeeded by promising the Comanches weapons, gifts, and admission to the annual Taos trade fair if they stopped fighting. Both Indians and Spaniards concluded that peace was preferable to war.

Apache pacification was less successful. Ferocious Spanish attacks and enslavement of Apache women and children stiffened the Indians' intransigence. The underlying source of friction was competition for the same marginal desert lands. Pushed from the southern Great Plains by Comanches and into regions with inadequate game and tillable land, Apaches resorted to stealing. Attempts to induce them to settle as farmers near *presidios* worked only to a limited degree.

Relative tranquility by the early 1800s, coupled with demands for food and hides from silver-mining regions in Mexico, stimulated New Mexico's commercial economy. Santa Fe became a bustling trade center. Wagon trails linked it with Tucson and San Antonio. The major commercial artery was *El Camino Real*, "The Royal Highway," from Santa Fe to Chihuahua. New Mexico grew from an outpost into an integral part of the economy of New Spain. Its economy did not rival that of the United States, but adventurous American merchants took advantage of porous boundaries to trade illegally along what would later become the Santa Fe Trail.

THINKING BACK

1. How had conditions improved for *nuevomexicanos*?
2. What was the nature of *nuevomexicano* and Indian relationships?

CONCLUSION

The transition from Federalist to Republican-controlled government during the first fifteen years of the nineteenth century represented an important step toward a more democratic society. Under the leadership of Jefferson and Madison, the Republican party embraced inclusiveness to a far greater degree than had the Federalists. They opened up the political system—voting, office-holding, and popular election of presidential electors—to the vast majority of adult white males. This was one of the most significant accomplishments of the Republican ascendancy. But the movement toward what Jefferson called the "empire of freedom" was neither complete nor painless. Factions within the Republican party, like urban radical democrats in the Middle Atlantic states and aristocratic "Quids" in the South, represented different shades of democracy. Those most conspicuously omitted from Jefferson's vision were African Americans, who had no place at all. Jefferson accepted Native Americans only if they became like white yeoman farmers. If they did, they lost their cultural identity; if they did not, they lost their land. After reducing the scope of government and protecting economic prosperity, Americans strode confidently toward the popular dream of a continental nation.

During the War of 1812, the United States successfully defended itself against a formidable foe in Great Britain, even if the triumph was not pretty. There was no conquest of Canada as many War Hawks had hoped, and there was the humiliating sack of Washington. Yet in 1814, the American navy more than held its own against the British, and early in 1815 Jackson's army crushed the veteran British force at New Orleans. The Treaty of Ghent offered legitimate grounds for celebration even if it said nothing about the issues that had brought on the war, for it was no more of a victory for Great Britain. Quids and Federalists had condemned the mobilization of national power, but the War of 1812 brought to the forefront of the Republican party— once the party bitterly opposed to Hamilton's centralization of economic and political power—a national identity. Republican nationalism, though, rejected deference to "ye well-fed, well-dressed. Chariot-lolling, . . . [and] levee-reveling [F]ederalists." Rather, it was a more democratic nationalism, and its leaders emerged from the ranks of working people whom Federalists had once ridiculed as "poor ragged democrats."

On the heights of Weehawken, Aaron Burr killed Alexander Hamilton. But Burr did not single-handedly destroy Federalism. The Revolution of 1800 marked the beginning of the end for the Federalist party; the Hartford Convention finished the job.

SUGGESTED SOURCES FOR STUDENTS

James M. Banner, *To the Hartford Convention: The Federalists and the Origins of Party Politics in the Early Republic, 1789-1815* (1967).

Ride along with the great exploration of the Louisiana Purchase in Bernard DeVoto, ed., *The Journals of Lewis and Clark* (1953). This abridged edition captures the many facets of the journey but is intended for the general reader.

Hundreds of scholars have studied Thomas Jefferson from every imaginable perspective. Joseph J. Ellis, *American Sphinx: The Character of Thomas Jefferson* (1998), illuminates the recesses of Jefferson's mind and psyche. It is not a full-blown biography but rather an attempt to demystify a great though very private individual.

To understand the dilemma of the Federalist party, see David Hackett Fischer, *The Revolution of American Conservatism: The Federalist Party in the Age of Jeffersonian Democracy* (1965).

An excellent account of the scientific aspects Lewis and Clark expedition is offered by William H. Goetezmann in *Exploration and Empire: The Explorer and the Scientist in the Winning of the American West* (1966).

The most thorough examination of the Jefferson-Hemings relationship, and more importantly of the complex nature of slavery in Virginia during Jefferson's time, is Annette Gordon-Reed, *The Hemingses of Monticello: An American Family* (2008). While generations of mostly male historians denied that any meaningful relationship between Thomas Jefferson and Sally Hemings ever existed, recent DNA tests have shown the presence of Jefferson chromosomes in Hemings' youngest son, Eston. Gordon-Reed musters sufficient circumstantial evidence to establish that the Jefferson chromosome belonged to Thomas Jefferson and not a Jefferson relative. Furthermore, the book leaves little doubt that he fathered all of Sally Hemings' children.

Pekka Hämäläinen, *The Comanche Empire* (2008), explains the rise of Comanche dominance on the southern Plains and the internal coherence as well as external power of Comanche hegemony.

For a quick, enjoyable, and reliable look at the Barbary War, see Part II of Robert Leckie's *From Sea to Shining Sea: From the War of 1812 to the Mexican War, the Saga of America's Expansion* (1993).

For an interesting new perspective on the origins of American democracy, see J. S. Maloy, *The Colonial American Origins of Modern Democratic Thought* (2009).

Peter S. Onuf, ed., *Jeffersonian Legacies* (1993), presents several insightful essays on Jefferson's continuing impact on American society.

For an important account showing James Madison 's role in staging the American approach to Spanish Texas see J. C. A. Stagg, *Borderlines in Borderlands: James Madison and the Spanish-American Frontier, 1776-1821* (2009).

The standard history of United States diplomacy during the period remains Bradford Perkins, *Prologue to War: England and the United States, 1805-1812* (1961).

On Anglo-American competition on the Pacific Northwest coast see James P. Ronda, *Astoria and Empire* (1990).

Native Americans predominated in the trans-Mississippi West during the first decades of the nineteenth century. Several histories of their experiences broaden our understanding of American history at that time. Donald E. Worcester, *The Apaches: Eagles of the Southwest* (1979), is one of the best.

Sean Wilentz, *The Rise of American Democracy: Jefferson to Lincoln* (2005), is a sweeping and eloquent exploration of the inception and early growth of democratic institutions.

BEFORE WE GO ON

1. What did Thomas Jefferson's statement "We are all Republicans, we are all Federalists" reveal about American nationhood and identity?

2. How and to what extent did Thomas Jefferson shift the debate over the virtues of democracy in the United States?

Building a Democratic Nation

3. How did the United States change between the "Revolution of 1800" and the "Second War for Independence" as some have called the War of 1812?

4. Thomas Jefferson envisioned the American West as an "empire for liberty." What could he have meant insofar as Native Americans and African Americans were concerned?

Connections

5. What differences and similarities do you see in the impeachments of Associate Justice Samuel Chase and President Bill Clinton?

6. In what ways is the United States today the result of Jefferson's vision of a continental nation?

The Global Perspective

The Era of Industrialization and Democratic Nationalism, 1815–1840

> **What four economic, political, social, and cultural developments transformed much of the world?**

The period between 1815 and 1840 was a time of tremendous change in the world. In Europe and North America, the preceding generation had experienced both political and economic revolution. The American Revolution in the 1770s, followed by the French Revolution twenty years later, had introduced the world to republican government. In the 1780s, England embarked on a journey of dramatic economic and social transformation. In 1815, peace came to Europe and the United States, but the extent of four major developments that followed was unprecedented.

The first of these developments came during the last years of the eighteenth century, England emerged as the world's leading industrial nation. By the 1830s, the term "**Industrial Revolution**" conveyed the extent of change that industry had brought to English life. Inventors discovered the key to dramatic improvements in productivity: an energy source greater than human or animal muscle. Steam power energized factory machines, boats, and railroad locomotives. Industry produced large cities as entrepreneurs built factories where an available workforce and shipping facilities existed. By the 1830s, London's population surpassed one million and English cities of 20,000 or more accounted for one-third of the country's population.

Similar transformations occurred in continental Europe, especially Belgium and Germany. Those countries imported English technology, and their governments protected infant industries. Massive industrialization triggered social reorganization throughout Europe, expanding the middle classes with factory-owners and industrial capitalists and producing classes of workers who toiled long hours under strict discipline at monotonous tasks that produced meager wages while generating enormous wealth for their employers. Friedrich Engels, a future **communist** revolutionary, charged industrial capitalists with "mass murder" and "wholesale robbery" of industrial workers (the **proletariat**).

The disruptions caused by European industrialization after 1815 touched off a second important development: the greatest migration of people in recorded history. During the first half of the nineteenth century, displaced peasants and obsolete craftsmen by the millions set out for Australia, Argentina, Asian Russia, and North America. A Chinese population that more than tripled to 400 million between 1750 and 1840, combined with the suppression of the African slave trade, drew many Chinese peasants into backbreaking labor on plantations and in mines in southern Asia and Latin America.

The year 1815 marked a milestone in the evolution of European political theory—a third important development. After Napoleon's defeat, a reactionary mindset took hold. Conservatives believed that revolutions in the United States and France had caused boundless suffering and destruction and that only aristocracy could maintain social order. The conservative **Quadruple (Holy) Alliance** of Austria, Prussia, Russia, and France (under the restored Bourbon monarchy) stood ready to thwart the forces of republican revolution.

On the other side of Europe's ideological fault line stood liberals committed to republican

Image © moenez, 2010. Used by permission of Shutterstock, Inc.

Ludwig von Beethoven. A contemporary said of Beethoven's music that it awakened personal longings that constituted the "essence of Romanticism."

change. For entrepreneurial, middle class republicans, progress meant free enterprise and **laissez-faire** (no government interference with market influences). But more radical democrats claimed that freedom could not exist without equality. They also championed **nationalism**. Every nationality, they believed, had the right to govern itself. But uniformity within nations augured ill for cultural and racial minorities. Nationalism led to independence movements in many Spanish colonies and Greece's liberation from Turkish rule. It also produced unified nations out of small principalities in Italy and Germany. In the 1830s, idealists like the French socialist Charles Fourier advocated the abolition of all forms of slavery (including marriage), and in 1848, Karl Marx and Friedrich Engels published *The Communist Manifesto* in which they predicted that the working classes would free themselves from the bondage of industrial capitalism.

These social, economic, and political changes in Europe were accompanied by a fourth significant development: a cultural revolution. Writers, painters, and musical composers cast aside structure and formality and indulged in uncontrolled emotion and free expression. These lovers of passion were called Romantics. Of the Romantic composer Ludwig von Beethoven, a contemporary writer exclaimed: "[His] music sets in motion the lever of fear, of awe, of horror, of suffering, and awakens just that infinite longing which is the essence of **Romanticism**." Another Romantic essence was a reverence for nature. Early nineteenth-century artists were awed by its uncontrolled power and inspired by its divine grandeur.

Industrial breakthroughs in Europe profoundly affected the world. Industrialists sought to obtain cheap raw materials from non-industrial countries in exchange for an appealing assortment of tools, weapons, and textiles. A gap opened between the standards of living in industrializing countries like Britain, Hungary, the United States, Canada, and Argentina and those in non-industrial countries in Africa, Latin America, and Asia. Historically self-sufficient China resisted the intrusion of "barbarian" merchants from Europe, confining foreign commerce to the southern port city of Gwangzhou (Canton). But in the 1820s, the English introduced opium to China. The resulting addiction and cash drain alarmed Chinese authorities who tried to stamp it out. The result was an "**opium war**" that ended in 1842 which ended with Great Britain forcing China to cede the island of Hong Kong.

After 1815, economic and military power in the Middle East began a rather sharp decline. Societies failed to match the industrial progress of Europe and consequently struggled to maintain their territorial integrity. In 1816, the Ottoman Empire succumbed to Serbian nationalistic aspiration, granting Serbs autonomy. In 1830, France launched its conquest of Algeria in North Africa. But while Islam lost ground in the Middle East, it gained substantially in regions of Africa. Muslim clerics led campaigns (*jihads*) against traditional African religions that helped to reunify African societies after centuries of the devastating slave trade. In West Africa, local merchants began to export palm oil (used for soap and candles). By mid-century, a mercantile middle class had emerged in many African coastal towns that began to replace traditional elites that had been accomplices in the slave trade.

The United States moved in the same direction as Europe. Expanding world and domestic markets after the War of 1812 inspired agriculturists to step up production. No longer satisfied with meeting their own needs, American farm families moved onto virgin land, purchased machines to help them cultivate and harvest larger crops, and sold their grain, hides, and cotton for cash. This "**Market Revolution**" in economic production led to changes in the structure of family units and to new definitions of men's and women's roles in society. By 1840, the United States was surging forward in industrial output.

The War of 1812 helped unify the United States, and after 1815 a stronger sense of nationality existed. In this "**Era of Good Feelings**," there was a strong effort to expand national boundaries, improve transportation, and build an integrated national economy. Nationalism was still in its infancy, however, and as the excitement of the American "victory" over the British in the War of 1812 abated, class, sectional, racial, and ideological differences resurfaced. This generated tension and allowed the resumption of bitter partisan conflict.

Even though Americans disagreed on the merits of aristocratic and democratic republicanism, the country moved steadily toward a more rather than less inclusive society. In the 1820s and 1830s, democratic changes made class lines less distinct, although they benefited women, African-Americans, and Native Americans very little. Reforms expanded the franchise to include virtually every adult white male in the country. Numerous social reforms attempted to make society more compassionate. From religious utopians to Romantic perfectionists, Americans more than ever assumed unlimited potential in the human condition and zealously sought its fulfillment. Unfortunately, idealism collided with the economic interests of northern industrialists and southern cotton planters who selfishly extracted labor from immigrants, women, and African Americans.

The decades between the War of 1812 and mid-century witnessed significant advances in economic development, national consciousness, and political growth. Virtually every change was controversial and manifest in heated political debate. The United States was approaching a crossroads on its way to becoming a unified nation.

THINKING BACK

1. How did the "Industrial Revolution" and "Market Revolution" alter peoples' lives in Europe, North America, Asia, and the Middle East?
2. How would you describe the tension between conservative and liberal political theory in Europe? Where was that tension manifest? Where would you place Romanticism and the "Era of Good Feelings" on the conservative—liberal axis?

Chapter 9

DEVELOPING A NATIONAL AGENDA, 1815–1830

A PERSONAL PERSPECTIVE: JEDEDIAH SMITH, MOUNTAIN MAN

Image © Ferenc Cegledi, 2010. Used by permission of Shutterstock, Inc.
Autumn was beaver hunting season for Rocky Mountain trappers.

> **How did Jedediah Smith exemplify the nationalistic spirit in the United States following the War of 1812?**

In July 1825, amid brilliant sunshine near the Green River in Wyoming, 120 mountain men kicked back after two arduous years combing the central Rocky Mountains and the Great Basin for beaver. These two-fisted guys had come to the Far West seeking freedom and adventure, but primarily fortune, in the fur trade. They found least of what they wanted most. In their pursuit they had nearly frozen to death, traded shots with Indians, and battled grizzly bears. Beaver fur thinned out during the summer and pelts were not worth much, so the trappers took time to relax, drink whiskey, and purchase supplies that merchant William H. Ashley had just brought up from St. Louis, the bustling gateway to the Far West.

Twenty-three-year-old Jedediah Smith, a New York native who had come to the mountains three years earlier, was among those present. "I started into the mountains," Smith later wrote, "with the determination of becoming a first-rate hunter, of making myself thoroughly acquainted with the character and habits of the Indians, of tracing out the sources of the Columbia river, and following it to its mouth; and of

making the whole profitable to me." He bore fresh scars from an encounter with a grizzly bear that had ripped open his scalp and nearly torn off his ear. With amazing calm, Smith had told his companion James Clyman to "stitch [it] up some way or another," which Clyman managed to do, but ever after Smith wore his hair long to hide the scars.

William Ashley was a wealthy St. Louis merchant, militia general, and Missouri's first lieutenant governor. He was also the headman (or "booshway" in the lexicon of the mountain men, derived from the French word "*bourgeois*" meaning entrepreneur) in a fur-trading company doing business with the Indians of the upper Missouri River country. Three years earlier Ashley had posted an advertisement in the *Missouri Gazette & Public Advertiser* offering to pay 100 "enterprising young men" to venture by boat up the Missouri and trade glass beads, guns, and liquor to the Indians for beaver pelts. Smith had spotted the ad and responded to it. But on the trip, Arikara Indians attacked the party, killing several of Ashley's men and destroying thousands of dollars worth of furs and trade goods. To minimize further financial losses and to provide the mountain men with incentive to acquire more beaver pelts, he turned them into **free trappers** who harvested beaver on their own. Ashley promised to *rendezvous* with them in the mountains once a year to buy their pelts and sell supplies. The Green River gathering that summer was the first of many such *rendezvous*.

The high-country *rendezvous* exemplified the rapid expansion, commercialization, and nationalization of the economy of the United States after the War of 1812. From St. Louis, Ashley shipped merchandise from New Orleans and Cincinnati to the trappers' *rendezvous*, transporting the goods initially by keelboat and then by steamboat up the Missouri River and then via horseback and wagon to the *rendezvous* sites. The mountain men purchased coffee, sugar, tobacco, cloth, buttons, woolen blankets, fishhooks, traps, ammunition, and whiskey using beaver pelts as money.

Smith, already highly regarded by the other mountain men for his courage, good sense, and organizational

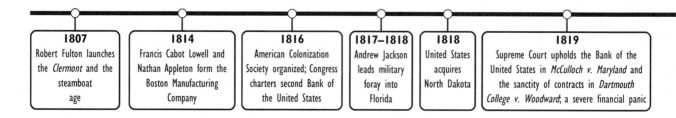

1807	**1814**	**1816**	**1817–1818**	**1818**	**1819**
Robert Fulton launches the *Clermont* and the steamboat age	Francis Cabot Lowell and Nathan Appleton form the Boston Manufacturing Company	American Colonization Society organized; Congress charters second Bank of the United States	Andrew Jackson leads military foray into Florida	United States acquires North Dakota	Supreme Court upholds the Bank of the United States in *McCulloch v. Maryland* and the sanctity of contracts in *Dartmouth College v. Woodward*; a severe financial panic

skills, became a "booshway" himself, leading parties of twenty or more free trappers. Indeed, he made significant contributions to the commerce and ultimate incorporation of the Far West into the United States. First, he rediscovered a low-grade pass through the Rockies, South Pass, known before but not fully appreciated until now as a wagon route over the crest of the Rockies and ultimately to the Pacific Coast. Second, by entering the valley of the Green River, a tributary of the Colorado River, he pushed the Far West fur-trade into the vast regions beyond the Continental Divide.

Free-spirited, enterprising, and patriotic, as most mountain men were, Jedediah Smith contributed importantly to United States expansion across the continent. His maps enhanced Americans' understanding of western geography, even though some of his discoveries only duplicated those of earlier Spanish and French explorers. And, of course, Native Americans understood the geography of the Far West best of all. But Smith and the other mountain men also grasped the West's geopolitics. As they roamed, the mountain men took into account tribal boundaries: Mandan, Arikara, Sioux, Crow, and Blackfeet. Distinguishing friends from foes could make the difference between a successful hunt and being killed unawares while wading in frigid streams.

Treaties between the United States and various western Indian tribes as well as federal licenses allowed whites to trade but not to trap beaver. The mountain men understood the rules, but they often ignored them, provoking not only the ire of many Indians but also rebuke from United States authorities. The distinction did not apply to the Blackfeet and other tribes beyond the Missouri with whom no treaties had ever been signed. Smith eagerly exploited the absence of legal restraints, bagging as many beavers as he could get away with. The editor of an influential Washington, D.C., newspaper, *Niles' Weekly Register*, complained about the practice, contending that the Indians' lands "must be regarded as their own." Whites had no more right to trap there than "Indians would have to enter our settlements

and carry off whatever they pleased." In 1824, Congress enacted a law sponsored by Missouri Senator Thomas Hart Benton authorizing new treaties with all the western tribes, but none of the agreements dealt effectively with trapping on Indian lands, and United States military presence was too thin in those faraway places to keep the peace.

Smith and the other mountain men were also aware of international borders in the Far West, alternatively respecting and disrespecting them as their business interests and nationalistic exuberance dictated. Since 1818, the United States and Great Britain had jointly occupied the Oregon Territory. For years, though, the British Hudson's Bay Company and the Canadian Northwestern Company had battled for domination of the fur trade in the Columbia River drainage while Americans had struggled to establish themselves on the upper Missouri. But Smith and his trappers confronted the British in Oregon, asserting an exclusive United States claim there. At best, Smith paid only nominal respect to Mexico's national sovereignty in New Mexico and California. Following the 1826 *rendezvous* near the Great Salt Lake, Smith led a party in search of the fabled **Rio Buenaventura**, supposedly a navigable river flowing across the Great Basin to the Pacific coast. He failed, because the Buenaventura River never existed, but in blazing the first overland trail to California Smith gave the new government of Mexico, recently independent of Spain, cause for concern about the security of its northern frontier against an expansionist United States.

At the annual mountain *rendezvous,* two out of three fur trappers were French or *metís* (French-Indian). Others besides men from Virginia, New York, and other locales back east included Canadians, New Mexicans, and even Hawaiians. An African-American named James Beckwourth, whose father was a white planter and mother was an enslaved black woman, earned respect not only from other mountain men but also the Crow Indians who adopted him. Indians also came to trade, compete in games, and smoke

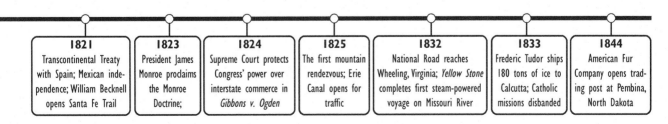

1821	1823	1824	1825	1832	1833	1844
Transcontinental Treaty with Spain; Mexican independence; William Becknell opens Santa Fe Trail	President James Monroe proclaims the Monroe Doctrine;	Supreme Court protects Congress' power over interstate commerce in *Gibbons v. Ogden*	The first mountain rendezvous; Erie Canal opens for traffic	National Road reaches Wheeling, Virginia; *Yellow Stone* completes first steam-powered voyage on Missouri River	Frederic Tudor ships 180 tons of ice to Calcutta; Catholic missions disbanded	American Fur Company opens trading post at Pembina, North Dakota

tobacco. Two-thirds of the mountain men were married, most of them to Indian women. Such unions produced children that tightened kinship relations and added to what the trapper Osborne Russell called the "mixed multitude" of the Rocky Mountains.

The *rendezvous* era lasted only fifteen years, from 1825 to 1840, and Jedediah Smith was gone from the mountains long before the market for beaver pelts dried up, dying at the hands of Comanche Indians on the Santa Fe Trail. He was thirty-two years old. Smith and the other 1,000 or so mountain men who plied the Far West's beaver streams heralded the arrival of a mighty entrepreneurial machine that substantiated ambitions in the United States for a continental nation, what Jefferson had characterized as an "empire for liberty." But for Indians, the march of Americans (a term that citizens of the United States appropriated for themselves) into their country had ultimately devastating effects, just as earlier expansion had transformed other Native American societies. The fur trade also severely damaged fragile mountain ecosystems. Penetration of the Southwest altered the way of life and the national identities of Hispanic North Americans. In the past, historians idealized this episode in Western history as a triumph of modern civilization and rugged individualism, a step in the process of building a democratic nation. More recently, however, they have seen it as a scene from a transforming Market Revolution and an example of domineering American nationalism.

THINKING BACK

1. Why did Jedediah Smith venture into the Far West?
2. How did Smith exemplify the exuberant nationalism in the United States following the War of 1812?

THE SPIRIT OF NATIONALISM

The War of 1812, Albert Gallatin observed, had "renewed and reinstated" a national identity. "The people . . . are more American; they feel and act more like a nation; and I hope that the permanency of the Union is thereby better secured." In the spirit of nationalism, or **patriotism**, Americans celebrated the young nation's achievements and ideals, and in a burst of expansionist zeal, the United States acquired Florida, moved closer to exclusive ownership of the Pacific Northwest, and claimed dominance in the Western Hemisphere. However, bitter ideological, sectional, and partisan disagreements broke the nationalistic spirit, and the nationalism that Gallatin observed still excluded significant numbers of Americans. African Americans, for instance, found themselves wedged between two identities.

Honoring America

Americans across most of the country reacted to the end of the War of 1812 with a collective sigh of relief, but soon thankfulness grew into boastfulness, especially in the South and West. Americans attributed their victory over Britain, a sheen they rubbed onto what had been a largely stalemated war, to the superiority of American culture, especially ordinary people's ingenuity, common sense, and republican ideals. Georgia Congressman George Troup praised the "the yeomanry of the country," marching to the nation's defense like the Minutemen of 1776, "leaving their wives and children and firesides at a moment's warning" to fight professional British Redcoats. Citizens characterized the late conflict as a "second war for independence," and like the Revolutionary War of 1776, this one produced a military hero who personified American ideals. Andrew Jackson rocketed to super-stardom by way of his masterful victory in the Battle of New Orleans. Old Hickory, as Jackson's troops called him, also came to embody the era's increasingly democratic form of republicanism.

The typical American soldier, an image drawn from the troops who had defended New Orleans, was a farmer and family man. He replaced an older national icon: the solitary wilderness Indian fighter. And Jackson was the ideal military officer—strict, self-disciplined, and tough—just like the mountain-man "booshway" Jedediah Smith but on a grander scale. Poems and popular songs retold the saga of Jackson and his men at the Battle of New Orleans. In May of 1822, a stage entertainer named Noah Ludlow sang "The Hunters of Kentucky" in front of a New Orleans audience. The tune described the British attack and the devastating American counterstroke.

> But Jackson he was wide awake, and
>
>   wasn't scared with trifles,
>
> For well he knew what aim we take
>
>   with our Kentucky rifles;

> How did the War of 1812 boost American nationalism?

So he marched us down to "Cypress Swamp";

The ground was low and mucky;

There stood "John Bull," in martial pomp,

But here was old Kentucky.

Ludlow's listeners broke into uproarious hurrahs as his song rose to its triumphant climax. The audience made him sing it three times before the performance ended.

Such expressions of national pride strengthened a heretofore weak sense of nationhood. In 1818, Congress mandated a uniform American flag: thirteen stripes, representing the original rebellious colonies, and a star for each state—fifteen of them that year. Independence Day celebrations featured fireworks, picnics, and an abundance of patriotic oratory. On the faraway New Mexico frontier, merchant Josiah Gregg brimmed with the same "harmony of feeling, and almost pious exultation, which every true-hearted American experiences on this great day." July 4, 1826, was particularly memorable, for eighty-three-year-old national icon Thomas Jefferson died at his beloved Monticello. Later that day, at his home near Boston, ninety-year-old John Adams also slipped into eternity. Across the country, Americans interpreted the passing of these two national icons, on the fiftieth anniversary of the Declaration of Independence, as a manifestation of God's watchfulness over the nation's destiny.

The Era of Good Feelings

The War of 1812 doused the fiery partisanship that had raged for a generation by precipitating the collapse of the two-party political system. Federalists' opposition to the war had branded them as disloyal which, at least outside of New England, reduced them to insignificance. Meanwhile, Republicans rode the crest of postwar exuberance. Subsequent events also broke the Republicans' way. In the late summer of 1815, Commodore Stephen Decatur led a successful naval campaign that finally ended Barbary pirate raids against American shipping in the Mediterranean. The Republican party became virtually unbeatable, as the 1816 elections proved. President Madison retired, underscoring the unofficial two-term presidential limit, and his Republican successor, James Monroe of Virginia, most recently secretary of state, defeated the Federalists' Rufus King of New York by 183 electoral votes to 34. In Congress, the Republicans captured 79 percent of the seats in the House of Representatives. The election results were so overwhelming in the Republicans' favor that the Boston Federalist *Columbian Sentinel* newspaper proclaimed the onset of an **"era of good feelings,"** meaning the onset of an era of one-party politics.

> **What did the phrase "era of good feelings" signify?**

The sixty-one-year-old Monroe marked the end of the Revolutionary generation of national leaders. His "retro" ceremonial wardrobe—knee-britches and powdered wig—defined him in some eyes as a relic. He was also the last of the "Virginia Dynasty," that string of Virginians, including Washington, Jefferson, Madison, and now Monroe, who had controlled the presidency since 1789, interrupted only by John Adams. Although clearly less illustrious than his predecessors, Monroe was a good-natured and well-intentioned man. His prior service to United States had been commendable, and he evoked confidence, if not awe, from the public.

More than a mere punctuation mark at the end of one generation of national leaders however, Monroe and most of his Republican colleagues had advanced beyond the elitist, agrarian, and limited government philosophies of the party's founders. A rising democratic tide, especially in the South and West, rejected

Courtesy of Library of Congress

James Monroe: last of the *"Virginia dynasty"*

the deferential politics of Jefferson's day and demanded more direct popular participation and equality. Even in staid New England, where ultra-conservative Federalists shuddered at even the mildest democratic reforms, Republicans and moderate Federalists combined to inch toward universal white manhood suffrage. A new constitution for Connecticut disestablished the powerful Congregationalist Church and put Episcopalians, Methodists, Presbyterians, and Baptists on comparable footing. Young Daniel Webster of Massachusetts, who like most Federalists believed that the republic's future depended on ensuring property rights against the landless masses, argued for a wider distribution of property as the best way to head off class conflict. Wartime struggles with finances and mobilization validated old arguments for big-government, leading Republicans to adopt nationalist economic policies once associated with Alexander Hamilton and other early Federalists.

Hoping to lead his party and the country away from old-style factionalism and partisanship toward a new brand of consensus politics, Monroe appointed to his cabinet mostly Republicans who held broadly national views. The key post of secretary of state went to John Quincy Adams of Massachusetts, who was dedicated above all to continental expansion. John C. Calhoun of South Carolina, the nationalist War Hawk, became secretary of war. In the interest of conciliation, Monroe selected William H. Crawford of Georgia, a traditional, limited-government Republican, to be secretary of the treasury. Speaker of the House Henry Clay of Kentucky, another powerful nationalist, helped bring Congress and the president into agreement on government policy.

Almost everyone welcomed the end of hateful party squabbling, and when in 1820 Monroe sought re-election, nobody opposed him. The Electoral College would have elected him unanimously had not a single elector from New Hampshire believed that only George Washington deserved such distinction. An "era of good feelings" seemed certainly at hand.

Seizing Florida

| Why and how did the United States acquire Florida and move closer to control of the Pacific Northwest? |

Nationalism caused Americans to extend their mental map of the United States to natural geographic boundaries, which at the time meant at least from Atlantic Coast to Pacific Coast. Special interests focused the country's acquisitiveness on particular territories. Expansionist logic dictated the acquisition of Spanish Florida, which Jefferson had unsuccessfully sought to include in the Louisiana Purchase. South Carolina and Georgia planters wanted it because the mostly ungoverned territory gave sanctuary to runaway slaves and marauding Seminole Indians, many of whom had been displaced by advancing white settlement into the trans-Appalachian West. Since Spanish authorities in Florida could not or chose not to check the raids, pressure built in the United States for annexation. In 1811, Congress had secretly authorized seizing Florida; now, circumstances provided a credible rationale.

In December of 1817, the War Department authorized General Andrew Jackson to pursue raiding Seminoles into Florida. Adhering to the principle that possession was nine-tenths of the law, Jackson told President Monroe to signal his desire for Florida and "in sixty days it will be accomplished." Jackson later said he received an affirmative response, so early the next year, in what was known as the **First Seminole War**, he led a small army of occupation into Florida, capturing Spanish garrisons at St. Marks and Pensacola and hanging a couple of renegade Indians and two British gun traffickers.

Jackson's audacity shocked some Washington officials but delighted others. Monroe expressed embarrassment and returned the garrisons to Spanish authorities. Calhoun advised a public rebuke of Jackson. Secretary of State Adams, however, defended Jackson, for despite angry complaints from Spain and Great Britain the incident actually strengthened Adams' hand in negotiations with Spanish minister Don Luis de Onís y Gonzales to purchase Florida. The Spanish government, harried by colonial revolutions, could clearly see the futility of trying to hold it.

The Adams-Onís talks actually centered on the Louisiana frontier, left undefined by the Louisiana Purchase. Onís would not relinquish Florida until he had located the Louisiana boundary a safe distance from Mexico, which he regarded as essential for protection against aggressive Americans. Adams suggested the Colorado River, which Onís rejected. The two finally struck a deal, settling on a line along the Sabine, Red, and Arkansas rivers and then northward to the 42nd parallel. (See map on p. 277.) In agreeing to that boundary, the United States relinquished any right to Texas, but by the same token Spain withdrew claims to the central Rockies and the Pacific Northwest. Then Onís assented to the transfer of Florida to the United States. In return, the United States dropped $5 million

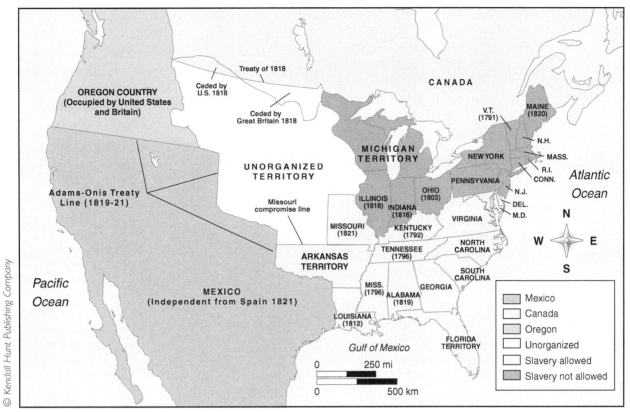

Political Boundaries of North America 1818-1821

in liability claims originating from Spain's earlier closing of the Mississippi River.

The **Transcontinental Treaty**, as the Adams-Onís agreement was known, was ratified by the Senate in 1821 and achieved two important territorial objectives. Florida rounded off the United States' southeastern boundary. The U. S. also moved closer to control of the Columbia River in the Pacific Northwest with Spain no longer a contender. Hope for a Northwest Passage to the Pacific Ocean remained alive. In 1818, Great Britain and the United States extended the Canadian boundary along the 49th parallel to the Rocky Mountains. British and American citizens, including fur trappers like Jedediah Smith, jointly occupied the Oregon country, from Spanish California to Russian Alaska. Americans would soon set their sights on the fertile farm lands of southern Oregon, but now they watched Spain's deteriorating situation in Mexico.

Envisioning the Hemisphere: The Monroe Doctrine

Spain was one of the casualties of the Napoleonic Wars. Napoleon had persuaded the Spanish king, Fernando VII, to allow French armies into the country for defense purposes, but in 1808 he double-crossed the Spanish monarch, deposing him and placing his brother Joseph Bonaparte on the Spanish throne. Rebellion soon broke out against French rule and in support of liberal reforms. Insurgents wrote a new constitution limiting monarchical power and providing for colonial representation in a Spanish parliament (the Cortes). After Napoleon's final defeat at Waterloo in 1815, Fernando VII returned to power, but he renounced the new constitution, and Spain staggered through years of bloody civil war.

> **What prompted the Monroe Doctrine, and what did it accomplish?**

During the turmoil in Spain, independence fever raged through Spain's New World colonies. Simón Bolívar and José de San Martín led patriot armies to victories over Spanish forces throughout South America as much of the Spanish empire disintegrated into independent republics. France, backed by the Holy Alliance of Russia, Prussia, and Austria, joined Fernando VII to quash the revolutions, and by the early 1820s, the prospect of armed European intervention in the Americas loomed large.

Both Great Britain and the United States objected to European interference in the Western Hemisphere. For strategic reasons, Britain opposed Europe's monarchial alliance while simultaneously benefiting economically from profitable trade with the new Latin American republics. The United States initially adopted a policy of neutrality regarding the revolutions taking place in the Spanish Empire; however, after ratification of the Adams-Onís Transcontinental Treaty, Congress declared its support for the newly independent republics and President Monroe recognized them. Furthermore, many Americans were concerned about the new Russian trading outpost at Ft. Ross located near Bodega Bay in northern California. In the aftermath of the War of 1812, Anglo-American relations improved, leading British Foreign Minister George Canning to propose that the two nations stand together against foreign intervention in the republics. Although Monroe thought well of the idea, Adams persuaded him that the United States should continue to heed George Washington's advice against alliances. Adams also suspected Britain of really aiming to thwart future United States territorial expansion. Adams composed a pronouncement denouncing all further European involvement in the Western Hemisphere, and in December 1823 Monroe incorporated it into his annual message to Congress. The declaration became known as the **Monroe Doctrine**.

The Monroe Doctrine contained two basic ideas. The first was clear and explicit. Europe and the Americas adhered to conflicting political systems—the former monarchical and the latter republican. Therefore, "the American Continents . . . are henceforth not to be considered as subjects for future colonization by any European power." The second idea was equally important although implicitly conveyed. The United States would protect the Western Hemisphere from all threats, and protection could mean annexation. Indeed, Adams believed that the natural "laws of political and physical gravitation" dictated that the United States would eventually absorb nearby territories.

Few people on either side of the Atlantic paid much attention to the Monroe Doctrine because the United States had little muscle with which to enforce it. But Britain was pleased to stand behind it because it served its national interests too. Although the Monroe Doctrine revealed more about Americans' intense nationalism and commitment to republican ideals than the nation's military and economic strength, the time would come when the United States could impose its will on others.

African or American?

Along with patriotic nationalism came measures that defined American nationality in terms of people with white skin. Southern state legislatures made it harder for masters to manumit slaves, thus keeping the vast majority of blacks enslaved. Several states considered banishing free African Americans, whom John Randolph of Virginia called "promoters of mischief." In many northern states too, programs of racial discrimination marginalized African Americans. Connecticut's new and otherwise liberal constitution disfranchised the state's small but growing black population. Ohio required African Americans to carry citizenship papers and to post bond insuring good behavior.

The culmination of efforts to ostracize free black people came in 1816 when Robert Finley of New Jersey along with Henry Clay of Kentucky and John Randolph of Virginia

> What were the goals of the American Colonization Society, and how did people react to them?

organized the **American Colonization Society** to transport freed slaves to West Africa. British abolitionists had already established the colony of Sierra Leone to promote emancipation. Many southern planters endorsed the project not to end slavery but to protect it, fearing that free blacks would inspire slaves to revolt. Most ACS supporters did oppose slavery but abhorred free blacks too. Clay characterized free blacks as "a useless and pernicious, if not dangerous portion of its population." He and others believed that African Americans would be better off and happier in Africa than in America. The ACS raised money to purchase slaves whom it then intended to emancipate and deport. The organization acquired territory through purchase and lease agreements with local African leaders and then ironically named it Liberia.

Most African Americans emphatically opposed deportation. Three thousand protesters, including Richard Allen, founder of the African Methodist Episcopal Church, gathered in Bethel AME Church in Philadelphia to register their objection to being expelled from "the land of our nativity" and to the "unmerited stigma" that Clay had attached to them. The protesters also resolved not to abandon the slaves who "are our brethren by ties of consanguinity, of suffering, and of wrong."

But some African Americans responded positively to the idea of voluntary emigration. In 1823, Haiti's president, Jean Pierre Boyer, offered to pay African Americans to help build that nation. Two thousand did emigrate, although conflicts with native Haitian citizens discouraged most of them and led to their eventual return to the United States. Other emigrants considered Africa. Their reasons varied: hope for better lives or a sense of duty to Africa. Absalom Jones wondered if the reason God had inflicted slavery on African Americans was so "that a knowledge of the gospel might be acquired by some of their description, in order that they might become qualified to be the messengers of it, to the land of their fathers."

Paul Cuffe of Massachusetts, whose father was an African slave and mother a Native American, had risen from hard-working seaman to become a successful ship-owner and the leading advocate of voluntary emigration. Prior to the War of 1812, Cuffe had begun to recruit settlers for Africa to release them from the "yoke of oppression." In 1816, he transported thirty-eight colonists to West Africa. Leaders of the American Colonization Society could see that at least some African Americans distinguished voluntary emigration from forced colonization and assured blacks no slaves whose freedom they purchased would be coerced into relocating. Four years later, Daniel Coker, an African Methodist Episcopal Church leader in Baltimore, led ninety-four colonists to Africa under the auspices of the American Colonization Society. The ACS settled several hundred African Americans in Liberia, the first colonists to do so. Others followed during the following decades.

Whether voluntary emigration or coerced colonization, the question of relocating to Africa caused African Americans to ponder their identities. Africa was in their consciousness, part of who they were. Africa permeated their culture, exemplified by the word "African" in the names of many black organizations. But in a nation of immigrants, African Americans were as American as whites, with family lineages reaching far back into the nation's history. Rather than emigrate to a foreign land, most African Americans wished to be treated as equal citizens of the United States, whose independence they had fought to achieve and recently to defend. Because of African colonization, many blacks used the word "African" less often. The First African Baptist Church of Boston, for example, dropped the word from its name because it was "ill applied to a church composed of American citizens." So, despite efforts to exclude them, African Americans grew even more aware of their American identity.

THINKING BACK

1. Why did the spirit of nationalism soar after the War of 1812, and how did Americans express it?

2. What particular dilemma regarding national identity did African Americans confront, and how did they reconcile it?

PRE-INDUSTRIAL AMERICA

After the War of 1812, the American population grew significantly, the result mostly of high fertility. The number of Americans doubled each generation and by 1830 had reached 12.8 million. One in five Americans was of African descent. Numerically, Native Americans declined sharply, although 110,000 still lived east of the Mississippi River. Nine out of ten Americans resided in rural areas; the men expected to produce food and the women expected to maintain their households and rear children. But cities were beginning to swell. Atlantic and Gulf coast trading centers maintained vital commercial links to Europe, and many merchants imagined expanding trade networks into Asia. The greatest growth spurt of all occurred in the trans-Appalachian West, the destination of a Great Migration from eastern regions of the country. Soon half the country's population resided between the Appalachian Mountains and the Mississippi River. These sweeping trends give us a big historical picture of American society, but they provided only the backdrop for the daily routines that made up the experiences of most people's lives.

Cities of Commerce

In 1820, only seven of every 100 citizens lived in communities of 2,500 or more, yet, cities claimed first-rank importance in the country's economic life. Over half the urban population crowded into New York,

> What were the most important American cities, what were they like, and what role did city merchants play in the nation's expanding economy?

Philadelphia, Baltimore, Boston, New Orleans, and Charleston. The population of both New York and Philadelphia exceeded 100,000 in 1820, but Baltimore with 62,700 residents was the fastest-growing city. Baltimore was the major market for the Chesapeake Bay region's wheat and tobacco production and an important gateway to the trans-Appalachian West. New Orleans was also entering a period of considerable expansion. And Cincinnati, on the Ohio River, burgeoned too. The Crown City's 9,600 residents in 1820 represented a 300 percent rate of growth over the preceding decade. Pittsburgh, Louisville, and St. Louis were other important trans-Appalachian cities.

Cities hummed with commercial activity. Those in the West served as inland centers for transshipping agricultural goods from surrounding areas and supplying farmers with tools and other merchandise. Cincinnati developed a meat-packing industry while iron foundries in the coal-rich area of western Pennsylvania and eastern Ohio manufactured nails, farm implements, and horseshoes for markets in Pittsburgh. East coast cities faced the sea, with their main streets leading to busy Atlantic piers. People poured into the cities looking for work on the wharves or in the many warehouses, shops, and stores. In 1818, five New York City merchants established the first sailing "**packet**" ships between New York and Liverpool, England. These vessels departed at preset and advertised times, a substantial improvement over the customary practice of departing only when cargo holds were full. Packet lines quickly augmented coastal routes as well.

City merchants largely managed the nation's economy. They bought the grains, hides, grains, and minerals shipped by wagon from the back country and distributed them to distant and even global markets. Early on, the wealthiest merchants like John Jacob Astor of New York, the richest man in the country, maintained their own fleets of ships, which served as common carriers for lesser merchants who paid for shipping. The age of economic specialization was fast approaching, however, and gradually, ship owning became a separate business. Merchants specialized too, many in wholesale business, some in retail, and others (known as factors) in buying and selling for Southern planters and Northern manufacturers.

The cities were the heart of the national economy. They pumped the products of farms, mountains, and woodlands, and mines to markets at home and abroad. Eventually many of them would move to the rhythms of factories and foundries, but now they depended on the ship manifests and mercantile accounting ledgers.

The Great Westward Migration

As Eastern merchants kept an eye on European markets, a great migration of settlers poured into the trans-Appalachian West. Fertile **Midwestern** soil, the best farmland on the continent, drew people away from the thin, stony earth of New England where farms had been subdivided among children for so many generations that plots had become too small to support families. Emigrants also came from the exhausted tobacco lands of the Chesapeake and cramped Appalachian valleys. They broke through the woodland fringe onto the rolling prairies of Illinois, Missouri, Iowa, and

Wisconsin. Few hostile Indians resisted the homesteaders now, but there was still plenty of danger in settling the country. Death rates from accidents, disease, and childbirth were fearfully high. Still, the immigrant flood continued. From 1810 to 1830, the Midwest's non-Indian population leaped from 670,000 to 2.9 million. Most settlers were white; however, by 1820 some 7,000 African Americans, many of them emancipated slaves, had homesteaded. Altogether, by 1816 enough people had made homes in Indiana to allow statehood, followed in 1818 by Illinois.

> **What enticed people to move west, and what cultural baggage did they bring with them?**

Most new Midwesterners were market-oriented. Economic prospects rose with the end of the War of 1812 and the resumption of international commerce. Furthermore, Eastern cities generated additional demands for wheat, corn, barley, beef, pork, wool, and hides. According to guidelines laid down in the Land Ordinance of 1785 (see p. 188-89), public land was available to private citizens in square mile sections (640 acres) at one dollar per acre. Cash payment was required. Such terms put the price (over $24,000 in today's money) beyond the financial resources of most homesteaders. Congress later adjusted the minimum purchase to 160 acres but raised the price to two dollars. Wealthy speculators stepped in, acquired large tracts, and sold it to settlers on credit. Eventually banks also loaned money for land purchases. In 1820, following the economic crisis (see the Panic of 1819 on p. 291), the government boosted homesteading in a major way by lowering the price of public land to $1.25 per acre and reducing the minimum purchase to 80 acres. Most Midwestern farms were under 200 acres, large enough for raising cereal grains and livestock and supplying timber for construction of houses, barns, and fences. Although the vast majority of the immigrant settlers were farmers, artisans also set up shops and mills—blacksmiths, boat-builders, grain and lumber millers, tanners, and carpenters. Merchants, lawyers, school teachers, and itinerant preachers added cohesion and permanence to community development.

New communities usually struggled for the first few years. Cash-starved and isolated local economies operated under a primitive barter system. Newly arrived farmers planted familiar crops brought from their previous homes but quickly learned what grew best in their new environments and adjusted accordingly: wheat near the Great Lakes and corn in

New Salem, Illinois. Settler James Rutledge helped found New Salem in 1828. Abraham Lincoln arrived three years later. Many believe Rutledge's daughter Ann was Lincoln's first love.

the Ohio Valley. Settler women from Virginia and North Carolina raised hogs and chickens while their New England counterparts tended cattle. As the men cleared more land and increased their crops, they hauled surpluses to regional markets like Cincinnati, Louisville, and St. Louis. From there, merchants hired riverboatmen to transport the products on flatboats down the Ohio and Mississippi rivers to New Orleans. By the middle of the nineteenth century, the Midwest was one of the most highly commercialized areas of the world.

Getting ahead does not totally explain the migration to the Midwest. Many newcomers wanted to reestablish lifestyles they had once enjoyed. They fled the destructive effects of commercialization on their families and communities back East and hoped to reestablish themselves as self-sufficient producers. In the spring of 1820, such a colony of Vermonters settled along the Illinois River, helping each other to survive adversity the way their Puritan forebears had. Daniel Brush recorded the settlement's growing prosperity in terms of the value of self-sufficiency rather than profit. "Provisions in abundance, was the rule in that Yankee Settlement, and no one needed to go supperless or [hungry] to bed." Across the upper Midwest, Yankee settlers established communities that looked very much like the New England townships they had left behind.

Economic life in the **Old Southwest** was also commercialized. The main crop, however, was cotton. Farmers could not eat it; therefore they had to sell it. And the voracious appetites of British textile factories

doubled the price of cotton, motivating planters to boost production and increase their earnings. Between 1815 and 1830, cotton exports jumped from 83 million to 298 million pounds, and revenue reached $30 million. Cotton-growers demanded Indian land in Georgia, Alabama, and Mississippi to convert into plantations. From 1815 to 1820, the government negotiated treaties with Creeks, Cherokees, Choctaws, and Chickasaws that transferred millions of acres to whites.

Public land policies intended for the old Northwest Territories did not apply in the Old Southwest. Many early homesteaders simply settled ("**squatted**") on unoccupied land, cleared trees, and planted food crops and perhaps a little cotton. Gradually, more substantial planters moved in, bringing families and slaves. They too built rough cabins and planted corn the first year. James Tait, a successful Georgia planter who moved to Alabama in 1817, wrote to his brother Charles, a congressman in Washington: "I am lost to reflect on the vast differences that exist between your situation and my own, . . . I in my humble cabin . . . You engaged in the noble business of legislating for a great nation." James soon began growing cotton, and a year later, Charles likewise became an Alabama cotton planter. Thus, Southeastern culture was transferred to the Southwest. By 1817 this wing of the Great Migration brought enough people into Mississippi for statehood, followed in 1819 by Alabama (see map on p. 277).

The **Great Migration** pushed the United States halfway across the continent. The dream of a continental nation was becoming a reality. And as people moved from one part of the country to another, they lost some of their provincialism and became more absorbed into a national identity.

The Intimacies of Life

Early nineteenth-century America was a dirty place. Foul odors filled the air. Even the rich and famous did

> **What did early nineteenth-century America look, feel, and smell like?**

not measure up to modern standards of cleanliness. Grime, sweat, and decayed teeth made most people obnoxious by today's standards. Livestock manure littered yards and caked men's boots and clothes, especially farm folk. Mothers hung soaked and soiled "nappies" (diapers) on hearths to dry. The scents of town and city were especially pungent, the result of concentrations of people and animals and their wastes. Privies, or "necessary houses," stood behind every house and were periodically emptied into wagons that hauled their dripping contents through the streets. Fashionable housekeepers furnished their bedrooms with English ceramic chamber pots to avoid night-time trips to the outhouse, but slave quarters and many rural houses had no facilities at all.

Gradually, cleanliness became a health consideration and a symbol of gentility. In July of 1799, sixty-five-year-old Elizabeth Drinker of Philadelphia, the wife of a prominent Quaker merchant, bathed in a shower stall her husband had recently erected in their back yard. "I bore it better than I expected," she told her diary, "not having been wet all over at once, for 28 years past." Drinker never became a regular bath-taker, but her daughter did. By the 1820s, public baths operated in most towns. Families who could afford them installed bathtubs, and wealthy households included china wash bowls in their bedroom furnishings. Hot water still had to be carried from the kitchen, and bathers used brushes rather than soap to clean their bodies. Bath soaps were scarce and expensive; however, in the 1830s William Procter and James Gamble developed a popular commercial laundry detergent that was milder than homemade lye soaps. Even by mid-century, though, those who practiced John Wesley's adage that "Cleanliness is . . . next to godliness" were outnumbered by those who did not.

Tobacco smoke and juice added to the generalized grime. Smokers puffed on clay pipes; cigars came into vogue too. Workers everywhere chewed plugs and dipped snuff. Slave rations typically included tobacco, and many women chewed and smoked. Horace Greeley remembered it being his boyhood duty "to fill and light my mother's pipe." People spit tobacco juice everywhere, often ignoring or missing spittoons. Sticky barroom floors testified to the "incessant, remorseless spitting." Although Southerners consumed more tobacco than people in other parts of the country, even the New England *Farmer's Almanack* instructed female dairy workers to "put your snuff box aside when you are working over your butter."

Travelers endured especially disgusting conditions. When John Melish stopped at a South Carolina house for a meal he heard a "violent retching" from the adjoining room that killed his appetite. Margaret Hall, an English traveler, collected assorted fleas and bedbugs on a journey from Washington to New Orleans. "We bring them along with us in our clothes and when I undress I find them crawling on my skin, nasty wretches." By the 1820s, however, many accommodations, especially in major cities along the eastern seaboard, had become more comfortable. Fine hotels like Boston's new Tremont House and New York City's Astor House offered luxurious beds and bath tubs.

An innovation in food preservation helped make menu items in restaurants and fashionable homes more palatable. Heretofore, people ate perishable food as quickly as possible because they had no effective way of preserving it. Ice was readily available in New England, but in the Deep South the story was different. In 1805, Frederic Tudor, a twenty-one-year-old Bostonian, began harvesting ice from frozen New England ponds and selling it in tropical climes. After experimenting with several insulating materials, Tudor constructed ice boxes in which less than 10 percent of the contents melted. For cutting the ice out of frozen ponds, Tudor turned to Nathaniel Wyeth, who designed a useful sawing mechanism pulled by horses. By the 1820s, Tudor's business had become a spectacular success. Southerners were refrigerating meats and dairy products and homemakers served chilled fruit and beverages in summer. In 1833, Tudor shipped 180 tons of ice to India, a feat that earned him the title "Ice King."

Spiritual Intimacies: The Second Great Awakening

In the Revolutionary era, only one American in ten had belonged to a church, but that changed at the turn of the century as the number of church-goers burgeoned. The number of congregations vaulted

What ignited the religious revivals known as the Second Great Awakening, and what impact did they have on Americans?

too, from 2,500 in 1780 to 11,000 in 1820. Although many factors contributed to the revival of religious fervor, the most important was a reaction against the Enlightenment's secularism, which did not satisfy people's spiritual needs. Also, clergymen, influenced by liberal theology, endeavored to shatter the complacency of non-religious persons about their spiritual destiny. Like earlier Great Awakening preachers, they reminded people that they were doomed to Hell but also promised God's forgiveness. Here they tapped into enormous latent religious energy emanating from the republicanism of the time, namely the acknowledgment of individual freedom. The oppressed most eagerly joined worship services that allowed free expression and celebrated salvation. And settlers on the western frontier, overwhelmed by the loneliness of isolated existence, welcomed intimate union with communities of born-again Christians.

From about 1800 through the 1830s, the "evangelical fires" of the **Second Great Awakening** swept the country. Fanned by the Great Migration, the flames burned a broad swath across the Appalachian Mountains and into the Mississippi River valley. Settlements multiplied faster than Protestant churches could find ministers for them. The Baptists resorted to lay preachers and the Methodists employed itinerant ministers who traveled circuits from one settlement to the next. All preached the Gospel of salvation through acknowledgment of sin, repentance, and acceptance of Jesus Christ as their savior.

Evangelists also held revivals to spread the Gospel. Although the Baptists typically conducted revivals inside their churches, Methodists invented the outdoor camp meeting. Participants pitched tents in forest clearings near streams and camped out for weeks. At the sites, benches filled with zealous Christians faced platforms occupied by platoons of ministers. Around-the-clock preaching, hymn-singing, and praying, illuminated at night by candles and torches, kept emotions at a fever pitch and exhausted nearly everyone. Sinners waiting for the divine spirit to purify their souls sat on the "anxious seat." Baptisms symbolized the death and resurrection of sinners as **born-again Christians**. As many as 20,000 worshippers and forty ministers attended the great Cane Ridge, Kentucky, camp meeting in 1801, the first of its kind.

Many people scorned camp meetings because of the uncontrolled emotionalism and disorder, and indeed, drunkenness and open sexual promiscuity often prevailed among outsiders who hung around the tent cities. But the revivals reinvigorated the Christian churches and helped double church membership.

The psychology of revival evangelism involved stirring people's deepest anxieties, especially the fear of death. James McGready exhorted with such intensity and vivid language that, according to one witness, his listeners "would tremble and quake, imagining a lake of fire and brimstone yawning to overwhelm them." The revivals also comforted with the prospect of salvation. It was a terribly exciting experience for the participants who shouted, succumbed to "the jerks," and frequently fainted from sheer exhaustion. These were interpreted as signs of God's powerful and redeeming presence.

The Second Great Awakening was both revolutionary and conservative. It uplifted the lowly with its populist doctrine of salvation for all who sought it. Evangelical churches openly advocated the emancipation of slaves. African Americans were attracted by the anti-slavery rhetoric as well as the spiritualism, emotionalism, and baptismal sacraments that resembled traditional African religious beliefs. Moreover, skin color and worldly status were no barriers to preaching, and many slaves became effective ministers, preaching to white audiences as well as black. Women comprised the vast majority of camp-meeting attendees and evangelical church members. Evolving sex roles accorded women privilege in matters of the conscience; thus, their status in church was higher than it was in the secular world, greatly enhancing their self-esteem. Egalitarianism eventually caused friction in the South, however. Powerful planters resented the churches' racial liberalism, and white ministers abhorred the African accents that blacks placed on Christianity. Blacks were segregated and denied power in church governance. Women threatened patriarchy, and therefore males, citing the Apostle Paul, rallied to deny them ordination.

Evangelism stirred Northeasterners too, but in different ways. It began as a reaction among Presbyterian and Congregational theologians against various eighteenth-century rational "isms" that undermined traditional churches. In *The Age of Reason* (1794), Thomas Paine had voiced Deism's denunciation of churches, calling them "human inventions, set up to terrify and enslave mankind." Univeralism meant that everyone was destined for salvation. And Unitarianism denied the Trinity (Father, Son, and Holy Spirit), representing Jesus as a teacher, not the Messiah. In the wake of these departures from conventional Protestant Christian doctrines, orthodox Presbyterians and Congregationalists revived Calvinist canons while liberals moved in the direction of "**free agency**." During the 1810s and 1820s, from churches in Litchfield, Connecticut, and Boston, Lyman Beecher presented a God filled with love and compassion. Beecher became the most eloquent spokesman for **New School Presbyterianism**. Great excitement spread through New England churches, although they did not exhibit the disorderliness of the western revivals, and church membership swelled.

The greatest evangelist of the time, either North or South, was the Methodist itinerant Lorenzo Dow. With his long hair parted in the middle, Dow cultivated the image of John the Baptist. His awe-inspiring theatricality as well as his religious passion drew seekers by the thousands as he barnstormed the country, from New England to Mississippi—and three trips to Great Britain. He ridiculed orthodox Calvinism's endless, confusing circularity.

> You can and you can't,
>
> You will and you won't;
>
> You'll be damned if you do,
>
> And you'll be *damned if you don't.*

The revivals of the Second Great Awakening not only transformed the face of religion in the United States but also pushed the country further toward its republican ideals. Democratic organization, antislavery doctrine, and gender equality represented the kind of nation that evangelicals hoped the United States would become. They promoted the formation of Christian communities living according to Scripture and an ascetic code of behavior that forbade drinking, gambling, smoking, and dancing. These evangelical fires consumed the orthodox Calvinism, which, according to the liberal Boston pastor William Ellery Channing, "has passed its meridian, and is sinking to rise no more." And at the same time, the Second Great Awakening defined the South as the Bible Belt.

THINKING BACK

1. How did life in America change during the early nineteenth century?

2. In what ways did the national government and Christian religion assist Americans in taking advantage of the new opportunities and meeting the great challenges that confronted them?

ECONOMIC GROWTH, DIVERSIFICATION, AND INTEGRATION

To some extent, the religious excitement of the early nineteenth century also reflected anxieties prompted by a number of economic upheavals, especially after the War of 1812. The economy boomed as producers strained to meet the rising demand for agricultural commodities both at home and abroad. A **Market Revolution** enticed people away from relatively stable subsistence production and into a more volatile, unpredictable economic environment. There was also a patriotic element to economic change, as wartime shortages of critical manufactured goods affirmed the connection between industry, banking, and the country's independence. A **Transportation Revolution** provided the essential infrastructure. Roads, canals, and riverboat steamers integrated the three major sections of the country—Northeast, South, and West—into a national economy. And finally, the Republican party adopted many nationalist measures previously associated with the Federalists. In the end, postwar economic expansion proved financially unsteady, underscored by the Panic of 1819 that foreshadowed the nation's boom and bust future.

Technology for Supply and Demand

The Market Revolution stimulated technological innovation that dramatically boosted both the demand for products and the supply of goods. In 1811, Elkanah Watson organized the country's first agricultural fair in Pittsfield, Massachusetts, introducing farmers to new implements and awarding prizes for the most outstanding farm produce. Between 1800 and 1850, several innovative farm tools hit the market. John Deere's sharp steel plow marked a significant improvement over iron blades that quickly became dull and clogged with sod. Various other mechanical devices made their entry into American agriculture as well, including hay rakes and threshing machines. In the early years of the nineteenth century, agricultural patents exceeded those issued for all other types of devices.

Although colonial Americans had developed a practical genius for improvisation in agricultural production, they had not been driven to invent complex machinery for manufacturing. Most early innovation occurred in England, where the Industrial Revolution spurred the development of power-driven machines. Americans became more inventive as market influences strengthened. In addition, many unappreciated English technicians immigrated to the United States, bringing with them critical manufacturing technology.

Title page from the Lowell Offering. Published from 1840 to 1845, the periodical contained fiction and on-fiction contributions from Lowell employees.

What new technologies boosted economic production?

Textile manufacturing attracted much of the innovative technology. The demand for clothing fabric grew in proportion to the population, and both urbanization and the expansion of slavery also increased the number of people who did not or could not make their own garments. For generations, farm women had operated a type of peddle powered device known as a "spinning jenny" to produce cotton and wool thread, but it was too slow for commercial use. Samuel Slater, an experienced British mechanic who immigrated to the United States in 1789, revolutionized that phase of textile production. Moses Brown of Pawtucket, Rhode Island, hired him to build an automated spinning machine, and within a year Slater had started up the country's first textile mill. The Embargo of 1808 motivated other entrepreneurs to expand the domestic industry. "Our people have 'cotton mill fever,'" Brown declared. Between 1808 and 1812, thirty-six mills began operation.

The key to machines was finding a power source greater than human muscles. Early American textile mills harnessed the Northeast's rushing rivers. Soon, however, steam replaced water-wheels. Here again, the basic technology came from England in the form of James Watt's **steam engine**. American ingenuity became apparent with the application of steam power to textile machinery. With the technology fitting into place by the beginning of the nineteenth century, the expansion of the American textile industry was set to begin.

The Lowell System

What were the main features of the Lowell System, and how did it characterize industrial organization in the United States?

The War of 1812, one industry advocate explained, "emancipated us from our former slavish dependence on the looms and anvils of Great Britain." Francis Cabot Lowell, a successful Boston merchant and Harvard graduate, was in England studying English power looms when the war broke out. He memorized what he saw and returned to the United States. In 1814 Lowell and fellow merchant Nathan Appleton, founded the Boston Manufacturing Company in 1814. They raised $400,000 in capital and built a textile mill with powered spinning and weaving machines in Waltham, just outside Boston. Soon, other investors joined the venture, which they called the **Boston Associates.**

The Associates began building an industrial complex on the Merrimack River, twenty-seven miles north of Boston, which they named Lowell. They poured $8 million (comparable to $150 million today) into the erection of multi-story textile factories. Lowell, Massachusetts, became the first genuine factory town in the United States. Other manufacturing centers emerged in neighboring New Hampshire and Rhode Island. From farm houses to small mill towns scattered throughout New England, manufacturing had commenced its move to the city.

Two characteristics of the **Lowell System** distinguished it from Slater's earlier textile mill. The first was the integration of carding, spinning, and weaving processes under one roof to produce bolts of finished cloth. The second was the employment of young, unmarried women to tend the machines. Drawn from surrounding farm families, the Lowell mill girls lived in boarding houses provided and supervised by the Boston Associates, took classes in the evening, and even published their own magazine, the *Lowell Offering*. The owners accepted responsibility for creating a proper, nurturing environment for the working girls that would eventually make them suitable wives. The opportunity for factory jobs, however, was not available to African Americans.

The domestic features of the Lowell System were designed to avoid producing the type of exploited and oppressed industrial working class that existed in England. The young factory women usually remained for less than two years before they married. But the nature of the work they performed hinted strongly at a new industrial order. For some, "the sight of so many bands, and wheels, and springs in constant motion, was very frightful." Factory whistles called the women to work at 5 o'clock in the morning and did not blow again to stop work, except for lunch, until 7 o'clock in the evening, six days a week with three holidays a year. The intense concentration required of the workers was exhausting, and mistakes caused by fatigue led to rebukes by factory managers and often serious injury. Lucy Larcum recalled that her machine "had to be watched in a dozen different directions every minute, and even then it was always getting itself and me in trouble."

The Lowell System revealed another important difference between early industrialization in the United States and England. English industrialists enjoyed an abundant supply of cheap labor; thus machinery was not as important. The use of technology to increase worker productivity came mostly from the United States. The Lowell System was the prototype for corporate-dominated industries that employed workers primarily to operate machines. The factory was not yet the norm in American manufacturing, which still relied heavily on the traditional "**put out**" home manufacturing system. In nearby Lynn, Massachusetts, for example, workers manufactured shoes at home and in small workshops using hand tools.

Revolutionizing Transportation

Market-oriented inventors and developers completed a number of greatly needed transportation innovations that amounted to a what historians have called a "**Transportation Revolution.**" Known at the time as **internal improvements**, roads, steamboats, and canals enabled farmers and manufacturers to produce for markets located miles away. They also helped cement national unity.

> What were the primary components of the Transportation Revolution, including their advantages and disadvantages?

Laying out a national network of roadways commenced before the war. By 1818, builders had completed a roadway through the Appalachian Mountains from Cumberland, Maryland, on the Potomac River, to Wheeling, Virginia (West Virginia today), on the Ohio. Work continued in stages, and by 1832 the **National Road** had reached Ohio and eventually the Illinois prairie. **Conestoga wagons** clogged the stone and gravel thruway, some carrying settlers and their belongings west and others filled with farm produce destined for eastern markets.

Shippers paid maintenance tolls to use the National Road, passing at intervals through turnstiles operated by tollhouse keepers. Most of the **turnpike roads** constructed after the War of 1812 operated this way. State governments issued charters to private corporations to build roads. The states usually purchased shares of the companies' stock, although most of the capital raised was private. Passengers in carriages and coaches enjoyed the comfort of the relatively smooth ride, but there were problems. Many large commercial freight haulers complained about the high tolls, and carriage drivers, or **teamsters**, often bypassed the tollhouses, reducing revenues and causing many of the companies to skimp on maintenance or abandon the turnpikes altogether.

Turnpikes usually required bridges for crossing rivers and gorges. Stone bridges sufficed in most parts of the country, but, covered bridges provided protection from ice and snow. Specimens of these early bridges can still be found today, especially in the Northeast and Midwest. By the 1830s, civil engineers using iron frame construction turned bridge-building into a science. The immigrant John A. Roebling pioneered in

Conestoga wagon, the primary means of transport for settlers moving along the National Road to new homes in the Midwest.

building wire-cable suspension bridges, the best-known of which was his famous Brooklyn Bridge.

The Transportation Revolution also utilized rivers, lakes, and coastal waters as thruways, applying steam power to boats to overcome the obstacles of one-way water currents and contrary winds that plagued sailing vessels. In 1807, after years of experimentation, inventor Robert Fulton teamed with New York land magnate Robert R. Livingston and launched *The North River Steamboat of Clermont,* sometimes referred to as simply the *Clermont.* This side-wheel paddleboat carried passengers between New York City and Albany on the Hudson River. Fulton's first steamboat, and the dozen other, more powerful steamers that followed, boosted New York City's standing as a market center for the agricultural products of upstate New York. As a result, New York City moved ahead of Philadelphia as the country's largest city. Passenger traffic dominated eastern steamboat travel, and the boats' sleek design emphasized speed. Packets helped make steamboats the preferred mode of travel along the Atlantic seaboard.

The most important commercial use of steamboats involved freighting bulky agricultural commodities on western rivers. Although sail-driven ships continued to dominate Great Lakes commerce, steamboats overcame powerful currents and turned the Ohio and Mississippi rivers into two-way thoroughfares. Using a Fulton design, Nicholas Roosevelt built the 148-foot steamboat *New Orleans* in Pittsburgh. In 1811 the vessel made its maiden voyage to New Orleans. Later, majestic stern-wheelers carried as many as 350 deck passengers as well as other customers in luxurious, first-class staterooms.

Riverboat entrepreneur Timothy Flint believed the steamboat age "ought to be estimated the most memorable era of the West." It was certainly one. Previously, crews of hearty boatmen required three months to pole, row, or pull flatboats up-river to Louisville; by 1820 steamboats completed the trip in a scant two weeks. Steamboat transportation gave a tremendous impetus to commercial development in the Ohio and Mississippi valleys, and sparked remarkable growth in New Orleans. By 1830, the Crescent City had become the second leading exporting city in the country, behind New York, and over the next decades hundreds of steamboats plied tributaries like the Red, Wabash, Cumberland, and Missouri rivers, reaching deep into the interior and turning subsistence homesteaders into market producers. By the Civil War, steamboats ran the rivers of Washington, Oregon, and California. In fact, by mid-century, more steamboats operated in the western United States than in any other part of the world.

Despite the steamboat's dramatic effect on transportation, it was many years before passengers and commercial customers could trust them. Because of frequent accidents, steamboats seldom lasted more than five years. Engine boilers frequently exploded, causing fearful loss of life. Only gradually did engineers develop steel boiler plates and welded joints that lessened the risk of failure. Underwater snags

Mississippi River steamboat. Such vessels turned rivers into two-way thoroughfares.

sank almost half of all steamboats lost on western rivers. Sparks often ignited cargoes of cotton and other combustibles, even the wooden planking of the boat itself. And reckless captains caused unnecessary accidents by racing and overloading their boats. Not until 1852 did Congress establish standards of construction and operation that made steamboats safer.

The greatest engineering feats of the Transportation Revolution created artificial rivers, or **canals**. Early canals improved natural waterways by bypassing obstructions and channeling between rivers and lakes. Canal-building in the United States actually began late in the eighteenth century, inspired by Europeans. In their heyday, from the 1820s to the 1850s, canals served three broad functions: linking upland areas with the tidewater along the Atlantic coast, establishing waterways through the Appalachians, and joining the Great Lakes with the Ohio-Mississippi river network. Horses and mules towed barges along the canals, the towpaths doubling as roadways for pedestrians, horses, and carriages.

The first canals were short. In 1785 a syndicate of Virginia and Maryland planters, including George Washington, founded the Potomac Company to circumvent the falls above Georgetown. They hoped to make the Potomac the gateway to the Ohio Valley and turn Washington, D.C., into a bustling emporium, but it never happened. In 1803, the Middlesex Canal, opened between the Merrimack River and Boston. Twenty-eight miles long, thirty feet wide, and three and a half feet deep, it took a decade to

construct. When it was completed, barges hauled lumber and foodstuffs down river from New Hampshire to Lowell and Boston through locks and stone aqueducts, while towboats carried passengers and finished products upstream.

Despite tremendous public interest, by 1816 only 100 miles of canals had been dug, and only three canals were as much as two miles long. But the **Erie Canal** heralded the coming of a new age in inland transportation. A man named Jesse Hawley, while in debtors' prison, had originally proposed a canal from Lake Erie through the Mohawk Valley to the Hudson River. In 1817 a bill backed by Governor De Witt Clinton (George Clinton's nephew) and authorizing construction passed an enthusiastic legislature. When "Clinton's Ditch," as critics derided it, opened in 1825, it sparked an explosion of national pride. It was indeed a phenomenal engineering accomplishment: 364 miles long, forty feet wide, four feet deep, and with eighty-four locks to enable boats to pass through the 600 feet of elevation between the Hudson River and Lake Erie. Pennsylvania followed suit with its Mainline Canal, which traversed the entire state. Ohio, Indiana, and many other states also undertook canal projects.

Between 1816 and 1840, immigrant, convict, and slave workers dug 3,200 miles of canals at a cost of $125 million (approximately $3.2 billion today). The Erie Canal was a stunning success; traffic grew steadily through the middle of the nineteenth century, more than recovering the original cost. Western New York state sprouted grain farms and milling centers like

Buffalo, Rochester, and Syracuse. New York City now vied with Montreal for the commercial traffic of the Great Lakes. Canals were a vital element in the expansion of the nation's market economy. Most Americans accepted public financing of these massive projects, recognizing both the enormous economic benefits and the mammoth costs. As one contemporary stated: "The canal has been more useful to the public, than to the owners." He might have added that citizens viewed the canals as monuments to their republican virtues. The Erie Canal not only opened the Midwest to international markets for agricultural commodities but it also demonstrated the benefits of public financing and led to a canal-building boom.

Henry Clay and Economic Growth

> **What did economic nationalism entail, who backed it, and how did it affect national identity?**

The War of 1812 taught many Americans to appreciate a diversified economy. Dependence on other countries for manufactured products compromised national security. Even President James Madison, once an arch opponent of Alexander Hamilton's economic measures, now supported industry and incentives for it. In 1811 the Bank of the United States' charter had expired, and in his 1815 annual message to Congress, Madison conceded that "a national bank will merit consideration." In addition, he thought a suitably high tariff would protect American manufacturing against "competitions from abroad" and thereby be "a source of domestic wealth and even of external commerce." And to facilitate the shipment of farm goods, minerals, and lumber to markets and the transport of manufactured products to consumers Madison suggested that Congress establish "throughout our country the roads and canals which can best be executed under federal authority." Exceeding even what Hamilton had advocated, government promotion of economic growth became Republican party policy.

Congress moved promptly to enact the Republicans' nationalist economic agenda. Backers came from all sections of the country: Daniel Webster of Massachusetts, John C. Calhoun of South Carolina, and Henry Clay of Kentucky. As Speaker of the House, Clay took charge of pushing measures through the Congress. Secretary of the Treasury Alexander J. Dallas, with the endorsement of leading capitalists, drafted a proposal for a new national bank. Early in 1816, over opposition from New England, where state banks functioned adequately to finance economic expansion, Congress passed a twenty-year charter bill creating a second Bank of the United States. The BUS soon opened for business with headquarters in Philadelphia and branches in eighteen cities. For all practical purposes the second BUS was identical to the first one, only with a larger capitalization.

A month later, Congress passed a modestly protective tariff law. Calhoun favored protectionism partly because he believed the southeast would industrialize and partly because he regarded manufacturing as a national benefit. However, another southerner, John Randolph of Virginia, signaled a storm of protest against protective tariffs among those who paid consequently higher prices for manufactured goods. "On whom bears the duty on coarse woolens and linens, and blankets, upon salt and all the necessaries of life," Randolph asked? "On poor men and on slaveholders."

Wide agreement, although certainly not consensus, existed on the need for internal improvements. Calhoun declared: "Let us . . . bind the republic together with a perfect system of roads and canals. Let us conquer space." Some controversy surrounded the constitutionality of federal government financing of the projects, especially those contained within a single state, and another question was where the money to pay for internal improvements would come from. Clay pointed out that Congress had required the BUS to pay the government a "bonus" of $1.5 million for its charter. Why not use that? In March of 1817, Congress passed the **Bonus Bill**; however, Madison vetoed the measure on constitutional grounds. Thus for at least the time being internal improvements had to rely on state funding.

Known as the **American System**, this package of nationalist economic programs reflected a broad, continental, big-government outlook rather than a narrow, parochial, limited government one. Its support indicated that more Americans thought of themselves as Americans than Virginians or New Yorkers. This was particularly true of persons involved in commerce. Nationalism of this sort, however, was not yet pervasive. Old Republicans, like the Virginia planter aristocrats John Randolph and John Taylor, remained committed to a traditional social order revolving around autonomous plantations situated on navigable rivers. They objected to taxes for distant projects that benefited others. Many

New Englanders and some residents of the southeast feared that development of the West would drain their population, reducing their political clout in Congress and in presidential elections. Their resistance to the American System revealed the continuing strength of local attachments even amidst growing nationalism.

The Law, the Courts, and the Market Place

How did legal and judicial changes promote commercial capitalism?

Several legal and judicial changes broke restraints on entrepreneurial activity, setting down in law the idea that economically successful individuals produced a prosperous society. Traditional common law had enforced morality; new statutory law encouraged free-wheeling accumulation and development of property. Complex economic transactions required lawyers to draft documents; likewise, economic policy demanded carefully crafted laws. Not surprisingly, the number of lawyers multiplied. By 1815, lawyers comprised half the members of Congress and increasingly dominated state and federal courts. In earlier times, few judges had been trained in the law, but now they were. Many of them had been raised in a commercial environment and embodied a market ethic that held that whatever was good for business was good for the community. More and more, lawyers put a pro-capitalist spin on the law.

Numerous judicial rulings deregulated how property could be used, giving entrepreneurs wider latitude. Judges reinterpreted the traditional common-law rule that property should be used for the common good in ways that privileged private enterprise. In 1805, a New York court excused a dam-builder from compensating farmers whose property was flooded. Judges also replaced ancient common-law precepts protecting consumers with the capitalist principle of "buyer beware" that favored the seller. Courts defined market transactions as binding contracts and granted entities that built canals and turnpikes eminent domain. Preferred enterprises could condemn farm property without just compensation.

Chief Justice John Marshall's long tenure on the United States Supreme (1801–1835), together with his charming personality and methodical mind, enabled him to forge a consensus favorable to a national market economy. He managed that despite the appointment of several Republicans to the high bench. Indeed, Marshall's staunchest ally was the erudite Justice Joseph

Story, whom Madison had appointed reluctantly because Story was too much of a "Tory" (Federalist). In the early years, Supreme Court justices seldom met to discuss cases, but Marshall convened them regularly as a group and established a sociable custom of sharing a bottle of wine. "We are all united as one," Story declared. Marshall is often ideologically linked with Alexander Hamilton, but he was not dogmatic; nor did he slavishly adhere to the principle of nationalism, although his philosophy tied in perfectly with the emerging national market economy.

In cases involving economic growth, Supreme Court rulings laid out a permissive interpretation of the federal government's powers under the Constitution. The issue of the Bank of the United States' constitutionality arose again, as it had in the 1790s. When the Maryland legislature imposed a tax on the Bank's Baltimore branch, cashier James McCulloch refused to pay it. The case ultimately came before the Supreme Court, and the ruling in *McCulloch v. Maryland* (1819) was a ringing endorsement of Hamilton's earlier argument that any federal economic policy not expressly prohibited was legitimate. As for the validity of a state tax on an agency of the national government, the Supreme Court declared that since taxes carry the potential for destruction, Maryland's levy was unconstitutional. The ruling reinforced federal government sovereignty.

In *Dartmouth College v. Woodward* (1819) the Marshall Court upheld the sanctity of contracts. In 1769 George III had chartered Dartmouth as a privately endowed college. It was now governed by a board of Federalist trustees. The Republican legislature of New Hampshire amended the charter expanding the number of trustees and putting the school under public control. The old trustees retained the noted lawyer Daniel Webster, a Dartmouth graduate, to challenge the state's action. Webster argued that corporate entities, like citizens, possessed rights under the Constitution that must be protected. The Supreme Court agreed, ruling that Dartmouth's charter was a contract and that the state's action violated the Constitutional ban on any state action "impairing the obligation of contracts."

The court also protected Congress' power to "regulate Commerce . . . among the several States," something that Marshall believed was essential to the formation of a national economy. The case of *Gibbons v. Ogden* (1823) involved the state of New York's grant of an exclusive charter to Robert Fulton and Robert Livingston for steamboat service across the Hudson River between New Jersey and New York

City. Fulton and Livingston in turn contracted with Aaron Ogden to operate the ferry. The New York monopoly conflicted with a federal government charter granted to another steamboat operator, Thomas Gibbons, whose attorney, Daniel Webster again, argued that the federal government's power to regulate interstate commerce was exclusive. The Supreme Court agreed that state regulation was improper in this instance. Marshall's opinion did not rule out state control of harbor and river pilots, health and quarantine issues, or bridge construction and maintenance but did broadly interpret commerce to include passengers as well as cargo.

State and federal statutes along with judicial interpretations of the law played a key role in the nation's economic development. They promoted competition, which lowered prices and raised the quality of goods and services. Supreme Court findings under Marshall's leadership helped to establish a national market by restricting state interference with interstate commerce. Nationalists claimed that this would result in prosperity for all, but they were overly optimistic.

The Panic of 1819

> What caused the Panic of 1819, why did the Bank of the United States fail to prevent it, and what were the consequences of the financial crisis?

Despite activity and optimism, serious problems threatened the economy. High cotton prices, which had driven much of the economic expansion, began to fall. British textile manufacturers began importing cheaper cotton from the East Indies. By 1819 prices for American cotton stood at less than half their peak. Foreign markets for other American export commodities also shrank as European agriculture recovered from a generation of war. In 1815 the eruption of an Indonesian volcano sent a mammoth dust cloud into the atmosphere, causing heavy rains and cold temperatures for several summers. New York City ponds froze in June, and accompanying rust and insect infestations blighted crops.

Feverish land speculation also clouded the economic picture. Developers had pushed up prices, and when commodity prices fell the land bubble burst. Property values dropped by as much as 75 percent. Bankers had contributed to inflated prices by offering easy credit to purchasers with slight regard for how much specie (gold and silver) their banks held in reserve. Between 1815 and 1819, the number of state-chartered banks doubled from 204 to almost 400. Most of the new banks operated in the West where they were mostly free from regulation. Countless "wildcat banks" operated without any licenses at all.

The Bank of the United States possessed the ability to regulate local banking and prevent unwise lending; however, it did not perform that duty well. Indeed, under questionable management, the BUS had actually fed the credit frenzy through its own unsound policies. In 1819 the bank's president, William Jones, resigned under allegations of showing favoritism to his friends. The BUS's governors attempted to tighten credit and dampen speculation by calling in loans, foreclosing mortgages, and demanding redemption of state bank notes, but instead of bringing the economy under control it precipitated a financial panic. Banks failed to meet demands for specie, developers went broke, and hard-working farmers could not repay mortgage loans and lost their homesteads.

The BUS did not single-handedly bring on the **Panic of 1819** and the depression that followed, but many people blamed it—especially in the West. The consequences of the collapse were noticeable everywhere, though not with equal severity. The West was especially hard hit, and farm prices fell sharply. In newly developing areas, however, the productivity of virgin land helped offset lower prices. Land values and rents continued to rise in growing cities—as much as 50 percent in Baltimore. It took half a decade for the national economy to recover from the economic downturn and longer than that for many people to recover confidence in banks and the market economy.

The Panic of 1819 left deep scars. Debate on the national political stage over the proper role of government in the economic life of the country resumed with even greater intensity. The episode confirmed long-standing skepticism about the Bank of the United States. The absence of an organized political party handicapped the government in responding to the depression, although it did extend some relief to farmers by dropping the price of public land and delaying due dates for debt payments. A higher tariff in 1824 afforded manufacturers greater protection from foreign competition. But the Panic of 1819 did not diminish the national commitment to economic growth nor to the territorial expansion of the country.

1. What changes did the Market Revolution bring to the country?
2. How was the Market Revolution tied to the spirit of nationalism?

CHANGES IN THE WEST

Like European colonization two centuries before, the United States explored, exploited, and populated the Far West. Entrepreneurs ventured to the frontier to commercialize its resources. From outposts along the upper Missouri River, they competed with the British for control of the fur trade. Merchants, trappers, and settlers moved into Texas, New Mexico, and California, all of which broke free from suffocating Spanish mercantilism with Mexico's independence from Spain in 1821. Almost immediately, Mexico began to gravitate toward the United States. "Where others send invading armies," observed one Mexican official, "[the United States] send their colonists." Big changes were in store for Native Americans, as they too entered the United States' trade network and fought with immigrant Indians displaced from eastern regions. The environment also began to show wear-and-tear from the fur trade. Too remote to be attractive to farmers, the Far West offered opportunity to keen-eyed commercial capitalists.

The Fur Trade and the Transformation of the Western Environment

How did the fur trade function, and what effect did it have on the West?

Eastern clothing fashions initiated the transformation of the Far West. Tailors in America and Europe used the short, silky under-hair on beaver skins to trim elegant men's and women's garments. Hat-makers fabricated stylish men's headgear from beaver felt. Wealthy customers in cold climates prized buffalo hides for rugs, robes, and sleigh blankets. Supplying these lucrative markets had long been a thriving North American business, but declining animal populations in the east drew enterprising individuals into the Far West.

The booming fur trade along the upper Missouri River was a cutthroat business. Among the competing firms were the Missouri Fur Company, founded by Manuel Lisa in St. Louis, and John Jacob Astor's giant American Fur Company. Both firms constructed trading posts near Indian villages on the northern Great Plains, where they exchanged tools, weapons, blankets, trinkets, and whiskey (despite a government ban) for animal skins. Indians dealt shrewdly with the American traders, shopping for the highest-quality at the lowest price and often demanding finer European products. The fur trade thus reached from the Far West in North America to Paris and Amsterdam in Europe.

Upper Great Plains commerce relied on the bison and Indian hunters, who followed customary seasonal rhythms and utilized traditional bow-and-arrow weapons. Men hunted the animals, but the preparation of marketable hides was female work. Women dressed the skins by scraping the flesh and rubbing them with oil to make them supple. A woman could process twenty buffalo robes during a season. Demand for such heavy labor encouraged men to take multiple wives, and partly for that reason some Indian women found indulgent and monogamous white trappers more attractive as mates than Indian men.

The new improvements in transportation helped boost the fur trade. St. Louis-based merchant companies initially shipped trade goods and furs in keelboats and crude flat-bottomed *mackinaws*. But in 1832, the 120-foot long steamboat *Yellow Stone* completed its first voyage up the Missouri River to Fort Union near the North Dakota-Montana border, belching smoke from its twin chimneys and laden with valuable supplies (including whiskey) for Indians and mountain men. Steamboats hauled more cargo faster than floating craft, especially against swift currents. The up-river trip still required two months, one less than before, but they zipped down stream in a mere two weeks. From St. Louis, steamboats carried furs up the Ohio River where canal boats and sailing craft on the Great Lakes took the pelts on to New York.

The celebrated Rocky Mountain beaver trade was in the hands of smaller companies who traded with white "free trappers." Ownership frequently changed hands. After a few profitable seasons, William H. Ashley sold his assets to Jedediah Smith, David Jackson, and William Sublette, three other famous mountain men, who formed the Rocky Mountain Fur Company. The mobile, low-cost *rendezvous* gave these small firms an advantage over larger ones that maintained expensive trading posts. These smaller companies seem like a throwback to an earlier time when the economy was less-heavily capitalized and more free-wheeling. Legend, however, has romanticized the "free-trappers" who, in reality, were pawns in a vast market network. Merchants exploited them, selling supplies at exorbitant prices and acquiring their furs at bargain-basement prices. They were not as "free" as they thought they were.

Veteran trapper Joe Meek explained how Astor's heavily capitalized American Fur Company finally drove the Rocky Mountain Fur Company, and others like it, out of business. "They tampered with the trappers, ferreted out the secret of their next *rendezvous*; they followed on their trail, making them pilots to the trapping grounds; they sold goods to the Indians, and what was worse, to the hired trappers." Competition eventually raised overhead costs while the supply of pelts diminished and, as Meek noted, "finally ruined the fur-trade for the American companies in the Rocky Mountains."

The collapse of the Rocky Mountain fur trade came in the 1840s. "It was time for the white man to leave the mountains," reads trapper Osborne Russell's journal, "as Beaver and game had nearly disappeared." Brigades of the British Hudson's Bay Company cleaned the Snake River region of present-day Idaho out of beaver, leaving behind a "fur desert." Furthermore, the whims of fashion shifted again, from felt to silk, and the beaver market shut down. This was far from the end of western commerce, however. The upper Missouri fur trade prospered for another generation. The commerce in buffalo robes remained robust until the bison neared extinction in the 1870s.

The fur trade had a significant impact on the Far West. St. Louis thrived as the gateway to the Missouri, but during the 1830s new mercantile centers sprang up at Independence and St. Joseph. And Fort Laramie did a thriving business in Wyoming. Few mountain men got rich, but nine out of ten of them lived the remainder of their lives in the West. They helped to map the area and served as guides and Indian agents. The fur trade affected the ecology. Beaver populations declined sharply, although they rebounded after the pressure of intense beaver trapping eased. The incidental destruction of beaver dams caused erosion and disturbed salmon spawning in Pacific Northwest rivers. Steamboats consumed twenty full-grown oak trees every day for fuel, contributing to the despoliation of fragile river eco-systems. Trading posts also contributed to deforestation as their residents cut wood for winter burning. These effects foreshadowed future degradation of the western environment.

Viva Mexico!

The political turbulence that rocked Spain and its American empire during the Napoleonic era touched off revolution in New Spain (Mexico). Mexico had never flourished economically. Despite rich silver mines and agricultural estates (*haciendas*) near Mexico City, most of New Spain was a dry, barren country. Spain had always shown more interest in extracting taxes and silver from Mexico than promoting the public's welfare. Wealth remained concentrated in the hands of government bureaucrats, large landowners, and Catholic bishops, while the vast mixed-race (*mestizo*) and Indian populations remained wretched and hopeless. The archbishop in Mexico City, for example, received the modern equivalent of a $2 million each year while most of his parishioners languished in grinding poverty. Social status favored the privileged *peninsulares*, who were Spaniards born on Europe's Iberian Peninsula (Spain). Subservient to them were Spaniards born in Mexico and called *criollos*, or Creoles. At the bottom were *indios*, or native Mexican Indians. This social system produced resentment but little national pride and less unity.

> **Why did Mexico rebel against Spain, and what was the immediate result of Mexican independence?**

Independence began to percolate on September 16, 1810, when Padre Miguel Hidalgo y Costilla, a humble parish priest, called for independence on behalf of the oppressed *indios*. This coincided with a Creole landowners' conspiracy to seize power from the Spanish-born elite *peninsulares*. But *indios* and *criollos* had conflicting goals. Hidalgo demanded land for the *indios*, which directly threatened *criollo* wealth. The two joined forces nevertheless. Spanish authorities trapped Padre Hidalgo near Monclova in 1811 as he rode toward the United States hoping to obtain assistance, and stood him before a firing squad. More executions and bloody reprisals created widespread chaos, and finally in February 1821, General Agustín de Iturbide toppled the Spanish government. A tricolor flag, symbolizing independence, the Catholic Church, and popular equality, now flew over Mexico. The country's name revived ancient Aztec (Mexica) glory, but Iturbide sensed trouble ahead in forging national unity. "Mexicans," he warned citizens, "now you have liberty and independence. It is for you to find happiness."

Unfortunately, no basic ideals united Mexican social

Father Miguel Hidalgo y Costilla. Because of his role in precipitating revolution against Spanish rule, Hidalgo is considered the "Father of Mexico."

groups the way republicanism had allied American patriots. And the pretentious Iturbide lacked the aura of George Washington. Conservatives demanded a monarchy, to which Iturbide easily acceded, but he could not harness powerful revolutionary forces. Stephen F. Austin, an American doing business in Mexico, sized up the political situation. "The political character of this country seems to partake of its geological features—all is volcanic." Swarms of peasant brigades forced Iturbide into exile, and authorities later executed him by firing squad when he tried to return. In 1824, an elected congress promulgated a liberal constitution, providing considerable autonomy for Mexican states, a two-house representative congress, and an independent judiciary. The new government functioned much the same as the United States under its own decentralized Articles of Confederation. Although it recognized only the Catholic Church, the constitution otherwise erased class and racial distinctions. For the first time, all Mexicans were citizens.

Without experience with republican government, Mexican citizens struggled to govern themselves. One attempt after another to establish an effective government— liberal followed by conservative— ended in forcible takeover. New national symbols and rituals like independence-day celebrations failed to inspire widespread patriotism. Instead of sculpting

a national identity, Mexican politics reinforced traditions of bitter factionalism among the states that passionately guarded their sovereignty.

Nationalism on the Mexican Frontier

In some respects, independence affected the northern borderlands less than Mexico itself. Distance hindered the formation of a Mexican nationality despite the efforts of many provincial leaders to promote it. Officials conducted elaborate ceremonies for pledging allegiance to the new government. A Catholic priest in Taos compared Padre Miguel Hidalgo to Jesus Christ. And the few local newspapers and schools generated awareness of national affairs.

Texas, the province closest to Mexico City, suffered acutely during the struggle for independence. Small, aggressive armed forces from the United States invaded Texas from time to time, adding to the disorder. Royalists retaliated fiercely, shooting 327 alleged insurgents in San Antonio and wreaking havoc in Nacogdoches. Many terrified residents fled to Louisiana, leaving the already under-populated province nearly deserted.

In the spring of 1821, news of independence reached the plazas of San Antonio, the largest Hispanic settlement in Texas and the provincial capital. San

How did Mexico's independence from Spain affect conditions in its northern territories?

Antonio's flat-roofed adobe and stick houses sheltered nearly 1,500 local residents, called *Tejanos*. Independence did not excite the Spanish-born governor, Antonio Martinez, however; he along with townspeople and church leaders dutifully swore allegiance to Mexico but did not celebrate. Since Texas possessed limited resources and was sparsely populated, Mexican authorities incorporated it into the neighboring state jointly named *Coahuila y Tejas*, much to the chagrin of *Tejanos*.

Mexican officials struggled with what to do with its other northern frontier provinces. New Mexico, Arizona, and California were poor. Approximately 30,000 ranchers and small farmers lived in squalid settlements scattered along the upper Rio Grande River, 2,500 in southern Arizona, and 3,200 in California. They were too weak to govern themselves but too far from Mexico City to be governed from the capital. The legal system showed the effects of this ambiguity. A new network of appeals courts eliminated the necessity of travel to Mexico City, but basic justice still depended on local magistrates who often possessed the barest knowledge of the law. New Mexico and California became dependent territories, while Arizona, not yet a separate political entity, remained part of Sonora. Town councils and provincial legislatures provided a measure of local government.

A significant change on the frontier came with the Mexican government's dismantling of the Catholic missions. The missions' purpose had been to introduce Christianity among Native Americans, but Mexican authorities declared that Indians and Hispanics alike should be members of regular parishes administered by regular priests and supported by local taxes. One important consequence of this change was the distribution of mission property to regular citizens. It mattered little in Texas and Arizona, where the missions were small and weak, and in New Mexico the missions had been located on Pueblo Indian land. But California missions were wealthy and powerful institutions, controlling Indian labor and provisioning the territorial government. Ranchers gained control of the extensive mission properties. The Indians, once exploited by the mission padres, now became hired workers on land that used to be theirs.

Following Mexican independence, the northern borderlands erupted in Indian warfare. Several factors brought this about. The peace agreements that Spanish authorities had cobbled together with gifts fell apart because the impoverished Mexican government could not afford presents. Comanches, Apaches, Utes, and Navajos raided farms and ranches to acquire horses, food, and other supplies. Intruding Americans disrupted Indian-Hispanic trade relations and sold firearms, ammunition, and whiskey to the Indians. As Mexican historian Carlos J. Sienna has written, "guides or pioneers of the so-called American West were spies in our territory and dealers in furs and arms—many of them were constant instigators of attacks on Mexican towns and villages." Mexico responded to Indian raids with savage attacks against the tribes, trading Spain's "velvet glove" Indian policy for an "iron fist." But that only continued the cycle of violence.

Anglo-American Colonization of the Borderlands

Why did Mexico allow commerce with the United States, and what were the consequences?

The biggest change in the borderlands resulted from economic penetration by the United States. Spain's ban on foreign merchants had never prevented bootleggers from slipping through porous perimeters, but now Mexico admitted American traders to vitalize border economies. In November of 1821, William Becknell, an Independence, Missouri, merchant, was shocked and delighted when Mexican officials allowed his freight wagons into Santa Fe unmolested. Thus encouraged, American merchants brought $15,000 in merchandise into Santa Fe the next year, and in 1826 imports quadrupled. By 1831, the son of a former French Louisiana official, Cerán St. Vrain, and two sons of a Louisiana Territory superior court judge, Charles and William Bent, dominated the Santa Fe trade through their firm Bent, St. Vrain and Company. Trade links also opened between Texas and New Orleans.

The Santa Fe trade richly rewarded customers as well as merchants. *Nuevomexicanos* obtained cheap, high-quality cotton and silk cloth; iron cooking pots and pans; efficient, durable tools; and window glass for their adobe homes. When the province ran out of cash, the Anglo (United States) merchants pushed their wagon trains into northern Mexico. By the early 1830s, they were hauling back to the United States annually $200,000 (roughly $4.8 million today) in Mexican silver. In fact, so much Mexican cash circulated in the western United States that the *peso* became a common currency. Hispanic merchants sniffed the profits, and taking advantage of community and kinship networks they soon entered business as married family members, controlling almost half of New Mexico's exports by the end of the 1830s. Anglos helped their Hispanic counterparts with markets in the United States, and Hispanics guided foreigners through local regulations. Anglos often married local women, which also greased entrepreneurial skids.

Anglos carried the Market Revolution into the borderlands. Jedediah Smith observed "that restless enterprise that . . . is now leading our countrymen to all parts of the world." New England shipping interests built docks and set up shops along the coast of California. They traded for sea otter and cowhides, which their schooners carried to China and the United States. During the 1820s and 1830s, American merchants acquired 6 million hides and 7,000 tons of tallow for candles. This produced a bonanza for California *rancheros*, whose lavish lifestyle became the envy of American visitors. Merchants also transported lumber to Hawaii and Tahiti, cotton from Texas to New Orleans, and wine from California to the East Coast. The Franciscan missionaries had originally planted the vineyards, and fancy Bostonians now enjoyed tasty California wines. Books like Richard Henry Dana's *Two Years Before the Mast* and later Josiah Gregg's *Commerce of the Prairies* beaconed a wave of Anglo-American settlers seeking to share in the idyllic life of the *rancheros* in these remote northern Mexican states.

Many Mexicans became alarmed as the frontier economies fell increasingly under United States control. A *Californio*, Juan Bautista Alvarado, reported: "All the ships that were trade carriers were foreign. The greater part of the capital in the territory was in the hands of foreigners." Foreign businessmen siphoned the profits from the frontier economy. American trappers took over the fur trade, plying the mountain streams and routinely wintering in Taos and Santa Fe. Their incessant pursuit of beaver took them all the way to California. Jedediah Smith, Richard Campbell, and James Ohio Pattie all blazed trails to California, an accomplishment that had eluded generations of Spanish explorers. Local artisans could not compete successfully against American merchandise or against American craftsmen (tailors, carpenters, blacksmiths, and shoemakers). Mexicans had never had the opportunity to develop their skills, but Americans unfairly chalked up their backwardness to laziness and stupidity. Some *Tejanos* like Juan Martín de Veramendi were

successful merchants, but their trade routes pointed directly to the United States, and they lacked access to American capital.

John Quincy Adams' "laws of political and physical gravitation" caused attachments in the borderlands to swing from Mexico and toward the United States. Lucas Alaman, the Mexican interior minister, explained that instead of sending conquering armies, the United States established hegemony through trade. "Then they demand rights that would be impossible to sustain in any serious discussion, and . . . little by little these extravagant ideas . . . become sound proofs of ownership." Mexico City attempted to tighten its grip, but it lacked decisiveness; moreover, the few customs officials were poorly paid and easily bribed. Thus, the provincial economies continued to expanded under irresistible influences from the north, and while Mexico's economy continued to stagnate, the inhabitants of Texas, New Mexico, and California grew more prosperous and acted little concerned about the consequences.

THINKING BACK

1. What economic, social, and environmental changes did the Market Revolution bring to the Far West?
2. In what ways did nationalism overtake New Spain, both in terms of Mexican nationalism and American nationalism?

THE LOCAL PERSPECTIVE: FOCUS ON NORTH DAKOTA

| What drew Europeans to (North Dakota? |

In the region of the Great Plains that is now North Dakota, temperature extremes are daunting. The greatest recorded yearly temperature extremes range from 121 F to minus 60 F. This United States borderland was never a pot of gold at the end of a rainbow; nevertheless, North Dakota attracted its share of fortune-seekers during the Market Revolution.

Even Native Americans had shunned North Dakota for centuries. Mandan Indians had lived there longer than anyone, occupying wood and earthen lodges along the western bank of the Missouri River in central North Dakota. Cree, Assiniboine, and Chippewa men, women, and children hunted game and harvested berries in the flat valley of the Red River, which flows northward along the eastern boundary into Lake Winnipeg in the Canadian province of Manitoba. Various bands of Lakota Sioux, the largest group of early North Dakota residents, moved out of the Great Lakes woodlands onto the plains only a few years before the first Europeans came down from Canada.

Those adventurous Europeans were French explorers. In 1738 they crossed Dakota, the first white men to do so. French traders hawked merchandise to Indians in exchange for furs, taking native women as wives to make commerce easier and fathering mixed-race (*metís*) children. The *metís*, like *mestizos* in the Southwest, shaped the culture and economy of this northern borderland. Their Creole French-Cree language, colorful calico shirts and blouses, dashing waist sashes, beads, and feathers, and traditional bark houses reveal their mixed cultural heritage.

England's victory in the Seven Years' War (1756–1763) altered the course of North Dakota's history. The British Hudson's Bay Company and its Canadian rival, the North West Company, took over the fur trade. North Dakota fur-bearers included beaver, otter, and fox, but the real attraction was bison. By 1801 both companies maintained trading posts with transient residents at Pembina, in the extreme northeast corner of the region. Pembina became the trail-food capital of the world, producing Indian pemmican—a pounded mixture of dried buffalo meat, buffalo fat, and cranberries—for Indians, trappers, and explorers.

Early in the nineteenth century, the Earl of Selkirk, a Scottish nobleman, established the first European colony in the Red River Valley as a home for landless Scots highlanders. The Hudson's Bay Company sold him 116,000 square miles of territory called Assiniboia, five times the size of Scotland, in present-day Manitoba and northeastern North Dakota. In promotional literature, Selkirk painted an unrealistically rosy picture of the area. A few hundred souls took the bait. In 1812, the first contingent of settlers arrived and, despite their bewilderment at what they saw and the tremendous hardships they endured, founded present-day Winnipeg. In 1813, a party led by Captain Miles Macdonnell moved seventy miles up the Red River to Pembina, where they established an outpost settlement.

In 1818 the nationality and economic importance of Assiniboia changed; Britain and the United States agreed on a United States-Canadian boundary at the 49th parallel (see map on p. 277). The intensely competitive fur trade made the northern plains valuable to both countries. The United States constructed Fort Snelling, on the Mississippi River in today's Minnesota, to protect its territory.

In compliance with the boundary agreement, the Hudson's Bay Company evacuated United States territory; however, a number of *metís* remained, happy to become United States citizens. They conducted annual bison hunts and offered valuable robes for trade. John Jacob Astor's American Fur Company was eager to draw this traffic southward and opened a trading post at Pembina in 1844. But the closest market was St. Louis, and there were no roads to the Mississippi River. Alexander Henry, a Pembina resident, had previously designed an ox-drawn cart with solid wooden wheels that could be removed and mounted under the body for floatation in crossing streams. Soon, these carts had opened a profitable commercial link from the Red River Valley to St. Paul, Minnesota.

Slowly but surely, North Dakota entered the commercial orbit of the United States and joined in the Market Revolution. Steamboat traffic on the upper Missouri to Fort Union steadily expanded, and the number of trading outposts multiplied. In the east by the early 1850s, approximately 2,500 carts, driven by the colorful *metís*, traveled the St. Paul road, bringing $100,000 in profit. They returned with tea, carpets, tobacco, medicine, and mail for the residents of the borderland. North Dakota, the "American Siberia," entered the Union as a state in 1889.

THINKING BACK

1. Who were the *metís*?
2. How and when did North Dakota enter the United States' commercial orbit?

CONCLUSION

The War of 1812 marks the arrival of a new stage in the evolution of the United States as a democratic nation. The war inspired a generation of Americans with deep feelings of national pride, a sense of nationhood that revealed itself in many ways. Self-consciously, Americans celebrated their collective achievements and sought common ground for a national consensus. The leaders of the country were still among the wealthiest citizens. The Era of Good Feelings was less harmonious than National

Republicans wanted to think, and conflicts over colonization of African Americans, the power of the South and its slaveholders, and the federal government's expanding role in economic life broke the mood of harmony and conciliation. Yet, as Americans pushed their political boundaries toward natural continental limits, moved about the country with unprecedented ease, and contributed their energies to an emerging national market, they were becoming more Americanized than they had ever been.

SUGGESTED SOURCES FOR STUDENTS

For a close look at community-building in the early Midwest read John Mack Faragher, *Sugar Creek: Life on the Illinois Prairie* (1986).

For fascinating description everyday life during the period see Jack Larkin, *The Shaping of Everyday Life, 1790-1840* (1988).

John Lauritz Larson, *The Market Revolution in America: Liberty, Ambition, and the Eclipse of the Common Good* (2009), presents a penetrating but readable account of the Market Revolution's impact, much of which was beyond the vision of those who benefited most.

Kirkpatrick Sale presents a fresh and provocative look at the development of steamboat transportation in *The Fire of His Genius: Robert Fulton and the American Dream* (New York, 2001).

To avoid coming away from a study of this exuberant time with too rosy a view, read Scott Sandage, *Born Losers: A History of Failure in America* (Cambridge, 2005).

Charles Sellers, *The Market Revolution: Jacksonian America, 1815-1846* (1991), has done more than any other work to clarify the transformation of the national economy from subsistence to commercial motivation. Brilliant and sweeping in scope, it places post War of 1812 America into this economic context.

Ronald Shaw surveys canal building across the country in *Canals for a Nation: The Canal Era in the United States, 1790-1860* (1990).

Andres Tijerina expertly examines Hispanic culture and communities in Mexican Texas in *Tejanos and Texas Under the Mexican Flag, 1821-1836* (1994).

A description and analysis of Fourth of July celebrations can be found in Len Travers, *Celebrating the Fourth: Independence Day and the Rise of Nationalism in the Early Republic* (1997).

Robert M. Utley, *A Life Wild and Perilous: Mountain Men and the Paths to the Pacific* (New York, 1997), studies the short but dramatic period of the Far West fur trade as conducted by mountain men such as Jedediah Smith.

To understand the effort involved in literally digging canals, see Peter Way, *Common Labour: Workers and the Digging of North American Canals, 1780-1860* (Cambridge, 1993).

There is no better way to grasp the important transition from patrician to democratic republicanism than reading Sean Wilenz's magisterial *The Rise of American Democracy: Jefferson to Lincoln* (New York, 2005).

BEFORE WE GO ON

1. What did being an American mean **to** people living in the United States after the War of 1812? What did it mean **for** those living along its boundaries?

2. Some historians have called the War of 1812 a second struggle for independence. Were Americans really more independent than they had been before? If so how, and if not why not?

Building a Democratic Nation

3. In what concrete ways did the United States develop more unified political and economic systems after the War of 1812?

4. Early in the nineteenth century, how did global events shape the development of the United States, and how did American nationalism impact other countries?

Connections

5. Did the United States become more or less democratic as a result of growing nationalism? Explain.

6. Two big issues in today's public discourse involve (1) the role of government in solving problems and maintaining a fair and prosperous economy and (2) the importance of religious faith. How were those basic issues framed and resolved in the early nineteenth century?

Chapter 10

FORGING A MORE DEMOCRATIC SOCIETY, 1820–1840

A PERSONAL PERSPECTIVE: FOCUS ON MARGARET EATON AND THE "PETTICOAT AFFAIR"

Photograph of Margaret "Peggy" O'Neal Timberlake Eaton. She was at the center of a controversy in Washington society that precipitated a crisis in President Andrew Jackson's Cabinet.

In February of 1829, Senator John Henry Eaton and his recent bride Margaret paid a social call on John and Floride Calhoun in Washington. Both men figured prominently in the approaching Andrew Jackson administration, and so did their wives. John Calhoun was not at home, but Floride, a polished South Carolina aristocrat, courteously entertained her guests. What happened next, however, known as the "petticoat affair," was anything but cordial. Floride Calhoun and other Washington society matrons considered Margaret Eaton coarse and immoral, and they shunned her. This infuriated Jackson, whose beloved wife Rachel had suffered public humiliation during the recent presidential election campaign. Embedded in the controversy were issues of democracy that deeply divided the young nation.

Andrew Jackson and John Eaton symbolized the rising tide of American democracy. Citizens living west of the Appalachian Mountains demanded a voice in national affairs commensurate with their rapidly-increasing numbers. They resented the inordinate and entrenched power of eastern aristocrats who regarded them as unsophisticated, combustible, and unfit to run the country. Jackson, from Tennessee, was the first president elected from beyond the Appalachians. Eaton, also from Tennessee, had served under Jackson during the War of 1812. The two had become fast friends, and Jackson was fiercely loyal. He appointed Eaton to head the War Department. Conversely, Jackson despised men who betrayed him, and he remembered that after his invasion of Florida Calhoun had urged President Monroe to reprimand him. Calhoun had supported Jackson in the 1828 presidential campaign and had just been elected vice president on the Democratic party ticket, but Jackson still held a grudge.

Margaret Eaton was another type of democrat who demanded personal freedom and flouted social convention with brazen, unladylike behavior. Her Irish father had operated a popular Washington hotel and tavern patronized by numerous political notables. Nicknamed "Peggy," her vivacious personality, keen intelligence, and honey-like beauty attracted male patrons with whom she enjoyed carousing. "I was always a pet," she said of herself. No mere barmaid, she was not a respectable young woman either, for respectable women did not frequent saloons. Peggy O'Neal married Navy officer John B. Timberlake, purser on the renowned USS Constitution, and the couple lived in her father's hotel where, as a member of Congress, John Eaton boarded. The three became good friends. Eventually Timberlake returned to duty at sea and during his long absences Margaret worked in the tavern. Murmurs of disapproval turned into malicious gossip. She slept around, people said, including with Eaton. Rumors alleged a miscarriage. In April of 1828, John Timberlake died at sea, apparently cutting his throat, and immediately gossips said it was due to Margaret's infidelity. Within a year she and Eaton married.

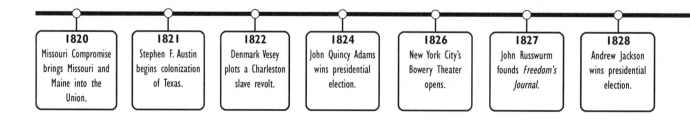

1820	1821	1822	1824	1826	1827	1828
Missouri Compromise brings Missouri and Maine into the Union.	Stephen F. Austin begins colonization of Texas.	Denmark Vesey plots a Charleston slave revolt.	John Quincy Adams wins presidential election.	New York City's Bowery Theater opens.	John Russwurm founds *Freedom's Journal*.	Andrew Jackson wins presidential election.

This was why Floride Calhoun refused to return the Eatons' visit. Personally disinterested in the affair, John acquiesced in his wife's position "though I foresaw the difficulties in which it would probably involve me." The "petticoat affair" furthered the alienation of the president and vice president that culminated in a national crisis. It also divided Jackson's administration, for most members of the President's cabinet joined the social boycott of the Eatons, as did Jackson's nephew Andrew Jackson Donelson, the President's personal secretary, and his wife Emily, whom Jackson adored and who served as official White House hostess. Jackson's main ally was Martin Van Buren, a widower and a Washington outsider. Washington's society women could not punish Eaton directly because they had little power in the male domain of politics. They persuaded their husbands to demand Eaton's resignation, but Jackson would have none of that. He steadfastly supported both John and Margaret.

The "petticoat affair" foreshadowed several key issues in Jacksonian America. Free-spirited Margaret flaunted conventional social mores at a time when conservative Americans could see aristocratic republican order dissolving into democratic chaos. Jackson too possessed a paternalistic passion for order, which made him protective of Margaret, the interests of the vast majority of Americans he believed he represented as president, and the Union he swore to uphold. But his need for control also led him to uproot Indians, veto more congressional bills than his predecessors combined, and rein in big government. Jackson also represented changing norms. His behavior during the controversy typified rough frontier ways. His legendary stubbornness in the face of contradictory facts—insisting that Margaret was "chaste as a virgin"—was both a strength and a weakness in political leadership. In his turbulent political career, Andrew Jackson won more battles than he lost, over bureaucrats with a sense of entitlement, the Supreme Court, nullifiers and secessionists, and the Bank of the United States. He dominated his opponents by uncommon shrewdness and monumental will power, and even the most critical historians admit that he helped revolutionize the political

life of the nation. But against the society ladies of Washington, Old Hickory was overmatched.

THINKING BACK

1. What does the Margaret Eaton story reveal about democracy in the United States?
2. How did the Eaton controversy affect the Jackson administration?

NEW DEMOCRATIC VALUES

In the wake of the Eaton hullabaloo, a keen-eyed French aristocrat named Alexis de Tocqueville visited the United States to study democracy, more advanced in America than anywhere in Europe. Did it have a future? he wondered. In his classic book *Democracy in America*, Tocqueville took note of an unusually large **middle class** with "**bourgeois**," get-ahead values. This was perhaps the first "me" generation, aggressively pursuing wealth, behaving in new-fashioned ways, and stamping their imprint on literature, music, and other forms of entertainment. Overhauled political systems amplified the voice of ordinary citizens. The democracy that Tocqueville beheld did not eradicate social distinctions or equalize wealth, but it did change the expectations of ordinary people and increased social and economic mobility. The stifling effect of middle-class conformity—remember Margaret Eaton—concerned Tocqueville. Democracy's light shined brilliantly, but the Frenchman wondered if it would burn itself out.

The Middle Class: Wealth and Respectability

Colonial Americans had recognized two economic classes: the rich and everyone else. The Market Revolution, however, produced a substantial middle class, located primarily in northern towns and cities. Always there had been a few extraordinarily successful urban artisans and professionals whose modest livings fell short of upper-class status; however, the new middle class encompassed a sizable segment of

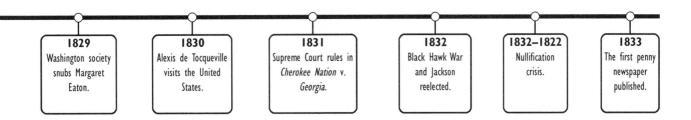

1829	**1830**	**1831**	**1832**	**1832–1822**	**1833**
Washington society snubs Margaret Eaton.	Alexis de Tocqueville visits the United States.	Supreme Court rules in *Cherokee Nation* v. *Georgia*.	Black Hawk War and Jackson reelected.	Nullification crisis.	The first penny newspaper published.

the populace united by their business occupations and materialistic ("bourgeois") values.

White-collar (non-manual) entrepreneurs—proprietors, salesmen, brokers, and even clerks—dominated the middle class. Many had once been artisans. Cyrus Alger of Boston, for instance, still called himself an iron founder after becoming the proprietor of a large Boston manufacturing firm. Ambition energized men like Alger and young Charles Grinnell, who rode miles on horseback through Virginia and Maryland every day representing the mercantile firm of Tiffany, Fite, & Company of Baltimore. Grinnell hoped to become a partner, and he must have been gratified the day the company's new letterhead read: Tiffany, Fite, and Grinnell.

> Who comprised the "middle class," what influence did it exert on public attitudes, and how did it foster a more democratic economy?

The middle class held novel ideas about progress that changed the thinking of many Americans. Striving to get ahead seemed natural and legitimate. After the disastrous Panic of 1819, optimism spread over the country. Burgeoning global markets, the transportation boom, and unplowed western land generated enormous excitement. An Episcopal priest, Calvin Colton, oozed middle-class expectancy. "Ours is a country where men start from . . . humble origin[s], and from small beginnings rise gradually in the world, as the reward of merit and industry." This bourgeois ethic contrasted sharply with feudal Calvinism, when common people worked for their masters and accepted their condition as ordained by God.

If this seems like crass materialism, note that middle-class status also required modesty, tastefulness, and piety, qualities that were not in Margaret Eaton's nature. Many in the middle class had begun humbly, without lessons in good manners; however, book shops sold them etiquette manuals, and peer pressure and role models also taught them how to behave. Dressing well, holding one's body stiff and erect, and speaking correct English helped earn respectability. The middle class surrounded itself with the trappings of refinement. Formal living rooms (called parlors), china tea sets, and upholstered furniture imitated the decor of the upper class, who remained the arbiters of good taste. Gradually, middle-class neighborhoods appeared in cities. But above all, middle class status required moral rectitude—a quality that Margaret Eaton defied.

The Market Revolution created opportunities for improvement but not an egalitarian economy. Traffic on the economic ladder moved both ways. Climbers often slipped and tumbled, with few protections to soften their landing. Prosperity depended on bankers, whose judgment often proved faulty and whose hearts could be stone cold. In the Panic of 1819, mortgaged properties fell wholesale into receivership, wiping out countless hard-working farmers, artisans, and entrepreneurs. The gulf between rich and poor grew wider not narrower. From 1774 to 1860, the share of the nation's wealth in the hands of the richest tenth jumped from 50 percent to 73 percent, most of it after 1820. Reverend Colton declared that "this is a country of *self-made men*," yet nine out of ten of the wealthiest citizens of New York, Philadelphia, and Boston came from rich families whereas only two of every hundred rose from the bottom. The economy remained in elite hands, a point of considerable debate in an increasingly democratic nation.

The Cult of Democracy

Along with economic liberalization, the 1820s and 1830s produced a cult of democracy whose longevity would have amazed Tocqueville. The eighteenth-century elite had been able to afford luxury and thought they deserved it, but distinctions that implied innate superiority clashed with nineteenth-century American ideas about democracy. As common people gained power, they buried the artifacts of aristocracy, including first-class accommodations. In the 1830s, even in the finest restaurants, customers seated themselves around common tables and took their food from common bowls and platters.

Rustic, democratic manners did not always impress foreign tourists. The acerbic British writer Frances Trollope scolded Americans in her book *Domestic*

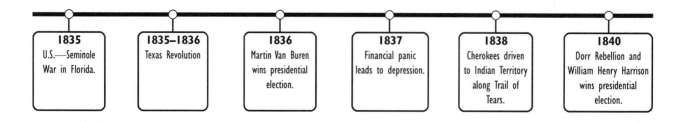

1835	1835–1836	1836	1837	1838	1840
U.S.—Seminole War in Florida.	Texas Revolution	Martin Van Buren wins presidential election.	Financial panic leads to depression.	Cherokees driven to Indian Territory along Trail of Tears.	Dorr Rebellion and William Henry Harrison wins presidential election.

This cooper (barrel maker) represented the ideal "Common Man" of the period. Clearly self-confident, he nevertheless occupied a lower rung rather than a higher one on the economic ladder.

<table>
</table>

| How did the democratic spirit reveal itself culturally? |

Manners of the Americans. The egalitarian American handshake had little charm, she complained, "when it presents itself in the shape of a hard, greasy paw, and is claimed in accents that breathe less of freedom than of onions and whiskey." Her famous son Anthony especially disliked the way American women behaved. "The men are dirty and civil," he said, but "the women are dirty and uncivil." Visitors were shocked at the lack of deference that servants showed to their employers. Americans attached less stigma to domestic service than Europeans did, but domestic workers objected to the use of the word "servant."

Democratic reformers pushed for more access to professions and businesses through fewer restrictive licenses and charters. In the 1830s, a medical practitioner named Samuel Thompson, who employed timeless Indian cures, argued that "people are certainly capable of judging for themselves" what was the best treatment for them. Sylvester Graham (the Graham cracker man) failed to win the endorsement of trained physicians for his progressive ideas about "holistic" medicine, but he did spawn a popular health movement. Lawyers came under attack too for deliberately keeping the law incomprehensible to ordinary citizens. Likewise, many religious people pleaded for the right to preach without a license. Of special concern to aspiring entrepreneurs were exclusive corporate charters granted to big shots with political connections. Democrats constantly harped on chartered bank and transportation "monopolies."

People devised various definitions of democracy, especially as it related to government. Some believed that less government created more democracy. On the one hand, **bourgeois democracy** meant the absence of government restraint. This was not synonymous with strict **laissez-faire**, however, as many business people were very comfortable with government assistance in the form of protective tariffs, monopoly charters, and public financing. Anti-business democrats, on the other hand, favored using the power of government to wipe out special privileges and favoritism. But all invoked the ideal of democracy to justify their particular interest.

Nature and Romanticism

The cult of democracy rooted itself in the land, although American attitudes about nature varied widely. Farm property had long been equated with independence. The forest clearing with a corn crop symbolized the American spirit. Trudging through the backcountry, Tocqueville felt overwhelmed by endless forest and was relieved when he heard the sound of an ax and caught sight of a settler's clearing. But others derived inspiration from undisturbed wilderness. Partly because eastern forests were receding at a disturbing pace and partly because the Enlightenment had spawned a deep appreciation of nature, many thoughtful citizens began to reconsider what the forest meant.

Whereas settlers often sensed evil and chaos in untamed nature, many philosophers and artists perceived divine order. Idyllic visions came easily with the Indians gone; furthermore, the intellectuals were usually city dwellers who did not have to contend with the forest's harshness. Since the eighteenth century, European writers had contemplated nature fondly. They originated an intellectual movement called **Romanticism**. The German philosopher Immanuel Kant signaled the new Romantic genre by denying that reason was the key to wisdom, stressing instead the human senses as the pathways to truth. Nature stimulated those senses. Crowded Europeans could only imagine untamed nature, since their countryside was largely settled, but in the United States it was real. Nature shaped American identity the way antiquities buttressed European nationalism. "There is nothing old in America," a French visitor observed, oblivious to millennia of Native-American

> **What was Romanticism, and how did it affect the way many Americans looked at their environment?**

Courtesy of Library of Congress

"*Farmers Nooning*," *painting by William Sidney Mount. America's first "genre" painter, Mount depicted scenes of everyday life, often using youth as a symbol for America.*

history, but the mountains and forests "are certainly the equivalent for monuments and ancestors."

Early American Romantic writers drew upon nature and regional cultures as they developed concepts of American nationality. Washington Irving, son of a New York City cutlery merchant, wrote stories about New York's Hudson River Valley, the Rocky Mountains, and the Pacific Northwest. His tale of Rip Van Winkle, from his acclaimed *The Sketch Book* (1820), was the first American short story. Irving was also the first professional American writer. James Fenimore Cooper decried the ecological impact of economic expansion. Natty Bumppo, the hero of his Leatherstocking novels (1823–1841), lived in harmony with nature, and his loyal companion Chingachgook, the "last of the Mohicans," represented the "noble savage" being destroyed by civilization. Lawyer-poet-journalist William Cullen Bryant composed many popular verses and edited the ideologically democratic New York *Evening Post*. He and other early Romantics affirmed the positive image that Americans had of themselves.

Just as writers conveyed Romantic ideas through words, painters brushed them onto canvas using form and color. Taught now in American art schools, they no longer depended on European training. Nature elicited conflicting images from them (wilderness forest *versus* pastoral landscape); however, most artists depicted a beneficent nature submitting to honorable human endeavor. Thomas Cole painted the awe-inspiring Northeastern countryside, showing few signs of bloody white-Indian conflict. John James Audubon, however, a self-trained ornithologist and a skilled field naturalist, reveled in the violence of nature. His breathtaking *Birds of North America* (1840–1844) remains the greatest work on American natural history. Another artist, Long Islander William Sidney Mount, portrayed everyday farm life, while George Caleb Bingham's pictures of Missouri featured solitary hunters (European and Native American), freedom-loving settlers, and democratic citizens. Bingham was the first significant Midwestern painter.

While Westerners battled to civilize wilderness, eastern urbanites visited natural places for recreation and meditation. Among those places were new rural cemeteries. Many traditional churchyard burial grounds were now surrounded by noisy, sprawling cities. Boston's Mount Auburn Cemetery, opened in 1831, was the country's first urban burial ground located on the outskirts of town. It offered visitors rural serenity. Affluent Americans vacationed in more distant scenic spots, like the Catskill Mountains of New York. But the biggest attraction of all was Niagara Falls. The Erie Canal gave travelers access to a wonder that until recently had been too remote and dangerous to enjoy. By the 1830s, carriage service from Buffalo, comfortable hotels, and viewing trails accommodated swarming tourists. Many viewed Niagara Falls as one of God's most awesome creations. To young Harriet Beecher, it was "like the Mind that made it." Niagara Falls soon became a popular honeymoon spot. Thus, in a variety of ways Americans used nature to redefine themselves culturally and to express fundamental values.

Producing and Selling Mass Culture

As plain people became more prominent in American life, purveyors of culture catered more to their tastes. Publishers utilized automated, steam-powered printing presses, cloth bookbinding (as opposed to more expensive leather), and faster paper manufacturing to mass-produce books, magazines, and newspapers. The Transportation Revolution and urban growth introduced economies of scale. Publishers produced five times as many novels in the 1820s as the previous decade, indicating an expanded readership. Editors employed large print and illustrations to appeal to less sophisticated readers. And the subject matter in popular literature revealed the changing face of American culture.

> **How did plain people influence American culture?**

Middle-class women read avidly (supposedly men were too busy at work). They especially enjoyed sentimental love stories and advice books by female authors. The best-known and most prolific woman writer was Lydia H. Sigourney, called "the sweet singer of Hartford" for her fifty-seven books and more than 2,000 poems. Lydia Maria Child circulated among eminent literary figures and wrote novels and biographies that emphasized women's moral leadership. Catharine Sedgwick sought to bring bourgeois refinement to the rising masses through novels of manners. Much of this popular women's literature appeared in magazines like *Godey's Lady's Book* and *Graham's Magazine*, both lavishly illustrated.

Regional folklore, laced with rough humor, appealed to male audiences. One of the era's most popular characters was Jack Downing, the creation of Portland, Maine, journalist Seba Smith. Downing was a country bumpkin with a piercing sense of humor whose specialty was parodying politicians. Outrageous folk tales emanated from the West. Davy Crockett became a national celebrity as a bear-killing Tennessee frontiersman and congressman. The ghost-written *Life of David*

Crockett of the State of Tennessee, Written by Himself (1834) went through seven printings in the first year and brimmed with folksy wisdom. Other masculine heroes whose daring-do appealed to popular tastes included riverboat man Mike Fink, "half horse, half alligator," and the muscle-bound African-American laborer John Henry.

Journalism changed significantly in 1833 when Benjamin Day began publishing the New York *Sun*, the first penny newspaper. Day intended "to lay before the public, at a price within the means of every one, ALL THE NEWS OF THE DAY, and at the same time afford an advantageous medium for advertising." In 1835 James Gordon Bennett followed with the New York *Herald*, from which he built a newspaper empire. Utilizing printing presses with continuous paper feeding mechanisms, Bennett pushed circulation into the tens of thousands. These early newspaper entrepreneurs attracted unsophisticated readers with sex scandals, lurid crimes, and natural monstrosities like two-headed babies. Another important breakthrough in mass journalism came when John Russwurm, the first African-American college graduate (Bowdoin College), founded *Freedom's Journal* in 1827.

Popular culture embraced the theater too. In fact, William Shakespeare's *Richard III* was the country's favorite play. Audiences also enjoyed Shakespearean parodies—*Julius Sneezer* and *Hamlet and Egglet*. Theater moguls erected large city theaters for equally popular song and dance shows. In 1826, New York's Bowery Theater opened its 4,000 seats to eager patrons in a neighborhood notorious for gangs of toughs, gambling, and prostitution. Audiences critiqued performances by applauding, booing, or tossing objects at the performers. Rowdiness turned tragic on the evening of May 7, 1849, outside of New York City's upscale Astor Place Theater, when devotees of the renowned American Shakespearean actor Edwin Forrest rioted against the English tragedian William Macready, both of whom were starring in separate presentations of *Macbeth*. Soldiers fired on the unruly crowd, killing at least 22 and wounding 150.

Theater often exploited prevailing ethnic and racial stereotypes. Dramatists idealized the disappearing Native American. John Augustus Stone's *Metamora*, based on the life of Metacomet (see King Philip's War in Chapter 4) debuted in 1829, starring Edwin Forrest—the country's first stage star. Comedy frequently ridiculed African Americans and rationalized racial oppression. Although African Americans occasionally appeared in stage roles, whites usually represented them in blackface. In 1828, Thomas Rice heard a black man sing: "Wheel about and turn about jus' so/Every time I wheel about, I jump Jim Crow." From that song, Rice developed a musical routine called "Jump Jim Crow" that became a hit in the United States and England. E. P. Christy and other showmen followed with popular touring minstrel shows that mimicked African Americans. Later, the term "Jim Crow" referred to racial segregation.

Common people enjoyed exciting, even brutal, entertainment. Cock-fighting, bear-baiting, and prize fighting drew large crowds eager to wager on the outcome. Circuses, peep shows, and other "attractions" regularly toured the country. Phineas T. Barnum, the son of a Connecticut farmer and tavern keeper, produced some of the era's most remarkable entertainments. Barnum got his start in show business when he discovered an African-American woman who claimed to have been George Washington's wet nurse. Taking her on tour, and demonstrating a great knack for publicity, Barnum became the prototype showman/promoter.

Democratizing the Political Game

Political institutions felt the brunt of democratic change. Most people still used the word "republican" to describe their political system, since "democracy" remained for many Americans as much of an epithet as when Martha Washington had blamed soiled wallpaper on some "filthy democrat." But for growing numbers, democracy resonated like the gospel.

Reformed voter requirements widened access to the franchise. Making taxpaying instead of property a qualification produced more voters from among the common people. New western states drafted constitutions with no property restrictions, and in the 1820s and 1830s many eastern states followed suit, fearing that their citizens would move to states that allowed them to vote. Many conservatives, however, resisted this "dangerous" innovation. Daniel Webster of Massachusetts insisted that "power naturally and necessarily follows property." In Rhode Island a democratic rebellion led by Thomas L. Dorr in 1840 forced the conservative legislature to expand the electorate. By 1840 the United States had achieved nearly universal, white, manhood suffrage.

Other liberalizing reforms further democratized the political process. Many appointed offices became elected; election districts diminished, making it easier

> **How did political systems change to reflect democratic values?**

for voters to reach the polling places; and secret ballots instead of voice voting lessened intimidation. The Electoral College itself remained unchanged; however, by the 1830s most states held public elections to choose electors. Only Delaware and South Carolina continued to choose electors by state legislatures. Presidential elections became the primary focus of political life, helping to promote a national identity.

Democratic-minded citizens sought to increase popular participation in nominating candidates for public office. The caucus system fell short of democratic standards; moreover, some parties did not have enough congressmen or legislators to hold them. Conventions provided an alternative. Several states pioneered the device, but the **Anti-Mason party** held the first national convention in 1831. The Order of Free Masons, with its mysterious rituals and secret handshakes, had become extremely popular among American businessmen. Masons used their fraternal connections for social, commercial, and political advantage, which struck non-Masons as unfair. The Anti-Mason party participated in the election of 1832, and their nominating convention helped stimulate public interest in it.

New tactics in political campaigning accompanied the other democratic reforms. Politicians motivated voters with rallies, barbecues, and torch light parades. Slogans, bombastic oratory, and personal attacks on an opponent's character (reviled today as "negative campaigning") worked too. Success in canvassing the vote, however, required great care, for the slightest hint of condescension could backfire. Not everyone approved of these electioneering innovations. One North Carolina newspaper editor lamented the "contemptible and degrading" campaigns in which "treating, fawning and courting" substituted for reasoned debate as in the old days. But they proved successful—from 1824 to 1828 voter turnout doubled—and politicians have used them effectively ever since.

More than anyone else at the time, Martin Van Buren helped political parties gain acceptance as democratic organizations. Van Buren, the son of a Kinderhook, New York, saloon-keeper, was a pragmatic political activist who understood how to mobilize popular will to overwhelm narrow special interests and bridge sectional divisions. The keys to party success, in Van Buren's view, were efficient grassroots organization, unswerving loyalty, a system of rewards, and effective electioneering. After the War of 1812, he organized a faction of New York democratic Republicans called **Bucktails** to challenge the entrenched power of Governor De Witt Clinton.

Bucktails combined a military style discipline with rewards of government jobs. As one Bucktail put it, "To the victors belong the spoils," and it was a powerful motivator. Bucktails captured the state government, which Van Buren controlled as governor through a cadre of lieutenants known as the **Albany Regency**. Aptly known as the Little Magician, the shrewd Van Buren revolutionized the party system.

THINKING BACK

1. How did popular democratic values influence social and cultural life?
2. What were the major democratic changes that took place in the realm of politics?

THE SECOND TWO-PARTY SYSTEM

By the late 1820s, the Era of Good Feelings had ended, and the intense post War of 1812 nationalism dissolved into sectional, ideological, and personal bickering. The triumphant Republican party needed lessons in managing success. Competing interests tore it apart. Pro-slavery and anti-slavery advocates vied for control of the western territories, and heated questions arose over certain aspects of the Market Revolution. After the Federalists' demise, Republicans succumbed to both apathy and arrogance. In 1816, for example, congressmen doubled their own pay, arousing public ire. Denouncing this example of corrupt extravagance, peevish voters turned two-thirds of the House and half the Senate out of office. Speaker of the House Henry Clay abjectly apologized, but John C. Calhoun sneered: "Well, then, has it come to this? Have the people of this country snatched the power of deliberation from this body?" Resentful people foresaw additional tax burdens foisted on them to advance the Market Revolution. Moreover, President James Monroe, who despised political parties, refused to groom his successor, inviting a mad scramble among presidential hopefuls.

Controversy Over Missouri

Disagreement over slavery contributed to the dissolution of the Republican party and the reordering partisan alignments. John Quincy Adams of Massachusetts and John C. Calhoun of South

> **Why was Missouri's request for statehood controversial, and how did congressional leaders resolve the issue?**

Carolina, both Republicans, stood together for national economic growth, but in the 1820s they parted over slavery. Their estrangement illustrated the Union's vulnerability to sectional divisiveness. Deepening Southern commitment to slavery coincided with simmering Northern resentment over slaveholders' inordinate power derived from the "three-fifths" rule (see p. 193). A controversy arising in 1819 over Missouri's request to enter the Union as a slave state ignited the first nineteenth-century slavery crisis.

Sixty thousand white settlers lived in Missouri, most of them from slave states, and they had dragged approximately 10,000 slaves with them to the territory. Heretofore, few voices had been raised against slavery in Missouri, but statehood would tip the balance between the eleven free and eleven slave states, carefully maintained since 1789, giving the slave states even more power. Moreover, Missouri's admission would open the way for slavery to expand into other parts of the Louisiana Purchase, further strengthening the slave states. Since they already had more votes in government than their white population warranted because of the Constitution's "three-fifths rule," the added power of two more senators and at least one congressman pushed Northerners too far.

To curb the expansion of Southern "slave power," New York Congressman James Tallmadge introduced two anti-slavery amendments to the Missouri statehood bill. One prohibited further slave imports and the other emancipated all slaves at age twenty-five. The House approved Tallmadge's measures in sectional voting, since free-state representatives outnumbered slave-state congressmen, but the slave states defeated them in the Senate. Congress adjourned for its autumn recess, giving representatives and senators additional time to think through their positions.

The public debate over Missouri grew to a climax. Protest meetings in the North hardened anti-slavery feelings while pro-slavery extremists in the South threatened disunion. Congressman Thomas W. Cobb of Georgia claimed that Tallmadge had "kindled a fire . . . which seas of blood can only extinguish." Representative John Tyler of Virginia spoke more moderately, suggesting that the diffusion of slaves into western territories might actually encourage emancipation, noting that slavery had ended in states where the number of slaves had been small. Efforts to organize the Arkansas Territory (Arkansas and Oklahoma) and prepare anti-slavery Maine for statehood provided the framework for a compromise

resolution of the dispute. Two pro-slavery congressmen, Senator Jesse B. Thomas of Illinois and Henry Clay, drafted a bill allowing Missouri to enter as a slave state, admitting Maine as a free state, and prohibiting slavery north of Arkansas (36° 30'). In 1820, enough Northerners and Southerners accepted this Missouri Compromise to pass it.

The Missouri controversy foreshadowed the sectional division that lay ahead. But the **Missouri Compromise**, also known as the **Compromise of 1820,** resolved the question of slavery in the territories for the next twenty-five years as Congress maintained the sectional balance. When Arkansas entered the Union as a slave state in 1837, Michigan followed as a free state the next year, reinforcing the balance and protracting the line between North and South. Slavery was indeed a weighty matter, but so was the Union (see map on p. 277). Political attention quickly shifted to the election to succeed President James Monroe.

The Election of 1824

Contenders for the presidency included three of Monroe's Cabinet officers. Georgian William H. Crawford identified with Old Republican aristocrats in his native Virginia. Crawford's highly organized campaign enjoyed the backing of Virginia planters and Martin Van Buren. The Republican caucus also favored Crawford, although only 66 of the 291 Republican congressmen participated in that now-discredited process. The other candidates sought state legislature endorsements. John C. Calhoun, a South Carolina cotton planter, touted nationalist economic policies. He failed to garner anti-slavery Northern support, however, and settled for the vice presidency. John Quincy Adams was an ardent nationalist, but in his own words "a man of reserved, cold, austere, and forbidding manners." He abhorred politicking; the people, he insisted, would choose him if they wanted him—which he desperately hoped they would.

> Who were the contenders in the 1824 presidential election, and how was the outcome determined?

Two western men chased the prize too. The gregarious Henry Clay, a gambling man and a hard drinker, counted on the support of commercial interests. Andrew Jackson, the "military chieftain" from Tennessee, was now a slave-owning bigwig recently elected to the Senate. Despite his charisma and shrewd political instincts, most political leaders discounted him. Jackson's stance on many issues was enigmatic, but he clearly distrusted banks and paper money. "Every one that knows me," he declared, "does know that I have been always opposed to the U. States Bank, nay all Banks."

In that crowded field, nobody could win the election outright. Jackson was the most popular nationally and gathered 99 electoral votes. Adams came in second with 84. Prior to the election, Crawford had suffered a crippling stroke that hurt his viability, but he still collected 41 votes. Clay trailed the field with 37. Jackson also led the popular balloting with 152,901 (42 percent of the total cast in the eighteen states that allowed popular voting) to 114,023 (32 percent) for Adams. Jackson carried the Old Southwest and Middle Atlantic areas. Adams won big in New England and along the trail of Yankee emigration from New York through the Upper Midwest. Clay captured Kentucky, Ohio, and Missouri, and Crawford showed strength only in Virginia and Georgia.

The Twelfth Amendment stipulates that if no candidate wins a majority of the electoral vote, the House of Representatives, voting by state, chooses from the top three. That eliminated Clay, but as Speaker of the House he could virtually pick the winner. Although he and Jackson had much in common, bad blood ran between them. Clay did not like Adams either, but he shared Adams' enthusiasm for national development. Moreover, Clay still hoped to be president, and it would be easier to succeed a Northerner than another Westerner. In the balloting on February 9, 1825, a stop-Jackson campaign delivered several Jackson states to Adams. Clay's support pushed Adams to within one state of a majority. It came down to New York's evenly divided delegation, and according to Van Buren, veteran Congressman Stephen Van Rensselaer, the last to make up his mind. The old man prayed for guidance, it is said, and when his eyes fell upon a discarded Adams ballot, he took it as a providential sign and put it in the ballot box. Thus, Adams carried the election.

John Quincy Adams' Difficult Presidency

> Why was John Quincy Adams' presidency so difficult?

Politics appealed to Adams, but the new democratic style did not suit him. Although he had abandoned Federalism during Jefferson's second term, skillfully represented the United States as a diplomat abroad, and outmaneuvered Spanish and British envoys as secretary of state, he was stubborn and impolitic. He refused make partisan loyalty a litmus test for administration appointments, carrying over most of Monroe's appointees, many of whom were his enemies. He had

offered Clay the state department in return for the Kentuckian's support, creating at least the appearance of a bribe and the worst political mistake either one ever made.

Allegations of a "corrupt bargain" actually preceded the House vote in the 1824 election, and should have alerted both men to the danger. "Rumors say," Andrew Jackson observed, "that deep intrigue is on foot." Jackson was enraged when Adams blandly announced Clay's appointment. "The Judas of the West," Jackson fumed at Clay, "has closed the contract and will receive the thirty pieces of silver." The "corrupt bargain" crippled both men politically, but Adams was oblivious to the consequences, insisting on the right to make appointments.

After his inauguration, the president and First Lady Louisa Adams settled into the redecorated White House. Soon, however, Adams' obstinacy and the fallout from the "corrupt bargain" brought frustration and gloom. Amid a revival of old-fashioned Republican states' rights dogma and growing resentment of corrupt, aristocratic power, Adams, a minority president, pushed a program of national economic

John Quincy Adams, sixth president of the United States.

development. His first message to Congress recommended expenditures for roads and canals, updated patent laws, a decimal system of weights and measures, and a national university. In proposing an astronomical observatory, he committed the heresy of comparing the United States unfavorably to Europe. This stunned the Cabinet; opponents of nationalist programs fumed. Adams had anticipated criticism, but rather than defusing it he arrogantly lectured those who represented opposition to economic nationalism. "The spirit of improvement is abroad upon the earth," and congressmen must not be "palsied by the will of our constituents." Such an insult to the public outraged democratic-minded citizens and hardened resistance to Adams' program.

Congress approved none of his initiatives, not even in the arena of foreign affairs. When Adams proposed sending a delegation to an international conference on American unity organized by Simón Bolívar in Panama in 1826, Southerners objected, citing Haiti's presence. Other opponents complained that Adams was sacrificing national sovereignty. Congress delayed appropriating money for the delegation until the conference had adjourned, and Adams slipped into despondency and began counting the days until the end of his term.

Adams's enlightened policy of recognizing Indian tribal rights clashed directly with local white bigotry. Prior treaties had promised the Indians government protection; however, Georgia's governor George M. Troup aroused popular demands for Creek lands. The Indians resisted the pressure, even imposing the death penalty on local chiefs who ceded territory. At first, Adams supported the Creeks, but Clay persuaded him that they "were destined to extinction" and "not worth preserving." Governor Troup turned up the rhetoric, calling Adams a traitor and threatening military campaign to seize more Creek land. Adams finally caved in, leaving the Creeks almost landless.

Insofar as accomplishments were concerned, John Quincy Adams was an abysmal presidential failure. And the "corrupt bargain" along with rising opposition to national economic development set the stage for an organized political opposition.

Rebuilding the Party System

A new generation of leaders in the 1820s and 1830s embraced New York Governor Martin Van Buren's ideas about political parties. Divisive sectional interests—especially slavery—threatened national integrity during the one-party "era of good feelings."

National parties were the best way to preserve the Union at this time of divisive sectional interests. An ambitious and enthusiastic party organizer before very many other statesmen appreciated the

> **What was the key to rebuilding the two-party system, and what political parties played major roles in the 1828 election?**

value of political parties, Van Buren started with the old New York/Virginia alliance that had elected Jefferson in 1800 and worked from there, turning to Andrew Jackson as a candidate in the 1828 election.

Jackson was becoming the most popular politician in the country. His hatred of Adams and Clay and their "corrupt bargain" motivated him to win what he thought was rightfully his (and the people's) and to restore republican virtue. Born on the Carolina frontier and with little formal education, Jackson did not read much, but he thoroughly absorbed republican ideology. Like Jefferson, he believed in limited government, civic virtue, and an economy based on agriculture and artisanship. His faith in common people even exceeded Jefferson's. His mother taught him that a man should behave honorably, that is, with strength and courage to protect those who depended on him. Van Buren recognized a strong leader in Jackson, someone around whom to build a national party. He used the name **Democratic Republican** for the organization.

John C. Calhoun also figured in this party even though he was still Adams' vice president. Ambitious himself for the presidency, he considered an alliance with Jackson and Van Buren useful. Willing to be Jackson's vice president and hoping to succeed him later, Calhoun signed on, putting the last key element in place for a campaign against the hapless but determined Adams.

Adams' honor and sense of duty demanded that he defend himself. Henry Clay stood by him, recognizing in Adams' campaign his best chance of promoting national economic development and succeeding to the presidency himself. The bourgeois interests who supported Adams called themselves **National Republicans**. They did not organize as effectively as the Democratic Republicans, but both parties established local organizations in all twenty-two states to build grassroots support. It would be wrong to think of these two parties merely as ego-driven organizations committed to personal power and vindication; however, the election of 1828 certainly made it seem like they were.

The Triumph of Democracy

The election of 1828 was one of the most exciting in American history. Neither candidate campaigned directly, but the Democratic Republicans pulled out the stops in canvassing voters. Old Hickory clubs, using the name Jackson's troops had bestowed on him, drummed up local enthusiasm. Old Hickory was the first presidential candidate to be known by an affectionate nickname, and the device was so effective that it started a fad.

Clear ideological issues divided the contestants, although they were not the focal point of the campaign. Adams bluntly advocated expansive government, internal improvements, and commercial growth, while Jackson danced around specific issues and registered general opposition to the Market Revolution. When queried about tariffs, for instance, Jackson said he favored "judicious" ones.

> **What modern campaign tactics emerged in the election of 1828, and how did common citizens figure into them?**

Instead of debating ideology, the campaigns resorted to backbiting, which degenerated into a mud-slinging free-for-all. Amos Kendall's *Argus of Western America* questioned Adams' morality because he had purchased a billiard table for the White House. Isaac Hill's New Hampshire *Patriot* topped that by suggesting that Adams had once procured a young American woman as a sex partner for the Czar of Russia. Adams partisans hammered on Jackson's reputation for violence. They recounted duels he had fought, men he had killed, and brawls he had participated in. A handbill illustrated with six coffins representing deserters Jackson had executed during the Creek Indian war in 1814 implied that he was bloodthirsty. Another attack alleged that Jackson's mother had been a prostitute and that his marriage almost 40 years earlier to Rachel Donelson had been bigamous, technically correct but more a consequence of frontier circumstances than moral failure.

Backed by a superior organization and popular support, Jackson won 56 percent of the vote. Not until the twentieth century did any candidate do better. He triumphed even more decisively in the electoral vote: 178 to 83. Except on Adams' New England turf, Jackson was overwhelming. The ever-active Van Buren's strategy had worked to perfection. A national alliance committed to popular democracy prevailed over another one supporting an expanding market economy. The results also demonstrated the emerging power of the West. For the first time, a candidate from beyond the Appalachian Mountains had won a presidential election. And also for the first time, someone other than a member of the established elite would occupy the White House. But the triumph was bitter sweet for Jackson. Rachel had been devastated by the personal attacks during the campaign. "The enemies of the General," she said, "have dipped their arrows in wormwood and gall and sped them at me."

Image © aceshot1, 2010. Used by permission of Shutterstock, Inc.

The Hermitage, the Jackson plantation near Nashville. Although Jackson's political persona was that of a "common man," he was actually a slave-owning planter and member of the Tennessee aristocracy. Jackson's wife Rachel died here shortly after the 1828 presidential election.

Three days before Christmas, she succumbed to an apparent heart attack. Jackson blamed the Adams campaign for her death, and his hatred escalated.

Ordinary citizens felt elation and empowerment, and they turned Jackson's inauguration into a democratic jubilee. Twenty thousand people clogged Washington's muddy streets to watch in respectful silence as Old Hickory, thin, erect, and grief-stricken over Rachel's death, walked from his hotel to the capitol. His barely audible inaugural address contained vague but pleasing principles: "proper respect" for the states, a cautious and compromising approach to the tariff issue, removal of "unfaithful and incompetent" officials from the civil service. "It was grand,—it was sublime!" exclaimed the Washington hostess Margaret Bayard Smith, who had similarly celebrated Jefferson's inauguration. But as the president made his way to the White House, somber restraint burst into jubilation. Boisterous crowds pushed their way into the mansion, climbed on the furniture with their muddy boots to get a better look at their hero, and shattered crystal and china. One newspaper described the scene as a "Saturnalia . . . of mud and filth." Even Mrs. Smith was appalled: *The Majesty of the People* had disappeared." Desperate White House staffers set up punch bowls on the lawn to draw the revelers outside. Said the dubious Supreme Court Justice Joseph Story: "the reign of King 'Mob'" had begun.

The old Republican party had now completely disintegrated. Some Southern planters adhered to its ideals of gentility and legislative prerogative, but a new political era had begun. Through Martin Van Buren's vision and boundless energy, the Democratic party had reached the pinnacle of national power. The only question was what the new president would do with it.

THINKING BACK

1. Why did the Era of Good Feelings come to an end?
2. How did a new two-party system come into being, and what modern political campaign techniques emerged from the 1828 election?

DEMOCRACY'S BOUNDARIES

Historians have long labeled the years that Andrew Jackson dominated national politics as "the age of the common man," suggesting era of egalitarianism. Recent scholarship, however, shows that the democrat-ic spirit was largely limited to white men. Women were regarded as too emotional and insufficiently intelligent to make rational decisions about property, business, or government. Similar prejudices held African Americans to be "a peculiar people, incapable . . . of exercising [voting rights] with discretion, prudence, or independence." Black women had double trouble. By and large, Native Americans did not seek inclusion in white society, but struggled instead for autonomy on ancestral lands. Their aim sparked a new round of conflict with land-hungry whites and a renewed dispute over states' rights. Women, African Americans, and Native Americans realized few immediate benefits from the rise of the common man.

Women Not Allowed

The Market Revolution and lingering, though diminished, patriarchy redefined women's status in national life without making it appreciably better. Women's direct political power remained nil because no state enfranchised them. And for all of Andrew Jackson's fuss over Margaret Eaton, praise of feminine virtue, and readiness to draw a pistol in defense of womanly honor, he did not lift a finger to extend them equal rights. Tocqueville found women and men living in separate spheres, a useful metaphor for modern analysis of women's history. His normally keen eye, however, failed to discern the nuances of women's degradation.

> What reduced women's power in relation to men, and how did the Cult of True Womanhood solidify separate male and female spheres?

The Market Revolution and incipient industrialization rewrote the script for working women. First, the new economy devalued women's work. Market-oriented agriculture emphasized field production—men's work—while factory machines took over the spinning, weaving, and sewing customarily assigned to women. Women thus contributed less to the family's finances and, consequently, commanded less power in relationships with men. Second, women who worked in factories generally labored in gender-segregated, unskilled jobs that offered few prospects for advancement. When President Jackson walked through the mills of Lowell, Massachusetts, he marveled at the technology but never inquired about the women employees.

Middle-class women had little opportunity for gainful employment other than renting rooms to boarders and teaching school. They were expected to devote themselves to raising children and instilling compassion, piety, and self-restraint in a society corrupted by competition, worldliness, and cupidity. Historian Barbara Welter has termed this the **Cult of True Womanhood**, and its advocates sought to substantiate it. Women, wrote a prominent Philadelphia physician, were moral, sexual, reproductive, and nurturing creatures. Their heads were "almost too small for intellect but just big enough for love." Christian evangelism deemed female domesticity a higher calling than the mundane business and political activities of men, and Catharine Beecher argued essentially the same thing in numerous books and speeches. This prescription reduced some women to doormats, but it also inspired a feminine politics of passive dominance coupled with moral leadership.

Political parties of the era harped on civic virtue while simultaneously excluding women, the paragons of virtue, from active involvement in the political arena. Partly, males just refused to share power, but some also feared female sexuality. Patriarchy ascribed original sin to women, who might make fools of men the way Eve had beguiled Adam. Males structured political parades and rallies as masculine, warlike activities with women confined to the sidelines, waving and cheering on their noble "soldiers." Political clubs like New York City's Tammany Hall were strictly male havens, free from all female influences.

Although the Cult of True Womanhood minimized women's involvement in civic life, it did not keep them out altogether. Wives, sisters, and daughters often influenced men. They participated in public events that celebrated American values—like the Fourth of July. When the Marquis de Lafayette visited New Orleans in 1825, the city's leading ladies read a welcoming address. An honorary procession passed two female statues representing liberty and justice—feminine icons for republican virtues. Women writers, of course, occupied a very public platform, as did teachers and church workers. These activities approximated women's home duties. In busy city streets, women of all ranks mixed with men, although in the 1840s cities began providing specific public spaces for ladies—sidewalks outside of department stores (for window shopping), parks, and promenades.

The era honored women, but usually in ways that rationalized their degradation. Their special calling carried protections from worldly cares. According to the Southern code of honor, men fought to defend helpless women; conversely, male sexual conquests of women were notches in their guns—a double standard that allowed male sexual activity outside of marriage while severely punishing "fallen" women. Northern society tried to establish that women were passionless in order to keep them attentive to their moral responsibilities. Immodest women, and others who were tricked by cruel, lustful men, risked humiliation, unwanted pregnancy, and disease. After John Eaton's death, fifty-year-old Margaret married a teenage gigolo who ran off with her daughter, looted her estate, and left her penniless. The Age of Democracy definitely excluded women.

Indian Removal

Indians were not included in the definition of democracy either. As the Plains Indians approached the pinnacle of their power early in the nineteenth

> **How did whites justify their demands for Native Americans' land, how did the Indians attempt to thwart their efforts, and what was the outcome?**

century, demoralized eastern tribes faced annihilation and expulsion. A few Indian towns remained in New England, their citizens participating marginally in the market economy. More autonomous Iroquois communities dotted the frontier of northwestern New York, grappling with painful schisms between Christians and traditionalists, male angst resulting from the abandonment of hunting, and pervasive alcoholism. In 1838, the New York legislature hoodwinked Senecas into trading their beloved woodlands for the treeless Kansas prairie. In the Midwest, native Algonquians and immigrant Iroquois struggled futilely to maintain their tribal identities, while Shawnees, Kickapoos, and Delawares fled across the Mississippi River. In 1832 a defiant warrior named Black Hawk led a handful of displaced Sacs and Foxes from Iowa back across the Mississippi to plant corn in Illinois. For a while, they resisted white pressure to leave, but federal troops, in what is called the **Black Hawk War,** attacked and routed them, virtually destroying the tribes.

Claiming that they were withholding land that whites could use more productively, President James Monroe had proposed that Congress relocate some 130,000 eastern Indians to the West. During the first two decades of the nineteenth century, federal treaties transferred 20 million tribal acres in the Southeast to the United States. Andrew Jackson personally negotiated several of them. Hoping to protect what land they still had, many Cherokees, Choctaws, and Chickasaws adopted elements of white culture, even becoming agricultural capitalists. Mixed-bloods, like the Cherokee John Ross, became successful cotton planters and large slave owners. In addition, Cherokees hoped to impress whites with their 80,000 domestic animals, 2,500 spinning wheels, 750 looms, 31 grist mills, 10 saw mills, and 8 cotton gins. Cherokee government closely followed the Constitution of the United States, their schools taught pupils English as well as Cherokee, using an alphabet devised by Sequoyah, and a tribal printing press enabled Cherokees to publish a bilingual newspaper.

The Indians' tactic failed. A sense of urgency overwhelmed Georgia whites following the discovery of gold on Cherokee land. Old Hickory's election emboldened the legislature, which dissolved the Cherokee constitution and extinguished their land claims. Mississippi did likewise to Choctaws and Chickasaws. Jackson feigned sympathy for the Indians but claimed he was powerless to help his "red . . . children." If they relocated beyond the Mississippi River, though, away from grasping whites and state authority, the government in Washington would protect them for "as long as the Grass grows or water runs." Some Indians accepted the inevitable and moved voluntarily; however, most refused to budge. In 1830 Congress passed the **Indian Removal Act** that authorized their relocation to Indian Territory in present-day Oklahoma.

The Cherokees took their case to the United States Supreme Court. In *Cherokee Nation v. Georgia* (1831), the Court ruled that the Indians were not dependents of the state, but Georgia simply ignored the ruling. The arrest of two missionaries for refusing to obtain a license to reside on Cherokee land, led to a second case. In *Worcester v. Georgia* (1832), the Supreme Court declared that Georgia had no authority over the Indians. Jackson, caring as little for the Supreme Court as he did for the Indians, refused to enforce the decisions, and some dismayed Indians began moving to new homes. In 1838, federal troops dislodged those who remained. On the trek, ever since known as the "**Trail of Tears**," approximately 4,000 of the 16,000 Cherokees succumbed to disease, hunger, or exposure. The scattered individuals who escaped removal were condemned to lives of much poverty, few rights, and eventually a small reservation in North Carolina. Most of the Creeks, Chickasaws, and Choctaws joined them in the new Indian Territory.

Seminoles in Florida resisted removal with armed force. Already pushed off fertile land in northern Florida, they took refuge in swamps in the central portion of the peninsula, and now they were required to move to Indian Territory. Under the leadership of Oceola and Wild Cat, they battled federal troops to standstill in the everglades. Among the Seminole fighters were African Americans, led by John Horse, a man

Image © gary718, 2010. Used by permission of Shutterstock, Inc.

Historic Indian village in the Great Smokey Mountains National Park. Cherokee Indians in Tennessee lived very much the way whites did, but that did not prevent President Jackson from ordering their forced removal.

of African-Seminole-Spanish descent who had escaped from slavery. Army commander General Sidney T. Jesup attacked Black Seminole villages and turned prisoners over to his Creek auxiliaries as slaves. White slave owners demanded the return of their property while the Black Seminoles rode among the slaves on Southern plantations urging rebellion. Jesup used treachery to lure Oceola, Wild Cat, and John Horse into his camp and captured them. Osceola died of fever, but Wild Cat and John Horse escaped and continued the fight. Only years later did they take their followers to Indian Territory. The **Second Seminole War** (1835–1842) cost the United States $30-40 million and more than 1,500 casualties but for all practical purposes brought Indian removal from the Southeast to a close.

Thus Jefferson's earlier policy of "tempting all our Indians . . . to the West" was brutally carried out by Jackson. Some 82,000 Indians were crowded together with about 9,500 indigenous Kansas, Omahas, and Osages in a territory 200 miles wide between the Platte and Red rivers. To keep the peace among resentful Indians and whites, the government built Fort Leavenworth and Fort Gibson. Instead of being incorporated into the democratic republic, Native Americans were being placed on isolated reservations.

African Americans on the Outside

What kind of democratic freedom did African Americans enjoy?

Indian removal put African colonization into the unmistakable context of racial cleansing. From time to time, whites even proposed creating African-American reservations. Banning free African Americans from states and territories was more common, however, and virtually every legislature considered it. Whites in Northern states bordering on slave states feared inundation by emancipated or fugitive slaves. An Ohio congressman warned that his constituents would line up "with muskets on their shoulders" to bar emancipated slaves. Even liberal Massachusetts considered a ban to avoid the burden "of an expensive and injurious population." Where anti-black laws were enacted but not enforced, as a Cincinnati lawyer told Tocqueville, "we annoy them [African Americans] in a thousand ways."

Whites despised African Americans more than Native Americans. In 1831, a Philadelphia Quaker explained: "The policy, and power of the national and state governments, are against them. The

popular feeling is against them—the interests of our citizens are against them. The small degree of compassion once cherished toward them in the commonwealths which got rid of slavery, or which never were disfigured by it, appears to be exhausted. Their prospects either as free, or bond men, are dreary, and comfortless." The goal in the North was to isolate African Americans in separate neighborhoods and public facilities. But educating black pupils at taxpayers' expense, even in segregated schools, provoked the most vigorous protest, especially in the Western states. Liberal private schools that admitted African Americans also felt community pressure. When twenty-eight white and fourteen black students started classes at the Noyes Academy in Canaan, New Hampshire, in 1835, angry townsfolk hitched up yokes of oxen and hauled the school building away.

African Americans did not benefit from political democratization. In fact, reforms drove African Americans out of the political system. Nine out of ten African Americans living in free states could not vote, and only in Massachusetts, Vermont, New Hampshire, and Maine could they vote on the same basis as whites. New York abolished the property requirement for white voters in 1826 but retained it for blacks. New Jersey, Pennsylvania, and Connecticut just took the vote away. "There can be no mistaking public opinion on this subject," observed a Pennsylvania delegate to its 1837 constitutional convention. "The people of this state are for continuing this commonwealth . . . a political community of white persons." Without voting power, African Americans could not earn the right to hold public office, participate in nominating conventions, or sit on juries.

"Pardon me if I feel insignificant and weak," said an African-American high school valedictorian in New York. "What are my prospects? To what shall I turn my hand? Shall I be a mechanic? No one will employ me . . . . Shall I be a merchant? No one will have me in his office . . . . Can you be surprised at my discouragement?" Far from bourgeois optimism, African Americans felt rampant pessimism. They advanced little in the Market Revolution. Although there were notable exceptions, the vast majority of African Americans toiled in service or menial jobs. "They submit themselves to do menial service," a white Pennsylvanian observed, "and we get the profit." According to white racial stereotypes, unchanged by democratic ideology, African Americans occupied their proper place at the bottom of the heap. This, of course, served white interests too, for as the white Pennsylvanian added: "If they would not do this, we ourselves would be compelled to do it."

Jacksonian democracy had fixed and visible boundaries. Jackson declared liberty only for white males. He and his followers had once been outsiders too, and their anxiety about their status bred hostility toward whoever threatened or rivaled them. By keeping women, Indians, and African Americans beneath them, white men could find equality.

THINKING BACK

1. Alexis de Tocqueville wrote that men and women in America occupied "separate spheres." What did that mean in terms of democracy?

2. How did Native Americans and African Americans fare in the "Age of Democracy"?

ANDREW JACKSON: THE PEOPLE'S PRESIDENT

Old Hickory rode into Washington with a reputation as a quick-thinking, hard-hitting man. He cared little for philosophical musings or ideological consistency. While he vilified the "moneyed power" he consorted

President Andrew Jackson.

with Tennessee bankers and developers. Jackson did hold dear some important principles: democracy, states' rights, and the Union, and by his second term had become rather doctrinaire. But what makes the Old Hero so compelling is his tenacity, which assisted him in dealing with the ravages of age (he was sixty-two when he became president), years of hard military campaigning, two bullets from earlier duels, and determined political opposition. Of course, he had a fiery temper too, which ignited political explosions on occasion. Historians have disagreed heatedly over what he stood for: working people against capitalists, rising entrepreneurs against the entrenched elite, or subsistence-level producers against advocates of the Commercial Revolution. Whatever motivated Andrew Jackson, though, he unquestionably dominated the politics of his time.

The Spoils System

Andrew Jackson made a democratic principle out of appointing loyal supporters to the civil service (government jobs). Nobody, he believed, owned a government job; yet, many bureaucrats acted like they did. "Office is considered as a species of property," he complained, "and government rather as a means of promoting individual interests than as an instrument created solely for the service of the people." Jackson scoffed at the idea that only the well educated were qualified for government employment. "The duties of all public officers are . . . so plain and simple" that anyone with good values and some horse sense could perform them. The more people who rotated into government, the more democratic it was.

> **How did Jackson justify the replacing civil servants with his political supporters?**

Jackson scrutinized department accounts and netted a few crooks, but he removed fewer than 10 percent of the bureaucracy's incumbents during his first term. Nevertheless, he made "rotation in office" an article of faith in staffing the bureaucracy. Skeptics denounced the **"spoils system,"** claiming that an office-holder's primary qualification was loyalty to the president; however, historian Sidney H. Aronson has found that Jackson appointed mostly honest men with qualifications virtually identical to their predecessors. Jackson was not an infallible judge of personal character, though, and one of his appointees, Samuel Swartwout, embarrassed him by skipping the country with $1.2 million in embezzled money.

With the exception of Secretary of State Martin Van Buren, Jackson's Cabinet appointments were not outstanding. A widower, Van Buren supported Margaret Eaton during the "petticoat affair," which Jackson greatly appreciated. As a result of that imbroglio, the president discontinued regular Cabinet meetings, instead, consulting personal friends derided as his "cronies." The inner circle included Kentuckian Amos Kendall, William B. Lewis, an army buddy from Tennessee, and newspaperman Francis P. Blair. Critics labeled this coterie Jackson's "**kitchen cabinet**," and he relied on them for advice. Jackson's nephew, Andrew Jackson Donelson, served as his private secretary and Donelson's wife Emily as White House hostess.

The Union or the States

Old Hickory regarded centralized government as expensive, easily corrupted by special interests, and a threat to individual freedom. He trusted state governments more, although their political machinery was corruptible too. Tennessee had been in the hands of land developers and bankers for years. When the chips were down, however, Jackson's patriotism outweighed his commitment to states' rights. He had fought for the Union and would not allow states' rights to destroy it.

States' rights caused Jackson to object to federal internal improvements when the projects were within state boundaries. In 1830, when Congress authorized the

> **How did Jackson conceive the relationship between the Union and the states?**

purchase of stock in a turnpike company constructing a road from Maysville, Kentucky, to Lexington, he vetoed it, alleging an unwarranted federal government intrusion into the state's affairs. He also knew that Henry Clay would benefit from the road, and still further, he wanted to apply all available funds to federal debt reduction. He actually eliminated the debt for the first and only time in history. Would the public agree with the Maysville Road Veto? "The line . . . has been fairly drew," Jackson ungrammatically declared, and they did. Subsequently he vetoed similar measures on the same constitutional grounds while approving coastal lighthouses on state property that clearly had strategic national value.

How much states' rights could the Union tolerate? In 1829, John C. Calhoun provided the answer. More than other states, South Carolina's economy produced cotton for European factories, but protective tariffs caused Europeans to retaliate by importing less cotton,

hurting South Carolina planters. Tariffs also raised consumer prices. Disgruntled planters painted a woeful scenario: cotton prices at depression levels, slavery coming under attack, and a bloody race war in the offing. In 1822, Charleston authorities had uncovered a plot to liberate slaves designed by a free black carpenter named Denmark Vesey, who had purchased his freedom with winnings from a lottery. Vesey, and thirty-four accomplices went to the gallows, but another conspiracy surfaced in nearby Georgetown in 1828. South Carolina planters felt victimized by a national majority that disregarded their vital interests. If they could not protect themselves against tariff exploitation, many wondered, how could they safeguard slavery? Thomas Cooper, president of South Carolina College, suggested seceding from the Union. "We shall ere long be compelled to calculate the value of our union and enquire of what use to us is this most unequal alliance."

Calhoun did not endorse secession, but he sympathized with fellow planters' feelings of victimization. In 1828, Congress had bumped tariffs even higher, a clever political maneuver by Martin Van Buren, then serving as a pro-Jackson New York senator, to build support for Jackson in the coming election. The new tariff, more political than economic in its conception, protected Mid-Atlantic and Midwest wool and hemp producers (hemp was used to make rope for ship rigging and material for cotton bales) as well as Pennsylvania iron makers. For that, voters in those areas would be grateful to Jackson. But the tariff hurt New England shipbuilders and rum distillers, and South Carolina planters worried that Great Britain would retaliate against Southern cotton. By tinkering with the bill's provisions, Van Buren got it passed. Planters thundered in protest over what they termed this "**Tariff of Abominations**," some hinting at secession. To calm the storm, Calhoun proposed "**nullification**" in a treatise called the *South Carolina Exposition and Protest*. Majority rule, he insisted, tyrannized minorities—sovereign states. The states had the right to protect themselves by nullifying within their boundaries any law they judged unconstitutional. If three-fourths of the states amended the Constitution to legitimize the law, then secession remained a lawful recourse.

South Carolina was not unique in objecting to the tariff. When in January of 1830 a Connecticut senator suggested limiting western land sales to slow emigration from the east, and to offset lost revenues with higher tariff duties, western states blasted it. Senator

Robert Y. Hayne of South Carolina joined the attack, hoping to forge a South-West alliance. The debate shifted abruptly when Daniel Webster attacked Southern slavery, prompting a rejoinder by Hayne, who invoked nullification to prevent the "deliberate, palpable, and dangerous exercise of . . . powers not granted by the Constitution." Webster, the most celebrated orator of the day, replied that the United States was a union of citizens not states. "Liberty and Union," he exclaimed, "now and forever, one and inseparable."

Everyone wondered where Jackson stood on these tangled issues. He believed the South's lamentations were exaggerated, but he also thought protective tariffs were unfair. Three months after the Hayne-Webster debate, at a banquet honoring Thomas Jefferson, Jackson took a clear stand on the question of sovereignty. Following a number of toasts to states' rights, Jackson raised his glass and declared: "Our Federal Union. It must be preserved." The crowd murmured expectantly, and, according to the diminutive Van Buren who had to stand on a chair to see, Calhoun trembled with fury as he delivered his toast. "The Union, next to our liberties, the most dear." The two men's positions were crystallizing: Calhoun for states' rights and Jackson for the Union.

The Nullification Crisis

> What sparked the nullification crisis, and how did political leaders resolve it?

President Jackson and Vice President Calhoun represented opposing extremes on federal authority even though both were ambivalent. Personal animosity amplified their differences—remember the Margaret Eaton affair. Also, during Jackson's foray into Florida in 1818 (see p. 276), Calhoun had recommended a reprimand, though never publicly. Jackson now learned the truth. When the *United States Telegraph*, heretofore the administration's voice, defended Calhoun, Francis P. Blair's Washington *Globe* spoke out for Jackson in a major media battle. Jackson eventually maneuvered Van Buren into the vice president's slot for the 1832 election, dumping the disloyal Calhoun.

A crisis for the Union and the *coup de grace* for the Jackson-Calhoun relationship came in 1832 when Congress passed another tariff law. A nullification convention in South Carolina declared the tariffs of 1828 and 1832 null and void. The ordinance charged unlawful discrimination, and the nullifiers threatened to resist "at every hazard" and ultimately to secede if the federal government used force. In the midst of these events,

Calhoun resigned from the vice presidency and the South Carolina legislature elected him to the Senate. In December, a resolute Jackson issued a proclamation dismissing the nullification argument, and in response to the threat of secession, which he declared "is *treason*," he dispatched military reinforcements to Charleston and asked Congress for a "**Force Bill**" to guarantee compliance with the law. Through the winter, the prospect of civil war loomed ominously.

Fortunately, few in the country relished armed conflict. There was little support, even in the South, for nullification, and Calhoun still nursed his ambition for the presidency. Jackson had little to gain from a showdown. He supported states' rights and identified with the South's planters on slavery. This was a crisis ready for a compromise, and Henry Clay provided it early in 1833 with a new tariff ending protection by 1842. Jackson hated giving Clay any credit, but he had no choice. Calhoun and the nullifiers went along because the compromise addressed their concerns. Jackson signed the tariff and the Force Bill on the same day, and South Carolina nullified the Force Bill, but that did not matter. The crisis had evaporated.

The immediate tariff issue was resolved, but not the fundamental issue of sovereignty. The future of Southern slavery was not clarified either. Resolution

John C. Calhoun, the leader of the nullification movement

of those important matters awaited the opening salvos of the Civil War.

Killing the Bank

The Bank of the United States towered over other banks. Its currency was like gold, and its director, Nicholas Biddle, kept close watch on local banking. By adjusting the money supply, Biddle could correct a variety of economic problems. Opinions on the Bank varied however. Conservative businessmen welcomed its stabilizing influence on the economy, but many democratic-minded citizens questioned the value of a private institution run for profit by non-elected officials. And while on the one hand Thomas Hart ("Old Bullion") Benton scorned "rag money" (as he put it, "Gold and silver is the best currency for a republic."), borrowers in the rapidly growing and cash-starved West craved credit and resented BUS constraints on paper currency. Nor were feelings about the BUS always clear and consistent. Richmond newspaperman Thomas Ritchie criticized the Bank in his editorials but borrowed freely from it, and Andrew Jackson spoke against the BUS in his early presidential speeches and then appointed pro-Bank men to his Cabinet.

> Why did people like Jackson dislike the Bank of the United States, what did Jackson do about the Bank, and what were the consequences?

The Bank War commenced in 1832 when Henry Clay persuaded Biddle to request congressional renewal of the BUS's charter, not due to expire until 1836. Clay figured the Bank had broad public support and that if Jackson vetoed the recharter bill he would lose the approaching election. "The bank . . . is trying to kill me," Jackson told Van Buren, "*but I will kill it.*" In an unprecedented veto message that ranged beyond questions of constitutionality, he denounced the BUS as a "hydra of corruption" and a direct threat to freedom. His language alluded to social revolution—the poor rising against the rich.

The election of 1832 thus became a referendum on the "monster" Bank and Andrew Jackson's leadership. The National Republicans nominated Henry Clay, but Biddle set the campaign's tone by characterizing Jackson as a mad animal spewing "all the fury of a chained panther biting the bars of his cage." As before, though, Jackson gauged public opinion on the Bank more accurately than Clay. In addition, the Democrats organized a massive grassroots campaign with parades, barbecues, and symbolic hickory sticks. Old Hickory smothered Clay and other minor opponents, receiving 219 electoral votes to Clay's 49. He bagged 55 percent of the popular vote to 42.4 for Clay.

Jackson's veto and re-election signaled the beginning of the **Bank War.** The "will of the people" was clear, and Jackson now claimed a mandate to destroy the BUS. He ordered the withdrawal of government deposits, placing them in seven selected state banks, known derisively as "**pet banks.**" Without government funds, the BUS would have to call in loans and scale back its operations. The plan hit a snag when Louis McLane, Jackson's pro-Bank treasury secretary, refused to obey. Jackson replaced him with William Duane, who also refused. Finally, Roger B. Taney agreed to write the necessary directives. The National Republicans were aghast. A censure resolution passed both houses of Congress, but the President was unfazed. The arrogant Biddle (called "Czar Nicholas") retaliated. "This worthy President thinks that because he has scalped Indians . . . he is to have his way with the Bank. He is mistaken." Biddle deliberately called in more loans than necessary, causing an economic stall-out that he tried to blame on Jackson. When desperate businessmen pleaded with the President for help, Jackson told them to go talk to Nicholas Biddle. Biddle finally surrendered, once again extending loans and allowing the economy to resume its growth. In 1836, the BUS's charter expired.

Jackson defeated the BUS, as he had the British, Indians, and nullifiers, but winning is not always everything. He deprived the country of useful banking controls during decades of tremendous economic expansion and nauseating ups and downs. Both Jackson and Biddle allowed personal animosity to cloud their vision and harm the country.

THINKING BACK

1. How did the spoils system and killing the BUS exemplify Jackson's commitment to democracy?
2. How did the nullification crisis clarify the difference between Jackson's genuine belief in states' rights and his ultimate devotion to the Union?

THE JACKSONIAN LEGACY

Old Hickory bequeathed a huge legacy, but it often contradicted his stated ideals. For example, he left the presidency stronger than he found it, odd for a disciple of Thomas Jefferson, and although he abhorred political parties, he contributed significantly to partisan politics as we know them today. Jackson's personal influence on the culture of his time, however, is easily exaggerated. After all, the "**second American party system**," that originated during his presidency, reflected social divisions and class consciousness for which no one person could be responsible. By 1836, two parties, Democrats and Whigs, had assembled mechanisms that incorporated unprecedented numbers of people into the political nation. Through them, citizens developed strong partisan identities, enthusiasm for political activity, and deep loyalty to their respective parties. Ironically, Martin Van Buren, mastermind of the new party system, had neither the charisma nor the administrative skills to capitalize on it. More importantly, a depression ravaged the economy. Ironically, Whigs, not Democrats, brought the modern campaigning tactics to the peak of perfection in the election of 1840.

Moderating Judicial Nationalism

How did Jackson's legacy impact the Supreme Court?

When John Marshall died in 1835, he created a vacancy on the United States Supreme Court and left economic nationalism without its most powerful judicial advocate. As John Adams had demonstrated in appointing him, judicial appointments projected ideology deep into the future. After much speculation, Jackson filled the position with Maryland's Roger B. Taney. Like Old Hickory himself, Taney was an inveterate foe of bourgeois privilege and intrusive federal authority. Conservatives characterized him as a "political hack," and denounced his appointment. In two important areas, the Taney Court backtracked from its predecessor.

The new chief justice's democratic trousers a stylistic innovation of the time announced the Supreme Court's retreat from Federalist knee-britches principles. Taney's first important decision came in the *Charles River Bridge Company v. Warren Bridge Company* case in 1837. The action involved an exclusive charter from the Massachusetts legislature in 1785 to the Charles River Bridge Company authorizing it to operate a toll bridge into Boston. In 1828, however, the legislature permitted the Warren Bridge Company to erect a toll-free bridge, which would slash into the older company's profits. Many wealthy Bostonians, even Harvard College, owned stock in the Charles River Bridge Company,

which sued on grounds of injury and that its charter had been improperly voided. Taney, writing for the majority, reversed the court's earlier *Dartmouth College* decision (see p. 290), and insisted that community needs prevailed over corporate profits. This ruling subordinated corporate property rights to community welfare.

A second area that Taney reviewed from a Jacksonian perspective was interstate commerce. The question involved the states' regulatory power in the absence of federal authority. In two ways, the court extended the rights of states. First, it allowed companies licensed in one state to conduct business in another, and second, it approved state regulation of commerce where no federal regulations existed. This ruling limited the impact of *Gibbons v. Ogden* (see p. 290).

Taney's initially radical departures from precedents caused the dejected National Republican Justice Joseph Story to consider resigning, and New York's Chancellor James Kent to lament the undermining of "the foundations of morality, confidence, and truth." But the overall impact of Jacksonian democracy on constitutional law was less extreme. The rule of *stare decisis*, which means that principles of law used in resolving one case apply to all subsequent ones based on similar facts, insures considerable judicial continuity. Moreover, considerations of slavery soon caused Taney and the other Southern justices to reevaluate their support for property rights.

A New Political Party System

Democratic Republicans and National Republicans had obsessed on Andrew Jackson: one on electing him and the other on defeating him. By the Bank War, however, opposing

What political parties emerged in the 1830s, what did they stand for, and to whom did they appeal?

ideologies had crystallized into two new parties. Both paid homage to democracy with their names: **Democrat** and **Whig** (a reference to Revolutionary War Whigs). Rhetoric and electioneering tactics also exemplified the growing respect for democracy.

As the wellspring of political controversy, the Market Revolution swayed the ideologies of both parties. Whigs applauded economic expansion and strong, positive government leadership on economic issues, saying that these would improve living standards and enhance liberty. They pushed protective tariffs, internal improvements, and a national banking system. Democrats opposed monopoly even if they did not always reject the Market Revolution. "Soft-money" Democrats, for instance, favored easy credit and hated a controlling national bank while "hard-money" Democrats denounced all banks and their "rag money." Thomas Hart Benton thundered, "I did not join in putting down the Bank of the United States to put up a wilderness of local banks." New York's anti-bank faction endeavored to unite "the producing classes," the "bone and sinew of the country," against the "monsters" of the new economic system: capitalist employers, sprawling cities, and big government. Democrats in the 1830s embraced the principle long before Henry David Thoreau published the aphorism "That government is best which governs least."

Class and religion also helped solidify the "second party system." Democrats demanded access to power and equal opportunity for the little guy; consequently, the working class tended to vote Democratic, as did Irish and German immigrants who gave the party a slight Catholic tinge. Bourgeois Americans, dismayed by the destruction of social order and a decline in morality, which they associated with Jackson and his policies, imparted their moral, evangelical Protestant values to the Whig party. Anti-Masons, with their abhorrence of corruption, merged with the Whigs after 1832, as did Southern planters concerned with Jackson's stance on nullification and the increasing prominence of the anti-slavery Martin Van Buren in Democratic councils.

Compared to preceding parties, Democrats and Whigs were better organized from the national level on down to counties and towns. Local conventions, state organizations, and national nominating conventions boosted participation and held people's interest between presidential elections, developed strong party identities, and generated enormous interest in elections. The class, ethnic, and religious differences intensified party loyalty. The two parties were very evenly matched as far as voter strength was concerned, so leaders concentrated on turning out their own supporters rather than winning converts.

Winning elections was the primary objective of the second party system, and the presidency was the big prize. The Democrats jumped out to a fast start with the enormously popular Andrew Jackson, but could they maintain their primacy when the Old Hero retired?

Van Buren and the Panic of 1837

His spirits unflagging but his body failing, Jackson announced his retirement and the hope that Martin Van Buren would succeed him. The ticket of Van Buren and Richard M. Johnson, who claimed to have killed Tecumseh and openly kept an African-American mistress, faced no single Whig candidate. Instead, three regional opponents hoped to throw the election into the House. Daniel Webster of Massachusetts attracted business-oriented voters; Hugh Lawson White, from Tennessee, appealed to Southern planters; and Indian-fighter William Henry Harrison of Indiana focused on the western vote. But not even triplets could weaken Old Hickory's aura, which helped "Little Van" to collect 170 electoral votes to 124 for the opposition. That was fewer than Jackson's 1832 total, and Van Buren received just 51 percent of the popular vote. The Whigs lost, but were optimistic.

Fate sabotaged the genteel, good-natured, but rather dull Van Buren. Jackson was a hard act to follow, but Van Buren's biggest problem was the economy. The Bank War had unleashed countless "**wildcat**" banks that fueled explosive economic expansion with paper money. Historians used to blame Jackson's Bank War for this volatile situation, but now they realize that the real causes were large quantities of Mexican silver and heavy British investment in American cotton. The government further excited the frenzy by distributing surplus revenues to the states—a Whig idea—which used them to finance transportation improvements. All parts of the country felt the boom, especially the West, where grain and land prices skyrocketed. Land-hungry settlers and speculators purchased over 30 million acres in 1836 and 1837, mostly with bank credit and paper currency. New towns sprouted everywhere. Chicago, now with access to New York and abroad via the Erie Canal, went crazy. One local hotel proprietor boasted: "on this kind of worthless currency . . . we are creating a great city, building up all kinds of industrial establishments, and covering the lake with vessels."

Bravado, however, could not prevent a bubble burst in 1837. The departing Jackson precipitated a crisis with his **Specie Circular** directing land offices to accept only gold or silver payments. Banks could not meet the sudden demand for specie and suspended exchanges. Paper money disappeared and land and commodity prices plummeted. Simultaneously, British banks halted cotton loans, causing trading firms from New Orleans to New York to fail. As prosperity vanished, a young New Yorker, George Templeton Strong, recorded

> **What problems did Martin Van Buren have to contend with, and how successful was his presidency?**

Martin Van Buren, the first president born under the flag of the United States, retired to the farm he called "Lindenwald" located in New York's Hudson River Valley. Although strongly antislavery, Van Buren employed Irish women for domestic labor, which introduced a measure of class tension within the supposedly harmonious and virtuous republican household.

the panic in his diary: "[April 21] Failure on failure . . . [April 27] Strong fears entertained for the banks, and if they go . . . political convulsion and revolution, I think, would follow." The **Panic of 1837** led to the severest and most prolonged depression Americans had ever experienced.

The meltdown was disastrous for President "Van Ruin," as people called him. Whigs blamed the Democratic Bank War and Specie Circular. Van Buren laid it to excessive borrowing and extravagant living—the loss of public virtue. When desperate businessmen appealed to him for a new national bank, he invoked *laissez-faire*: "All communities are apt to look to government for too much." Instead, he presented a plan for taking government funds out of banks altogether and putting them in independent treasuries. But that could not solve the immediate problem, and the Whig-controlled Congress blocked it anyway. Fist fights and weapons in the House and Senate chambers raised the ante. One Whig and one Democrat dueled with rifles at

eighty yards—both survived. Not until 1840 did an independent treasury bill become law.

Van Buren could do nothing right. Another panic shocked the economy in 1839. In Florida, the Seminoles kept the United States Army at bay, and along the still undefined and disputed border between Maine and Canada bloody skirmishes threatened to ignite an Anglo-American war. Andrew Jackson could not have succeeded without the Democratic party, and now it seemed that Van Buren and the Democrats could not succeed without Old Hickory.

"Tippecanoe and Tyler Too"

Even though circumstances favored them, Whigs still needed to act democratic if they hoped to win the 1840 election. The depression made Van Buren a

> **Why did the Whigs win the election of 1840?**

sitting duck, but the Whigs had to find a candidate and design a campaign that could nail him. Above all, they had to convince voters that economic nationalism was consistent with democratic freedom.

Henry Clay enjoyed the most name recognition of any Whig, but he also bore the black eye of a loser and was a slave owner closely associated with the BUS. Thurlow Weed of New York, a cigar-smoking party manager, told him bluntly that he was unelectable and would not be nominated. Several other names surfaced, but William Henry Harrison's topped the list at the party's nominating convention. He had demonstrated popularity in 1836, embodied Andrew Jackson's frontier-military virtues, and contrasted favorably with Van Buren despite being descended from a prominent Virginia family that included a signer of the Declaration of Independence. Political pragmatism led the Whigs to choose for vice president John Tyler of Virginia, a states' rights Democrat who deserted Jackson over nullification.

"Tippecanoe and Tyler too," snorted New York aristocrat Philip Hone about the reference to Taylor's victory over the Shawnees in 1811 (see p. 254). The ticket had "rhyme, but no reason in it." Maybe not, but it made an effective slogan. Another cynical quip by a Democratic newspaper reporter suggested how the Whigs would package Harrison. "Give him a barrel of hard cider, and . . . he will sit out the remainder of his days in his log cabin . . . and study moral philosophy." A simple, virtuous democrat and family man who despised hack politicians—that was the Whig image. Women responded positively to it and participated in the Whig campaign like never before, cheering avidly at rallies and torchlight parades. Whigs portrayed Van Buren as an extravagant aristocrat while lambasting Jackson for turning the federal government into a monarchy. Van Buren tried futilely to draw the campaign back to monsters, monopolies, and paper money. It was an uphill fight, however, and the Democrats faltered.

The Whigs swept to victory. Harrison carried 19 of 26 states with an electoral vote margin of 234 to 60. The real significance of the election, however, was the turnout—an astounding 80 percent of the eligible voters. Although he suffered defeat, Van Buren's concept of parties and what it took to win elections triumphed. "They have at last learned from defeat the art of victory," a Democratic newspaper moaned. "We have taught them how to conquer us." It was a hollow victory, however. On March 4, 1841, the sixty-seven-year-old Harrison read the longest inaugural speech in history. Underdressed for the chilly Washington weather, he contracted pneumonia and died a few weeks later. Presidential leadership shifted to John Tyler, the first vice president to assume office on the president's death. A Democrat in Whig clothing, Tyler did not buy into the Whigs' legislative agenda. Thus, the Whigs' next political battle would be with themselves.

THINKING BACK

1. What were the major differences between Democrats and Whigs?
2. How did the Whigs defeat the Democrats in 1840?

THE LOCAL PERSPECTIVE: FOCUS ON TEXAS, THE LONE STAR REPUBLIC

| What caused the revolution in Texas? |

The occupation of Texas by Anglo-Americans in the 1820s and 1830s was indicative of American support for territorial expansion. Andrew Jackson and Southern slave owners were particularly enthusiastic about Texas, reasserting the claim that John Quincy Adams had negotiated away in the Transcontinental Treaty (see p. 277). Colonization resonated with American chauvinism.

During the 1820s and 1830s, Texas was a complex borderland of multiple and contrasting cultures.

Native Americans, *Tejanos*, and Anglos (immigrants from the United States) formed an uneasy coexistence. Political boundaries meant little at that time; people crossed and re-crossed them with relative ease. National identities were fuzzy too. Texas was a huge territory, yet most *Tejano* and Anglo residents were settled into a triangle formed by San Antonio, Goliad, and Nacogdoches in the southeast portion of the territory. Indians presided over the rest. Each culture group kept a distrustful eye on the others.

The ripples of President Andrew Jackson's Indian removal policy could be felt in Texas. Bands of displaced tribes chose Texas over Indian Territory because Mexico had a better reputation for dealing with Indians than the United States. The largest contingent comprised Cherokees who crowded onto the traditional lands of various native Caddos along the Sabine River. The Caddos actually welcomed the powerful newcomers as useful allies. Cherokees also offered their services to the Mexicans who were defending themselves from marauding Comanches.

Most *Tejanos* were peasant farmers and stock raisers huddled around San Antonio and Goliad. A tiny military garrison at Nacogdoches ostensibly guarded the border with the United States, and a few ranchers owned herds of longhorn cattle that grazed on the dry prairies of South Texas. *Tejanos* were actually a mixed population of Spanish settlers, Canary Island immigrants, and *mestizo* soldiers (many of ancient Aztec ancestry). But a common *Tejano* culture and sense of community had emerged by the 1820s and are clearly evident today. Women grilled flat *tortillas* from stone-ground corn meal and *tamales* filled with chopped beef, beans, and hot cayenne pepper. *Tejanos* consumed beef like the Comanches utilized buffalo, crafting carpets, chair bottoms, beds, packs, and ropes out of the rawhide. They interacted with peaceful Indians and Anglos to such an extent that a member of a Mexican government inspection team in 1828 observed that "they are Mexican only by birth, for even the Castilian language they speak with considerable ignorance."

By 1830 some 7,000 Anglos resided in Texas, twice the number of *Tejanos*. Stephen F. Austin had been the most successful of the *empresarios* (or contractors) that the Mexican government had hired to bring 300 settler families from the United States. Indeed, Austin negotiated four more colonization contracts that brought an additional 900 families into Texas. Most of them were upstanding citizens content to mind their own business, farming and ranching in eastern and central Texas, but others dreamed of annexation by the United States or of an independent Texas republic. In 1826 Haden Edwards, a small-time *empresario*, led an unsuccessful revolt against Mexican authority, and in 1832 one of Andrew Jackson's Tennessee army companions, Sam Houston, entered Texas with dreams of conquest. Despite Austin's efforts to keep the Anglos under control, many of them violated Mexican law, sold land illegally to other immigrants, and openly smuggled through clandestine coastal landings. In response, alarmed authorities in Mexico passed the Law of April 6, 1830, which suspended further colonization and prohibited the importation of additional slaves. Illegal adventurers and vagabonds continued to pour into Texas, however, and by 1835 some 27,000 Anglos and 3,000 African-American slaves resided in Texas.

Political upheaval in Mexico City boded ill for Anglo Texans. Mexico's federal system of government could not improve the economy, so in 1834 General Antonio Lopez de Santa Anna disbanded the national congress and the constitution, assumed dictatorial power, and began centralizing authority in Mexico City. This action rankled the democratically minded Texans, Anglo and *Tejano*, who wanted local control—

a situation similar to the conflict between Democrats and Whigs in the United States. Circumstances continued to worsen. In response to a Mexican military buildup in Texas, a militant faction led by William B. Travis, a hot-headed Alabama lawyer, demanded independence. Stephen F. Austin urged patience; he traveled to Mexico City and persuaded Santa Anna to grant more autonomy for Texas. But that did not placate the militants, and in 1835 an armed force of Texans overran a Mexican military garrison at Anahuac near the Gulf coast.

Santa Anna acted forcefully to suppress the Texas revolt. He arrested Austin, who returned to Texas and published a call for armed resistance. Santa Anna then led a major military assault on the disorganized rebels. In March of 1836, Santa Anna ordered an assault on a Texan garrison in the Alamo in San Antonio, killing all of the approximately 200 defenders, including Davy Crockett, William Travis, and a number of native *Tejanos*. He also ordered the execution of 371 Texans captured at Goliad. The Texans used the cry "**Remember the Alamo**" to rally support for independence. Believing that he held the upper hand, Santa Anna swept with his army toward the coast, foolishly overextending his supply lines. In April of 1836, Sam Houston, commanding a Texan force, surprised and annihilated the Mexicans in a

Image © Christopher Eng-Wong Photography, 2010. Used by permission of Shutterstock, Inc.

The front of the Alamo mission in San Antonio, Texas, scene of the battle that became a rallying cry and symbol during and after the Texas Revolution.

battle near the San Jacinto River. Afterward, Santa Anna, who had been taken prisoner, signed a document acknowledging Texas independence.

Most Texans assumed that President Jackson and the Democratic-controlled Congress would act promptly to bring Texas into the United States. And that no doubt would have happened if it had not been for slavery. But Martin Van Buren was seeking election to succeed Jackson as president, and Old Hickory and Van Buren both believed that the annexation of a slave state would split the party along sectional lines and might give election victory to the Whigs. Thus, Texas remained the Lone Star Republic. A slave-based plantation system developed that supplied cotton to British factories. In 1841, Texas launched a military invasion of New Mexico to lay claim to the entire Rio Grande River to its headwaters as well as Santa Fe. But nothing the Texans tried succeeded in establishing a viable economy.

Like the Jacksonian Democrats in the United States, Anglo Texans had demanded freedom for themselves alone. They brought more slaves into Texas and harassed free African Americans unmercifully. Anglos also turned against the *Tejanos*, including those who had fought alongside them for independence, pushing them off their land. Loyal *Tejano* leader Juan Seguin ultimately fled with his family after several racially motivated threats and attempts on his life. Thus, the Lone Star Republic incorporated many of the characteristics of the Jacksonian democracy that swept across the United States at that time.

THINKING BACK

1. Why did the citizens of Texas rebel against Mexican authority?
2. What role did *Tejanos* play in the Texas Revolution?

CONCLUSION

Democracy took a firm grip on American society during the 1820s and 1830s. Andrew Jackson, who led the movement to eliminate special privilege and regarded himself as the common citizens' steward, proved to be correct on several key points in dispute about the economy. The tariff was helpful but not crucial to economic development. Commercial production and industrialization continued and even gathered strength despite the elimination of tariff protection. The war against the Bank of the United States revealed the BUS's arbitrary power, although it too had been useful in managing the economy. In opposing nullification, Jackson had not intended to oppose Southern slavery. He was, after all, a slave owner himself. In fact, his simultaneous refusal to block the removal of Native Americans opened additional land for plantation agriculture. Jackson claimed victory in the crisis with South Carolina, but in the process he opened fissures in the party. Southern Democrats did not trust Martin Van Buren, and many of them went over to the Whigs. Democrats did succeed to a considerable extent in uniting farmers, planters, and laborers on the basis of limited government, self-sufficient rather than market-oriented production, and the powerful symbol of Andrew Jackson—a common man who embodied democratic values. Whigs kept the Market Revolution going and government partnership with business alive. But even they, clearly an elitist party, had to acknowledge the democratic changes in American culture were profound and irreversible.

SUGGESTED SOURCES FOR STUDENTS

Stuart M. Blumin, *The Emergence of the Middle Class: Social Experience in the American City, 1760-1900* (1989), uses quantitative analysis to define and describe the emerging middle class.

Nancy Cott, *The Bonds of Womanhood: "Woman's Sphere" in New England* (1977), argues that confinement in a separate sphere generated a supportive sense of sisterhood.

Carl N. Degler, *At Odds: Women and the Family in America from the Revolution to the Present* (1980), maintains that women gained power within their domestic sphere at the expense of patriarchal authority.

Daniel Walker Howe, *What God Hath Wrought: The Transformation of America, 1815-1848* (2007), presents America emerging from the multi-interest chaos of its inception into a nation still divided but not crippled by the competing aspirations for modernization and increasing inclusiveness.

Mary Kelley, *Learning to Stand and Speak: Women, Education, and Public Life in America's Republic* (2006), explores how expanding their intellectual growth helped women learn to take positions in the Republic's public life.

For the details of the Petticoat Affair, see John F. Marszalek, *The Petticoat Affair: Manners, Mutiny, and Sex in Andrew Jackson's White House* (1997).

Jon Meacham has authored the latest Jackson biography, *American Lion: Andrew Jackson in the White House* (2008). As the title suggests, it is a political biography (and a Pulitzer Prize winner) that presents Jackson as he would have wanted to be seen: a rough populist from the West who spoke for the vast majority of heretofore unrepresented people.

Michael Paul Rogin offers a harsh critique of Jackson's Indian policy in *Fathers and Children: Andrew Jackson and the Subjugation of the American Indian* (1975).

Robert V. Remini has written extensively about Andrew Jackson and his times. For a good look at one of Jackson's arch political opponents see his *Henry Clay: Statesman for the Union* (1991).

Mary P. Ryan has corrected the impression of isolation that can easily be drawn from the "sphere" metaphor by showing connections to the "male sphere" in *Women in Public: Between Banners and Ballots, 1825-1880* (1990).

The most probing contemporary analysis of democratic America is Alexis de Tocqueville's classic *Democracy in America*, edited by J. P. Mayer (1969). Since the 1960s, historians have focused on social dynamics more than outstanding political figures. That is why we began with an examination of Jacksonian America rather than with Andrew Jackson himself.

For the rise of democracy from the 1820s to 1840 (before and after as well), see Sean Wilentz, *The rise of American Democracy: Jefferson to Lincoln* (2005).

BEFORE WE GO ON

1. Alexis de Tocqueville expressed concern about the suppression of individual liberty by an unrestrained democratic majority. What examples can you give of that particular problem in the Age of Jackson?

2. The metaphor of "separate spheres" is often used to analyze gender relationships in early nineteenth-century America. Can you apply that model to racial and ethnic groups? If so, how, and if not, why not? What problems does the concept present in helping us to understand society at that time?

Building a Democratic Nation

3. What changes can you see in American society from the era of the Revolution to the era of democracy?

4. What political techniques worked the best in the Age of Jacksonian?

Connections

5. Considering as many details as possible, how democratic had the United States become by the middle of the nineteenth century?

6. What democratic campaign tactics developed in the 1820s and 1830s can you say are still used effectively today?

Chapter 11

STRIVING FOR A BETTER AMERICA, 1815–1860

PERSONAL PERSPECTIVE: FOCUS ON REBECCA GRATZ

CL: Courtesy of Library of Congress

Rebecca Gratz.

> **How did Rebecca Gratz personify the idealism of the early nineteenth century?**

Rebecca Gratz's intelligence, elegance, and piety graced Philadelphia society for nearly eighty years. Born seventh among twelve siblings, "Becky" grew up in a close-knit family that nurtured deep religious values and a commitment to freedom. Her adult life fit the pattern of the sentimental women's novels she adored and the gender role of moral leadership and compassion that the **Cult of True Womanhood** defined for American females. But while Rebecca Gratz exemplified the Romantic era's "True Woman," she stood out as exceptional in two important ways:

she never married, and she remained devoted to her Jewish faith.

Like her female contemporaries, Gratz depended on men for her livelihood. Both her father and her uncle made their fortunes in international commerce. Young Becky's father provided well for his children, including their education. Doing so enhanced their prospects for good marriage matches, defined in Jewish tradition as individuals of uncommon piety, wealth, and education. The nature of Rebecca's formal schooling is unclear; most girls of her generation received little education, but evidence suggests that she attended Philadelphia's exclusive Young Ladies' Academy, one of the few such schools in existence at the beginning of the nineteenth century. When Michael Gratz died, his sons redirected the family business toward the expanding inland commerce. Following her mother's death, Rebecca served as the matron of the family household, which she shared with two of her bachelor brothers and an unmarried sister.

Early nineteenth-century America's 3,000 Jews experienced relatively little of the discrimination that characterized **anti-Semitism** later in the century. They suffered no voting disabilities, although in Pennsylvania one had to swear belief in Christianity in order to hold a public office. Rebecca circulated easily among non-Jews, including the celebrated Romantic writer Washington Irving, yet she remained firmly grounded in traditional Jewish culture. She observed a kosher diet, supported the local synagogue, and embraced Jewish domesticity, which was similar to the Cult of True Womanhood. When later German immigrants, desiring assimilation, rejected customary rituals, Jewish national identity, and the goal of a restored Israel (Zion), Gratz was dismayed. How could they deny their culture?

Religious freedom, however, did not shield Jews from all forms of anti-Semitism. A movement to restrict non-religious activities on Sundays, mounted by Christian evangelists during the 1830s, hurt many Jewish businesses. Furthermore, Rebecca felt pressure from her Christian friends to convert, but she believed that the route to salvation lay through

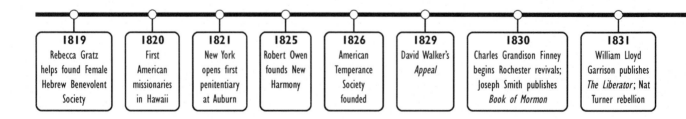

1819	1820	1821	1825	1826	1829	1830	1831
Rebecca Gratz helps found Female Hebrew Benevolent Society	First American missionaries in Hawaii	New York opens first penitentiary at Auburn	Robert Owen founds New Harmony	American Temperance Society founded	David Walker's *Appeal*	Charles Grandison Finney begins Rochester revivals; Joseph Smith publishes *Book of Mormon*	William Lloyd Garrison publishes *The Liberator*; Nat Turner rebellion

obedience to God rather than by following the evangelical formula. "[W]hat a pity," she lamented, "that the best and holiest gift of God . . . should be perverted into a subject of strife." Anti-Semitism worsened with the rising number of Jewish immigrants at mid-century. Even Philadelphia's otherwise sophisticated literary journal *Port Folio*, to which Gratz subscribed, published a piece that referred to "FILTH[Y] . . . Jews."

Rebecca Gratz single-mindedly sought to prove her piety and moral purity to non-Jews who believed that only Christians could be righteous. This may actually have influenced her decision to remain unmarried. Many Americans stereotyped Jewish women as passionate and wanton. To counter that image, Rebecca might have cultivated a "sexless" persona, even though her striking beauty suggested otherwise. In any event, Gratz avoided romantic relationships and dutifully nurtured dozens of nieces and nephews. She described her life as humble, domestic, and useful to others—faithful to the Cult of True Womanhood.

Middle-class women of the early nineteenth century often led religious charities and moral improvement societies. Rebecca used them to bridge Christian and Judaic communities. In 1801, at age twenty, she joined a score of Christian and Jewish women in organizing the **Female Association for the Relief of Women and Children in Reduced Circumstances** (contemporary style did not favor short names). This was the first women's charitable organization in the City of Brotherly Love. With donations from benevolent men, the society supported "gentlewomen" who, through the unfortunate loss of male providers, faced the poorhouse. She added to her social responsibilities in 1815 by helping to found Philadelphia's first orphan asylum. Enterprises like these proliferated through the nineteenth century.

Since religious humanitarianism was assumed of respectable women in those times, Gratz believed that it was important for Jews to organize charities and assist people to realize their full potential and make America a better place. She helped to found the

Female Hebrew Benevolent Society in 1819, the first independent Jewish women's charity in the country. It provided food and other basic necessities to needy Jews, religious instruction, medical care, travelers' aid, and employment counseling. In 1830 she led in the formation of the **Hebrew Sunday School**, part of a widespread effort at that time to expand educational opportunities and teach religious values.

Rebecca Gratz exemplified the optimistic crusade undertaken prior to the Civil War to reform American society. For legions of pious and visionary crusaders, making America into a paradise on earth was not only a figurative but also a literal goal. They believed that men and women were capable of perfection. This was a time of boundless idealism, which flowed from both secular and religious sources: the Second Great Awakening's evangelical revivalism, Jacksonian egalitarianism, and literary Romanticism. All these "isms" emphasized unlimited potential for human and social improvement. Many of the reformers were women like Rebecca Gratz, and not the least of their targets was slavery. Women played prominent roles in the abolitionist movement. From their activities on behalf of others came an impetus to work for their own liberation. "No slaves," observed the South Carolina plantation mistress Mary Boykin Chesnut, are more enslaved than "wives." Few periods in American history have witnessed such a profound commitment to progressive change.

THINKING BACK

1. In what specific ways did Rebecca Gratz personify the idealism of the early nineteenth century?
2. In what specific way did Rebecca Gratz's background suggest the limitations of that idealism?

STOKING THE EVANGELICAL FIRES

If Rebecca Gratz resented the arrogance of Protestant evangelism, she also admired its success in converting heathens and organizing campaigns to stamp out

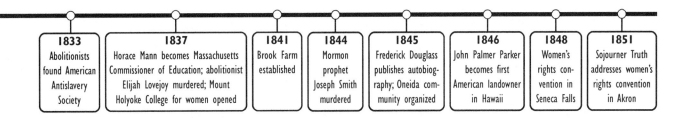

1833	1837	1841	1844	1845	1846	1848	1851
Abolitionists found American Antislavery Society	Horace Mann becomes Massachusetts Commissioner of Education; abolitionist Elijah Lovejoy murdered; Mount Holyoke College for women opened	Brook Farm established	Mormon prophet Joseph Smith murdered	Frederick Douglass publishes autobiography; Oneida community organized	John Palmer Parker becomes first American landowner in Hawaii	Women's rights convention in Seneca Falls	Sojourner Truth addresses women's rights convention in Akron

sin. Revivals gave poor lives rich new meaning and fostered comfortable feelings of belonging to a righteous community. By the 1830s, **Great Awakening** revivals had touched the middle class, bestowing on Protestant evangelism, particularly in the North, a distinctly bourgeois, **Whig** quality. Protestant denominations multiplied even faster than the country's exploding population. The tally of Methodist congregations leaped from 2,700 in 1820 to 20,000 in 1860, Baptists from 2,700 to 12,150, and Presbyterians from 1,700 to 5,400. They endeavored to make Americans healthier and more compassionate. As Protestant churches became more secular in their concerns, however, they no longer satisfied some that God was real. This resulted in a number of Spiritualist spin-off movements at the margins of Protestant Christianity.

Democratizing Religion

How did New Light evangelism blend with democratic idealism?

The revivalists' theatrical methods succeeded in arousing the masses and democratizing religion, but they shocked conservative ministers. The Presbyterian Lyman Beecher (see p. 283) and kindred Congregationalists abhorred the tactic utilized by some uneducated preachers of appealing to people's emotions without reasoning with them. "Illiterate men have never been the chosen instruments of God to build up his cause," Beecher harrumphed. However, the "fire and brimstone" Baptist and Methodist evangelists did not equate formal education with righteousness. "[L]arnin' isn't religion, and eddication don't give a man the power of the Spirit," the Methodist evangelist Lorenzo Dow retorted. Perhaps uncouth by Yale standards, the radical evangelists touched common anxieties. One thoughtful Bostonian attributed Dow's phenomenal success to the fact that he "understood common life, and especially vulgar life—its tastes, prejudices, and weaknesses."

With their common touch, many evangelists preached an explicitly democratic gospel. They often employed provocatively political language. In a pamphlet entitled *Analects upon the Rights of Man*, Dow proclaimed that equal rights derived from "the great and universal 'law of nature.'" Such phrases resounded with Revolutionary republicanism. Dow frequently quoted Thomas Paine and copied Thomas Jefferson's rhetorical style. "By what rule of right can one man exercise authority with a command over others?" Why, he wondered, in such a bountiful country "one hath thousands, gained by the labour of others, while another hath not the assurance of a day's provision." Such rhetoric was loaded with class conflict and mirrored the mass revolt that characterized Jacksonian Democracy.

Electrifying revivals further democratized Christianity by winning busy middle-class converts in the North. More than anyone, Charles Grandison Finney successfully tailored the coarse, frontier camp meeting to the refined sensibilities of the bourgeoisie, heretofore preoccupied in their counting houses and factories. The young, sandy-haired ex-lawyer flashed his ice-blue eyes and simultaneously warmed the souls of listeners with his endearing personality. In 1821 he had abandoned a promising legal career and turned Presbyterian following a shattering religious conversion experience. Defying church authorities, he preached without benefit of formal theological training, circulating through the booming mill towns that hung like ornaments along the Erie Canal. During the winter of 1830–1831, his evangelism culminated in a series of highly publicized revivals in Rochester, New York, a flour-milling center and the fastest-growing town in the country.

The evangelical fires that Finney ignited scorched western New York state so much that it became known as the "burned-over district." Uprooted Yankee immigrants, mostly young single males, had poured into the area looking for jobs in newly opened mills and shops. Many had failed and become despondent and unruly; those who succeeded found that capitalism and the obsession with profit had dissolved the old patriarchal responsibilities of employers toward their employees, leaving workers precariously on their own. Both types of newcomers embraced Finney's Protestant gospel, which promised ultimate redemption and the immediate comfort of a supportive congregational family. Merchants and mill-owners embraced Finney too. They regarded his lessons on self-denial and the Protestant work ethic as just the ticket not only for their own advancement but also for shiftless, undependable, and often inebriated employees, turning them into a more reliable and productive workforce.

Like the vaunted political orators of his time, Charles Grandison Finney understood the first rule of persuasion: know your audience. He eschewed the typically dull, hair-splitting Presbyterian sermons. "Nothing is more calculated to make a sinner feel that religion is some mysterious thing that he cannot understand." Finney did not encourage the same level of emotional display that marked frontier and

Southern revivals, but he did sanction public prayer, intense protracted meetings, and the "anxious bench" for those hoping for a powerful conversion experience. He mixed the precise style of a lawyer's plea with emotional theatricality to create a virtual reality for his audiences. In fact, in 1832 he opened a Presbyterian church in a converted New York City theater.

Finney's revivals democratized Christianity in two other ways. First, he preached that God "made man a moral free agent" and not innately wicked. Life, he said, was a succession of moral choices, and with God's help a person could make correct ones. Every man and woman possessed the capacity for perfection. Finney envisioned a society of saints, as foretold in the New Testament's Revelation of Saint John. Christ would return to earth and reign for a thousand years over a sinless world. Finney was not alone in this belief. William Miller, a Baptist minister from New York, gained nationwide attention by predicting that this **Holy Millennium** (the second coming of Christ) would commence in 1843. He and numerous followers waited expectantly for Christ's return. Disappointed but solid in their faith, the Millerites organized the **Seventh Day Adventist** church in 1860. Without predicting a date, Finney believed that Christian conversion would bring forth the second coming.

Finney's second major contribution to democratic Christianity was in promoting women's active participation in the revival experience. He prompted them to pray and testify to their spiritual conversion in public. The evangelist shrewdly used women, who as a whole were more responsive to revivals than men, to reach their husbands. Once they had converted they would prod their spouses to do likewise. Elevating women's status in the church opened opportunities for leadership in many auxiliary church activities.

Given this kind of encouragement, many women explored the boundaries of freedom within the evangelical movement. The African Methodist Episcopal churches, like other Protestant denominations, barred females from the pulpit, but Julia Foote demanded the right to preach. She believed that spiritual conversion was only the second stage in the process of salvation. In the third and final phase, the Holy Spirit liberated men and women from sin, producing complete harmony and inner peace. "Sanctification" dissolved any obligation to obey ecclesiastical rules that obstructed God's will—like the sexist barrier against gospel preaching. After achieving the "sweet peace" of sanctification, Foote joined the African Methodist Episcopal Zion Church in Boston. But when she persisted in trying to mount the pulpit, church authorities expelled her. For the next few years, Julia Foote traveled from New England to Ohio organizing women for religious work and preaching the doctrine of sanctification.

Populist trends in Christian religion horrified crusty orthodox Calvinists and dismayed even moderates like Lyman Beecher, who praised Finney for igniting the greatest revival of all time while condemning him for unleashing non-Christian passions. As for women's liberation, one horrified husband spoke for countless others when he complained that Finney had "*stuffed* my wife with tracts, alarmed her fears" and led her to the "miraculous discovery, that she had been 'unevenly yoked.'" By the 1840s, even many evangelical ministers thought democratization had gone far enough. But firebrands continued to stoke the evangelical fires, in the process redirecting Protestant Christianity away from punishing sinful behavior toward persuading sinners to make the right choices.

The fervent religious revivals of the Second Great Awakening prompted responses outside of the churches. Numerous jokes targeted unlearned preachers. The foreign visitor Frederick Marryat poked fun at one earnest but uneducated minister who addressed his prayer to the "Almighty and diabolical God." Evangelical fires ignited religious intolerance too, as Rebecca Gratz experienced in a mild form and later Jewish immigrants suffered acutely. Most Americans, even those who were not particularly religious, equated Protestant Christianity with freedom. Finney, like Lorenzo Dow, employed the vocabulary of democratic politics. "Vote in the Lord Jesus Christ as the governor of the Universe," he implored. Ironically, Irish Catholic immigrants associated with the Democratic party while Protestant evangelicals typically voted for more elitist Whigs. The growing number of Catholic immigrants after 1840 was the source of considerable tension and produced ugly Protestant anti-Catholicism.

Spreading the Word

The democratic thrust in American Christianity mandated carrying the gospel far and wide. Previously, responsibility for spreading the word fell to itinerant ministers on horseback. But the new

How did the evangelical movement spread the Christian Gospel?

churches capitalized on modern means of mass communication: organization and technology. The first task, however, was to provide seminaries to train more ministers.

Harvard and Yale had stood foremost for generations in educating the clergy. Both had endured theological crises early in the nineteenth century. Radical free thinking had taken over Yale in 1800, when only one member of the graduating class belonged to a church. But Timothy Dwight, grandson of the venerable Jonathan Edwards, took over the school's presidency and instituted regular campus revivals. "Wheresoever students were found," wrote one undergraduate of his experience at Yale during Dwight's presidency, "—in their rooms, in the chapel, in the hall, in the college-yard, in their walks about the city—the reigning impression was, 'surely God is in this place.'" Unitarianism had entrenched itself at Harvard; reacting against "the insidious encroachments of *innovation*," orthodox Congregationalists

CL: Courtesy of Library of Congress

Rev. Lyman Beecher, Presbyterian minister and first president of Lane Theological Seminary for training Christian missionaries. Beecher's daughter, writing under her married name Harriet Beecher Stowe, authored the famous antislavery novel Uncle Tom's Cabin.

established Andover Theological Seminary. Fire and brimstone filled the atmosphere. "There will be a prayer meeting," Andover's headmaster explained in dismissing classes one day; "those who wish to lie down in everlasting burning may go, the rest will stay." Most remained, and later as ministers they diffused the evangelical gospel. Out West, evangelists founded Lane Seminary in Cincinnati and hired Lyman Beecher to guide it. Oberlin College in Ohio and Knox College in Illinois became famous locations for evangelical revivals.

The tremendous enthusiasm for evangelism in the North also led to the formation of numerous societies to mobilize mass proselytizing enterprises. Born-again businessmen brought deep pockets and specialized talents to the projects, and wives to manage them. **The American Bible Society** (1816) and the **American Tract Society** (1825), both headquartered in New York City, acquired high-speed printing presses and blanketed the country with Testaments and pamphlets. The results were phenomenal. By the end of the 1820s, they had published more than 300,000 Bibles and 6 million tracts. Hundreds of traveling agents, local auxiliary organizations, and local ministers pledged to place a Bible in every home and one new tract each month in the hands of every family in every city and hamlet in the country.

In their zeal to hasten the coming Millennium, Christian denominations organized missionary societies to reach Native Americans, African-American slaves, the urban poor, and heathen populations around the world. Presbyterians had organized a Home Missionary Society as early as 1789 and teamed with Congregationalists to form the Board of Commissioners for Foreign Missions in 1810. Baptists and Methodists shared in the missionary work. One of the prime targets of evangelical enterprise was Hawaii (see The Local Perspective pp. 358-60). American ship captains often sent Hawaiian boys to school in New England. One of them, named Opukahaia, appeared on the steps of Yale College in 1809. The students called him Henry Obookiah and President Timothy Dwight himself cared for the boy. Obookiah studied to become a missionary, and although he died before he could return to the islands, he inspired the Board of Commissioners to send two Yale men, Hiram Bingham and Asa Thurston, and their wives to Hawaii in 1820. The evangelists built schools that enrolled 52,000 pupils in 1831 and acquired the first printing press west of the Rockies.

Missionaries aimed to convert not only heathens but also Catholics and Jews like Rebecca Gratz. The path to the Millennium, they believed, extended from Protestant churches. The effort to proselytize was massive by the standards of the day. By 1850, all the evangelical denominations combined spent $600,000 on mission work. Spreading the word was a logistical challenge successfully met; changing people's lives by purifying their souls and correcting their behavior, however, required heavy-duty coercion.

Stamping Out Sin

What were some of the social sins that Northern reformers sought to stamp out?

Northern evangelical Christians, more than Southerners, followed a theory that the best way to redeem sinful souls was through a network of benevolent societies dedicated to stamping out evil. Jacksonian political culture in the South discouraged external control of personal behavior. Even in the North, Democratic masses had little tolerance for Whig do-gooders legislating their conduct. Instead, reformers relied on the power of persuasion, including direct, hard-hitting confrontation.

Of all the temptations that led people into lives of vice and destruction, "Demon Rum" was the most insidious. Liquor dissolved the bonds of individual self-restraint, a key attribute of respectability, and was the root of other evils as well. Drunkenness loosened the bonds of family by disabling men folk (the breadwinners) and prompting the abuse of wives and children. Heavy drinkers poured household earnings into the liquor trade and received little, if any, benefit from it. Drunkenness contributed to an upsurge of urban social disorder in the 1830s. As cities grew larger and more impersonal, individuals sought companionship in taverns and solace in liquor. Inevitably, outbreaks of mayhem worsened under the influence of heavy drinking. Yuletide merrymaking often started in taverns and turned into drunken rampages against people and property. Drunkenness was also linked to poverty. One study in Rochester showed that 70 percent of the city's poorhouse inmates were alcoholics, as were 90 percent of the convicts in the local jail. Whiskey in the hands of despondent or, worse still, armed Indians posed threats to Native American and settler societies on the frontier.

Farmers and artisans worked hard in those days, but not always soberly. Micajah McGehee planted a peach orchard when he homesteaded in Georgia.

He made peach brandy from the fruit and drank it from morning until he collapsed drunk into bed at night. Almost every master artisan served ale and grog (rum and water) to his employees throughout the workday. Hard drinking had characterized colonial America too, but nothing like after the War of 1812. The expansion of grain farming led to the production and consumption of staggering quantities of distilled, fermented, and brewed beverages. The average American over the age of thirteen guzzled 9.5 gallons of hard liquor and an additional 30.3 gallons of cider, beer, or wine every year, almost three times as much as today. Drinking was a popular social activity irrespective of class. Colleges served it in dining halls. Dinners, parties, and balls usually included copious amounts of liquor, as did Fourth of July parades and other festivities. Bear in mind, however, that liquor was more healthful than polluted water, and even milk and unfermented juices contained disease-bearing organisms.

Alcoholism was unquestionably a serious health and moral problem, and the **Benevolent Empire** mobilized to stamp it out. The **American Temperance Society**, founded in 1826, promoted moderation in drinking as a matter of self-control and attempted to persuade people to avoid saloons. Lyman Beecher, one of the society's founders, published *Six Sermons on the Nature, Occasions, Signs, Evils, and Remedy of Intemperance* as an inspiration, and by the early 1830s the society had over 6,000 local affiliates and better than a million members. In 1836, leaders of the temperance movement reorganized as the **American Temperance Union** and pushed the more radical goal of total abstinence. Teetotalers set an example of self-discipline by taking a "cold water" pledge; the once hard-drinking Henry Clay took it, and Charles Grandison Finney declared it a requirement for Christian conversion. Pious Whigs, comfortable with the idea of government intervention, lobbied state and local authorities for regulations on distilleries and saloons.

Success for the anti-drinking crusade was mixed, but a few Northern state legislatures did ban the sale of liquor in small quantities to keep it out of the hands of the working poor. Their idea was "Let those who can afford it drink." That attitude bred considerable resentment. No state, except Maine, prohibited liquor altogether, and no Southern state passed any kind of restrictive measure. The pious middle class did significantly reduce their own alcohol intake—at least moving liquor out of their homes—and ordinary working people drank less on the job. Saloons flourished in working-class neighborhoods; still, overall, liquor consumption by 1845 had declined by 75 percent.

A religious campaign to preserve the sanctity of the Sunday Sabbath, once a common practice in colonial New England, ran into stiff opposition. Zealous Sabbatarians sought to prohibit all non-religious activity, even travel, on Sunday. One such minister in 1829 advised President-elect Andrew Jackson to revise his schedule so as not to arrive in Washington on Sunday. Lyman Beecher submitted a petition later that year to have the government suspend Sunday mail service. The notably profane Senator Richard M. Johnson, in announcing its rejection, suggested that a better way of making human beings better was to seek God's assistance in "purifying their hearts." Observing a Sunday Sabbath was not a social issue like temperance; it was a matter of doctrine and raised the question of religious freedom. Designating Sunday rather than Saturday as a day of rest and devotion to God involved Scriptural interpretation. Eventually, the Sabbatarians prevailed in keeping Sunday mostly free of commercial activity, much to the chagrin of Jewish and non-religious businessmen.

Sexual immorality troubled evangelical reformers too, particularly prostitution but also fornication (sex between unmarried persons) and adultery (sex involving married persons not married to each other). Illicit sex was another case of self-indulgence and disorder that conflicted with bourgeois values. It undercut families, corrupted women, and supposedly drained men's productive energy and made them lethargic. Commercial sex became more widespread as young, single men and women flooded the cities. Prostitution was not illegal in New York City, unless it caused disorder, and usually had police support. Wholesale merchants often provided traveling salesmen with paid visits to brothels as inducements to handle their products. Boston outlawed prostitution; nevertheless illicit sex flourished with official tolerance. An estimated 2,000 women in 1820 sold sex in the city's expanding red-light district. Southern cities like Charleston and New Orleans also contained thriving sex businesses.

Reformers disagreed over who was the predator and who the prey in this world of passion and deception. Men accused women of seducing weak but basically guileless men. During the 1820s, males in New York and Philadelphia organized Magdalen

Societies to reform these "fallen women." Militant female reformers, however, asserted that women had been lured into prostitution by "the treachery of man." A group that included Lydia Andrews Finney, the great evangelist's wife, organized the **New York Female Moral Reform Society** in 1834 with hundreds of auxiliaries from Maine to Michigan. Their stratagem was to identify brothel customers, especially married men, and publish their names in their newspaper, *The Advocate of Moral Reform*. This, by the way, was one of the first newspapers owned and operated entirely by women and had a circulation of 2,000.

Through the 1830s, efforts to eliminate prostitution failed. A New York woman could earn $200 a month serving ten customers per week, far more for less work than a decent mill girl made, and there were always men willing to risk discovery for a sexual adventure. Gangs periodically broke into brothels scaring the madams and their employees but not shutting down the businesses; neither did occasional police sweeps demanded by angry neighbors. The sensational hatchet murder of a young New York City prostitute in 1836 received wide publicity in the penny tabloids. The subsequent trial of one of her young customers triggered a heated public debate with male and female moral reformers taking turns placing blame on the victim and the murderer. The case disclosed the dangers involved in prostitution but no remedy for the problem.

Persuasion succeeded better than coercion in stamping out sin, and in the South it was the only method employed. Temperance provides the best example. Although Whigs accepted government intervention to hasten the Millennium, Democrats objected to being controlled by others. The moral crusades showed gathering support for the theory that environment determined behavior, a striking contrast to the Calvinist belief that sin was inherent in human nature. Improve the environment and you improve the person. Attacking the causes as well as the symptoms of improper behavior would purify society and bring on the Millennium.

Religion on the Edges

"What would I have said six years ago," New York lawyer George Templeton Strong asked himself, "to anybody who predicted that . . . hundreds of thousands of people in this country would believe them selves able to communicate with the ghosts of their grandfathers?" Strong was referring to an 1846 claim by two sisters,

Margaret and Kate Fox, that spirits knocked on the walls and floorboards of their upstate New York house. The mysterious "rapping" caused a national sensation, and subsequent demonstrations of spirit contact drew thousands of interested witnesses. Some attended for the same reasons they paid to see P. T. Barnum's freak shows (in fact, the famous showman promoted the Fox sisters). Others, like George Templeton Strong, scoffed at the notion of talking ghosts. But many were convinced that the dead communicated with the living.

Spirit contact did not seem far-fetched in early nineteenth-century America. Many people believed in witches, and ghosts haunted African-American culture. Folks everywhere and from various backgrounds used divining rods (called "water witches") in digging water wells. Fortune-tellers and astrologers abounded. Given such widespread belief in the supernatural, we should not be surprised that "mediums" conducted seances to contact the spirit world. There was enough interest in the occult even in the little town of Waterloo, Iowa, to keep two mediums busy.

The Fox sisters popularized a religious phenomenon called **Spiritualism**. In a materialistic society that seemed disconnected from its primordial origins, people used contact with the spirit world to bring a living God back into their lives. Spiritualism was not a cult with specific rites and an acknowledged leader; rather, it was a movement among Christians who acknowledged divine intercession through spirits. People struggling against difficult economic conditions were most susceptible to its appeal. Spiritualism's fountainhead was an eighteenth-century Swedish scientist and theologian named Emanuel Swedenborg who claimed the ability, "in a perfect state of wakefulness," to "converse with the angels and spirits." Spiritualists also drew from the practitioners of mesmerism—the use of hypnosis from which the term "mesmerize" originated. The man who drew these ideas together was Andrew Jackson Davis, an otherwise unsuccessful young man residing in the "burned-over district" of New York during the 1830s. Spiritualism also embraced science and technology. Robert Hare, a professor of chemistry at the University of Pennsylvania and a frequent contributor to the *American Journal of Science*, theorized that "spirit" was actually matter that could be scientifically analyzed.

The essence of Spiritualism was that the universe was an entity unified by spirits who linked God and humankind. Spirit contact came through seances conducted by special persons known as "mediums." Although some participants just wanted to communicate with departed loved ones, the philosophical goal of Spiritualists was cosmic harmony. "By spiritual intercourse," Davis explained, "we learn that all men shall ultimately be joined into one Brotherhood, their interests shall be pure and reciprocal; their customs shall be just and harmonious; they shall be as one Body, animated by Universal Love and governed by pure Wisdom."

Spiritualism of another sort took hold of fifteen-year-old Joseph Smith of Palmyra, New York, a descendent of the earliest Puritans whose family had long since fallen on hard times. Smith showed no signs of precociousness. As one neighbor later recalled, "Joe was the most ragged, lazy fellow in the place." But in 1819 he began receiving visions in which an angel commanded him to found a new church and directed him to buried golden tablets containing inscriptions laying out the "latter days" of the world with instructions for gathering believers for the coming Millennium. In 1830, Smith published the transcriptions as the *Book*

Image © Melissa Dockstader, 2010. Used by permission of Shutterstock, Inc.

Mormon Temple in Salt Lake City, Utah.

of Mormon and began attracting hundreds of converts, or "latter day saints," whom he organized into what became the **Church of Jesus Christ of Latter-Day Saints.** Smith dispatched disciples to Missouri to locate a Mormon Zion there and to follow God's commandment to convert Native Americans. On the way to Missouri, the Mormon vanguard established a community of converts in northwestern Ohio. Smith joined them and established his religious authority as God's sole Prophet, but the Panic of 1837 brought financial disaster to the Ohio settlement, and Smith led the Saints on to Missouri.

Although most residents of Missouri were not averse to religious experiments, they resented growing Mormon militancy and political activism. During the 1838 elections, flaming rhetoric and armed clashes forced the Mormons to move once again, this time across the Mississippi River into neighboring Illinois where they established a prosperous community named Nauvoo. Smith aligned himself politically with the ruling Whig party, promising to deliver Mormon votes in return for a town charter that allowed the community's nearly 15,000 Saints to govern themselves. This enraged local Democrats. Finally, in 1844 anti-Mormon hostility exploded against the practice of plural marriage (polygamy). Authorities jailed Smith, and on June 27, a mob dragged him out and murdered him. Smith's family and one faction of Mormons renounced polygamy and settled in Iowa, but the larger group chose to follow Brigham Young to the Far West. Reaching an agreement with Mexican authorities to settle on the remote New Mexico frontier, in 1847 they began their Great Migration to the Great Salt Lake.

The evangelical revivals of the 1830s inspired many people to contemplate a world free from sin and tribulation, resulting in an upsurge of religious activity and social reforms. Southern and frontier evangelists dealt with the issue of sin on a personal basis and held out the prospect of heavenly salvation, whereas Northern evangelical Whigs organized societies to address not only individual but also collective transgressions against God in order to perfect an imperfect world. Spiritualists and Mormons in somewhat different ways exemplified another approach: making direct contact with a spiritual world that was closer to the Divine or, short of that, separating from a corrupt society on earth and creating something akin to the early Puritans' beacon guiding sinners to a safe haven where they might await the Second Coming of Christ.

THINKING BACK

1. How did Christian evangelism blend with democratic trends of the period?
2. What was the connection between religious revivalism and social reform?

UTOPIAN DREAMS

Scores of religious communities appeared in New England and across the Midwest in the 1830s and 1840s. Many were Spiritualist and Millennial; all disdained a society that seemed to have lost its sense of religious and social responsibility in the Market Revolution. These believers shared with more secular visionaries the goal of human and social perfection. Instead of the coercive measures, however, they taught by example. Their ideas seemed weird and ridiculous to others, and their communities rarely attracted more than a few hundred residents; scarcely any of them outlived the generations that founded them. But each was a tableau representing the intense idealism of the time and the almost desperate attempt to replace shattered social institutions with new ones built on Christian ethics and respect for labor.

Religious Communities

A few radical religious communities had existed in the eighteenth century, but scores of them came into existence in **antebellum** (pre-Civil War) times. Pious groups retreated from the sinful world both literally and figuratively, like the seventeenth-century Pilgrims. Part of their motivation was psychological: the structure and discipline of their commonwealths provided shelters from the chaos and disorder of the Market Revolution. But they were also driven by religious conviction. Invariably, individuals of extraordinary piety inspired others to follow. Participants established authoritarian regimes, mirroring God's Kingdom, and because the residents believed that private property fostered selfishness and inequality, they renounced individual ownership. In other words, they were communists preparing for Christ's return and the inauguration of the Millennium.

Shakers were the most successful of these radical religious sects, establishing more than twenty communities prior to the Civil War, some of which survived well into the twentieth century. A Quaker offshoot, the Shakers acquired their name from a peculiar dance in which they shook their hands to rid

What were the common goals of religious communities, and what were some of the defining characteristics of specific ones?

themselves of sin. The sect originated in England, from where a handful came to America in 1774 following Ann Lee Stanton, a former mill worker who claimed to embody the feminine side of God. Mother Ann, as she was known, died in 1784; however, Shaker communities continued to grow by recruiting revival converts during the Second Great Awakening. They entered their period of greatest prosperity in 1830 when membership reached 6,000.

Shakers strove for perfection defined by such virtues as faith, hope, charity, simplicity, and equality. Converts pledged to observe strict gender equality. Men and women worked separately and practiced celibacy. Certain of the approaching Millennium, they saw no reason to reproduce, and sex for pleasure was self-indulgent. They maintained their numbers by admitting new members. A central ministry, evenly divided between women and men, dictated and enforced rules. Shaker societies were not democratic, but they were entirely voluntary and few people left them.

Nothing stands out more conspicuously than the Shakers' passion for simplicity and order. Their houses contained only necessities, carefully constructed and arranged: no pictures or curtains (they collected dust); occasional hand-woven rugs on clean, hardwood floors; beautifully austere yet functional chairs and tables; and rows of wooden wall pegs for hanging coats and hats. The Shakers' practical ingenuity was evident in devices that pumped cool spring water through metal coils for refrigeration and hot water for radiated heat in winter. Interestingly, Shakers adapted to the market economy by selling medicinal herbs and assorted handicraft products like brooms, palm-leaf bonnets, and furniture.

Other religious communities relied on immigrants for new members. George Rapp, a German grape grower involved in protests against liberalism in the Lutheran Church, settled with his followers in the United States in 1804. They sought a haven where they could practice their religious beliefs, including renunciation of marriage and sexual intercourse. **Rappites** were not communists in principle, but they had to pool their meager assets in order to purchase land. Six hundred settled in western Pennsylvania; however, the area was not good for grapes and in 1815 Rapp moved them to Indiana, establishing a community called **Harmony**. Another group of German pietists founded the **Amana Society** in 1843 on land near Buffalo, New York. Distracted by commotion of the busy Erie Canal, they resettled on 26,000 acres in Iowa. Amana residents lived simply and democratically on farms and villages, prospering

Image © Jeffrey M. Frank, 2010. Used by permission of Shutterstock, Inc.

Shaker Meeting House, Canterbury, New Hampshire.

through hard work and rising land values. Both groups spoke only German, which meant that only German-speakers entered the communities; that and Rappite celibacy stunted growth.

Experiments such as these, regardless of their eccentricities and insubstantial followings, symbolize a widespread longing for a sense of spiritual community in a bustling country given to selfish competition, material obsession, and individualism. Rules and rituals aimed at building harmony, self-sacrifice, and charity. **Perfectionism**, as they understood it from the Bible, was their goal. They knew how God wanted them to live and possessed the devotion to commit themselves to that ideal and the reward of salvation.

Intellectual and Agrarian Visionaries

Other visionaries drew concepts of perfection from secular as well as religious sources. The swirl of republican ideologies, for example, offered numerous definitions of equality, each of which provided a basis for utopian experiment. In all, more than fifty visionary communities existed for longer or shorter periods of time in pre-Civil War America. They turned away from the changing national economy and back toward an ideal of subsistence farming and artisanship.

What was the main difference between visionary and religious communities, and how did specific visionary communities seek to achieve their goals?

Residents of **Hopedale**, a small collective farm established in 1841 in Milford, Massachusetts, subscribed to equality "irrespective of sex, color, occupation, wealth, rank, or any other natural or advantitious peculiarity." They purchased shares in the enterprise. Begun by a Universalist minister, Adin Ballou, Hopedale was committed to "practical" social reforms. An insurmountable problem, however, was disagreements over everyday details. William Ellery Channing, a warm supporter, applauded the community's efforts to "live together as brothers" instead of "preying on one another," but noted the "difficulty of reconciling so many wills, of bringing so many individuals to such a unity of feeling and judgment as is necessary to the management of an extensive common concern." Hopedale failed, after sixteen years, because of what Ballou confessed was "a deficiency . . . of those graces and powers of character which are requisite to the realization of the Christian ideal of human society."

Some social experimenters were too fuzzy-headed to succeed. Bronson Alcott, a naive Boston schoolteacher and intellectual, tried to found a "second Eden" with a crabby Englishman named Charles Lane. Mostly with Lane's money, the two purchased a small farm called **Fruitlands** in a picturesque Massachusetts valley some fifty miles from Boston. In the spring of 1843, they settled in with their families and a small group of eccentrics. The Lane banned gaiety or frivolity, causing Alcott's daughter Louisa (author of the novel *Little Women*) and most of the others to hate him. He also decreed a diet of potatoes, apples, whole wheat bread, and acorns. Workers could not use beasts of burden (animal abuse), wear cotton (slave labor) or wool (deprivation of the sheep's property), or bathe in warm water (self-indulgent). The experiment broke up in less than a year with the despondent Alcott lying face-to-the-wall wishing he were dead.

All the intellectual firepower and cheerfulness that Fruitlands lacked was present in the famous **Brook Farm** experiment. Organized in 1841 by George Ripley, a Unitarian minister, Brook Farm enjoyed the support of such luminary reformers as Ralph Waldo Emerson, Margaret Fuller, and Horace Greeley, all intelligent, learned, and deeply humanitarian. Brook Farm aimed to establish a natural union between intellectual and manual labor. Simplicity, egalitarianism, and democracy were its guiding canons—fittingly so in Jacksonian America. Residents employed no servants and eagerly pitched in to accomplish daily chores. When the acclaimed writer Nathaniel Hawthorne joined the colony, he received a pitchfork and the task of disposing of a pile of manure.

Brook Farm barely sustained itself economically, since this brainy community possessed more good will than practical skill, but the intellectual stimulation excited everyone. Lectures by distinguished scholars, artists, and social activists enlivened evenings. Brook Farm's philosophy underscored informality and spontaneity, and that also characterized the community's approach to education. "It was a perpetual picnic," said Emerson, a frequent visitor though never a resident, "a French Revolution in small, an Age of Reason in a patty-pan."

If any utopian experiment should have succeeded it was Brook Farm. As one of the teachers later wrote, "there were never such witty potato-patches and such sparkling cornfields before or since." However, not everyone who lived there liked it, including the disillusioned and aforementioned Hawthorne. A devastating fire and an ill-advised venture into socialism doomed Brook Farm, and in 1847 its members amiably closed it down.

The most sensational and controversial utopian experiment of the era took place at **Oneida**, New York. A young lawyer, John Humphrey Noyes, one of Charles Grandison Finney's converts, sought perfection through the wedding of revivalism and socialism. But the most outlandish of Noyes' tenets was his rejection of traditional marriages. Husbands exploited wives, he asserted, and conventional marriages united two individuals to the exclusion of all others and thus were antisocial. Noyes' remedy was "complex marriage," whereby every man in the community was married to every woman. To numerous complaints that he was promoting promiscuity and "free love" Noyes responded by pointing out that sex was by mutual consent. Noyes also urged men to practice withdrawal before ejaculation to limit pregnancies and counseling before engaging in intercourse. Few people paid much attention to the community's other beliefs and practices, but they protested mightily against Oneida's complex marriage.

Noyes and his followers prized harmony and cooperation more than competitive zeal. Frank encounter sessions helped alleviate conflict within the community. Residents did not believe in hard work in their farming and logging enterprises. Even after the development of a profitable silverware industry, for which Oneida is still known, its residents ambled casually in their search for perfection. Parents indulged their children, and the community's school pioneered in what later would be known as progressive education. "It was never, in our minds an experiment," commented one Oneida woman, adding that "we believed we were living under a system which the whole world would sooner or later adopt." In fact, each of the utopian experiments was based on the same assumption—like the Puritans' city on a hill. When few followed their examples, discouragement ensued and the communities disbanded. But while they lasted they demonstrated an intense idealism and a major commitment to progress and perfectionism.

Socialist Experiments

Some radical social experiments sprang from anti-capitalist ideological currents in Europe. They were not just non-religious; most were anti-evangelical. Some humanitarians hoped to establish models of cooperation and harmony based on the social theories of the French reformer Charles Fourier. They organized **Fourierist** "phalanxes," each with numerous specialized work groups and democratically elected leaders. Over twenty phalanxes surfaced in the 1840s with several hundred total members.

> What in particular did the socialist experiments attempt to accomplish, and what became of them?

A wealthy Scottish industrialist, Robert Owen, developed the most ambitious plan for a socialist community in the United States. The son of a Welsh saddler and ironmonger, Owen ascended the economic ladder to a position of great power, but unlike other factory tycoons he developed a sensitivity to the workers' plight. After building a model factory town in Lanark, Scotland, and achieving an international reputation as a reform-minded industrialist, the charming Owen decided to locate an experimental community in the United States based on the concept of cooperative ownership of property.

After a popular speaking tour that included two addresses to the House of Representatives in Washington, Robert Owen purchased the Rappites' property in Indiana (George Rapp moved his people again to Pennsylvania), brought some 900 settlers, and christened the community **New Harmony**. Owen's architectural plan was nothing if not grandiose, an enclosed square compound a thousand feet on each side. Within, he intended to construct mills, shops, houses, schools, and eventually a university. From this beginning, Owen hoped to engineer a new society along socialist theory. Observing, as Adam Smith and other liberal British economists had, that labor was the major source of wealth, he denigrated capitalist parasites. Owen's name eventually came to be associated with militant anti-capitalism.

One of Robert Owen's most ardent disciples was Frances Wright, a flamboyant, free-thinking daughter of a Scottish tradesman and a noted socialist. "Fanny" Wright met Owen in the United States in 1825, soon joining the New Harmony community and publishing a journal called *Free Enquirer*. Soon her interest turned toward antislavery. She purchased a plantation called **Nashoba** near Memphis, Tennessee, and established an experimental farm that would teach slaves to labor independently. The profits from Nashoba could be used to purchase the slaves' freedom. In 1829 she moved on to New York and a career on the lecture circuit, advocating Owenism, feminism, and Deism. Admirers called her the "female Tom Paine;" critics branded her the "Priestess of Beelzebub" because of her libertine ideas and flowing white robes. Wright, acting with Owen's son Robert Dale Owen, finally turned to educational reform.

Alas, the socialist experiments worked no better as agents of social change than the religious utopias. Residents of the communities failed to live up to the idealistic expectations of their dreamy founders. Disillusion and dissension plagued New Harmony and Owen's dream never materialized. Frances Wright failed to generate enough interest in her plan to end slavery to sustain Nashoba.

Individualism and the zeal for commercial capitalism eclipsed these communal visions. Communal living required prodigious self-sacrifice, but too much opportunity existed within the capitalist commercial economy for the accumulation of wealth and luxury, even with the unsettling cycles of boom and bust. The visionary communities failed to change society in the ways their members had planned, but their ideals survive even today as is evident in a popular political vocabulary that includes terms like "compassion," "charity," and "cooperation."

THINKING BACK

1. What kind of perfection did religious evangelists seek?
2. What kind of perfection did the secular visionaries hope to attain, and how were their goals and tactics different from the religious reformers?

THE FLOWERING OF ROMANTICISM

Reforming zeal in the decades preceding the Civil War expressed itself simultaneously in evangelical revivals and Jacksonian Democracy. Those two sources of progressive change, opposite to each other in European-based cultures that separated spiritual from natural objects, merged in Romanticism (see The Global Perspective, pp. 268-70). Like Christians, some Romantics avowed that living people possessed a divine spirit. And just as Charles Grandison Finney preached the doctrine of human perfection, Romantics imagined a world as it could be—a paradise. Like Jacksonian Democrats, they praised the individual and were optimistic about her or his advancement. This rosy outlook gripped the United States during the 1830s, 1840s, and 1850s. It constituted a rich environment for the writers and scholars who brought the Romantic Movement to full bloom.

Transcendentalism and Individualism

Some free thinkers on the fringe of Protestant Christianity drifted entirely out of organized religion because it was too thought-confining. Among them were a handful of intellectuals who felt constrained by ultra-liberal Unitarian doctrines. All rejected standard conceptions of God and held to the mystical belief that humanity and divinity touched through the soul.

> What were the key elements in Romantic literature, and how did the Transcendentalists and the poet Walt Whitman exhibit those characteristics?

Intuition (which they called "reason") allowed women and men to understand God (they often used euphemisms like "eternal Center," "Unity," and "Over-Soul). They believed that people could transcend themselves and become divine. By 1836 this particular group had formed the **Transcendentalist Club**, meeting frequently for lofty discussions in the Concord, Massachusetts, home of their guru Ralph Waldo Emerson. They published their views, including opposition to the economic competitiveness associated with the Market Revolution, in a journal called the *Dial*, edited by the feminist Margaret Fuller.

Ralph Waldo Emerson gave fullest expression to the Transcendentalist philosophy. The son of a Unitarian minister, a Harvard graduate, and one-time Unitarian himself, Emerson made a living lecturing, writing, and teaching about Transcendentalism. He explained that nature linked all existence, including humanity and God. In an essay entitled "Nature," published in 1836, he wrote: "Standing on the bare ground, . . . I see all. The currents of the Universal Being circulate through me; I am part or particle of God." Like other Romantics, Emerson invested nature with supreme beauty, wisdom, and freedom.

Transcendentalism was all about individual freedom to achieve unity with God. People must be who they are, and consistency and conformity were prisons that prevented self-actualization and transcendence. "A foolish consistency," Emerson stated in his most famous essay, "Self-Reliance," is the "hobgoblin of little minds." "I must be myself," he said. "I cannot break myself any longer for you, or you." Thus, Emerson never joined the Brook Farm community, even though he shared their ideals and supported their goals because to do so would compromise his freedom to think and act as an individual.

The naturalist Henry David Thoreau practiced transcendental philosophy even more than his friend and mentor Emerson. For sixteen months in 1845–1846, he lived alone by the shore of Walden Pond on Emerson's property outside of Concord. Thoreau scorned material possessions beyond essentials. The key to spiritual fulfillment, he said, was "simplicity." His book *Walden* (1854) was his masterpiece, demonstrating how to strip life down to its bare necessities and heighten one's sensitivity to the beauties of nature. Thoreau lived up to his belief in individualism by refusing to conform to rules that violated his conscience. He declined to pay taxes to the federal government because it supported slavery, and in an essay on "Civil Disobedience" he put forth a theory of passive resistance to immoral authority that influenced modern civil rights leaders such as Ghandi and Martin Luther King, Jr.

Walt Whitman, the son of a Brooklyn carpenter, worked as a journalist in preparation for the greatest celebration of human life in American literature, his poem *Leaves of Grass* (1855). This splendid work was actually a series of poems unified by their radical individualism, as can be seen in the title of one of them: "Song of Myself," which begins: "I celebrate myself, and sing myself." What makes the composition unique, beside its sexual subject matter (Whitman was homosexual), was its unrhymed, free verse form. Whitman freed himself from the conventions that gripped early nineteenth-century literature, and doomed his book to slow sales. Always on the edge of poverty, Whitman nevertheless felt confident of his work's importance, which has been widely recognized since his death in 1892.

Soaring optimism, the perfection of nature, and the worth of the individual human being were key elements in Romantic literature. They also ruled over American culture in Jacksonian America. Transcendentalists took all three to the conclusion that American society could be improved. Along with evangelical revivalists and utopians, they pushed the United States toward the ideal of perfection.

A Less Sunny Outlook

Optimism about individual perfection did not show itself in all Romantic writers. Individualism can become arrogance, and its pursuit can lead to destruction. Caution, some writers advised, should be taken about pushing it too far. And nature, including human nature, had its dark and dangerous side.

Other Romantic writers dramatized the destructiveness of nature and anti-social individualism. Herman Melville, who first went to sea as a merchant sailor at age nineteen and sailed again in his early twenties aboard a whaler in the South Pacific, accumulated a wealth of experiences for his famous adventure tales. *Typee* (1846), his first novel, was an instant success, but his masterpiece, *Moby-Dick* (1851) tells more about the obsessive side of human nature and what the author thought about the thralldom of nature. Captain Ahab, the novel's central character, puts his personal vendetta against the great white whale, Moby-Dick, above the welfare of his ship's crew. In the end, the whale destroys Ahab and nearly all the men who depended on him. Likewise, Nathaniel Hawthorne criticized Romanticism's glorification of individual ego. In numerous novels and short stories, Hawthorne, who wrote mostly about colonial New England society, betrayed his innate skepticism of transcendentalism and other forms of celebrating the individual and nature without rejecting them altogether.

> Who were the major critics of Romanticism's sunny outlook, and what did they say?

The essence of Romanticism was to view the world in positive terms. Even where evil existed, good triumphed in the end. Romanticism was a metaphor for the morality that antebellum Americans believed in and the impetus for reform that marked the early nineteenth century.

Early Environmentalism

In Transcendentalist thinking, nature uplifted the soul. It also supported economic growth. Considering all the attention that farmers, entrepreneurs, and philosophers paid to the environment, sensitivity to changes in its health and to its preservation came naturally.

> What early expressions foreshadowed modern environmentalism?

Economic expansion wreaked havoc on woodlands. By 1850, over 100 million acres of forest land had been cleared for farming, most of it since 1800, and commercial timber consumption added to forest depletion. Fuel needs, housing material, and ship-building material constituted the bulk of the commercial lumber market. Steamboats burned 500 cords of firewood on each round-trip from Louisville to New Orleans.

Thoreau wrote, "Wilderness is the preservation of the World," but what would preserve the wilderness? That question troubled a former Vermont sheep raiser and now successful businessman, George Perkins Marsh. Marsh had observed disturbing effects of human activity on the landscape. "Wherever he plants his foot, the harmonies of nature are turned to discords." When Marsh was born in 1801, over 90 percent of Vermont was forested; in 1850 less than half was wooded. In a book that marks the inception of the conservationist mentality, *Man and Nature* (1864), Marsh observed that "of all organic beings, man alone is to be regarded as essentially a destructive power." The "harmonies of nature," he believed, could be maintained through reasonable management of the land and its resources. Marsh was America's first environmentalist, recognizing nature as an organic entity composed of many integrated parts. Damage to one part affected others. This was a very modern concept that placed Marsh ahead of others concerned only with forests, land erosion, or the depletion of animal populations.

Only later, however, with further human demands on the land and its resources, would conservation become a major influence on public policy. Most concern in pre-Civil War America was with people and their condition.

THINKING BACK

1. Where did American Romantic literature find its primary themes, and what were those themes?
2. How did Romanticism give rise to efforts at natural preservation that foreshadowed modern environmentalism?

SOCIAL REFORMS

Americans' faith in progress burdened them with responsibility for social change. Old institutions reflected the elitist notion that only a few possessed wisdom and good character, but in the Romantic Era the idea took hold that environment rather than human nature dictated behavior. A man became a criminal because he never received an education or possessed the skills to succeed in an occupation or profession. A woman fell into prostitution merely because her parents died and left her in nobody's care. Reformers now urged society to accept the burden of rehabilitating misfits rather than locking them away. Citizens acted together in a massive crusade to alter the basic institutions of American society in order to realize the ideal state of perfection.

Progressive Education

Antebellum society placed new demands on schools, traditionally employed to teach basic literacy skills that enabled children to read and understand holy scripture (the Bible or Talmud). A popular primer published in Boston in 1800, for example, taught the alphabet along with religious principles. To learn the letter A, pupils read that "In Adam's Fall/We sinned All." But a democratic political system required educated citizens; new immigrants needed instruction in citizenship; a commercial economy necessitated educated clerks; True Womanhood implied female education; and freethinkers clamored for reasoning over rote memorization. These thrusts combined in a major push for educational reform.

> **What ideas about progressive education emerged from the era of reform?**

Although public schools had functioned since colonial times, communities did little to support them. Even New Englanders typically provided only dingy shacks for schools, hired teachers barely more literate than their pupils, and paid them meager salaries. Wealthy Southern planters hired tutors for their children, and public schools operated only in a few cities in the South. Most rural white children in the South, and virtually all blacks, were deprived of formal schooling. Along Sugar Creek in Illinois, Samuel Williams, a farmhand and rail splitter who had only recently learned his ABCs, taught thirty of the local landowners' children in the winter of 1823 in return for food and board. Using Noah Webster's *Spelling Book* and McGuffey Readers, teachers stressed values as well as the "three R's." Discipline under the administration of male teachers was universally harsh. "As for those boys and girls that mind not their books," Webster observed, "they will come to some bad end, and must be whipt till they mend their ways." Cornelius Lyman, an Illinois schoolmaster, used the rod so viciously that one boy's body provided proof, said a school investigator, that "he had been placed under the tuition of one who knew how to torture as well as teach."

The movement for teacher training gained momentum during the 1830s. Samuel Read Hall opened a normal (teacher training) school in his home in Concord, Vermont, in 1823. He introduced the blackboard and the use of illustrations as teaching methods as well as courses in geography and history. Hall not only taught the classes but he also wrote the texts. His fame spread throughout New England where he became a consultant in the establishment of other normal schools.

Massachusetts became the first state (1837) to create the position of state superintendent of education, and the lawyer Horace Mann was the first person to hold it. Friends criticized his decision to sacrifice his budding career for such a meaningless position, to which he replied: "If the title is not sufficiently honorable now, then it is clearly left for me to elevate it." And that he did, working slavishly for twelve years. Mann compiled exhaustive reports to the legislature calling for reforms, to which grudging lawmakers responded by doubling state appropriations, improving school buildings, adding a month to the school term, and authorizing teacher training. Mann inspired action in other states too, and gradually the concept of free public schools took hold in the Northeast. By 1860, three-fourths of the school-age population attended school. In the South and Midwest, the rural population, transient nature of communities, and more primitive economies slowed progress and school attendance was much lower.

Some of the most innovative teaching methods developed in utopian community schools. Progressive teachers followed the theories of the Swiss educator Johann Heinrich Pestalozzi, who argued that learning was a natural process that teachers should facilitate. The Transcendentalists encouraged free thinking, physical activity as well as mental discipline, and individual learning at Brook Farm. Progressives also believed that learning should be exciting and not painful. Such principles eventually found their way into public education.

Opportunities for women as schoolteachers expanded along with their responsibility for nurturing moral character. And teacher training received growing emphasis. Emma Willard earned acclaim for her pioneering normal school for women in Troy, New York, which opened in 1821. A major breakthrough in female higher education came with the opening of

During the 1820s and 1830s, a growing awareness of childhood as a time of nurturing and learning coupled with the inability of the working poor to educate their children at home led to a public school movement. In addition to literacy skills, students in schools such as this received lessons in the Protestant ethic of hard work and prudent living.

Image © Infomages, 2010. Used by permission of Shutterstock, Inc.

Mount Holyoke College in 1837. It offered education equal to that of men's colleges even though the school did not receive formal recognition as a college until 1888.

Expansion of higher education came largely through the efforts of religious denominations, whose mission expanded to providing liberal arts education. Many colleges implemented manual labor programs to cover the students' tuition. The Methodists founded Emory College in Georgia in 1837 and it soon rivaled the state university as an educational center. Oberlin College in Ohio helped lead the way not only in progressive education but also in social reform. It was among the first colleges to admit women and it played a significant role in the antislavery crusade.

The importance of education also showed itself in the amount of money and effort expended on creating learning opportunities for adult citizens. Over 50,000 libraries operated on the eve of the Civil War. The vast majority were school libraries, but approximately 3,000 towns and cities maintained public libraries. John Jacob Astor donated a major collection to the New York Public Library, and other philanthropists also endowed libraries. Public lyceums sponsored lectures by prominent figures like Ralph Waldo Emerson and Frances Wright. Most prominent in New England, lyceums existed in half the states by 1840. Massachusetts that year held 137 local lyceum lectures attended by 33,000 "lecture addicts."

Belief in the transforming power of education inspired a program of schools among Native Americans. If Indians were to be civilized, reformers contended, it would be through education. Christian missionaries conducted schools in the designated Indian Territory (Oklahoma) and as far west as the Oregon Territory in the 1840s. Despite a general failure to inculcate European values among Native Americans, however, educational reforms succeeded in making the United States the most literate country in the world by the Civil War. But what about those whom Noah Webster had warned would come to a bad end if they did not study their lessons?

Prisons to Penitentiaries

> **How did perfectionism influence the way society treated criminals?**

On a frigid February morning in 1823, William Gross walked from the Walnut Street jail in Philadelphia to Logan Square, one and a half miles away, accompanied by the sheriff, the coroner, and a hangman in a black mask. After Gross advised onlookers to look upon his fate as the result of a life of crime, the executioner sprung the trap and the young man dropped to his death. Gross' execution for the murder of Keziah Stow was the last such public ritual in Philadelphia. Within months, the state of Pennsylvania ended public executions as part of a series of reforms that brought in new ideas about the treatment of criminals. Many other states did likewise.

Although capital punishment (hanging in most instances) remained common for crimes such as murder, penal reformers began to shift the emphasis from vengeance against criminals to rehabilitation. Whipping and other corporeal punishments resembled slave masters' plantation tyranny. Increasingly, penal codes prescribed imprisonment. Reformers also criticized jails that mixed together all sorts of offenders: men and women, delinquent children, paupers and debtors, and hardened criminals. Prison inspectors in Pennsylvania argued that "the petty thief becomes the pupil of the highway robber; the beardless boy listens with delight to the well-told tale of daring exploits and hair-breadth escapes of hoary headed villainy, and from the experience of age derives instruction which fits him to be a pest and terror to society."

Reforms did not result in coddling criminals. Many advocates of reform urged solitary confinement, believing that a man or woman would suffer more from total isolation than from being in work gangs or general lock-ups. Solitary confinement also offered abundant opportunity to contemplate wrongdoing and experience conversion. "I will venture to say," wrote one reformer, "that one year passed in this way would have more effect upon criminals, than ten years passed in the continual society of numerous fellow convicts." This approach required new prison design. In 1821, New York constructed the first new "penitentiary" (the name suggested remorse and reform) at Auburn and then another at Sing Sing. Solitary confinement, however, caused physical deterioration, severe mental stress, and suicide. Officials modified the system, using work assignments during the day, silence during labor and meals, and solitary confinement at night. Pennsylvania built the ultra-modern Eastern State Penitentiary outside of Philadelphia, which contained roomy cells, running water, and toilet facilities. Inmates were kept in solitary confinement.

A controversy raged over the Auburn and Pennsylvania systems, but in the end most state legislatures followed

Eastern State Penitentiary, Philadelphia

the more economical Auburn model. By 1840, twelve Auburn-style corrections facilities had been constructed with 5,000 cells, some with separate women's units, profitable industrial departments, and permanent chaplains and Sunday schools. They certainly represented a great advancement in the treatment of criminals; however, the severity of the discipline in some ways marked no improvement at all over previous jail conditions.

One of the most sensible prison reforms involved debtors, many of whom were unfortunate victims of economic depression. Imprisoning them prevented them from paying off their debts, some of which were trivial amounts. One Vermont man landed in jail for owing a business establishment fifty-four cents, and in Philadelphia in 1828, 1,000 debtors were in prison for average debts of $25 although it cost the prison twelve times that amount to keep them. Reforms began slowly with legislatures establishing minimum indebtedness that could result in imprisonment, then exempting women (which must have pleased Rebecca Gratz), and finally abolishing debtors' prison altogether.

Treating Mental Disorders

Treatment of the insane had once been as cruel as dealing with criminals. In fact, authorities usually imprisoned severely disturbed individuals along with thieves and murderers. The famous reformer Dorothea Dix found that in Massachusetts the insane were "confined . . . in cages, closets, cellars, stalls, pens! Chained, naked, beaten with rods, and lashed into obedience." The common assumption was that they had reverted to an animal state. Puritans had regarded all disability as the will of God—a punishment for wrongdoing or a test of faith. Revised perceptions of God emanating from the evangelical revivals, however, regarded Him as loving and forgiving. An optimistic and more compassionate society believed it owned the insane a comfortable environment and every scientific treatment available. Curing or overcoming an infirmity resembled progress toward perfection.

> **How did the treatment of mental disorders change during the early nineteenth century?**

Two approaches to mental illness combined in antebellum America to transform standard ways of treating it. The eighteenth-century physician and statesman Benjamin Rush had pioneered the field of psychiatry in the United States. Instead of locking patients away, Rush experimented with diet, water therapies, shock treatment, and humane care. The other innovation came from Europe, where specialists had begun using retreats to create soothing asylums (a sanctuary or refuge) for mentally ill patients. Between 1815 and 1840, seven states from Maine to Ohio had built insane asylums.

Dorothea Dix became the champion of insane asylums. Rocked in the cradle of humane New England evangelism, she taught school in her home as a young woman and engaged in charitable endeavors. In the 1840s, the plight of the insane captured her attention, and she successfully lobbied several state legislatures to build mental hospitals. Her method involved traveling extensively, inspecting prisons, hospitals, and almshouses, and then reporting in great detail to lawmakers. "I am the Revelation of hundreds of wailing, suffering creatures," she exclaimed. Critics from taxpayers to prison and hospital officials derided this snooping woman and denounced her "sensational and slanderous lies," but fifteen states responded by opening or expanding facilities.

Such prodigious efforts produced generally favorable assessments of their effectiveness. In 1832, an investigative committee told the Massachusetts legislature that "with appropriate medical and moral treatment, insanity yields with more readiness than ordinary diseases." More sober analysis, however, revealed that behind the relatively few showcase asylums, most severely disturbed patients were still locked up in windowless rooms or even in cages. Eventually, optimism regarding the treatment of mental illness gave way to the gloomy conclusion of a doctor who said that "when a man becomes insane, he is about used up for this world."

Care for unfortunates, including Rebecca Gratz' **Female Association for the Relief of Women and Children in Reduced Circumstances**, orphanages, and homes for "fallen women," like the host of other reforms reflects the humanitarian crusade undertaken by antebellum Americans. The zeal of the reformers was not always matched by the generosity of ordinary citizens. The plight of society's unfortunates remained wretched, but society had at least recognized the difference between the criminal, the mentally disturbed, the parentless child, and the ordinary debtor, and it began to deal with each one separately in ways that corresponded with their particular needs.

THINKING BACK

1. How did perfectionism influence methods of educating children and the treatment of criminality and mental disorders?
2. What successes and what failures did educational and social reformers experience?

CRUSADING AGAINST OPPRESSION

The moral reformers also targeted slavery. Massachusetts, western New York, and northern Ohio became strongholds of **abolitionism**, but support elsewhere built very slowly. In fact, slavery existed in New York down to 1827, and in 1830 approximately 2,200 New Jersey African Americans remained enslaved. In 1824, Illinois nearly became a slave state as pro-slavery advocates fell short by a vote of 6,822 to 4,950. The first modest steps to liberate slaves took place in the upper South, but in 1831, the movement turned distinctly radical. Abolitionists debated methods, timetables, and priorities, and their ranks were laced with racism. In the end, their efforts proved inadequate to overcome the determination of white Southerners to maintain their "Peculiar Institution."

Southern Emancipationists

Early Jacksonian-era agitation against slavery began in the upper South where farmers did not grow cotton. Cereal grains and livestock, raised on moderate-sized farms in most parts of Virginia and Maryland, required only seasonal labor, and growers preferred free white laborers. Ordinary farmers resented the inordinate political power of the fairly small number of plantation tycoons in coastal Virginia and Maryland, where half the population was slave. The slave owners' strength derived from the three-fifths rule that gave their counties extra legislative votes.

> Why were some Southerners interested in emancipation, and how did they propose to accomplish it?

Moral considerations also played a part in the antislavery feelings of whites in the upper South. Many whites in Virginia and Maryland believed slavery was wrong and should eventually be discarded. Farther west in the border state of Kentucky, James G. Birney spoke publicly for abolition. An intemperate man in his youth, Birney had gambled away his plantation and most of his slaves. Then in the 1820s, he converted to Christianity during one of the evangelical revivals; consequently, he freed his remaining slaves and became a leading crusader for freedom and in the 1840s the presidential candidate of the antislavery Liberty party.

An 1831 Virginia slave rebellion amplified white fears about large slave populations. A trusted household slave and preacher named Nat Turner, who resided on a plantation in Southampton County, knew of the whites' two-mindedness about slavery. But Turner would take responsibility for his own emancipation. He had a vision "of white spirits and black spirits engaged in battle, and the sun was darkened, the thunder rolled in the Heavens, and blood flowed in the streams." Turner planned the attack for the Fourth of July, but illness caused a postponement. In mid-August, an eclipse signaled the beginning. In the dead of night, slaves slipped into the houses and slit the sleeping people's throats. In all, there were fifty-seven victims—many of them women and children. Before soldiers could reach the scene, most of the rebels had vanished. Enraged whites took revenge on any blacks they found, slaughtering over 100. Someone flushed Nat Turner out of hiding and authorities held him in jail until his execution. Stoic and unrepentant, Turner went to the gallows as the symbol of the rebellious slave waiting behind a placid face.

In the wake of Nat Turner's rebellion, the Virginia legislature debated slavery's future. Several proposals came forward for a gradual emancipation that included removal of all African Americans from the state. Lawmakers from western counties supported the proposals, but those from eastern, plantation areas blocked them. Divisions among Virginia's white citizens closed, however, as sectional tensions deepened so that by the time of the Civil War the ranks of white Virginians were solid in support of slavery.

Further north, support for gradual emancipation was stronger. Whites in Maryland and Delaware, both of which bordered on Pennsylvania, could observe that state's use of segregation, disfranchisement, and job discrimination to control African Americans. In 1832, the state legislature debated the future of slavery, which a representative from the state's most heavily enslaved county called "an admitted and awful evil." Unlike Virginia, however, Maryland passed a law encouraging owners to free their slaves. Delaware moved even faster, reducing the number of slaves by 60 percent. The Democratic *Gazette* in Delaware pointed out that "Slave labor is far more unprofitable . . . than free labor." But the key was that whites were satisfied that either deportation or discrimination would take care of slaves after they were freed.

Radical Abolitionists

Who were some of the leading abolitionists, and what inspired them to action?

In the North, abolitionists inspired by religious revivals emphasized that slavery was a sin against God. If not ended, it could prevent the Millennium. Radical abolitionists paid no attention to the property rights of slave masters and had no patience with dawdling. Sin required immediate action. This introduced a measure of urgency that had been absent heretofore in the mostly genteel and philosophical debates about slavery.

Thunderous signals of a radical turn in the abolitionist movement commenced at the close of the 1820s. David Walker, a free African American from Boston, published an *Appeal* to all African Americans calling for the use of any necessary force to end slavery. Then on January 1, 1831, Boston's William Lloyd Garrison, a slim, balding, bespectacled printer of ferocious determination published the first edition of his newspaper *The Liberator*. Steeped in revivalist fervor, Garrison proclaimed: "I *will be* as harsh as truth, and

as uncompromising as justice." On the subject of abolition, "I do not wish to think, or speak, or write with moderation . . . . I am in earnest . . . AND I WILL BE HEARD." Garrison helped to establish a militant tone for the abolitionist crusade. His stridency shocked white readers but won the respect of blacks.

In 1833, Garrison organized the American Antislavery Society with over sixty other abolitionists, one-third of them Quakers, some wealthy, and many of them women. All were inspired and encouraged by the success of British liberals in persuading Parliament to outlaw slavery in the empire. The organization deplored the wicked racism that had soaked the core of society and denounced deportation of blacks who were as much Americans as whites were.

Never before had a national publicity campaign been conducted so effectively. Employing modern marketing strategies and printing technology, the **American Antislavery Society** sent its message through newspapers, tracts, posters, and even wrapping paper. A convert and protégé of Charles Grandison Finney, Theodore Dwight Weld, incorporated the abolitionist crusade in his Christian revivals. Weld taught aboli-

Frederick Douglass, an abolitionist who had himself been enslaved.

Courtesy of Library of Congress

tionism to students at Lane Theological Seminary in Cincinnati. As ministers, Lane students carried the torch of immediate abolition throughout the Midwest. When Lane's trustees banned antislavery activity on campus, Weld and his students moved to Oberlin College. The success of the abolitionist crusade can be measured in the growth of the American Antislavery Society, which by 1838 had 1,350 local auxiliary societies with as many as 250,000 supporters.

In 1838, the abolitionist movement received a great boost with the participation of a refugee slave named Frederick Douglass. Born in Maryland, Douglass escaped to Massachusetts. His brilliance as an orator made him a natural for the lecture circuit. He bonded black and white abolitionists and stood as proof that if released from the oppression of slavery African Americans could achieve perfection. Publication of Douglass' autobiography, *Narrative of the Life of Frederick Douglass* in 1845, was an enormous success and added to his sensational career as a lecturer on behalf of equal rights in the United States and abroad.

Dissension in the Movement

Race, gender, and doctrine were at the same time sources of unity and dissension within the abolitionist movement. For the first time in a major way, whites and African Americans demonstrated an ability to break through prevailing concepts of race that degraded persons of color. The presence of women in the antislavery vanguard endowed it with even greater moral authority. And the linkage of abolitionism with the popular acceptance of religious and Romantic humanitarianism carried the potential of producing a truly mass assault on the bastions of slavery that could be irresistible. But in fact, all three became issues that divided antislavery forces.

> **Why and how did dissention fracture the abolitionist movement?**

William Lloyd Garrison was the dominant personality in the abolitionist movement and was at the center of controversies that divided the antislavery forces. Through the 1830s, Garrison became steadily more radical, charging that all social and political institutions in the country were corrupt and racist. He shocked even his closest allies with his anger and perplexed them with the assertion that all forms of coercion, even government action to abolish slavery, were wrong. Garrison advocated passive resistance. His disavowal of political action precipitated a rift with Douglass, who believed that constant political pressure was necessary.

Garrison also disagreed with most abolitionist men about the place of women in the crusade. He outraged his male counterparts by helping elect Abby Kelley to a committee seat during the American Antislavery Society's 1840 annual convention.

The antislavery movement broke into parts that were either radical or moderate. Gradualists were convinced that the end of slavery would come only through Christian conversion. The liberation of millions of slaves would not happen overnight. The set their sights high—"immediate abolition"—but were prepared to settle for less—"gradually accomplished." In the late 1840s, many moderates abandoned abolition altogether and concentrated on keeping slavery out of newly acquired territories. Containing the evil institution, they maintained, would lead to decline and eventual collapse. After all, slavery was already dying out in the Chesapeake.

Meanwhile, militants kept up the pressure for immediate abolition. Inflammatory literature sought to bring to light the horrible experiences of slaves in the shadows of Southern plantations. Abolitionists published first-hand accounts of slave life as told by runaways. They helped to maintain sanctuaries known as "way stations" along several routes of escape out of the South that slaves called the "Underground Railroad." The American Antislavery Society deluged Congress with a flood of abolitionist petitions that filled a twenty-by-thirty-foot room to the ceiling and sent thousands of pieces of abolitionist literature to Southerners through the mail hoping to generate a ground swell of antislavery pressure in Dixie.

Fragmented as it was, abolitionism never organized itself into a political party. Northern Whigs were inclined to support abolitionist aims and Southern Whigs were not, putting a tremendous strain on the Whig party during the elections of the 1840s and early 1850s. The Democrats, likewise, felt the tension over the slavery question. Although none of their political activities brought about the end of slavery, the abolitionists succeeded in forcing the country to confront the great contradiction between slavery and its most cherished ideal—freedom.

Obstacles to Emancipation

Neither the abolitionists' most blunt attacks nor their most eloquent appeals managed to convince more than a minority of Americans that the time was right to end slavery. In

> **How did opponents obstruct the abolitionist movement?**

1840, membership in antislavery societies reached a peak of less than a quarter of a million, and that included a large percentage of women who could not vote and exercise direct political power. The antislavery assault actually closed the ranks of white Southerners in slavery's defense. Those who considered phasing the system out could not stand somebody else telling them when and how to do it, and attacking their character to boot. And in the North, self-interest often came between white communities and the ideal of universal emancipation.

Pro-slavery white Southerners fought back against the abolitionists. They rationalized slavery by insisting that they had not created it and were doing the best they could to make it work. They claimed that Southern slavery was more humane than Northern "wage slavery," meaning an exploitative factory labor system. "A merrier being does not exist on the face of the globe," a professor at the College of William and Mary proclaimed, "than the negro slave of the U. States." Southerners also tried to silence the abolitionists. President Andrew Jackson ordered the interception of abolitionist literature sent by mail. In 1836, Democratic congressmen passed a "gag rule" to table all petitions on behalf of the abolition of slavery without being read on the floor of the House or Senate. Nor were white Southerners opposed to violence to stop the abolitionists—or even suspected abolitionists. Between 1830 and 1860, some 300 hundred assaults against whites suspected of being abolitionists occurred in the South.

Northern hostility to abolitionism was no less intense. Outside of strongholds in prosperous commercial towns, where middle-class evangelicals resided, abolitionists found little support. Especially among the working class and in cities in southernmost parts of the North, fear ran rampant that ending slavery would produce a mass influx of African Americans who would compete for jobs. Mob violence targeted abolitionists. In 1834, a hostile crowd in Philadelphia burned the local abolitionist meeting house to the ground and then rampaged against black residents. William Lloyd Garrison barely escaped being lynched in Boston, but Elijah Lovejoy, an abolitionist newspaper editor in Alton, Illinois, was not so fortunate. In 1837, a mob burned his newspaper office and shot him to death.

The moderate Charles Grandison Finney warned that militancy would lead to bloodshed. Long before Northern and Southern armies faced each other on Civil War battlefields, inflamed passions unleashed by the moralism clashed with deep-seated anxieties both North and South in a preview of what was to come.

The Feminist Revolt

The presence of women in the ranks of moralist abolitionist crusaders created a dilemma for many men. Women were a moral inspiration, but they were supposed to remain in the background rather than engaged in public political activity. Some women believed they had as much right to platform speaking on behalf of abolition as men. In 1837, Sarah and Angelina Grimké, the feisty daughters of a South Carolina slave owner, did just that, lecturing in Massachusetts. When criticized, Sarah exclaimed: "The Lord Jesus defines the duties of his followers . . . without any reference to sex." When they were denied, they began to see more clearly the similarity between their condition and that of the slaves they agitated to free.

> How was the women's rights movement linked to abolitionism?

In 1840, a crisis arose at the first annual international antislavery convention in London. When officials refused to seat women delegates, Americans Elizabeth Cady Stanton and Lucretia Mott resolved to return to the United States and fight for the rights of women and slaves to be equal citizens with white men. Mott, a Quaker, had studied the radical Englishwoman Mary Wollstonecraft's feminist manifesto since its publication forty years before. But Stanton had just recently come to an awareness of her inferior status and was, she said, "slowly sawing off the chains of my spiritual bondage." Their constant agitation deepened the fissures within the abolitionist movement, but that was not their concern.

In 1848, Mott and Stanton gathered 100 activists in Seneca Falls, New York, for a women's rights convention. They demanded complete equality and encased their argument in a **Declaration of Sentiments and Resolutions** that echoed the Declaration of Independence signed over seventy years earlier. "We hold these truths to be self-evident: that all men and women are created equal." Men, they said, had endeavored to establish an absolute tyranny over women, and they now insisted on all the rights of citizens of the United States. Men across the country hooted in derision and did not come close to conceding the right to vote or any others that the Seneca Falls women demanded. But the women kept up the pressure. Annual women's rights conferences reiterated their stand. Radical feminists donned ensembles

Elizabeth Cady Stanton's house in Seneca Falls, New York, the site of the first women's rights convention in 1848 and now part of the Women's Rights National Historical Park.

of short skirts over baggy pantaloons called "bloomers," named after their designer Amelia Bloomer, as a symbol of their rebellion.

Ironically, when in 1851 a former slave evangelist who went by the name Sojourner Truth tried to speak to the women's rights convention in Akron, Ohio, it became clear that many of the white feminist abolitionists could not overcome race bigotry and accept a black woman colleague. Hisses rained down on the thin black woman as she pointed out that men claimed that women were fragile and gentle and dependent by nature and should be treated with indulgence and respect. But nobody ever lifted her into a carriage or helped her over a mud puddle, "And a'n't I a woman?"

It would be a while before a majority of Americans would accept the abolition of slavery. It would be longer still before men would acknowledge gender equality. And it would be even longer still before race prejudice would give way to color blindness.

THINKING BACK

1. How was the movement to abolish slavery part of the ongoing effort to make the United States a more democratic nation?

2. What principles and what personal interests drove the opposition to abolition?

THE LOCAL PERSPECTIVE: FOCUS ON HAWAII

The arrival of Henry Obookiah at Yale College in 1809 and the resulting missionary activity in Hawaii during the 1820s and 1830s inspired new American interest in the lovely Pacific islands. Intense revivalism and a commitment to social reform looked for objectives abroad as well as at home. Not always, however, did native Hawaiians regard growing American involvement in their affairs with enthusiasm.

> Why did Americans settle in Hawaii?

Peopled by Polynesians between 100 and 600 C. E., the Sandwich Islands, as the British had named them in the eighteenth century, had first come to the attention of people in the United States with the publication of the journals of Captain James Cook. That famous British navigator had landed on the island of Kauai in 1778 and died the next year at the hands of resentful natives on the big island of

The landscape of Hawaii appealed to Americans for its agricultural potential.

Hawaii following a dispute over allegedly stolen goods.

In 1790, the first American ship to sail to Hawaii docked at Honolulu. It carried a cargo of sea otter skins, hunted along the northwest coast, from California to China. American Pacific Coast commerce naturally moved toward China since there was as yet no overland trade route to Eastern cities and the sea passage to east-coast ports involved a long and dangerous voyage around South America. Hawaii was conveniently situated in the middle of the Pacific, allowing vessels from North America to stock up on provisions, repair ships, and obtain crew members from among the native population. Yankee merchant adventurers dominated this extremely lucrative trade. During the Market Revolution after the War of 1812, enterprising Americans on the lookout for profits also shipped Hawaiian sandalwood to the massive Asian market. In the Chinese port of Canton by 1820, sandalwood shipments yielded $100,000 annually. This opened the way for an even more diverse trade with China that earned American merchants $1 million during the first two decades of the nineteenth century.

Native Hawaiians generally welcomed foreign merchants and their enterprises. They participated in the expanding Asian commerce and in Hawaiian economic development. Hawaiian men worked as seamen, dock laborers, loggers, and herders. Many native women married American seamen, producing mixed-race children whom their fathers often took back to the United States for education. The principal restraint on foreigners was that they could not own land, but local leaders encouraged the expansion of American commerce. In the 1830s, a fleet of whaling vessels, like the one on which young Herman Melville sailed, was based in Hawaii, and between 400 and 500 ships called at Honolulu and Lahaina on Maui.

Cattle provided beef for the whalers. In the 1790s, the British explorer George Vancouver introduced cattle to Hawaii, many of which became feral and an enormous nuisance to the local inhabitants. An American sailor, John Palmer Parker of Massachusetts, jumped ship in Hawaii in 1809, married Hawaiian king Kamehameha I's granddaughter, and raised the king's personal cattle herd. Mexican herdsmen (*vaqueros*) also came to Hawaii from California. In 1846, Kamehameha II made an exception of Parker by giving him two acres of land, the beginning of the famous Parker Ranch, which remains in operation today and is the largest cattle ranch under a single owner in the United States. By the early 1840s, approximately 400 Americans resided in Hawaii, two-thirds of all the foreigners in the islands, and most of them resided in Honolulu.

A large number of those Americans had come as Protestant Christian missionaries, like the Yale graduates mentioned earlier in this chapter, or were descended from them. American missionaries provided not only religious instruction but also reading and writing lessons that would presumably advance native Hawaiians toward perfection. By 1840, some 20,000 Hawaiians had converted to Christianity. More than 50,000 Hawaiian pupils attended mission schools where they learned English and to read native Hawaiian using an alphabet. To supply natives with reading material, the missionaries obtained a printing press—the first one in the Pacific islands. Such a positive reputation had the American missionary schools acquired by the 1840s, that an American merchant in California, Thomas O. Larkin, sent his children there for their early education. The missionaries also began the transformation of Hawaii into a constitutional republic like the United States. In the 1840s, the Hawaiians, under strong missionary influence, adopted a constitutional monarchy.

Thus, the United States extended its commercial realm halfway across the Pacific while its most reform-minded, evangelical citizens attempted to perfect the native residents of this island paradise. The reforms did not please all Hawaiians. Conservatives protested against social upheaval and the emigration of other Hawaiians to the Pacific Northwest in the 1840s. But they clearly showed the energy and dedication to profit and righteousness.

THINKING BACK

1. Who were the first Americans to settle in Hawaii?
2. How did the Americans change Hawaii?

CONCLUSION

Converging currents of reform in the 1830s aroused Americans' social conscience and an uncommon sense of humankind's ability to achieve perfection. This faith in human progress grew out of their belief in divine power that was latent in everyone, ready to lift people above themselves. Definitions of divinity and just how, when, and where perfection would be achieved varied widely, but in the decades before mid-century, many Americans tried to behave according to what they believed was morally correct—defined in religious terms. This attitude was not altogether new, of course, and the reforms of that time were not sharp breaks with the past as much as the culmination of efforts to improve society that extended back to the eighteenth century. Pragmatism and compromise, however, particularly with respect to slavery, which had been the watchwords of early republican politics, now gave way to rigidity and moral resolve. "I will not equivocate," said William Lloyd Garrison, "I will not excuse—I will not retreat a single inch." The consequences of this approach for the United States were profound.

SUGGESTED SOURCES FOR STUDENTS

Robert Abzug challenges the contention that religious revivals were responses to social situations in *Cosmos Crumbling: American Reform and the Religious Imagination* (1994).

Arthur Bestor, *Backwoods Utopias* (1970), focuses expertly on the career of Robert Owen.

The fullest coverage of Spiritualism is Bret E. Carroll, *Spiritualism in Antebellum America* (1997). Carroll places Spiritualism in the context of Christian theology.

Frederick Douglass' autobiography, *Narrative of the Life of Frederick Douglass* (1845), has been published in many editions and is readily available in paperback.

Several historians have examined the utopian community phenomenon from different perspectives. Together they afford a good understanding of the movement. See Michael Fellman, *The Unbounded Fame* (1973), for a discussion of the tension between freedom and community.

An insightful look into the origins and tactics of the women's rights movement is Lori D. Ginzberg, *Untidy Origins: A Story of Women's Rights in Antebellum New York* (2005).

For an excellent and very readable treatment of social conditions and Charles Grandison Finney's revivals in Rochester see Paul E. Johnson, *A Shopkeeper's Millennium: Society and Revivals in Rochester, New York, 1815-1837* (1978).

School reform is treated effectively in Michael B. Katz, *The Irony of Early School Reform* (1968).

Louis J. Kern's *An Ordered Love* (1981) examines sex roles in utopian communities. And Carl Guarneri explores Fourierism in *The Utopian Alternative* (1991).

Michael Meranze, *Laboratories of Virtue* (1996), examines the evolution of punishment in Philadelphia from the eighteenth into the early nineteenth centuries.

The subject of reforming correctional institutions is treated thoughtfully in David J. Rothman, *The Discovery of the Asylum* (1971).

The literature on abolitionism is extensive. An excellent overview of the abolitionist movement is James Brewer Stewart, *Holy Warriors* (1976).

Kathryn Kish Sklar and James Brewer Stewart, *Women's Rights and Transatlantic Slavery in the Era of Emancipation* (2007), looks at feminism, slavery, and freedom from a global Perspective.

Alice Felt Tyler's classic *Freedom's Ferment* (1944) remains the most complete survey of the social reforms of the antebellum period, including utopian experiments. It is dated but still an extremely useful reference and easy to read.

Ronald G. Walters, *American Reformers, 1815-1860* (rev. ed. 1997), is more up-to-date. Arthur Bestor, *Backwoods Utopias* (1970) focuses expertly on the career of Robert Owen.

Equally useful for a start in researching the abolitionists is Ronald G. Walters, *The Antislavery Appeal* (1976).

For other African-American abolitionists see Shirley J. Yee, *Black Women Abolitionists* (1992).

BEFORE WE GO ON

1.   What were the common links between and contrasting features of evangelical reformers, utopian visionaries, and Romantic idealists?

2.   What inspired early environmentalism?

Building a Democratic Nation

3.   Could abolitionists have been any more effective in persuading Southern slave owners to emancipate their slaves? Explain.

4.   How did social reforms aimed at education, criminals, and person suffering from mental disorders exemplify the country's faith in human progress?

Connections

5.   What do you think Frederick Douglass and Sarah Grimke would say about the status of African Americans and women in the United States today?

6.   Did the building momentum for making the United States better create a more democratic society? Explain.

Chapter 12

FACTORY AND PLANTATION: INDUSTRIALIZATION NORTH AND SOUTH, 1840–1860

A PERSONAL PERSPECTIVE: FOCUS ON CELIA, A SLAVE GIRL

Slave cabins were no refuge for enslaved women like Celia from predatory masters like John Newsom.

Why did Celia kill her master?

On the night of June 23, 1855, in Callaway County, Missouri, a pregnant, nineteen-year-old slave named Celia killed her master, a middle-aged widower named John Newsom. She stuffed his body into the fireplace of her cabin and incinerated it. After Newsom's children reported him missing, authorities launched an investigation that eventually led them to Celia's cabin and to the gruesome discovery of his charred bones. Under intense questioning, she confessed to the killing. Following a trial in which her attorney mounted a spirited defense, an all-white jury convicted her of murder and condemned her to death by hanging. A reporter who witnessed the execution wrote afterward: "Thus closed one of the most horrible tragedies ever enacted in our county."

Most white citizens of Callaway County believed that justice had triumphed. After all, Newsome had been a respected neighbor. Celia, who had received many special favors from him, had done the thing that whites feared most—she murdered her master. But what most people did not know, or would not admit, was that Newsom had purchased Celia when she had been just fourteen to be his sex partner. He also wanted her to provide him with slave children so as to increase his wealth and status in the community. Toward these ends he had repeatedly raped her, starting the day he brought her to his farm, and threatened to kill her if she resisted. Celia had built up an intense loathing of this man, and she could not make him stop abusing her.

Celia's life became more complicated when she fell in love with George, another slave on the Newsom place. Although Missouri law did not recognize slave marriages, Celia and George vowed to be faithful to each other. George knew about Celia's relationship with Newsom. It made him angry and frustrated him, but what could he do about it? When Celia became pregnant, George did not know whether it was by him or Newsom. George finally reached the end of his rope and demanded that Celia reject Newsom. He told her that if she did not he would break off with her.

A sense of entrapment overwhelmed her. She loved George and cared for his wounded feelings, yet she feared Newsom and knew he would continue to force himself on her. She had to make a choice; her psyche could not tolerate the stress any longer. When Newsom entered her cabin on that fateful night, Celia refused to have sex with him. He persisted and then, as she later testified, "the Devil got into me." She snapped; she grabbed a piece of heavy timber and bludgeoned him until his body lay still and lifeless.

When George learned what Celia had done, he too lost his bearings. George could not cope with the consequences of Newsom's murder. He faced certain execution if convicted of complicity. Forsaking Celia, George ran away, leaving her in the hands of fate. Celia never implicated him, insisting always that she had acted alone. At her trial, her attorney argued that, based on Missouri law, her actions could be interpreted as self-defense, but such a defense stood

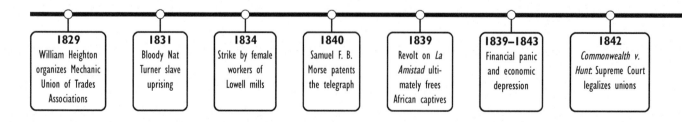

1829	1831	1834	1840	1839	1839–1843	1842
William Heighton organizes Mechanic Union of Trades Associations	Bloody Nat Turner slave uprising	Strike by female workers of Lowell mills	Samuel F. B. Morse patents the telegraph	Revolt on *La Amistad* ultimately frees African captives	Financial panic and economic depression	*Commonwealth v. Hunt*: Supreme Court legalizes unions

little chance of saving her life. The white judge refused to allow testimony challenging the absolute authority of a slave master over his enslaved human property.

Celia's case dramatically points out the awful, dehumanizing realities of life for enslaved people in a country that professed to be a democratic nation. Slavery brutalized millions of men, women, and children. Most were severely whipped at some point in their lives, and no enslaved person possessed the legal right to protect themselves against exploitation. Enslaved women could not defend their bodies against male predators, and neither could they count on sympathy and understanding from white women who knew or suspected that their husbands were having sex with them. Even though laws restricted slave owners' treatment of slaves, enforcement usually favored the masters. The system victimized women like Celia and men like George, whose behavior reveals the enormous psychological pressures that slaves suffered.

Slavery in the antebellum or pre-Civil War United States developed as part of a new industrial order. *Noblesse oblige* (the obligation of honorable behavior associated with high rank) was less common than in Thomas Jefferson's day. And as far as the organization of workers was concerned, differences between the slave states and the industrial states grew a little dimmer. Control of the industrial workforce in the North took on the same level of importance as it did for Southern planters. Plantations functioned like farm factories. Slave masters and industrialists, like masters, squeezed every ounce of work out of their employees. The organization of work played a key role in shaping the lives of Americans in the decades before the Civil War.

THINKING BACK

1. What does Celia's story say about the nature of slavery?
2. How would you have responded to Celia's and George's predicament?

INDUSTRIALIZATION OF THE NORTHEAST

By the 1840s, industry was revolutionizing economic and social life in the Northeast. Factories popped up everywhere, their mechanized systems of production taking manufacturing out of the hands of skilled artisans. Steam engines allowed factories to break free of the rivers that powered earlier mills, allowing plants to locate in towns and cities. Growing numbers of Americans lived off their labor rather than the land's bounty. Highly competitive markets encouraged employers to exploit their workers. Conflict defined employer-employee relationships, and the term "**boss**" came into common usage. During the **Industrial Revolution** the factory became strictly a place of business and not a place to learn a trade.

Expansion of the Factory System

By the 1840s, factory production had gathered a full head of steam. Cloth manufacturing relocated from scattered mills and workshops to completely automated factories. Even artisans worked more and more with tools and machines. Factory machines

> How did the factory system differ from earlier methods of manufacturing, and how widespread was it by mid-century?

had few adjustable settings; workers mainly turned them on and off. The factory was noisy, the air within textile mills heavy with lint, and the work monotonous. The steam engines and leather drive belts kept the machines whirring at accelerating speeds. In 1855, the fifty-two textile mills in Lowell, Massachusetts, employed 13,200 workers, mostly women, and turned out 2.25 million yards of coarse cloth every week.

Mechanized production took over handiwork in other industries as well. Factories, forges and foundries manufactured cast iron wheels and other railroad hardware, plus iron fittings for ships, guns, and most of all for heating and cooking stoves. This

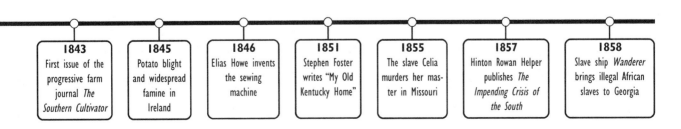

1843	1845	1846	1851	1855	1857	1858
First issue of the progressive farm journal *The Southern Cultivator*	Potato blight and widespread famine in Ireland	Elias Howe invents the sewing machine	Stephen Foster writes "My Old Kentucky Home"	The slave Celia murders her master in Missouri	Hinton Rowan Helper publishes *The Impending Crisis of the South*	Slave ship *Wanderer* brings illegal African slaves to Georgia

triggered activity in iron works located in the Delaware and Hudson River valleys.

Shoe manufacturing implemented mechanical stitching after Elias Howe invented the sewing machine in 1846. A government report called it the industry's "crowning invention." Women had traditionally stitched shoes in their kitchens in their spare time, but manufacturers now hired them to operate sewing machines in factories. Here their work could be more easily regulated; as a consequence, their productivity increased. Over a twenty-year period starting in 1855, machines reduced the workforce by 2,000 people and allowed those who remained to manufacture 7 million more shoes. By the end of the 1850s shoemaking was the country's number one industry.

Clock and gun manufacturers specialized in large-scale production using interchangeable parts. In 1800, fewer than one adult in fifty owned a clock; they were expensive and not really necessary on farms. With the onset of factory discipline, however, people needed to keep track of time—their jobs and profits depended on it. Connecticut clock makers like Seth Thomas cranked out 80,000 clocks a year by the 1830s, mostly with wooden movements. Standardized and interchangeable brass gears made their appearance in the 1840s. By the 1850s manufacturers produced and sold hundreds of thousands of timepieces each year, and incidentally the price dropped from $10 to $2.

Eli Whitney actually pioneered the use of interchangeable parts back in the 1790s in the manufacture of muskets. Later gun makers adopted the method to meet military needs for large numbers of weapons that could be easily fixed on the battlefield.

Image © Refat, 2010. Used by permission of Shutterstock, Inc.
Clock manufacturers were among the first to rely on interchangeable parts.

Federal arsenals in Harpers Ferry, Virginia, and Springfield, Massachusetts, stamped out and assembled the parts. Inspectors using precision gauges ensured that components met exacting specifications. By the 1850s an admiring Englishman heralded the "**American system of manufacturing.**"

Reliance on machinery gave rise to machine shops, another sort of factory. They specialized in the production of machine tools required to build looms, locomotives, gears, and other mechanical devices. These machine tools included steam hammers, lathes, and drills. Smaller machine shops specialized in repairs. Long ago American industrialists had relied on English machine technology, but by the 1850s, American machinists were second to none in innovation and creativity.

The term "factory" usually brings to mind images of massive buildings and labor-saving machines, but the factory system involved much more than that. It generated a totally new attitude toward work and innovative ways of managing labor. Profit-hungry capitalists, who could afford to buy expensive machinery, replaced master craftsmen as employers in many industries. These new industrial capitalists no longer provided their employees with room and board, educational opportunities, and a supportive environment. Their attention was riveted to the bottom line of the profit ledger. Instead, they demanded long hours on the job (as many as fourteen hours a day, six days a week) and punctuality. They paid as little in wages as necessary to lure people into factory jobs. Management and discipline fell under the responsibility of "overseers," whose earnings depended on productivity.

These industrial changes did not sweep away shop and home production overnight. On the eve of the Civil War only a third of the working class toiled in factories. Skilled craftsmen, working with the aid of tools and machines and no longer independent entrepreneurs, applied their skills to transforming metal, stone, and wood. Philadelphia weavers, producing fancy cloth and blends beyond the ability of power looms, still worked in small shops. Many rural women continued to weave straw hats at home. Carpenters in New York's shipyards routinely took a break from work at 8:30 a.m. when Arlie McVane hawked her hot turnovers, cookies, and cakes. "In the afternoon, about half-past three, we had a cake-lunch, supplied by Uncle Jack Gridder, an old, crippled, superannuated ship carpenter." And thus it went until sundown, and home to supper.

Rapid Transit and Instant Communication

How did improvements in transportation and communication speed up the Industrial Revolution?

Growing markets stimulated industrialization, and the nation's infant railroads provided the key link between consumer and factory. They also made it easier and more economical to ship raw materials. The Baltimore and Ohio Railroad, the United States' first common rail carrier, officially opened for business in 1830. Time was money, old Ben Franklin used to say, and it took four days by canal to haul coal sixty miles from Reading to Philadelphia. By train it took only four hours. And trains cut travel time from New York to Chicago from three grueling weeks by stagecoach to a mere forty-eight hours. Steam locomotives cruised at fifteen to twenty miles per hour, like a "lightning flash" according to Caroline Fitch of Boston. Snow and ice, which blocked rivers and canals during winter, did not shut down the railroad. Canals cost enormous sums in maintenance and repair, and the high-pressure steam engines on riverboats frequently blew up. Railroads cost less and were safer. Railroads cut travel time considerably and made transportation more reliable. But they also put businessmen on their toes; they had to be prepared to send and receive shipments according to exact train schedules.

Communication improved dramatically too. The artist Samuel F. B. Morse revolutionized communication with his electric telegraph, patented in 1840. Congress granted him $30,000 to build a telegraph link between Washington and Baltimore, which he demonstrated during the presidential election campaign in 1844 using a special code. By the 1850s, railroads were using the telegraph to announce train arrivals. Merchants ordered goods by telegraph and farmers could instantly determine commodity prices in faraway markets.

Newspapers contributed as well to the Industrial Revolution. *Niles' Weekly Register* and the New York *General Shipping and Commercial List*, catered to businessmen and politicians. With one out of ten Americans living in cities by the 1840s, the market for cheap dailies grew rapidly. Dailies did not specialize in business news, but through advertisements they certainly boosted business.

An Immigrant Work Force

Where did most European immigrants come from, what made them leave their homes, and how did they change the face of the country's industrial workforce?

An adequate supply of workers was one of the important keys to industrial expansion, and many laborers entered the American workforce from abroad. In 1820, about 8,400 immigrants crossed the Atlantic—a dribble that scarcely anyone noticed. During the 1840s and 1850s, however, a flood tide swept across the nation's shores. One and a half million arrived in the 1840s. During the next decade a quarter million entered the country every year. Not since early colonial times had the population grown more from immigration than from natural increase.

Several factors brought about this sharp increase. In Ireland the commercialization of agriculture drove peasants off the land, and factory and construction jobs lured them to the United States. Then in 1845 a fungus blighted Ireland's vital potato crop. At least 750,000 people starved and another 2 million fled the country. From 1840 to 1860, nearly 3 million impoverished Irish men and women emigrated. They came from other countries too. Artisans and farmers from Germany and Scandinavia joined the flood of newcomers.

Bosses turned eagerly to job-hungry immigrants for cheap labor. Drawing native-born Americans into the industrial workforce had been difficult, especially when economic conditions were rosy. Farm-bred men and women disliked the regimen of clocks and

Image © Anyka, 2010. Used by permission of Shutterstock, Inc.

Telegraph operators sent electrical currents through wires to distant receiving stations by opening and closing circuits. Operators on the other end heard corresponding clicks on their receivers. By varying the spacing between clicks, the sender created "dots" and "dashes," which, if arranged according to the "Morse code" developed by Samuel F. B. Morse and his associate Alfred Vail, allowed for the instant transmission of information.

factory whistles. Moreover, they worked mainly to earn a few extra dollars or until planting time. The incompatibility of the rural work routine with industry demands doomed many would-be manufacturers. One group of entrepreneurs erected a textile factory on Nantucket Island off the coast of Massachusetts and hired the wives and daughters of local whalers to operate the machines. But after a month the women grew tired of the work and went back, as one of the exasperated owners put it, to "their shore gazing and to their seats by the sea." The mill ultimately shut down.

Most immigrants had few options, especially the penniless Irish. They accepted jobs regardless of the pay or circumstances. During the depression of the late 1830s and early 1840s, native-born workers returned to farms, leaving the Irish to dominate the industrial workforce. One New England factory worker recalled that her employer shifted to Irish immigrants because "they take no vacations, and can be relied on at the mill all year around."

Frederick Douglass voiced the frustration of African Americans whom the Irish squeezed out of the menial jobs traditionally reserved for them. "White men are becoming house-servants, cooks and stewards, common laborers and flunkeys to our gentry." Blacks and Irishmen engaged in desperate and sometimes violent competition on the margins of employment. Armed clashes broke out between groups of railroad employees, coal miners, and dock workers. During anti-black demonstrations in New York in 1850, Irishmen shouted: "Let them go back to Africa, where they belong."

The Irish crowded into sprawling factory towns. As much as half the population of New York City in 1850 were immigrants. They crowded into squalid tenements and shanties. Disease, malnutrition, and exposure resulted in a frightfully high death rate. Men took jobs digging canals, building railroads, hacking away in coal mines, and working in factories. Women abandoned family responsibilities for wages in factories and domestic service.

Other immigrants moved west after their arrival in the country. Germans, for example, often came with enough money to buy land. After disembarking in ports like Baltimore and New Orleans they settled in the Midwest and Southwest. Germans became the majority in St. Louis and nearly so in cities like Milwaukee and Cincinnati. German settlers founded a number of small farming communities in the hill country of central Texas.

As miserable as conditions might be for the immigrant poor, life in America turned out better in most cases than it had been in Europe. John Parks, a recent immigrant from Great Britain, wrote to friends back home: "You would be surprised to see provisions so cheap." But according to Parks, immigrants worked harder in the United States than they had in Europe. "Day labor demands a more strenuous exertion than

Faced with starvation, thousands of Irish peasants emigrated, leaving their abandoned cottages behind.

we are used to." Some laborers managed to struggle up the ladder of success. Employers usually selected job foremen from the ranks of the laborers. Richard Kelley became a successful storekeeper, but most workers like him found themselves locked into an emerging industrial working class.

A Fair Wage

> To what extent did the Industrial Revolution generate a working-class consciousness and cause labor unrest?

Industrial capitalism influenced the way workers thought of themselves. A distinct line divided businessmen from workers, and people on both sides were increasingly aware of it. Industrialization depersonalized labor, turning human beings into market commodities, which profit-minded manufacturers sought to purchase at the lowest possible price. With the steady elimination of small shops, artisans slid into the expanding working class, and apprenticeship evolved into child labor.

People at the time spoke of the "working classes" because of the many different groups of wage earners, determined largely by ethnicity, gender, race, and skill. Although antagonistic toward one another, each group developed a working-class consciousness. They felt alienated from manufacturers, whom they condemned as "leeches" and "parasites." Labor added value to raw materials, but industrialists grew rich. The women shoemakers of Lynn exclaimed: "these *things ought not so to be!*" More and more workers demanded "equality." This was, after all, the "age of democracy."

Although workers sought fairness, the heartless law of supply and demand was against them. The greater a commodity's quantity, the lower its price. The labor market became overstocked, enabling employers to set wages. Anybody refusing an offered wage could look elsewhere. Manufacturers slashed payrolls, and while they were at it they lengthened the workday and withdrew benefits, such as room and board.

Laborers protested against these changes in their livelihood. The term "strike" was unknown then, but workers participated in work stoppages called *turn outs*—more than 150 in the 1830s. Many of them involved women who comprised eight out of every ten textile workers and one third of the total industrial work force. Women especially felt "a want of justice" since they earned less than men. For a week in February 1834, women employees of Lowell's textile mills refused to work, a protest against anticipated wage cuts. But the Lowell strike, like most turn outs, failed and the women went back to work. Most industrial workers did not plan to remain in the labor force long anyway, so when conditions worsened enough they returned to their farms or households.

Some workers organized groups to protect their interests. **Workingmen's parties** first appeared in 1830. They aimed at broad social reforms like free public education, the abolition of debtors' prisons, and welfare services. Although the parties elected some candidates to public office, larger political organizations quickly absorbed them. In 1829 a shoemaker named William Heighton founded the Mechanics Union of Trade Associations, the first federation of unions in the United States. And shoemakers organized the Female Society of Lynn and Vicinity, one of the first women's labor organizations.

Neither working-class solidarity nor labor unions, however, had evolved to such a point by mid-century that workers could protect themselves. The manufacturers clearly held the upper hand. Organized labor did enjoy one victory though. In 1842 the Massachusetts Supreme Court ruled in the case of *Commonwealth* v. *Hunt* that unions were legal. This did not mean, however, that employers were obliged to negotiate with them. An age that idealized free enterprise did not look favorably upon labor unions.

A New Way of Life

Some of the most important implications of industrialization affected the family. Urban living and industrial jobs weakened family cohesion, particularly among the working classes. Because of the necessity for women and children to go out and earn money, the working-class family showed signs of disintegration. Typical of industrial societies, upper-class men and women married later and had fewer children. Comfort and Lucy Freeman of Sturbridge, Massachusetts, had nine children between 1772 and 1790, and their son Pliny and his wife Deliah produced seven offspring. But their children averaged only four children each in the 1830s and 1840s.

Freed from the need to make her family's clothes because of factory ready-to-wears, the middle-class housewife spent more time on other domestic chores. Meal preparation was

> How did people's domestic lives change with industrialization?

one. With new cast-iron stoves that provided regulated heat, unlike pots hung over open hearths, cooks prepared a range of meals more varied than soups and stews. Susan Blunt's family in Manchester, New Hampshire, boasted the town's first stove. Her mother "was quite pleased with it; it was easier to cook on than the fireplace." The neighbors scoffed at first, but in a year or two they all enjoyed cooking on stoves too. The new emphasis on serving varied meals inspired the writing of cookbooks. At least two or three new ones appeared every year in the 1830s and 1840s.

The wives of businessmen took charge of decorating and managing the home and their husbands moved their work out of the house and into business offices. Likewise, the seats of government relocated from governors' mansions to state capitols. The appearance of commercial office buildings in Northeastern cities signified the growing separation of domestic and economic power. It also symbolized the diminishing role of middle- and upper-class women in industrial America.

In the new industrial order, the gap between the haves and the have-nots increased. By 1860 less than 1 percent of the population possessed one quarter of the North's wealth. An aristocracy comparable to those of Great Britain and European countries included old and distinguished families, but it added the *nouveau riche* (newly rich) who made their fortunes in industry, banking, and commerce. The elite built mammoth houses in Philadelphia, New York, and Boston, wore the finest clothes, and drove around in fancy carriages.

In between the rich and the working poor, an enlarged middle class of prosperous farmers, merchants, clerks, and professionals testified to the growing opportunity for upward mobility. The middle class displayed their refinement in modest houses modeled after the mansions of the rich. They painted them attractively, usually white with dark trim. They received guests in formal parlors, serving tea in silver and china tea sets just as upper-class families did. Carpets on floors, cornstalk brooms for cleaning, and comfortable furniture, including an American innovation, the rocking chair, were representative of middle-class gentility.

The growing disparity between social classes conflicted with the nation's democratic ideals. The idea of the day held that equalization could be accomplished through the spread of good manners. Taste and delicacy, in other words, could elevate the lowly. African Americans put the theory to the test. Although nine out of ten African Americans worked at unskilled or domestic jobs, several African-American families had achieved prominence in Northern cities. Their wealth came not from industry directly but through success as barbers, merchants, physicians, ministers, and teachers. They adopted the manners and dress of refined whites but remained outcasts.

James Forten of Philadelphia converted his youthful experience on board a Revolutionary War naval vessel and skill as a businessman into a $100,000 fortune. Respected by leaders of white society for his success and for his refinement, Forten nevertheless could not vote or hold political office after the legislature withdrew voting rights from blacks in 1838. When white ruffians humiliated a group of African-American women attending a dance by pushing them around and ripping their gowns, the *Philadelphia Gazette* ridiculed the "sable divinities" and their pretensions. Obviously race mattered more than refinement.

Concern About the Assault on Mother Nature

Industrialization of the economy and a burgeoning population placed new strains on the natural environment of the United States. In his novel *The Pioneers* (1823), James Fenimore Cooper had condemned the sickening wastefulness of settlers in frontier New York who slashed through forests and netted lake trout and bass by the thousands and slaughtered birds by the millions simply for sport. The protagonist was Natty Bumppo, who lived in harmony with nature and never killed beyond his needs, observes the wanton destruction and remarks: "This comes of settling a country." Environmental degradation had worsened by mid-century.

> **What impact did industrialization have on the ecology of the Northeast?**

A shift to coal in the 1830s did little to reduce the cutting of trees but added a new environmental problem—air pollution. Emissions that today threaten to raise global temperatures to dangerous levels began with the Industrial Revolution. Burning coal released sulfur, phosphorous, and carbon dioxide into the atmosphere. These and other emissions trap heat close to the earth's surface, alter the climate, and pollute the air that people breathe. Anthracite, a hard and relatively pure form of coal, emitted fewer pollutants than "dirtier" bituminous coal. Deposits of anthracite, however, were smaller and less accessible than bituminous coal, found plentifully in western Pennsylvania and Ohio. Burning coal not only fouled the air but further damaged the environment by depositing coal dust that destroyed trees, diminished soil fertility, and contaminated water supplies. The English novelist Frances Trollope, who visited the United States in the early 1830s, reported never having seen places "so dyed in black" as towns like Wheeling (then in Virginia).

Even the flow of rivers adjusted to the domineering rhythms of the factory. Dams on the Concord River in Massachusetts, built to energize machines in textile mills, allowed water to flow Monday through Saturday. But on Sunday, when the factories stood empty, the river slowed to a trickle. Henry David Thoreau quipped, "So emasculated and demoralized is our river that it is even made to observe the Christian Sabbath."

Concern about Mother Nature led only slowly to efforts to fend off the assaults. In 1838, New York passed a law forbidding batteries of guns in commercial bird hunting. The measure was later repealed because it was ineffectual. Many plumed birds faced extinction. The great auk, a flightless bird that inhabited islands in cod fishing waters off the northeast coast, unfortunately had no fear of humans and disappeared. In 1843, John James Audubon noted a decline in the size of some buffalo herds and mentioned the plight of the bison and the passenger pigeon, which were being slaughtered literally by the millions. An Englishman, Henry William Herbert, immigrated to the United States in 1831 and began publishing conservationist magazine articles under the pen name Frank Forester. His biggest concern was the hunting of game animals. Forester criticized commercial hunters for destroying wildlife and habitat. He urged sportsmen to organize to protect against the devastation of professional hunting.

THINKING BACK

1. What changes took place in the way products were produced, and why do you think those changes constituted an Industrial Revolution?
2. What improvements did industrialization bring to Americans, and what hardships?

THE SOUTH'S ECONOMIC DEVELOPMENT

In 1836 James Davidson, a twenty-six-year-old Virginia attorney, told his diary: "Any young man of energy and good character in the South can make a fortune."

Davidson's optimism reflected the South's rebound from the Panic of 1819 and the subsequent market slump that had pushed agricultural prices down by as much as 70 percent. During the three decades prior to the Civil War, known by historians as the **antebellum period**, the South's economy grew at a rapid clip. Factory demand for raw cotton in England and New England stimulated production, and Mississippi, Louisiana, and Texas offered fertile land to hordes of profit-seeking planters and their hard-working slaves. By the 1850s, the South was richer than every nation in Europe except Great Britain. However, the expansion of Southern agriculture came at the expense of land that was wastefully farmed and slaves who performed the back-breaking labor.

Agricultural Capitalism

The Old South's planters coupled proven methods with innovative techniques to rank among the world's most successful agriculturists. Southerners had always managed to take care of themselves, even hard-pressed backcountry farmers. And throughout the colonial era successful planters grew fabulously rich exporting rice, indigo, and sugar. But by the 1840s, even small farmers turned from subsistence to cash-producing crops.

Not all Southerners grew the same crops. Characteristics of the soil and climatic conditions determined the possibilities. The high cost of slaves and machinery kept the production of some crops in the hands of rich planters. Rice, for example, requiring capital outlays for dikes, processing mills, and a large labor force, grew on large plantations in the South Carolina and Georgia low country. Similarly sugar production, introduced to southern Louisiana in the 1790s by émigrés from Haiti, remained in the hands of substantial planters.

> What cash crops did Southerners raise and where did they grow them?

Until the 1840s, however, Maryland, Virginia, and North Carolina harvested most of the country's tobacco, but after 1843 the western states of Kentucky and Missouri dominated tobacco cultivation. Not only did the growing of tobacco shift westward, but growers raised it on smaller farms. Small-scale farmers took over the bulk of tobacco production. In Virginia and North Carolina the typical farmer planted five and a half acres in tobacco and required only a few extra hands to work it. Chesapeake Bay tycoons did not suffer from this shift in tobacco culture. Many Maryland planters turned to wheat production, for which a growing demand existed in the burgeoning population centers of Baltimore and Philadelphia. Planters on the Eastern Shore, like the Lloyds, masters of the magnificent Wye House plantation mansion, functioned as local mercantile outlets for Baltimore trading firms and as marketers (factors) of their neighbors' crops. Although farther away from marketing centers, Virginia planters successfully diversified too.

Of all the Old South's cash crops, however, short-staple cotton ranked number one. "Cotton *is* king," enthusiastic Southerners proclaimed. Requiring only 200 frost-free days a year, cotton grew in a variety of soils, from the sandy loams of the up-country to the rich, black earth of the Gulf South's "black belt." By the 1850s the **Cotton Kingdom** encompassed the area from southern Virginia to Texas. Steamboats and railroads carried the fluffy white gold to waiting markets. In 1830, states along the lower Atlantic seaboard had produced most of the South's 750,000 bales of cotton, but five years later three-fourths of the yield emerged from the Gulf states and Arkansas. In 1860 production topped 4.5 million bales, and King Cotton topped the list of United States exports.

Wasteful Farming

The gluttonous King Cotton devoured land insatiably on his westward march. Cotton absorbed the soil's vital nutrients, and successive plantings left the land barren. Continuous cultivation also led to damaging erosion. Many planters exhibited little concern about environmental degradation. When the land gave out they simply pulled up stakes, leaving behind what a Georgian described as "a dreary desolation."

> What impact did intensive commercial farming have on Southern soil, and what efforts did planters make to preserve the land's fertility?

But it would be unfair to characterize all Southern farmers as land rapists. Agronomists worked hard to improve agricultural methods. Some Virginia planters converted to wheat, rotated crops, and developed new varieties of seeds. Edmund Ruffin, the antebellum South's leading agricultural reformer, carefully analyzed soil chemistry and found that marl, an alkaline substance derived from seashells, neutralized soil acidification caused by growing tobacco. Southerners also applied fertilizers, including imported Peruvian bird-droppings, to rejuvenate mother earth. Agricultural societies and journals like *The American Farmer* (founded in Baltimore in 1819) and *The Southern Cultivator* (begun in 1843) conveyed these new ideas to farmers throughout the South.

Down Yonder in the Land of Cotton

Cotton was the lifeblood of the antebellum South's capitalist economy, and slavery kept it flowing. Never before had the prosperity of white Southerners depended so much on the forced labor of blacks. As the cotton South flourished the number of slaves multiplied. In 1808 a million slaves toiled in the South. By 1860 the number had quadrupled. Slaves accompanied King Cotton on his westward march. Mississippi gained 10,000 slaves a year during the antebellum period, and in Texas between 1846 and 1860 the number grew by 265 percent. Slaves were valuable assets. Demand drove their market value up from $500 before 1820 to $1,800 by 1850. Prices varied according to age and sex, with healthy males in their twenties being generally the most valuable. Healthy women of child-bearing age, however, possessed the potential of adding to the slave owner's assets. Thus they were often as highly prized as males. By 1860, the market value of the South's 4 million slaves stood at $3 billion, more than all of the South's agricultural land.

> How important was slavery in the Cotton Kingdom?

Despite the antebellum boom, however, the Cotton Kingdom remained 25 percent poorer than the industrialized Northeast. Southerners invested too much capital in land and slaves, and not enough in more profitable manufacturing, marketing, and transportation enterprises. This concentration of capital is understandable during those flush times when cotton prices peaked. And although prices actually declined overall by two-thirds over the first half of the nineteenth century, investment in cotton agriculture still yielded a substantial return. Money invested in railroads, mines, and factories produced profits generally three times as much, but a powerful attachment to a rural, agricultural way of life in the South discouraged diversification.

The Profitability of Slavery

The Charleston *Mercury*, a prominent newspaper, responded to Northern critics by asserting that without slavery "civilization, society, and government" as Southerners knew it would cease to exit. But whether planters needed slavery to make a profit is a different question. Generations of historians have grappled with the profitability issue; however, incomplete records and racial attitudes have complicated the economic analysis.

**How profitable
was slavery?**

After the Civil War white Southerners dominated the writing of southern history. Depicting slave owners as benevolent masters, they concluded that the plantation system produced meager profits at best. Some plantation records showed lots of red ink. Many masters grumbled that "tho' I take every care, . . . they [the slaves] make me comparatively nothing." It might seem that slavery would have eventually collapsed of its own weight, and that the Civil War might have been avoided. But there were other types of slave owners too—some who were ruthlessly exploitative, as well as other good businessmen who profited from the system.

Much of the data from antebellum plantations has been lost or was never kept; however, a great deal of information remains. Using that available data, modern analysis suggests that well-managed plantations made a substantial profit. The 10 percent that they earned encouraged continued investment in the system. To the extent that plantations failed to profit, other factors bear responsibility: extravagant spending, soil depletion and erosion, and variable climatic and market conditions.

Buying and Selling Human Beings

The clamor for plantation labor sustained a lively slave trade. Since Congress outlawed the importation of Africans in 1808, the only way planters could obtain them was by

**How did planters
maintain an ade-
quate supply of
slaves?**

smuggling. In 1858 the ship *Wanderer* deposited 300 to 400 Africans on the Georgia coast. Slave traders also brought Africans in illegally from Mexico. Although we can only guess at the extent of this illicit commerce, it was enough, numbering at least in the tens of thousands, to lead the federal government to join with Great Britain in patrolling the west coast of Africa in an attempt to suppress it.

One of the most dramatic episodes in the history of the Atlantic slave trade occurred in 1839. Fifty-three West Africans victimized by slave hunters and transported to Cuba in violation of international agreements overpowered the Spanish crew of the schooner *La Amistad* as it sailed along the Cuban coast. Ordered by the mutineers' leader, Cinque, to steer toward Africa, the whites instead navigated toward the United States. A navy cutter intercepted the vessel

Courtesy of Library of Congress

UNITED STATES SLAVE TRADE.
1830.

From an abolitionist tract, this illustration from 1830 suggests the buying and selling of enslaved Africans while other black slaves work, all within eyesight of the nation's capitol in Washington.

off Long Island and took it, along with its starving and dehydrated passengers, into port.

A monumental legal battle ensued over the Africans' fate. Spanish authorities, claiming the mutineers were slaves born in Cuba, demanded their return under provisions of the Pinckney Treaty of 1795. The Africans, jailed in miserable conditions, denied they were slaves. "Make us free" they pleaded. Abolitionists took up their cause and provided legal defense. For publicity they retained 73-year-old ex-President John Quincy Adams as counsel. President Martin Van Buren supported the Spanish in order to retain Southern Democratic support for his coming reelection campaign. But the Supreme Court, ironically dominated by Southern slave owners, decided that the captives were free people who had been "kidnapped" and ordered their release.

The *Amistad* case was the first and only successful legal challenge to the notorious African slave trade in over 300 years. It generated popular support for the abolitionist movement and contributed to Van Buren's defeat. As for Cinque and the thirty-four other surviving captives, the abolitionists hired a ship to return them to Sierra Leone.

With Africans hard to come by, antebellum planters in the Gulf South turned to domestic slave markets. Slaves generally came from the Upper South, where unsteady tobacco prices, small-farm production, and a shift to less labor-intensive wheat production encouraged whites to sell off surplus slaves. Between 1830 and 1860, slave markets sold some 425,000 people. The historian Herbert G. Gutman found that owners who sold slaves made as much money as those who employed them on their plantations.

Buying and selling human beings outraged abolitionists. It brought into public view the most heart-wrenching and dehumanizing aspects of the peculiar institution: children separated from their parents and spouses from one another; human beings reduced to merchandise sold to the highest bidder. One slave out of every three was put on the auction block at some time in his or her life. Slave owners insisted that they resorted to selling slaves only during financial stringency or to rid themselves of troublemakers. But it was a rare owner who did not realize that each slave birth represented a valuable capital asset, and many owners engaged in slave breeding. Edmund Ruffin admitted that it made sense for owners "to turn the increase . . . into money at the highest market price."

Industrial Slavery

The image of endless cotton fields disguises the existence of Southern industry and the employment of slaves in non-agricultural labor. J.D.B. De Bow, publisher of the influential *De Bow's Review*, recognized an excessive concentration of capital and labor in the production of cotton. To balance the economy and soften the effects of the ups and downs of the cotton market, De Bow urged Southerners to invest in manufacturing.

William Gregg did not have to be persuaded. He had already caught the factory fever. Following the pattern set by Samuel Slater in Waltham, Massachusetts, Gregg built a textile mill at Graniteville, South Carolina, in the 1840s. Similar to the New England industrialists, Gregg employed white women to operate his machines. He doubted that slaves could learn the skills or the discipline to work in the new industrial system. Most Southern industrialists, however, employed slave labor. By 1860 about 20 percent of the nation's industrial capital was invested in the South. And if the South had been an independent country it would have ranked among the top five industrialized nations in the world.

> To what uses besides raising cotton did Southerners put enslaved laborers?

By the 1850s, about 5 percent of all slaves worked in industrial jobs. Slaves provided reliable and economical labor in the South's major iron foundry, the Tredegar Iron Works in Richmond, in salt, iron, and coal mines, granite and marble quarries, tobacco factories in Virginia and North Carolina, and textile mills, sawmills, and gristmills nearly everywhere in the South. Canals employed slave laborers, and railroads relied almost exclusively on slaves to clear rights-of-way, lay track, and erect bridges and trestles. Many mechanics and artisans employed slaves as assistants. Suggesting the value of slave workers in non-agricultural endeavors, one visitor noted that "the Negro is a third arm to every working man, who can possibly save money enough to purchase one."

Although the antebellum South was largely a rural society with only a handful of cities of 10,000 or more (there were none of that size in the trans-Appalachian region), many professional and business people lived in towns. A number of them owned slaves. Most were not large slave owners—except to the extent that they owned plantations in the country and employed slaves as plantation hands. Most urban slave owners owned only one or two slaves and employed them as personal or household servants, as gardeners, or as skilled craftsmen. Urban businesses often employed slaves as stevedores, draymen, store clerks, washerwomen, and manual laborers.

The South was indeed rich. The expansion of the Southern economy, however, depended on land that was being rapidly exhausted and on labor that had little incentive to work. Even more serious was the concentration of the South's economic resources. Time would tell what a problem this would be.

THINKING BACK

1. Why did the South's economy remain agricultural instead of industrial, and did that make economic sense?
2. Why did the South develop a commitment to slavery? Were there any alternatives?

LIFESTYLES OF THE RICH AND NOT SO RICH

Certain images sometimes leap to mind when we think about the Old South: sprawling plantations, lovely mansions, elegantly dressed men and women, and legions of devoted slaves. Musical composers like Stephen Foster wrote songs like "Swanee River" (1851), "My Old Kentucky Home" (1853), and "Old Black Joe" (1860) that idealized plantation scenes. The twentieth-century novelist Margaret Mitchell and Hollywood motion picture producers immortalized the romantic Old South in *Gone with the Wind*. These images contain a grain of truth but grossly distort the reality of antebellum Southern society. They reflect the way some but not most Southerners, not even a majority of wealthy ones, really lived.

Moonlight and Magnolias

The magnificent tobacco, rice, and cotton plantations of the Chesapeake and the coastal Carolinas and Georgia represented the highest achievement of Southern aristocracy. Their owners attained great opulence. They prided themselves on their gentility and dominated social and local political affairs. Historians do not agree on whether the antebellum South was essentially feudal or capitalistic, that is governed by tradition and paternalism or profit and exploitation, but at least along the Atlantic coast a group of wealthy planters lived amid distinctly aristocratic pretensions.

> **How did the South's planter aristocracy live?**

Masters and mistresses of some Virginia and Carolina plantations presided over holdings of thousands of acres and occupied elegant homes. Their slaves (by definition plantations employed twenty or more) produced an abundance of food, and the ample revenues from cash crops paid for fine clothes, fashionable furnishings, expensive works of art, and the children's private tutors. The estates of the most prominent families, like the Lees, Carters, Byrds, and Rutledges, originated in the seventeenth century. They had been handed down to the latest scions of Southern gentility.

An antebellum plantation mansion in Florida. The opulence of the South's planter aristocracy was indeed magnificent.

Traditional gender roles defined who did what on these palatial estates. The masters controlled the business side of things, deciding what to plant, how many slaves to buy or sell, and where to market the plantation's products. Mistresses managed the household. They took charge of the domestic slaves, supervising their work and disciplining them. The planters' wives oversaw the cooking, sewing, and cleaning. As the symbols of domestic gentility, women planned and conducted the many social activities associated with plantation life.

The Old South's aristocracy boasted the latest generation of the "first families," but in the Old Southwest (Mississippi, Louisiana, and later Texas) sheer wealth more than heritage and refinement determined social rank. This type of society is defined as a *plutocracy*. Plantation agriculture in the Southwest was strongly capitalist. Many of the Southwest's grandees had ascended from lower classes through the shrewd accumulation and investment of cash and credit. And since their ventures were highly speculative they occasionally lost their fortunes before they could pass them intact to their children.

These planters of the Old Southwest were entrepreneurs, practical men, who put business above refinement. The men, but not necessarily women, were coarser than their eastern counterparts. Those on the frontier built simpler houses and spent less time and money on luxuries. Illiteracy was more common among them. They lived stressful lives and often transferred the tension to their wives and children through verbal and physical abuse.

Regardless of where they lived, the planter elite owned the vast majority of slaves. At mid-century, approximately 350,000 Southern families, one quarter of all white families, owned slaves, but most slaveholders owned five or fewer. They were not particularly rich. In fact, only one out of five slaveholders met the definition of a planter. Roughly 10,000 slaveholders in a total white population of 8 million owned fifty slaves or more and barely 3,000 owned in excess of 100. One out of eight slaveholders owned more than half the South's slaves and an even larger percentage of its overall agricultural wealth.

Ordinarily, planters employed managers called **overseers**, comparable to managers in Northern factories, to supervise day-to-day operations. Overseers organized the labor force and disciplined slaves. Their employers provided them with detailed instructions specifying their responsibilities and what, if anything, they could not do. They were not, for example, supposed to abuse the slaves. But their jobs depended on whether they produced a profit; consequently overseers were quick with the lash.

Overseers bore an unsavory reputation, even among the planters who employed them. One Mississippi planter described them as "a worthless set of vagabonds." In reality, however, they were probably no more flawed morally and no more brutal by disposition than people generally. They operated in an inhumane system, one that often brought out the worst rather than the best in the human character.

What You May Not Know About Slave Owners

Slave ownership was not limited to white males. Despite restrictions that limited the property rights of antebellum

> **What other types of persons owned slaves?**

Southern women, they did own slaves. Indeed, one slave owner in every ten was a woman. In most cases, however, they were widows who had inherited slaves from their husbands. Women as a rule did not actively engage in the purchase or management of slaves.

Native Americans also owned black slaves. In 1861 Choctaws and Chickasaws owned approximately 5,000 slaves. One Native American, Greenwood Leflore, a chief of the Mississippi Choctaws, owned more than 400 slaves. Although few Native Americans owned very many, slaveholding established a strong bond between Indians of the Southeast and white Southerners. When secession forced Indians to choose allegiances between the Union and the Southern Confederacy, many sided with the Confederacy, proclaiming support for "our Southern friends."

The Southeastern Indians' involvement with African-American slavery began in colonial times. Their customs included enslaving war captives, but during the conflicts with white settlers in the Carolinas and Georgia they stole African-American slaves. Eventually they entered the lucrative slave trade, stealing from one owner and selling to another. As groups like the Cherokees adopted white methods of commercial agriculture, they employed slaves as field hands. The Cherokee government passed strict laws governing slaves and free African Americans who lived among them. With their removal to Oklahoma during the 1830s the Southeastern Indians took slaves and the institution of slavery with them into the West.

A number of free blacks owned slaves as well. Some had managed to purchase members of their families.

John Meachum of Virginia purchased his freedom and moved to St. Louis. There he married a slave. As he prospered as a carpenter he bought his wife's freedom. Meachum acquired other slaves too, taught them his trade, and let them purchase their freedom. Other African Americans owned slaves for strictly economic reasons. Artisans employed them as hod-carriers, wagon-drivers, and delivery-persons. William Johnson, a wealthy barber in Natchez, Mississippi, owned fifteen slaves. That these slave owners were black did not prevent slaves from resenting them. As a Texas slave put it, "one nigger's no business to sarve another." Black slave owners tended to come from the ranks of mixed-race mulattoes, especially in places like Louisiana where since French colonial days race played less of a role in determining social status than in other parts of the United States.

Neither Slave Nor Free

The anomaly of African-American slave owners accentuated the important division between slaves and free blacks. For the most part they existed on the margins of Southern society, seen by whites as troublesome.

| How did African Americans who were not enslaved fit into the social system of the antebellum South? |

Nine out of every ten black Southerners were slaves, but more than 260,000 occupied an ambiguous middle ground between slavery and freedom. As a result of manumission (Virginian John Randolph freed all 400 of his slaves in 1833), escape, and natural increase, those African Americans were technically free; however, no state allowed them to vote, hold public office, or testify in court, although slaves could give evidence against them. Whites prevented them from engaging in trades or professions where they might directly compete. For offenses as minor as failure to pay taxes they could be sold into bondage. "Quasi" or "semi" free fits the status of this group of African Americans

Free, or quasi-free, blacks occupied an ambivalent position between slaves and whites. Their legal status separated them from slaves and yet racial ties bound the two together. Elite free blacks, especially *mulattos* (people of mixed race), avoided association with slaves out of fear of their own debasement. Whites generally did not approve of free blacks. They worried that free African Americans would encourage slaves to rebel. But, on the other hand, "if blacks see all their color slaves," a Virginia lawmaker explained,

"it will seem to them a disposition of Providence, and they will be content."

As whites marginalized them, the South's free blacks looked to their churches, schools, and social organizations for support. Most free African Americans resided in larger towns, and African Methodist and Baptist churches appeared there. Savannah's African Baptist Church grew so large that it divided into three separate congregations. In Charleston, the elite Brown Fellowship Society, which admitted only free mulattoes, held literary sessions and provided insurance benefits for its members.

These self-help mechanisms worried white slaveholders, however. They represented a degree of freedom that could undermine slavery, so whites cracked down on them. In the 1830s Daniel Alexander Payne had conducted a school for free black children in Charleston, but when the legislature banned such schools Payne emigrated to Pennsylvania, exactly what most whites wished all free African Americans would do. Authorities also banished the African Methodist Church. For most white Southerners, the solution to the problem presented by free Africans was to enslave or expel them.

Whites Who Did Not Own Slaves

Three out of four white southerners had no direct connection with slavery. Most of those fell into a social stratum of hard-working "plain folk" known as **yeomen**. They possessed no money buy slaves.

| What did white Southerners who did not own slaves think about slavery? |

These non-slaveholding whites typically struggled on small parcels of marginal land in the pine barrens or sand hills of the South's back country. They could scarcely raise their own food let alone quantities of cotton, sugar, or rice. They accumulated only one tenth as much wealth per capita as slave owners and usually lived in crude log cabins.

The white non-slave owners constituted a distinct economic class in Southern society. And the disparity in wealth between them and slave owners bred resentment. Poorer whites hated the slave owners' monopoly of the best land. The use of slave labor prevented them from hiring out as farm hands and limited their opportunities in skilled trades.

Yet, most yeoman farmers dreamed of owning slaves, whether to help them with hard labor or as status symbols, or both. Especially in the face of abolitionist criticism, the slave owners neutralized much of the yeomen's hostility by pointing out that slavery benefited both groups. By enslaving only African Americans, the system ensured the freedom of all whites. With some exceptions, slave owners succeeded in plastering over the cracks in white solidarity.

Hinton Rowan Helper, however, a non-slaveholder from western North Carolina, blasted away at the fissures. Helper condemned slavery as an un-progressive labor system. It stifled economic expansion, he contended, and took honest labor out of the hands of ordinary whites. In 1857 he fired a bombshell in a book entitled *The Impending Crisis of the South*. He not only attacked slavery but African Americans too, who, he argued, should be colonized outside of the country. Helper raised a furor in the South by urging yeomen to topple the "slaveocracy." Southern leaders demonized him, regarded him as at least as great a threat to the Southern way of life as any Northern abolitionist.

THINKING BACK

1. What proportion of the antebellum South's white population owned slaves, and why did whites who did not own slaves support the system, or did they?
2. What sort of situation did free African Americans live in?

EXPERIENCING ENSLAVEMENT

Custom and law in the antebellum South, both of which bore the unmistakable mark of racism, narrowly defined the world that African American slaves inhabited. Yet within those confines slaves built complex and dynamic societies. From sunup to sundown their lives belonged to their masters, but within the slave quarters, mostly hidden from the prying eyes of whites, black men, women, and children laughed, worshipped, grieved, celebrated, and rewarded themselves in treasured ways.

Slave Codes: The Badges of Degradation

How did the slave laws work?

After the American Revolution, states enacted laws that defined slavery. During the 1830s legislatures revised the statutes to tighten controls. The slave codes established a dual character. As property, the slaves' "time, labor and services" belonged to their masters; as human beings they were responsible for their behavior and would be punished for it.

At the heart of the definition was the understanding that only African Americans could be slaves. Moreover, the laws presumed that any African American was a slave unless he or she had proof to the contrary. Masters enjoyed absolute legal control over their slaves; they could sell them as well as inflict punishment upon them. Slaves could not sue or testify against whites, bear arms, or move about without passes from their owners.

The slave codes established slavery as an inherited condition. Slaves lived as a caste, which meant that they were locked into that status forever, as were all of their posterity. A child took the status of its mother, so the children of slave women were automatically slaves. The only way slaves could become free, according to the law, was by manumission, and that became rarer as lawmakers made it more difficult for masters to free their slaves.

The World of Work

A strict regimen governed slave labor, beginning at sunrise and ending at sundown Monday through Friday, and usually half a day on Saturday. Slaves were generally given Sundays off. The workday commenced with the peal of a wake-up bell. After breakfast the hands marched to the fields. A northern journalist, Frederick Law Olmsted, witnessed the scene on a Mississippi plantation. First came "forty of the largest and strongest women I ever saw together," followed by the plow-hands, "thirty strong, mostly men, but a few of them women," and then "a lean vigilent white overseer, on a brisk pony." On another plantation the hands were already at work. One Northern traveler observed field work on a Southern plantation.

What was it like to work as a slave?

"We found in the field thirty plows, moving together, turning the earth from the cotton plants, and from thirty to forty hoers, the latter mainly women, with a black driver walking about among them with a whip, which he often cracked at them, sometimes allowing the lash to fall lightly upon their shoulders. He was constantly urging them also with his voice. All worked very steadily, and though the presence of a stranger on the plantation must have been a most unusual occurrence, I saw none raise or turn their heads to look at me."

Masters assigned each slave a daily task or organized the workforce into gangs. Slaves preferred the task system because they could quit when they completed their assignments. Planters did not like it though because slaves might work sloppily to finish early. In the gang system slaves remained on the job until the day ended. Unlike on small farms, work on the large plantations was highly specialized. Field hands became cotton-pickers, ditch-diggers, or tobacco-cutters. Others learned the skills of artisanship: blacksmiths, carpenters, and stone masons. Slave owners highly-valued such skills, as did the slaves. Few planters could afford to maintain a full complement of artisans. Those who could hired them out to neighbors.

Slaves also performed various jobs in and around the plantation household. Cooks, nursemaids, seamstresses, and personal servants comprised an army of domestics. Household slaves constituted a privileged upper class. Masters and mistresses trained them to perform the required tasks and to comport themselves well. "I want him to acquire a *house look*," wrote a Georgia slave owner, "which you know is not the acquisition of a day."

Slaves submitted to this regimen under the threat of punishment freely applied. The slave codes theoretically regulated slave punishment, but in reality only the self-restraint of master or overseer prevented punishment from turning into torture and death. Flogging was the most typical form of corporal punishment, although whites employed a variety of hideous devices to inflict physical pain. By confinement, withholding food or clothing allowances, and selling incorrigible slaves, planters pressured workers into becoming obedient and productive.

Food, Clothing, and Shelter

The amount of care that slaves received varied widely. Most states enacted guidelines for masters. Texas' slave code required masters to provide "necessary food and clothing."

> How well did slave owners provide for their enslaved laborers?

Such laws, however, were too vague to be effective. No doubt some masters minimized their slaves' provisions, but most provided enough food to supply minimum energy needs and to keep the slaves relatively healthy.

Nobody ate particularly well in the South, including slaves. Southern cooking, a writer for the popular women's magazine *Godey's Lady's Book* pointed out, "is fat bacon and pork, fat bacon and pork only, and that continually morning, noon, and night, for all classes, sexes, ages, and conditions." Most masters allowed their slaves to maintain gardens, and hunting yielded deer and varmints that supplemented the standard ration of three pounds of salt pork and one peck of corn meal per week. Peas, yams, turnips, possum, and rabbit turned up in the slaves' cooking pots, as did poultry and beef pilfered from the masters' livestock. Treats included molasses poured over cornbread and into coffee.

Ample in calories and seasonally balanced, the slaves' diet overall was deficient in many vitamins and minerals. But they did not suffer from diet-related maladies any more frequently than ordinary whites did. Health problems stemmed as much from a general

Image © Joyce Chapman, 2010. Used by permission of Shutterstock, Inc.

Cabins in the slave quarters on a plantation in South Carolina

ignorance of nutrition as from the master class' stinginess.

Clothing allowances were less adequate. Field hands typically received two allotments of clothing each year. Men acquired two shirts, two pairs of pants, and a hat along with a pair of shoes and a woolen jacket once a year. Women's allowances included two dresses, two chemises, and a pair of shoes. Children, Frederick Douglass remembered, wore sackcloth "made into a sort of shirt, reaching down to my knees."

The wealthiest planters dressed their household servants as fashionably as possible. Masters wanted their domestic servants to reflect their gentility. So they decked them out in fancy dresses, pants, shirts, and waistcoats. Although mostly cast-offs from the masters' and mistresses' wardrobes, their clothes nevertheless made household slaves to stand out from other plantation hands.

Slave cabins on well-managed plantations lined up in regimented rows, a short distance from the main house or the overseer's cottage. Like the other provisions, the slaves' living quarters ran the gamut from cabins to hovels. Olmsted saw "neat and well-made" cabins, but more run-of-the-mill habitations stood "in the most decayed and deplorable condition." Even the best of them were drab, drafty, and cramped.

After Sundown

> How did enslaved people maintain a sense of their identity, self-worth, and community?

From sundown to sunup slaves lived their own lives. Never totally secure from the intrusions of white people, as Celia's tragic life exemplifies, slaves shared their own thoughts and feelings, sang, played, prayed, loved, and suffered together inside the quarters. African-American culture flourished there throughout the long history of slavery. The echoes of African languages could be heard in slave dialects. Healing methods, burial rituals, and housekeeping had African antecedents.

Music and dance allowed slaves to express a range of emotions and ideas that they could not reveal to whites. West Africans commonly communicated through song. As they danced, slaves complained about "ol' massa."

We raise de wheat,

Dey gib us de corn;

We bake de bread,

Dey gib us de crust;

We sif the meal,

Dey gib us de huss;

We peel de meat,

Dey gib us de skin;

And dat's de way

Dey take us in;

We skim de pot,

Dey gib us de liquor,

And say dat's good enough for nigger.

Work songs set the rhythms of hoeing, digging, and chopping. They also made the time go by a little faster and easier. As it had for their West African ancestors, singing helped slaves maintain a sense of community that in turn encouraged and strengthened them against life's hardships.

Folk tales gave immense pleasure to young and old. Trickster tales like those involving "Bre'r Rabbit" and "Bre'r Fox" taught valuable lessons. Wiley critters representing slaves outwitted larger, more powerful animals, thinly disguised masters and overseers. The tales not only entertained but also reinforced values. Justice ultimately prevailed in them. They instructed children how to behave in the presence of whites and how to survive in the face of the lethal power.

Religion too provided comfort as well as the strength to endure. It is hard to know how many slaves were religious, but there was certainly a large proportion. Partly due to Christian evangelists, especially Baptists and Methodists, and partly to the fact that many masters urged them to attend church services, many slaves had accepted Christianity. Masters wanted their slaves to hear the gospel message of submission, but slaves mostly responded to the Christian promise of salvation, which they interpreted as including freedom. Christianity, in other words, gave slaves a vocabulary for expressing their desire to be free. Biracial worship was common, but slaves also enjoyed their own religious meetings. They listened to slave preachers who did not exhort them to obey their masters. And they sang hymns like "Swing Lo, Sweet Chariot" and "Steel Away to Jesus," which carried the message of escape to the "Promise Land."

Although their marriages had no legal basis, slaves established families and built lasting relationships.

Whenever and wherever possible, slaves gathered in their own churches, as far away from whites as they could get. Worship services reinforced the sense of community that helped sustain them. Sermons, drawn from Protestant Christian gospels, emphasized liberation rather than submission.

In many ways slavery threatened the integrity of slave families: spouses being sold away from each other, having to share living quarters with non-family members, and the sexual abuse of slave women. Nevertheless, a majority of slaves grew up in two-parent families, not unlike conditions today. They maintained as stable a family life as they could.

Slave Resistance

> **What forms did resistance to enslavement take?**

Masters maintained the pretense of paternalism by referring to their slaves as part of their extended families, sort of like dependent children. They and their wives liked to use the phrase "our Negroes." The model served the master's purpose because it justified their use of stern discipline. But their constant complaints about how hard it was to get slaves to work, and especially their fear of organized slave rebellion or individual acts of violence, tell us that they regarded them as most unruly children.

To be sure, some were submissive, exhibiting a "Sambo" personality that historians have compared with prisoners in concentration camps. Others coped by working hard and taking pride in their jobs. They cared for their families as best they could and sought

security and advancement. But these characterizations, though accurate in many instances, divert our attention from the many faces of slave resistance.

Slaves seldom rebelled outright, primarily because the odds of success were too small. Even armed, they were no match for trained and even better-armed white militias. Whites maintained constant vigilance and punished conspirators severely. The testimony of two slaves in 1800 disclosed a plot to arm 1,000 others in Henrico, County, Virginia. The ringleader was a twenty-four-year-old blacksmith named Gabriel Prosser (see pp. 239-40). Officials executed Prosser and two dozen of his followers. Whites uncovered another slave revolt in South Carolina. They arrested the plotters, including a preacher named Denmark Vesey, and hanged a total of thirty-seven. In 1831 Nat Turner, who believed himself God's agent on a mission to deliver African Americans from bondage, mobilized over seventy slaves in Southampton County, Virginia, in a rampage of killing (see p. 354).

Nat Turner lent his name to the rebellious type of slave. "Nats" attacked the system and the whites who maintained it. Hundreds of assaults and murders filled court dockets while countless others went unreported. How tempting for a cook or dining room servant to poison food served to the master and his family. Uncontrollable anger or humiliation led slaves like Celia to strike out in violent rage.

Far more frequently than they committed acts of violence, however, slaves engaged in subtle gestures of defiance. They undertook massive campaigns of sabotage, abused and killed work animals, stole livestock and poultry, or destroyed farm tools and machines. They feigned illness or injury in order to slow down plantation operations. How many slaves must there have been who vented their anger like Delia, a household servant, who could not count the times she "spit in the biscuits and peed in the coffee just to get back at them white folks."

THINKING BACK

1. How did the white regimes of the South control the lives of enslaved people?
2. How did enslaved people control their own lives, fortify themselves against the stresses and abuses of enslavement, and resist their condition?

THE LOCAL PERSPECTIVE: FOCUS ON THE WASHINGTON TERRITORY IN THE AGE OF SLAVERY

In the 1830s, the misty and thickly forested Pacific Northwest coast was a world way from the factories and cotton plantations of the East. It was a distant frontier from the standpoint of the United States. To reach it from St. Louis required an arduous and dangerous 1,500-mile journey up the Missouri River and overland along trails blazed by early explorers and mountain trappers. The alternative involved a 20,000-mile sea odyssey around stormy Cape Horn. Yet, today's Washington state was one of the most densely populated regions of North America with extensive economic development, commercial trade, and even slave labor.

What form did slavery take in the Washington Territory?

Exploration of the Pacific Northwest coast had begun only a few decades before. Eight days after the Declaration of Independence, Captain James Cook sailed from England in search of the Pacific end of the fabled Northwest Passage. Cook and his crew landed at Nootka, on the west coast of Vancouver Island, just to the north of present-day Washington, where they made repairs and traded trinkets to local Indians for the thick, silky fur of the sea otter. This foreshadowed the coast's early economic development.

Subsequent Spanish, Russian, and British explorations during the 1780s accumulated a wealth of information about the native people, geography, and ocean currents from southern Alaska to California. In 1792, one of those explorers, Britain's George Vancouver, sailed through the Strait of Juan de Fuca and into Puget Sound, the latter named for one of his officers. He assigned names to other familiar

Image © KennStilger47, 2010. Used by permission of Shutterstock, Inc.

Columbia River Gorge. In 1821, the Hudson's Bay Company built Fort Vancouver, a gateway to the territory jointly occupied for twenty-five years by British and American trappers, merchants, and settlers.

places: Bellingham Bay, Whidbey and Vashon islands, and mounts Baker and Rainier. The Europeans also introduced small pox and other diseases that devastated Indian populations.

Large-scale economic development of the far Northwest involved the fur trade. The sea otter soon became depleted, but the Cascades and the Columbia River basin yielded abundant beaver. Following Lewis and Clark's expedition, American and British fur-trading companies entered the area. The Montreal-based North West Company built trading posts at Spokane and Walla Walla. When the venerable Hudson's Bay Company absorbed the North West Company in 1821, it constructed Fort Vancouver on the Columbia River, which quickly became the largest community in the territory. It contained a hospital, a jail, a sawmill, and several grist mills along with orchards and vegetable and grain fields. Its cosmopolitan population, in addition to company employees, included *metis* from the prairies to the east, Hawaiians, and local Chinook Indians. The company also commenced commercial farming on the south end of Puget Sound and built Fort Nisqually at today's Tacoma.

The Native Americans who inhabited the coastal region of Washington, including Chinooks along the Columbia River, Puyallup-Nisqually communities at the southern end of Puget Sound, and Skagits near present-day Seattle, traditionally supplied themselves with seafood and meat from the abundant resources that were readily available. To be sure, hunting, fishing, and foraging for berries and other plant foods required a great deal of drudgery work. So did processing animal hides for clothing and cutting the red cedar and other trees that craftsmen used to build boats and houses. To perform the most onerous work, Indians relied on slaves. Over the generations that preceded contact with Europeans, Northwest coast Indians developed slave labor systems that functioned in many ways like slavery in the Southern United States. In the 1820s, Sir George Simpson of the Hudson's Bay Company recorded that Indian slaves "are made to fish, hunt, draw water and wood[,] in short all the drudgery falls on them."

Slaves among Northwest coast Indians came mostly from raids against other communities. But once a person became a slave, he or she usually remained in that condition for life, as did their children. It was possible for the family of a captured slave to pay a ransom, and occasionally owners manumitted their slaves. They had no rights or privileges, usually bore some kind of mark that distinguished them from non-slaves since

this was not racial slavery, and lived under the complete control of their masters. Indeed, slave owners could kill slaves. Killing was usually ritualized, but the death rate was much higher than among African-American slaves in the South. During the 1840s, in one community along the British Columbia coast, at least nineteen slaves in a population of 160 slaves, were killed by their masters. That would have been 52,000 killings had the slave population there equaled that in the antebellum South. Death rates in other communities were probably similar. Although Indian slavery was not commercialized and capitalized like it was in the Southern United States, it was still brutal and exploitative. Sir George Simpson believed that the slave who was unfortunate enough to live among the Chinooks along the Columbia River was "the most unfortunate wretch in existence."

Religious revivals ignited American passions for missionary activity in the Northwest. Misunderstood reports that some Indians flattened the foreheads of their infants (as in the Flathead tribe) aroused disgust and compassion for what seemed like an unenlightened people. When a group of Nez Perces in 1831 asked for teachers and missionaries to be sent among them, the call was too much for pious eastern reformers to resist. The American Board of Commissioners for Foreign Missions dispatched Congregational, Presbyterian, and Dutch Reformed missionaries to the far Northwest. Among them were Marcus and Narcissa Whitman, who established a mission among the Cayuse Indians a short distance from Walla Walla.

Not satisfied with Christianizing the natives, the Whitmans sought to remake them in their own images. The Cayuses grew resentful. "They are an exceedingly proud, haughty, and insolent people," Narcissa wrote to her mother. Settlers passing through on their way to the Willamette Valley used the Whitman mission as a way station and made the Indians jumpy. On a foggy November day in 1847, the Cayuses murdered Narcissa and Marcus with their tomahawks. This tragic episode effectively ended missionary work among the Indians. They had brought more acres under cultivation than converts to Christianity.

In the two decades before the Civil War, 53,000 hardy pioneers poured into Oregon, mostly settling in the fertile Willamette Valley south of the Columbia. That and the British withdrawal to the 49th parallel in 1846 spurred Congress to establish a territorial government. Only 3,000 non-Indians lived above the Columbia River, many near sawmills in the fledgling towns of Tacoma and Seattle. But these northern

Oregonians chafed under the domination of the Willamette farmers. Moreover, a government survey demonstrated the superiority of Puget Sound over the Columbia River estuary as a port. In 1853, Congress created a new territory. Some residents preferred the name Columbia; however, they settled on Washington and located the capital in Olympia.

Washington's first territorial governor, an under-sized, over-achieving West Point graduate named Isaac Stevens, moved quickly to stimulate economic development. Regarding the territory's 17,000 Indians as an impediment, he coerced most of them into moving onto confined reservations. The bait he offered was a guarantee of fishing rights and a government annuity.

Washington's growth remained slow though. Statehood did not come until 1889. Its remoteness retarded its growth. The next great transformation, a heavily capitalized lumber industry in western Washington and commercial agriculture in the Yakima Valley and on the eastern plateau, awaited the arrival of the railroad and its opening of vast eastern markets.

THINKING BACK

1. What attracted people from the United States to the Washington Territory?
2. Who were Marcus and Narcissa Whitman, and what caused Cayuse Indians to kill them?

CONCLUSION

Factory industry in the North and the plantation system of the South shared common traits. Both were dynamic, expanding, and market oriented. Capitalist incentives drove both of them. And in particular ways, both widened the gap between rich and poor, impeding the growth of democracy. But at the same time these two economic systems differed sharply from one another. One carried the distinctive marks of modern societies: machines to do the work, wage laborers, a strong middle class, and an urban environment. The other was distinctly traditional: agricultural production, unfree labor doing work by hand, and a rural population dispersed over the land. These characteristics symbolized diverging paths of economic and social development for North and South. The North pointed boldly to the future, to the type of society we live in today, while the South sought to maintain an old way of life. By 1860, institutional slavery existed legally in only three countries in the Western Hemisphere. Most white Southerners were determined that they would not follow in the path of other societies that had once relied on slavery but had cast it aside. In fact, they were determined to expand their dominion. In many unfortunate ways, slavery scarred America. Its consequences are evident today in the remnants of racism and the lingering effects of generations of oppression.

SUGGESTED SOURCES FOR STUDENTS

The historical literature on the slave experience is extensive, but the most modern treatment that brings together regional and generational differences is Ira Berlin, *Generations of Captivity: A History of African-American Slaves* (2003).

Mary H. Blewett, *Men, Women, and Work: Class, Gender, and Protest in the New England Shoe Industry* (1988), is a superb analysis of gender and class in the emergence of a working class.

Shearer Bowman, *Masters and Lords: Mid 19th Century U.S. Planters and Prussian Junkers* (1993), addresses the controversy over the nature of the planter class. His conclusion: they were capitalists.

But anyone beginning a study of industrial America would want to look at Thomas C. Cochran, *Frontiers of Change: Early Industrialism in America* (1981). It offers a brief, easy to read introduction to industrialization.

Steven Deyle, *Carry Me Back: The Domestic Slave Trade in American Life* (2005), explores several aspects of the marketing of slaves as commodities, noting the different perspectives taken in slave-exporting and slave-importing regions as well as the importance of the slave trade to overall wealth creation in the antebellum South.

Thomas Dublin, *Women at Work: The Transformation of Work and Community in Lowell, Massachusetts, 1826-1860* (1979), puts working women into a social and political setting.

Tiya Miles and Sharon P. Holland eds., *Crossing Waters, Crossing Worlds: The African Diaspora in Indian Country* (2006), present fifteen essays that examine the intersecting experiences of African Americans and Native Americans.

William W. Freehling, *The Road to Disunion: Secessionists at Bay, 1776-1854* (1990), is the first volume in a larger work detailing the growth of Southern nationalism. Here he highlights differences and conflicts between the Upper and Lower South.

Elizabeth Fox-Genovese and Eugene D. Genovese, *Slavery in Black and White: Class and Race in the Southern Slaveholders' New World Order* (2008), masterfully examines the slaveholders' contention that "slavery in the abstract" represented the world's most progressive, bourgeois, moral, and efficient labor and social system, certainly when compared to the exploitation and misery associated with wage labor systems throughout the industrialized world.

For an engaging examination of the day-to-day experiences of Americans, and how they changed with economic developments, the best bet is Jack Larkin, *The Reshaping of Everyday Life, 1790-1840* (1988).

For a brief description and analysis of industrialization see Walter Licht, *Industrializing America: The Nineteenth Century* (1995). It is easy to comprehend and highly interpretive.

For a clear and readable explanation of the role of technology in the Industrial Revolution see Brooke Hindle and Steven Lubar, *Engines of Change: The American Industrial Revolution, 1790-1860* (1986).

Albert Raboteau, *Slave Religion: The "Invisible Institution" in the Antebellum South* (1978), describes the origins, practices, and importance of African-American slave religion.

For an examination of African Americans in the workforce see David Roediger, *The Wages of Whiteness: Race and the Making of the American Working Class* (1991).

Sean Wilentz, *Chants Democratic: New York City and the Rise of the American Working Class, 1790-1865* (1984), describes the emergence of a working-class consciousness.

The best analysis of Southern economic development is still Gavin Wright, *The Political Economy of the Cotton South* (1978).

BEFORE WE GO ON

1. Why did economic growth in the North and South move in such different directions?

2. In what ways was the United States in the 1840s different from the way it had been at the close of the War of 1812?

Building a Democratic Nation

3. How might the antebellum South's economy be described as agricultural capitalism? How were Southern plantations similar to Northern factories?

4. Overall, how was the North different from the South?

Connections

5. Did the factory and the plantation move the United States in a more or less democratic direction? Explain.

6. How does the American experience with slavery affect us today, or does it? Explain

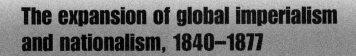

THE GLOBAL PERSPECTIVE

The expansion of global imperialism and nationalism, 1840–1877

During the tumultuous decades of the mid-nineteenth century, the rapid expansion of European power precipitated changes in the lives of people around the world. Liberal idealism, romantic nationalism, and the steady growth in industry—particularly in Great Britain—influenced the course of events. In 1848, these elements produced dramatic though mostly unsuccessful revolutions in several European countries. Afterward, they contributed to the formation of unified nation-states. Industrial expansion led to renewed colonial enterprises in nearly every corner of the globe. European economic penetration of traditional societies forced new ways of life and often bred indigenous nationalism. Some changes, however, were more positive. Medical advances contributed to a 50 percent increase in the world's population.

> **How did global imperialism ignite revolutionary nationalism?**

Aggressive industrial capitalism wrecked existing social structures in which mutual obligation bound various classes of people together in ordered, locally-oriented societies. Capitalist employers (the bourgeoisie) exploited factory employees (the proletariat), and both groups began to recognize themselves as distinct classes. Karl Marx, the German son of a Jewish lawyer, believed that the working class would overthrow capitalism. Marx formulated a theory that every age produces a dominant set of ideas (a **thesis**), which provokes an opposing set of ideas (the **antithesis**). The result is a new ideology (a **synthesis**) for the next era. From that process, Marx concluded that **class conflict** was inevitable. In the capitalists' exploitation of the working class, he saw the seeds of a **communist** revolution. "The proletarians have nothing to lose but their chains," he and fellow socialist Friedrich Engels wrote in *The Communist Manifesto* (1848). They have a world to win. WORKING MEN OF ALL COUNTRIES, UNITE!"

Not Marxist communism, however, but romantic idealism, grinding poverty, and the yearning for independence generated the immediate demands for liberal reforms in Europe. In Great Britain, reformers attacked the **Corn Laws**—measures limiting imported wheat (called corn in England). Landowners had contrived ways to keep grain prices high despite widespread hunger among Britain's poor. But, Parliamentary reforms gave industrialized regions more representation and empowered the working class; in 1846, the government of Prime Minister Robert Peel adopted the principle of **free trade**, without protective tariffs, to allow greater food imports and averting a potential revolution. In 1833, Great Britain abolished slavery throughout the empire.

France and various central European countries did not escape revolution. In Paris in February of 1848, workers and shopkeepers demanded the right to vote. They took up arms and erected barricades in Paris's narrow streets to show their determination. When the monarch Louis Philippe abdicated, the revolutionaries proclaimed the Second French Republic. Universal male suffrage and abolition of slavery and the death penalty throughout the French empire quickly followed. But Paris' middle-class would not support socialist reforms; nor would conservative rural landowners and peasants. In June, **revolutionary socialists** once again threw up barricades, but this time government armies crushed them, at the cost of 10,000 casualties. In a reaction against the Paris upheavals, a national constituent assembly constructed a new government with a strong executive. Voters chose Louis Napoleon, Bonaparte's nephew, as president, and in 1852, in keeping with family tradition, he became Emperor Napoleon III.

Economic improvements reduced political tensions in France, and the modernization of Paris with broad boulevards and beautiful parks improved living conditions. But the disastrous Franco-Prussian War (1870-71) reignited bitter class conflict. In 1871, another uprising, led by radical visionaries, declared something called the **Paris Commune**. The conservative government sent in the army, as it had in 1848, and once again Paris was subdued.

The 1848 tremors also shook the Austro-Hungarian Empire. The ruling Habsburg monarchy abolished serfdom but reacted harshly against Hungarian patriots (**Magyars**) who sought independence. In 1849, teen-aged King Francis Joseph, with help from Czar Nicholas I of Russia, vanquished the Hungarians. In 1866, Francis Joseph finally agreed to a separate Hungarian monarchy; however, neither Austria nor Hungary accorded equal rights to their ethnic citizens. In Austria, anti-Semitism mounted as Jews flocked to Vienna and began transforming its culture and economy. The ruling Magyars in Hungary suppressed Serbian, Croatian, and Romanian nationalism in the Balkans but could not completely douse the embers of independence.

In Prussia, the second largest German-speaking country in Europe, liberal reformers had two objectives: constitutional limits on monarchical power and unification of the thirty-eight German-speaking states. In 1848, efforts to achieve those ends failed; however, in 1866, the powerful aristocrat Otto von Bismarck forged a partial German confederation. "Might makes right," he declared, and his triumph in the Franco-Prussian War drew the remaining states into modern Germany—an emerging industrial and imperial giant.

Industrial demands for raw materials and markets drove Germany and other European countries into nonindustrialized countries. Sometimes the penetration was peaceful because the Europeans had products that local people desired. In most instances, however, the Europeans forced capitalism on unwilling populations which often suffered acutely.

Historically, China had supplied Europe with more goods than it imported, a situation that began to change in the 1840s when Great Britain forced the ruling Qing (Manchu) Dynasty to allow the importation of opium. The Chinese government attempted to confine growing foreign commerce to Hong Kong and the southern city of Gwangzhou (Canton). In 1856-60, however, the British and French forced open additional Chinese markets. This contributed to the **Taiping Rebellion** (1850-65), which brought the Qing Dynasty to the verge of collapse before the formidable empress dowager (the elderly widow of the deceased emperor) Tzu Hsi rescued the government for the time being. Meanwhile, hundreds of thousands of Chinese peasants sought economic advancement abroad. Between 1853 and 1873, some 130,000 Chinese workers migrated to Cuba while others went to Dutch, British, and French colonies in Southeast Asia. Large numbers came to the "**Mountain of Gold**" in California. Most Chinese emigrants hoped to earn quick money and return to their families in China.

Japan's response to intrusive foreign enterprise took a different path. While a figurehead emperor presided over Japan's feudal society, a series of strong-armed *shoguns* and their warrior *samurai* actually ruled Japan. In 1853, Commodore Matthew Perry of the United States sailed his squadron of ships into Edo (Tokyo Bay), breaching the wall of Japanese insularity. Between 1858 and 1863, the *samurai* reacted by terrorizing foreigners. They turned against the *shogun* as well and in 1867 restored imperial power (the **Meiji Restoration**). Instead of destroying all foreign influences, however, the reinvigorated imperial government modernized Japan. "Enrich the state and strengthen the armed forces" officials urged, and the United States became one of the models. Railroads, factories, and a market-oriented economy soon emerged. Foreign scientists and engineers arrived in Japan and Japanese students began studying abroad.

The effects of European expansion around the globe also registered dramatically in India and Egypt. Partially colonized by Great Britain in the eighteenth century, India fell under complete British control. A small cadre of British civil servants and military officers backed by native Indian troops and trained bureaucrats introduced many desirable changes: secondary education, systems of irrigation, and railroad networks. But the cost to traditional Indian culture and self-esteem was stiff: an artificial state that fused Hindus and Muslims; segregation from British society; and the imposition of the English language. Furthermore, the masses of Indians benefited little from the commercial production of cotton, tea, and jute. In Egypt, the Albanian-born ruler Muhammad Ali initiated modernization. His policies drew tens of thousands of European businessmen, engineers, physicians, and government officials. In the 1860s, under Muhammad Ali's grandson Ismail, Europeans invested heavily in irrigated cotton production and in the construction of the Suez Canal (completed in 1869) which eliminated the need for ships to sail around the tip of Africa. Cairo took on a distinctly European appearance with hotels, restaurants, and broad boulevards. "My country is no longer in Africa," Ismail observed. "We now form a part of Europe." Indeed, by 1876 Egypt could not pay the interest on its enormous foreign debt and European creditors took control of Egypt's public finances.

In many ways, Americans were influenced by these global developments as they advanced down the path toward becoming a democratic nation. In pursuing their "Manifest Destiny," they merged romantic ideals with national pride and economic motives, and were sometimes inspired by the revolutionary upheavals of 1848. The United States transformed or shoved aside Native American and Hispanic societies that stood in the way. In some ways, the struggle over slavery resembled clashes between the European industrial bourgeoisie and traditional agrarian aristocracies. Europe played a role in the American Civil War, and Reconstruction involved unifying the nation and the triumph of industrial capitalism. In studying the history of the United States in the middle of the nineteenth century, we benefit from a global perspective.

THINKING BACK

1. How did industrial imperialism fuel class consciousness, class-conflict, and revolution?
2. What kind of resentment did global imperialism produce in the Middle East and Asia, and how did that resentment manifest itself?

Chapter 13

MANIFEST DESTINY, 1835–1850

A PERSONAL PERSPECTIVE: FOCUS ON BENT AND ST. VRAIN

How did Charles Bent and Cerán St. Vrain contribute to the fulfillment of America's Manifest Destiny?

In the 1840s, Americans found a new slogan to represent the old process of territorial expansion: **Manifest Destiny**. With those words, Americans expressed their indomitable spirit and their commitment to establishing a divinely sanctioned "empire of liberty." Far from foreordained, however, America's Manifest Destiny often became readily apparent only after war, and the consequent fate of many of the Far West's residents was not always to live under republican institutions but rather to lose their most valuable possessions, including freedom. Charles Bent was an agent of Manifest Destiny, as a partner with his brother William and Cerán St. Vrain in Bent, St. Vrain, and Company. The mercantile firm was heavily involved in commerce between the United States and Mexico on the Santa Fe Trail. Bent's personal experiences in many ways illustrate Manifest Destiny's intricate and ambiguous reality.

During the 1840s, no more than 1 percent of all New Mexicans were Anglo Americans, but Anglos dominated the territory's commercial economy, which heavily depended on foreign trade. The American traders had commercial experience, connections to markets in the United States, and above all money. They carefully cultivated the support of New Mexico's *ricos*, an elite of large landowners, sometimes by marrying into their families.

Charles Bent was one of the more successful American businessmen in New Mexico. The son of a judge on Missouri's supreme court, Bent brimmed with ambition and good business sense. He followed standard practice by marrying Maria Ignacia Jaramillo of Taos, who opened doors into the family-based New Mexico trade network. However, Bent's insistence on remaining a United States citizen and a Protestant drew bitter resentment from the local Catholic priesthood who hated growing foreign influences. Bent's partner, Cerán St. Vrain, was the grandson of a refugee from the French Revolution and the son of a man who had commanded a Spanish naval fleet on the Mississippi River. The young

Bent's Fort. Operated by Bent, St. Vrain, and Company, it was key to the company's commercial operations along the Santa Fe Trail. From the fort, traders exchanged goods with Cheyenne and other Plains Indians and did business with travelers.

1844 Mormon leader Joseph Smith murdered	**1845** U.S. annexes Texas	**1846** Oregon Treaty resolves dispute over occupation of Oregon; Congress declares war against Mexico; U.S. army occupies New Mexico	**1847** Mexico signs armistice

St. Vrain learned the principles of Western commerce in the office of a St. Louis fur-trading tycoon. In the 1820s, he took his knowledge and language skills to Taos, where he became a Mexican citizen, established connections with resident fur-trappers like Christopher "Kit" Carson, and married the daughter of a prominent *Nuevomexicano*.

From its Taos headquarters, Bent, St. Vrain, and Company operated trading posts throughout the southern Rockies. Between 1831 and 1834, it constructed Bent's Fort alongside the crystal-clear Arkansas River, flowing eastward out of the mountains and astride the Santa Fe Trail. Charles Bent's younger brother William selected the site, near the location of a busy Cheyenne Indian bartering center. His marriage to Owl Woman, daughter of a respected Cheyenne leader, further enhanced his status within the tribe's kinship network. By adopting Indian rituals in the conduct of his business, William made Bent's Fort an important cultural intersection in the dynamic social world of the central Plains. In the summer of 1840, roaming bands of Cheyenne, Arapahoe, Kiowa, and Comanche Indians gathered there to make peace after years of bloody warfare. As part of the peace process, they exchanged American-made brass cooking kettles, guns, dried bison meat, and New Mexican corn meal sweetened with molasses from New Orleans.

Notable travelers along the Santa Fe Trail found comfortable accommodations at Bent's Fort. In the summer of 1846, James Magoffin, a wealthy Missouri merchant, and his wife Susan rested there on their journey to Santa Fe, just ahead of an American army of conquest at the start of the U. S.–Mexico War. Guests dined on elegant porcelain and ceramic dishes and drank fine French wine. After dinner, the men entertained themselves in the upstairs billiard room. Teamsters, blacksmiths, carpenters, and assorted other Bent, St. Vrain, and Company employees maintained busy workshops and storerooms.

With the commencement of the U. S.–Mexico War in 1846, Bent, St. Vrain, and Company's intricate relationships with Hispanics and Indians in New Mexico unraveled. Trouble erupted when New Mexico's governor Manuel Armijo granted 1.7 million acres of prime land to some of the company's closest associates, including St. Vrain's *rico* father-in-law. Many poor *Nuevomexicanos* resented this huge giveaway, as did Taos Pueblo Indians whose own land holdings were infringed by the grant. U.S. General Stephen W. Kearny's appointment of Charles Bent as provisional governor of New Mexico, ignited a revolt in Taos. In January of 1847, Indians swept into town and murdered Bent. Bent's friends and family accused Antonio José Martínez, a local Catholic priest, of instigating the bloody attack; however, Martínez's actual role in the affair remains in dispute among historians.

Charles Bent's death and Cerán St. Vrain's subsequent retirement precipitated a sharp decline in the fortunes of Bent, St. Vrain, and Company. Manifest Destiny unleashed other forces of change as well. Thousands of people from the United States moved into Far West, people with little understanding or tolerance Native American ways of life. Heavy wagon traffic along western trails damaged the fragile natural environment upon which Indians depended. Garbage from Bent's Fort accumulated in dumps located close to the river, polluting the once-clear stream. In 1849, a deadly cholera epidemic, caused by tainted water, broke out among the Cheyenne near Bent's Fort killing Indians agonizingly and compelling William Bent to destroy the facility.

In the 1840s, the United States fulfilled its Manifest Destiny, and in the process destroyed or marginalized the Hispanic and Native American residents of the Far West. Scores of thousands trekked along the overland trails from Missouri to Oregon, and even more migrated to California in the famous 1849 Gold Rush. Those migrations altered relationships with the plains Indians living along the overland trails. Moreover, expansion put a new face on the sectional debate over slavery. Could immigrants from the South bring slaves into the new lands? That question turned into an irreconcilable conflict.

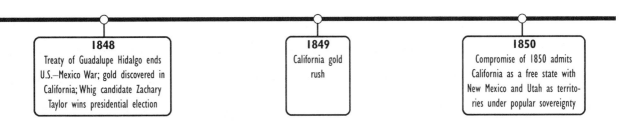

1848
Treaty of Guadalupe Hidalgo ends U.S.–Mexico War; gold discovered in California; Whig candidate Zachary Taylor wins presidential election

1849
California gold rush

1850
Compromise of 1850 admits California as a free state with New Mexico and Utah as territories under popular sovereignty

Charles Bent's home was here in Taos, New Mexico. His wife, Maria Ignacia Jaramillo, was the sister of Kit Carson's wife. The Carsons also resided in Taos. Charles Bent was murdered in his home during the Taos Pueblo uprising in January of 1847.

THINKING BACK

1. By what means did Americans like Bent and St. Vrain insert themselves into the economic and social organization of territorial New Mexico?
2. What evidence do you see that Bent, St. Vrain, and Company succeeded in its business endeavor, and what evidence suggests its failure?

FULFILLING MANIFEST DESTINY

Before fleets of "prairie schooners" transported thousands of pioneers from the United States across the western prairies, Native American immigrants sought their destiny along the western Great Plains. They exchanged commodities with other Plains Indians and with American traders in places like Bent's Fort. During the 1840s, American emigrants and United States Army patrols crossed this Indian territory toward Oregon and California. The impulse to advance motivated the overland pioneers, but politicians like Missouri's spread-eagle expansionist senator Thomas Hart Benton aroused the nation with declarations about gaining territory to promote freedom and republican institutions. Twenty million Americans crowded into the United States, and untilled land was becoming scarcer. If anyone doubted the practicality of a continental republic, they only had to ponder the capabilities of railroads and the telegraph to bind the country with ribbons of rail and wire to have their minds changed. The rationale for continental expansion had distinctly religious overtones too. In 1845, a thirty-two-year-old New York newspaper editor named John L. O'Sullivan coined the phrase "Manifest Destiny." He proclaimed that Providence had blessed "the development of the great experiment of liberty . . . and self-government," and made emigrants and businessmen its missionaries. But undertones of racism and bigotry were present as well. Popular pseudo-scientific theories asserted the superiority of the "Anglo-Saxon race." Mid-nineteenth-century Americans and later historians extolled Manifest Destiny as the culmination of civilization's inevitable westward march and the triumph of American nationalism. In reality, however, there was nothing inevitable about Manifest Destiny, and much of it was divisive.

The Called Out People

Until the 1830s, two human domains dominated the western Great Plains. The **Lakota** (Sioux) prevailed in the area above the Platte River, and a **Comanche-Kiowa** alliance held sway below the Arkansas. Like

Great Plains people for thousands of years, these Native Americans hunted bison (buffalo) and lived in portable deerskin *tipis* that enabled them to follow the migrating herds of shaggy mammals. Between 1829 and the mid-1850s, the Great Plains Indian population doubled as other Native Americans looking for new homes filled the gaps in between. Not long after Lewis and Clark, **Cheyenne** bands left their villages and gardens along the Missouri River in North Dakota and migrated southward.

> **What kind of economy did the Plains Indians maintain, and how did it change?**

The Cheyenne followed a vision into this nomadic hunter's world. By trading horses, guns, and buffalo robes, they hoped to acquire items that would enable them to live more comfortably. Horses were a valuable commodity on the Great Plains. Hunters mounted them to chase down the large but speedy bison, and the Plains Indians maintained up to ten horses per family. Bitter winters devastated horse herds, however, and every spring the Lakota waited for the arrival of Comanche bands who sold them horses stolen from ranches in Texas and New Mexico. The Lakota paid for the horses with guns acquired from Canadian and American dealers. The enterprising Cheyenne entered this vital market exchange as agents representing both the Lakota and Comanche.

To facilitate their new lifestyle, the Cheyenne restructured their society. They formed small, mobile bands for better hunting and learned to make *tipis* out of animal skins. Cheyenne women specialized in animal-hide processing. The Cheyenne situated themselves between the Black Hills of South Dakota, which remains today the holiest of Cheyenne places, and the Arkansas River. They even took a new name, the "**Called Out People.**"

The early years of the nineteenth century were especially good to the Cheyenne. Abundant rainfall turned the plains lush and green. The bison fattened on nutritious Grama grass. Twenty-five to thirty million buffaloes grazed the boundless ranges. Countless elk, deer, antelopes, and grizzly bears also populated the plains, providing the Cheyenne with plenty of meat and valuable skins. Their horses grew strong and the rivers and streams flowed fully, freshening the cottonwood trees and grasses that grew in the basins. The Cheyenne liked to camp there during the winters, protected from deadly blizzards and supplied with fuel for cooking and forage for their horses. The market for buffalo robes was good too.

But unfolding events clouded the Cheyenne vision and altered their way of life. Friction developed with their neighbors. The powerful Lakota regarded them as intruders and drove them from the Black Hills. Comanche and Kiowa bands, driven northward out of Texas by white settlers and dislocated Cherokee immigrants, pushed hard against the Cheyenne. In the 1830s, fighting along the Arkansas River was frequent and bloody. In 1840, the agreement among several of the Plains tribes near Bent's Fort brought peace to the western Great Plains; however, cooperative hunting seriously reduced the buffalo population, forcing Cheyenne and Arapaho hunting parties eastward into Kansas and Iowa where they clashed with indigenous tribes and displaced eastern Indians hard-pressed to make do in an already crowded area.

In these troubled times, white people and their cultures entered the Cheyenne's world. Merchants like Bent and St. Vrain introduced attractive trade goods: lightweight woolen blankets, cotton cloth, combs, metal cooking utensils, coffee, sugar, tobacco, and, of course, whiskey. The Cheyenne swapped buffalo robes and various other animal skins for the merchandise and in the process entered the expanding commercial economy of the United States. To obtain prized trade goods, the Indians killed more animals. In order to gain access to Indian customers, white traders like William Bent often married Indian women. These marriages and their "half-breed" offspring altered Indian cultures and societies, frequently raising troublesome issues of identity. In addition to the white traders, white travelers passed through Indian country in wagon caravans. Forty thousand crossed the Plains in the 1840s, and over the next decade 200,000 pioneers lumbered across the prairie. Their wagons, draft animals, and livestock trampled or devoured the vital grasses on which the Indians' horses grazed, and they cut down the sparse trees for firewood. Pioneers and their animals introduced deadly diseases—cholera that devastated Indian societies and anthrax and brucellosis that destroyed buffaloes.

The Cheyenne, like other Native Americans, felt the frustration of a dream turned nightmarish and focused their anger on whites who, as one Cheyenne man complained, "destroyed our buffalo, antelope, and deer, and have cut down our timber." This was a repeat of an old story, one destined to replay again and again. And as the hordes of pioneers descended on the Far West, the United States Army undertook a systematic reconnaissance.

Western Reconnaissance

Coincident to the rising spirit of Manifest Destiny, Congress in 1838 authorized the creation of the United States Army **Corps of Topographical Engineers**. This small unit of thirty-six officers, all trained in science and engineering, completed special projects that the president and Congress assigned to it. Its commandant was Colonel John Abert; however, the greatest influence on its activities was Senator Thomas Hart Benton, the ardent advocate of Western expansion, and its most celebrated officer was Benton's son-in-law, Lieutenant John C. Fremont.

> **Why did Congress create the Army Corps of Topographical Engineers, and what did they accomplish in the Far West?**

For centuries, explorers had charted the Pacific coastline and probed the interior of the North American continent. The difference between those earlier explorations and the expeditions of the Topographical Engineers was the latter's commitment to scientific techniques. The engineers' maps, catalogues, and narrative descriptions were more reliable than any that preceded them. Although intended to advance scientific knowledge, the Topographical Engineers became a vital element in the development of Western expansion by gathering information of strategic military importance.

John C. Fremont's greatest assets were his charisma and boundless energy, which brought recognition to him and the Topographical Engineers. In 1842, Fremont accepted his first command: a mapping expedition to the Rocky Mountains beginning at present-day Kansas City and following the Missouri and Platte rivers. In recording locations and elevations using the best instruments of the day, Fremont demonstrated the precision of the scientist. His measurement of the distance to the expedition's western-most point was only three miles off. Yet, from the summit of what he took to be the highest peak in Wyoming's Wind River Mountains (Fremont's measurements were not always accurate), he responded with the emotion of a Romantic: "Here a view of the utmost magnificence and grandeur burst upon our eyes."

In 1843–1844, Fremont led his most famous and spectacular reconnaissance, taking a party of thirty-nine hunters, guides, scientists, and artists to Oregon and California and back. His equipment included an artillery piece, hinting at a political-military objective into territory claimed by rivals

COL. FREMONT
PLANTING THE AMERICAN STANDARD ON THE ROCKY MOUNTAINS.

Courtesy of Library of Congress

Illustration of John C. Fremont planting the flag of the United States at the crest of the Rocky Mountains.

400   Chapter 13—*Manifest Destiny, 1835–1850*

Great Britain and Mexico. Traversing the Great Basin, Fremont and his men mapped the Great Salt Lake before proceeding to the Hudson's Bay Company's headquarters at Fort Vancouver, situated near the confluence of the Columbia and Willamette rivers in the Oregon Territory. After a harrowing wintertime crossing of California's Sierra Nevada mountain range, the expedition returned to the United States in 1845, resting at Bent's Fort before marching on to Missouri.

Congress published Fremont's illustrated report and made it available to citizens of the country. Fremont had discovered very little on his reconnaissance that individual explorers of various nationalities had not previously observed; however, the comprehensiveness of his investigations, the reliability of his measurements, and the presentation of his reports added factual detail to the general wealth of knowledge about the Far West, and earned Fremont fame as "The Pathfinder." More importantly, though, the reconnaissance undertaken by the Topographical Engineers inspired great excitement among the American public about the Far West and encouraged many citizens to undertake the journey West themselves.

Traveling the Overland Trails

> **What drew pioneers to the Far West, and how did they get there?**

Following the spring thaw in 1840, Joel P. Walker, his wife, and their children loaded the family belongings into a wagon and joined a Christian missionary caravan headed for Oregon, which then included today's Oregon, Washington, Idaho, and British Columbia. Fewer than fifty Americans—trappers and missionaries mostly—lived in the territory at the time, particularly in the valley of the Willamette River (see The Local Perspective, pp. 416–18). The Walkers were among the first American settlers to embark on this arduous overland journey. The main trail westward ran along the Platte River into Wyoming, crossed the Rocky Mountains, and then hugged the Columbia River into the Oregon country (see map on p. 408). In 1841, John Bidwell and John Bartleson, who captained a party organized by the Western Emigration Society of Missouri, steered their wagon off the trail in modern Idaho and headed to California. In 1845, approximately 400 emigrants arrived in California, and by the end of the decade, the Western trails had become a major transcontinental thoroughfares carrying thousands of travelers.

These nineteenth-century Argonauts followed their dreams to carefully planned destinations. The earliest pioneers aimed for Oregon's fertile Willamette Valley and central California's Sacramento and San Joaquin valleys. Later adventurers sought out the California gold fields (see pp. 422–23). Some travelers hoped to escape from economic strife, religious harassment, family responsibilities, or the law. Wanderlust, a thirst for adventure, or some "wild goose chase" motivated others to pack up and head west. Men usually made the decision to move; their wives and children, more often reluctant to uproot themselves, had little choice.

"Oh, I wish we never had started," lamented one pioneer woman as she trudged and bumped across the hot, dusty plains. Overland travel was especially hard on women. On top of the physical strain of the 2,000-mile journey and debilitating ailments like dysentery, colds, or the flu, women contended with gender-related maladies such as complications from pregnancy. They also had responsibility for maintaining their mobile domiciles. Like many pioneer women, Charlotte Pengra herded the family's livestock and collected dried buffalo dung for the evening cook fire. Her journal reads: "Kept busy in preparing . . . for the morrow. I baked cracker pudding, warm biscuits and made tea, and after supper stewed two pans of dried apples, and made two loaves of bread, got my work done up, beds made, and child asleep . . . . Pretty tired of course." Most women bore their burdens stoically, but when Lavinia Porter's husband refused to veer off the trail to a timber grove for wood for the cook fire, her temper erupted. If he wanted a hot supper, he could get the fuel himself "and cook the meal also." Conditions on the overland trail distressed many women because they undermined the gender-based "separate spheres" that ordered their lives. Women often had to perform "men's" work, relinquish control of the "home," and compromise the Sabbath due to the demands of the onward caravan.

Most of the emigrants owned some kind of serviceable wagon and livestock. Those who did not bought their equipment and draft animals—usually at inflated price—from outfitters in trailhead towns like Independence and St. Joseph. Canvas stretched over the wagon bed made the famous "**prairie schooner**" pulled by oxen, which Indians were less likely to steal than horses. The beasts also helped the homesteaders plow new fields after their arrival. Inventive sorts experimented with vehicles that supposedly shortened

A "prairie schooner" like those that carried emigrant families from Missouri along the Oregon and California trails to their new homes. In addition to the water keg, wagon gear typically included ropes and block-and-tackle for hoisting and a feed-bag for horses and mules.

the two-month trip. One man alleged that his "wind wagon," rigged with a mast and sails, attained speeds of fifteen miles an hour. Others crossed the plains pushing handcarts and wheelbarrows.

Most travelers depended on guides. Some of the guides were veteran mountain men who knew their way around; others, unfortunately, were less reliable. A number of guide books described the routes and advised travelers about what time of year to go and what to take. The most popular was young Lansford Hastings' *Emigrants' Guide to Oregon and California.* None of the guidebooks was totally reliable, and Hastings, in cahoots with the old mountain man Jim Bridger, urged travelers to take a dangerous route, explored by Fremont, that passed by the old mountain man's fort located off the beaten trail so he could hawk supplies at exorbitant prices.

During the 1840s, the number of wagon caravans multiplied. Many travelers commented on the endless streams of white canvas ahead of and behind them. Caravans usually began as tightly organized companies with elected captains for the maintenance of discipline and order. Various situations, however, caused wagons to drop off the pace: broken wheels or axles, illness, and injuries. Disagreements over what route to take also broke up caravans. Overall, large trains were the safest; they carried more food, medicine, and equipment and afforded greater protection against Indians.

Indian molestation was the pioneers' greatest fear. The emigrant trains were heavily armed, and as the trickle of emigrants turned into a torrent, conflicts with Indians did become more frequent. But in contrast to Hollywood movie images, Indian depredations usually involved no more than stealing or killing livestock. Murders did occur, especially after the gold rush in 1849; however, the victims were usually Indians not travelers. From 1840 to 1860, approximately 360 whites and 425 Indians died violently along the Oregon and California trails. Most Indian murders of pioneers involved stragglers and avenged some particular outrage, but Indians also lashed out against the mounting number of pioneers. Most of the time, travelers recorded peaceful, even helpful, encounters with native people, and many never saw Indians at all.

Disease, injury, and starvation harmed the emigrants more than Indians did. The greatest risk involved taking one of the touted "shortcuts." These often turned into dangerous "longcuts" on which travelers ran out of food and water and were victimized by accidents. The bleached bones of dead animals, castoff belongings, and unmarked graves offered grisly testimony to the hazards of overland travel. The most dramatic disaster involved the George Donner party of Illinois. These eighty-seven pioneers and their twenty wagons broke away from a larger caravan in Wyoming, lured by the notorious Lansford Hastings to a cutoff he misleadingly advertised as the shortest route to California. After choking of thirst on the barren alkali flats of Nevada, the Donner group found itself stranded in heavy autumn snows in the Sierra Nevada Mountains. Unable to advance or retreat, the emigrants encamped for the winter. When their food gave out, animals and people died. The survivors resorted to cannibalism before rescuers arrived.

The many horrible incidents associated with overland travel brought calls for federal government protection. Oregon and California businessmen worried that reports of Indian atrocities would discourage emigration. "Oregon," claimed local leaders, "may write her own epitaph" in disaster reports. Newspapers demanded that the army free the trails from the Indian menace. In response, the federal government built and garrisoned several forts along the Oregon Trail, starting with Fort Kearny in Nebraska, Fort Laramie in Wyoming, and Fort Hall in Idaho. Dragoons patrolled the trail and mapped and graded other roadways to lessen hazards and reduce travel time. Few people today realize the important role that government played in the peopling of the Far West.

By the end of the 1840s, the heavy volume of traffic and the presence of many government and private service stations made the wayfarers feel less vulnerable in the wilderness. For California-bound travelers, Mormon settlements in the Great Basin between the Rockies and the Sierra Nevada Mountains provided welcomed stopovers, with opportunities to purchase supplies and make repairs on their equipment. Without them, many pioneers would have met disaster.

The Mormon Emigration

> **What was the Mormons' "Manifest Destiny," and how did they attempt to fulfill it?**

In the 1840s, thousands of Mormons abandoned their homes in Nauvoo, Illinois, (see p. 344) and embarked for the Far West. After murdering Joseph Smith in 1844, the Mormons' hostile neighbors burned their barns and fields, forcing the beleaguered Saints to seek refuge in the West to preserve their beliefs and institutions as they awaited Christ's Second Coming. Brigham Young, the martyred Smith's chief disciple and a man of extraordinary organizational talent, led the exodus. Under his authoritarian brand of leadership, the Mormons established prosperous communities from the Rockies to California.

Brigham Young laid careful plans for the relocation, based on his reading of John C. Fremont's report on the valley of the Great Salt Lake. In 1846, the emigrants set up an outfitting center at Council Bluffs, Iowa, and a camp across the Missouri River at the site of present-day Omaha, Nebraska. The following year an advance party of 1,700 men, women, and children steered their wagons near the Oregon Trail to South Pass in Wyoming, where they turned southward. In July, they peered down from the Wasatch Mountains into the Salt Lake Valley. "This is the place whereon we will plant our feet and where the Lord's people will dwell," Young proclaimed as he lay recovering from a near-fatal attack of mountain fever. Another 12,000 Mormon refugees soon followed, as the vanguard constructed stockades and erected the first buildings of Salt Lake City. As more immigrants poured in, including some 22,000 Europeans, Young and the Church of Latter-Day Saints ordered that missions and settlements be set up throughout the Great Basin.

Image © Gary Witton, 2010. Used by permission of Shutterstock, Inc.

Much of the Great Basin was desert and a difficult place for homesteaders. This Mormon settler's dug-out cabin was located near Pipe Spring in the northern part of today's state of Arizona.

The land the Mormons chose was harsh and unforgiving, but Brigham Young viewed it as "a good place to make Saints, and . . . a good place for Saints to live." Here the Mormons might be left alone, and under Young's regime they set themselves to the task of making the high desert bloom. The first winter was miserable, and the following summer swarms of grasshoppers devoured the Mormons' crops. But then flocks of sea gulls swooped down and devoured the insects. Mormon communalism also carried the settlers through the hardest times. They dug irrigation ditches from the rivers that flowed from the mountains; however, water was scarce, and the settlers followed a strict system of rationing.

Mormon isolation demanded self-reliance. It took twice as long to reach St. Louis by wagon from Salt Lake City as it did to reach London by ship from Boston. The settlers met their needs for agricultural products with little difficulty; however, coal, copper, iron, lead, silver, and gold resources went undeveloped because the Mormons lacked necessary mining and processing skills. Efforts to grow cotton and develop a viable textile industry in southern Utah likewise failed. Thus, whether they liked it or not, Mormons found themselves less self-reliant than they wanted to be and more dependent on the national economy, for instance, through commerce with passing wagon trains.

The Mormons' relationship with Native Americans was shaped by the belief that Indians descended from one of the tribes of Israel. Mormons thus regarded Indians as subjects of religious conversion. Relatively few Native Americans occupied the Salt Lake Valley, but as the Mormons established outlying settlements they encroached on Indian land, leading to periodic conflicts. Brigham Young proclaimed a policy of conciliation rather than aggression in dealing with the Indians, taking the practical view that it was less expensive to feed and clothe the Indians than to fight them. Mormon communities typically maintained storehouses that supplied starving Indians with food, and a **Women's Indian Relief Society** made clothes and blankets. Legend tells of one grateful Indian man who testified that "Mormon *bueno* [good]. White man, son-of-a-bitch."

Although the Mormons had retreated from the United States, they shared in the American spirit of Manifest Destiny. Young expected that Utah would become a state in the Union, safeguarded by the fact that the Mormon settlers constituted "a vast majority of the people" in the territory. In 1849, after the Mexican War transferred the territory from Mexico to the United States (see pp. 413–15), the Latter-Day Saints established the state of **Deseret** (a term derived from the Book of Mormon meaning "honeybee"). They adopted a constitution in common with most other states and petitioned Congress for admission to statehood. Mormon polygamy, clannishness, and tendency toward bloc voting under Church influence, however, made lawmakers in Washington leery. Deseret's status was deferred, along with other related issues.

The Lone Star Republic

Most Anglo Texans felt the spirit of Manifest Destiny. At the conclusion of the Texas Revolution (see pp. 327–29), a referendum showed that Texans overwhelmingly favored joining the United States. Stephen F. Austin wrote to his brother-in-law: "I have *full confidence* that all will go right, and that by next March we shall belong to the U.S." But subsequent events did not go as Austin predicted. In Washington, issues relating to possible war with Mexico and slavery raised political obstacles. In the Lone Star Republic's first presidential election in 1836, which Austin was confident of winning, Sam Houston, the hero of the Battle of San Jacinto, defeated him handily. Worn out physically from years of hardship, Austin contracted pneumonia and died. Despite the spirit of Manifest Destiny, Texas' future appeared quite uncertain.

How did people in Texas and the United States feel about annexation?

Politicians in Washington looked upon the annexation of Texas as a political mine field, with war with Mexico and slavery serving as the explosive devices. The Mexican government had communicated clearly to the United States that it would consider any attempt to annex Texas an act of hostility justifying war, an outcome both Andrew Jackson and Martin Van Buren chose to avoid. And John Quincy Adams warned members of Congress that everyone in the northern United States had a "deep, deep, deep" interest in keeping Texas out of the Union because Texas' constitution recognized and protected slavery. So, for the time being, Texas remained the independent Lone Star Republic.

Texas' best prospects for economic viability lay with cotton and commerce. From the standpoint of antebellum Southern culture, successful cotton plantations required the labor of slaves. In the late 1830s, approximately 15,000 African Americans, fewer than in tiny Delaware, were enslaved in Texas, a territory comparable in geographic size to the Deep South. This translated into an acute labor shortage that limited the development of plantation agriculture. In 1837, only one in forty acres of Texas' prime farm land had felt the blade of a plow. But planters in other Southern states where cotton fields were becoming less productive were reluctant to risk bringing their slaves to the rugged Texas frontier. Low land values and resulting tax income coupled with the high cost of governing such an expanse of territory saddled the Houston administration with a $1.25 million debt ($32 billion in today's money).

President Houston's successor, the belligerent Mirabeau B. Lamar, hoped to remedy the problem by laying claim to the Rio Grande River, thereby capturing the lucrative commerce of the Santa Fe Trail and turning the river into the Texas equivalent of the Mississippi or Hudson. In 1841, an ill-fated invasion of New Mexico targeting Santa Fe by 300 Texans ended in disaster, as Mexican troops captured the contingent and marched the men to a Mexican prison. An attempt to gain control of the lower Rio Grande the following year yielded similar results. The failure of the **Santa Fe Expedition** and other military operations against Mexico demonstrated not only Texas' inability to expand its boundaries but also the importance of annexation to the United States.

Although Mexico refused to recognize the Rio Grande as the boundary of Texas and even Texas' independence, civil strife and financial chaos hamstrung the Mexican government and prevented it from recovering its lost property. Antonio López de Santa Anna returned to Mexico after a prolonged Texas confinement following his defeat at San Jacinto and once again claimed presidential power. Twice in 1842 he dispatched armies to occupy San Antonio, more as a gesture of intent than a sign of Mexico's ability to reestablish its authority and control over Texas. In 1843, Sam Houston, reelected to a second term as Texas' president, negotiated a truce with Santa Anna, anticipating annexation by the United States.

The Issues of Annexation

What made the annexation of Texas so controversial, and how was it finally accomplished?

Several political issues grew out of the push for westward expansion, generating controversy over an otherwise popular concept. Did Manifest Destiny justify the invasion and conquest of a friendly neighbor, struggling to secure its own democracy? The theoretical answer was no. Expansion should be altruistic in motive and voluntary on the part of all parties involved. Yet selfishness and prejudice often drove expansionism over troubled consciences. Many cotton belt Southerners demanded additional territory that would eventually become states and add to the proslavery bloc in Congress. Many white people across the country cited Anglo-Saxon superiority as a rationale for running roughshod over Mexico's largely *mestizo* population. "The inferior must give way before the superior race," declared Ashbel Smith of Texas. John C. Calhoun actually objected to adding more people of color to the United States.

Partisanship added more controversy to the discussions of expansion. Democrats claimed that expansion benefited hard-pressed yeoman farmers. Whigs, who favored missionary activity over conquest and annexation as the preferred method of advancing Protestant Christianity and democratic principles, countered that expansion risked destructive wars. Most Northern and even some Southern Whigs believed that overly aggressive expansionist Democrats had conspired with Texans to steal Texas from Mexico, and that Mexico had every right to be angry and to demand the its return. Manifest Destiny generated internal strains within national parties that threatened to pull them apart. Whig president John Tyler, a pro-slavery Virginian, revived the issue of Texas annexation and supported it while Whig senator Henry Clay opposed it. After extended political conflict, Clay and the other Whig leaders drummed Tyler out of the party. Tyler's entire cabinet, except for Secretary of State Daniel Webster, resigned.

Exhibiting typical Whig moderation in the area of territorial expansion, Webster remained in the administration to finalize delicate negotiations with Great Britain over a Canadian boundary dispute. He and a special British emissary, Lord Ashburton, were trying to define the line between New Brunswick and Maine, left undetermined since the Revolutionary War. A conflict over the timber-rich Aroostook Valley spanning the Maine-New Brunswick frontier had recently raised the urgency of the issue. Bellicose bands of Canadian and American citizens threatened a blood bath. But in 1842, the **Webster-Ashburton Treaty** quieted the disturbance by establishing an acceptable boundary. Webster conceded forested lands in northern Maine, and Ashburton agreed to relinquish claims to lands with iron ore deposits west of Lake Superior. Thus both Great Britain and the

United States made concessions in order to avert a potentially disastrous conflict neither country wanted. With this diplomatic success tucked away, Webster abandoned Tyler, whose administration then adopted a more aggressively expansionist policy.

Uncomfortable as a Whig, Tyler flirted with the idea of a Southern-oriented political party, and to that end he renewed efforts to annex Texas. Meanwhile, Republic of Texas president Sam Houston exploited British intrigue in Texas to accomplish their common goal. Early in 1843, Houston disclosed a British offer to send settlers to Texas and help defend it against Mexico. In return, Great Britain expected Texans to abolish slavery. This aroused patriotic as well as pro-slavery furor in the United States. The aging and ailing Andrew Jackson condemned Britain's thinly disguised attempt to thwart American expansion. Southerners expressed alarm that Texas without slavery would lure slaves away from their plantations. Pennsylvania's Democratic senator James Buchanan put a contorted antislavery spin on annexation by suggesting that Texas "will be the means of gradually drawing the slaves far to the South," from where they would "finally pass off into Mexico." Tyler banked on this pro-annexation coalition as the basis for his new party.

In the spring of 1843, Secretary of State Upshur commenced secret negotiations with Texas. Just before submitting the completed treaty to the Senate for ratification, however, he was fatally injured in an explosion on board a new warship. Tyler replaced Upshur with another Southerner, John C. Calhoun, who early in 1844 sent the treaty to the Senate under a cover letter explaining its necessity to Southern slave owners. By baldly linking Texas annexation with Southern slave owners, Calhoun doomed any Northern support for the treaty, although their support for ratification had been consistently weak. **Anti-slavery "Conscience" Whigs** in the North commanded enough votes to kill it, dousing the embers of Tyler's election hopes.

In the 1844 presidential election campaign, however, Texas annexation was the major issue. Former president Martin Van Buren seemed to be the heir apparent to the Democratic nomination, but Northern and Southern Democrats took opposite positions on annexation. The "Little Magician" employed sleight-of-hand in an attempt to unite them, denouncing Tyler's treaty to appeal to Northerners but promising to solicit Mexico's approval to placate Southerners. But delayed annexation satisfied nobody, and Van Buren failed to close the nomination. In desperation, the party's nominating convention turned to a "**dark horse**"—a little-known person hidden in the pack of contestants. His name was James K. Polk, and he was a pragmatic politician from Tennessee. But he was also a protégé of Andrew Jackson, a slave owner, and an ardent expansionist without obligations to narrow sectional interests. Polk's nationalism was just the ticket for a divided Democratic party. Inventor Samuel F. B. Morse tapped out the announcement of Polk's nomination on his new telegraph, to the amazement of the American public.

"Young Hickory," as Democratic campaigners nicknamed Polk, unleashed rivers of rousing rhetoric. He demanded the "re-occupation" of Oregon, implying that he would force Great Britain out of the jointly occupied territory. "**Fifty-four forty or fight**," shouted vociferous Democratic campaigners—a reference to the line separating Oregon from Russian Alaska. Polk also insisted on the "re-annexation" of Texas, suggesting that Texas had been part of the Louisiana Purchase and then bargained away in the Transcontinental Treaty. In his aggressive stance toward Great Britain and Mexico, Polk provided national momentum for the annexation bandwagon.

"Who is James K. Polk?" Whigs smugly asked, posing their candidate, the formidable Senator Henry Clay, as unbeatable. But the Whig party was broken into quarreling factions too. To cater to powerful antislavery Northern Whigs, the moderate Clay strongly opposed annexation, acknowledging only the remotest chance that Mexico would ever accede to it. Above all, Clay wished to avoid the "hazard of foreign war." But Polk's pro-war rhetoric registered high marks on the scale of public approval. He won nearly everywhere, but by the slender margin of 38,000 votes out of the 5.3 million cast.

Although the election results did not establish a clear public preference on the annexation question, John Tyler interpreted the outcome as a mandate to push a joint resolution through Congress inviting Texas to join the Union. Such a measure required only a simple majority. The resolution allowed Texas to divide itself into five states and to retain its public lands but compelled Texas to pay off its debt. The government of the United States would settle any issues with Mexico over a Rio Grande boundary. In March of 1845, six days before Polk's inauguration, Congress passed the resolution. Instead of deferring to Polk, as Congress no doubt expected he would, Tyler immediately dispatched a courier to

James K. Polk's birthplace, a 150-acre farm near Charlotte, North Carolina. Known as "Young Hickory" after he moved to Tennessee, Polk entered politics and as speaker of the United States House of Representatives strongly supported Andrew Jackson's policies. Polk's parents had taught him intense patriotism, and he became an avid proponent of Manifest Destiny. His wife, Sarah Childress Polk, helped write his speeches and advised him on political matters.

Texas, inviting the Lone Star Republic to enter the Union. On July 4, 1845, a convention in Texas unanimously accepted.

James K. Polk had precipitated Texas annexation, but he also brought on a crisis with Mexico. Responding to public outrage, the Mexican government of President José Joaquín Herrera immediately suspended diplomatic relations with the United States. President Polk hoped for peace; however, he was prepared to unsheathe the sword to achieve his expansionist goals.

THINKING BACK

1. What did Manifest Destiny mean insofar as it was conceived and as most ordinary Americans understood it?
2. How did the reality of Manifest Destiny play out for Native Americans of the Great Plains, and what stood in the way of the annexation of Texas?

BUILDING A WESTERN EMPIRE

The election of 1844 led the United States to the brink of war with both Great Britain and Mexico. The notion that God ordained Manifest Destiny helped salve the consciences of citizens who might have winced at snatching foreign territory. Besides, scarcely anyone felt guilty about forcing arch-rival Great Britain out of Oregon, or compelling Mexico, widely regarded in the United States as an inferior nation with friendly relations with rival Britain, to relinquish California's magnificent and underdeveloped harbors. Settlers in Oregon pressed the Polk administration to terminate the joint-occupation agreement with Great Britain, in the spirit of Manifest Destiny. For twenty-five years on the southwestern frontier, Mexicans had anxiously watched the "Colossus of the North" encroach on their frail country's northern perimeter. The war that commenced in 1846 became a living nightmare for Mexico. Ironically, Mexicans had clamored for war, and at the start, the outcome would have been difficult to predict. The two belligerents matched up fairly evenly with their particular strengths and weaknesses, but the short conflict proved disastrous for Mexico and richly rewarding to the United States. As humiliating as the final peace terms were to Mexico, they could have been worse.

"Fifty-four Forty or Fight"

For a generation, American and British trappers, traders, and missionaries had shared the vast, ecologically diverse Oregon territory. At that time, Oregon included most of the Pacific Northwest from

California to Russian Alaska and from the Rocky Mountains to the Pacific coast. Neither the United States nor Great Britain had possessed sufficient strength in the region to push the other out, nor any compelling reason to try. By the mid-1840s, however, Manifest Destiny had changed the international dynamics of the territory. "Oregon fever" began filling the area with homesteaders from the United States,

How, and on what terms, did the United States and Great Britain resolve the issue of who owned Oregon?

and British authorities looked for ways to block further American expansion.

Since the mid-1820s, the Hudson's Bay Company governed British citizens residing in Oregon. The company's Oregon headquarters were at Fort Vancouver, at the confluence of the Willamette and Columbia rivers, some ninety miles inland from the coast. The fortress enclosed numerous workshops, soldiers' quarters, and laborers' cabins situated along spacious streets that reminded one visitor of "a very neat and beautiful village." It was the Pacific Northwest's version of Bent's Fort. Although the

The American demand for exclusive ownership of the entire Oregon Territory was largely a manifestation of the idea of Manifest Destiny. But by the mid-1840s thousands of pioneers were traveling the Oregon Trail, sharpening interest in the Willamette Valley and making it relatively easy to accept the compromise Oregon Treaty.

Hudson's Bay Company traded primarily in furs and hides, officials encouraged farming to make Fort Vancouver a self-sustaining outpost. Retired company employees, many with Indian spouses and mixed-blood (*metís*) children, operated farms that supplied the traders' food needs. In 1840, Britain's hold on Oregon seemed secure. One official reported that Britain had "little to apprehend from [American] Settlers in this quarter." Nor did Native residents pose a threat. The British commander, John McLoughlin, had seen that Indian attacks on whites were severely punished. Moreover, nearly 90 percent of the 14,000 Indians who once lived in the Willamette and lower Columbia river basins had succumbed to disease in the preceding half-century.

In the middle of the 1840s, however, conditions in Oregon changed radically. The number of Americans, flushed with Manifest Destiny, multiplied. Oregon City, only a few miles up the Willamette River from Fort Vancouver, hummed with activity. The newcomers, who governed themselves with a hodgepodge of laws taken from their home-state statutes, petitioned Congress to assert United States authority over the territory, claiming they were "the germ of a great State." British attitudes toward Oregon were changing too. Since Hudson's Bay Company trappers and traders had depleted the Columbia basin of fur-bearing animals, the southern portion of the territory was less valuable, and the commitment to holding it less than in earlier times. The firm planned to move its headquarters north to Fort Victoria, at the southern end of Vancouver Island. Still, Great Britain was not ready to hand all of Oregon over to the United States. The British foreign office hoped the United States would accept a division of the territory along the Columbia River.

In his annual message to Congress in 1845, President Polk reasserted the United States' "clear and unquestionable " right to Oregon, a position consistent with the Democratic party's commitment to "Fifty-four Forty or Fight." But he actually favored compromise on the Oregon question. Polk did not feel strongly enough about all of Oregon to risk a war over it, especially with a conflict with Mexico looming over the annexation of Texas, so he privately suggested to British officials the extension of the 49th parallel international boundary from the Rocky Mountains to the Pacific coast. The British held out for a Columbia River boundary, however, and Polk returned to his earlier demand for the entire territory.

Ultimately, the overwhelming reasonableness of a compromise compelled a negotiated settlement. In June of 1846, the two governments initialed the **Oregon Treaty**, which extended the 49th parallel to the Strait of Georgia and then dipped below Vancouver Island and west through the Strait of Juan de Fuca (see map p. 422). Cries of betrayal arose among extreme expansionists in the United States, but they quickly subsided. No Americans lived above the boundary line, and few had any interest in going there. Moreover, in May Congress had declared war on Mexico, and there was much valuable territory and the superb harbors of California at stake, more than enough to keep the fires of Manifest Destiny burning.

The U.S.–Mexico War

Although James K. Polk was not a brilliant man, he was a compulsive worker and an audacious leader. Polk became one of the United States' most successful presidents by taking complete charge of his administration and accomplishing virtually everything he set out to do in one four-year term—quite a feat for any president under any circumstances. Undoubtedly, eager expansionists would have pursued Manifest Destiny even if Polk had not been present to lead them; however, "Young Hickory" managed to acquire more territory than any other president in American history. Over the years, historians have debated Polk's priorities. Some say that he hoped to smooth over the rift with Mexico without resorting to war; others contend that he aggressively maneuvered Mexico into a war that he then exploited to acquire California and New Mexico. There is plenty of evidence to support both contentions.

While Polk negotiated with Great Britain over Oregon, he trained a keen eye on the Southwest, hoping to secure access to the Pacific coast and thus the profits of Asian trade. Texas was already in the fold, but proud Mexicans now threatened to take it back. Adding insult to injury, Polk reinforced Texas' claim to the muddy Rio Grande River boundary, rather than the Nueces, as Spanish and Mexican maps had historically shown. The dry, rocky plain that lay between the two rivers was not in dispute here; rather, the issue was control of the Rio Grande itself and the valuable commerce it might carry. But more than the Rio Grande, President Polk coveted California, a rich province ripe for American expansionist ambitions. Ownership of California would

> **What caused the U.S.–Mexico War?**

give the United States the superb harbors at San Francisco and San Diego. Acquiring New Mexico made sense because it lay in between Texas and California and would allow overland transportation between the two. Polk hoped for peaceful negotiations with Mexico, but he was prepared to take the territories by war.

Mexican newspapers printed bitter denunciations of American aggressiveness and condemned beforehand any craven submission by their government to the further theft of Mexican territory. President José Joaquín Herrera, however, invited negotiations with the United States on the Rio Grande boundary issue. In November of 1845, Polk dispatched a special envoy, John Slidell of Louisiana, to Mexico City with an offer to assume $2 million in claims that United States citizens held against the Mexican government in return for the Rio Grande boundary. In addition, Slidell was authorized to tender $25 million for California and New Mexico. Polk worked another angle as well, a proposition from the wily Antonio López de Santa Anna, once again living in exile from his turbulent country. Santa Anna solicited Polk's help in regaining power in Mexico; in return he would sell California and New Mexico. Political and media leaders in Mexico stormed against Slidell's mission and set off a drumbeat for war. "We have more than enough strength to make war," one Mexican newspaper sounded. "Let us make it, then, and victory will perch upon our banners." Bending before enormous political pressure, Herrera turned Slidell away without a hearing. But his opponents forced him from power anyway.

To pressure the Mexican government into negotiating, Polk ordered General Zachary Taylor (known fondly by his troops as "Old Rough and Ready") with 4,000 dragoons, infantry, and artillerymen to camp for the summer at Corpus Christi at the mouth of the Nueces River. He then ordered Taylor to move to the Rio Grande, cognizant, of course, that Mexico regarded this disputed land as Mexican territory. Taylor's Army of Occupation met no resistance, however, and after fortifying a bluff overlooking the river, he trained his batteries on the Mexican troops bivouacked near Matamoros on the other side of the Rio Grande. On April 25, as Polk busily drafted a war message in the White House, Mexican cavalry crossed the Rio Grande and ambushed a company of Taylor's troops, killing and wounding sixteen soldiers. Polk received word of the incident two weeks later, and on May 11 asked Congress for war on the grounds that Mexico "has invaded our territory, and shed American blood on American soil." Two days later Congress voted for war by 214 to 16.

Even before the war declaration, Mexican and American soldiers fought two pitched battles just north of the Rio Grande that primed soldiers and civilians alike for the conflict that lay ahead. Taylor's troops defeated the attacking Mexicans at Palo Alto and Resaca de Palma, inflicting heavy losses. The victories stirred American pride. In New York, the novelist Herman Melville noted that "people here are in a state of delirium . . . Nothing is talked of but the 'Halls of the Montezumas.'" New York's popular Bowery Theater staged "The Campaign on the Rio Grande" for all who wanted to imagine the scene of the great triumph. As yet, however, the public gave little thought to the seriousness of what they were undertaking. They felt only the excitement of war. And all the hoopla disguised the bitter disagreement that divided Americans over the moral correctness of the war.

A Bitter Debate

The decision for war drew a narrow but intense opposition, mostly from Whigs. Daniel Webster, the era's oratorical titan, condemned it as "a most

> What were the issues in the debate over the U.S.–Mexico War?

unnecessary and therefore most unjustifiable war." John Quincy Adams, the only ex-president to sit in Congress, denounced the "unrighteous war" used to advance the evil of slavery. In February 1848, the aged and feeble Adams suffered a fatal stroke while rising to speak against the war on the floor of the House of Representatives. The philosopher Henry David Thoreau went to jail for refusing to pay a tax to finance the war. There he wrote his famous essay *Civil Disobedience*, which inspired protests against racism and the Vietnam War in the 1960s. Thoreau's dear friend Ralph Waldo Emerson remained aloof from the political fray. Visiting Thoreau in jail, Emerson reportedly asked: "Henry, what are you doing in there?," to which Thoreau replied, "Waldo, what are you doing out there?" Much of the opposition was sheer partisanship. Whigs enjoyed referring to "Mr. Polk's war."

Despite the impassioned opposition, public support for the war ran high, especially in western, heavily Democratic locales closest to the action. Even most Whigs who lambasted Polk's war message voted for the war, perhaps remembering what happened to the Federalist party for opposing the War of 1812. Walt

Whitman, then the Democratic editor of the *Brooklyn Eagle*, reflected the popular view when he observed that "miserable, inefficient Mexico" should not be allowed to interfere "with the great mission of peopling the New World with a noble race."

Romantic symbolism and publishing for the masses also helped to generate popular support for the war. For the first time, American troops fought under the "Stars and Stripes," which the United States Army officially adopted in 1834. Brass regimental bands pumped up enthusiasm with renditions of the *Star Spangled Banner, Hail, Columbia!,* and *Yankee Doodle*. Writers equated the Mexican War and the American Revolution. In one example of the day's extravagantly patriotic rhetoric, novelist and journalist George Lippard claimed that "the American people are in arms for the freedom of a Continent." Lippard pointed proudly to the "Symbol of our destiny— THE UNSHEATHED SWORD OF WASHINGTON RESTING UPON THE MAP OF THE NEW WORLD."

Another emblem of rampant martial spirit was the extent to which citizens volunteered for military service. The regular army contained only 6,500 officers and enlisted men. Congress immediately authorized the recruitment of 50,000 volunteers and nationalized an equal number of state militia who otherwise could not be ordered to fight on foreign soil. Neither the national nor the state governments encountered much difficulty in raising their quotas of troops.

As the war progressed, many American soldiers lost their enthusiasm for war because of the conditions in the army and persistent moral questions about the war. Over 9,000 soldiers deserted during the war, the highest percentage (8 percent) of any of the United States' foreign conflicts. Among the first troops to go "over the hill" were members of Zachary Taylor's army in Texas. One homesick and disgruntled Georgian complained that the state was "distinguished, above all other particulars by its myriads of crawling, flying, stinging and biting things." An Irish private soldier named John Riley deserted Taylor's force and became a lieutenant in the Mexican army, where he earned five times the pay as an American soldier. Riley was instrumental in organizing other deserters into the St. Patrick's Battalion, Irish Catholics who reacted against racist attitudes and atrocities committed by Anglo-American troops. The *San Patricios* fought for Mexico for the remainder of the war.

Despite the opposition to the initial concept of war, the majority of Americans supported their soldiers in the field. And most of the troops, regardless of where they came from, caught the patriotic fever that suffused their invasion of Mexico. Indeed, fighting on foreign soil, exposure to alien people and cultures, and being thrown together with other Americans from diverse backgrounds boosted their national consciousness—a typical response to such wartime circumstances. "Here we are," reported one soldier, "from all quarters of our glorious Union, acting in the same concert as if all were the children of one state or family."

The understated reality behind the patriotic exuberance was the atrocities committed against Mexican civilians. Rogues and cutthroat bandits operated on both sides of the war, but reports of atrocities committed by American volunteers, said General Winfield Scott, were reason "to make Heaven weep" and every American of Christian morals to "*blush* for his country." The Texas Rangers, a unit formed to fight Indians on the Texas frontier, carried strong prejudices against Hispanics. The Rangers' reputation for undue violence, however, was little worse than the Mexican guerrillas who preyed on off-duty American soldiers and hired civilian teamsters. Zachary Taylor was not much of a disciplinarian; however, American commanders eventually brought unruly volunteers under considerable control by inflicting harsh military punishment.

The war gained widespread American support despite problems because it was a small price to pay for the prized territories of Manifest Destiny. Seizing the borderlands was the easiest part of the war to accomplish because of its remoteness from Mexico and the relatively few Mexican citizens and soldiers who resided there. Furthermore, armed American citizens already resided in those territories in significant numbers. Americans began planning quickly and almost spontaneously for the occupation of New Mexico and California.

Occupation and Rebellion

After Congress declared war on Mexico, President Polk immediately ordered the occupation of New Mexico and California. With war at hand, "by the act of Mexico herself" as the President had claimed in his war message, Polk justified the occupation the Mexico's borderlands as compensation. Generations of historians have told the story of the conquest of the Southwest territories as though it came with little local resistance. In truth, however, neither *Nuevo Mexicanos* nor *Californios* universally welcomed the Anglo conquerors.

How did the residents of New Mexico and California respond to United States occupation?

President Polk directed General Stephen W. Kearny and his 1,700-man Army of the West to march from Fort Leavenworth in Kansas to Santa Fe and take possession of New Mexico. As Kearny's force approached Santa Fe in August, having stopped to rest and repair equipment at Bent's Fort, Governor Manuel Armijo massed the New Mexico militia to resist them. Overcome by a sense of futility, Armijo, a successful merchant with many connections with American businessmen, abandoned the defense. Kearny's troops entered the provincial capital without a shot, proclaiming United States sovereignty and installing Charles Bent as provisional governor. Then, leaving a detachment of his troops to garrison the town, Kearny led a column to California to join with American military and naval forces already there.

Despite President's Polk's assertion that the borderlands were just compensation for a war he had sought to avoid, the United States had earlier shown its readiness to seize California. In October of 1842, a United States naval squadron had taken possession of Monterey, thinking war had broken out. After two days, the embarrassed commander discovered his mistake and withdrew with his apologies. But Missouri's senator Thomas Hart Benton, one of the most ardent expansionists in the United States, felt no need to apologize. He assumed that the American settlers who were pouring into California would take over the territory eventually. Unlike earlier merchants, trappers, and consular officials who generally resided in villages along the coast and entered local societies, the recent emigrants settled in remote interior valleys, did not learn Spanish, and had no intention of becoming Mexican citizens. Thus, a situation similar to Texas now existed in California. Uneasy Mexican authorities in California began to restrict further immigration from the United States, causing settlers in the Sacramento and Sonoma valleys to fear their expulsion from the territory.

In December of 1845, "Pathfinder" John C. Fremont brought another exploring party from the Army

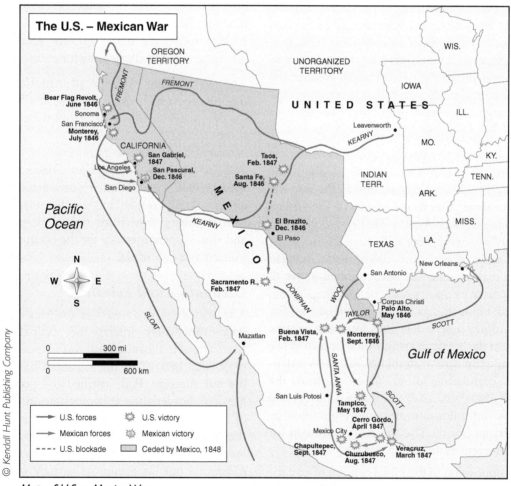

Map of U.S.—Mexico War

Corps of Topographical Engineers to California. Ostensibly, their mission was to locate potential railroad routes from the east; however, Fremont had Manifest Destiny on his mind. In May of 1846, he set up a military camp on the Sacramento River estate of the prosperous Swiss immigrant John Sutter and encouraged surrounding settlers to rebel against Mexican authority. In June, the Americans raided the town of Sonoma, captured the military garrison there, and proclaimed the independent Bear Flag Republic. Local resistance to this foreign takeover commenced immediately, even though the *Californios* were out-manned and out-gunned. Juan Bautista Alvarado and many others of the local elite admired the Constitution and republican institutions of the United States, but they also "loved our country most dearly." Even some of the foreign *rancheros* aided the resistance. California's governor, Pío Pico, and commanding general José Castro, organized a militia campaign to defeat the foreigners and throw them out of the province. But with little support from Mexico, the odds against success were high.

In July of 1846, the United States opened military operations in California. Commodore John D. Sloat and the Navy's Pacific Squadron arrived in Monterey harbor. Local authorities quickly surrendered, and the Americans raised the "Stars and Stripes" above the town. Sloat and Fremont joined forces and seized San Francisco, forcing the California militia to withdraw southward to Los Angeles, the provincial capital. The civilian population, including Abel Stearns, an American who had arrived in 1829 and became the richest *ranchero* in the territory, supplied the resistance fighters with food and shelter while slowing down the advancing Americans. Commodore Robert F. Stockton, who took over naval command from Sloat, sailed to Los Angeles while Fremont marched his troops overland. In August 1846, Los Angeles' defenses collapsed under the superior American firepower. Stockton and Fremont, feeling a false sense of security, left a small garrison behind and returned to Monterey. The *Californio* resistance had not died, and in September the militia retook the Los Angeles. For the next three months, they retained control of the southern portion of California.

In the autumn of 1847, however, the Americans received reinforcements. Fremont led a battalion of 430 soldiers, settlers, and Indians (including nine Delawares from Missouri and some Miwoks from the Sacramento Valley) to San Diego, where he joined with Stockton and General Stephen W. Kearny's col-

umn from New Mexico. In the bloodiest battle of the war in California, fought at San Pascual on December 6, the Americans suffered a stinging defeat. But the *Californios* were unable to obtain additional weapons or reinforcements, and in January of 1848, they evacuated Los Angeles and signed an armistice that brought the resistance to America's Manifest Destiny in California to a close.

By force of arms, the United States had acquired the California and New Mexico territories that James K. Polk had been determined to possess. To put pressure on the Mexican government to acknowledge this situation, Polk ordered an invasion of Mexico itself.

The Invasion of Mexico

> **How did Mexico and the United States measure up militarily, what was the United States' strategy in the war, and what was the military outcome?**

Unlike the conquest of Mexico's remote border provinces defended by civilians and ill-equipped militia, the invasion of Mexico threw United States military forces directly against a sizable and professional Mexican army defending its homeland. At the outset, the strengths and weaknesses of both sides seemed to balance each other out. Mexico's 30,000-man army was five times larger than the United States army. Moreover, Mexican soldiers were trained and battle-ready. The London *Times* newspaper thought them "superior to those of the United States." Surprisingly, however, the war produced relatively little patriotic spirit in a factious and economically ravaged Mexico, and the troops, who included draftees and prisoners, sometimes wilted in the heat of battle. Commanders, especially Antonio López de Santa Anna, were not good at making the correct decisions in the field. In the United States by contrast, where the martial spirit prevailed, discipline was often lacking, but never *élan*. The war served as valuable training for talented West Point graduates like Albert Sidney Johnston, George B. McClellan, Robert E. Lee, and Ulysses S. Grant, all of whom played important roles in the Civil War fifteen years later.

The United States' war effort benefited enormously from industrialization. Factories mass-produced uniforms, knapsacks, weapons, ammunition, and wagons that kept the troops well supplied. Railroads and steamboats helped immensely in mobilizing men and delivering necessary equipment. Although distribution snarls, contractor profiteering, and staggering waste boosted the cost of the war, Lieutenant Henry

W. Halleck stated correctly that "no army [up to that time] was better supplied than ours in all matters of subsistence, clothing, and medical and hospital stores, and in means of transportation."

Americans at home experienced the Mexican War as no civilian population previously had experienced war. The penny press covered it from top to bottom; war correspondents accompanied the armies and reported from the scene of the action, and high-speed printing presses and the telegraph kept civilians at home informed about the activities of their armed forces. Many journalists set up local newspaper offices in Mexico. As citizens read about the exploits of their husbands, sons, brothers, and other loved ones, they collectively cheered every victory and mourned together their losses. These experiences did much to forge a bond of national unity throughout the war.

Military strategy against Mexico dictated three lines of advance. Zachary Taylor and his army pushed into northern Mexico from the Rio Grande. In September of 1846, American troops took Monterrey after bloody street-fighting and costly tactical blunders. Meanwhile, a regiment of Missouri volunteers under Colonel Alexander Doniphan, a lawyer with no military experience but a lot of grit, marched through southern New Mexico's lunar landscape and the blistering deserts of northern Mexico. Their remarkable feat symbolized the courage and physical strength of the citizen soldiers and resulted in a victory at Sacramento and the capture of Chihuahua.

Polk's plan was to squeeze Mexico City between two offensives, the first bearing down from the north. Taylor's troops pushing southward from Monterrey collided with a powerful Mexican army commanded by General Santa Anna, who had been allowed to slip through the American naval blockade at Vera Cruz. On February 22, 1847, in a spectacularly beautiful mountain pass near Buena Vista ranch, the two armies fought a bloody two-day engagement. Surprisingly, Santa Anna withdrew his forces with the outcome still in doubt. Buena Vista solidified American control of northern Mexico and confirmed "Old Rough and Ready" as a genuine war hero. Americans at home erupted in celebration upon hearing of the American victory, although many mourned their loses, including Henry Clay, whose son was among the Americans who fell.

As Americans rejoiced, General Winfield Scott, a veteran of the War of 1812 and the United States' most renowned military officer, prepared a daring amphibious assault on the vital port city of Vera Cruz

on Mexico's east coast. Over 8,600 troops sloshed ashore on March 9, 1847, without a single casualty. "It is wholly inexplicable to us," commented one amazed soldier, "why the enemy did not oppose our landing." Meanwhile, Santa Anna had seized the Mexican presidency. He privately advised Scott to exert military pressure on Mexico City so that he could persuade pro-war politicians to accept a peace treaty. With 9,000 wagons of food and other supplies, Scott and his men trudged up the same winding road that Hernán Cortez's *conquistadores* had followed into the high central valley of Mexico 328 years earlier. In a crucial battle at Cerro Gordo on April 17 and 18, the Americans cleared the road of Mexican resistance and continued deliberately toward the Mexican capital.

In August, as Scott's army approached the outlying fortifications guarding Mexico City, a state department clerk named Nicholas Trist began peace negotiations with the Mexican government. Trist, who spoke Spanish fluently, had joined the American army at Vera Cruz with authorization to strike a bargain with Mexican authorities. Polk's wariness of Whig generals who might become presidential candidates dictated Trist's selection as chief negotiator. The haughty and vane Scott complained bitterly of this affront to his honor and snubbed the equally belligerent Trist. The two finally made friends over a case of guava marmalade, and Trist communicated to Santa Anna Polk's demand for the Rio Grande boundary, upper and lower California, New Mexico, and transit rights across southern Mexico at the Isthmus of Tehuantepec. Trist was authorized to pay Mexico up to $15 million in compensation. During a brief armistice, the Mexicans considered and then rejected these terms, and the campaign against Mexico City continued.

The climax came during the second week in September. Costly but decisive American victories at Churubusco and at the fortress of Chapultepec, whose defenders included young cadets from a Mexican military academy, led to the surrender of Mexico City on September 14. In Mexico, the cadets who died fighting for their country were commemorated as the "Heroic Sons" or the *Niños Heroes.* Attention in the United States now shifted to the diplomatic front, and to Nicholas Trist.

The Treaty of Guadalupe Hidalgo

Despite the collapse of Mexico City's defenses, Nicholas Trist made no progress in his negotiations on a peace treaty. Partly, the problem lay in the disarray

What was the United States' goal in the peace negotiations, and to what extent did the Treaty of Guadalupe-Hidalgo meet that goal?

and incessant political infighting within the Mexican government, which relocated to Querétaro. Santa Anna resigned the presidency following the fall of Mexico City, and factions favoring peace wrestled with those urging continuation of the war for control. In addition, a proud and resentful Mexican populace still objected to American territorial demands. In October, Polk ordered Trist to break off negotiations and return to Washington. The President was responding to building pressure in the United States to annex all of Mexico.

The "**All Mexico**" campaign derived from the intoxication of military victory and extreme expansionism in some quarters in the United States. The penny press and ardent Democrats in the urban Northeast argued that Mexico's stubborn resistance to the United States' Manifest Destiny demanded greater compensation. The frenzy swept up President Polk too, but gradually it became clear that most Americans had little stomach for absorbing all of Mexico. Furthermore, annexing a nation of 6 million mostly mixed-race people was objectionable. "We do not want the people of Mexico," explained Lewis Cass of Michigan, "either as citizens or subjects. All we want is a portion of territory which they nominally hold [California and New Mexico], generally uninhabited, or, where inhabited at all, sparsely so, and with a population which would soon recede, or identify itself with ours."

The headstrong Trist also rejected the "All Mexico" movement and disobeyed his recall instructions. His insubordination infuriated Polk, who fumed at Trist's arrogance. In the meantime, though, attitudes in the Mexican government softened, and in February 1848, Trist met with Mexican peace commissioners in the beautiful Villa of Guadalupe Hidalgo, on the outskirts of Mexico City. There, they initialed a treaty. Trist dropped the demand for transit rights across Mexico and lower California. The final agreement acknowledged the Rio Grande boundary of Texas, the cession of upper California and New Mexico to the United States, and a $15 million indemnity payment to Mexico. To protect the residents of the ceded territory, the treaty guaranteed United States citizenship and property rights to all Mexican citizens of the ceded territories.

The **Treaty of Guadalupe Hidalgo** cost Mexico half of its territory and gave the United States the

Courtesy of Library of Congress

American troops assaulting the fortress of Chapultepec, September 13, 1847. Taking the castle was part of General Winfield Scott's campaign to capture Mexico City. Its defenders, including Los Niños Heroes, fought valiantly but were overpowered by superior numbers. Several American officers, including Robert E. Lee and Ulysses S. Grant, who opposed each other in the Civil War, gained combat experience in Mexico.

present states of California, Arizona, New Mexico, Nevada, Utah (Deseret), and portions of Colorado and Wyoming. Along with the Oregon Treaty, it made the United States a continental nation. Work began almost immediately on stagecoach lines and pony express mail service. On the recommendation of government engineers, the United States asked Mexico for additional territory below the Gila River to facilitate overland travel to California. The **Gadsden Purchase** (named after negotiator Christopher Gadsden of South Carolina) added 45,000 square miles across today's New Mexico and Arizona for $15 million, the same amount the United States had paid for half a million square miles in the **Mexican Cession**.

Despite the triumph of American expansionism, explosive issues of race, national identity, and slavery raised during the U.S.–Mexico War dampened the enthusiasm for territorial expansion. Manifest Destiny had come with a heavy political price tag. Incorporating the Mexican Cession into the Union proved in some ways more difficult than the war itself.

THINKING BACK

1. What concrete objectives did the proponents of Manifest Destiny have in the 1840s, what obstacles did they face, and how and to what extent did they achieve those objectives?
2. How did the U.S.–Mexico War change the way the United States had previously gone about expansion? How was it similar?

THE LOCAL PERSPECTIVE: FOCUS ON OREGON

What changes did settlers from the United States bring about in Oregon?

In the 1840s, the fertile Willamette River Valley, stretching south toward California from present-day Portland, represented dream fulfillment for thousands of settlers (see map on p. 408). As they loaded their possessions into covered wagons for the 2,000-mile trek to the Pacific Coast, emigrants pictured an Eden in the Oregon country, a place where they could be prosperous and secure. In 1830, a New England schoolteacher and Oregon booster named Hall Jackson Kelley helped in forming that mental picture. Although he had never

seen the Pacific Coast, Kelley published a popular sketch of the Willamette Valley. Using the florid language of the Romantic era, Kelley wrote exaggerated descriptions of "sublime" mountains, "salubrious" climate, and "well watered" farms, "nourished by a rich soil, and warmed by a congenial heat." Anticipating a migration of farmers to the Pacific Northwest, Kelley assessed the country as "exactly accommodated to the interests of its future cultivators."

In 1852, Esther Hanna, an eighteen-year-old minister's wife, arrived in Oregon apparently expecting everything Kelley had described. Reality probably set in as she crossed the dry, treeless prairies of eastern Oregon on the famous Oregon Trail. When Hanna and her traveling companions reached the "grand and sublime" Columbia River, she felt disappointment. "Instead of trees with luxuriant foliage, you see massive rocks, pile upon pile . . . The only green shrub I saw was a weed." For some 22,000 immigrants like Hanna, who arrived between 1843 and 1855, the leg of the journey from the Columbia River to the Willamette Valley was the final, and most dangerous portion of the most exciting adventure in their lives. Ahead lay their personal Manifest Destiny.

Half a century before Esther Hanna arrived in Oregon, Lewis and Clark reported being harassed by local Indians who resisted intruders; in the 1840s, however, settlers hired peaceful Indians to lead their wagons and teams of draft animals along the portage road that paralleled the river. A small Methodist mission station and six log houses situated at The Dalles gave footsore overlanders an opportunity to rest, wash and mend their clothes, and repair equipment. In 1850, the United States Army established a fort, and by 1855 a thriving town prospered through the overland trade. Like tourist towns of today, greedy merchants at The Dalles "skinned" the travelers. "Instead of being received by the Oregon people with open hearts and arms . . .," one immigrant complained, "we are fleeced without mercy." The formation of local cultures and the complex identities of residents of frontier regions showed among the local Indians. Entering the commercial network that developed after the Oregon Treaty gave the United States exclusive authority of the Oregon country, Indians at The Dalles traded provisions, horses, and canoes to the immigrants for articles of the newcomers' clothing. The Catholic missionary Pierre-Jean De Smet observed some Indians "in the full dress of a wagoner, others in a mixture composed of the sailor's, the wagoner's, and the lawyer's, arranged

This white clapboard church in Oregon's Willamette Valley suggests the large number of settlers who arrived from New England and the upper Midwest.

according to fancy." They were adapting to cultural influences and struggling with the pressures of identity exerted by a new national sovereignty.

From The Dalles, Oregon immigrants chose between two possible routes to their final Willamette Valley destination. The overland road was a comparatively short 100 miles, but the rigors of cresting the Cascade Mountains made it more difficult than most of the previous portions of the Oregon Trail. Many people chose to boat down the roiling river that knifed through the snow-capped Cascades. Fooled by river guides and outfitters into expecting a short, easy ride, many travelers were stunned by their encounter with nature at its wildest and most dangerous. Disasters were frequent. In 1843, a canoe carrying members of the Jesse Applegate party capsized, drowning two boys and one man. By the early 1850s, experience, and the appearance of the steamboat *James P. Flint* made the trip through the Columbia River Gorge much easier.

Settlement of the Willamette coincided with the rapid decline of the Native American population. In the 1840s, the *Oregon Spectator*, the first local newspaper, noted: "The Indian retreats before the march of civilization and American enterprise; the howling wilderness is fast becoming fruitful fields." Such was the perception, part truth and part romance, that underlay the spirit of Manifest Destiny. Settlement of the Willamette Valley introduced intensified use of the land for commercial purposes. Cleared fields planted with wheat, lumber and flour mills, cattle in fenced pastures were the measures that settlers, and Americans generally, used in determining progress. Killing predators like wolves, bears, and cougars altered the valley's ecology, leading to increases in game animals that competed with livestock for pasturage.

Other settler developments were also regarded as signs of progress, like the presence of towns. Oregon City, a few miles up the Willamette River, was the first sizable white settlement in Oregon, but Portland, at the juncture of the Willamette and Columbia rivers, became the largest and most important town economically. A sandbar at the mouth of the Columbia River prevented the building of a port there, but the site of Portland, named by an emigrant merchant from Maine after his hometown, was well-suited for docking vessels. The first houses went up in 1844 on the west side of the river, but soon a ferry shuttled back and forth between settlements on both sides. Stores, blacksmith shops, a tannery, a sawmill, and a hotel supplied the needs of some 700 Portland residents in 1848. Ships from California, Hawaii, and the East Coast brought merchandise, mail, and newspapers; they also carried off wheat and hides from Willamette Valley farmers. The discovery of gold in

California in 1848 siphoned off much of Oregon's male population, creating a severe labor shortage; however, "gold fever" boosted demand for Oregon produce, which in turn stimulated rapid growth not only in Portland but also in other Willamette Valley towns like Corvallis and Salem.

Another development that settlers and Americans back East recognized as signs of "civilization" was the publication of books and newspapers. The first book printed in Oregon was produced by a printing press imported from Hawaii—one of six presses that Christian missionaries had shipped there in the 1820s. Judged to be too worn out for further use, that surplus, hand-operated printing press made its way to the Oregon country. In 1839, it was unloaded at Fort Vancouver and transported to Henry Spalding's Lapwai Indian mission in present-day Idaho (then part of the Oregon territory). In 1846, the Lapwai press, as it was known, arrived in the Willamette Valley. During its Oregon career, the press printed various reading books for use in missionary schools, newspapers, and the *Laws and Statutes* of territorial Oregon.

The statutes were a welcome sight to Oregon citizens. Prior to the Oregon Treaty in 1846, Americans had been bound by no particular legal authority. The Hudson's Bay Company, Great Britain's agent in the Oregon country, governed only British subjects. Early American settlers enforced the statutes of their home states for a semblance of law and order. But the murder of missionaries Marcus and Narcissa Whitman in 1847 (see p. 385), dramatized the isolated and dangerous circumstances of citizens residing in Oregon. Residents sent former trapper Joe Meek to Washington to petition for federal authority. Congress responded in 1848 with a territorial organization act that authorized an elected legislature and a governor appointed by the president. The first territorial governor was Joseph Lane, a proslavery Democrat from Indiana and a close ally of President Polk's. In 1850, Congress encouraged further immigration by passing **Donation Land Claim Act**, a homestead law that granted settlers 320 acres if they resided on it and cultivated it for four years. Within five years, 8,000 settlers had claimed almost 3 million acres, mostly in the Willamette Valley.

The Donation Land Claim Act excluded African Americans and Hawaiians. Issues of race and slavery penetrated even this remote corner of the Pacific Northwest. A majority of Oregon's settlers were prejudiced against African Americans and did not want free blacks living in the territory. A few settlers, however, were slave owners, and many considered the fertile land of the Willamette Valley and the temperate climate suitable to a slave-labor system. The debate over slavery, which dominated national discourse by the end of the 1840s, divided Oregonians. During the 1850s, voters rejected statehood, in part because they could not resolve questions relating to slavery, and when they finally voted overwhelming for admission to the United States in 1857, they opposed slavery by a margin of three to one and against allowing African Americans to enter the state by eight to one.

Oregon exemplified the theme of Manifest Destiny that ran through the United States in the 1840s. Oregon's experience illustrates not only the continental scope of American thinking but also the emerging debates over slavery and the complex issue of identity. For a large number of Americans, skin color and culture defined who was an American and who was not.

THINKING BACK

1. What part of the Oregon Territory was most attractive to settlers from the United States, and why was that so?
2. How did the influx of settlers affect the Native American population of Oregon?

THE MEXICAN CESSION

The Mexican Cession came with a host of problems. Cultural influences from the United States stressed Hispanics and Native Americans. Many adapted to new ways of living; however, most found themselves on the margins of society—if they survived at all. Questions immediately arose about the status of the new territories. To American politicians, the issue of slavery in California and New Mexico was the most explosive one, and it touched off a fierce debate in and out of Congress. The California gold rush put additional pressure on Congress to resolve the question. A stop-gap compromise in 1850 decided the status of slavery in the Mexican Cession, but not the broader questions of slavery, ethnicity, and national identification in the United States.

The New Americans

For generations, historians and popular writers believed Manifest Destiny brought civilization to backward and untamed lands. In 1927, novelist Willa Cather claimed in her best-selling historical novel *Death Comes for the Archbishop* that progress in the Southwest began with the U.S.–Mexico War. In truth, not all of the new Americans benefited from becoming a part of the United States.

The new political situation in the Southwest confused Apache Indians. They could not understand why the government of the United States wanted to protect Hispanics. For decades, Apaches had fought against Spaniards and Mexicans. During the Mexican War, they regarded the American army as an ally. Now the United States attempted to subdue them. The Army constructed forts along the trails through the Southwest to protect travelers against deadly Apache attacks. The government sought to locate the Apaches on reservations where they would be supplied with provisions.

In northern New Mexico, serious trouble brewed among the Pueblos and the entrenched Hispanic elite. The hostility of those new Americans focused on Governor Charles Bent and associates who had received extensive land grants from the Mexican government. During the autumn of 1846, American troops garrisoned at Fort Marcy in Santa Fe caused further resentment by abusing local residents. Bent wrote to General Stephen W. Kearny that the commander of the Santa Fe garrison must learn to "conciliate and not exasperate" the local populace. Bent's own murder soon after proved his point (see p. 397).

Over in California, American officials adopted policies intended to give Hispanic and American landowners control of Indian labor. Many Indians adapted to the new circumstances they faced by earning wages working for local ranchers and farmers, and abandoning traditional patterns of hunting, gardening, and raiding for food. The war, however, had crippled the California economy, and as jobs became scarce, Indians resumed raiding. United States officials attempted to halt the raids by punishing the culprits rather than addressing the causes. The United States military commandant even attempted to revive the old mission system, requiring Indians to work on missions or be arrested—a system of peonage. Meanwhile, the enterprising John Sutter ordered two wheat threshing machines, a

portent of future technological changes that would replace Indian manual labor. And the notorious Indian livestock raider José Jesus turned to capturing other Indians and selling them as laborers to missions and farms that had not yet mechanized. In the Treaty of Guadalupe Hidalgo, the government of the United States had promised citizenship to all Indian citizens of California; however, in practice, that did not happen.

The transfer of territory from Mexico to the United States produced ambivalent political identities for Hispanics. The arbitrary political boundaries that separated the United States from Mexico also bisected regional societies. In Los Angeles, a weekly Spanish-language newspaper called *El Clamor Público* ("the public clamor") recognized the persistence of an ethnic Mexican identity. Using the term *nuestra raza* ("our people"), the paper not only distinguished Hispanics from Anglos but also described an Hispanic population in the United States that maintained strong national ties to Mexico. In New Mexico, crafty Anglos alienated Hispanics by manipulating the land laws of the United States to cheat Hispanics out of communal properties. Likewise in Texas, Hispanics were uprooted and driven from their communities. Such losses contributed to border banditry that had broad social implications. Seen as a bandit by Anglo lawmen, one *Tejano*, Juan Cortina, justified violence against Anglo ranchers who "rob us, without any cause, and for no other crime than that of being of Mexican origin." The enemies of Hispanics, proclaimed Cortina, "shall not possess our lands until they fatten it with their own gore."

Thus, the rationale for Manifest Destiny—the happy advance of civilization and republican principles—did not accurately describe the situation in the Mexican Cession. Not only was there considerable resistance on the part of the local citizenry to being annexed by the United States, but also the "empire for liberty," as Thomas Jefferson had envisioned the Far West, was in danger of becoming "an empire for slavery." Had Manifest Destiny spread democracy and liberty, or did it bring racism and slavery?

Slavery in the New Territories

Rancorous though the transition from Mexican control to the sovereignty of the United States proved to be, it was matched in vituperation by the war of

California's Santa Barbara mission. After the war, the United States commandant attempted to revive the old mission system of exploiting Indian labor.

What were the interests and the arguments pertaining to slavery in the territories acquired from Mexico, and how were the issues resolved?

words over the status of slavery in the newly won territories. "The slavery question is assuming a fearful aspect," President Polk confided to his diary. Whereas the debate on the Mexican War had largely followed party lines, the subsequent argument over slavery divided Americans along more sectional boundaries. As Northerners and Southerners formulated positions pro and con, they left precious little room between them for compromise.

In the summer of 1846, as the House of Representatives prepared to vote money for the war against Mexico, a Democrat from Pennsylvania, David Wilmot, submitted an amendment to the appropriations bill stating that "neither slavery nor involuntary servitude shall exist" in any land the United States might acquire. Wilmot was not an abolitionist who cared what slavery did to African Americans, but he was dead set against allowing slave labor to drive free, white, wage labor from the Western lands. Historical precedent stood on his side. Congress had outlawed slavery in the Northwest Territory in 1787 (see pp. 188–89), and in the Compromise of 1820 (see pp. 311–12) Congress had banned it north of 36° 30' in the Louisiana Purchase territory. Northern Whig abolitionists supported Wilmot's amendment, adding a moral ingredient to the **free-soil** argument. The House passed the amendment in a strictly sectional vote; however, the Senate, in which Southern states constituted half the votes (Iowa had not yet been admitted to the Union), rejected it. But the **Wilmot Proviso**, as it came to be called, symbolized the principle of banning the extension of slavery into the territories. "As if by magic," observed the *Boston Whig*, "it brought to a head the great question that is about to divide the American people."

Immediately, Southern slave owners voiced their constitutional right to take their slave property into territories won by the blood and treasure of all the states. Even though John C. Calhoun had opposed the war, he now led the campaign to defend what he deemed **Southern rights**. In the tightly reasoned style that characterized his constitutional theories, Calhoun pointed out to fellow senators in a series of resolutions in 1847 that the Constitution protected citizens' property against seizure by the government without due process of law. To deny Southern slave owners access to common territories while granting it to other property owners violated the 5th Amendment. In addition to their constitutional rights, white Southerners tried to convince the nation that slavery was, in Calhoun's words, "a positive good" to slave, master, and white laborer. But the proponents of slavery in the territories rankled most at what they regarded as the degrading "moral taint" that free-soil advocates fastened on the South. "Death," cried one Southerner, "is preferable to acknowledged inferiority."

Democratic party leaders searched for some pragmatic way to resolve the question. A worried President believed the issue "cannot fail to destroy the Democratic party, if it does not ultimately threaten the Union itself." An easy solution, as he saw it, lay in extending the 36° 30' line all the way to the Pacific coast; however, Northerners were tired of compromising with the South. Lewis Cass of Michigan proposed another solution. Let the citizens of the territories decide whether they wanted slavery. This idea, known as **popular sovereignty**, had an seductively democratic ring; however, it satisfied neither ardent Northern antislavery advocates because it allowed the possibility of slavery expansion nor the extreme Southern slave owners who would listen to no suggestion about keeping slavery out of the territories.

The question of slavery in the territories, of course, was a political one, and politicians were hard-put to find answers that satisfied more than they offended. After the final ratification of the Treaty of Guadalupe Hidalgo, and Congress' failure to come up with a solution, Americans went to the polls to choose a new president.

The Election of 1848

How did the two major political parties deal with the slavery issue during the 1848 election?

In the 1848 election, with no solution to the slavery problem at hand, both parties looked for ways to dodge it. The U.S.–Mexico War had exhausted the workaholic Polk; he withdrew from consideration for a second term and died just four months after leaving office.

The Democratic party felt the sectional tension over slavery, but many believed that some kind of compromise solution could be found. Popular sovereignty might be just the ticket to election victory. It was ambiguous enough so appeal to those who wanted slavery in the territories and those who wanted to keep it out. So, the party turned to Lewis Cass. Ominously, however, delegations from Alabama and New York walked out of the nominating convention,

signifying the sectional opposition to the party's candidate and platform.

The Whigs valued ambiguity too, and searched for it in the corps of military heroes who had achieved fame in the war that the party had opposed. Winfield Scott was a possibility; his successful campaign against Mexico City led Great Britain's famous Lord Wellington to crown him "the greatest living general." He was too pompous, however, and had too many enemies. Zachary Taylor, more amiable than Winfield Scott, possessed all the necessary credentials. The hero of Resaca de la Palma and Buena Vista, Taylor held moderate views on slavery and was outspokenly nonpartisan. "Old Zach" carried liabilities—a Southern birth and ownership of 100 slaves on Louisiana and Mississippi plantations—, but his military career had made him a strong nationalist, and his heroes were the border state nationalists like Henry Clay. His uncertainty on the slavery question cinched his nomination.

Alas, Taylor could not prevent major defections by Northern "Conscience" Whigs. Nor could Lewis Cass prevent pro-Wilmot Proviso Northern "Barnburner" Democrats from bolting their party. The dissenters formed a coalition with the minor Liberty Party, which stood squarely in opposition to slavery in the territories, to form a new **Free Soil party**. Advocates of free-soil nominated Martin Van Buren for president. Van Buren had not forgiven Southerners for blocking his nomination four years before. No longer catering to the slave owning crowd, he led a ticket that included Charles Francis Adams for vice president.

Most voters chose between the ambiguous popular sovereignty platform of the Democratic party and the equally ambiguous Zachary Taylor. Taylor proved to be stronger in the South than Cass was in the North. He carried eight of the fifteen slave states and seven of the fifteen free states. The Whigs tallied just over 47 percent of the popular vote and 163 electoral votes to Cass' 42.5 percent and 127 electoral votes. Van Buren and the Free Soil party did not win a single state, but as one Free Soil party member, Charles Sumner of Massachusetts, observed, "the public mind has been stirred on the subject of slavery to depths never reached before."

So, there still was no resolution to the debate over slavery in the Mexican Cession. But even as the election campaign unfolded, dramatic events in California changed the political situation completely, adding new urgency to the search for a formula that both Southerners and Northerners would find acceptable.

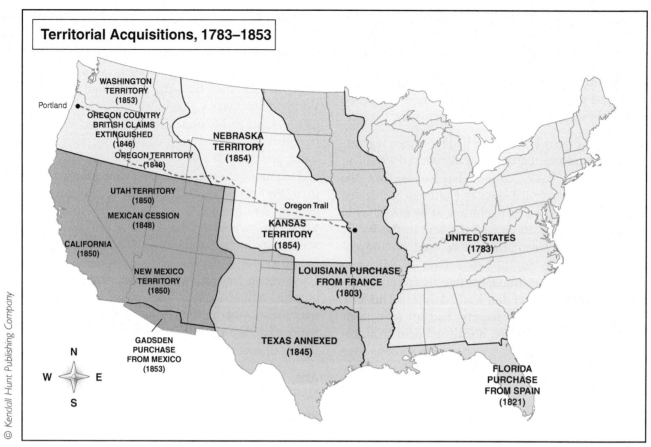

Map of Territorial Acquisitions and Boundary Changes, 1821-1853

The California Bonanza

What effect did the discovery of gold in California have on the debate over slavery in the new territories?

The debate over slavery in the newly won territories gained urgency as the election campaign of 1848 unfolded. The discovery of gold in California earlier in the year set off a mass migration to the territory. The California gold rush was one of the most tumultuous events of the nineteenth century, profoundly affecting the economy of the United States and accelerating the pace of settlement on the Pacific Coast. Almost overnight, California's population topped 100,000. Statehood was imminent, but what would be the possibilities for slavery?

The dramatic discovery of gold happened on the American river flowing down the western slope of the Sierra Nevada Mountains. John Sutter had formed a partnership with James Marshall to construct a sawmill on the river near Sutter's vast estate on the site of present-day Sacramento. On the morning of January 24, 1848, as he inspected the mill site, Marshall saw tell tale golden sparkles among the tailings and exclaimed: "Boys, by God I believe I have found a gold mine." Word spread rapidly, all the way to the East Coast, and 5,000 feverish miners staked their claims. Newspapers ran daily stories, and Governor Richard Mason confirmed the reports: "The discovery of the vast deposits of gold has entirely changed the character of . . . California." Those who could, left their homes, families, farms, and jobs and headed for "Californy" to strike it rich. Some booked rail or steamer passage to Missouri and then formed wagon companies for the overland trek. Others sailed to Panama, crossed by land to the Pacific coast, and thence to San Francisco.

The California "gold fever" reached a frenzy in 1849. Some 80,000 eager "49ers" descended on the gold fields—eight times as many people as resided in the territory at the time of Marshall's discovery. The "49ers" mined $10 million in gold, and between 1848 and 1855, miners dragged $300 million in gold from rivers that carried nuggets from the Mother Lode buried below the surface of the mountains. San Francisco burgeoned, from a few hundred residents to 20,000 in 1850. Fire destroyed most of the town in December of 1849, but citizens rebuilt it almost immediately.

The Compromise of 1850

How did Congress hope to resolve the great issue of slavery in the new territories?

As gold fever raged in California, the intense heat of sectional conflict seared the nation. Californians were ready for statehood and had little interest in slavery. In Washington, however, members of the House and Senate tightened their fists and pointed their pistols at one another defending the free-soil doctrine or threatening secession. In Nashville, Tennessee, a convention of Southern secessionists, called "fire-eaters," gave credence to threats of disunion. President Taylor shocked his fellow Southerners by proposing to admit both California and New Mexico as free states. The stage was set for one of the most dramatic public debates in American history. "There is a bad state of things here," a congressman from Illinois reported. "I fear this Union is in danger."

The speeches on the floor of the United States Senate early in 1850 focused on a series of conciliatory resolutions that Henry Clay, the "Great Compromiser," introduced. Clay, John C. Calhoun, and Daniel Webster faced the ends of their long and brilliant careers in public service. Clay's proposals called for admitting California as a free state and organizing New Mexico as a territory without "any restriction or condition on the subject of slavery." He addressed two other concerns with resolutions banning the slave trade in the District of Columbia and urging enactment of tough federal legislation providing for the return of fugitive slaves. Finally, Clay addressed Texas' insistent demand for eastern New Mexico to the Rio Grande River. His resolutions rejected that claim and offered to assume the state's public debt as compensation. Just days away from death and too feeble to speak himself, Calhoun asked James Mason of Virginia to read his response to Clay's compromise. Claiming that "the equilibrium between the two sections has been destroyed," Calhoun insisted that the only hope the Union had was for the North to cease its attacks on the South. If California entered as a free state, the Southern states could not "remain in the Union

consistently with their honor and safety." Three days later, Webster spoke eloquently "for the preservation of the Union." He pleaded that the North not "taunt or reproach" the South. As for secession, it could no more take place without apocalyptic destruction than "the heavenly bodies [could] rush from their spheres . . . without causing the wreck of the universe."

Despite early favorable reactions to the pleas for compromise and conciliation, prospects for Clay's proposals dimmed. Backers of the compromise package tried putting the major components together in an **omnibus bill**; however, combined opposition to each measure doomed the entire bill. Moreover, Governor William H. Seward of New York suggested that "a higher law than the Constitution" was operating to end slavery. And President Taylor threatened to veto the compromise anyway. The logjam began to break in the summer of 1850. President Taylor, after becoming overheated during the daylong Fourth of July celebration at the still unfinished Washington Monument, consumed huge amounts of vegetables and cold milk and died five days later of acute intestinal inflammation. The new president, Millard Fillmore, backed the compromise. When the despondent and ailing Clay retired from Washington to recuperate, young Stephen A. Douglas led an effort to divide the omnibus bill into its constituent parts, where a series of majorities could be assembled to pass each measure separately.

In its final form, the **Compromise of 1850** admitted California as a free state and organized two territories, New Mexico and Utah, without commitment about slavery. A decision on slavery there would come later using a mechanism based on the principle of popular sovereignty. The slave trade (not slavery itself) would cease in the District of Columbia, and a **Fugitive Slave Act** would help slave owners recover runaway slaves. The Texas and New Mexico land dispute was settled in favor of New Mexico, with Texas receiving $10 million to help extinguish its public debt.

THINKING BACK

1. Who were the new Americans of the Mexican Cession? How were they like the Americans living east of the Great Plains, and how were they different?

2. What political issues arose with regard to the Mexican Cession, how did discovery of gold in California change the context of those issues, and how did the Compromise of 1850 attempt to resolve them?

CONCLUSION

Manifest Destiny evoked both Americans' highest aspirations and basest instincts. In the Far West, a nation committed to democracy and largely committed to Protestant Christian teachings regarding sin and redemption sought to spread a culture of freedom across the North American continent, braving personal suffering and even death to achieve what they believed was God's will. Yet, they no more than later generations of Americans and other nationalities could free themselves from the limits of their culture. Manifest Destiny for citizens of the United States certainly did not hold the same rewards as it did for Native Americans. Historians once rhapsodized about the westward expansion as though the fulfillment of continental nationhood was inevitable and altogether a good thing, but a **New Western History** shows us that it was actually the result of conquest, and that *Tejanos, Nuevo Mexicanos, and Californios* had little choice in the matter. Oregon came into the Union as a result of pioneer settlement backed by the threat of war.

Behind Manifest Destiny lurked the deeply divisive issue of slavery. Since the U.S.—Mexico War had been a common national effort, Southerners argued, they deserved their share of the rewards—slavery into the new territories that would ultimately become slave states. Most Northerners opposed extending slavery. The issue threatened to tear the nation apart. In 1850, many members of Congress hoped the often used method of compromise would once again resolve the slavery question. Time would tell.

SUGGESTED SOURCES FOR STUDENTS

Richard L. Bushman, *Joseph Smith: Rough Stone Rolling* (2005), is a balanced, comprehensive, and scholarly biography of a man who has mostly provoked either condemnation or unjustified praise.

Christopher Corbett, *The Poker Bride: The First Chinese in the Wild West* (2009), uses the lives of a white saloon keeper and his Chinese bride to illuminate the lives of early Chinese immigrants.

Amy Greenberg, *A Wicked War: Polk, Clay, Lincoln, and the 1846 Invasion of Mexico* (2012), criticizes the U.S. war with Mexico, as did most Americans at the time.

For the experiences of men and women, including why they uprooted themselves in order to settle in the Far West and the difficult experience of getting there, see John Mack Faragher, *Women and Men on the Overland Trail* (1979).

Michael F. Holt explores in grand fashion the struggle of the Whig party over the slavery question in the 1840s, as well as the battle over the Compromise of 1850, in *The Rise and Fall of the American Whig Party* (1999).

An excellent overview of the 1840s along with careful and detailed analysis appears in Daniel Walker Howe, *What God Hath Wrought* (2007).

And Reginald Horsman, *Race and Manifest Destiny: The Origins of American Racial Anglo-Saxonism* (1981), emphasizes race as a rationale for conquering Mexican territory.

Patricia Nelson Limerick, who launched the New Western History, offers an unvarnished look at the Far West in *The Legacy of Conquest: The Unbroken Past of the American West* (1987).

James M. McCaffrey presents the U.S.—Mexico War from the perspective of the combatants in *Army of Manifest Destiny: The American Soldier in the Mexican War, 1846-1848* (1992).

Frederick Merk, *Manifest Destiny and Mission in American History, A Reinterpretation* (1963, new edition 1995), explained some of the other motives behind Manifest Destiny, particularly the expansion of Southern slavery.

Andrés Reséndez presents the Texas Revolution as a transnational event in *Changing National Identities at the Frontier* (2005).

The old standard treatment of American expansionism is Albert K. Weinberg, *Manifest Destiny, A Study of Nationalist Expansionism in American History* (1935). Weinberg equated Manifest Destiny with progress, an outdated notion today; however, the book is still useful for the information it contains.

BEFORE WE GO ON

1. The impression persists that in the Far West, government has played a limited role in people's lives. What evidence do you see that such a notion was either true or untrue?

2. Recently, historians have begun to look at history in transnational terms, maintaining that many developments can be understood only by going beyond national boundaries. How can "Manifest Destiny" be better understood by such a transnational approach?

Building a Democratic Nation

3. How did Native Americans fare in the wake of United States expansion westward?

4. How did *Tejanos, Nuevo Mexicanos, and Californios* respond to the concept of Manifest Destiny?

Connections

5. Did the United States become more or less democratic as a result of Manifest Destiny? Explain.

6. What sources of the border issues that confront the United States and Mexico today do you find in the annexation of Texas and the outcome of the U.S.—Mexico War in the 1840s?

Chapter 14

THE UNION IN CRISIS, 1850–1861

A PERSONAL PERSPECTIVE: FOCUS ON MARGARET GARNER

Courtesy of Library of Congress

Illustration from Harper's Weekly, May 1867, showing Margaret Garner, two of her children lying on the floor, and the four white men who had pursued her. The caption compares Garner to the character Medea from Greek folklore who murders her two children.

> **Why did Margaret Garner murder her young child?**

Margaret Garner and her husband Robert were enslaved in Kentucky. Margaret was twenty-three, Robert a year younger. The Garners parented four children even though they lived on separate farms. Margaret was one of about a dozen enslaved people who resided at Maplewood, the prosperous hog and grain farm of prominent Boone County landowner Archibald Gaines. Margaret performed ordinary domestic tasks like grinding wheat and corn, carding and spinning wool, cooking, and nursing the children of the master and mistress. Robert belonged to another owner in the vicinity and labored as a farm hand. In many respects, the lives of this African-American family paralleled those of thousands of enslaved Kentuckians—hard-working parents trying to raise and protect their children in a society that despised them. There was also the telltale, and all too common, sign of the Southern white male's sexual hegemony over enslaved women—the extraordinarily light skin of three of Margaret's children, including two-year-old

Mary, who was "almost white" and very likely Archibald Gaines's child. Soon, however, the Garners' ordinary wretchedness turned singularly dramatic and tragic as they made a desperate dash for freedom.

The Garners knew about the Underground Railroad—a network of compassionate white people and kindred blacks who helped enslaved people escape to freedom in the North. Margaret and Robert had both been to Cincinnati before and had seen African Americans who were free, some of them escapees living under the protection of the state's **"personal liberty"** law. In 1852, Cincinnati abolitionist Harriet Beecher Stowe had published a blockbuster novel, *Uncle Tom's Cabin*, in which she told about an enslaved mother named Eliza who darted for freedom across the half-frozen Ohio River with her infant in her arms. On Sunday, January 26, 1856, ice on the Ohio River was several inches thick. Robert had stolen two horses, a sleigh, and a six-shooter from his master. That night, the Garners, Robert's father Simon, his mother Mary, and eleven others made their way to the river. A steady snowfall muffled their sounds and kept neighborhood dogs from alerting whites. At dawn, they crossed the river on foot and entered Cincinnati just as the local citizenry began filling the streets. The band broke up to avoid calling attention to themselves, and Margaret and Robert sought out Margaret's uncle Joe and cousin Elijah Kite. The two men, both formerly enslaved, lived in Cincinnati and had connections with the **Underground Railroad**.

According to a plan worked out in advance, the Kites would take them to Levi Coffin, a conductor on the Underground Railroad who would "punch their ticket" through to Canada. The Garners could not relax, for the federal Fugitive Slave Act, part of the Compromise of 1850, helped slave owners recover runaways. In the first year and a half of the law's existence, authorities returned eighty-four fugitives and released only five. Cincinnati was polarized on the slavery question—the nation in microcosm. Many whites, like governor Salmon P. Chase, were active in

1850	1851	1852
Congress makes the Fugitive Slave Act part of the Compromise of 1850; a federal land grant to the Illinois Central Railroad sets a precedent for government aid to railroads	Narciso Lopez leads filibustering expedition to Cuba; Edward Gorsuch, a Maryland slave owner, is killed attempting to retrieve a runaway slave in Pennsylvania; *Uncle Tom's Cabin* appears in serial form; Fort Laramie Treaty with Plains Indians guarantees safety of passing wagon trains	Franklin Pierce elected president of the United States

antislavery Republican politics. Equally vocal pro-slavery Democrats and Irish immigrants felt hostility toward African Americans.

As the Garners made their way to the Kites' cabin, an infuriated Archibald Gaines stormed into Cincinnati and alerted local authorities. On a hunch, or perhaps by following the Garners' tracks in the snow, Gaines and a posse surrounded the Kite house as the fugitives finished breakfast. The deputies called for the Garners to surrender and battered the cabin door open when they refused. Amid shouts, screams, general pandemonium, Robert fired his pistol and wounded a deputy. Then, in one helter-skelter moment, Margaret grabbed a butcher knife and slit her little two-year-old daughter Mary's throat, nearly decapitating her. She slashed away at her two sons and bashed her infant's head with a coal shovel. But before she could actually kill them, the posse subdued her. After her arrest, Margaret confessed "that her determination was to have killed all the children and then destroy herself rather than return to slavery" and the "cruel treatment" of her master.

Astonishingly, the state of Ohio never tried Margaret Garner for homicide. Archibald Gaines' property rights and the federal Fugitive Slave Act took precedence over Ohio's murder statute. And Margaret Garner became a *cause célèbre* among opponents of slavery and the object of vilification by pro-slavery racists. That horrifying moment of Margaret's infanticide spotlighted slavery's pathological evil. Abolitionists pointed out that slavery had driven this desperate mother to slay her helpless child. Abolitionists especially hated the fact that the slave laws of Kentucky extended to the free state of Ohio. Pro-slavery Southerners refused to take responsibility for Margaret's behavior. Abolitionists, they said, provoked runaways, thereby subverting the Constitutional protection of property rights that safeguarded liberty.

Surrounded by angry and armed crowds that threatened to ignite a civil war, a federal commissioner, as provided by the Fugitive Slave Act, heard arguments about whether Margaret Garner and her family should be returned to their Kentucky masters. Under the Fugitive Slave Act, Margaret and Robert could not testify, nor were they entitled to a jury trial. But Margaret's lawyer, John Tolliffe, argued that she and Robert not be returned to slavery because they had previously been to Cincinnati and from that time had been technically free. Archibald Gaines denied that the two had ever been out of Kentucky, and the special federal commissioner, whose ruling could not be reversed, ordered Margaret and her family returned to their masters.

During the 1850s, uncompromising moral certitude and confrontational strategies replaced conciliation and compromise as the governing principles in dealing with the vexing issue of slavery. Extremism, both self-serving and altruistic, led directly to secession and the Civil War. The plight of Margaret Garner and hundreds of other fugitive slaves caused support for the Compromise of 1850 to evaporate. Congress had not intended the compromise to apply to territories besides those acquired from Mexico in 1848, and with "Young Americans" keeping the spirit of Manifest Destiny alive, the question of slavery in other territories was bound to surface. Indeed, the Kansas-Nebraska Act and the controversial case of another slave who had been to free soil, Dred Scott, sparked a firestorm that led directly to disunion. "We live in revolutionary times," wrote a Northern proponent of free soil at the close of the decade, "& I say God bless the revolution." That statement could just as easily have come from the pen of a pro-slavery Southern extremist ("fire-eater"), or the lips of Margaret Garner.

THINKING BACK

1. What drove Margaret Garner to murder her young child?
2. What does this episode reveal about slavery and about public opinion, particularly regarding the Fugitive Slave Law?

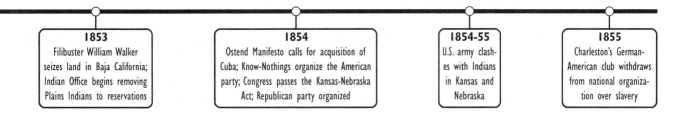

1853	1854	1854-55	1855
Filibuster William Walker seizes land in Baja California; Indian Office begins removing Plains Indians to reservations	Ostend Manifesto calls for acquisition of Cuba; Know-Nothings organize the American party; Congress passes the Kansas-Nebraska Act; Republican party organized	U.S. army clashes with Indians in Kansas and Nebraska	Charleston's German-American club withdraws from national organization over slavery

AMERICA AT MID-CENTURY: FLUSH TIMES TO FRAGMENTATION

In 1850, the United States stood unsteadily at the threshold of greatness. Over the preceding half-century, the country's population grew to 23 million and at a rate six times faster than the world average. Although partly attributable to natural increase, this explosion came mostly from the steady stream of new arrivals from distant shores. Population growth went hand-in-hand with economic expansion. Stimulated by the opening of new land for farming, the Transportation Revolution, a growing labor supply, and the infusion of California gold, the Gross Domestic Product (the total value of goods and services) doubled every fifteen years over the first half of the century, creating more agricultural and industrial jobs, greater incomes for farmers, laborers, and business-owners, and longer and healthier lives. Differences between the economic structures of North and South, however, widened the gap between those two sections and threatened national integrity. In the North, where 60 percent of the workforce toiled in industry, republicanism meant free, wage-labor, while in the South, it translated into property rights—particularly in the form of slaves. The **Fugitive Slave Act**, and the plight of people like Margaret Garner, evoked moral outrage in the North even as Southern slave owners acclaimed it as a valid protection of their constitutional rights. As tension mounted, the time-tested strategy of harmonizing sectional interests gave way to entrenchment and confrontation.

Young America

The battle over slavery in the territory recently acquired from Mexico (the **Mexican Cession**) had an important impact on the spirit of Manifest Destiny. It made expansionism a divisive rather than a unifying policy by equating it to slavery expansion. Most of the energy for acquiring new territory now came from the South. Slave owners constituted a distinct minority in the country, but they enjoyed exceptional power because of the "three-fifths rule." Not particularly optimistic about the prospects for establishing slavery in what remained of the Western territories, slave owners looked south of the border, where slavery already existed or might be reestablished.

Youthful, aggressive Democrats, many of them from the South and calling themselves **Young Americans**, persisted in the pursuit of foreign territory. They drew new inspiration from the 1848 liberal and nationalist revolutions in Europe (see The Global Perspective). Flushed with patriotic zeal and romantic spirit, they also embraced technology and the market economy, dismissing "old fogy" Jacksonians and their fearful opposition to expanding capitalism. Thus, Young Americans grafted business enterprise onto the nationalistic ideology of territorial expansionism. Stephen A. Douglas of Illinois emerged as **Young America**'s most dynamic spokesman, but Southern slave owners wholeheartedly backed expansionism. *De Bow's Review* proclaimed that "we have a destiny to perform ...all over Mexico, over South America, over the West Indies." Swashbuckling **filibusters** (a term derived from a Spanish word meaning "free-booty" or "pirate" and applied to small, private armies that often functioned as mercenary soldiers) carried the banner of Young America into foreign lands. With the tacit support of Democratic administrations, and usually with Southern financial backing, filibusters raised private armies to invade neighboring countries.

> **Who were "Young Americans," and what did they stand for?**

Cuba was the most inviting target for expansion, lying just ninety miles from the southern tip of Florida. If Cuba, with its half a million slaves, could be reeled into the Union, it would add two senators and several representatives to the slave states' representation in Congress. "Cuba must be ours," exclaimed Senator Jefferson Davis of Mississippi. In the 1840s, President James K. Polk had considered paying as much as $100 million for Cuba, but the Spanish foreign minister had spurned the offer, remarking that he would just as soon see the island sunk into the ocean. Attempts to ignite a revolution in Cuba, like the ones that had resulted in annexing Texas and California,

---

1856
Margaret Garner flees to freedom; William Walker seizes power in Nicaragua; "border ruffians" sack Lawrence followed by Pottawatomie Massacre; Preston-Brooks canes Charles Sumner; James Buchanan elected president of the United States

1857
Supreme Court ruling in *Dred Scott* case; railroad completed from Baltimore to St. Louis; Lecompton constitution drafted; Mountain Meadows Massacre in Utah, followed by Mormon War.

1858
Lecompton constitution rejected by Congress; Lincoln-Douglas debates

Cuban tobacco plantation. Cuba was attractive to planters in the American South as a potential slave state.

met stiff opposition, both from Spanish authorities in Cuba and the Whig administration of Zachary Taylor in Washington. Southerners persisted, though, and in 1851 they backed an invasion led by a Cuban exile named Narciso Lopez. When the filibuster ended in defeat and with the public executions of Lopez and fifty Americans in Cuba, rioters in New Orleans sacked the Spanish consulate and Spanish-owned shops. "Our brethren must be avenged!" declared one belligerent New Orleans newspaper. "Cuba must be seized!"

The spirit of Young America aroused not only patriotic feelings but also passions concerning the issue of slavery in the territories. The presidential election of 1852 would test the healing effect of the Compromise of 1850.

The Election of 1852

As the presidential election of 1852 approached, however, leaders of both major parties side-stepped the volatile issues of slavery and expansion into Cuba. Whigs had trouble finding a candidate acceptable to Northern and Southern wings of the party. Northern "Conscience" Whigs objected to the incumbent Millard Fillmore, whom they regarded as too conciliatory toward the South, and not until the fifty-second ballot did the nominating convention settle on General Winfield Scott, another Mexican War hero. Scott was a Virginian by birth; however, he owned no slaves and was mostly apolitical. The Democrats, experiencing the same kind of sectional tension as the Whigs, adopted a different tactic. They nominated Franklin Pierce, a good-natured former senator from New Hampshire and a Mexican War veteran himself. Pierce was not widely known, having failed to distinguish himself either in combat or the hallowed halls of Congress, but neither did he have many enemies. His greatest appeal was that he sympathized with the South. Whig detractors branded him a "**doughface**," a derogatory term

> **How did the major parties try to avoid the controversial slavery issue?**

1859
South Carolina legislature considers bill to enslave all free African Americans; John Brown raid on Harpers Ferry

1860
Abraham Lincoln elected president of the United States; South Carolina secedes from the Union

applied to Northern politicians who had Southern sympathies.

In order to avoid the quicksand of slavery, both candidates ran on platforms that reprised the issues and the rhetoric of the 1830s, when "special privilege" had battled "King Andrew" Jackson. The Whigs called for protective tariffs and internal improvements while the Democrats demanded free trade and states' rights. Democrats condemned Scott as "an old-fashioned federalist" who would "clothe the national government with dangerous powers." On a matter of growing importance, they accused Scott of hostility toward immigrants—a charge that fit many bourgeois Protestant Whigs. For their part, Whigs dismissed Pierce as a second-rate party hack and blasted the anti-entrepreneurial Democratic party for renouncing "all the essential powers of the Constitution."

In the end, the Whigs could not straddle the Mason-Dixon line. Like a magnet, the Free-Soil party (whose candidate was the unknown John P. Hale of New Hampshire) attracted Yankee "Conscience" Whigs away from Scott, while many Southern "Cotton" Whigs, remembering Zachary Taylor's disloyalty during the debate over slavery in the Mexican Cession, stayed home rather than vote. The election was a yawner; Pierce won by a landslide in the Electoral College (254 to 42). His popular vote, however, registered only a slight majority (50.9 percent to 44.1 percent for Scott and 5 percent for Hale).

Democrats were now in a position to pursue the goals of Manifest Destiny. Cuba was a primary attraction for the Pierce administration while others looked to Mexico and beyond.

Expansion Into Latin America

> **How did the United States attempt to acquire Cuba and other Latin American territories, and what was the outcome?**

President Pierce sought to capitalize on the Young America spirit in order to steer attention away from potentially troublesome domestic matters. Unfortunately, his main objective, Cuba, sparked a wildfire of sectional controversy. In 1854, Pierce's minister to Spain, Pierre Soulé of Louisiana, carried an offer of $130 million (equivalent to $3.7 billion today) to purchase Cuba. In Ostend, Belgium, Soulé consulted with two other United States diplomats, James Buchanan of Pennsylvania and James Mason of Virginia, and the three penned a dispatch declaring that "Cuba is as

necessary to the North American republic as any of its present ... states." Possession of the island, they argued, would not only provide the South with another slave state but also prevent a slave rebellion in Cuba and another African-American republic like Haiti in the Caribbean. When this **Ostend Manifesto** appeared in the press, angry protests forced Pierce to repudiate it.

Although President Pierce had failed to acquire Cuba, his efforts inspired filibusters, of whom William Walker was hands down the most notable. Raised in Tennessee and trained in medicine and the law, Walker craved excitement. In its pursuit, he joined the California gold rush, settling in booming San Francisco. An ardent expansionist and a tireless schemer, Walker concocted a plan to seize Baja, California and Sonora from hapless Mexico and turn them over to the United States. In 1853, he landed in La Paz, the peaceful capital of Baja, with an assortment of vagrants and adventurers whom he styled a "liberation" army. After proclaiming the Republic of Lower California, Walker imposed the pro-slavery laws of Louisiana. He failed to look after his troops, however, and insufficient supplies led to desertions and the escapade's collapse. Walker returned to California, where a sympathetic jury acquitted him of charges of violating the federal neutrality law.

Despite the Mexican fiasco, filibustering had entered William Walker's blood. In 1854, as federal authorities winked their assent, he recruited 2,000 men for an expedition to Nicaragua, where he joined rebels in a civil war. In 1856, Walker took over the presidency and opened the country to slavery, drawing rousing applause from Southerners. But his grip on power was tenuous, and not even the arrival of reinforcements from New Orleans could prevent factions from overthrowing him. In 1857, he fled the country, but Southerners continued to egg him on. After two aborted tries he launched another expedition, this time to Honduras. In 1860, Walker's romantic career ended in front of a Honduran firing squad.

A majority of Americans still supported expansionism in principle; only now, sectional perspectives predominated over national ones, and the implications were deeply divisive. Similarly, the economic boom that once boosted nationalism now contributed to more sectional tension.

Railroads and Rising Sectionalism

If anything could bind the nation together symbolically as well as concretely it was railroads. The achievement of continental status pointed more directly than ever before to the importance of speedy and reliable transportation to link the population centers of the East with the rapidly developing West. The impetus for railroad construction, however, came more from sectional than national considerations and actually intensified sectional competition.

During the 1850s, railroad construction jumped significantly. At the beginning of the decade, the country had 9,000 miles of iron rails; by 1860, that had tripled to 30,000—four and a half times the mileage of Great Britain and eight times that of France. Even Oregon got in on the act with railroad projects linking the upper Columbia River basin to Portland. Private railroad companies tackled most of the building projects in the country, selling stock to investors to generate necessary capital. However, in the cash-starved Midwest, liberal assistance from state and federal governments subsidized the work. Although Whigs were the primary backers of government aid, Illinois' Democratic senator Stephen A. Douglas also got behind federal land grants. These grants provided not only right-of-way for laying track and sites for stations and maintenance facilities but also choice tracts near the rail lines that homesteaders would eagerly purchase. Douglas particularly favored grants to foster railroad construction in western areas. In 1850, he backed a federal grant to the Illinois Central Railroad that provided six acres of land for each mile of track. That measure established a pattern for federal government support for railroad building that lasted through the nineteenth century.

Instead of cultivating national unity, however, railroads isolated the South economically and socially. Not that the South refused to engage in railroad building; to the contrary, during the 1850s, the slave states quadrupled railroad mileage as planters settled in remote, interior areas that had no access to navigable rivers. However, Southern rail lines ran mostly from the Upper South to the Gulf Coast, linking Louisville, Memphis, and New Orleans. No railroads ran from Arkansas or Texas to the Southeast. And importantly, Southern railroads did not connect with Northern lines. No national standard for track gauge existed as yet, so railroad builders laid rails at whatever distance apart suited local needs, and travelers and shippers had to switch trains if they moved from one intermediate destination to another. In other words, Southern railroads were not plugged into the developing national rail network. Despite Southern efforts to catch up with the North in railroad construction, the South lagged significantly behind. Southern investment capital remained locked into land and slaves in order to capitalize on an expanding cotton market and rising prices in the 1850s.

In the North, trunk lines linked the wheat fields of the Midwest with the urban market places and manufacturing centers of the East. In 1857, the year after the ordeal of Margaret Garner's flight for freedom, Cincinnati celebrated the opening of the Ohio and Mississippi Railroad, which completed a 900-mile trunk line from Baltimore to St. Louis. By 1860, Chicago had become the bustling railroad hub for a dozen lines that brought farm produce into the city for distribution to the Northeast. Improvements in efficiency dropped shipping costs for Midwestern farmers dramatically, shrinking the price differentials between Midwestern suppliers and Northeastern consumers. During the decade, the difference between wholesale pork prices in the slaughter houses of Cincinnati and markets in New York City shrank from $9.53 to $1.18 per barrel. Food now cost nearly the same in the kitchens of Northeastern homes and restaurants as on Midwestern farms hundreds of miles away. This boosted the economies and populations of both areas.

Thus, the impact of railroad development was not uniform in all sections of the country. The Northeast and Midwest benefited more than the South. Midwestern commerce, which in the past had moved slowly south along the Ohio and Mississippi rivers to New Orleans, now sped rapidly eastward along corridors formed by railroads and freighters plying the Great Lakes. As economic ties between the Northeast and Midwest strengthened, so too did the social and political connections. People came in contact with each other and formed friendships and alliances. Meanwhile, Southerners were left out of this developing pattern and, as a consequence, felt increasingly alienated and vulnerable.

Railroads constituted one of the most powerful forces forging national unity in the nineteenth century. Yet, they also reinforced sectional divisions. But sectional conflict was not the only source of dissension in the country; differences in class and ethnicity also splintered the country into multiple identities.

Nativists Lash Out Against Immigration

Why did native-born Americans resent the rising tide of immigration, and what did they attempt to do about it?

During the 1840s and 1850s, the stream of immigrants produced deep strains in the American population. Poor foreigners competed with native-born workers for jobs and housing in crowded cities. Often heavy drinkers, the Irish immigrants were thought to be contributors to zooming crime rates and welfare costs, as in Cincinnati, for example, where crime tripled coincident with the rise in immigration. Irish and German Catholics annoyed the native Protestant majority. Reacting to the European revolutions of 1848, the Roman Catholic Church hierarchy became the hardened enemy of social reform. And in 1850, Archbishop John Hughes of New York, in a highly publicized message, proclaimed that the church's mission was "to convert the world—including the inhabitants of the United States" and every official of the government—to the Catholic faith and subservience to Rome.

In the Far West, refugees from over-populated China, torn by the anti-foreign Taiping Rebellion (see the Global Perspective p. 392), sought their fortunes on California's Mountain of Gold. In 1852, as many as 20,000 Chinese immigrants arrived in San Francisco, most making their way to the gold diggings. Their clannishness, distinctive clothing and food preferences, and willingness to work harder and for less pay than citizens of the United States caused native-born Americans to resent them. Most of the relatively small number of Chinese women were indentured as prostitutes in West Coast boom towns. That fact, plus the widespread but exaggerated association of Chinese with opium led native-born Americans, including Hispanics, to see them as threats to moral values. Prejudice often turned into violence directed at the Chinese.

Once the immigrants obtained voting rights, their partisan affiliations influenced how native-born Americans responded to them. The Irish tended to affiliate with the Democrats, a party that embraced working people and tolerated their fondness for beer. Germans, fewer in number, more stand-offish, and generally antislavery, gravitated to the Whig party. Thus, anti-immigrant, anti-Catholic, and anti-liquor sentiment whiplashed the political party system. Skilled, blue-collar workers, Protestants, and temperance advocates spoke out most vocally against the rising tide of immigration. In time, these "nativists" formed organizations such as the Order of United Americans and the Order of the Star Spangled Banner, to give voice to their feelings. They promoted patriotism and Protestant values, but usually shrouded their activities in secrecy. Members, estimated to have been as many as 1 million, pledged to vote only for native-born candidates for public office, and to answer "I know nothing" to any inquiries from outsiders. Thus, they became known as "**Know-Nothings**."

In 1854, Know-Nothings organized the **American party**, with a concrete, anti-immigrant platform based on ethnic prejudices. For instance, the party sought to minimize the influence of immigrant voting by lengthening the residency requirement for citizenship and voting rights. The American party achieved its greatest measure of political success in state elections, particularly in Massachusetts, where the reaction against a heavy Irish Catholic immigrant population resulted in the election of American party candidates in the gubernatorial, state senate, and congressional elections. Indeed, the American party controlled the state's government. Most of the party's support came from Northern Whigs.

By 1855, as nativism spread across the country, the American party stood poised to replace the crumbling Whig party in the country's two-party political system. The Compromise of 1850 had seriously weakened the cohesion of the Whig party. The part of the compromise that Northern Whigs found most galling was the Fugitive Slave Act.

The Compromise of 1850 Falls Apart

Although the Compromise of 1850 had unified the moderate majority of the country, it did little if anything to mollify the diehards on either side of the

What caused the spirit of compromise to evaporate?

slavery question. Only three of 60 South Carolina and Mississippi congressmen had voted for California statehood, which they called a "sellout" and a "defeat." Conversely, just 37 of 261 Northern Conscience Whigs had voted for the Fugitive Slave Act, which they called "immoral" and unconscionable. The **Fugitive Slave Act** had made the Compromise of 1850 possible by heading off Southern secession, but by the mid-1850s it had become the component that caused the spirit of compromise to disappear.

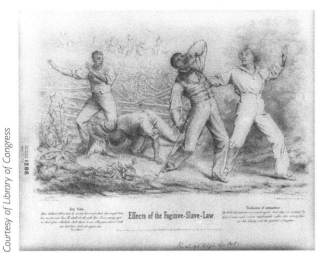

An antislavery print condemning the Fugitive Slave Act. The drawing shows African Americans, perhaps free persons, being attacked and apprehended by a posse of white slave hunters. Below are two quotes, one from Deuteronomy and the other from the Declaration of Independence, that establish a moral basis for resisting the law.

For years, runaway slaves had threatened the stability of the plantation workforce. The Constitution and a federal fugitive slave law enacted in 1793 authorized slave owners to recover runaway slaves, but success depended on local enforcement—a serious weakness in the law. The Northern free states not only refused to cooperate with Southern planters but also enacted countervailing "personal liberty" laws that blocked efforts to recover fugitives. The Supreme Court of the United States had opened the way for these laws in *Prigg v. Pennsylvania* (1842). The financial losses sustained through runaways were significant (perhaps 1,000 slaves escaped each year, mostly from the Upper South), but more than that, Southern slave owners believed that the federal government ignored their rights. "Although the loss of property is felt," explained Virginia planter James Mason, who sponsored the Fugitive Slave Act of 1850, "the loss of honor is felt still more."

The Fugitive Slave Act shifted the threat of loss away from the slave owners and onto the runaways themselves. A slave owner, like Archibald Gaines, could sign an affidavit stating that an African American (like Margaret or Robert Garner) was a fugitive and a special federal commissioner would hand over the fugitive—no jury trial, no appeal. The commissioner received ten dollars for every fugitive he returned to slavery and five dollars for every one he set free. Ninety percent of the 332 alleged fugitives brought to trial under the law were returned to the South as a result of what abolitionists regarded as legalized bribery.

The Fugitive Slave Act outraged antislavery Northerners. It set up an open season for slave catchers to hunt legally free African Americans as well. The law required Northerners to serve on slave-catching posses or risk a $1,000 fine. Because it enjoined the free states to respect slave laws, and even to enforce them by helping masters recover enslaved people, antislavery Northerners defied the law. In 1851, Edward Gorsuch, a Maryland slave owner, and his son sought to retrieve two runaways from the Quaker community of Christiana, Pennsylvania, a well-known stop on the Underground Railroad. Local African Americans, armed and organized as a vigilance committee, protected the runaways in a house. When the Gorsuches approached the hideaway, a hail of bullets killed Edward and severely wounded his son. Whites then sped the fugitives on their way to Canada. In all, forty-five residents of Christiana were arrested, including a local Quaker charged with treason. Nobody was convicted.

Resistance did not always succeed, as in the Margaret Garner case, but even the failures galvanized Northern antislavery feeling, sometimes even more than the successes. In 1854, authorities in Boston apprehended Anthony Burns, a Virginia fugitive, and held him for extradition. President Franklin Pierce, bending over backward to placate Southerners, ordered the employment of all means necessary "to enforce the law." Angry abolitionists stormed the jail in an attempt to rescue Burns. In the ensuing gunfire, a deputy was fatally shot, but Burns remained incarcerated. A company of federal troops marched Burns through streets lined with protesters waving flags turned upside down to an awaiting naval vessel for transportation back to Virginia. It had cost the federal government $100,000 to return a single fugitive slave. Industrialist Amos Lawrence testified that he and others went to bed before the Anthony Burns extradition as conservative "Union Whigs" and awakened as "stark mad Abolitionists."

The determination of Southerners to force the government to recognize their constitutional right to slave property and the bitter Northern reaction illustrated the deep rift that had developed between South and North. The spirit of compromise that had sealed the truce of 1850 was evaporating in the cauldron of sectional controversy. The conflict transcended slavery per se; North and South were becoming separate nations.

Undoing the Bonds of Nationhood

Nothing tormented antislavery Northerners more than fugitive slaves risking their lives for freedom and being thwarted by a republic whose history contained Patrick Henry demanding liberty or death during the Revolution. The reality of the fugitives' plight was moving enough, but in the hands of powerful polemicists writing in the sentimental genre of the Romantic era, their dramas were overwhelming. In the 1850s, accounts of enslaved people's daring escapes proliferated in the North, including a new edition of Frederick Douglass's inspiring autobiography with its description of his flight from enslavement in Maryland. Their premise was the moral superiority of Northern society and culture. With equal doses of emotion, Southerners sought to counteract the dishonor that sensationalized accounts of slavery attached to the South. Through the decade, the bonds of nationhood weakened under the powerful strains of sectionalism, and some snapped.

> **How did popular culture excite and reflect growing sectional animosity?**

In June of 1851, the first installment of Harriet Beecher Stowe's *Uncle Tom's Cabin, or, Life Among the Lowly* hit the streets in an antislavery weekly newspaper. It became an instant sensation, and in 1852 the book version sold 300,000 copies. Stowe's father, Lyman Beecher, had been the most famous and influential evangelist-theologian of his day, and instantly his daughter became the most famous and influential author of hers. Growing up in Cincinnati, she had felt the intensity of local abolitionism and witnessed the dramatic escapes of enslaved people from plantations across the river in Kentucky, near where Margaret and Robert Garner lived. Her marriage to Calvin Stowe, an abolitionist professor at Bowdoin College in Maine, and the responsibility of rearing seven children left her little spare time; however, during the 1840s, she managed to publish a few short stories. Her outrage over the Fugitive Slave Act and the encouragement of her family to write about it led to the book that Abraham Lincoln reportedly said caused the Civil War. By then, over a million copies of Stowe's blockbuster circulated around the world in twenty languages.

Although Harriet Beecher Stowe had never been to the South, she brought the scenes of Southern slavery to life for her readers. Writing in terms of moral absolutes, she introduced the enslaved man Tom who forgave all those who abused him. She gave Eliza the indomitable courage to cross the half-frozen Ohio River with her child in her arms in a desperate bid for freedom, just as

Harriet Beecher Stowe, daughter of evangelist Lyman Beecher and sister of the writer and educator Catharine Beecher. Stowe published the serialized, antislavery novel Uncle Tom's Cabin in 1851.

Courtesy of Library of Congress

the real-life Margaret Garner did five years later. Stowe also showed how slavery corrupted even kind-hearted masters. "Ten thousand thanks," wrote the Northern poet John Greenleaf Whittier to Stowe for revealing the truth about the horrors of Southern slavery.

Southern readers did not appreciate Stowe's depiction of slavery. In fact, they condemned *Uncle Tom's Cabin* as outrageous slander and railed against this "vile wretch in petticoats." One reviewer pointed out that the only realistic white person in the story was the odious Simon Legree, a transplanted Yankee. Southern writers published their side of the story, painting a contrasting, more sympathetic picture of honorable, benevolent masters and loyal, contented slaves. An eccentric Virginian named George Fitzhugh drew sharp distinctions between paternalistic Southern society and the greedy North. In *Cannibals All!* he claimed that industrial capitalism devoured its workers, whereas enslaved Southerners and their masters lived in mutual dependency and harmony.

As American literature became decidedly sectional in nature, other historically national institutions also split along sectional lines. In 1844 Southern Baptists had withdrawn from their Northern co-religionists, followed a year later by the Methodists. And during the 1850s, the political parties splintered into fragments that drifted in and out of various sectional coalitions. Not a unified nation, but a deeply divided one emerged from the bitter debates over slavery and the Fugitive Slave Act.

THINKING BACK

1. What issues strained national unity and threatened the integrity of the Union?
2. How did the Young Americans hope to overcome sectional tension and promote national unity? Why did they not succeed?

THE LOCAL PERSPECTIVE: FOCUS ON SOUTH CAROLINA

> **Why did South Carolina become the hotbed of secession?**

By the 1850s, South Carolina had become the hotbed of Southern secessionism. From John C. Calhoun during the nullification controversy to a new generation of fire-eaters like Robert Barnwell Rhett, South Carolinians mounted the barricades in defense of slavery. In 1856, Congressman Preston Brooks added to the state's notoriety by caning Massachusetts abolitionist Charles Sumner on the floor of the United States Senate (see p. 444). The impression lingers that all whites in the Palmetto State were fanatics, but through the 1850s,

One of the fine homes that arguably made Charleston, South Carolina, the most beautiful city in the United States.

devotion to the Union among residents of the South Carolina upcountry remained strong. Much of the state's radicalism grew out of its vulnerability. Although once the center of Britain's North American empire, Charleston now anchored a collapsing Southern universe.

South Carolina's social structure and economy reveal much about its political culture. It was the most aristocratic state in the Union. The "Three-fifths" rule (where three-fifths of the slaves were counted as population) gave coastal rice and cotton planters and slave owners inordinate power. Beginning in the 1840s, their wealth reached spectacular levels, due to skyrocketing world cotton prices. Prosperity partly explains why, in 1850, radicals could not generate widespread support for independence. To take full advantage of the economic upswing, however, planters required enslaved laborers. South Carolina planters were prepared to go to whatever lengths necessary to defend slavery.

In the 1850s, storm clouds cast dark shadows over South Carolina's fiefdoms. For one thing, people were moving out of the state, reducing South Carolina's voting power in Congress. Out-migration had continued for several years. In 1834, the *Camden Journal* lamented that "the old and the young are preparing to emigrate, and the inquiry is not whether you are going, but when do you go." In 1820, South Carolina had been the most populous state in the Lower South and carried considerable clout in the region; however, by 1860 only frontier Florida, Arkansas, and Texas had fewer residents. Neighboring Georgia had grown six times faster. Planters abandoned the state's worn out land for unplowed and fertile places. Those who departed included the state's best and brightest. In 1854, five graduates of South Carolina College served as governors of other states. For proud South Carolinians, this decline in status was hard to swallow.

African Americans left the state too, although not by choice. During the first half of the century, as many as 179,000 enslaved South Carolinians emigrated with their masters. African Americans still constituted the majority of the state's population, making race an especially important issue there, but by the 1850s, the black majority was smaller than before. Wealth and slave ownership were directly correlated in antebellum South Carolina; most of the accumulated wealth in the state was in enslaved people, and the backbreaking labor they performed produced the valuable rice and cotton crops that supported the aristocracy's luxurious lifestyle. By 1860, almost one half of the state's white families owned enslaved people, and 20 percent of those owned twenty or more, almost twice the percentage in the slave states generally. South Carolina's ten richest districts were more than 60 percent black, and two coastal counties, Beaufort and Georgetown, were over 80 percent black. The departure of enslaved African Americans represented a substantial decline in the state's wealth and ability to produce valuable crops.

Some of South Carolina's leaders, especially progressive journalists like Benjamin F. Perry, knew that an economy too heavily dependent on decaying agriculture had a dim future. Cotton prices were unpredictable. Entrepreneurs tried unsuccessfully to crack the hard-shell agrarian-republican dogma that equated freedom with land. In 1856, a meeting of concerned planters agreed on the need to channel capital and other resources into manufacturing and railroad building, but as one participant put it: "Like the Christian religion, everybody agrees that it is good, but few endorse it." In 1849, Charleston jeweler and importer William Gregg had opened a huge cotton textile mill in Graniteville, but he could not hire enough workers to make the operation sufficiently profitable to start a trend. People refused to work in factories; furthermore, the presence of a white working class in a slave society might blur the important distinction between enslaved African Americans and free white people. This mentality stifled enterprise in the state and contributed to an agrarian culture that set South Carolina apart from the democratic capitalist societies of the North.

But if the state as a whole suffered from self-doubt, most of Charleston's 40,000 residents exuded confidence. The city's grandeur, with its Classical Revival public architecture, lovely, fragrant gardens, and charming homes situated end-wise along a stretch of waterfront called "The Battery," pleased visitors. Beneath the graceful surface of elegant aristocracy, however, existed a world of working class men and women that resembled many grimy Northern cities. One striking difference was the absence of public schools—"a disgrace to an enlightened people" according to Governor James H. Hammond. Over 3,000 of Charleston's entrepreneurs, tradesmen, and laborers were unbound African Americans. Nearly three quarters of them were the offspring of mixed-race unions, and they constituted the city's dark-skinned elite that maintained its own churches, schools, and social clubs.

Charleston also contained one of the largest enclaves of German-Americans in the antebellum South. Uncommon among Southern communities, where nativism led to the Know-Nothing phenomenon, Charleston readily assimilated German American newcomers. Most were Protestant Lutherans rather than Catholics or Jews, which provoked a less negative reaction among native-born Charlestonians, and the immigrants readily embraced the city's rich cultural heritage. In 1855, when a national German-American social organization called the Turnverein passed a resolution against slavery, Charleston's local Turnverein club seceded from the national body. When the ultimate test of loyalty came in 1860, however, Charleston's German Americans overwhelmingly supported South Carolina's secession from the Union.

Considering South Carolina's high proportion of African Americans and its dependence on slavery, the almost hysterical white defense of slavery is not hard to comprehend. Anxiety also made white South Carolinians leery of free African Americans. By 1860, new restraints caused free African Americans' already-constricted world to tighten more closely around them. The state clamped down on manumissions, making it virtually impossible for enslaved people to become free without escaping. Whites simultaneously pressured free black people to leave the state. In 1859, the legislature even considered a bill to enslave all free persons of color. Passage of the measure failed, but many saw the handwriting on the wall. "It is plain now," said one free African American, "all must go."

By 1860, a vast majority of whites in South Carolina were ready to abandon the Union even if it meant doing so without the cooperation of other Southern states. John Brown's raid on Harpers Ferry, Virginia, (see pp. 449–50) and the election of an antislavery Republican, Abraham Lincoln, as president of the United States allowed the fire-eaters to prevail over the Unionists. From Charleston, the correspondent for the London *Times* newspaper reported: "There is nothing in all the dark caves of human passion so cruel and deadly as the hatred the South Carolinians profess for the Yankees."

THINKING BACK

1. Who were the political, economic, and social leaders of South Carolina?
2. Why was South Carolina ready to leave the Union by 1860?

THE HOUSE DIVIDES

As the Union's cohesion weakened, people increasingly responded to major issues from their slave-state or free-state points of view. Although slavery was not the only source of friction during the 1850s, it certainly was the overarching one. In 1854, Congress voted on a controversial bill intended to facilitate the construction of a transcontinental railroad. Earlier, such a project would have generated national excitement; now it splintered the national parties and divided the nation. From the wreckage of a political system that had been designed to conciliate opposing sectional interests emerged one that encouraged militant confrontation. As a preview of the onrushing national crisis, a bloody civil war erupted in Kansas. Vicious clashes also broke out between whites and Indians in Kansas and neighboring Nebraska. Symbolizing the way Americans regarded each other across free-state/slave-state boundaries, Kentucky slave owner Archibald Gaines horsewhipped his arch-enemy John Jolliffe, the Cincinnati attorney who defended Margaret Garner. The presidential election of 1856 demonstrated that the South depended on Northern "doughface" presidents to protect its peculiar slavery institution, an unsettling realization.

Senator Stephen Douglas of Illinois

Courtesy of Library of Congress

"A Hell of a Storm"

"How are we to develop, cherish and protect our immense interest and possessions on the Pacific," asked Young American senator Stephen A. Douglas, "with a vast wilderness fifteen hundred miles in breadth, filled with hostile savages, and cutting off all communication?" In attempting to incorporate the Far West more fully into the economy of the United States, Douglas touched off an ugly chain of events that tore apart the divided Union and cast a pall over his presidential aspirations.

> **Why did Stephen Douglas want to organize a formal territorial government in Nebraska, why did Southerners object, and how did Douglas appease them?**

Stephen A. Douglas (called the "Little Giant" because of his diminutive stature, pugnacious personality, and prodigious energy) was eager for a railroad linking the East to the rapidly developing Pacific Coast. As a loyal Illinoisan, however, he also looked out for his home state. The Army Corps of Topographical Engineers had mapped several potential railroad routes, including a southern one from New Orleans through the relatively easy terrain, mild climate, and politically organized New Mexico Territory. Douglas favored a mid-continent railway that would connect with the web of iron rails radiating from Chicago. The main disadvantage of Douglas's route was that it passed through the unorganized Nebraska Territory, a remnant of the old Louisiana Purchase that Congress had permanently reserved for Indians. Before the railroad could go forward, this obstacle that had to be cleared away.

The federal government had already begun to help by negotiating transit agreements with the Plains Indians. In 1851, a treaty with representatives of the Lakota (Sioux), Cheyenne, Crow, Assiniboine, Mandan, and Arikara Indians at Fort Laramie pledged protection for passing wagon trains. Ex-mountain man Thomas "Broken Hand" Fitzpatrick, who negotiated the Fort Laramie Treaty, pointed out that the agreement would allow railroad trains to pass through too. Fitzpatrick saw as clearly as anyone the treaty's inevitable impact. "[A]t no distant day the whole country over which those Indians now roam must be peopled by another more enterprising race." As a matter of fact, at that very time the Office of Indian Affairs, which moved from the War Department over to the new Interior Department in 1849, was developing an Indian reservation policy. Officials could see no more expanses of vacant land for relocating Indians in the rapidly developing West, but small reservations in out-of-the-way places would hasten the Indians' "civilization" by forcing them to adapt to agriculture and educating them for citizenship. This, they believed, would prevent the final destruction of Indian societies.

The government began liquidating the Plains Indians' Nebraska land claims through new treaties. In 1853, well-intentioned Indian commissioner George W. Manypenny visited the Nebraska tribes, including the previously relocated Shawnees and native Otoes, Missouris, and Omahas, and persuaded them to exchange their larger landholdings for smaller reservations supported by government annuities to Indian families. The Indian Office encouraged Indian families to take from the reservations 160-acre allotments for farms. Congress appropriated money to help the Indians move to the reservations, supply them with farm tools, and build lumber and flour mills for them. The ultimate goal was to destroy Native American cultures and remake the Indians into farmer-citizens.

With the Indian obstacle to railroad construction across Nebraska being cleared away, Senator Douglas drafted a bill to establish a territorial government on the central Plains. The measure easily passed the House, where widespread support existed for railroads; however, it met stiff opposition from various factions in the Senate, including a powerful group of pro-slavery senators led by South Carolina's Andrew Butler and Missouri's David Atchison. These senators objected to Douglas's bill because Nebraska lay north of the 36° 30' Missouri Compromise line, meaning that slavery was forbidden there. Why should they support a bill that would create a free territory and eventually another free state? To break the logjam, Douglas agreed to repeal the Missouri Compromise line, opening the territory to slavery, and divide it into Kansas and Nebraska. Settlers would vote on whether they wanted slavery. Douglas favored local autonomy over congressional authority on the slavery question and hoped that Northerners and Southerners would accept Popular Sovereignty as a legitimate means for regulating slavery in the territories.

Douglas expected the Kansas-Nebraska bill to "raise a hell of a storm" in the North, and it did. Free-soil proponents exploded in expressions of wrath. Whigs especially regarded the Missouri Compromise as a sacred barrier against the advance of slavery. The morally soft concept of Popular Sovereignty was cer-

tainly no substitute for an uncompromising congressional ban on slavery. Summoning his considerable energy and remarkable political skills, the "Little Giant" managed to cobble together a majority in favor of the Kansas-Nebraska measure, and in May of 1854, it passed by a largely sectional vote. Both parties split down the middle, but the Whigs were more bitterly divided than the Democrats. Every Northern Whig voted "No" while two-thirds of the Southern Whigs voted "Yes." On the Democratic side, only five of the twenty-three Northerners broke party ranks to vote against Douglas's measure. President Franklin Pierce, who sought to appease the South, signed the Kansas-Nebraska bill into law. Shrieks of anger immediately rained down from the North, where citizens rebuked Douglas, the Southern Slave Power, and the "**dough-face**" Pierce for turning Kansas and Nebraska into a "dreary region of despotism, inhabited by masters and slaves."

The **Kansas-Nebraska Act** brought the country measurably closer to disunion by destroying the national two-party system. "The Whig party has been killed off effectually by that miserable Nebraska business," assessed a disgusted Connecticut senator. Once and for all, Northern Whigs parted ways with "Cotton" Whigs. Although most Northern Democrats had stayed in line, they paid a stiff price for their collaboration with the Slave Power, most of them losing their seats in the 1854 congressional elections. So, even though the Democrats remained fairly united, they were becoming a distinctly pro-Southern party. Douglas was severely wounded too by the flack from the Kansas-Nebraska Act. Northerners now regarded Popular Sovereignty as a smoke screen for the Southern Slave Power, and besides that, Douglas had failed to gain a railroad. Congress did not authorize its construction until after the start of the Civil War. All in all, Douglas's chances for the presidency were seriously diminished.

The Heyday of Sectional Parties

Fallout from the Kansas-Nebraska Act produced a new, sectional political party. From a fairly stable political system dominated by two national organizations, both balancing Southern and Northern points of view, the Kansas-Nebraska Act created a polarized political universe in which sectional coalitions advanced more localized values and interests.

> How did the Republican party come into being, and what did it stand for?

In 1854, various antislavery types gathered in Ripon, Wisconsin, to organize a new political party. Many Northern Whigs, members of the Free Soil party, and some antislavery Democrats rushed to join. They called themselves **Republicans** (suggesting that they advocated an ordered society based on personal freedom) and swore an oath to "free soil, free labor, and free men." Although Republicans trumpeted an antislavery message, they included both abolitionists who hoped to marshal political power to eliminate slavery and advocates of free-soil who cared primarily about keeping slavery out of the territories. Republican rhetoric emphasized the moral bankruptcy and economic backwardness of slavery, often attacking not only the institution but also the individuals who defended it. Unburdened by any obligation to gain Southern support, Republicans concentrated on winning elections in the Northern free states, where a majority of the people and electoral votes resided.

The strictly sectional Republican party soon dominated the political landscape of the Northern free states, but the Democrats retained strength in particular areas. For instance, in New York City, Boston, and other areas where Young Americans or Irish immigrants held sway, Democratic appeal remained strong. Stephen A. Douglas emerged as the most popular national political figure of the 1850s despite the Kansas-Nebraska fiasco, because of his emphasis on Western economic development. He was least appealing in the Upper North; however, Douglas Democrats were numerous in states like Indiana, Ohio, and Pennsylvania that bordered on slave states. So even though the Democratic party held itself together in the aftermath of the Kansas-Nebraska Act, it became more of a Southern foil to the new Republican party of the North.

Bitter Strife In "Bleeding Kansas"

The Kansas-Nebraska Act unleashed terrible forces in Kansas. Situated in the same latitude as the slave state of Missouri, Kansas seemed more suited to slavery than Nebraska, and thus it became a battleground for pro-slavery and antislavery partisans. William H. Seward of New York expressed the determination of Northern free-soil advocates to carry the battle for control of Kansas to the territory itself, "and God give the victory to the side which is stronger in numbers as it is in right." Southerners strapped on their armor to meet the challenge head-on.

Settlers who entered Kansas after the Kansas-Nebraska Act were the agents of anti- and pro-slavery interests elsewhere. They brought preconceived ideas about slavery with them into the territory instead of developing indigenous responses to it. Northern free-soil societies sponsored emigrants who sought to ensure that Kansas

> How and why did the battle over slavery in Kansas turn violent?

voted to ban slavery. During 1854 and 1855, the **New England Emigrant Aid Society** sponsored over 1,200 Kansas homesteaders, most of whom actually hailed from the Midwest. Similarly, Southerners backed pro-slavery emigrants, although few slave owners risked bringing their valuable human property into the troubled territory. Missouri slave owners, already hemmed in by the free states of Illinois and Iowa, were the most concerned about a free-soil Kansas. Runaways to free territory would bleed slavery to death in Missouri. Senator David R. Atchison characterized the battle for Kansas from the Missouri slave owners' perspective. "If we win we carry slavery to the Pacific Ocean, if we fail we lose Missouri, Arkansas, [and] Texas." Atchison's hyperbole reflected the urgency felt by pro-slavery Southerners generally.

No sooner had Franklin Pierce inscribed his signature on the Kansas-Nebraska Act than these converging streams of settlers into eastern Kansas sought to organize a territorial government. Popular Sovereignty assumed an honest, republican process; however, fraudulent elections produced two tainted governments. Pro-slavery settlers, bolstered by Missourians who stayed in Kansas only long enough to vote, reached the territory first. "Enter every election district in Kansas," one of their leaders exhorted, "and vote at the point of a Bowie knife or revolver." With nearly 5,000 phony votes, they elected a pro-slavery delegate to Congress and a legislature that promptly outlawed even the discussion of free soil. The antislavery minority established a rival government. Kansas thus had two governments but no law and order.

In May of 1856, the no-holds-barred struggle over Kansas exploded into a full-blown civil war. Missouri's belligerent David Atchison made no bones about what the pro-slavery faction needed to do: "shoot, burn & hang." On May 21, a gang of 800 hard-drinking "border ruffians" from Missouri, armed with rifles and cannons and deputized as a posse by a pro-slavery judge, rode into the free-soil town of Lawrence. Their purpose was to intimidate antislavery settlers and drive them from the territory. They burned the Free State hotel, wrecked local newspaper offices, and looted stores and shops. Fortunately, the only fatality was one of the raiders, who died when a burning building fell on him, but the antislavery press characterized the "sack of Lawrence" as a "massacre."

Retaliation from the antislavery settlers came swiftly. A militant, Bible-toting emigrant named John Brown swore revenge on all pro-slavery Kansans. Brown believed in an eye for an eye, and with four of his sons (he had twenty children altogether) and three other comrades armed with revolvers and razor-sharp swords, he set out to "strike terror in the hearts of the pro-slavery people." On the night of May 24–25, Brown's gang abducted five pro-slavery settlers, including James Doyle and two of his teenage sons, who lived along Pottawatomie Creek. None of the men had participated in the attack on Lawrence, or in any other act of violence against antislavery settlers; nevertheless, Brown and his men shot and hacked them to death. Such a level of lawlessness existed in "Bleeding Kansas" that no indictments followed the "Pottawatomie Massacre." Afterward, the ghastly violence escalated as bloodthirsty bushwackers on both sides took as many as 200 lives.

The crossfire caught Kansas and Nebraska Indians in the middle. The rush of settlers onto the well-watered, grassy prairies of eastern Kansas and the absence of any land surveys due to the general chaos cost the Indians their promised new homes. Moreover, as Indian Commissioner Manypenny reported, "they have been personally maltreated, their property stolen, their timber destroyed, their possessions encroached upon, and divers other wrongs and injuries done them." The result was deepening Indian hostility. Farther out on the Plains, Lakota and Cheyenne raiders took out their frustrations on emigrant wagon trains. In August of 1854, a Lakota Indian killed an emigrant's cow near Fort Laramie. A greenhorn lieutenant named John Grattan marched a detail of soldiers to a nearby village to punish the culprit. When the Indians failed to hand him over, the impetuous Gratten killed the chief. The enraged Lakotas then wiped out Grattan and his entire command. The next summer, the Army launched punitive attacks on a Lakota village in western Nebraska and a Cheyenne encampment in western Kansas. To protect emigrants, the government built more forts on the overland trails; however, travel across the Plains remained extremely dangerous until after the Civil War.

In some ways, the most shocking episode of violence following the Kansas-Nebraska Act occurred hundreds of miles to the east, in the stately chamber of the United States Senate. There, abolitionist senator Charles Sumner of Massachusetts nursed a fearful hatred of Southern Slave Power, particularly the individuals who were responsible for "The Crime Against Kansas." "My soul is wrung by this outrage," Sumner seethed, "& I shall pour it forth." For two solid days beginning on May 19, 1856, he assailed the "murderous robbers from Missouri," but he spewed his most hateful venom on South Carolina's aged senator Andrew Butler, who had been partly responsible for the Kansas-Nebraska Act. Sumner's personal remarks insulted Southerners. Butler's nephew Preston Brooks, a congressman from South Carolina, felt bound to defend his uncle's wounded honor. Two days after Sumner's speech, Brooks approached the senator, seated at his desk on the Senate floor, and beat him over the head with a stout wooden cane. Sumner's injuries required a long convalescence.

The **Sumner-Brooks** incident had brought lawmakers face to face with the passion that slavery aroused. The antislavery press was aghast. "Has it come to this?" asked William Cullen Bryant of the *New York Evening Post*. "Are we to be chastised as they chastise their slaves?" Southerners, however, feted and justified Brooks. The *Richmond Enquirer* noted that Northern abolitionists "have grown saucy, and dare to be impudent to gentlemen! . . . They must be lashed into submission."

Rancor had reached such a level in this age of passion that violence seemed an appropriate way to express anger and commitment to moral principle. For many Americans, physical force to uphold fundamental civic values was the *sine qua non* of moral citizenship. And if the nation's leaders lashed out violently against an immoral opponent, how was the rest of the country going to resist? "Bleeding Kansas" was certainly an ominous context in which to conduct a presidential election. The Republican party was prepared to wage an all-out crusade against slavery. What would the South do if the federal government fell into the hands of Republican abolitionists?

The Election of 1856

As the election of 1856 approached, both Know-Nothings and Republicans vied for the spot vacated by the defunct Whig party. The relative importance of nativism and antislavery would determine which one prevailed. As it turned out, a decline in immigration during the mid-1850s helped push anti-Catholicism into the background, and when Northern Know-Nothings walked out of the party's June nominating

What were the primary issues in the 1856 election, who won and why, and what did the election signify for the South?

convention after Southerners blocked a resolution condemning the Kansas-Nebraska Act, the party went into a precipitous decline. Southern Know-Nothings nominated Millard Fillmore; however, his campaign failed to catch fire.

The first tests for the Republicans were writing a platform that set forth its values and objectives and selecting a candidate to stand on it. Since antislavery appealed to everyone in the party, the platform writers condemned the Kansas-Nebraska Act, called for the admission of Kansas as a free state, and denounced the Ostend Manifesto, all presented in rousing rhetoric. But the platform also included standard Whig economic policies—promoting commerce and advocating government aid to railroads. Republicans carefully selected their candidate. William H. Seward, a former Whig of New York, and Salmon P. Chase, an ex-Democrat from Ohio, both high-profile abolitionists, had made enemies in their public careers. Seward seemed fanatical in referring to "a higher authority," and Chase, as governor, had dragged his feet when abolitionists urged him to block Margaret Garner's extradition to Kentucky. Republicans turned instead to the senator from California, John C. Fremont. The Pathfinder's antislavery record was impeccable. Besides, his connection with the old Jacksonian Thomas Hart Benton might win over a few Democrats, and his wife Jessie had shrewd political instincts that would assist his campaign.

Democrats faced the thorny task of uniting Northern and Southern wings of the party. Finding an acceptable candidate was especially difficult since the party required a two-thirds vote of convention delegates for nomination (a rule first adopted in 1844). The obsequious incumbent Franklin Pierce and the flamboyant, hard-drinking Stephen A. Douglas had crippled themselves by their roles in the Kansas-Nebraska episode. Antislavery Northerners objected to both of them. As an alternative, the party turned to the drab but inoffensive James Buchanan, a bachelor from Pennsylvania and another "doughface." He had been abroad since 1853 and avoided being tainted by the Kansas-Nebraska Act, although he had affixed his signature to the controversial Ostend Manifesto. Democrats extolled the virtue of Popular Sovereignty in dealing with the slavery question but spent most of their time, as they had in 1852, touting Jacksonian principles like states' rights, limited government, and opposition to a new national bank.

The heated election campaign spotlighted the deepening sectional nature of national politics. Southern-leaning Democrats attacked Republicans as a dangerously sectional party (which was like the pot calling the kettle black) and one that advocated racial equality (a Southern hot-button). Republicans effectively parried the disunion implication by pointing out that Southern Democrats were the ones who continuously threatened secession; however, the charge that they were "Black Republicans" who embodied "a wild and fanatical sentimentality toward the black race" was hard to wipe off.

When the votes came in, Buchanan carried the Electoral College by a comfortable margin of 174 to 114 (and 8 for Fillmore). But he was a minority president, receiving just 45 percent of the popular vote. Analysis of the returns shows that there had actually been two elections. In the South, Buchanan defeated Fillmore everywhere except in Maryland, with Fremont not even on the ballot in most states. In the North, Buchanan beat Fremont, although the Pathfinder won the Upper North by a wide margin. Fremont lost most of the Lower North (Illinois, Indiana, Pennsylvania, and New Jersey) because voters distrusted his liberal views on race (racism and antislavery existed side-by-side in those states). The lesson in the election was that had Fremont would have triumphed if he had won just two more Northern states. Since population had grown much faster in the free states than in the South during the preceding decades, the free states contained a majority of the electoral votes.

Because of Buchanan's victory, Southerners did not wring their hands in despair; yet, the realization that a sectional party could assemble majorities in Congress and in presidential elections without slave-state support disturbed them. Since the inception of the Republic, conventional wisdom had dictated carrying the South to win the presidency. Southerners could usually count on sympathetic presidents to veto unwanted legislation. But now the rules had changed, and Southern strategists would have to recalculate the value of remaining in the Union.

THINKING BACK

1. How did the Kansas-Nebraska inflame sectional controversy? What did the violence associated with it signify about the new political culture of the country and nature of political issues?

2. How was the political balance between North and South shifting by mid-century, and why might that shift have encouraged the South to consider secession?

PLUNGING INTO THE STORM

Little chance remained of avoiding a catastrophic showdown over slavery. Southern planters resolved to resist the free-soil movement while Northern Republicans dedicated themselves to thwarting what they regarded as an immoral pro-slavery conspiracy. William H. Seward called conflict over slavery "irrepressible." The federal government was deadlocked. Republicans held majorities in Congress, but Democrats controlled the executive and judicial branches. In August of 1857, a financial panic sharpened the edge on people's feelings. Withdrawal of European investments triggered a round of bank closings, suspension of specie payment, and business failures. The Chicago *Tribune* put the **Panic of 1857** in human terms: "The failure of this or that cotton or iron mill means the failure of so many human beings in the terms of food, fuel and shelter. Failure is but another word for famine and suspension is synonymous with starvation." Any faint hope that the next presidential election might occur in an atmosphere of conciliation crashed with an attempt to ignite a slave uprising. Two sections, one North and the other South, brought the United States to its most crucial and defining moment since 1787.

The Case of Dred Scott

In his March 1857 inaugural address, President James Buchanan asserted his belief that the question of slavery in the territories was essentially a judicial one. The Supreme Court, he added, would soon resolve it. Inappropriately kept abreast of the court's deliberations by the Democratic and pro-slavery Chief Justice Roger B. Taney, Buchanan was actually announcing the upcoming decision in the *Dred Scott case*. In the guise of a judicial ruling, the President and the court's pro-slavery majority rendered a decision conceived to allay Southern anxiety about slavery's future.

The plaintiff in this famous litigation was an enslaved man named Dred Scott. Born in Virginia around 1800, Scott eventually became the property of a United States Army surgeon named John Emerson who was stationed for a time at Fort Armstrong, on the Illinois frontier, and then at Fort Snelling, the site

of present-day Minneapolis in the old Louisiana Purchase. Emerson had kept Scott enslaved during these sojourns, even though the Northwest Ordinance in 1787 had banned legal slavery in Illinois and the Missouri Compromise in 1820 prohibited it north of 36° 30′. While at Fort Snelling, Scott married Harriet Robinson, a woman enslaved by a local justice of the peace who ignored federal law. The Scotts did not claim their freedom at that time, however, perhaps not realizing that state courts frequently freed slaves who had resided in free states or free territories. But in 1846, after Emerson died, Dred and Harriet Scott, then residents of Missouri, sued Emerson's widow for their freedom, encouraged to do so by a local black minister and the antislavery attorney who handled their case.

What was the Dred Scott case about, why did President Buchanan hope it would help preserve the Union, and, instead, what was the reaction to it?

Dred Scott, his wife Harriet, and their daughters Eliza and Lizzie

Courtesy of Library of Congress

In his lawsuit, presented before the Supreme Court in February 1856, Dred Scott argued that from the time he and Harriet had set foot on free soil they had been legally free. At the same time, John Jolliffe was making that argument on behalf of Margaret Garner in Cincinnati. Missouri courts had previously held in favor of plaintiffs in such circumstances, and although the court ruled against Scott on a technicality, a retrial freed the couple. Emerson's widow appealed that decision, however, and the Missouri Supreme court reversed it, going directly against legal precedent. "Times are not as they were when the former decisions on this subject were made," declared the state's chief justice.

Scott and his supporters moved the case into federal court. When the federal district judge upheld the Missouri finding, Scott appealed to the United States Supreme Court. Of the nine justices, seven supported slavery, including Chief Justice Taney. This old Jacksonian was a bitter and implacable foe of abolitionism, free soil, and racial equality. He was also determined to render a comprehensive and irreversible decision on two issues: whether African Americans could be citizens, and whether Congress possessed authority under the Constitution to ban slavery from a territory.

Tossing aside dissenting arguments from the court's two Northern justices, Chief Justice Taney left no room for doubt on either score. Because he was an African American (not just because he was enslaved), Dred Scott possessed "no rights which the white man was bound to respect." Therefore, Scott had no business suing in a federal court. But instead of dismissing the case for want of jurisdiction, Taney proceeded to declare that Congress had acted unconstitutionally in attempting to bar slavery from the territories. To do so, he claimed, violated the property guarantees laid down in the Fifth Amendment. In other words, for Congress to permit the owner of one type of property (a wagon or a mule) access to a territory while prohibiting another type (an enslaved human being) constitutionally discriminated against slave owners.

It was a stunning decision. Republicans called it "wicked" and "abominable." Horace Greeley's New York *Tribune*, the party's leading newspaper, said Taney's opinion carried the same authority as the utterances of drunks in a "Washington barroom." Pro-slavery Democrats were gleeful. Political leaders and newspaper editors proclaimed that the *Dred Scott* decision would "settle these vexed questions forever, quiet the country, and . . . perpetuate our Union."

Dred and Harriet Scott eventually were freed by their owners, but the case inflamed Northern antislavery opinion. The ruling hardened Republicans' resolve to defend free soil against a Democratic conspiracy. If anyone doubted the Republicans' take on the situation, they had only to read the steady stream of newspaper articles about the hoax being perpetrated in Kansas.

The Lecompton Swindle

By the time the Supreme Court announced that congressional bans on slavery in the territories were unconstitutional, the violence in Kansas had diminished. Franklin Pierce's third territorial governor, a tall, tough, and fair-minded Pennsylvanian named John W. Geary, had cleared out the "border ruffians" and brought an end to the worst violence in Kansas' horrible civil war. Slowly, government crews surveyed homesteads and federal land offices registered titles to property. As more free-soil emigrants made their way into Kansas, they became a substantial majority of the territory's population. Only a handful of enslaved people lived there, and the pro-slavery settlers began to concede that they would remain a minority. Before capitulating, however, the pro-slavers took advantage of their control of the territorial legislature to push through a constitution that would make Kansas a slave state.

> How did the pro-slavery minority in Kansas try to impose the Lecompton Constitution on the citizens of Kansas—and the country?

The only way they could bring off their plan, however, was through fraud, of which they were more than capable. Early in 1857, the pro-slavery legislature called for fall elections, for which pro-slavery officials would compile voter lists and serve as election judges. Governor Geary vetoed the election bill because of its obvious potential for mischief, but the legislature overrode his action. Disgusted by a lack of support from President Pierce and worn down by constant death threats, Geary resigned. When the equally pro-Southern James Buchanan took office, he appointed former Mississippi senator Robert J. Walker as territorial governor, but Walker, who did not own slaves and had moved to Mississippi only recently, immediately offended the slave-state faction by offering the opinion that slavery would never take root in Kansas because it was too far north. This statement pleased free-soilers, but they still refused to participate in the bogus elections for convention delegates. Approximately 1,800 pro-slavery citizens voted while 17,000 qualified antislavery voters stayed home. The result was a convention composed entirely of slave-state delegates, who gathered in Lecompton. The outcome of their work was a foregone conclusion, a state constitution that protected slavery.

Governor Walker demanded that the Lecompton constitution be submitted to a popular vote. Otherwise, as he said, Popular Sovereignty would become a farce "too monstrous to be tolerated." Buchanan concurred—willing to accept the rigged convention elections if the voters had an opportunity to judge the final constitution. The convention, recognizing that they could not win an open plebiscite, submitted to a vote only the question of whether the constitution was acceptable "with" slavery or "without" slavery. But a negative vote only meant that no additional slaves could be brought into the state. So, slavery would exist either way. Disgusted free-state voters again refused to vote. Slave-state leaders then sent the **Lecompton Constitution** to Washington "with slavery."

The arrival of the Lecompton Constitution in Washington drew impassioned outbursts from antislavery advocates. Buchanan now faced a dilemma. Supporting the Lecompton Constitution would legitimize cheating, and the result could be a return to civil war in Kansas. Rejecting it would deeply wound Southern Democrats, his major constituency, and perhaps cause secessionists to destroy the Union. Buchanan chose loyalty to the South and preservation of the Union over a fair process and urged Congress to accept Kansas as a slave state under the fraudulent Lecompton Constitution. Senator Stephen Douglas, however, would not endorse this perversion of Popular Sovereignty. During a nasty confrontation between the Democratic leaders in the White House, Buchanan reminded Douglas of how President Andrew Jackson had once crushed a group of Democrats who had opposed him. "Mr. President," an angry Douglas retorted, "I wish you to remember that General Jackson is dead." After a titanic battle in Congress, Douglas and the opponents of the Lecompton Constitution prevailed. Congress sent the constitution back to Kansas, where voters rejected it overwhelmingly. Thus, the free-staters won the battle for a democratic process in Kansas. Kansas became a state in 1861.

The political ramifications of the Lecompton Constitution battle were enormous. Buchanan's stance further discredited Popular Sovereignty in the eyes of Northerners. Douglas's dwindling prospects for the nomination of a united Democratic party in the 1860 presidential election evaporated. Southerners now

viewed him as a turncoat and Northerners did not regard Popular Sovereignty as an acceptable alternative to free soil in the territories. As a unifying principle within the Democratic party, Popular Sovereignty had failed, and soon Republicans took the opportunity of Douglas's reelection to the Senate from Illinois to point that out.

The Lincoln-Douglas Debates

Despite Stephen A. Douglas' strong stand against the Lecompton Constitution, the question was, could he and the tainted doctrine of Popular Sovereignty help the country avert a catastrophic conflict over slavery? Not only had the Lecompton

> **What was the occasion for the Lincoln-Douglas debates, and how did they affect the political careers of both contestants?**

Constitution perverted Popular Sovereignty, but the Supreme Court had also nullified it.

In 1858, Douglas faced an untimely Senate reelection campaign. His Republican opponent was a prosperous railroad attorney and former Whig congressman, Abraham Lincoln. The contest between the two candidates developed into a classic confrontation: the lanky, homespun, local politician against the most recognizable political figure in the country. In a series of public debates held up and down the Prairie State, Lincoln and Douglas discussed all sides of the slavery question. Lincoln disliked slavery and flatly rejected Popular Sovereignty, along with the notion that the country could exist "half slave and half free." He declared that "a house divided against itself cannot stand," and added that he did not expect it to fall. Douglas did not like slavery either, but he did not believe that the issue mattered enough for Americans to fight about. His goal was to unify the country through conciliation and compromise.

The most famous part of the **Lincoln-Douglas debates** was the question that Lincoln posed: "Can the people of a territory, in any lawful way, . . . exclude slavery from its limits?" It was a pertinent question in light of the Dred Scott decision, and Douglas, had a ready response. Yes, they could simply refuse to enact slave laws. Nobody volunteered for slavery, nor was anyone naturally a slave. Laws enslaved people, and without them slavery could not exist. Thus, Popular Sovereignty could still work.

But the real importance of the Lincoln-Douglas debates was that they gave these two capable men an

Abraham Lincoln, a photograph taken two weeks prior to the final Lincoln-Douglas debate

opportunity to discuss the issue of slavery with intellectual rigor as the nation read about it in the newspapers. "If slavery is not wrong," Lincoln declared in response to Douglas's temporizing, "then nothing is wrong." The two candidates' feelings about slavery seemed poles apart, and yet, they represented the moderate branches of their respective parties. So, if the moderates differed so radically, what hope was there for national reconciliation? The last, best hope for the Union perhaps lay in the fact that both embodied a Romantic nationalism that abhorred disunion. Neither advocated abolition of slavery in the states, although Lincoln said that he favored a national policy that would put slavery on "the course of ultimate extinction." Many slave owners in the Upper South could support that goal. And as far as the rights of free African Americans were concerned, Douglas and Lincoln embodied the views of most white Americans everywhere. Douglas agreed with Chief Justice Roger Taney that African Americans had no citizenship rights. Lincoln acknowledged the abstract concept of racial equality but at the same time expressed the belief that white people should occupy a position in society superior to black people.

The result of the election was a mixed victory for Stephen Douglas. In Illinois at that time, voters did not directly elect senators, the state legislature did, so the campaign was technically for legislative seats. The November balloting resulted in a Democratic majority, which in turn led to Douglas's reelection. Lincoln had forced Douglas to affirm Popular Sovereignty, which had worked against slavery in Kansas, instead of the Dred *Scott* decision. This strengthened Douglas among Northern antislavery Democrats but reinforced his negative image among Southern Democrats. Lincoln was stung by the defeat but his cogent antislavery arguments had transformed him into a formidable national figure.

John Brown's Raid on Harpers Ferry

Early in the autumn of 1859, the next-to-last electrifying scene in the pre-Civil War slavery drama unfolded in the mountain town of **Harpers Ferry**, Virginia. The site of a federal arsenal, Harpers Ferry contained hundreds of rifles stored in the local armory. In this secluded place with few large farms or enslaved people, the ne'er-do-well abolitionist John Brown launched an ill-conceived plan to spark a slave uprising that would bring slavery down in one gigantic explosion.

> **What was John Brown's objective, and what did he accomplish at Harpers Ferry?**

After his vicious attack on the pro-slavery settlers on Pottawatomie Creek in Kansas three years before, Brown had traveled through the Northeast meeting with illustrious intellectuals and wealthy business tycoons, trying to persuade them to subscribe to his crusade against slavery. Many nodded in sympathy; however, in the end, only a tiny and timorous group, the "Secret Six," provided him with any money. With it, Brown managed to procure a few weapons, including steel-tipped pikes (spears), with which he intended to arm enslaved people. He figured that they would use the weapons to free themselves. With a cadre of twenty-two devoted followers, including several of his sons, Brown set up a camp on a nearby farm. On the evening of October 16, 1859, they cut the telegraph line into Harpers Ferry and slipped into town, occupying the armory. A small detail of men captured two local slave owners, one of whom was the great-grandnephew of George Washington, and a handful of bewildered slaves. Brown's men also hijacked a Baltimore and Ohio railroad train as it passed through town, accidentally killing a baggage handler before letting it go. Then the naïve Brown waited for slaves to join him. They, of course, knew

John Brown ascending the scaffold to be hanged for his attack at Harpers Ferry

better than to trust a stranger in such a risky endeavor. Instead, the terrified train crew alerted authorities, and by the end of the next day, Virginia militia and a company of United States marines commanded by Lieutenant Colonel Robert E. Lee had descended on Harpers Ferry. Only then did everyone learn the attackers' identity. An assault by the marines killed ten of Brown's men, including two of his sons. Authorities apprehended Brown himself, painfully but not seriously wounded.

The botched slave revolt typified John Brown's life, one filled with erratic and frequently violent behavior. Many commentators have called him crazy, pointing to his extremism and the piercing eyes that look out from his most famous photograph. The eminent historian David M. Potter, who rejected such a simplistic assessment, conceded some years ago that he "was not, as we now say, a well-adjusted man." In any event, Virginia indicted Brown for treason and inciting a slave revolt, and within a week his trial began in Charlestown. A jury convicted him and passed a sentence of death by hanging.

As he awaited his fate, John Brown wrote to his wife: "I feel quite determined to make the utmost possible out of a defeat." Brown showed uncharacteristic dignity during the pre-execution vigil. He also knew that he could become a martyr to the cause of emancipation "by only hanging a few moments by the neck." On December 2, John Brown dropped through the trap door on the gallows. Northern flags flew at half-staff in his honor, newspapers eulogized him, and Ralph

Waldo Emerson, comparing Brown to Christ, said that he had made "the gallows as glorious as the cross." Abraham Lincoln, however, did not want the party identified with fanaticism and denounced Brown's methods. In fact, Stephen A. Douglas sought to brand the Republicans just so; the Harpers Ferry raid, he said, was the "natural, logical, inevitable result of the doctrines and teachings of the Republican party."

In the South, despite some grudging acknowledgment of Brown's courage, a consensus emerged that the Harpers Ferry raid betrayed the Republican party's hostile intentions. Mississippi's Jefferson Davis declared that the Republicans were "making war" on the South. Expressions of alienation had seldom been this strong previously. White South Carolinians were virtually unanimous in their belief, as Governor William Gist said, that the South must "now unite for her defense," and the Upper South was more in tune with the Lower South than before. One Richmond, Virginia, newspaper reported that "There are thousands upon . . . thousands of men in our midst who, a month ago, scoffed at the idea of a dissolution of the Union as a madman's dream, but who now hold the opinion that its days are numbered, its glory perished."

In the December 1859 session of Congress, Southerners and Northerners came armed and itching for a fight. For two months they battled over who should be elected speaker of the House, although no shots were fired. Senator Jefferson Davis of Mississippi proposed a national slave code for the territories, which the free-soil majority angrily rejected. During the acrimonious debates, Southern fire-eaters made it plain how they would react to the election of a Republican in the upcoming presidential election. Lawrence Keitt of South Carolina vowed to shatter the Union "from turret to foundation."

The Election of 1860

How did the 1860 presidential election unfold, and why did Abraham Lincoln and the Republican party win?

In this highly charged atmosphere, the political parties prepared for the most crucial presidential election in the history of the Republic. Extremists rejected any compromise, preferring disunion to a government in the hands of their opponents. Democrats divided along the Mason-Dixon line and faced almost certain defeat. Republicans were excited about their prospects, knowing they could win without Southern support. They needed only a candidate who could balance antislavery Unionists and all-or-nothing abolitionists.

The Democrats held their nominating convention in Charleston, South Carolina. Delegates from the Deep South, demanded a resolution calling for a national slave code for the territories. They squared off against Stephen A. Douglas's supporters who pressed for an endorsement of Popular Sovereignty. Through more than fifty agonizing ballots, Douglas's backers failed to line up the two-thirds vote necessary for nomination, but they did reject the Southerners' slave-code resolution, whereupon the extremist delegates from South Carolina to Texas marched out of the convention. The convention reassembled in Baltimore after Douglas's supporters recruited new pro-Douglas delegations from the states that had bolted. The convention proceeded to nominate Douglas for president and Georgian Herschel V. Johnson for vice president. The anti-Douglas Democrats nominated a ticket of John C. Breckenridge of Kentucky and Oregon's senator Joseph Lane. Thus, the Democrats had fractured, and this virtually guaranteed defeat in the November elections.

Some border-state Democrats allied with former Southern Whigs and Know-Nothings in an effort to save the floundering Union. Finding a neutral name to go by was their major problem, since Whigs and Democrats, as someone put it, had grown up hating each other "as the devil is said to hate holy water." They chose to call themselves the **Constitutional Union party**, and adopted no platform other than vowing to uphold the Constitution and preserve the Union. They nominated two old Whigs, John Bell of Tennessee for president and Edward Everett of Massachusetts for vice president.

Exuberant Republicans held their convention in the newly constructed Wigwam in Chicago. No longer a "one-idea," antislavery party, Republicans were also committed to tariff protection, federal support for a Pacific railroad, and a homestead policy. Republican strategists concentrated on winning the moderate states of the Lower North (Illinois, Indiana, Ohio, and Pennsylvania). A statement denouncing John Brown's attack on Harpers Ferry helped enhance the party's appeal to those states. William H. Seward of New York was the leading presidential candidate, but he retained his reputation for extremism. Several alternatives emerged, including Abraham Lincoln. If Seward failed to win on the first ballot, delegates would look elsewhere. He did come up short, and on the third ballot the convention nominated Lincoln. Hannibal Hamlin of Maine, the vice presidential nominee, balanced the ticket geographically.

The campaign electrified the nation. The Breckenridge Democrats demanded federal protection of slavery in all the territories, whereas the Douglas Democrats maintained Popular Sovereignty. Lincoln and the Republicans demanded the outright congressional exclusion of slavery from the territories. The prospect of disunion after the election pushed the stakes to the highest level, although many in the North did not take Southern threats of secession seriously. "The people of the South," said Lincoln, "have too much of good sense, and good temper, to attempt the ruin of the government." Employing proven methods of electioneering, the parties organized campaign clubs to turn out the vote. Republican **Wide Awakes** marched by torch light through towns and cities carrying split rails as symbols of "Honest Old Abe." Voter turnout was astounding by today's standards—three out of every four qualified voters went to the polls.

With four contenders in the field, chances were good that nobody would win a majority. The final tally revealed again, as it had in 1856, two distinct races. In the North, Lincoln bested Douglas, and in the South, Breckenridge outscored Bell. Lincoln garnered 180 electoral votes, a clear majority. He received just 39 percent of the popular vote, but it was concentrated in the free states and that yielded the electoral majority. Breckenridge won 55 percent of the popular vote in the slave states, and carried ten of them, but they produced only 72 total electoral votes. Douglas, who won nearly 30 percent of the popular vote overall, could defeat neither Lincoln nor Breckenridge. He carried only Missouri over Bell by a hair's breadth.

The Republican victory was ominous for the Union. Sectionalism was triumphant, and the Republican party, which was not even on the ballot in ten slave states, would now run the government. Southern fire-eaters had vowed to secede from the Union if such a "Black Republican" should be elected, and ten days after Lincoln's victory the Augusta, Georgia, *Daily Constitutionalist* proclaimed: "The only hope for its [Georgia's] preservation, therefore, is out of the Union." The nation waited breathlessly as the secessionists planned their course of action.

Secession

> **Why did the slave states of the lower South declare their independence?**

Despite the triumph of sectionalism, Unionism in the South was not dead. A majority of the voters in the slave states had voted for one of the Unionist candidates in the 1860 election. In the upper tier of slave states, where slavery was not an economically vital force, the vote had gone for either Douglas, the Unionist Democrat, or Bell, the Constitutional Unionist. Southern separatism derived from a sense of betrayal by the Republican party that disregarded the Constitution as white Southerners interpreted it.

In the Lower South, however, where slavery was a central economic, social, and political concern, fear of remaining in the Union with the government in the hands of that "foul, God-defying [Republican] party" overwhelmed devotion to the Union. Fire-eaters warned fellow Southerners of rivers of blood flooding the South if the Republicans unshackled millions of slaves to ravage and pillage. Their rhetoric dripped with hyperbole, but immediate and total destruction of slavery was indeed the avowed goal of the radical wing of the Republican party. In South Carolina, the response to the election came swiftly and angrily. Federal district judge Andrew G. Magrath ripped off his robes and stormed out of his courtroom. The state's congressional delegation resigned in unison. And on December 17, voters chose delegates to a secession convention that convened in Charleston. Three days later, South Carolina's convention voted 169 to 0 to dissolve "the union now subsisting between South Carolina and other States." Over the next six weeks, secession conventions in Georgia, Florida,

Alabama, Mississippi, Louisiana, and Texas also took the plunge. (See map on p. 466). In each state, some secessionists argued against moving without pledges of cooperation from other states, which caused some delay, but in every instance the momentum was unstoppable.

In the Upper South, moderates prevailed in debates over secession. For years, slave owners and non-slave owners alike had considered gradual emancipation. Although accepting the right of any state to secede, leaders in the Upper South chose to wait for some act of coercion from the Lincoln administration before they took any action to leave the Union.

The crisis had finally come, and it remained to be seen what the federal government would do about it. President James Buchanan was a "lame duck," meaning that he occupied the presidential oval office only until the new president took over, and that weakened his authority. President-elect Lincoln remained in Springfield, relatively powerless until his inauguration. As the nation looked anxiously on, the last bonds holding the Union together had begun to snap.

THINKING BACK

1. What attempts did national political leaders make to conciliate the South's slave owners in order to preserve the Union?
2. Why did conciliation and compromise fail to stop disunion?

CONCLUSION

One insightful observer pointed out that North and South "have been so entirely separated by climate, by morals, [and] by religion . . . that they cannot longer exist under the same government." Such divergent paths of development yielded fundamentally different civic values. The plantation system of agriculture placed ultimate importance on land and labor. Traditional Southern planters held firmly to the Jeffersonian ideal of freedom through property and the absolute necessity of constitutional protection of property rights; moreover, they had fully developed the argument that enslaved people were property in which owners had considerable sums of capital invested and a constitutional right to possess. Threats to their property propelled the Lower South's conservative planter aristocracy into the revolutionary act of secession much like the agrarian patriots of 1776.

Northern society, meanwhile, had advanced down the path of dynamic commercial capitalism. Wages provided individuals with opportunities for advancement—including the capital needed to begin their own businesses and to hire others to fill jobs. Freedom, from their Northern perspective, depended on access to wages. Slave labor would drive free labor from the market. Southern society was based on an aristocratic model while Northern society was based on a more democratic and bourgeois one. Furthermore, most Northerners considered freedom a national value, embedded in the Constitution, whereas slavery was seen as an aberration, unique to the Southern minority.

These conflicting values, expressed in rigid terms, led to the crisis of secession. The rapidly developing West was the precipitating agent. Would the West follow the Northern pattern or the Southern one? The politics of compromise and conciliation gave way to the politics of confrontation and absolute standards and principles. Some historians have blamed the crisis on incompetent leadership, but that minimizes the strength of conviction on both sides of the Mason-Dixon line.

SUGGESTED SOURCES FOR STUDENTS

The best one-volume Lincoln biography is David Herbert Donald, *Lincoln* (1995).

Nicole Etcheson, *Bleeding Kansas: Contested Liberty in the Civil War Era* (2004) shows that "Bleeding Kansas" raised fears of being enslaved more than compassion for the already enslaved.

A nice, brief summary of the *Dred Scott* case and extended excerpts from relevant documents is Paul Finkelman, *Dred Scott v. Sandford: A Brief History with Documents* (1997). For more extended coverage of the issues raised in the Dred Scott case see Finkelman's *An Imperfect Union: Slavery Federalism, and Comity* (1981).

The best treatment of the broad issue of slavery versus free soil is Eric Foner, *Free Soil, Free Labor, Free Men: The Ideology of the Republican Party Before the Civil War* (1970).

For different perspectives on the political parties of the era see William E. Gienapp, *The Origins of the Republican Party, 1852-1856* (1987).

The fragmentation of the Whig party following the enactment of the Compromise of 1850 symbolized the political condition of the Union at mid-century. Michael F. Holt's *The Rise and Fall of the Whig Party: Jacksonian Politics and the Onset of the Civil War* (1999) is the definitive treatment of that subject.

The best biography of the "Little Giant" is Robert W. Johannsen's *Stephen A. Douglas* (1973).

To understand the rise of Southern nationalism, see John McCardell, *The Idea of a Southern Nation: Southern Nationalists and Southern Nationalism, 1830-1860* (1979).

An insightful and readable probe into Lincoln's personal ethics, including where and how his moral principles intersected with practical politics, is William Lee Miller, *Lincoln's Virtues: An Ethical Biography* (2002).

The dramatic and poignant story of Margaret Garner received national attention after a century of oblivion when Toni Morrison fictionalized it in her Pulitzer Prize-winning novel *Beloved* (1987).

The most thorough examination of John Brown is Stephen B. Oates, *To Purge This Land with Blood: A Biography of John Brown* (1970).

Steven Weisenburger tells the historical story of the Garner's desperate flight from slavery and its symbolic effect on sectional politics in *Modern Medea: A Family Story of Slavery and Child-Murder from the Old South* (1998).

BEFORE WE GO ON

1. Why did the Compromise of 1850 fail to prevent the renewal of sectional conflict?

2. Why did the Kansas-Nebraska Act raise such a furor? What steps did the country take from that point that led directly to the break-up of the Union?

Building a Democratic Nation

3. Some historians have blamed disunion on incompetent political leadership. Where might different policies have resulted in different consequences? Or perhaps more significantly, should the federal government's policies on slavery been different?

4. Both North and South framed their arguments on the slavery question in terms of democracy. Southern secessionists contended that secession was legal, based on a type of democracy called state sovereignty. Does the Constitution say anything about secession, that is, giving states the right to vote with their feet on staying in the Union? Do you believe the Union was perpetual or voluntary? Explain. Republican party leaders argued that territories should be kept free, but how much freedom and democracy would Native American residents of Kansas and Nebraska enjoy?

Connections

5. The sectional crisis of the 1850s is usually understood as a North-South conflict. But what role did the West play in the great debates over the nation's future?

6. If the argument over slavery was really about democracy, how could the South hold millions of African Americans in bondage? And how could Abraham Lincoln say that the government of the United States had no power to free people held as slaves in the Southern states?

Chapter 15

CIVIL WAR: THE NATION'S ORDEAL, 1861–1865

A PERSONAL PERSPECTIVE: FOCUS ON THE FRONT-LINE SOLDIER

Courtesy of Library of Congress

Portrait of Pvt. Walter Miles Parker, 1st. Florida Cavalry, C.S.A.

Although the Civil War was a public war, often understood as a romantic struggle between opposing societies holding cherished values, it was experienced personally and usually painfully. And whereas government officials, newspapers, and official histories from Maine to Georgia and from Virginia to California usually pictured the war in terms of massed armies, the young men in blue and gray who filled the ranks of those armies were in a very real sense fighting alone. Each front-line solder, Union and Confederate, faced hailstorms of musket balls and rifle bullets, whistling waves of jagged iron and screaming cannon balls fired by an enemy trying to kill them. In those horrifying moments, they had only their courage and their natural fear to spur them on and keep them from "skedaddling."

As with most wars, adults started the Civil War but children fought and died in it. In the war's first year, eighteen-year-old boys comprised the largest age group among soldiers in both armies. As casualties

mounted, even younger children were enlisted. Fourteen-year-old Charles Bardeen of Fitchburg, Massachusetts, was aware of the gathering secession crisis, and "when [Ft. Sumter] was fired upon . . . I was excited." He later remembered "walking up and down the sitting room, puffing out my breast as though the responsibility rested on my poor little shoulders, shaking my fist at the South, and threatening her with dire calamities which I thought . . . of inflicting on her myself." Youngsters like Bardeen sometimes suffered wounds and always lost the innocence of their childhoods. "I was certainly scared, . . . and the one thing I wanted was to get where no more shells would burst around me." No doubt deeply scarred by the scenes of death that he witnessed, Bardeen could find the words to describe them when making entries in his diary. "My first battle is over and I saw nearly all of it. . . . I saw the Irish Brigade make three charges. They started with full ranks, and I saw them, in less time than it takes to write this, exposed to a galling fire of shot and shell and almost decimated."

Day in and day out, Bardeen suffered the same grinding hardships that challenged front line troops of both sides: long marches, bivouacking in rain and mud, and eating moldy crackers and spoiled meat—or worse, when scarcely any food was available at all. In camp, between battles, soldiers fought boredom, homesickness, and the insidious germs that silently attacked, sickened, and killed more of them than enemy bullets. Those who were captured experienced the most hideous conditions.

Midway through the war, governments of both the United States and the Confederacy began drafting men roughly between the ages of seventeen and forty-five. For the draftees, finding the courage to face death was especially difficult. They deserted more often than volunteers, and they were more likely to run from the enemy or shoot themselves in the hand or foot in order to obtain a discharge.

Civil War officers commanded their troops from in front of the ranks rather than from the rear.

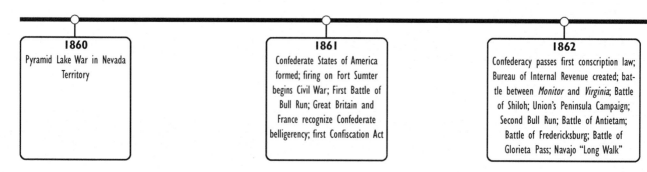

1860	1861	1862
Pyramid Lake War in Nevada Territory	Confederate States of America formed; firing on Fort Sumter begins Civil War; First Battle of Bull Run; Great Britain and France recognize Confederate belligerency; first Confiscation Act	Confederacy passes first conscription law; Bureau of Internal Revenue created; battle between *Monitor* and *Virginia*; Battle of Shiloh; Union's Peninsula Campaign; Second Bull Run; Battle of Antietam; Battle of Fredericksburg; Battle of Glorieta Pass; Navajo "Long Walk"

Consequently, 15 percent more officers than private soldiers were killed in combat. Even generals exposed themselves to enemy fire: They were special targets and were 50 percent more likely to die in battle than enlisted men. Officers established credibility among their troops by demonstrating their own courage. The visible signs of courage were fearlessness and showing no sign of pain when wounded. During one heated battle, an officer of an Illinois regiment coolly rode up and down the line, stopped to ask a soldier for a match, nonchalantly lit his pipe, and then led the attack. One of the men later recalled: "How I admired his wonderful coolness."

The deadliness of a new generation of weapons was another reason for the ghastly Civil War casualty rate. Most infantry soldiers carried a .58 caliber muzzle-loading rifle that fired a conical bullet called a "**minié ball**," named after its French inventor Claude-Etienne Minié. These weapons were far more accurate than the older smooth-bore muskets. Concentrated rifle fire from thousands of infantry decimated exposed attacking troops, whose commanders were slow to adjust their offensive tactics to account for these new deadly weapons. By the end of the war, the United States equipped many of its troops with breech-loading rifles that cut down the reloading time and in some cases even repeating carbines that, Rebels said, the Yanks could load on Sunday and fire all week.

In Civil War battles, soldiers usually attacked in close order, totally exposed to enemy fire. In those days, no technology existed enabling commanders to communicate with troops scattered about and concealed for protection. The telegraph existed and allowed quick communication between armies and between field headquarters and respective political capitals, but not close in to the fighting. Frontal assaults often resulted in horrifying casualties, testing the courage and honor of soldiers forced to overcome the fear of instant and seemingly certain death. "I saw wounded men brought in by the hundred and dead men lying stark on the field . . . and I am discouraged."

The Civil War that soldiers in blue and in gray experienced personally was the most destructive armed conflict in the nation's history. Never before, or since, have Americans had to suffer death and destruction on such a massive scale. Perhaps, in the spring of 1861, had they known what lay ahead, they would have worked harder to avoid it. But through the course of the long and difficult struggle, the United States redefined itself as a democratic nation

HOME BY CHRISTMAS, 1861

During the weeks following Abraham Lincoln's election, cities, towns, and the rural countryside of the North and South pulsated with excitement. Southern nationalism soared. Southerners geared up to fight for their right to own slaves, and they believed that God would bless them. Northerners vowed to preserve the United States intact. Ironically, many of them saw no point in fighting and dying to abolish the very thing that most threatened it—slavery. They too were certain of the justness of their cause. Nearly everyone assumed that the crisis would quickly pass, primarily because they all believed the other side had no stomach for war. "So far as civil war is concerned," proclaimed an Atlanta newspaper, "we have no fears." Even President-elect Abraham Lincoln believed the great majority of Southerners wanted the Union to survive.

Making the Confederate States of America

Early in February 1861, delegates representing the seven seceded states gathered as a constitutional convention in Montgomery, Alabama. Within a month they had established a new union called the **Confederate States of America.** Despite the presence of several fire-eaters, the convention set a moderate tone, hoping

> How was the Confederate Constitution similar to and different from the Constitution of the United States?

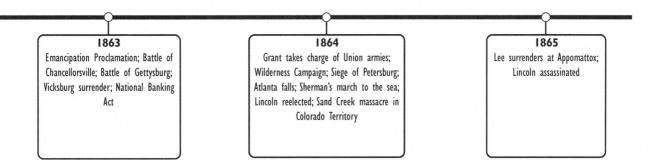

1863	1864	1865
Emancipation Proclamation; Battle of Chancellorsville; Battle of Gettysburg; Vicksburg surrender; National Banking Act	Grant takes charge of Union armies; Wilderness Campaign; Siege of Petersburg; Atlanta falls; Sherman's march to the sea; Lincoln reelected; Sand Creek massacre in Colorado Territory	Lee surrenders at Appomattox; Lincoln assassinated

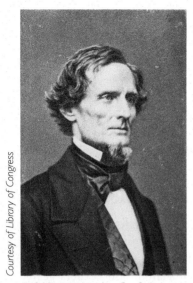

Jefferson Davis of Mississippi, the Confederate president, was probably more qualified than Lincoln to lead a nation into war. But that was not enough to win.

to win the support and perhaps the eventual inclusion of those states in the Upper South that had held back during the first wave of secession.

In setting forth the philosophical foundation of the Confederacy, the drafters of the Confederate Constitution clearly stated their commitment to white supremacy. Responding to Thomas Jefferson's famous statement in the Declaration of Independence that "all men are created equal," Alexander H. Stephens of Georgia proclaimed: "Our new government is founded upon exactly the opposite idea; its foundations are laid, its cornerstone rests, upon the great truth that the negro is not equal to the white man; that slavery—subordination to the superior race—is his natural and normal condition."

In erecting the structural framework of the new nation, the Confederacy borrowed liberally from the Constitution of the United States. The Confederate government contained three branches with a president, a bicameral Congress, and a judiciary. But convinced that the United States had betrayed the hallowed principle of property rights laid down by its Founders, the drafters of the Confederate Constitution underscored states' rights (but also proclaimed "a permanent federal government"), guaranteed citizens' right to own slaves (no hedging on the word) as property both in the states and in territories, and prohibited protective tariffs. The Confederate Constitution outlawed the African slave trade, an implicit appeal to the Upper South, which supplied many Southern cotton plantations with slaves. And it

limited the presidency to one six-year term, reverting to the traditional republican ideal of legislative rather than executive dominance.

In selecting persons for executive positions, the Confederacy's organizing convention again took into account the sensitivities of the Upper South. For provisional president, they eschewed hotspurs like South Carolina's Robert Barnwell Rhett and Alabama's William Loundes Yancey and selected instead Jefferson Davis of Mississippi. A West Point graduate and veteran of the U.S.—Mexico War, Davis would have preferred a military command; however, his status as a gentleman planter and his experience as a senator and secretary of war under President Franklin Pierce qualified him better for civilian leadership. The convention elected a former Whig, Douglas Democrat, and reluctant secessionist Alexander H. Stephens as vice president. The song *Dixie* became the Confederacy's unofficial national anthem. Elections for full presidential and vice presidential terms were set for November.

President Davis had not only to lead the new Confederate government but also to make it operational the way George Washington had seventy years earlier. The Confederacy's devotion to states' rights allowed state governors like Joseph E. Brown of Georgia and Zebulon B. Vance of North Carolina to withhold resources for Confederate operations. The absence of political parties made organizing opposition to government policies difficult and thereby reduced accountability. Davis supervised the taking over of United States properties within the boundaries of the Confederate states, including post offices, court houses, customs offices, mints, and military posts. The individual states had begun doing this as soon as they withdrew from the Union. To keep the economy going, the Confederate treasury issued new currency, and the Congress convened to begin the process of lawmaking. With a functioning government and a growing national consciousness, the Confederacy existed in fact, even though many in the North denied that secession from the Union was legally valid. But the Davis government's main objective was to expand the Confederacy by incorporating the Upper South.

Waiting for Something to Happen

At his home in Springfield, Illinois, President-elect Lincoln could only wait for his inauguration in March and hope that secession fever did not spread to the Upper South and border states. In the

After his election, how did Lincoln respond to secession?

meantime, the lame duck President James Buchanan sat paralyzed by indecision. In his December message to Congress, Buchanan forcefully denied that a state possessed a constitutional right to secede from the Union, asserting that the framers of the government back in 1787 "never intended to plant in its bosom the seeds of its own destruction." But he refused to prevent seceding states from seizing federal property. Government in Washington effectively went on hold insofar as the South was concerned.

Lincoln used this time to assemble his Cabinet. Seeking unity among moderates and abolitionists within the Republican party, Lincoln included all of his rivals for the recent presidential nomination. The key position was secretary of state, which went to William H. Seward. The New Yorker held particularly strong and well-known antislavery views and expected to be the power behind the throne, like a European prime minister, but when during the first weeks of the administration he attempted to take the reins of government, Lincoln firmly put him in his place. He told his private secretary: I can't afford to let Seward take the first lick." Seward quickly came to acknowledge Lincoln's wisdom and strength. None of the other appointees challenged Lincoln although they were eccentric and sensitive and often tried Lincoln's enormous patience: the cheerless but able abolitionist and former Democrat Salmon P. Chase as secretary of the treasury, Edward Bates from the slave state of Missouri as attorney general, and Simon Cameron, a political hack from Pennsylvania, as secretary of war. One of Lincoln's shrewdest appointments was Montgomery Blair to the position of postmaster general, an important appointment partly because of the large number of local postmasterships that could be awarded to loyal supporters. Blair resided in Maryland, a key border state, and his brother and father, Francis P. Blair junior and senior, had been and still were influential figures in Missouri, another border state. The senior Blair had been a member of Andrew Jackson's "kitchen Cabinet." All in all, Lincoln's "team of rivals" proved to be exceptionally loyal and capable.

While everyone waited for the other shoe to fall, Northern and border-state moderates devised a number of compromises they hoped would avert an armed clash. Buchanan urged the Northern states to repeal their "personal liberty" laws, enforce the Fugitive Slave Act, and endorse what he believed was the constitutional right of Southerners to own slaves in the territories, all as one big goodwill gesture toward the South. He got nowhere. Northern newspaper editorials condemned his "wretched drivel," branding it a "shameful surrender." Senator John J. Crittenden of Kentucky, successor to the Great Compromiser Henry Clay, revived the idea of a dividing line along 36° 30', adding to it a guarantee of slavery in future territories, both of which he asked Congress to make into constitutional amendments that could never be altered or repealed. Few if any Northerners supported compromise. Most regarded it as spineless capitulation to slave owners that would only encourage them to renew efforts to annex new territory. Lincoln explained that voters had registered a desire to keep slavery out of the territories. "The tug has got to come, & better now, than any time hereafter." Giving in would only postpone the inevitable battle because the South would keep up its demands for more territory and within a year "we shall have to take Cuba as a condition upon which they will stay in the Union." Congress voted down the **Crittenden Compromise**.

Compromises would probably not have made any difference. The Lower South had already chosen its path. One secessionist declared: "We spit on every plan to compromise." And the Upper South was keying on Lincoln, looking for any sign of hostility on his part toward the Confederate states. Citizens of the Upper South and the border states generally believed that secession was a state's legitimate right even if it was not yet their policy. Knowing that all eyes were upon him and that an action seen as aggressive toward the Confederacy could cause the Upper South to secede, Lincoln moved deliberately and uttered mostly platitudes as he slowly made his way by rail to Washington. In Baltimore, a hotbed of secessionism with a tradition of rioting, he secretly changed trains because of an alleged assassination plot. Thus the man whom many saw as a country bumpkin over his head in this crisis slipped into Washington by his own admission "like a thief in the night."

If Lincoln's arrival in the capital was inauspicious, his inaugural address, delivered on March 4, 1861, more than made up for it. Deftly, he offered an olive branch to the recalcitrant southern states with one hand while holding a sword in the other. He promised not to "interfere" with slavery in the states where it already existed and to enforce the Fugitive Slave Act. But he also vowed to "hold, occupy, and possess" all property such as court houses, post offices, and military installations still in government hands and to maintain federal authority everywhere. He concluded with an impassioned appeal for reconciliation based on shared traditions and a common national identity. "We are not enemies, but friends. We must not be enemies. Though passion may have strained, it must not break our bonds of affection." Americans, he declared, are united by the "mystic chords of memory" that stretch "from every battle-field, and patriot grave to every living heart and hearthstone," and the chorus of Union will ring "when again touched, as they surely will be, by the better angels of our nature."

The Confederacy Attacks Fort Sumter

> **How did Lincoln attempt to contain secession while maneuvering the Confederacy into firing the first shot?**

But deeds carried more impact than "honeyed phrases," as the unmoved Frederick Douglass characterized Lincoln's speech. Lincoln had long hated slavery on moral grounds, as being utterly incongruous within a democratic nation. Ultimately it would have to be extinguished, but in the short term slavery took a back seat to secession as the President's foremost concern. By taking the presidential oath of office, he had sworn to preserve the Constitution, in which he read no explicit or inherent right to secede. Once a state entered the Union it remained forever. His logic rested on **The Articles of Confederation and Perpetual Union**, the nation's first formal constitution. In Lincoln's view, secession was rebellion, and the Constitution assigned the president responsibility for enforcing federal law and suppressing rebellion. Lincoln had to be careful, though, because coercion might drive the Upper South into the Confederacy and make restoration of the Union practically impossible.

The remaining federal properties on Confederate soil held great symbolic value in this face-off over sovereignty. The most important ones were military bases, Fort Pickens in Florida's Pensacola Bay, and the recently constructed **Fort Sumter**, situated on a small, man-made island commanding the entrance to Charleston harbor. Lincoln felt a particular sense of urgency about Fort Sumter, with its forty-foot walls and emplacements for 146 heavy guns but dwindling supplies of food and fresh water. In fact, its commanding officer informed Lincoln that if not resupplied within weeks, he would be compelled to surrender.

Lincoln looked at three choices in this situation, none of them particularly good. He could resupply Fort Sumter—a non-threatening move—and hope that negotiations with the Confederacy would resolve the crisis. Sending reinforcements along with supplies was another option; however, that would clearly be an aggressive act certain to provoke a

An aerial view of Ft. Sumter today

Confederate attack and push the Upper South into secession. If Lincoln evacuated Fort Sumter, the third alternative, he might appear weak, even cowardly. Most members of the Cabinet, including Seward, favored evacuation. When word leaked that this was under consideration, one incensed New Yorker exclaimed: "The bird of our country is a debilitated chicken, disguised in eagle feathers." Seward did even more damage by informing a delegation of Confederate commissioners that abandonment was imminent. Furious but, as always, calm, Lincoln told Seward that he, not Seward, would decide.

The president had no intention of turning over Fort Sumter. Demonstrating masterful ability, he sent word to Governor Francis Pickens of South Carolina that he was dispatching a small, non-threatening squadron with "food for hungry men." The ships would carry no reinforcements, weapons, or ammunition. If the Confederates ordered guns to open fire, then they would bear the onus of starting the war.

Davis had placed General Pierre G. T. Beauregard in command of the militia and artillery batteries trained on Fort Sumter. Davis felt enormous pressure to do something heroic in order to rally the Upper South into joining the Confederacy. "If you want us to join you," proclaimed a Virginia fire-eater, "*strike a blow!*" Davis ordered Beauregard to bombard Fort Sumter, and shelling commenced before dawn on April 12, just as the Union relief vessels approached. Curious and cheerful residents of the city watched from their balconies and rooftops. Under bombardment, the supply ships withdrew, and thirty-three hours and 4,000 rounds later, Fort Sumter's garrison lowered the Stars and Stripes and stood down.

Charleston's citizenry erupted with ecstasy. "During this time," wrote Mary Boykin Chesnut, the wife of a Beauregard's staff officer and member of the Confederate Congress, "the excitement . . . was so great I had never a moment to write." Lincoln used the attack on Fort Sumter to call for 75,000 volunteers to enlist for three months to help quell an insurrection that could not be managed peacefully. The North responded with similar euphoria. "I never knew what a popular excitement can be," exclaimed a Harvard professor. "The whole population, men, women, and children, seem to be in the streets with Union favors and flags." The scene was much the same in Illinois, where Stephen A. Douglas told a Chicago audience a month before his death: "There can be no neutrals in this war, *only patriots—or traitors.*" In the Upper South, however, the choice did not seem so clear cut.

The Upper South Secedes

Most citizens of the Upper South interpreted Lincoln's mobilization against the Confederacy as an act of unwarranted aggression. Although they had not felt

> **How did the Upper South react to the outbreak of fighting?**

right about seceding because of Lincoln's election alone, they now believed there was reason to reconsider the matter. The Upper South was crucial to Confederate success, containing half the South's population and three-quarters of its industrial capacity. Tennessee's governor declared that his state "will not furnish a single man for the purpose of coercion, but fifty thousand if necessary for the defense of our rights and those of our Southern brothers."

Virginia was vital to both the Union and the Confederacy because of its location, resources, and prestige. Virginia contained the South's largest iron foundry, Richmond's Tredegar Iron Works, as well as important salt mines (salt still being the primary means of preserving food). In April, less than a week after Fort Sumter surrendered, the home state of Washington, Jefferson, and Madison voted to secede from the United States. Militia forces promptly took control of the rifle factory at Harpers Ferry and transported the machinery to Richmond. They also seized the shipyard at Norfolk and captured a damaged wooden frigate, the *USS Merrimack*. The state invited the Confederate government to make Richmond its permanent capital, audaciously located only 100 miles from Washington, D.C.

Another valuable resource that Virginia brought to the Confederacy was Colonel Robert E. Lee, whom Commanding general Winfield Scott rated as the United States Army's best officer. Lee's father had fought with Washington in the Revolutionary War, and Lee himself had spent his entire career in the military, seeing action during the U.S.—Mexico War and serving as superintendent of West Point. He disavowed slavery and secession but declined an offer to take command of the armed forces of the United States. "I cannot raise my hand against my birthplace, my home, my children," he explained as he broke his oath of allegiance to the United States, left his stately Arlington plantation overlooking the Potomac River (now a national military cemetery), and offered his services to the Confederacy.

Despite strong secessionist sentiment in most regions of the state, Unionism prevailed in the mountainous western counties, where few plantations existed and

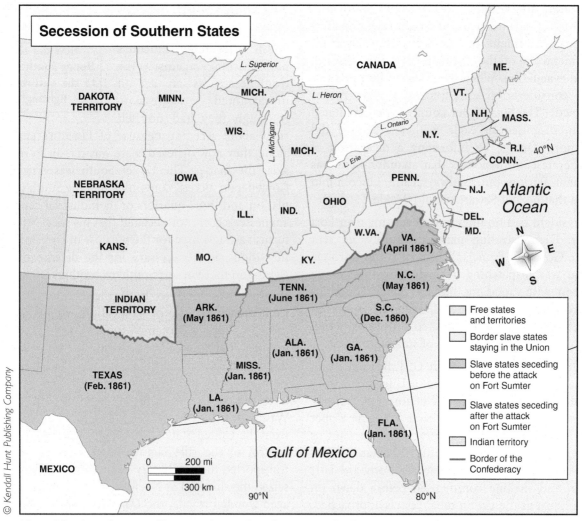

Secession of Southern States

CANADA

DAKOTA TERRITORY
MINN.
MICH.
L. Superior
L. Heron
ME.
VT.
N.H.
MASS.
WIS.
L. Michigan
MICH.
L. Ontario
N.Y.
R.I.
40°N
CONN.
NEBRASKA TERRITORY
IOWA
L. Erie
PENN.
N.J.
Atlantic Ocean
ILL.
IND.
OHIO
DEL.
MD.
KANS.
MO.
KY.
W.VA.
VA. (April 1861)
INDIAN TERRITORY
ARK. (May 1861)
TENN. (June 1861)
N.C. (May 1861)
S.C. (Dec. 1860)
ALA. (Jan. 1861)
GA. (Jan. 1861)
TEXAS (Feb. 1861)
MISS. (Jan. 1861)
LA. (Jan. 1861)
FLA. (Jan. 1861)
MEXICO
Gulf of Mexico

0   200 mi
0   300 km

90°N   80°N

Legend:
☐ Free states and territories
☐ Border slave states staying in the Union
☐ Slave states seceding before the attack on Fort Sumter
☐ Slave states seceding after the attack on Fort Sumter
☐ Indian territory
— Border of the Confederacy

Map of Southern Secession: This map depicts the relative strength of secession sentiment by the date when states in the lower South and upper South adopted ordinances of secession.

slaves comprised only a tiny fraction of the population. Indeed, the region's farmers had always resented the slave owning nabobs of the eastern Tidewater and Piedmont and were oriented more toward the markets and culture of Pittsburgh than Richmond. In July 1863, after agreeing to abolish slavery, West Virginia joined the United States, but Confederate sympathizers kept up a savage campaign of terror throughout the war.

Virginia's secession influenced decisions in other states. In May of 1861, Arkansas and North Carolina both seceded, followed in June by Tennessee. Like West Virginians, however, citizens of eastern Tennessee lived in mountainous country that never supported plantation-style slavery and opposed secession. The Lincoln administration tried to restore loyal government in Tennessee by recruiting Unionists like United States Senator Andrew Johnson and Knoxville newspaper editor and former

Methodist minister William G. "Parson" Brownlow. Both men hated planter aristocrats and secessionists. Johnson was the only senator from a seceded state not to resign. The famously profane Brownlow swore he would "fight the Secession leaders till Hell freezes over, and then fight them on the ice." But the Lincoln government could not provide the Unionists with military support. Confederates severely punished them, and Brownlow was lucky to be expelled to Union lines.

Maryland was strategically important because it surrounded Washington on three sides (Virginia occupied the other). Secessionists constituted a minority of the state's population but a passionate one that even predominated in areas like Baltimore. On April 19, fury against Lincoln erupted when the 6th Massachusetts Regiment, the first to answer Lincoln's call for volunteers, passed through Baltimore on the way to Washington. As the troops marched from one railway station to another (remember that most railroads were not yet linked), an angry mob attacked them with brickbats and firearms. When the angry and panicky Yankees fired back, a horrible riot ensued, ending with four soldiers and twelve citizens dead. Lincoln declared martial law in Maryland and arrested thirty-one legislators to prevent them from holding a secession convention. Gradually the Unionist majority prevailed, and two-thirds of the white Marylanders who fought in the Civil War did so in blue.

Kentucky, situated along the Ohio River, could provide the Confederacy with a natural defense perimeter if it chose to secede. In line with the state's tradition of compromise, most Kentuckians hoped for reconciliation, and Kentucky's legislature passed a resolution of neutrality. But others were more divided in their sympathies than neutral. Both Davis and Lincoln were Kentucky natives. Lincoln tried to honor Kentucky's wishes, even turning his back on the state's flourishing commerce with the Confederacy, in order to keep it from seceding. In September of 1861, however, a Confederate army under the command of General Leonidas Polk seized the Mississippi River town of Columbus, and in response a force of Illinois volunteers commanded by Union General Ulysses S. Grant occupied Paducah and gained control of the strategically important Cumberland and Tennessee rivers. The initial violation of Kentucky neutrality by the Confederacy helped hold the state in the Union. The poignant tragedy of the Civil War was illustrated by the four of Henry Clay's grandsons who fought for the Confederacy and the three who joined the Union army.

Missouri's lead mines were invaluable for the manufacture of bullets, and secessionists moved quickly to align the state with the Confederacy. Governor Claiborn F. Jackson and General Sterling Price, a U.S.—Mexico War veteran who commanded the state's militia, squared off against Unionists who stood behind Francis P. Blair and Nathaniel Lyon, commander of federal troops stationed in St. Louis. In heavy fighting in June, Lyon's Union forces drove Price and his secessionists out of the state in the first significant encounters of the Civil War. Like West Virginia, however, Missouri suffered through years of brutal guerrilla war.

The great concern about the Upper South and border states that Lincoln and Davis shared was justified. If all eight had seceded, the outcome of the war would most likely have been different. As it was, they contributed 425,000 troops to Confederate armies, approximately one-half of the Confederate total, and

320,000 to the Union, or fifteen percent of its total manpower.

What They Fought For

Civil War armies depended heavily on volunteers rather than professional soldiers and sailors. The issues that had brought on the conflict were the great public concerns of the day—discussed by citizens regardless of their place in society and including those who joined the armed forces of both sides. "When the South becomes an enemy to the American system of government . . . ," a Pittsburgh Democratic newspaper declared, "and fires upon the flag . . . our influence goes for the flag, no matter whether a Republican or a Democrat holds it." A North Carolinian put his views more succinctly: "I had rather be dead than see the Yanks rule this country."

> What motivated men to join their countries' armed forces?

And just as citizens voted in elections that set directions for both the United States and the Confederacy, so they joined the military ranks to implement those policies. Civil War soldiers were politically informed citizens.

Recruits proudly donned their blue or gray uniforms and had their photographs taken to document their role in the epic event. Families and sweethearts watched proudly and with apprehension as their soldiers marched off to war. The unifying sentiment on both sides of the battle lines was the obligation to defend something dear. "Johnny Reb" and "Billy Yank" had been indoctrinated in civic duty through schools, churches, local newspapers, and popular literature. Soldiers on both sides declared the same basic purpose: "My whole soul is wrapped up in this our Country's cause." Ambiguous, high-blown notions usually had very specific personal meaning. A captured North Carolinian replied to his Yankee interrogator: "I'm fighting because you're down here." Union soldiers felt and expressed similar feelings. After Gettysburg, Sergeant William Henry Redman wrote his mother: "I am only satisfied nowadays when I am fighting the enemy. The proper time to fight him is while he is on our northern soil. I shall kill every one of them I can."

For African-Americans, whose entry into the ranks of the Union armed forces as combat troops came in 1863, the cause related closely to the Emancipation Proclamation. As many a soldier stated, they fought for

"God, race, and country." In addition, because blacks suffered more atrocities at the hands of Confederates, vengeance and retribution provided additional motivation to fight against and to kill the enemy.

Women also responded to patriotic appeals, although sometimes with ambivalence and concern. "What do I care about patriotism?" declared one South Carolina woman. "My husband is my country. What is country to me if he be killed?" Typically, however, women's patriotism equaled men's and in some cases was what encouraged men to do their duty. Women in one Texas community sent bonnets and skirts to local males who refused to enlist. Bringing honor to family and community was a strong motivator. Dying a "**good death**" was important to soldiers on both sides of the battle lines. In an overwhelmingly Protestant Christian society, it was important to die in Christian faith, ready to meet one's maker. And martyrdom to the cause of country was equally important. An Indiana volunteer wrote to his wife that "if it should be that I do not Return I wish you to instruct My little Boy that I die a Martyr to my country, without any sympathy for traitors."

Bull Run: The First Major Test Under Fire

What were the initial military objectives of both sides, and how did they work out in the first major engagement?

In the weeks after Fort Sumter, neither the Lincoln nor the Davis administration had had enough time to develop a comprehensive plan for victory. In some ways, the Confederacy had an easier task. Largely ignoring the clamor in the press to "utterly destroy" northern farms and cities, Davis reflected on history and George Washington's goal as commander of the Continental Army to avoid being annihilated by the British. To that end, Davis attempted to concentrate his forces, shifting them along **interior lines** as needed to meet an advancing Union army. By prolonging the war he hoped to eat away at the North's morale and eventually force Lincoln to relent and allow the South to secede in peace. The Confederacy could win if it simply did not lose. State officials complicated that strategy, however, by reserving troops for their own defense, which amounted to dispersing rather than concentrating forces.

In the United States at the outset of the war, no single, clearly defined strategy emerged. Like Davis, Lincoln spent his first months in office clarifying his war aims while trying to devise an overarching plan. His primary goal was to reestablish a peaceful and relatively harmonious Union and to avoid a social and political revolution in the South. The present and future of slavery, he believed, should be determined by laws enacted through normal democratic processes, not by executive dictate or armed force. Yet at the same time Lincoln felt pressure from abolitionists to destroy slavery and from the public to strike quickly against rebels and traitors. Newspaper headlines blared: "On to Richmond" and hang "Old Jeff Davis." He moved cautiously, mainly to avoid offending the loyal border states; furthermore, he sensed that victory would require destroying the Confederacy's armies, not merely chasing off its government. This was a fairly new concept in warfare and markedly different from the traditional military tactic of out maneuvering one's opponent to gain strategic advantage. Conquering the Confederacy would be difficult, comparable in magnitude to Napoleon's 1812 invasion of Russia, which failed utterly, yet many of Lincoln's military officers felt confident of a quick victory given the United States' success in the war with Mexico.

General-in-Chief Winfield Scott, the seventy-four-year-old commander of the invasion of Mexico, did not imagine a glorious three-month rout of the Confederacy, but as a native Virginian he hated the prospect of a prolonged war and a devastated South. Scott favored a naval blockade of the South's ports, a plan that would strangle the Confederacy (critics ridiculed it as the "Anaconda Plan") and bring reunion without massive destruction and bloodshed. He also proposed joint naval and military operations on the Mississippi River that would be like plunging a sharp dagger into the heart of the rebellion. But Lincoln could not ignore the political imperatives. Why not try to take Richmond? Besides, many of the volunteers who joined the army after Fort Sumter had signed up for only ninety days. So he approved both Scott's plan and an assault against Richmond.

General Irvin McDowell, in command of Union forces headquartered in Washington, developed the specific plan to march 35,000 men directly across northern Virginia to the Confederate capital. The operation promised a quick end to the war if it succeeded, but it also involved considerable risk. McDowell's recruits had no combat experience and little training, and McDowell himself could boast few military accomplishments. Lincoln gave the green light, hoping for the best. To defend Richmond, Confederate forces had drawn up near a railroad junction at Manassas, along Bull Run Creek, some thirty miles southwest of Washington (see map on

p. 470). Pierre G. T. Beauregard, of Fort Sumter fame, commanded 25,000 troops with another 10,000 men under General Joseph E. Johnston in the Shenandoah Valley available as reinforcements.

On Sunday, July 21, McDowell's men attacked the waiting Confederates, who had been alerted by an espionage network maintained by a Confederate sympathizer named Rose O'Neal Greenhow. Johnston brought his troops by train, arriving just in time to turn an evenly fought battle into a rout. Among the heroes of the day was Confederate General Thomas J. Jackson, a Bible-toting former professor at Virginia Military Institute whose brigade repulsed a Union attack by holding steady, as someone reportedly said, like a stone wall. Jackson was known ever after as **"Stonewall."** The Yankees panicked as the Confederates charged with their guns blazing and famous "rebel yell." Joining McDowell's men in the mad dash back to Washington were scores of United States congressmen, their wives, and other prominent citizens who had ridden down from the capital to watch what they thought would be a glorious Union triumph.

By Civil War standards, the **Battle of Bull Run** (or **Manassas**, as the Confederates called it) was small but enormously significant. Like a douse of cold water, the battle aroused Northerners to the reality that the Confederacy would not fold its tents anytime soon. Some 900 soldiers died that day, and 2,700 suffered wounds—shocking numbers at the time. Although stunned by the defeat, Lincoln immediately authorized the raising of a million troops for enlistment terms of three years and placed General George B. McClellan, a masterful organizer and disciplinarian, in charge of what was called the **Army of the Potomac**, the most powerful military force the United States had ever assembled. In the Confederacy, pride and confidence soared after Bull Run, sustaining both civilian and military morale that was at once crucial to any chance of an ultimate Confederate victory and yet detrimental in the sense that it led to unrealistic assessments of their opponents. Union troops and commanders improved as time went on, even as the bitter memory of Bull Run and the "rebel yell" fed their self-doubt.

THINKING BACK

1. How did a political crisis in 1860 become a military conflict in the spring of 1861? Why did proposed compromises fail to reconcile differences between North and South?

2. After Fort Sumter and the commencement of the Civil War, what assessment did both sides make of their chances of winning? What did both sides have to do to win, and whose chances looked better after Bull Run?

TOTAL WAR, 1862

Early in 1862, one of "Stonewall" Jackson's men wrote to his family back home that "the romance of the thing is entirely worn off." Not necessarily an indication of defeatism, his statement nevertheless acknowledged that a limited war had begun to turn into a long, exhausting, and often horrifying nightmare. Lincoln clearly understood now that victory called for total war against the South—its armies, its resources, and ultimately its institution of slavery. Consequently, the North's greater human and industrial resources came increasingly into play. Time became the Union's friend, yet, as battlefield losses mounted, demands for peace grew. In Richmond meanwhile, Davis confronted a different set of challenges. For any strategy to work, the Confederacy needed help from friends abroad, just as the patriots of 1776 obtained assistance from France. By the end of the second year of fighting the Civil War had taken on new dimensions.

Revised War Aims and Strategies

After Bull Run, strategists in Washington and Richmond developed more aggressive and comprehensive military plans. Davis and his fellow Confederates continued to follow a mostly defensive strategy, due largely to state governors' insistence that their states' defense deserved top priority. However, Davis personally favored an aggressive war, and twice the South took the fight into the North, hoping further to undermine civilian morale: the invasions of Maryland in September of 1862 and Pennsylvania in July of 1863. "My early declared purpose and continued hope," Davis told a supporter, "was to feed upon the enemy and teach them the blessings of peace by making them feel in its most tangible form the evils of war."

> How did strategies change in 1862, and how effective were they?

The Union naval blockade remained in place and grew steadily tighter, but after Bull Run Lincoln reassessed the military situation. Up to that time, most Union generals followed the eighteenth-century maxim of massing one's forces to capture territory rather than destroying enemy armies, but

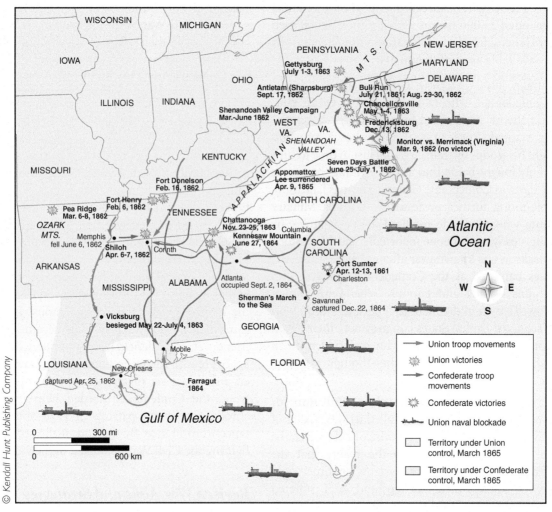

Map of the Civil War, 1861–1865, showing major Union and Confederate troop movements, pivotal battles, the extent of the Union's naval blockade, and areas of strategic control by each side by the spring of 1865.

Lincoln determined to negate the Confederates' advantage of interior lines. By launching multiple, simultaneous offensives into the South from Virginia and the Carolinas in the east to the Mississippi River in the west he could force the Confederates to spread their limited resources. In addition, he sought to reduce substantially the Confederacy's capacity to wage war by destroying or severely damaging its armies and railroads and even its factories, foundries, and plantations. Lincoln looked for generals who shared his views, and when he found them he interfered very little with them.

To accomplish his goal, Lincoln sought to dismember the Confederacy. In February of 1862, Union forces struck into the heart of the Confederacy from the Ohio River. General Ulysses S. Grant teamed with Admiral Andrew Foote to capture Fort Henry on the Tennessee River and Fort Donelson on the Cumberland River, both of which had been

constructed to defend Tennessee against river-borne operations. Those two losses forced Confederate General Albert Sidney Johnston, commander of the Military Department of the West, to withdraw some 42,000 troops into northern Mississippi. But as Grant's Army of the Tennessee advanced southward along the Tennessee River, expecting to be joined by another Union army under General Don Carlos Buell, Johnson sprang a furious surprise attack through a peach orchard near a country church called **Shiloh**. Fighting on April 6 nearly routed the Yankees, but Johnson was killed. The next day, General William Tecumseh Sherman helped Grant rally their troops, defeating the Confederates and forcing them to retreat into Mississippi.

Later that month, Admiral David Farragut, commander of a Gulf Coast blockading squadron, ran his vessels past Confederate guns on the lower Mississippi to capture New Orleans. Although critics accused Grant of having been drunk at Shiloh and demanded that Lincoln relieve him of command, the President liked what he saw. "I can't spare this man," said Lincoln; "he fights." Shiloh and New Orleans were the first important Union victories of the Civil War, both occurring in the West. Together they foreshadowed a gradual turnaround for the United States.

What They Fought With: Supplying the Troops

> What advantages and disadvantages did Union and Confederate forces have in a total war?

Shiloh revealed the disparity between the resources available to Union and Confederate forces, a gap that became increasingly important as the war dragged on. Early on, a reporter for the London *Times* expressed the widely held European belief that the North could not prevent secession, for the same reason that Great Britain had failed to subdue the United States in the American Revolutionary War. "No war of independence ever terminated unsuccessfully," he averred, "except where the disparity of force was far greater than it is in this case."

But clearly, the Union did enjoy crucial material advantages over the Confederacy. Lincoln led a country of 22 million people, more than double the South's 9 million, a margin that from a military standpoint was functionally greater since the Confederacy's population included 3.5 million slaves who were not permitted to bear arms. In all, the Union put approximately 2 million men into military uniform, the Confederacy half as many. But gross numbers do not tell the whole story. By 1864, nine out of ten white Southerners between the ages of 18 and 60 had entered the armed forces, leaving few able-bodied men behind, along with enslaved African Americans, to keep the country going. By contrast, less than half the North's male population entered the military, leaving a large civilian workforce to operate farms and factories.

At the outset of the war, more young men volunteered for military service than either side needed or could equip, but as the conflict grew in scope, as casualties mounted, and as war weariness deepened, both Lincoln and Davis faced the necessity of **conscription**, that is, forcing individuals into military service. One Virginia soldier wrote that if he survived his enlistment he would not reenlist. "I don't think I could stand it another year." In April of 1862, after trying bounties and various other incentives to rekindle voluntarism, the Confederate Congress passed the first conscription law in American history, and an extremely unpopular expansion of government into the lives of Confederate citizens. Under the law, all male citizens between eighteen and thirty-five could be drafted for three-year duty. Congress exempted certain categories of men due to their work's presumed value to the war effort: Confederate and state officials, railroad and river workers, telegraph operators, clergymen, and teachers. A draftee could also hire a substitute for the equivalent of three years' wages, which bred the kind of resentment conveyed in the saying: "A rich man's war but a poor man's fight." Abuse of the substitute provision, like substitutes immediately deserting and hiring themselves out again, caused Congress eventually to repeal it while adding other refinements like increasing liability to age forty-five and exempting one white man (an overseer most likely) for every plantation with twenty of more slaves in an attempt to keep agricultural production up.

In July 1862, the United States Congress also enacted a conscription law that authorized the president to set enlistment quotas for state militias that could be met by volunteers or by draftees. The act represented a significant expansion of federal power at the expense of the states, and despite Secretary of War Edwin Stanton's efficient administration of the militia draft (Lincoln had replaced the troublesome Simon Cameron with Stanton), Union manpower shortages by summer of 1863 resembled those in the Confederacy. So in March, Congress passed a national conscription act with a draft lottery. Even if a man's name was drawn, however, the chances of his actually entering service were remarkably small. More than one-fifth never reported for induction, and three-fifths of the remainder received personal exemptions for disabilities or hardship on their families. Others paid for substitutes or a commutation. Ultimately, of 776,000 men whose names were drawn in four draft lotteries, only 46,000 wound up in the army.

In addition to manpower disparities, economic productivity favored the Union. The North possessed six times as many factories as the South and manufactured seventeen times as much cloth for uniforms, haversacks, tents, and blankets and thirty-two times as many rifles, cannons, and mortars. In the production of food, too, the North outstripped the South, fourfold in the quantity of wheat, two times in the production of corn, and one-and-a-half times in processed meat and poultry. Throughout the war Confederate soldiers ate less well than their Union counterparts.

Railroad bridge on the Orange and Alexandria (Virginia) railroad. Railways provided vital transportation to both sides. Confederates destroyed railroads rather than have them fall into Union hands. This bridge had been damaged and then repaired by Union army engineers.

Strategic advantage was not only a matter of productivity; it was also a matter of distribution. Over the preceding two decades, Northern railroad companies had laid down 22,000 miles of track, mostly of the same gauge (the space between parallel rails) which allowed short lines to connect over great distances. The South had only 9,000 miles of track in various gauges so that local rail lines did not connect to each other in any kind of effective network. No Confederate railroad spanned the Mississippi River; consequently, railroads could not convey imports from Mexican ports like Matamoros, which were at least partially open, through Texas and Louisiana and into the heart of the Confederacy, thereby circumventing the Union naval blockade. Carrying capacity was another significant factor. Of 470 locomotives built in the United States in 1860 to pull trains, only nineteen came from Southern factories. Nevertheless, Confederate railroads did help move troops and supplies, and the Union expended considerable effort in capturing them or knocking them out.

Southern agriculture produced great quantities of cotton, which the Confederacy counted on to secure foreign intervention that might offset some of its material deficiencies. Davis and Secretary of State Judah P. Benjamin of Louisiana looked primarily to Great Britain for help in breaking the Union blockade, figuring that British textile factories would shut down without Southern cotton, causing massive unemployment and economic disaster. Early in 1861, Davis attempted to precipitate Anglo-French action by deliberately withholding cotton, citing the blockade. Unfortunately, the timing was critically off. Surpluses from a bumper cotton crop in 1860 kept British factories running, thus avoiding unacceptable levels of unemployment. Then beginning in 1862, rapidly developing cotton production in India and Egypt made up for declines in imports from the South (see The Global Perspective, pp. 392–94). And finally, crop failures in Europe made Great Britain dependent on corn imports from the North. In the end, the British government chose not to risk a United States grain embargo in retaliation against intervention in the Civil War.

"King Cotton Diplomacy" also aimed at coercing Great Britain and France into extending diplomatic recognition to the Confederacy and perhaps supplying it with rifles, ammunition, and other military hardware. Ironically, by blockading the Confederacy and expecting other nations to respect it, the United States implicitly acknowledged the Confederacy's international status as a belligerent nation. Nevertheless, Secretary of State Seward forcefully stated the Lincoln administration's policy that formal recognition by the European countries was intolerable and could lead to war. Prospects for recognition were not very good anyway; Britain had abolished slavery thirty years earlier and the British public supported the Union's republican, free labor ideology over the Confederacy's slave labor system. France's Emperor Napoleon III signaled a willingness to recognize the Confederacy, hoping that the South might in return support his plan to establish a protectorate in Mexico. But he preferred to follow Great Britain's lead rather than to act alone.

An incident in November of 1861, however, nearly reversed British reluctance to recognize the Confederacy and took Britain and the United States to the brink of war. A Union warship intercepted the British steamer *Trent* on the high seas and removed two Confederate diplomats on assignment to Europe to press for recognition. This curious twist brought to mind American complaints about British interference with neutral American ocean ships during the 1790s. Howls of outrage and protest emanated from the British press and from Prime Minister Viscount Palmerston, who told his cabinet: "You may stand for this but damned if I will." Lincoln defused the situation, reportedly murmuring "One war at a time." Authorities released the Confederates, and U. S. minister to Great Britain Charles Francis Adams, son and grandson of former presidents, skillfully soothed wounded feelings in London. When all was said and done, Great Britain and France recognized Confederate belligerency but withheld formal recognition and turned down requests for alliances.

Even without foreign intervention, Confederates found ways around the Union blockade. Swift blockade runners, many of them built in England and operated by British sea captains, slipped into Confederate ports with cargoes ranging from rifles, ammunition, and shoes to liquor, tea, and hoop skirts.

Material deficiencies were somewhat offset by intangible advantages, including the psychology of defending hearth and home. Even non-slave owners fought ferociously to defend white supremacy. The Confederacy's defensive strategy required less of its armies than did the Union's total war effort. On the one hand, civilians fed, sheltered, and provided valuable intelligence to Confederate forces. On the other hand, Yankee armies operating in hostile territory had to supply themselves, which required extending supply lines deep into Southern territory and employing thousands of horses, mules, and wagons for transport. Furthermore, once rail lines, depots, and support bases were established, Union armies had to detach units of troops to guard them. All in all, the Union's requirements for invading and subduing the Confederacy's vast area, insofar as troop strength and supplies were concerned, far exceeded those of the Confederacy.

Historians and Civil War buffs have argued heatedly over which side had more competent soldiers. Some of the best officers in the United States army came from the South, where seven of the eight existing military training schools, including Virginia Military Institute and The Citadel, were located and where more males than in the North received military training. When secession came, many of these men joined the Confederacy. But it would be hard to prove that the Confederacy enjoyed a superior officer corps. Debate rages over whether Lee was ultimately an asset or a liability; he won many battles but lost over 103,000 men, fewer casualties than he inflicted but more than he could replace. And attrition hurt the Confederacy, which lost Albert Sidney Johnston at Shiloh in 1862 and "Stonewall" Jackson, at Chancellorsville, one year later. Union command improved as the war progressed. Ulysses S. Grant, William Tecumseh Sherman, and Philip Sheridan emerged to give Lincoln generals who perfectly fit the North's aggressive strategy.

There was no shortage of valor among the citizen-soldiers on either side even though desertion increased in proportion with sagging morale and after implementation of the military draft. Rebel troops probably entered the war with greater raw skill, especially horsemanship, partly because Southern culture placed great emphasis on manly honor, defined in terms of martial arts. As the war progressed, however, and the Yankees gained more combat experience and discipline, the gap between Union and Confederate soldiering lessened. By the end of the war, many crack infantry and artillery units performed heroically and effectively on both sides of the battle lines.

The question of which side would win the Civil War ultimately came down to who managed to sustain the fight longer. And that was a function not only of material resources and military skill but of civic resolve and political leadership. Neither side fought with a professional army. Thus, the Lincoln administration had to project the North's commitment to the Union onto the battlefield through volunteers and draftees. Likewise, Jefferson Davis had to persuade Southerners that independent nationhood was worth fighting and dying for. In the end, the Civil War demanded more of the South than the North, and probably more than Southerners were able to give.

Managing the Politics of a Changing War

The Civil War put the Lincoln and Davis governments to many extraordinary tests. Both heads of state along with their respective cabinets and other officials brought strengths and weaknesses to the table, but political imperatives also influenced how they responded to crises and limited what they could accomplish. Both governments adjusted strategies and policies to meet changing circumstances.

> What political factors did the Lincoln and Davis governments have to consider?

Many members of the North's elite thought of Abraham Lincoln as a simpleminded hayseed. Snobby journalists poked fun at his fondness for homespun stories as well as his tall, gawky frame and ill-fitting clothes. But in truth, Lincoln was an exceptionally intelligent person, a shrewd judge of character, and an adroit politician. His humble roots and deep sense of compassion connected him to ordinary citizens. Lincoln frequently visited soldiers in camp, praising their courage and lifting their spirits with pithy speeches about the Union. Mostly unaffected by the religious revivals that had raged during his youth, he read the Bible more for "quotable quotes" than for inspiration. His mother's stern Calvinism instilled a fatalism that occasionally brought on episodes of melancholia. He could be thankful, however, for having an established government with working relationships with state officials and two healthy political parties to give voice to legitimate opposition.

The most profound political issue confronting the Lincoln administration involved the very nature of the war, whether to focus exclusively on preserving the Union and allow regular political processes to resolve the issue of slavery or to destroy slavery as part of waging war and reconstructing the United States. Although Lincoln started out on the side of preserving the Union, in 1862 political pressure along with his own moral and constitutional scruples drew him to the other side. Abolitionists, including ex-slave Frederick Douglass, argued hard for the destruction of slavery. "To fight against slaveowners, without fighting against slavery," Douglass declared, "is but a half-hearted business." Lincoln resisted, partly because an abolition war would alienate many Northerners as well as citizens in loyal border states but also because the Constitution protected slavery within the states. Yet, if abolition went beyond his war aim, confiscating enemy property, including slave property, used to destroy the Union did not.

In May 1861, three enslaved African Americans who had been working on Confederate fortifications in Virginia escaped and entered Union-held Fortress Monroe. Commanding officer General Benjamin F. Butler refused to return them to their owner, declaring them "**contraband of war.**" The Lincoln administration endorsed Butler's policy although without stating whether the escapees were free. On August 6, Congress passed a **Confiscation Act** declaring that contraband slaves could be freed if they were employed by the Confederate military, laying down the principle of emancipation by **military necessity**.

Without consulting Lincoln, John C. Frémont, military commander of the Department of Missouri, went farther, issuing an order in August that all slaves owned by Confederate supporters in Missouri were free. Lincoln immediately remanded Frémont's order and relieved him of command. In May of 1862, David Hunter did the same thing in coastal South Carolina, where Union forces had established control the previous November, and again Lincoln countermanded the order with a rebuke. Republicans, led by Senator Charles Sumner of Massachusetts and Representative Thaddeus Stevens of Pennsylvania, used their congressional majority to abolish slavery in the District of Columbia and prohibit it in the territories. By the summer of 1862, it was clear to the government in Washington that Confederate forces were employing slaves effectively in erecting fortifications, in driving wagons along vital supply lines, and in maintaining production on plantations and in the South's factories and mines. Therefore, in July of 1862, Congress passed the **Second Confiscation Act** that declared that the slaves of all rebels "shall be forever free." Total war now promised revolutionary change.

As expected, as the war intensified and war aims changed, dissenters grew more vociferous. Antiwar Democrats, known as **Copperheads**, demanded that Lincoln allow the Southern states leave in peace. Their leader, an Ohio congressman named Clement L. Vallandigham, charged that Republican "fanaticism," not Southern perfidy, had brought on the crisis. "Stop the war." Antiwar dissent jeopardized the war effort by eroding morale and encouraging resistance to military service. In this situation, the distinction between free speech and treason became ambiguous. "Must I shoot a simple-minded soldier boy who deserts," Lincoln asked, "while I must not touch a hair of a wily agitator who induces him to desert?" The government eventually arrested Vallandigham and banished him to the Confederacy.

Lincoln actually showed remarkable forbearance in the face of ordinary criticism, but when he believed that opposition to his war aims represented a clear and present danger to the country he acted aggressively to suppress it. In the spring of 1861, federal officials arrested Maryland secessionists for attacking Union soldiers and destroying vital telegraph lines, holding them without formal charges. This violated the constitutional right of *habeas corpus*, acknowledged in common, statutory, and constitutional law as a basic civil liberty. In *Ex parte Merryman* (1861), a case involving one of the detainees, Chief Justice Roger Taney, a partisan Democrat who abhorred the expansion of federal government power, condemned Lincoln's conduct as an abuse of power. Supported by an opinion by Attorney General Bates, Lincoln ignored the ruling, and in an address to Congress that summer asked: "Are all the laws, but one, to go unexecuted, and the government itself to go to pieces, lest that one be violated?" Congress eventually authorized the suspension of *habeas corpus*. Lincoln also approved military court trials of Indiana citizens accused of fomenting rebellion. In 1866, after the war was over, the Supreme Court ruled in *Ex parte Milligan* that the government must try citizens in civilian courts whenever possible. Despite these excesses in the name of national security, Lincoln acted with compassionate indulgence in his treatment of captured Confederate soldiers. Instead of charging them with treason and possibly putting them to death, he treated them as prisoners of war and even allowed paroles and exchanges.

Jefferson Davis's personality complicated his leadership. Sometimes hard to get along with, Davis made enemies more easily than friends among both soldiers and politicians. His critics used terms like "cold, haughty, peevish, narrow-minded, and pig-headed" to describe him. Even his wife, Confederate First Lady Varina Howell Davis, conceded that "if anyone disagrees with Mr. Davis he resents it and ascribes the difference to the perversity of his opponent." Building bridges to those opponents, who became more vocal and organized as Confederate prospects for winning the Civil War grew dimmer and hardship on the home front mounted, was not his forte. Davis constantly quarreled with political and military leaders and failed to reach consensus on overall policies. Davis refused to acknowledge Vice President Stephens as a contributor to administration policy, causing Stephens to note Davis' resemblance to "my poor old blind and deaf dog."

Contention between states' rights and central authority plagued the Confederate government. In addition to implementing military conscription, the Davis administration evoked the wrath of staunch states' rights advocates by proclaiming martial law and suppressing civil liberties, holding Unionists in eastern Tennessee in jail and executing some of them without benefit of a court trial. Opponents accused Davis of tyranny. Georgian Robert Toombs, originally the Confederate secretary of state, complained that "we have more to fear from military despotism than from subjugation by the enemy." And worsening economic conditions produced even more dissension. In the 1863 congressional elections, voters elected forty-one (out of 106) representatives and twelve (of twenty-six) senators who openly opposed the Davis administration. For Davis, the Civil War was an endless internal battle with jealous governors, leading one historian some years ago to quip that the Confederacy died of states' rights.

The absence of two functioning political parties further stymied the Confederacy. Without parties to channel criticism into alternative government policies, dissent degenerated into carping and bitter personal quarrels. Abraham Lincoln had a more functional political system to work with, and that made it easier for the Union to mobilize the resources to prosecute the war.

Because of Davis's military training and experience, he put himself directly into high command decision making. In practical terms, he was his own secretary of war. As a result, he found himself awash in the details of a large and complicated war and also continuously involved in feuds with field commanders. Davis' fondness for Albert Sidney Johnston, whom he had known at West Point and fought with in Mexico, and respect for Robert E. Lee, caused such deep resentment in Joseph Johnston, who regarded himself as a better officer and deserving of a higher rank, that the two seldom communicated directly.

Paying the Bills

The price tag on a total war was much higher than on a limited one, and both the Confederacy and the Union struggled to pay the bills. The South, however, operated on a weaker economic basis despite beginning the war with 30 percent of the total wealth of the United States.

> **How did both governments pay for the war?**

The main problem for Christopher Memminger, the Confederacy's talented treasury secretary, was a shortage of liquid assets. Most of the South's wealth was tied up in land and slaves, leaving very little money available to invest in Confederate bonds. Planters resisted taxes, even though this method of raising revenue carried the least potential for price inflation. With no mechanism in place for collecting local taxes, the makeshift Confederate government had to rely on the states, and they usually found ways to avoid taxes. Consequently, the Confederacy had to resort to printing valueless paper currency. In all, the government printed 1.5 billion Confederate dollars, but it did not make the currency legal tender. Counterfeiting and state issues added to the deluge of "shinplaster" paper money and resulted in staggering inflation—12 percent *per month* at the end of 1861. By the end of 1863, prices had multiplied seven-fold, and the situation continued to worsen with Confederate reverses on the battlefield. By the end of the war, inflation had reached 9,000 percent.

Inflation was the result of excessive paper money and chronic shortages of consumer goods. With the men folk off fighting the war, women and children struggled to provide themselves with food. The Confederate government exacerbated the problem by requisitioning food, and passing armies simply took what they needed. The situation worsened as the war dragged on. Desertion increased as desperate soldiers returned home to care for their families. "We are poor men and are willing to defend our country," explained a Mississippi volunteer, "but our families [come] first." Looking for someone to blame for these woes, frustrated citizens turned against their political leaders and assorted profiteers. Jewish merchants became easy scapegoats. "If we gain our independence," remarked a government clerk, "instead of being the vassals of the Yankees, we shall find all our wealth in the hands of the Jews."

The Lincoln administration had a vibrant economy to work with; thus, financing the war was less problematic. Ready cash made it relatively easy for Treasury Secretary Salmon P. Chase to borrow money. Following the advice of Philadelphia banking wizard Jay Cooke, the administration raised two-thirds of the money it needed through war bonds sold to individual investors as well as bankers. The government raised an additional 20 percent of needed revenues through taxes, including the first income tax in American history. In 1862, Congress created the Bureau of Internal Revenue to collect the assessments. Chase met the remainder of the government's monetary needs by printing currency. The Union "greenbacks" were legal tender and had the public's confidence. Limited paper, a reasonable tax policy, and increased economic productivity kept inflation at relatively modest levels, 80 percent for the entire war period.

Having a strong economy and a large population to draw from added immeasurably to the Union's enormous advantage over the Confederacy. And another crucial element in the clash between the Blue and the Gray was sea power. The Union blockade of the South accentuated the Confederacy's weaknesses.

The Naval War

A key element in Union strategy for victory was a naval blockade to prevent the Confederacy from importing and exporting valuable products. At the same time, the Lincoln administration sought to control the important rivers west of the Appalachian Mountains that served as vital shipping arteries. The Navy Department, under eccentric Secretary of the Navy Gideon Welles, directed the blockade along the Atlantic and Gulf coasts; however, the War Department and the irascible but hard-working and efficient Edwin Stanton oversaw the river operations in the West. Since the United States started with a respectable navy and the Confederacy with none, the advantage lay with the North. Most of the South's

| What were the primary naval operations in the war? |

naval vessels, including two frigates, the *Alabama* and *Florida*, were constructed in British shipyards.

The blockade entailed controlling of 3,500 miles of Confederate coastline and ports in a dozen cities. Five hundred vessels of various types went into blockade service. Late in 1861 and early in 1862, joint naval and amphibious task forces captured several key Confederate ports. The blockade never totally eliminated Confederate trade; indeed, in the first year only one out of twelve blockade runners was captured, and Wilmington, North Carolina, and Charleston, South Carolina, handled more traffic than before the war. But, by the end of 1864 the blockade had become more effective, and only one half of the blockade runners got through. One Confederate naval officer admitted after the war that the blockade ultimately "shut the Confederacy out from the world, deprived it of supplies, [and] weakened its military and naval strength."

The Civil War helped usher in a new era in naval warfare with the advent of ironclad warships. In July of 1861, Confederate shipbuilders in Virginia went to work attaching heavy iron plates manufactured at the Richmond Tredegar Iron Works to the hull of the frigate *Merrimack*, captured in the seizure of Norfolk (see p. 465). They installed a rickety steam engine, protected it and ten heavy cannons with more iron plates, and mounted a heavy, iron ram on its prow below the waterline. Officials christened the monstrosity the *Virginia*, and people who saw it said it looked like a floating barn with only its roof above water. Meanwhile, President Lincoln and Navy Secretary Welles accepted a radical design for a Union ironclad that looked like a short tin can mounted on a shingle. The vessel was called the *Monitor*.

On March 8, a titanic battle between the two ironclads took place off Hampton Roads on the Virginia coast. The *Virginia* steamed out from Norfolk on a test run, its feeble engine clanging and its boiler hissing as the pilot steered her toward a squadron of five Union vessels on blockade duty. The *Virginia* rammed one of the Union ships, punching a gaping hole in its hull and sinking it. Its guns then blasted another helpless Union ship to bits. Enemy cannon balls ricocheted harmlessly off *Virginia*'s sloping sides. As night fell, horrified Federal sailors could only wait for the Confederate monster to resume its attack. But daylight disclosed the *Monitor*, which had steamed from the naval yard in Brooklyn and engaged the *Virginia* in combat. All day, they pounded each other with cannon balls. At dusk, the battle ended, both vessels battered but neither destroyed.

A Union "Monitor" (ironclad) class vessel on the James River, Virginia.

The epic clash of the ironclads ended the long era of wooden warships, although neither the *Monitor* nor the *Virginia/Merrimack* survived the year. The Confederate vessel's creaky engine gave out right after the battle, and the crew scuttled it. On New Year's Eve of 1862, the *Monitor* sank in a gale off of Cape Hatteras, North Carolina. However, both sides built and deployed many more ironclads during the course of the Civil War.

Oceangoing ironclads were not the only such warships introduced during the Civil War. Both sides experimented with submarines but with little effect. To gain control of the important rivers that cut through the Confederacy from the Ohio to the Gulf of Mexico, the United States built a fleet of armed gunboats. During the spring of 1862, after taking forts Henry and Donelson as well as the Tennessee state capital of Nashville, Union forces gained control of long stretches of the Mississippi River. Moving down from the Mississippi's junction with the Ohio, Foote's flotilla of gunboats assaulted a Confederate stronghold known as **Island Number 10**, and after reducing it moved down river to Memphis. There, on June 6, Union and Confederate gunboats battled as anxious residents watched from overlooking bluffs. The Confederate fleet was pulverized, and Union troops raised the Stars and Stripes over this important commercial city. Meanwhile, David Farragut advanced his squadron upriver after capturing New Orleans. After Baton Rouge and Natchez fell, Vicksburg was the only strategic point on the river remaining in Confederate hands. Foote's and Farragut's flotillas attempted to take the city, but steep bluffs prevented an infantry assault and subsiding river levels threatened to strand the Union gunboats. The capture of Vicksburg required another plan and a prolonged siege.

By the summer of 1862, the Union had regained control of 1,000 miles of river, two Confederate state capitals (Nashville and Baton Rouge), and the South's largest city (New Orleans). It was an ominous beginning for the Confederacy in the Western theater of the war. And the military situation did not improve.

From Shiloh to Fredericksburg

The principal battles of the Civil War were fought in two theaters of action divided by the Appalachian Mountains. Other areas were important but decidedly secondary to these. Military engagements

> How did the military situation in the East differ from the West?

in 1862 clearly demonstrated how the Civil War had changed since its first few months when young men had marched confidently off to defend their countries.

Courtesy of Library of Congress

General Ulysses S. Grant at his headquarters at Cold Harbor, Virginia, 1864.

In the trans-Appalachian West, Lincoln found a fighting general who shared his understanding of how the war would be won. When the war began, Ulysses S. Grant had been nobody's hero. The thirty-nine-year-old veteran of the U. S.—Mexico War was clerking in a dry goods store in Galena, Illinois, after losing his battle with alcohol and resigning his army commission in disgrace. The bearded, laconic, and sad-faced Grant volunteered when the war broke out, and because the Union army needed experienced officers he was given command of an Illinois regiment, and he began to regain his confidence. He realized the importance of relentlessly hammering at the Confederates until they were exhausted, even if it meant sustaining large numbers of casualties. Union losses could be easily replaced; Confederate losses could not. Grant had led the infantry attacks that took Fort Henry and Fort Donelson and received credit for the bloody victory at Shiloh, for which Lincoln promoted him to major general and second in command in the Mississippi Valley.

Back east, however, the story was different, where George B. McClellan disappointed Lincoln as commander of the grand Army of the Potomac. A superb administrator, motivator, and strategist, the diminutive McClellan looked as much like a general as Grant looked like a slouch. He was arrogant, which Lincoln could deal with, but deep inside McClellan harbored serious self-doubt that caused him consistently to overestimate enemy strength and delay engaging in combat. This perplexed Lincoln, who complained that McClellan suffered from "the slows." Lincoln wanted a direct overland campaign against Richmond, but during the winter of 1861–1862 McClellan only drilled and drilled his 120,000-man force in its camp outside Washington. "If General McClellan does not want to use the army," the exasperated president remarked, "I would like to borrow it." Then, claiming that Confederate positions were too strong and that he was outnumbered, McClellan insisted on an amphibious assault from Chesapeake Bay.

The truth of the matter was that Joseph E. Johnston had only 45,000 Confederates troops to defend Richmond. In the spring of 1862, McClellan left a detachment to guard Washington and transported 100,000 men, 300 cannons, and 25,000 horses and mules by ship to the Virginia peninsula between the James and York rivers. For two months, he inched toward Richmond. On May 31 at **Fair Oaks**, the Rebels slammed into McClellan's army, halting the Yankee advance. Jefferson Davis replaced Johnston, who had been grievously wounded, with Robert E. Lee. In a series of battles known as the **Seven Days** (June 25–July 1), Lee's newly-named Army of Northern Virginia drove McClellan back on the Chesapeake, from where he eventually returned to Washington. Lee's dashing style, aided by cavalry commander James E. B. ("Jeb") Stuart, captured the imagination of Southerners.

A frustrated Lincoln removed McClellan from command of Federal forces in the Eastern theater and turned the task of taking Richmond over to John Pope. The boastful Pope had participated in the highly successful river campaigns in Kentucky and Tennessee, where, he said, "we have always seen the backs of our enemies." But in August, Lee brashly divided his army, sending "Stonewall" Jackson's corps circling around behind Pope. When the Yankees attacked the entrenched Confederates near Manassas on August 29, they lost fearfully. The **Second Battle of Bull Run** (or Manassas) resulted in a Union pullback to the outskirts of Washington and left Lee's army in position to attack the capital.

Lee's exhausted, barefoot soldiers were hardly in shape for an offensive. Nevertheless, Lee's disposition was to attack unexpectedly, which was one reason Davis liked him. In September he led his troops across the Potomac into western Maryland, where he expected to find a sympathetic population and food for his hungry men. Lee developed a plan that, if successful, could dislodge the Lincoln administration, destroy Northern morale, and persuade the British government finally to recognize Confederate independence. The stakes were high, as Lincoln understood, and having nowhere else to turn, he ordered McClellan to meet the challenge. The Army of the Potomac contained three times as many men as Lee's Army of Northern Virginia, and a Union soldier discovered some of Lee's orders that had been accidentally dropped, giving McClellan a clear picture of the Rebel plan of attack. But his slowness and timidity cost him and his men dearly. On September 17, Yankee brigades attacked the Rebels along a broad front beside Antietam Creek and near the tiny town of Sharpsburg. But instead of simultaneous assaults, McClellan advanced against only one Rebel sector at a time, giving Lee an opportunity to shift units from quiet areas to meet each offensive. The results were horrifying. At the end of the day, 24,000 men had fallen—the highest casualty figure for a single day's fighting in American history and four times the number of American killed and wounded on the Normandy beaches during D-Day in World War II. Both armies were left reeling, but Lee's smaller force was weaker. Still, Lee considered an attack on the following day, although he finally decided against it. McClellan failed to order another assault that almost certainly would have destroyed Lee's army, thus allowing Lee to withdraw unmolested into Northern Virginia.

The **Battle of Antietam** had no decisive strategic outcome. Lee sustained losses the Confederacy could ill-afford and was lucky to escape with his army intact, but McClellan failed to capitalize on a wonderful opportunity to shorten if not to end the war. Totally exasperated, Lincoln finally fired his reluctant general, but he still had no competent alternative, which became horribly apparent in December. Ambrose E. Burnside, who replaced McClellan, marched the Army of the Potomac toward Richmond in an unusual midwinter campaign. On December 13, he hurled his men against Lee's entrenched Confederates outside of Fredericksburg. At the end of the **Battle of Fredericksburg**, nearly 13,000 Yanks lay dead or wounded along with 5,000 Rebels. Northern morale plummeted. One Yankee soldier spoke for many others: "Why not confess we are worsted, and come to an agreement." Lincoln too was shaken. "If there is a worse place than Hell, I am in it." In the November elections, Democrats won governorships in New York and New Jersey along with thirty-four congressional seats. On the other side of the North's partisan and ideological divide, a caucus of Republican senators mounted a campaign to reorganize the Cabinet in order to expand the war's aims to include emancipation. Lincoln parried the attempt.

But Antietam did have one profoundly important impact insofar as the nature of the Civil War and the future of the United States were concerned. It gave Lincoln an opportunity to bring African Americans into the conflict.

"Free the slaves . . . or be subdued"

By 1862, most Republicans were ready to assail the heart of the rebellion. This was, after all, a war, and as one Union army officer put it: "The iron gauntlet must be used more than the silken glove to crush this serpent." Lincoln agreed. "We must free the slaves or be ourselves subdued."

> What did the Emancipation Proclamation do, and how did people react to it?

In the summer Lincoln had decided to issue a proclamation emancipating slaves. No longer concerned about the constitutionality of abolitionism, he had moved decidedly toward the abolitionists' position on the subject and to use his war-making authority. Those who were fighting to destroy the Union, he said, "were subject to the incidents and calamities of war." Three considerations led him to that decision. The first was political: the need to hold control of the government. The second, more military in nature, was the scale of the bloodletting happening on the battlefields and its chilling effect on the recruitment of volunteer soldiers. By linking the war to emancipation, Lincoln provided a basis for African-American participation in the conflict. So, instead of helping the Confederacy as forced laborers, slaves could be armed by the Union as soldiers. And the third factor, also a military concern, was the support that Great Britain provided the Confederacy. The British public mostly opposed slavery but did not choose sides in the American Civil War because abolition was not an issue. If the conflict became a crusade against slavery, public pressure might force the British government to refrain from tacitly permitting shipments of military and naval hardware the Confederacy.

In July, Lincoln consulted Cabinet members about an emancipation proclamation. Secretary of State Seward gave his strong endorsement, raising only a question of timing. In the aftermath of defeat on the battlefield, an emancipation proclamation might appear like a "*shriek*" from a desperate government "on the retreat." Lincoln agreed to wait for positive results, especially in the Eastern theater of the war on which many eyes were trained. Antietam, while not a decisive victory, provided Lincoln with the best opportunity that he had to make his move. On September 22, he announced that as of January 1, 1863, all slaves in rebellious states, or portions of states then in rebellion against the authority of the United States, "shall be then, thenceforward, and forever free." The wording was clear: if the Confederates laid down their arms by the first of the year, they could resume their normal places in the Union with slavery intact. Had Lincoln's priority changed? No not completely He was offering the Confederacy generous terms of surrender. However, he had become more revolutionary than at the beginning and was prepared to abolish slavery if the Southern states persisted in conducting war against the United States because he believed that slavery was wrong and he had the constitutional authority to abolish it as a war measure.

Jefferson Davis and the other Confederate leaders would not accept reunion and spurned Lincoln's surrender offer. They condemned the **Emancipation Proclamation** as an attempt to incite slaves to rise up and slaughter defenseless women and children. So, the Civil War continued. The Emancipation Proclamation freed no slaves immediately, but as Union armies won victories and established federal authority across the South, slaves became free. The Emancipation Proclamation did not apply to loyal slave states; however, individual state action in Louisiana and the border states eventually did end slavery there, and in 1865 the Fifteenth Amendment to the Constitution abolished slavery everywhere in the United States, a step Lincoln urged Congress and the loyal states of the Union to take.

Political reaction to the Emancipation Proclamation, both abroad and at home, came swiftly. Liberal opinion in Great Britain turned solidly in favor of the Union and against any further encouragement from the Palmerston government to the Confederacy. Shipments of weapons to the Confederacy ceased. Northern reactions were divided. Some abolitionists applauded the new policy while others condemned it as a halfway

Courtesy of Library of Congress

With the Emancipation Proclamation, African Americans were permitted to bear arms to fight against slavery. Their role proved crucial in the Union military success by increasing the number of men under arms.

measure. William Lloyd Garrison compared Lincoln to "a wet rag" with no strength of conviction. Nor was Frederick Douglass impressed with Lincoln's "allowing himself to be . . . the miserable tool of traitors and rebels." The potential for political disaster appeared in Democratic opposition and an anti-emancipation backlash that threatened the Republicans' congressional majority in the fall elections. Republican senator Lyman Trumbull of Illinois acknowledged that Midwesterners "want nothing to do with the negro." In many cities, angry anti-black workers took to the streets to protest against the Emancipation Proclamation. In Cincinnati, employers replaced striking Irish dock workers with African Americans, and it started a riot.

One Illinois soldier spoke for many Yankees when he said: "I am not in favor of freeing the negroes." A marked decline in volunteer enlistment led to the military draft, and conscription only added fuel to the fires of resentment, especially among poor workers who could not afford to hire substitutes. Why, many asked, should they risk their lives to free slaves who would then migrate to the North and compete for their jobs. Anger exploded into anti-draft rioting in several Northern cities, the worst occurring in New York City. For four days in July of 1863, the city erupted in flames and murders that took over 100 lives.

"Let the black man . . . get an eagle on his button and a musket on his shoulder," declared Frederick Douglass, "and there is no power on earth which can deny that he has won the right to citizenship." African Americans, slave and free, were willing to fight for emancipation. In August of 1862, Secretary of War Stanton had authorized the enlistment of slaves freed from plantations on the sea islands of South Carolina. This was part of a highly publicized experiment in revolutionary reconstruction of the South. But the Emancipation Proclamation explicitly authorized the incorporation of free black and slave units into Union armies. One of the first African-American regiments was the 54th Massachusetts, composed of free men. Other outfits included liberated slaves. By war's end, approximately 186,000 African Americans had served in the military. Most were assigned to labor and guard details, but some, including the 54th saw combat. In July of 1863, it participated in the assault on **Battery Wagner** near Charleston. Half the regiment, including Colonel Robert Gould Shaw, the unit's white commanding officer, fell in the attack. Overall in the Civil War, black troops suffered 40 percent more casualties than white soldiers, in part because of the rage of Confederates against them. Rebels commonly executed black prisoners and gave no quarter to their white officers.

The contributions of African-American soldiers to the war did not result in any more favorable treatment of black people by whites in the United States. Despite collecting twenty-one Congressional Medals of Honor, black troops received half the pay of white soldiers and were not permitted to become commissioned officers. They won a measure of respect from white Northerners who, like Abraham Lincoln, conceded to them the rights to life, liberty, and the pursuit of happiness proclaimed in the Declaration of Independence. But even Lincoln could not envision whites and blacks living together harmoniously. In August of 1862, Lincoln invited a group of prominent African Americans to the White House, a notable symbolic gesture. But what he told them was not comforting. Bluntly, he said: "Your race suffer very greatly, many of them, by living among us [whites], while ours suffer from your presence." The only solution Lincoln could conceive was emigration. "This is our country as much as it is yours," retorted one black Philadelphia man, "and we will not leave it."

Throughout most of the war, the Confederacy refused to employ African Americans as soldiers, even as manpower shortages became acute. Arming slaves and relying on them for independence contradicted the ideology of slavery. Yet, expediency was hard to ignore, especially late in the conflict. The Davis government proposed arming slaves with the promise of freedom and suggested that emancipation might cause Great Britain to recognize Confederate independence. Britain did not respond, but in March of 1865 the Confederate Congress authorized the enlistment of black troops, although much too late to impact the outcome of the Civil War.

The Emancipation Proclamation changed the war aim of Lincoln's administration and seemed to substantiate the charge that rebels had been making since the beginning of the war that the Republican party was determined to destroy slavery. The negative reaction in the North combined with redoubled resolve in the South to continue the war made the goal of defeating the Confederacy more difficult. But by neutralizing Great Britain, Lincoln had tightened the stranglehold on the Confederacy while clarifying the cause of freedom for which the Union was fighting.

THINKING FURTHER

1. How did the Civil War change during 1862?
2. What advantages and disadvantages, strengths and weaknesses, did both sides have in a total war?

THE LOCAL PERSPECTIVE: FOCUS ON NEVADA

Nevada, the Silver State, came into being basically because of three developments: the breakdown of the territorial system of government in the Far West during the 1850s, the discovery in 1859 of the fabulous gold- and silver-bearing **Comstock Lode**, and the secession of the South from the Union.

> **Why was the Lincoln administration eager to add Nevada to the Union as a state?**

Volcanic and seismic activity millions of years ago gave the state its corduroy-like appearance. Row after row of north-south fissures in the earth's crust pushed up rock and minerals to form a series of mountain ranges and intervening valleys. The mountains prevented drainage from the melting of ancient glaciers, resulting in massive inland lakes, particularly in the western portion of the state. Eons of aridity have diminished their size, but remnants are still visible in **Pyramid Lake** and in the **Humboldt** and **Carson** sinks that were landmarks on the emigrant trails.

Pyramid Lake, Nevada

Water evaporation at lower elevations deposited salts that crusted the earth and rendered it suitable only for shrub vegetation like greasewood, sagebrush, and Joshua trees; however, at higher elevations, where moisture fell more plentifully, organic soil content produced excellent range land for animal grazing.

Nevada's first known city—and ghost town—was located not far from modern Las Vegas. Nearly a thousand years ago, as many as 20,000 men, women, and children lived in stone pueblos, raised crops, mined minerals, and exchanged goods with other people through an extensive trading network. In the middle of the twelfth century, they inexplicably disappeared, and by the nineteenth century, Shoshoni, Paiute, and Washoe people had developed lifestyles adapted to this stingy country. They lived portably, fishing for trout in lakes and streams, hunting foxes and other small game, and harvesting wild berries and grains. Whites who entered the area in the eighteenth and nineteenth centuries called them "Diggers" because they incorporated wild roots into their diet.

Until the 1850s, white people in Nevada were an assortment of passers-by. Trappers, explorers, and emigrants from the East on their way to the California gold fields crossed Nevada along the Humboldt River. Enterprising merchants set up roadside businesses in the Carson Valley on the western end of the emigrant trail. As the flood of prospectors in California reduced the odds of striking it rich,

some of the emigrants simply stayed put in the valley, tracking through the nearby mountains for signs of gold. At that time, Nevada was part of the Utah Territory, and Brigham Young ordered Mormon settlements in the Carson Valley. In 1854, the Mormons organized a county government to bring law and order to the region. But authorities in Salt Lake City paid little attention to the remote Nevada settlements, especially after 1857 when Young recalled the settlers in anticipation of war with the United States. The non-Mormon residents petitioned Congress for territorial status, but Southerners blocked it because of strong antislavery sentiment there. Not until 1861, when Southern session had cleared the way, did Congress establish a separate Nevada Territory with its capital in Carson City (named for the famous mountain man and guide Christopher "Kit" Carson).

Territorial status corresponded with the discovery of significant gold and silver deposits. Over several years, prospectors had drawn nearly $650,000 (approximately $17.3 million today) in ore from the mountains; however, in 1859, two Irishmen, Patrick McLaughlin and Peter Riley, tapped into the main vein. Their claim was challenged by Henry P. Comstock, who forced a partnership with the two prospectors and lent his name to the Comstock Lode. The ore from the Comstock veins was assayed at a phenomenal $3,900 per ton, or about $104,000 per ton in today's money. Soon eager prospectors from California were pouring into western Nevada. The mining camp of Virginia City quickly became a roaring boom town with hotels, saloons, churches, and newspapers. The young writer Samuel Clemens, known as Mark Twain, was one of Virginia City's residents.

The Comstock Lode dominated Nevada for the next two decades. Between 1859 and 1880, its mines yielded nearly $310 million ($5.25 billion) in gold and silver. As in the California gold fields, prospectors located the deposits, but more sophisticated organization and capital resources were required to extract the ore locked deep in the ground and process it for transportation to San Francisco. In 1860 several claim-holders sold out to a syndicate of San Francisco capitalists who in turn organized the Ophir Silver Mining Company. Such enterprises provided machinery, hired miners, and encouraged solutions to many technical problems like smelting (reducing ore to pure metal). Comstock Lode companies also developed framing and ventilating techniques for deep mine shafts that became commonplace in later mining operations throughout the Far West.

The influx of thousands of prospectors and settlers into the Comstock area alarmed local Indians, whose margin of subsistence could not bear the destruction of food sources. Miners polluted streams, reduced fish populations, and hunted game animals to depletion levels. The result was the **Pyramid Lake War**. In May of 1860, angry Paiutes gathered at Pyramid Lake while nervous whites prepared a preemptive attack. A militia force of 105 men marched toward Pyramid Lake, and right into a well-planned ambush. Seventy-six whites were killed and most of the rest wounded. In a second battle later that month, whites routed the Indians, who afterward avoided pitched battles. The Pyramid Lake War touched off a series of Indian raids against stagecoaches and isolated white settlements that continued for two decades.

In 1863 efforts mounted to transform Nevada from a territory into a state. This was despite the fact that the territory's population, excluding Native Americans, was only 16,000. But statehood ran into opposition from Southern-born residents who resented the overly pro-Union provisions in the proposed state constitution. For example, the constitution denied political rights to anyone who had taken up arms against the United States and specifically disclaimed any right to secede. That, plus the fact that the constitution authorized the taxing of mine properties,

led to its defeat by a popular vote margin of four to one. However, the national Republican party, and especially President Lincoln, desired an additional Republican state in the critical 1864 election. They also desired support for a constitutional amendment to abolish slavery. Early in 1864, Congress passed a Nevada enabling bill, which Lincoln signed into law. Another state constitution, identical to the one already defeated with the exception that only mine proceeds and not the mines themselves were taxed, won by a ten-to-one vote. Lincoln proclaimed Nevada a state in October of 1864, just in time for the November elections. The state not only supported Lincoln but it also chose two Republican senators who rushed to Washington and cast their votes for the Thirteenth Amendment abolishing slavery. In February of 1865, the Nevada legislature ratified the abolition amendment.

Despite being a new state and having a population smaller than neighboring Utah (which was not allowed into the Union until 1890), Nevada's influence on the politics of the Civil War was significant. Its history during this period also suggests the importance of the Far West to the economic development of modern America, as well as the environmental consequences of the Far West's capitalization and industrialization.

THINKING BACK

1. What was the importance of the Comstock Lode, and what issues did it raise?
2. What impact did Nevada statehood have on the Civil War?

THE CIVIL WAR OUT WEST

Some of the cruelest fighting of the Civil War took place beyond the Mississippi River. In Kansas and Missouri, issues that had led to the bloody conflicts of the 1850s extended into the Civil War. The gold and silver of California, Nevada, and Colorado became the basis for intense competition by the Union and the Confederacy. Some Native Americans favored one side or the other in the war and participated as auxiliaries to Rebel and Union armed forces. The worst conflicts between whites and Native Americans took place on the western edge of the Great Plains, where the dual attraction of gold and fertile land brought more settlers and threatened the livelihood of Plains Indians.

Guerrillas and Jayhawkers

What was the reason for guerilla warfare in Missouri and Kansas?

The Civil War took on its most bloodthirsty aspect in Missouri and Kansas. Plundering, burning, and bushwacking terrorized civilian populations as they had in "Bleeding Kansas." In fact, much of the violence was a continuation of the vengeful feuding from earlier times perpetrated on behalf of South and North. Marauding guerillas affiliated with the Confederacy attacked pro-Union towns while Union "**Jayhawkers**" murdered and pillaged in the name of antislavery.

The most infamous Confederate guerilla band followed a cold-blooded killer named William Quantrill, whose gunmen included future gang leaders Jim and Cole Younger and Frank and Jesse James. Opposing them were "Jennison's Jayhawkers," who included the brother of feminist Susan B. Anthony and John Brown, Jr. These bands wreaked havoc along the Missouri-Kansas border.

Missouri's value to the Union and Confederacy lay in its lead mines and stretches of the Missouri and Mississippi rivers. In March of 1862, a Confederate army, comprising Cherokee regiments from Indian Territory, had attempted to retake the state. Cherokees still hated the United States for banishing them from their homelands a generation before. At Pea Ridge, along the Arkansas-Missouri border, Federal forces routed the Rebels. By 1863, the removal of all but a few Union troops to eastern battle zones had left most of western Missouri unprotected. Quantrill's raiders had easy going with food and shelter provided by accommodating Confederate women. The Union commander in the area arrested several women and detained them in Kansas City. In August, the building that housed them collapsed, killing five. Quantrill went on a rampage of revenge. With 450 men, he swooped

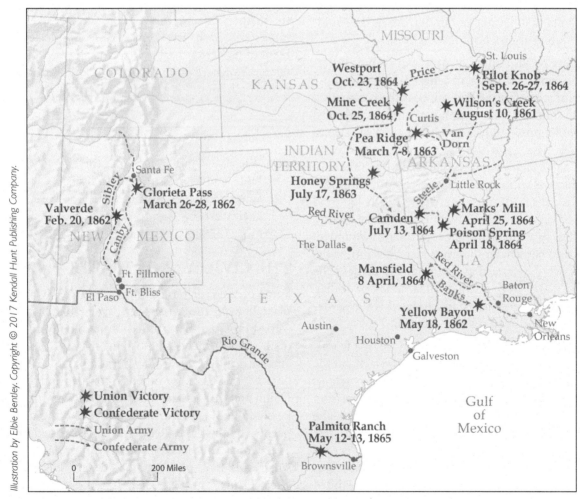

Illustration by Elbie Bentley. Copyright © 2017 Kendall Hunt Publishing Company.

Western states such as Arkansas and Missouri, along with the territory of New Mexico, were important to both sides due largely to their mineral resources.

down on Lawrence, Kansas, a Unionist bastion, to "kill every male and burn every house." He just about did; in all, 182 persons died during three hours of mayhem. A year later, Confederate General Sterling Price invaded Missouri from Arkansas and joined with local guerillas to take St. Louis. Turned back by a makeshift force of Union troops and local militia, Price withdrew from Missouri, leaving it firmly in Union hands.

Quantrill eventually rode east into Kentucky, where a patrol of Union cavalry killed him. When the Civil War ended, the James and Younger brothers turned to bank and train robbery, keeping parts of Kansas and Missouri in turmoil. Further West, Civil War armies fought over gold and silver.

In Pursuit of Western Gold

> **Why was the Confederacy interested in the Far West, and what was its plan to take control of it?**

Western gold and silver mines were of great value to a Confederate government desperate for cash. In 1858, prospectors had found traces of gold along a tributary of the South Platte River, near the site of present-day Denver. The next year, 100,000 excited miners hit the trails for the gold fields. In 1859–1860, the fabulous Comstock Lode in Nevada began to yield huge amounts of precious metal. If the Confederacy could gain control of the Rocky Mountain ore production, its ability to purchase needed supplies abroad would be greatly enhanced. Scattered Confederate sympathy existed in the Far West; however, Union loyalty prevailed, and Federal cavalry and infantry units dotted the west in forts built previously to protect emigrants on the cross-country trails.

Soon after Fort Sumter and Lincoln's call for volunteers, the Confederacy launched a campaign to seize the Colorado gold fields. The invasion route went through New Mexico. Texans maintained a special interest in the New Mexico campaign because it afforded an opportunity to make good on their long-standing claim to the entire Rio Grande River to its headwaters in Colorado. In July of 1861, a regiment of Texas volunteers under John R. Baylor had entered New Mexico from El Paso and captured a small Federal garrison. Baylor proclaimed the Confederate territory of Arizona comprising the southern portions of present-day New Mexico and Arizona before joining a Confederate command under Henry H. Sibley. The Confederates marched north along the Rio Grande, where resistance from Edward R. S. Canby's

Department of New Mexico was light, and by March had occupied Santa Fe. The local populace, mostly Hispanic and Indian, was Unionist in sympathy. Many of the Pueblo leaders received gold-headed canes from the Lincoln administration symbolizing their loyalty to the United States.

In April of 1862, as the Confederates crossed **Glorieta Pass** a short distance east of Santa Fe, they encountered a force of Federal troops along with Colorado militia. The Rebels had the best of the fighting on the first day of the battle, but the Coloradoans attacked their supply train and destroyed it. Stranded in hostile territory without food and ammunition, the Confederates fell back toward Texas as another small force of Confederates moved toward Tucson, Arizona. California officials became alarmed about a possible Confederate invasion of their state. Some 17,000 Californians, many of whom had been gold prospectors, had answered Lincoln's first call for volunteers, and Colonel James H. Carleton marched a brigade of 2,300 infantry and artillery troops across the desert to intercept the Rebels and reinforce the Union troops in New Mexico. By the time the **California Column** reached the Rio Grande River, the Confederates had gone, but Carleton declared martial law, enabling him to ravage the farms of Confederate sympathizers and force the men to work on Union fortifications.

Carleton's primary duty as commander of the Department of New Mexico was to punish Indians for attacking Anglo and Hispanic settlers. Most of the offending Indians were Apache and Navajo. Carleton's orders to his field commanders were brutally harsh: "All Indian men . . . are to be killed whenever you can find them; the women and children will not be harmed, but you will take them prisoners." He ordered Mescalero Apaches removed from their fertile mountain homelands in central New Mexico and placed on a cramped reserve in a dry and desolate area along the Pecos River and cleared other Apaches out of the upper Gila River drainage, where in 1860 gold had been discovered. In 1863 he turned to the Navajos, whose homeland was in the northern part of the department, appointing "Kit" Carson to lead a group of soldiers in burning Navajo crops, killing all the men who resisted, and marching the captives to the Pecos River reservation. The Navajos suffered horribly on their "**Long Walk**," and even more on the reservation where the lack of sanitation brought disease and death.

The Southwest and its mineral resources remained securely under Union control. The Civil War also provided the United States an opportunity to implement its Indian policy of locating Indians onto reservations. In doing so, the well-being of Native Americans was made secondary to the interests of those non-Indians who would exploit the land for its mineral resources or convert it into farms and ranches. The Civil War had much the same effect on the Great Plains.

Indian Battles on the Western Plains

How did the Civil War contribute to conflict between whites and Indians in the Far West

In the summer of 1858, Green Russell of Georgia joined a hundred or so other prospectors looking for gold along the eastern slope of the Rocky Mountains. Mule skinners and cattle drovers had reported traces of gold from Pike's Peak to the South Platte River. By July, most of the others had given up, but Russell struck pay dirt. Word spread—"The new Eldorado!"—and by the following spring another Far Western gold rush was on. Among the "fifty-niners" were merchants, lawyers, and ranchers. They founded the boom town of Denver to supply miners with necessities and to ship their gold to Kansas City and St. Louis.

The first gold seekers had not seen any Indians, but in the autumn Arapaho and Cheyenne hunters returned from their fall buffalo hunt to make winter camp in the sheltered river basins. The sight of miners' tents, ranchers' cattle, and military forts disturbed them. "Go away," Niwot (Left Hand) told the whites. "You come to kill our game, to burn our wood, and to destroy our grass." White miners, freighters, ranchers, and farmers were not interested in building peaceful relationships with Indians like old fur traders had. Niwot, Little Raven, and Black Kettle were elders who wanted peace, but younger warriors favored driving the white newcomers away. Attacks against the whites increased.

The Civil War led to even more conflict on the Plains. White authorities encouraged Indians to settle down to farming in return for annual payments from the federal government; however, pressing war needs delayed the annuities, contributing to disease and starvation among the Indians. Furthermore, fewer Union soldiers were on hand to deal with the militants. In the Indian Territory, Cherokee and Creek warriors attacked one another. Confederate-supporting Cherokees drove pro-Union Creeks into southern Kansas, where they suffered terribly from the bitter cold and from starvation. In Texas, Comanche men took advantage of the absence of soldiers to attack ranchers who had pushed them off their land. The Comanche often made peace with Unionists but punished Confederates.

In the newly organized Colorado Territory, whites prepared for a climactic war with the Cheyenne and Arapaho, whose raids on ranches and stagecoaches in the Platte and Arkansas river valleys increased during the Civil War. Black Kettle brought his band, including some with blood on their hands, to Fort Lyon on the Arkansas River, where they had been promised protection. But the fort's commander, citing inadequate supplies, suggested that the Indians camp at nearby Sand Creek. At dawn on November 29, 1864, a regiment of Colorado volunteers swept down on them. Ordered to kill every Indian they found, the troopers slaughtered 133 Indians, mostly women and children, and mutilated their corpses. Cheyenne warriors retaliated by murdering whites and destroying ranches along the South Platte River.

Thus the Civil War had important implications for whites and Native Americans living far away from the scenes of the war's bloodiest battles. During the 1860s, the United States moved deliberately forward with a policy of clearing away the western tribes. The result would be more exploitation of the Far West's natural resources and the reduction of bio-diversity.

THINKING FURTHER

1. What interest did the Lincoln and Davis governments have in the Far West?
2. How did the Civil War affect Native Americans in the Far West?

CIVIL WAR FROM BEHIND THE LINES

From the front lines to the back lines, the Civil War transformed the lives of Americans. The more than 600,000 deaths from battle wounds and disease reduced by one fourth an entire generation of American men, leaving widows to pick up the work of their dead husbands on farms, plantations, offices, and shops. The pressing need for supplies placed heavy demands on the workforce, jobs that many women filled as they sought to keep household incomes up with zooming prices. The Civil War did not remove all the gender barriers to full participation in the life of the nation, North and South, but it opened opportunities that many women, especially in the North, eagerly explored. The gathering of men in camps and prisons, along with the ghastly experience with wounds and sickness, added greatly to the need for improved hygiene, more hospitals, bandages and medicine, and sanitation. Medical departments in the United States and the Confederacy confronted the challenges. And although in some ways the Civil War set back economic progress, in many others it pushed Americans further down the road to commercialized industry and agriculture.

A Drag for Women

> **What functions did women perform, and what obstacles and hazards did they face?**

The Civil War was not exclusively a male experience. Women's involvement was an extension of their traditional domestic responsibilities. They encouraged men to enlist, cheered as they marched off to war, and wrote letters steering them down the straight and narrow moral path. In addition, they sent cookies and cakes, knitted socks, prepared linen bandages, succored the sick, and nursed the wounded. But total war also drew women out of the Cult of True Womanhood and into the male world of business, government, and the battlefield.

With so many men away in the army, disabled, or in their graves, women filled vital gaps in the work force. One traveler in Iowa met "more women driving teams on the road and saw more at work in the fields than men." Southern plantation women seldom entered the fields, but they assumed the difficult task of managing field slaves. Texan Lizzie Neblett urged her soldier husband to sell his troublesome slaves. "I'll . . . work with my hands, as hard as I can, but my mind will rest." Northern women ran shops and took jobs in factories, sewing uniforms, tents, and haversacks. Many Southern women worked as clerks in government departments. The absence of male teachers provided women with additional employment opportunities.

Of all the new occupations, nursing seemed the most compatible with women's customary role as domestic nurturers. Their model was England's famed nurse Florence Nightingale. Women nurses encountered strong opposition, despite the fact that patient mortality declined by half when they were in charge. Furthermore, many Confederate females, confined by rigid notions of womanhood, had to overcome their discomfort with touching male bodies, although they often cared for sick and wounded relatives at home and visited recuperating soldiers in hospital wards. African-American women served more frequently than white women in Confederate hospitals as cooks and laundresses. More Northern women than Southern women performed as wartime nurses—some 3,400 in all. In June of 1861, Secretary of War Simon Cameron appointed the noted reformer Dorothea Dix superintendent of professional women nurses for all Union armies. Other women, like Clara Barton, free-lanced, showing up on battlefields as well as in hospitals to comfort the injured. Phoebe Pember, a South Carolina widow, became the Confederacy's first professional matron.

Nurses ran a considerable risk to their own health. They were susceptible to the same diseases that ravaged the men they nursed. The author Louisa May Alcott contracted typhoid after only a month as a volunteer, and the Maine abolitionist and feminist Hannah Ropes, matron of Georgetown's Union Hotel Hospital, died of typhoid pneumonia.

The existence of feminism in the North, and its relative absence from the South, influenced how women responded to the exigencies of the times. Northern women greeted their new responsibilities as opportunities for growth, whereas elite women of the Confederacy often found work in schools, government offices, and hospitals inconsistent with the "dignity" of their gender and status. Southern society defined womanhood as a vulnerable and dependent condition, and many women resented having to fend for themselves. Others began to criticize their place in Southern society. "What a drag it sometimes is on a woman," remarked Catherine Edmondston of North Carolina, "to 'lug about' the ladder upon which man plants his foot and ascends."

Treating the Sick and Wounded

> **What caused the horrors associated with Civil War hospitals?**

Despite the tenderness with which female nurses treated the casualties of war, the fear of being wounded and hospitalized was often greater for Johnny Reb and Billy Yank than taking a bullet in the brain. Medicine and hospital practice were primitive before the development of the germ theory of disease. Wounded soldiers often lay on battlefields for hours, and it could be several days before they received treatment. In the meantime, infection made relatively minor wounds life-threatening. Stomach wounds were almost always fatal. Amputation was the standard treatment for arm and leg wounds, and half the patients died. Ether and chloroform were used as anesthetics during surgeries, but

Nurses and officials of the United States Sanitary Commission in Virginia, 1864

shortages often meant doses of whiskey or "biting the bullet." In all, one out of six Civil War soldiers succumbed to their wounds, compared to one in four hundred during the Vietnam War.

The problem was twofold: the staggering number of wounded men who needed treatment after battles and insufficient medical knowledge. Mangled soldiers poured into hospitals by the thousands. Over 20,000 wounded men were brought into Richmond after the Fair Oaks and Seven Days' battles. One Richmond woman wrote: "We lived in one immense hospital." Overwhelmed surgeons could not have provided adequate treatment even if they had known about germs and how to prevent deadly infection. They performed surgeries, including amputations, without antiseptics. Nurses washed but did not disinfect bandages.

At the start of the war, hospitals were few and far between, and ambulance services did not exist. At the beginning of the war, both sides tried using existing hospitals, but as fighting intensified, they had to build special ones. Armies set up field hospitals near battlefields for emergency treatment of wounds. In 1862, the Army of the Potomac established a trained ambulance corps, and other armies followed the example. The Confederacy's medical service moved in the same direction, although with fewer resources.

Women took the lead in organizing medical treatment of wounded Union soldiers. A society for the training of nurses became the basis for the **United States Sanitary Commission**. The "Sanitary" assisted hospitals and army camps in improving hygienic

conditions. By 1862 it had become a major lobby in Congress and challenged the medical establishment in defining criteria for physicians within the United States Medical Bureau.

As massive as was the problem of treating the wounded, curing the sick was even greater. Poor sanitary practices made military camps cesspools of infection. Confederate prisons, especially the notorious Andersonville prison in Georgia, were nothing more than stockades where up to 30,000 captured Union soldiers were held with no shelter, little food, and contaminated water. Illness was the greatest cause of disability and death among soldiers during the Civil War. Two men died of disease for each one killed in battle.

The massive experience in treating gunshot wounds and dealing with sanitation resulted in lessons that were good for the future. In this way too, the Civil War marked the beginnings of modern America.

Preparing a Modern America

The absence of Southerners from Congress during the Civil War years gave Republicans the ability to enact a number of old Whig measures that Democrats had been blocking for years. Easily overcoming the opposition of anti-capitalist Northern Democrats, Republicans established the principle of federal government support for industry and agriculture as well as the ideals of bourgeois capitalism. As the Civil War progressed, the Republican party pushed the United States toward a modern America of industry, continental transportation systems, and large-scale banking.

> **How did the Civil War point America toward the future?**

Economic programs that Whigs and Democrats had battled over for three decades became reality in the Civil War's political environment. In 1862, for example, Congress passed the **Homestead Act** that granted 160-acre tracts of public land free to settlers who improved their claims within five years. The **Morrill Act**, also in 1862, set aside public land in each state for public education. Among the uses to which these land grants were put was the establishment of "land-grant" colleges for the promotion of agriculture and technology. The **Pacific Railroad Act** of 1862 authorized the federal government to issue bonds and grant tracts of public land to subsidize the construction of the country's first transcontinental railroad. In addition, Congress approved loans of $16,000 per mile for construction across the flatlands of the Great Plains and

Great Basin and $48,000 per mile to traverse mountain ranges. And in 1863 Congress passed the **National Banking Act,** creating federally-chartered banks and the basis for a national banking system.

In some ways, the Civil War retarded economic growth, but in other ways it stimulated expansion. The loss of Southern markets early in the war hampered Northern industry. So many deaths reduced the size and skill of the work force, although the North rebounded through immigration and natural increase. Stimulated by wartime demands, however, economic productivity increased in the North. By the end of the war, production of coal and iron had reached record highs. Merchant ship tonnage exceeded pre-war levels, as did railroad and canal traffic. In the South, however, demolition of railroads, mills, and foundries destroyed the little industry that the war had generated. Furthermore, devastation of Southern agriculture produced an economic wasteland.

Northern economic policy during the Civil War set down what one historian called a "blueprint for modern America." The pattern for economic growth emerged in the North, and the end of the war initiated the process of transforming the Southern economy.

THINKING BACK

1. How did the United States and the Confederate States deal with the massive problems caused by battlefield wounds and communicable diseases?
2. In what ways did the Civil War propel the United States toward a future of big government and industrial growth?

THE TIDE TURNS, 1863-1865

Two years after the war began, optimism still abounded in the South about the Confederate cause. In 1863, however, Rebel defeats on battlefields in Pennsylvania and Mississippi inflicted devastating losses that continued throughout the following year. But those Northern victories also came at appalling cost. By the end of 1864, Union forces had suffered 300,000 deaths, and the gloom that those casualties imparted inspired a peace movement that seemed strong enough to force the Lincoln government to seek an armistice. In fact, as the presidential election approached, one Republican leader said flatly that "Lincoln's election is an impossibility." The capture of Atlanta turned the tide, and by early 1865, as Union troops pressed down on Richmond, even Lee and his weary but game army

knew the cause was hopeless. As spring awakened in Virginia, Lee and Grant met at Appomattox and agreed to terms of surrender. Days later, an assassin's bullet ended Lincoln's life.

The Turning Point: Union Victories at Gettysburg and Vicksburg

Mending from a wound received at Antietam, Yankee soldier Oliver Wendell Holmes, Jr., observed that "the army is tired . . . . I've pretty much made up my mind that the South have achieved their independence." Although on New Year's Day 1863, Union forces repulsed a Confederate invasion of Kentucky at the **Battle of Stones River**, the victory did not bode well for the Union. In April of 1863, Grant's troops were bogged down across the Mississippi River from Vicksburg as defiant citizens of that town strategically situated high on a bluff above the Mississippi River celebrated with a fancy dress ball.

In Virginia, after the slaughter at Fredericksburg, Joseph Hooker assumed command of the demoralized Army of the

> **What was won and lost at Gettysburg and Vicksburg?**

Potomac. The arrogant "Fighting Joe" had suggested that the United States needed a dictator. "Of course it was not *for* this," Lincoln told him, "but in spite of it, that I have given you the command . . . . What I now ask of you is military success, and I will risk the

Courtesy of Library of Congress

Some of the Union dead at the Battle of Gettysburg, July 1863. Four months later, President Lincoln delivered the "Gettysburg Address" at the dedication of the Soldiers' National Cemetery there. In this brief, profound, and beautifully crafted speech, Lincoln attempted to help Americans cope with the agonizing and unprecedented scope of suffering and death inflicted on them by the Civil War.

dictatorship." Hooker took "the finest army on the planet" to nearby Chancellorsville. Lee, with half as many men, once again divided his army, sending "Stonewall" Jackson with 30,000 troops through dense, tangled woods to attack the Union right flank. At dinner time on May 2, the Confederates crashed into the unsuspecting Yanks. As night fell, Union resistance stiffened, but Hooker never counterattacked. Instead, he retreated, and his troops lost heart.

Despite Lee's tactical brilliance, the **Battle of Chancellorsville** was a costly victory. The thirteen thousand irreplaceable Confederate casualties comprised 22 percent of Lee's army. Worst of all was the loss of "Stonewall" Jackson, accidently killed by his own men during the twilight fighting. Jackson had been Lee's "right arm," and the Confederate cause would miss him. Still, the triumph regenerated a sense of invincibility among Lee's troops and influenced his next move.

Always ready to attack, Lee proposed striking at Pennsylvania—Harrisburg or maybe Philadelphia. A dispirited North, he believed, would not tolerate devastation of its own farms and communities and would demand an armistice. A victory might also bring foreign recognition. Davis, despite misgivings, approved the plan. In the summer, Lee's 75,000-man army crossed Maryland into southern Pennsylvania brimming with confidence. Detachments fanned out, foraging for food, demolishing farms and shops, and capturing African Americans and sending them to Virginia as slaves. Lincoln placed General George G. Meade, a competent but unknown commander, in charge of the Army of the Potomac, and Meade quickly moved to intercept the Rebels.

The Civil War's biggest and most famous battle happened by accident. Lee's normally reliable cavalry failed to locate the enemy, and on a steamy July 1, Confederates collided with Union cavalry near the small town of Gettysburg. Lines of blue and gray quickly converged across a stretch of farmland south of town. On July 2 Lee ordered several attacks against Union defenses along Cemetery Ridge and Little Round Top but found no weaknesses. On July 3, eager and confident, Lee ordered divisions under George Pickett to assault the Union center. As Pickett's valiant infantry withered under sheets of Yankee lead, Confederate hopes for a climatic victory evaporated. A somber Lee admitted: "It's all my fault." He then ordered his army to retreat into Virginia. Lee had lost one-third of his men and would never regain offensive capability. But Meade, instead of counterattack-

ing, held his position as another Union opportunity for a decisive victory vanished.

As Union forces repulsed the Confederates at Gettysburg, Yankees finally overwhelmed Southern resistance at Vicksburg. Unable to scale the city's steep riverside bluffs or breech its defenses, Grant devised a daring plan. On the evening of April 16, Federal gunboats and troop transports ran past Confederate batteries while Grant took his infantry along the west bank of the Mississippi River and recrossed downstream. Cut loose from his own supply base, Grant's 40,000 troops faced 30,000 Confederates under transplanted Yankee John C. Pemberton. Rather than attacking directly, Grant sent part of his men eastward toward Jackson, where they sliced up Confederates under Joseph E. Johnston and then tore apart the city's railroads, foundries, shops, and mills. Then, on May 16, Grant's Midwestern farm boys mauled Pemberton's Rebels at Champion's Hill, driving the survivors into Vicksburg, where they dug in and waited.

After unsuccessful attempts to penetrate the stout Confederate defenses, the Yankees laid siege to the city. Initially, civilians and soldiers inside the town remained defiant. By the end of June, however, starvation and discouragement set in as people ate dogs, cats, and rodents and took refuge in caves against artillery bombardment. On July 4, Pemberton surrendered his entire army, and as Grant later asserted, "the fate of the Confederacy was sealed."

The surrender of **Vicksburg** and nearby **Port Hudson** five days later gave the Union control of the Mississippi River, splitting the Confederacy in two and isolating Arkansas, Louisiana, and Texas. Moreover, Grant had proven himself a shrewd and dogged fighter. "Grant is my man," Lincoln declared. The paired Union victories at Gettysburg and Vicksburg turned the military tide irreversibly and buoyed Northern spirits. European intervention was totally out of the question, and the chances of the Confederacy winning independence became infinitely slimmer.

"If It Takes All Summer": Exhaustion in Northern Virginia

In the spring of 1864, Lincoln appointed Grant lieutenant general, making him the first to hold that rank since George Washington, and placed him in command of all Union armed forces. Grant in turn put William T. Sherman in charge of Union forces in the West and Philip H. Sheridan in command in Virginia's Shenandoah Valley while he personally led the Army of the Potomac. All three men believed in total war against enemy resources and morale, a strategy that called for superior forces to pound the Confederacy into submission.

How did Grant change the war in the East?

In May of 1864, Grant launched his offensive with 115,000 men through the same dense forest, known as the **Wilderness**, where Hooker had been whipped the year before. Lee, with half as many Confederates, chose to fight in the thick underbrush where superior Union numbers would be less of a factor. After two days of brutal combat, the Yankees had suffered 18,000 casualties (killed and wounded) to the Confederates' 7,000, but instead of retreating as previous Union generals had done, Grant slipped around Lee's flank. "I propose to fight it out on this line if it takes all summer."

As the Union offensive continued, Lee dug in at **Spottsylvania**. Grant attacked, and a week of savage, hand-to-hand fighting (May 7-12) yielded another 12,000 killed and wounded. Once more, Grant skirted Lee's right flank. On June 3, at **Cold Harbor**, Grant ordered a charge reminiscent of Burnside's futile assault at Fredericksburg, and 7,000 more Yankees fell. And yet again, Grant circled around the Confederates, crossing the James River below Richmond. Lee's men dug trenches and built breastworks around **Petersburg** in order to defend the Confederate capital. Suddenly, the Civil War in Virginia settled into a siege and trench warfare that foreshadowed World War I. The psychological effects of constant artillery bombardment and sniping were new but would be acknowledged later as battle fatigue or **combat stress reaction**. "Many a man," wrote Oliver Wendell Holmes, "has gone crazy since this campaign began from the terrible pressure on mind & body." In a month, the Union army had suffered 60,000 casualties. Shocked Northerners referred to Grant as the "butcher," but he refused to lift the pressure on Lee's bloodied and exhausted troops.

Lincoln tried to bolster Northern resolve. "We accepted this war for [the] worthy object . . . of restoring the national authority over the whole domain . . . and the war will end when that object is obtained." He received cheers when he spoke to audiences, but would the voting public accept the war as Lincoln and Grant were fighting it?

In July, Confederates swooped out of northern Virginia's Shenandoah Valley and across the Potomac River, to the outskirts of Washington. Union troops turned them back, but the Copperheads made much of the raid. If news from William T. Sherman's campaign in Georgia was no better, the fall elections could turn against Lincoln and the Republicans in a rout.

Marching Through Georgia

Grant had ordered Sherman to advance from Chattanooga, Tennessee, which the Union took in November of 1863, to Atlanta, a railroad hub and a manufacturing center in the heart of the Confederacy. By June of 1864, Sherman's army

What effect did Sherman's offensive in Georgia have on the war and on public opinion in the North?

had entered northern Georgia, defended by Confederates under Joseph E. Johnston. The opposing generals differed markedly from Lee and Grant. Johnston preferred the defensive and Sherman hated frontal assaults. Sherman's Civil War career had started off bumpy, with a nervous breakdown, but he and Grant had formed a solid friendship. "He stood by me when I was crazy," Sherman said, "and I stood by him when he was drunk." Now by taking **Atlanta**, Sherman could cut off supplies to Lee in Virginia and hammer a major nail in the Confederacy's coffin.

The Yankees drove cautiously through the mountainous terrain of northern Georgia. In July, Davis, frustrated by Johnston's refusal to attack the Yankees, replaced him with the reckless John B. Hood. In three battles, Hood lost more than twice as many men as Sherman. Finally, on September 2, after heavy artillery bombardment, Hood evacuated Atlanta and the Yankees took control.

After surrendering Atlanta, Hood led a desperate Confederate offensive in Tennessee in an attempt to lure Sherman out of Georgia. But instead, Sherman and his men marched southeast to Savannah on the coast, cutting a path of destruction sixty miles wide to "make Georgia howl!" Sherman meant to deprive Confederate armies of the supplies they needed to continue fighting and to crush civilian support. "War is hell," he once famously remarked, and he intended to make it so hellacious that generations would pass before anyone would choose war over peace. When he reached **Savannah** in December, Sherman offered the city to Lincoln as a Christmas gift.

The result of the Georgia campaign was a great boost to Northern spirits and to Lincoln's prospects of reelection. Instantly the gloom of the preceding summer lifted and victory seemed finally at hand.

"Fire in the Rear": The Election of 1864

What determined the outcome of the 1864 election?

"Glorious news this morning—Atlanta taken at last!!!" Prominent New York Republican George Templeton Strong was ecstatic. "It is (coming at this political crisis) the greatest event of the war." Not even a month before, Lincoln had expressed certainty that he would be beaten in the November election—and beaten badly. Focusing on Grant's bloody Virginia campaign and what was still a stalemate in Georgia, the North yearned for peace. The popular song "When This Cruel War is Over" was 1864's best-seller. "Stop the war!" Democratic newspapers demanded. But word from Atlanta changed all that.

At the Democratic nominating convention, unity was the keynote. The election platform called for an immediate cessation of hostilities and the initiation of peaceful means of preserving the Union. The party nominated for president George B. McClellan, still widely popular despite his battlefield disappointments. McClellan condemned Lincoln's suppression of civil liberties, the Republicans' expansive economic policies, and the Emancipation Proclamation. The Republicans remained disunited, with abolitionists still dissatisfied with the Emancipation Proclamation and Lincoln's tendency toward pragmatic reconciliation. Chase made a run; however, Lincoln retained enough control over the party's apparatus to secure the nomination. For effect, Republicans selected a Southern War Democrat, Andrew Johnson of Tennessee, for vice president.

Victory at Atlanta turned the contest into an easy Republican victory. Lincoln received 55 percent of the popular vote and a solid majority in the Electoral College.

On to Appomattox

How did the Civil War finally end?

The end of the war came quickly but not without more pain. In December Hood's foolhardy invasion of Union-controlled Tennessee ended with his army's virtual destruction at the Battle of Nashville. Following a scorched-earth policy, Sherman marched his army from Savannah into the Carolinas for an anticipated convergence with Grant in Virginia. Confederate resistance was almost non-existent until Johnston scratched together a small army in North Carolina.

At Petersburg, the Union siege tightened into a strangle hold as the Yankees captured the remaining rail access upon which Lee's starving troops depended for survival. Combative as ever, however, Lee finally abandoned Petersburg and moved westward, hoping to link up with Johnston. Confederate officials, including Davis, fled Richmond ahead of occupying Union soldiers, and Grant moved quickly to block Lee's escape. On April 9, Lee considered attacking but decided that further bloodshed was useless and agreed to meet Grant in a private residence in the village of **Appomattox**. The two adversaries exchanged cordial greetings and agreed to terms of surrender. The erstwhile Confederates would be allowed to return to their homes, and those with horses or mules could keep them for spring planting. Shortly afterward, Johnston surrendered, and over the succeeding weeks other Confederate forces did likewise. The final battle, generally regarded as a Confederate victory, occurred on May 12-13 at Palmito Ranch along the Rio Grande River near Brownsville in south Texas.

After visiting Richmond, Lincoln returned to Washington to finalize the Union's reconstruction. On the evening of April 14, however, as he and First Lady Mary Todd Lincoln watched a play at Ford's Theater, a Confederate sympathizer named John Wilkes Boothe, brother of the famous actor Edwin Boothe, entered the presidential box and shot Lincoln once in the head with a pistol. Lincoln was taken to a residence across the street where he died early the next day. In the final tragedy of the Civil War, the man who had asked so much of other Americans also gave his "last full measure" of devotion to the Union.

CONCLUSION

The Civil War was one of the defining moments in American history. The identity, core values, and the future direction of the United States were all given shape in the crucible of the most horrifying war Americans have ever fought. The Union prevailed, and although emotional attachments to states remained strong, state sovereignty bowed to national supremacy. African Americans were now free, although nothing that happened in the Civil War guaranteed their citizenship or any measure of equality. Likewise, women achieved a greater amount of freedom without the removal of degrading political and legal disabilities. The North triumphed because of its greater resources and superior capacity to organize, support, and sustain its effort. Confederates performed amazing feats of courage and resourcefulness, but in the end they were whipped by overwhelming power and determination.

The Civil War preserved the Union; however, it did not unify the country. Devastation left the South a resentful economic dependent. A quarter of its white men, in their prime of their lives, were dead and scores of thousands more were permanently disabled. The South's labor system was destroyed, along with two-thirds of its wealth. In 1860 Southerners had owned 30 percent of the nation's wealth, and in 1870 just 12 percent. Reconstruction of the Union would require prodigious effort, and direction would come from the North.

SUGGESTED SOURCES FOR STUDENTS

An overstated but still important critique of Lincoln's role in the emancipation of enslaved people is Lerone J. Bennett, *Forced into glory: Abraham Lincoln's White Dream* (2000).

The most comprehensive single-volume biography of Abraham Lincoln is David Herbert Donald, *Lincoln* (1995).

Don H. Doyle, *The Cause of All Nations: An International History of the American Civil War* (2015), places the American Civil War, as it evolved into a war against slavery, squarely into a transatlantic global context.

Eric Foner, *The Fiery Trial: Abraham Lincoln and American Slavery* (2010), focuses on the evolution of Lincoln's ideas about slavery.

Also, Drew Gilpin Faust's *Mothers of Invention: Women of the Slaveholding South in the American Civil War* (1996) is imaginative and delightful to read.

Drew Gilpin Faust's *This Republic of Suffering: Death and the American Civil War* (2008) takes readers into the country's struggle to come to grips with the hugely unprecedented amount of physical and psychological pain caused by the Civil War.

Gary Gallagher defends the Confederate icon in *Lee and His Generals in War and Memory* (1998).

Lincoln's management of his Cabinet is the subject of Doris Kearns Goodwin, *Team of Rivals: The Political Genius of Abraham Lincoln* (2005).

For a readable and insightful study of Lincoln's mind, see Allen C. Guelzo, *Abraham Lincoln: Redeemer President* (1999).

The best one-volume treatment of the Civil War is James M. McPherson, *Battle Cry of Freedom: The Civil War Era* (1988).

James M. McPhersonn *Embattled Rebel: Jefferson Davis as Commander in Chief* (2014), is an objective and balanced account that highlights Davis' energy and determination to provide effective leadership.

Kathryn Shively Meier, *Nature's Civil War: Common Soldiers and the Environment in 1862* (2013), shifts focus away from how many Civil War soldiers died from disease and toward the incredibly high number of fatalities one would expect in a day before the discovery of germs.

For criticism of Robert E. Lee's generalship, see Alan T. Nolan, *Lee Considered: General Robert E. Lee and Civil War History* (1991).

For insight into the concept of total war, read Charles B. Royster, *The Destructive War: William Tecumseh Sherman and the Americans* (1991).

Elliott West brilliantly analyzes competition between whites and Indians on the Great Plains during the Civil War years in *Contested Plains: Indians, Goldseekers, and the Rush for Colorado* (1998).

BEFORE WE GO ON

1. Why did the Civil War happen? What were the rationales put forth by both sides? Do you agree with those rationales? If so why, and if not why not? How did both sides organize their war effort to attain their aims?

2. Did the United States emerge from the Civil War more or less democratic? Explain.

Building a Democratic Nation

3. Did the North win the Civil War, or did the South lose it? Explain.

4. Some scholars contend that wars are essentially destructive and that nothing constructive can result. How does the Civil War support or refute that contention?

Connections

5. Most historians maintain that the Civil War represents a transformation from an old style of warfare to a modern type of war. How would you support or refute that proposition?

6. Many historians see the Civil War as a revolution in America. Looking at the social, economic, and political aspects of the war, would you agree or disagree? Explain.

Chapter 16

EQUALITY BEFORE THE LAW: RESTORING AND EXPANDING THE UNION, 1865–1877

A PERSONAL PERSPECTIVE: FOCUS ON HENRY MCNEAL TURNER

In December of 1865, a thirty-one-year-old Union army chaplain named Henry McNeal Turner arrived in Atlanta, Georgia. An African American, Turner entered a city still showing the deep wounds of the Federal bombardment the year before. He was an agent of the Freedmen's Bureau, an agency that Congress had recently established to provide emergency relief to the emancipated slave population of the South and to supervise transactions between freed people and their former masters. General Davis Tillson was in charge of the agency's operations in Georgia, and he was not particularly sympathetic toward the plight of ex-slaves, so, after just two weeks, Turner resigned his army commission and devoted himself full-time to missionary activity.

> **How did Henry M. Turner define emancipation's full meaning?**

Henry Turner had never been enslaved. Born in South Carolina, his teenage mother had been a free woman. Turner's father, who died shortly after the boy's birth, was the son of a white plantation-owning woman and her black employee. When his mother married and moved to Abbeville, South Carolina, young Turner swept the floors of a local law office. Some of the lawyers taught him to read and write and instructed him in history, astronomy, and religion. Turner became a Methodist preacher and discovered that in the South "God's word had to be frittered, smeared, and smattered to please the politics of slavery."

Just prior to the Civil War, Henry Turner migrated to the North. After joining the African Methodist Episcopal Church, he became pastor of Israel AME Church in Washington, D.C. Among his acquaintances in the nation's capital were prominent abolitionist Republicans, including Thaddeus Stevens, Charles Sumner, Salmon P. Chase, and Benjamin Wade. Stevens, a congressman from Pennsylvania with a deep personal and political commitment to racial equality, and Wade, an Ohio Senator, both spoke from the pulpit of Turner's church.

During the Civil War, Turner criticized Abraham Lincoln's reluctance to push emancipation. But when Lincoln finally signed the Emancipation Proclamation on January 1, 1863, Turner extended his enthusiastic support even though the question of why both whites and blacks suffered so terribly in such a righteous cause troubled him. He comforted himself with the idea that the Civil War would mark the destruction of slavery and the beginning of a new Christian era in which freedom and equality would come to "oppressed humanity." He told his congregation: "God often sends affliction upon us for our own good," to prepare for Christ's second coming. By 1865, however, after he had helped raise a regiment of black troops and accompanied them to Virginia and North Carolina as their chaplain, Turner no longer believed that the United States was the location of Christ's millennial kingdom. He saw and felt too much fierce white racism for that. The South had surrendered but had not yet been redeemed, and in 1866 President Andrew Johnson attempted to reestablish traditional Southern society with its racial hierarchy intact.

In Georgia, Turner marshaled his enormous energy, faith, and intelligence to organize African Americans into the AME Church. During slavery, most blacks in the South had worshipped together with whites, seated separately inside churches and preached to by white ministers admonishing them to be obedient to their earthly masters. Turner, like many other black church missionaries who came to the South in the wake of Union armed forces, the Emancipation Proclamation, and the Thirteenth Amendment, endeavored to free African Americans from subservience to whites—spiritually, politically, and socially. The response from African Americans was overwhelming. They longed for freedom not just from slavery but in every aspect of their lives. Turner conducted a series of evangelical revivals. The exciting camp meetings gave blacks opportunities for giving thanks to God and to celebrate their liberation.

1863
Lincoln proclaims the policy of Amnesty and Reconstruction; Treasury Department initiates the Sea Island experiment with freed African-American labor

1864
Lincoln pocket vetoes the Wade-Davis Bill; W.T. Sherman orders distribution of Confederate land to freed people

1865
Congress creates the Freedmen's Bureau and the Freedmen's Savings Bank; Southern states enact Black Codes; Andrew Johnson proclaims Reconstruction complete; Congress refuses to recognize representatives from former Confederate states

In 1867, Georgia and the other rebellious states of the ex-Confederacy, entered a turbulent period called Radical Reconstruction. Congress took control of Reconstruction from President Johnson and installed a new Republican-dominated regime. Henry Turner, like many ministers, became actively involved in Reconstruction politics. As an educated and articulate member of the light-skinned, free-born African-American elite, Turner was a natural leader. Voters, including large numbers of freedmen, elected him to the state's constitutional convention where over half the black delegates were preachers. The resulting constitution extended voting rights to African Americans while denying suffrage to former Confederates. In 1868, Turner was elected to the state legislature.

Unfortunately for African Americans, Georgia's experience with Reconstruction was short. Whites despised the new politics that turned the traditional racial hierarchy upside down. Many resorted to fraud and violence in order to drive blacks out of the electorate. Blacks along with white Republicans (former Unionists along with recent immigrants from the North) who supported black suffrage, suffered beatings and murders. Turner and a white Republican named George Ashburn participated in a political rally, and thirty minutes after the meeting, a gang of whites murdered Ashburn, and probably would have killed Turner too if they had found him. In 1868, some thirty-two political assassinations were reported in Georgia, along with 212 non-lethal assaults. A year later, Turner received a note addressed to "Radical H. M. Turner: Your course of conduct is being closely watched by the owls of the night; do not be surprised if you should be aroused from slumber ere long by a boo hoo, boo hoo." The note was signed: "K.K.K."

The Era of Reconstruction marked the most extensive social revolution in American history. As the Civil War came to a close, 4 million African Americans became free. But the Emancipation Proclamation did not define the full meaning of freedom. A range of opinion from the conservative assertion that African Americans were not fit for citizenship to the most radical idealism embracing complete social and political equality found

expression. The postwar years were also a time of tremendous economic expansion. As the North consolidated its economic power over the country, entrepreneurs sought ways to integrate the South's war-torn economy into the nation's capitalist, free wage-labor system. Great opportunity for investment and profit, coupled with a devil-may-care attitude, produced a free-wheeling environment filled with fraud and abuse. It was a time of restoring and expanding the Union.

THINKING BACK

1. What did freedom mean for Henry M. Turner?
2. What does Turner's career say about the role of African-American churches?

CLASHING VISIONS OF RECONSTRUCTION

Historians like to organize events in ways that make them easier to understand. For instance, they usually study the Civil War and **Reconstruction** as separate episodes in American history—one primarily military and focusing on disunion and the other mostly political about restoring relationships among the states and the federal government. But this way of organizing the past is fuzzy around the edges. Abraham Lincoln's goal throughout the Civil War had been to reconstruct the Union—"With malice toward none; with charity for all," as he wrote in his second inaugural address. He wrapped Reconstruction into his effort to crush the rebellion. By defining the Civil War as a rebellion, Lincoln assumed responsibility for laying down the framework for Reconstruction because his duty as president was to defend the Constitution and ensure that the laws were "faithfully executed." **Radical Republicans** disputed Lincoln's claim. They wanted to seize the "golden moment" of victory over the Confederacy to revolutionize the South. Radical Republicans contended that secession had amounted to "state suicide" and considered the former Confederacy as conquered territory to be governed by the will of Congress. In 1865, most

1866
Johnson vetoes Freedmen's Bureau and Civil Rights Act, but Congress repasses them; Congress proposes Fourteenth Amendment; race riots break out in Memphis and New Orleans; Radical Republicans win massive majorities in Congressional elections; Congress passes Southern Homestead Act; Ku Klux Klan organized in Tennessee

1867
Congress passes Reconstruction Acts that begin Radical Reconstruction; Congress passes Tenure of Office Act

ex-Confederates promised future loyalty, but would these "white-washed rebels" accept Henry M. Turner and other African Americans as their equals before the law? When given the opportunity, they answered with a resounding "No!" And that led to what historians call Radical Reconstruction.

Lincoln's Lenient Reconstruction Plan

> **What exactly was Lincoln's Reconstruction plan?**

Midway through the Civil War, Abraham Lincoln devised a Reconstruction plan for the South that was remarkably forgiving, considering the intense suffering that the war caused. Rather than revenge, Lincoln hoped to "bind up the nation's wounds" as quickly and painlessly as possible.

In December of 1863, following the crucial Union victories at Gettysburg and Vicksburg, Lincoln proclaimed a policy of Amnesty and Reconstruction and applied it first in Louisiana. Whenever 10 percent of the qualified voters in 1860 pledged future loyalty to the Union they could draft a state constitution and conduct elections for governor, state legislators, and representatives to Congress. Lincoln did not permit Confederate civilian and military leaders to participate without a presidential pardon, but he only required the new state governments to establish republican structures and processes (a Constitutional requirement), abolish slavery, and provide for public education. He made no public mention of civil rights for African Americans, although privately he suggested suffrage for educated African Americans and those serving in the military.

Lincoln's Reconstruction plan blended compassion with political savvy. Leniency, he hoped, would encourage Confederates to surrender, shortening the war and saving countless lives. But Lincoln also understood that the Republican party was a sectional rather than a national organization; by wooing antislavery white Southerners with an easy reentry into the Union, he might broaden the party's popular base for the future. It was a long-shot, but 10 percent was only a beginning. "We shall sooner have the fowl by hatching the egg than by smashing it."

As long as the Confederacy remained at war with the United States, Lincoln's Reconstruction plan generated little enthusiasm. Only a few white Southerners took the loyalty oath, although enough did for the President to recognize reconstructed governments in Louisiana, Arkansas, Virginia, and Tennessee. Radical Republicans in Congress also rejected Lincoln's plan because they could not see in it a guarantee of civil rights for African-Americans. "The eggs of crocodiles," said Radical Republican senator Charles Sumner of Massachusetts in response to Lincoln's metaphor, "can produce only crocodiles." Radical congressmen refused to recognize Lincoln's reconstructed states and advanced their own formula that carried distinctly revolutionary overtones—freedom and equality for African Americans.

The Radicals' Alternative

"What is freedom?" Ohio congressman and Civil War veteran James A. Garfield asked. "Is it the bare privilege of not being chained? . . . If this is all, then freedom is a bitter mockery."

> **How did the Radicals' Reconstruction plan differ from Lincoln's**

Radical, and even most moderate, Republicans believed that true freedom meant more than emancipation from slavery, but they did not see eye to eye on how much more. Most Republicans asserted that African Americans possessed the right to sell their labor to the highest bidder in a free market, but Frederick Douglass went further in declaring: "Slavery is not abolished until the black man has the ballot." And after suffrage, what? Something more must be done, insisted the flinty but idealistic Thaddeus Stevens, to safeguard African Americans against economic dependency, exploitation, and a return to bondage. "This Congress is bound to provide for them until they can take care of themselves." Radical Republicans, most of whom had been abolitionists, envisioned an extensive transformation of Southern society. Carl Schurz, a German-American from Missouri, declared that "a free labor society must be established and built up on the ruins of the slave labor society."

1868
Fourteenth Amendment ratified; House of Representatives impeaches Andrew Johnson but Senate acquits; Wyoming organized as a territory; Henry McNeal Turner and other blacks expelled from Georgia legislature; Ulysses S. Grant elected president of the United States

1869
Congress proposes Fifteenth Amendment; Central Pacific and Union Pacific railroads meet at Promontory Point in Utah, completing first transcontinental railway

1870
Radical Reconstruction declared complete; Fifteenth Amendment ratified

In March of 1865, Congress established the **Bureau of Refugees, Freedmen, and Abandoned Lands** to provide basic relief for former slaves. Staffed mostly by military personnel, the **Freedmen's Bureau**, as it was known, distributed food, clothing, and fuel among the refugees, arranged for school buildings to educate them, and supervised the signing of work contracts between Southern planters and black laborers. Congress intended the Freedmen's Bureau as a temporary measure, with a one-year lifetime, to assist the freed people until they could get on their feet. Congress also chartered the **Freedmen's Savings Bank** to promote habits of thrift among former slaves inexperienced in the ways of capitalism.

With their bourgeois backgrounds, Republicans promoted economic independence among African Americans. In a highly publicized 1863–1864 experiment in the occupied Sea Island district of South Carolina, the Treasury Department sold abandoned Confederate plantations at public auction. Few freed slaves had the money to purchase these lands; nor did treasury officials want them to. Accepting popular African-American stereotypes, most Northern whites, including many Radicals, assumed that the freed slaves were not aggressive enough to become successful commercial farmers. So, treasury officials sold most of the land to Northern capitalists who hired the freedmen as wage laborers. According to this **Sea Island plan**, African Americans would absorb bourgeois values from Northern teachers and missionaries, save their hard-earned wages, and eventually purchase land and become independent, yeoman farmers. In this way, Republicans hoped to demonstrate the superior virtues of a free labor, bourgeois capitalism.

In 1864, however, William Tecumseh Sherman instituted a land redistribution program that many Radical Republicans espoused. During his infamous march through Georgia, Sherman ordered confiscated plantations divided into forty-acre parcels and distributed to freed slaves, each parcel with a mule to work it. In September of 1865, Thaddeus Stevens called for an expansion of this initiative through the seizure of 400 million acres from the wealthiest ex-Confederates. Moderate Republicans rejected this revolutionary innovation, however. Seizing civilian property violated bedrock Republican principles. Thus, "forty acres and a mule" remained only a dream for African Americans.

As they disagreed over land distribution, moderate and Radical Republicans also clashed over how to guarantee loyal governments in the Southern states. Finding President Lincoln's 10-percent plan way too generous toward the former slave owners that had tried to destroy the Union, Radical Republicans offered an alternative idea. In 1864, Senator Benjamin Wade of Ohio and Representative Henry Winter Davis of Maryland sponsored a bill requiring a majority of Southerners to pledge allegiance to the Union before commencing the Reconstruction process. Furthermore, the **Wade-Davis Bill** limited voting to those who swore an "ironclad oath" of past loyalty. Only white Unionists and ex-slaves could honestly pass such a test.

Congress approved the Wade-Davis Bill on the final day of the session. But when President Lincoln failed to sign it (what is called a "pocket veto"), the measure died. We cannot know how this conflict between Lincoln and the Radicals would have turned out because John Wilkes Boothe's bullet took the President's life; however, at the end of his life, Lincoln indicated he was moving toward a stricter Reconstruction plan. This suggested, perhaps, a closing of the gap between moderates and Radicals. But, in the spring of 1865, the real question was how Lincoln's successor, Vice President Andrew Johnson, planned to handle Reconstruction.

Presidential Reconstruction

Andrew Johnson's notions about Reconstruction arose both from personal feelings and from philosophical principle. Johnson had grown up poor and barely educated in eastern Tennessee, where as a young man he had

> **What did Andrew Johnson's Reconstruction plan entail?**

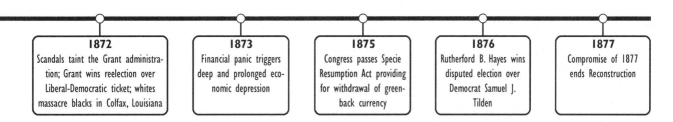

1872	1873	1875	1876	1877
Scandals taint the Grant administration; Grant wins reelection over Liberal-Democratic ticket; whites massacre blacks in Colfax, Louisiana	Financial panic triggers deep and prolonged economic depression	Congress passes Specie Resumption Act providing for withdrawal of greenback currency	Rutherford B. Hayes wins disputed election over Democrat Samuel J. Tilden	Compromise of 1877 ends Reconstruction

President Andrew Johnson. Johnson, a Southern Unionist, succeeded to the presidency upon Abraham Lincoln's assassination.

earned a living as a tailor. He was convinced that African Americans were suited for bondage, and he had managed to purchase a handful of slaves during his lifetime, but he detested bigwig planters who lorded it over both slaves and poor whites like himself. Entering politics as a champion of the common man, Johnson won election to Congress and remained a Unionist when Tennessee seceded. Lincoln rewarded Johnson's loyalty with an appointment as the military governor of Tennessee and in 1864 placed Johnson on the Union ticket as the vice presidential nominee. But despite a lengthy career in politics, the stubborn and quarrelsome Johnson developed few political skills. He differed strikingly from Lincoln in temperament.

Radical Republicans hoped that Andrew Johnson would become their ally. "Treason must be made odious," Johnson had said, "and traitors must be punished and impoverished." Radicals liked that, but in May of 1865 he announced his Reconstruction plan, and it was nothing like what the Radicals expected. It carried the tone of Lincoln's forbearance. Furthermore, Johnson did not share the Radicals' belief in coercive federal power over the states—he had grown up a Democrat—nor their commitment to the advancement of African Americans. Instead, he hoped to rebuild the South in partnership with moderate white

Southerners, like Georgia's Alexander Stephens, who had initially opposed secession. The President granted amnesty to those who had been reluctant Rebels and restored their confiscated property (except for their slaves). He excluded from the general amnesty all Confederate diehards and anyone who owned property worth $20,000 or more, but granted most of them individual pardons—over 13,000 in all. President Johnson did demand that new, loyal state governments abolish slavery, renounce secession, and repudiate Confederate debts.

The effect of Johnson's **"Presidential Reconstruction"** was that the same people who had once controlled the South regained power. Only Jefferson Davis was barred from holding public office. White Southerners had no intention of giving African Americans political or economic power. Indeed, newly elected state legislatures in all the former Confederate states except Tennessee enacted highly prescriptive laws known as **Black Codes**. While ostensibly protecting the ex-slaves' freedom by requiring planters to offer work contracts that specified wages and work conditions, the Black Codes severely limited black freedom. Mississippi law, for instance, prohibited blacks from owning guns and allowed authorities to auction off as forced labor any black "vagrant" who did not have a contract. While not reinstituting slavery per se, these discriminatory laws consigned African Americans to agricultural and domestic labor. By the time Congress reconvened in December of 1865, the President had proclaimed loyal governments in each of the former Confederate states and pronounced Reconstruction complete.

What a tonic it was for demoralized white Southerners who had resigned themselves to a much worse fate. But Republicans in Congress refused to accept this state of affairs. Both Radicals and moderates concluded that Presidential Reconstruction was unacceptable.

Johnson Versus the Radicals

Republicans were not unified on the details of their alternative to Presidential Reconstruction, however. Radical idealists wanted to employ federal power to secure citizenship and voting rights for African Americans. Moderates balked at black suffrage as well as the concept that the states were conquered territories devoid of rights. But against President Johnson's Reconstruction measures, Radicals and moderates

> How did Andrew Johnson and Presidential Reconstruction unite Republicans?

THE CRUEL UNCLE AND THE VETOED BABES IN THE WOOD.

Courtesy of Library of Congress

A political cartoon showing mean "Uncle Johnson" dragging the Civil Rights Act and the Freedmen's Bureau renewal bill into the darkness of the "veto wood," from where he expected they would never return to see the light of day. From Frank Leslie's Illustrated Newspaper

closed ranks. The resulting confrontation between Johnson and congressional Republicans not only reshaped Reconstruction but also threatened the constitutional balance between the executive and legislative branches of government.

In December of 1865, the showdown began when Congressional Republicans refused to recognize the representatives from the former Confederate states. In practical terms, that simply meant that the Union was not yet restored. Congress then voted to extend the Freedmen's Bureau with enhanced funding and authority and early in 1866 passed the **Civil Rights Act** establishing African-American citizenship, stipulating their rights as citizens, and punishing anyone who violated them. Johnson vetoed both of these measures, arguing that the federal government had no responsibility to care for "indigent persons" and that the measures favored blacks over whites. Shocked and angered by Johnson's belligerence, the Republicans re-passed the bills by the two-thirds vote necessary to override a presidential veto. Although Johnson won the praise of Northern and Southern Democrats for his defiance, he also galvanized Moderate and Radical Republicans into a powerful Congressional majority against presidential authority over Reconstruction.

The Republicans proceeded to etch African-American citizenship and equality under the law into the Constitution of the United States. In June of 1866, Congress presented the **Fourteenth Amendment** to the states for their ratification. The first part of the amendment proclaimed that all persons born or naturalized in the United States were citizens of the United States as well as the particular states in which they resided, with the rights to "life, liberty, and property." This was not limited to but certainly included African Americans. The second article said that any state that denied the vote to qualified "male citizens" would suffer a proportional reduction in its Congressional representation. The third section disqualified from public office anyone who had taken an oath of loyalty to the United States and then engaged in armed rebellion against the country. The fourth item invalidated all Confederate debts, and the fifth granted Congress authority to enforce the amendment.

Bold and sweeping as the Fourteenth Amendment later became, it was actually a compromise that pleased few in the country at the time. It disappointed many Radicals because it fell short of guaranteeing black suffrage. A state could refuse to allow African Americans to vote if it was willing to accept reduced representation in Congress. Feminists bitterly complained about placing the term "male" in the Constitution. Elizabeth Cady Stanton complained that "it will take us a century at least to get it out." President Johnson, most white Southerners, and many Northern whites as well condemned the proposed amendment because it pushed civil rights for African Americans well beyond the bounds of acceptance. Ten of the former Confederate states refused to ratify it (Tennessee was the lone exception), as did several Northern states.

The issue of black citizenship rights, especially voting rights, ignited passions, grimly illustrated by two horrible episodes of racial violence against African Americans. In May of 1866, a wagon driven by a black man down a Memphis street collided with another driven by a white man, touching off three days of rioting led by angry whites. During the rampage, at least forty-eight people died, almost all of them black. In July, New Orleans erupted in similar rioting. In both cities, white authorities did little to protect the black victims. Hostility toward African Americans and their Republican supporters raged across the South. For many Northerners, who did not support black voting rights and whose states did not enfranchise African Americans either, racial violence further discredited Andrew Johnson's "reconstructed" Southern governments.

The Congressional elections in the autumn of 1866 highlighted the clash between Johnson and the Radical Republicans. To counteract the mounting chorus of criticism directed at Presidential Reconstruction, Johnson took a campaign "**swing around the circle**," a speaking tour by railroad, during the Congressional elections in the autumn of 1866. Traveling through upstate New York and through the Midwest to St. Louis, his goal was to drum up support for Democratic Congressional candidates. At whistle stops, he launched fierce verbal attacks upon the Radicals. But intemperate comments—like "Why not hang Thad Stevens" in response to hecklers who demanded hanging Jefferson Davis—backfired, appalling even some of the President's most ardent supporters. One New York newspaper called his behavior "thoroughly reprehensible." The elections resulted in a total Democratic wipeout. Radicals won enough seats to guarantee veto-proof majorities in both houses of Congress. Republicans also won every Northern statehouse and majorities in most Northern state legislatures.

"This is the most decisive and emphatic victory ever seen in American politics," declared an influential news magazine called *The Nation*. Radical Republicans were now in charge of Reconstruction, and the process of restoring the former rebel states to the Union started all over again.

THINKING BACK

1. What were the consequences of Andrew Johnson's Reconstruction program?
2. What steps did Republicans in Congress take in attempting to ensure citizenship rights for African Americans?

RADICAL RECONSTRUCTION

"A great work of reconstruction is before us," declared the New York *Herald*. For Republicans, the key to that work was enfranchising African Americans and forging Republican electoral majorities in the Southern states. When the newly elected Congress convened early in 1867, Radicals demolished the Johnson-approved governments, erased the Black Codes, and imposed a military regime on the former Confederacy. New Republican state governments broke ground by incorporating African Americans into the civic life of the South. Bitter whites and later historians labeled this the era of "Black Reconstruction," although African Americans never dominated the politics of the Southern states. In addition to acknowledging African-American citizenship, Radical Republican governments undertook sweeping social and economic reforms. They were never popular among Southern whites, however, and the high taxes and inefficiency that they introduced made Radical Reconstruction vulnerable to criticism in the North as well as the South.

Congress Takes Command

In March of 1867, Congress passed **the first Reconstruction Act** over another of President Johnson's vetoes, and in doing so heralded the beginning of Radical Reconstruction. **Three additional Reconstruction acts** set up mechanisms for implementation and enforcement of Radical Reconstruction. The measures divided the former Confederacy (except for Tennessee, whose government had already passed Radical muster) into five military districts, each under the rule of a Union army general. Those commanders supervised elections of delegates to constitutional conventions, ensuring that African Americans voted and occupied seats in the conventions. Ex-Confederates generally boycotted the constitution-making process, and, of course, some were disqualified by the Fourteenth Amendment. The commanding generals scrutinized the resulting constitutions to ensure that they adequately provided for African-American suffrage. Finally, Radical Republicans required the new governments to ratify the Fourteenth Amendment. Only then did Congress receive the rebellious states into the Union, bringing Reconstruction to completion. By 1868, enough states had ratified the Fourteenth Amendment to add it to the Constitution, and by 1870, all the Southern states had been readmitted to the Union.

> How did the Radical Republicans in Congress take charge of Reconstruction, and how did they threaten the Constitutional balance of power between Congress and the presidency?

Certain that even the Northern public felt that Radicals had gone too far with their social engineering in the South, Andrew Johnson encouraged white Southerners to defy Congress while he obstructed Reconstruction by what means he could. The President vetoed every Reconstruction bill that crossed his desk, although

Congress easily overrode them. Johnson was more effective in removing military commanders who favored Radical policy and replacing them with generals who did not, but this maneuver triggered a crisis. To strip him of the power to remove appointed government officials, Congress passed the **Tenure of Office Act**, a measure that prohibited the president from removing from office appointees who had received Senate approval until a replacement acceptable to the Senate had been named. The law also declared, and this was a key provision, that a president could not dismiss Cabinet officials before the end of the term of the president who had appointed them, again without the Senate's consent. Johnson met the challenge by firing Secretary of War Edwin Stanton, his biggest enemy in the Cabinet, and early in 1868, the House of Representatives impeached him.

The spectacle of the President of the United States being hauled before the Senate on impeachment charges was unprecedented in American history. The specific grounds for removing the president from office were unclear—except for treason and bribery. House impeachment managers, led by Thaddeus Stevens, argued that the ambiguous "high crimes and misdemeanors" phrase in the Constitution included objectionable behavior, but Chief Justice Salmon P. Chase, whom Lincoln had appointed to the bench in 1864 and now presided over the trial, kept all testimony narrowly confined to the specific issue of whether Johnson had violated the Tenure of Office Act. This weakened the Radicals' case because Johnson had not appointed Stanton in the first place, Lincoln had. The Radicals seemed to be trying to strip from the chief executive its Constitutional authority to appoint his own executive subordinates.

In April, Washington bettors favored Johnson's acquittal. And while a majority of the Senate (35 to 19) voted for conviction, that was one vote shy of the two-thirds required for removal. Impeachment not only failed, but it split the Republicans. Seven Moderates sided with the Democrats for acquittal to avoid politicizing the impeachment process and because they figured that Radical Senator Benjamin Wade of Ohio, who stood next in line to become president, would be even worse than Johnson.

Andrew Johnson's impeachment trial also resulted in setting a higher standard than extreme partisanship or gross offensiveness for removing the president of the United States from office. This precedent played a major role in the later case of

Thaddeus Stevens and John A. Bingham from the House of Representatives bring impeachment charges before the Senate, February 25, 1867. From Frank Leslie's Illustrated Newspaper

Courtesy of Library of Congress

President Bill Clinton. It also preserved the political independence of the executive branch of the federal government. If the Radicals had succeeded, it would have been much easier in the future for a strong majority to remove the president any time the chief executive opposed the Congress. As it was, the impeachment ordeal intimidated Andrew Johnson, who suspended his war of sabotage against Radical Reconstruction. Indeed, executive leadership in government remained dormant for a generation.

The Fifteenth Amendment

The final component in the Radical Republicans' Reconstruction package was an African-American suffrage amendment. African-American voting was too important to be left to the swirling winds of racial politics. As a matter of fact, thirteen Northern and Border states, unaffected by the Reconstruction Acts, had not yet extended the ballot to African Americans. Inserting voting rights into the Constitution would make them secure and universal throughout the country. In February of 1869, Congress sent the Fifteenth Amendment to the states for their ratification.

> **What specifically did the Fifteenth Amendment do, and what did it fail to do?**

Simply and directly, the **Fifteenth Amendment** said that the right to vote "shall not be denied or abridged by the United States or by any state on account of race, color, or previous condition of servitude." But that language was not as tough as many Radicals had wanted it to be. Thus worded, the amendment did not prohibit restraints that, while not explicitly based on race, might fall disproportionately on particular racial or ethnic groups. This was less an oversight than a deliberate attempt to appease Northern and Western states that wanted to withhold the franchise from immigrants—including the immigrant Chinese in California. Resourceful Southern Democrats later took advantage of the amendment's "lame and halting language" to use literacy and property to exclude African Americans.

The most vociferous objections to the Fifteenth Amendment, though, came from women who felt betrayed because it did not extend political equality to women. Feminist leaders like Elizabeth Cady Stanton and Susan B. Anthony, who had supported the abolitionist movement, condemned enfranchising black males in the name of freedom while leaving women, black and white, dependent and unfree. Frederick Douglass tried to justify the Fifteenth Amendment by arguing that without it the entire race of African Americans, male as well as female, would be unrepresented. White women, he said, were already represented through their husbands and fathers. Most feminists were unconvinced, Stanton concluding that woman "must not put her trust in man." Although the American Woman Suffrage Association, which for years had been fighting for women's right to vote, backed ratification as a step in the right direction, Stanton and Anthony broke from the group and formed the rival National American Woman Suffrage Association. This fragmentation of the women's suffrage movement hampered the feminist cause for many years.

By March of 1870, Radical Republican pressure on four recalcitrant Southern states that had not yet been reconstructed forced them to ratify the Fifteenth Amendment, thereby accomplishing its adoption. Most Republicans now believed that Congress had done enough for African Americans. "The Fifteenth Amendment," declared James A. Garfield, "confers upon the African race the care of its own destiny. It places their fortunes in their own hands." The Northern commitment to justice for African Americans had gone as far as it would go.

Radical Reconstruction in the States

With the framework for Radical Reconstruction in place, attention shifted to the Southern states where Republicans hoped to complete a genuine political and economic revolution. African Americans enthusiastically entered the body politic, as did lower-class white farmers and artisans and Northern immigrants drawn to the South like moths to a candle. These groups, mostly from the lower ranks of society, formed a political pastiche that dominated Southern public affairs for a decade. "All society," one former Southern leader observed, "stands now like a cone on its apex."

How did the Republican party reorganize Southern society?

Ex-slaves comprised the majority of the incipient Southern Republican party. Local organizations known as Union Leagues recruited and mobilized black voters on behalf of Republican candidates. Meetings, often conducted by Northern blacks who had come South as soldiers or missionaries, were held in African-American churches, schools, and shops. League rallies turned out up to 90 percent of the African-American electorate. Ironically, African Americans' numerical superiority in the plantation districts allowed them to represent areas that once were the fiefdoms of their former masters.

African Americans not only voted but also occupied public offices in the South (more than 600 state legislative seats, sixteen Congressional seats, and numerous sheriff's offices, school commissioner's posts, and

Radical members, black and white, of the first Reconstruction legislature in South Carolina.

municipal alderman's positions). However, the number of black office-holders never reflected the percentage of African Americans in the Southern population. Nor did African Americans control Radical Reconstruction governments, as their critics and many racist legends maintained. Only in South Carolina, Louisiana, and Mississippi did African Americans hold positions as high as lieutenant governor, and only in South Carolina did they constitute a majority in even one house of the state legislature. Initially, the former free-black, light-skinned elite occupied most of the offices held by African Americans—men like Henry McNeal Turner. But by the end of Reconstruction, successful and intelligent ex-slave businessmen, landowners, teachers, artisans, and ministers typified African-American officials. By and large, African Americans were as qualified for the positions of public trust they held as whites were.

In most states, Southern white Republicans dominated state government. Hated by the ex-Confederate Democrats for their disloyalty to the Southern cause, local Unionists bore the name "**Scalawags**," a negative label Southerners usually attached to no-account scamps. In truth, the Scalawags were mostly solid yeoman farmers and artisans, and occasionally even local businessmen who favored the Republican party's pro-business policies. One such man was James L. Alcorn, one of the largest plantation owners in Mississippi. A third element in the Southern Republican coalition was the Northern "**Carpetbaggers**." That name, also applied by resentful white Southerners, suggested that these Republicans were good-for-nothing opportunists who had packed all their worldly belongings in cheap suitcases made of carpet material and had descended on the defenseless South to grab whatever political and economic plums they could find. The label fit in some instances; however, many more Carpetbaggers were idealistic army veterans, schoolteachers, or church missionaries. Others were wealthy men intent on investing in the modernization of the Southern economy. The Carpetbagger Henry C. Warmoth arrived in New Orleans with the Union army in 1864 and helped organize the Republican party in Louisiana. He was elected governor of the Radical regime. Because of their knowledge and leadership skills, Carpetbaggers often dominated Reconstruction politics, particularly in states like South Carolina, Florida, and Louisiana that had relatively few native white Republicans. Carpetbaggers held most of the highest offices.

The Republican coalition was not tension-free. Scalawags did not feel comfortable with their African American allies, disagreeing with them mostly over black suffrage. In 1868, Georgia's white Republicans joined with Democrats in the legislature to expel Henry McNeal Turner and other African-American legislators. The episode radicalized Turner, who had consistently voted on the basis of class rather than race on measures to protect the rights of property-owners, limit taxes, and establish educational requirements for voting. "Anything to please the white folks," he said. Now he felt betrayed. In 1870, Radicals in Washington helped him reclaim his seat, whereupon he regularly hurled verbal "thunderbolts" at persons who challenged his manhood and citizenship as an African American. Turner eventually became a vigorous proponent of African-American emigration from the United States.

Under the rules of Radical Reconstruction, Southern state conventions drafted new constitutions, most of which disenfranchised ex-Confederates. Between 1868 and 1870, reconstructed governments under Republican party control began operating in most of the states of the former Confederacy. They ratified the Fourteenth Amendment, held elections for United States senators and congressmen, and had reestablished their representation in Congress. Next they tackled the social and economic problems that confronted their states.

Radical Reconstruction's Record

Antebellum Southern state governments had served primarily the wealthy planters and thus had been limited in scope, concentrating on protecting slavery and costing the taxpayers relatively little. Ambitious Radical Reconstruction state governments changed the role and scope of state government. Their goal was two-fold: to protect the freedom of African Americans and modernize the Southern economy. Legislatures and executives spent enormous amounts of money, levied and collected taxes that fell heavily on white Democratic property owners, and, as a result, drew down upon them the bitter hatred of most white Southerners. Radical state governments ultimately failed to win lasting public support, either in the South or in the North.

Radical-led state governments instituted several liberal reforms in Southern society. For instance, they significantly increased popular participation in politics and government. In addition to enfranchising

> How did Radical Republican governments reform politics and the economy in the South?

African-American males, they increased the number of elected offices, removed property qualifications for voting and office-holding, and provided for the direct popular election of the president of the United States (South Carolina had been the last holdout for legislative selection of presidential electors). Equality before the law, regardless of race, made justice more color-blind than before. Whites were more likely than before to face punishment for crimes they committed against blacks; blacks and whites served together on juries; and blacks participated in law enforcement. For example, in 1870, one-half of the police forces of Montgomery, Alabama, and Vicksburg, Mississippi, were African Americans, and in Tallahassee and Little Rock blacks became chiefs of police.

Following the pattern of social reform begun in the North prior to the Civil War, Reconstruction governments established public hospitals, asylums, and orphanages. In the domestic realm, they expanded the grounds for divorce (making it easier for women to escape from abusive husbands), enhanced women's property rights, and forced white fathers to accept greater responsibility for their mulatto children. But the most important innovation of the Radical governments was in public education. Republicans believed that universal literacy was the cornerstone of an egalitarian society. Accordingly, legislatures provided for statewide school systems that, although under-funded, racially segregated, and generally less effective than Northern public schools, signified Southern acceptance of the principle of public education.

One of the greatest challenges facing the new governments was reconstructing a Southern economy devastated by the Civil War. That entailed repairing the massive destruction to farms, factories, and railroads and developing more efficient means of transportation that would help transform the South into a prosperous section of cities, industries, and diversified agriculture employing free wage laborers. Between 1868 and 1871, state and local governments poured millions of dollars into economic development, much of it into paving city streets and grading rural roads. In various ways, states assisted railroad construction: direct subsidies to railroad companies, purchase or endorsement of railroad company bonds, tax exemptions, and the use of convict labor in grading roadbeds and laying track. In addition, legislatures chartered banks to generate credit and appropriated money for strengthening river levees and reclaiming swamp land for agricultural expansion.

The cost of these reforms was steep, both in terms of dollars and the credibility of the governments that undertook them. To serve the needs of 4 million new African-American citizens and to support economic recovery and modernization required enormous financial outlays. State governments pumped property taxes from landowners and financed much of the remaining expenditures with bond issues. Economic activity drew developers eager to make a profit. Carpetbagger Daniel H. Chamberlain, who became governor of South Carolina, confessed: "I hoped to make money—dreamed of thousands." Corruption flourished in this hothouse environment because there was plenty of incentive and little regulation. Railroad and manufacturing executives spent hundreds of thousands of dollars in bribes to buy millions in government subsidies. Not only the rich, but also the poor drank from the public trough. One black South Carolina legislator sold his vote in the election of the state's United States senator because he needed the money. "I was pretty hard up, and I did not care who the candidate was if I got two hundred dollars." There probably was no more corruption in the South during Reconstruction than in other times and places before and since, but it was conspicuous in that era because it involved unpopular governments that were under close scrutiny.

The achievements of the Radical state government were significant, but they came at the expense of outrageous fraud and were desirable mainly to those Southerners who embraced change. Most white Southerners were conservatives who wanted things to remain as much as possible like they had been before the Civil War. For them, Radical Reconstruction was more humiliating and offensive than Lee's surrender of Confederate forces at Appomattox.

Reaction Sets In

Unpopular reforms, widespread corruption, and racism, all interrelated, brought Radical Reconstruction under harsh attack. The vast majority of white Southerners refused to accept the Republican plan for transforming Southern society. Bitterness spilled out in violence directed against Republican party leaders, teachers and missionaries who sought to uplift African Americans, and even against the entrepreneurs who sought to revamp the South's traditional agrarian economy.

> **Why and how did whites in the South and the North react against Radical Reconstruction?**

A cartoon showing three whites, one a former Rebel with a knife and a CSA belt buckle, the second an Irishman raising a club and carrying a whiskey bottle in his pocket, and the third a Northern capitalist waving a wallet filled with cash for Southern economic development. All three declare: "This is a white man's government" and Congress' Reconstruction Acts are "usurpations, and unconstitutional, revolutionary, and void." All three have their feet on the back of a prostrate black soldier while a school and an orphanage for freedmen burn in the background. From Harper's Weekly, September 5, 1868.

Reconstruction politics became a very dangerous activity. In 1866, Tennessee whites, including former Confederate cavalry hero Nathan Bedford Forrest, formed the **Ku Klux Klan**, an organization that launched a program of systematic terror directed at blacks, Scalawags, and Carpetbaggers. Gangs of white thugs roamed through the South, beating, killing, and burning. Military forces, severely reduced in size as Civil War enlistments expired and Indian wars in the West demanded increasing attention, and often commanded by men who did not support the goals of Radical Reconstruction, did little to stop the bloodshed.

The presidential election of 1868 marked a turning point in Radical Reconstruction. The Republican party turned to the enormously popular Civil War hero Ulysses S. Grant for leadership, adding Schuyler Colfax, a former Radical whose ardor had cooled, to the ticket for vice president. Andrew Johnson returned to the Democratic party, seeking its presidential nomination; instead, though, Democrats chose Horatio Seymour, a former New York governor backed by wealthy and conservative Northeastern business interests. His running mate, Francis P. Blair, Jr., whipped up racial hatred by ridiculing African Americans and condemning racial equality. Grant supported the goals of Radical Reconstruction, but he was a poor political leader. He relied on the platitudes, like his campaign slogan, "Let us have peace," which referred as much to Indian issues in the West as racial antipathy in the South. Republicans generally capitalized on the party's role in saving the Union. They waved the "**bloody shirt**," meaning that they reminded voters of the wounds inflicted on patriotic citizens by the disloyal, Democratic South. Grant's military reputation, not his idealism, carried him to victory in all but eight states. Yet, his 300,000-vote margin of victory (53 percent of the total) was smaller than the 450,000 African-American votes cast in the election. Seymour was the choice of a majority of whites in the country.

The outcome of the 1868 election, along with the death of Thaddeus Stevens, who had been the conscience of Radical Republicans and demanded to be buried in a black cemetery, signaled the gradual waning of Northern support for Reconstruction. Social and economic progress in the South could not sustain the North's commitment in the face of spiraling costs and rampant disorder. Political uncertainties scared away Northern investors, and Southern state legislatures began to cut back on their aid programs as they ran out of money. Increasingly, African Americans would have to advance on their own, with diminishing assistance from local governments or from Washington.

THINKING BACK

1. How did Congressional Republicans set up Radical Reconstruction? What did Radical Reconstruction accomplish? Where did it fail?
2. What led to President Andrew Johnson's impeachment, and what was the outcome of the Senate trial?

Courtesy of Library of Congress

THE MEANING OF FREEDOM

If Radical Reconstruction did not completely revitalize the South's economy, it dramatically reshaped race relations. Freedom and equality forged new relationships between black people and white people. Former slaves could do what they pleased without the approval of their former masters. Many African Americans withdrew from the social and economic connections with whites that reminded them of their enslavement. Freedom from slavery and opportunities for personal growth led to an expansion of the African-American middle class, and produced an elite that enjoyed genuine wealth. But freedom from slavery and the noble principle of justice before the law did not add up to social equality. White Southerners, Republican as well as Democrat, ostracized blacks. "For whites only" signs branded black persons (known as "Jim Crow") with the unmistakable badge of inferiority.

Bitten By the Freedom Bug

Because emancipation had come to African Americans at different times and in different ways, the former slaves' immediate responses to being free varied widely. No doubt, apprehension blended with excitement as liberating Union soldiers approached. White masters had often told slaves that the Yankees would kill them or ship them off to Caribbean slavery. Indeed, some of the Yanks had treated blacks monstrously. Although terrified individuals hid out, scores of thousands fled to refugee camps set up near the armies and maintained by the Freedmen's Bureau. Others stayed put until blue-coated officials read the Emancipation Proclamation to them. Some remained with their former masters even after they were free, out of affection or a desire for security. But once the dream of freedom came true, most former slaves broke into emotional celebrations.

How did freed slaves exercise their freedom?

After emancipation, Charlie Davenport of Mississippi said he "was right smart bit by de freedom bug." So were hundreds of thousands of other freed people. In March of 1865, 4,000 exuberant African Americans marched through the streets of Charleston, South Carolina, carrying a banner proclaiming "We Know No Master but Ourselves." Elsewhere, freed people celebrated with parades, picnics, barbecues, and church services, and continued to do so in annual commemorations of freedom day. Many ex-slaves yielded to an impulse to leave the plantations where they had lived and toiled. This sudden migration included people looking for spouses, parents, and children from whom they had been separated during slavery. Others sought jobs in Southern towns and cities. Between 1860 and 1870, Atlanta's black population jumped from 1,900 to nearly 10,000, boosting the African American proportion of the local citizenry from 20 percent to 46 percent. Most ex-slaves did not have the resources to travel far, but almost all of them moved away from their masters' farms and plantations.

Freedom allowed African Americans to scrap the fawning, servile mannerisms that the white master class had demanded from them. "I expect white folks to be waiting on me before long," one black woman harrumphed. They no longer felt the need to lower their eyes, doff their caps, or use terms like "Massa" or "Mistus" when addressing white people. African Americans were equal to white people now, at least insofar as the law was concerned. In establishing their new identities, freed people took last names. As slaves, they had not had them, but government agents required family names for record-keeping. Most people refused to adopt the last names of their former masters; instead, they named themselves after people they respected—like Washington and Lincoln.

Although the priority for Southern whites was putting African Americans back to work growing cotton, liberated blacks set their minds and energies to establishing solid domestic relationships. The Freedmen's Bureau insisted that African-American couples legally marry, reflecting the middle-class Protestant values that prevailed in the North as well as the bureau's commitment to voluntary but binding contracts as symbols of freedom. Legions of Northern church missionaries, thinking of the freed people as shiftless, also pushed them to legalize their marriages. But African Americans did not need government agents or missionaries to teach them lessons in moral commitment. Devoted couples who had been denied the opportunity to marry during slavery eagerly sought out ministers and civil officials to sanctify and legalize their unions.

The marriage contract, however, was in reality a lopsided arrangement that extended considerably more freedom to men than to women. Typical of the marriage relationships at that time, African-American marriages perpetuated the hoary principle of patriarchy. They provided men with the right to rule their wives and women with the right to relinquish their identity, their property, and their independence. Northern schoolteachers taught young African-American girls their proper place in marriage. With quotes from the Bible, one commonly-used spelling book drilled pupils in both ciphering and submission: "Wives, sub-mit your-selves un-to your own hus-bands."

In every way possible, African Americans disentangled themselves from the web of white dominance and formed separate black communities. African Americans chose to interact with other African Americans in ways that gave each other pleasure and satisfaction. Black churchgoers, for instance, withdrew from churches controlled by whites. In 1860, Georgia's bi-racial Baptist churches counted 27,700 African-American worshippers, but in 1870 there were only 5,700. Conversely, membership in all-black Baptist churches zoomed from a few hundred to 38,900. "Praise God," exclaimed a black man, "for the day of liberty to worship God." Most African Americans joined independent African-American Baptist and Methodist denominations. During the 1860s and 1870s, Baptist missionaries, former slave preachers, and women active in African-American community-building organized thousands of Baptist congregations into district associations and state conventions. Later (in 1895) they organized the **National Baptist Convention**, which became the largest African-American religious organization in the country. African Methodist Episcopal missionaries like Henry McNeal Turner expanded the AME and AME Zion churches throughout the South.

Independent black churches not only provided satisfying religious experiences with African-American music and preaching but also education in Sunday schools, financial assistance and emotional comfort to the needy, and business experience and leadership skills for men and women. The sense of community that had developed within the old plantation slave quarters transplanted itself into independent black churches, fraternal societies, and other social organizations.

Despite the rise of independent black churches, some freed women and men remained associated with white denominations. The noted Methodist missionary James Lynch envisioned a racially integrated South. In some instances the lure of property kept blacks attached to white-controlled churches. For example, the **Colored Methodist Episcopal Church**, formed in 1870, remained closely affiliated with white Southern Methodists who gave the CME Church buildings for worship. The Northern Methodist church promised racial equality and no segregation.

When questioned by a special congressional committee as to whether separate black churches were signs of African Americans' desire for autonomy or the result of forced segregation, an African-American minister assured the lawmakers that blacks preferred their own social institutions. He was correct. Pride, an overwhelming desire to be free of white people, and bad memories from slavery dictated the voluntary separation of black people from white people. That was evident in the freed people's attitude toward churches and schools.

Education: Another Key to African-American Advancement

Ex-slaves hungered for the ability to read and write. "There is one sin that slavery committed against me," stated a freedman, "which I will never forgive. It robbed me of my education." African Americans understood the practical value of literacy. They needed to read and to understand work contracts, as one freed person put it "so that the Rebs can't cheat me." They also had to be able to read election ballots in order to vote intelligently. And although Reconstruction governments provided for public education, it was over the deep-seated conviction of Southern whites that educating African Americans was a bad thing.

> What type of education did African Americans desire, and why did whites in the South oppose education for blacks?

Planters believed that learning would "spoil" African Americans for work. They wanted a compliant workforce, and one that included children; whites had no use for schools that would teach African Americans to be independent and that would keep children away from the cotton fields. But the Carpetbaggers insisted that free labor—the Republican mantra—and mass literacy went hand-in-hand. Their conviction and the African Americans' intense desire for schooling overcame entrenched planter resistance; however, the Radical Reconstruction governments tried to appease Southern whites by keeping public school terms so short that black pupils barely had time to learn. Terms often did not begin until December so that African-American children could participate in

Courtesy of Library of Congress

John Mercer Langston. Born free in Virginia, he moved to Ohio and became an abolitionist and political activist before the Civil War. Langston moved to Washington, D.C., in 1868 as the first dean of Howard University's law school. He later served as U.S. minister to Haiti and as a member of the House of Representatives from Virginia.

African-American inferiority. Ultimately, the AMA could not meet the crying need for teachers; indeed, by the early 1870s, Northern financial support for private schools for Southern blacks all but dried up, creating more dependence on segregated public schools. But as much as African Americans appreciated the efforts of white teachers on their behalf, they really wanted black teachers in black schools.

African Americans desired white assistance in training teachers, but not white control. Self-reliance was their goal. The primary sources of trained teachers were colleges and normal schools operated by the Northern religious societies and the African-American churches. **Howard University** in Washington and **Fisk University** in Nashville were founded by the AMA. African-American churches established schools specifically for teacher and minister training. The African Methodist Episcopal (AME) Church operated **Wilberforce University** in Ohio and soon Baptists and the other Methodist denominations founded colleges throughout the South. By 1880, over half of the 3,000 teachers in African-American schools were black, a source of great pride and feeling of autonomy.

Land and Labor

The ultimate source of freedom and improvement in the quality of freed people's lives was economic security. But this proved to be most elusive.

the fall cotton-picking. And in 1870, only one black school-age child out of four in the South attended school on a regular basis.

Northern whites, mostly women and men sponsored by church missionary societies and organized by the Freedmen's Bureau, taught in hundreds of schools established for freed children after the Civil War. The most important agency for educating freed African Americans was the **American Missionary Association**, an organization of Congregational and Presbyterian churches. Teachers not only instructed pupils in reading and writing but also imparted Northern bourgeois values. Despite their commitment to universal literacy, however, Northern teachers and their reading and spelling books, written specifically for the freed children, conveyed stereotypes denoting

Raised in an agricultural environment, most freed people yearned for a piece of land upon which to grow food crops and livestock and raise families. Least of all did they want to go back to plantation work gangs growing cotton. Even a good wage did not sub-

> **What was the ultimate source of freedom for African Americans in the South, and why was it so difficult to realize?**

stitute for the satisfaction of owning a farm. However, the dream of forty acres and a mule quickly evaporated for most freed persons. Except in the sugar-growing district of Louisiana and the rice-growing lowlands of South Carolina where antebellum plantations did not survive the devastation of the Civil War, the white planter class retained control of Southern farm land. Even where the cost of restoring plantations to their prewar conditions was prohibitive, whites refused to sell land to African Americans because it would give them a measure of independence that whites found objectionable. A few Southern blacks managed to acquire land, including some 4,000 who filed claims for poor public land offered through the Southern Homestead Act (1866). But in 1880, only one black farmer in twenty owned land (including over 9,000 black women).

By 1870, whites and blacks had settled on **land tenancy** for African Americans. This was a compromise arrangement. Whites had wanted to operate their plantations as they had prior to the Civil War, with black laborers working in disciplined gangs—men, women, and children—and living in the old slave quarters. Most planters believed that African Americans would not work without coercion, but freed blacks simply refused to submit to direct control, and their mobility made the agricultural workforce unreliable. Indeed, they reduced the available workforce by as much as a third, thereby coercing planters into adopting an alternative system of structuring Southern agriculture. Landowners rented African Americans (and poor whites) parcels of land, usually thirty-five to forty acres. Moneyless tenants usually paid the rent with a share of the crop—typically half, depending on what tools and animals the landlord provided. And since cotton was the most marketable crop, most Southern landlords demanded that the tenant raise cotton. It was an imperfect situation, but **sharecropping** allowed freed families to live in cabins that they built themselves on farms they more or less controlled.

The shortage of cash forced tenants into a credit system that seriously compromised their freedom. Throughout the cotton South, merchants opened stores in scattered small towns and rural crossroads. By 1880, more than 8,000 country stores did business in the South, offering seed, hardware, cloth, and processed foods to local farmers on credit. The merchants took liens on the farmers' crops as collateral. High prices for the merchandise, exorbitant interest rates, and declining cotton prices resulting from expanded production left most tenants in debt at the end of the year.

But not all freed men and women became farmers or farm laborers. Men found skilled and unskilled work in various industries under development during Reconstruction: loading and unloading cargoes in port cities; hauling cotton, grains, and manufactured goods in wagons; laboring in the iron foundries of Virginia and Alabama; and operating machines in North and South Carolina textile factories. As a clear sign that African Americans were determined not to go back to the way things had been during slavery, women and children generally withdrew from the agricultural labor force. Children spent more time in

school while women tried to establish themselves in their own households. Women who were required by economic circumstances to find work outside of their own households labored as domestics.

Feeling free was the former slaves' dream; actually being free, especially in economic terms, became a dream deferred. It would take time for poor people with limited skills to advance in a highly competitive economic system where capital and resources were concentrated in white hands. But time was running out on the Reconstruction experiment.

THINKING BACK

1. Why did many African Americans in the South prefer to separate themselves from whites, and how did voluntary separation differ from forced segregation?
2. How did African Americans dream of freedom, and why were their dreams so controversial and difficult to realize?

ABANDONING RADICAL RECONSTRUCTION

The notion persists that Radical Reconstruction began in 1867, lasted for a decade, and ended with the **Compromise of 1877**. The truth is that Northern support for Reconstruction began to wane almost as soon as it began. Not until 1870 had Mississippi, Georgia, and Texas been officially reconstructed, but as early as 1869, a conservative government had been elected in Virginia marking the end of Reconstruction there. In one former Confederate state after another, Democrats took government away from Republicans in what white Southerners called "**Redemption**." That word meant that God, through the agency of the Democratic party, had saved the South from the evil of Radical Reconstruction. Reconstruction's demise was partly the result of fatigue, which set in after years of exhausting crusades to modernize the South. Abolitionism, the Civil War, and Reconstruction all exacted a heavy toll on the psychic and physical resources of the country. Besides, there was too much corruption associated with the Reconstruction. Also, a conservative ideology took hold, first in the Supreme Court and then in the elected branches of the federal government. The federal government had no proper role in defining social relationships. Thus, Washington retreated from Reconstruction. Simultaneously, white Southerners attacked Radical Republican state governments. Following the disputed presidential election of 1876, the federal government withdrew its troops from the South, bringing down the final curtain on Reconstruction.

A Fumbling President and the Odor of Corruption

> **How and why did the Grant administration become so bogged down in corruption?**

As president, Ulysses S. Grant fell into the ineptitude that had clouded his career prior to becoming the Union's commander during the Civil War. The clear-sightedness and resolve that he had shown on the battlefield dissolved into bewilderment in the world of politics. Grant assumed that the politicians who fluttered around the Oval Office cared for him the way his wartime subordinates had; in fact, they just used him for their own enrichment. Although he stated his support for Radical Reconstruction, Grant failed to back it up. He became one of the personal tragedies of the Reconstruction era, and his administration caused an erosion of public and congressional trust in the worthiness of Radical Republican governments in the South.

Lax standards of conduct, perhaps one of the consequences of the Civil War, unbridled personal greed and ambition. The result was widespread corruption. Just as contractors and speculators had cheated for personal gain during the war, so members of Congress took bribes from a railroad construction company called the **Credit Mobilier**. Directors of the **Union Pacific Railroad Company**, which was constructing the first transcontinental railway, used the Credit Mobilier to skim public money from government subsidies. They then paid Congressmen in Credit Mobilier shares to head off an investigation of their fraud. Other knots of venal public officials, known as Whiskey Rings, operated in St. Louis and Milwaukee, siphoning revenue from whiskey excise taxes. Grant's private secretary, Orville H. Babcock was in the middle of the scandals, and Vice President Schuyler Colfax also became tainted. Grant himself was not involved, but he would not believe the evidence of widespread corruption and refused to do anything about it.

William Marcy Tweed and his Democratic friends in New York City's **Tammany Hall** bilked city and county treasuries of millions of dollars. Tweed's scam involved issuing exorbitant city and county

Courtesy of Library of Congress

HON. HORACE GREELEY,
Our Next President.

"Hon. Horace Greeley: Our Next President." A campaign portrait produced by backers of Greeley's unsuccessful run for the presidency as the candidate of the Liberal Party in the 1872 election.

government contracts to construction companies that he and his cronies owned. For instance, to build a courthouse that should have cost $250,000, the county paid $13 million, which included $1.5 million to Tweed's favorite plumber and $2.9 million to the plasterer. Millions of dollars of taxpayers' money thus fell into the hands of grubby politicians.

The odor of corruption influenced the presidential election of 1872. A group of high-minded Republicans organized the **Liberal party** and pledged to clean up the widespread fraud. They expressed disgust with the Grant scandals as well as the extravagance and graft associated with Southern Reconstruction governments. The Liberals nominated for president the famous journalist Horace Greeley, editor of the New York *Journal*. Democrats nominated Greeley too, hoping that a coalition could not only win the White House but also bring an end to Reconstruction in the South. But as much as voters loathed the chicanery associated with the Grant administration, they remained fond of the President himself, whose 56 percent share of the popular vote was the greatest margin of victory in a presidential contest since Andrew Jackson.

The Money Question

How did the currency question and economic depression affect Reconstruction?

Besides Reconstruction, the question of what to do with all the greenbacks issued as currency during the Civil War occupied the political stage. The Johnson administration had begun to withdraw them from circulation, returning the country to a gold and silver money system. Economic expansion, however, had cast new light on the greenbacks. Various interests, particularly credit-starved Westerners and manufacturing and commercial entrepreneurs in the East, objected to retrenchment. Bankers and other creditors, however, especially the holders of government bonds, urged a hasty retreat from soft money and the redemption of the national debt through specie. Neither political party was able to capitalize on the money issue because both parties included hard-money and soft-money advocates.

The currency issue moved to the forefront of public concern following a financial panic and a resulting depression that plagued Americans throughout most of the reminder of the decade. Feverish economic expansion drove reckless entrepreneurs beyond the limits of good sense. Jay Cooke, a prominent Philadelphia banker, overextended credit to finance railroad construction, and in 1873, his bank folded, sending shock waves through financial markets and then widely into the economy. The subsequent **Panic of 1873** led to massive unemployment and plunging prices for manufactured and agricultural products. Responding to the crisis in 1874, Congress passed a measure modestly increasing the number of greenbacks in order to stimulate economic activity, and inflationists hoped, restore prosperity. Grant initially supported the bill; however, he was bombarded with arguments from moneyed men that the bill represented an unwanted intrusion of government into the workings of the capitalist economy. The pressure worked on Grant, who vetoed it. A year later, Congress passed the **Specie Resumption Act**, sponsored by Senator John Sherman of Ohio, which provided for the gradual withdrawal of greenbacks to be completed in 1879. Grant and the Republicans did not suffer politically as a consequence because the Democrats were not unified on the issue. However, a **Greenback party** organized on the soft-money issue and participated in the 1876 elections.

The distraction of corruption and economic issues brought a waning of federal government support for Reconstruction. Priorities were changing, and as white Southerners recognized the lack of Northern support for the Republican state governments, they asserted themselves and regained control of political power in the South.

The Resurgence of White Democrats

How did white Democrats regain power in the South?

The campaign of racial violence directed at black and white Republicans in the South eventually sucked the vitality out of the Reconstruction governments. As the victims of the Ku Klux Klan turned to Washington for protection, they found little sympathy. Instead, white Republicans and Democrats worked to build a New South, and as they did, Reconstruction governments fell and a new order took their places.

In 1870 and 1871, the Ku Klux Klan, the **Knights of the White Camelia**, and other white terrorist groups targeted white and black Republicans, particularly in the upland districts of South Carolina, Georgia, and Alabama, where blacks comprised a minority of the population and the balance between Democrats and Republicans was even. Early in 1871, near Spartanburg, South Carolina, hundreds of African Americans were whipped and had their cabins burned and livestock destroyed. Following the election of 1872, in Grant County Louisiana, black Union army veterans tried fighting back. They fortified the county seat of Colfax and drilled as a militia, but whites, armed with rifles and a cannon, stormed the town, killing more than 250 defenders, and then massacred fifty African Americans who had raised the white flag of surrender.

The violence weakened the Southern Republican party. The killing had an intimidating effect on some Republicans, who chose not to vote or run for public office. It also drove the wedge of race deeper between blacks and whites. Many governors refused to call out state militias, which included blacks, as a conciliatory offering to white Democrats to end the violence. In 1871, reports of Klan violence moved Congress to crack down on Ku Kluxers by passing the Ku Klux Klan Act. Hundreds of whites were prosecuted and more held without benefit of habeas corpus; the Klan's power was effectively broken. But this was the last time that the federal government would use muscle in defense of the South's Republican regimes.

By and large, Northern sentiment asserted that African Americans had received all the tools that Washington had to give them in order to maintain their freedom and to advance in society. Most of the hard-line Radical idealists—Thaddeus Stevens, Charles Sumner, and Salmon P. Chase—were dead. Others, like Benjamin Wade, had been voted into retirement. Northern whites were more interested in ending the bacchanal of extravagance and corruption and in promoting economic development than protecting African Americans' civil rights. In one final initiative, Congress passed the **Civil Rights Act of 1875**, outlawing racial discrimination in public accommodations. However, the Supreme Court undermined the effort. In 1873, the *Slaughterhouse* cases established that the Fourteenth Amendment protected only rights derived from United States citizenship and not the freedoms and privileges conferred by the states. The effect of this narrow interpretation was to hog-tie Washington. In the *United States v. Cruikshank* (1876), the Supreme Court undercut the Civil Rights Act of 1875 by ruling that Congress could only legislate against the violation of civil rights by state governments, not individuals.

The federal government sent the message that it would no longer interfere with social, economic, or political affairs in the South. Whites were free to assert their power, and blacks were on their own to defend themselves.

The Triumph of White Supremacy

> **How did "Redemption" come about, and what did it mean for the South?**

It can be safely said that never in American history have governments been so unpopular with so many people as the Radical Republican governments were in the South. An embarrassment to most Northern Republicans because of their inefficiency and corruption, reviled by the white majority in the South as symbolic of despotic "bayonet rule" and chaotic "negro rule," they retained the support only of African Americans whose political clout was insufficient to maintain them. By the middle of the 1870s, Radical Reconstruction had nearly run its course.

Radical Republicans had promised the economic revitalization of the South; however, the South had fallen further behind the rest of the country. Between 1868 and 1872, many Southern railroads had been rebuilt and workers had laid over 3,000 miles of track, but that paled in comparison with the rapidly expanding railroad networks in the North.

Race became the Democrats most effective issue in toppling the Reconstruction regimes. Their strategy was two-fold: unify whites of both parties against blacks and use whatever means were necessary to drive African Americans out of the political process. The fusion of whites aimed at forging a new majority. Democrats lured white Republicans by defining themselves as the party of the "proud Caucasian race" and by promising to halt the Republican spending spree that had driven property taxes up to as much as four times their pre-Civil War levels. Whites who did not respond to the appeals were shunned, forced, as one white Republican said, "to live a life of social isolation." The strategy worked effectively in several states, leading to Democratic "Redemption" in elections in Georgia (1872), Texas (1873), and Arkansas and Alabama (1874). In Mississippi, South Carolina, and Louisiana, whites constituted a minority of the population, and Democrats resorted to violence to reduce the number of black voters and office-holders. The "**Mississippi Plan**" included throwing black tenants off their farms for voting Republican and using night-prowlers to beat, murder, and burn African Americans and their property. In 1875, violence became so widespread throughout the state prior to the fall elections that Mississippi's governor Adelbert Ames pleaded with the Grant administration for additional troops to protect African-American citizens. But Grant's attorney general refused, saying the people "are tired of these annual autumnal outbreaks in the South." The Democrats won the elections, bringing Reconstruction in Mississippi to an end.

In 1876, another presidential election year, only three Southern states remained in Republican control—Louisiana, South Carolina, and Florida. All three governments were defended by federal troops. The entire country slogged through the ongoing economic depression. Democrats hoped to capitalize on the hard times and the circus of fraud that infused the Grant administration by nominating a reformer, Samuel J. Tilden of New York. As the prosecutor who had finally nailed "Boss" Tweed and broken up the Tammany Hall's embezzlement caper, Tilden enjoyed enormous popularity. Republicans selected Rutherford B. Hayes, a liberal-minded politician himself, but one who waved the "bloody shirt" with great energy during the campaign. When the popular votes were tabulated, Tilden had 4,284,020 to Hayes's 4,036,572. But, there was a glitch in the electoral vote count. Fraud in

Louisiana, South Carolina, and Florida caused both parties to claim the nineteen electoral votes cast there. There had been enough monkey business on the part of both parties to make it impossible to decide whether they belonged to Hayes or Tilden. Without them, Tilden was one vote shy of a majority; Hayes required all of them to win by a majority of one.

Such a dispute had never occurred before; thus there was no established procedure for resolving it. Congress decided to establish a special election commission to investigate the irregularities surrounding the disputed votes and then to canvass them. The commission had to be non-partisan, so, the Democratic-controlled House of Representatives chose three Democrats and two Republicans; the Republican-dominated Senate selected three Republicans and two Democrats; and the Supreme Court picked two Republicans, two Democrats, and an independent—Justice David Davis. Unfortunately, as the commission began its work, Davis resigned his seat (Illinois had elected him to Congress), and his replacement was a Republican. Early in 1877, to nobody's surprise, the commission voted eight to seven to award each one of the disputed electoral votes to Hayes, giving him the election.

Democrats were outraged, and many threatened to resume the Civil War rather than accept the results of the obviously biased electoral commission. Hastily, however, Hayes and the Republicans offered a bargain. In return for their acceptance of a Republican election victory, Democrats would receive a spot in Hays's cabinet and the South would receive federal government financial assistance for economic development. But more importantly, this so-called Compromise of 1877 included a tacit pledge that Hayes would withdraw the remaining federal soldiers propping up Reconstruction governments. And with that, the Democratic "Redeemers" took over in Louisiana, Florida, and South Carolina, and Reconstruction finally came to an end.

THINKING BACK

1. What new priorities took attention away from Reconstruction?
2. How did the campaign of violence directed at black and white Republicans in the South contribute to the end of Reconstruction? And what was the final settlement that "redeemed" the South?

RECONSTRUCTING THE WEST

The triumph of Union and Republican economic policies during the 1860s and 1870s led to the integration of the West more fully into the nation. During the Civil War, two Republican-backed legislative programs, the Pacific Railroad Act (1862) and the Homestead Act (1862), pointed the way for future national development. Business opportunities opened up from the Great Plains to the Pacific Northwest, where economies had traditionally been local and subsistence-based. The lure of money beckoned individuals—mostly males, but a few females as well. **Transcontinental railroad companies** heralded the feverish development the West. Thousands of Civil War veterans and Irish and Chinese immigrants, armed with shovels and sledgehammers, laid track across plains, desert, and towering mountains. By the end of the 1870s, there were 75,132 Chinese in California. Some families also sought a fresh start in the West. Against the onslaught of people, animals, and machines, Native people fought desperately to preserve their traditional ways of life, but the Army hunted them down and stashed them on remote reservations, making way for the powerful "iron horse" and all the new things it would bring.

The Transcontinental Railroad

In the 1860s and 1870s, railroad lines replaced wagon tracks between the Atlantic and Pacific coasts and united the East and West into a single continental nation. In 1861, Mark Twain had bumped along in a leaky stagecoach for fifteen wearying days between St. Joseph, Missouri, and Carson City,

> What roles did government and private enterprise play in the construction of the nation's first transcontinental railroads?

Nevada; ten years later, the trip took four days—and much more comfortably—by train. Constructing a railway across 2,000 miles of seemingly endless plains and mammoth mountain barriers—the Sierra Nevada and Rocky mountains—was one of the most phenomenal feats of engineering and finance in the nineteenth century. Such enterprises exceeded the resources of private businessmen alone, and government aid proved essential to their success. In return for the assistance, the federal government expected the transcontinental railroads to carry soldiers and the U.S. mail at specially reduced rates.

The **Pacific Railroad Act of 1862** authorized the federal government to issue bonds and grant tracts of public land to subsidize, passed in the midst of the Civil War, Congress designated two railroad companies to receive federal aid to help meet the staggering costs of construction. Each company would receive 6,400 acres of public land per mile of track laid and loans ranging from $16,000 per mile across flat terrain and $48,000 per mile across mountain ranges. The **Union Pacific Railroad Company**, under the leadership of the wheeling and dealing physician-turned-railroad magnate Thomas C. Durant and Grenville M. Dodge, a Union Army general and highly regarded railroad engineer, was to build west from Omaha, Nebraska. The **Central Pacific Railroad Company**, formed by another engineer, Theodore D. Judah, fell into the hands of a quartet of enterprising shopkeepers from California who called themselves "**The Associates**": Collis P. Huntington, Mark Hopkins, Leland Stanford, and Charles Crocker. The Central Pacific started in Sacramento, California, and pushed east over the Sierra Nevada Mountains. The original plan was for the two railroads to meet at the California state line, near present-day Reno, Nevada; however, Congress changed the rules and allowed them to build as fast as they could and join wherever they might. That juncture came at a place called Promontory, in Utah, just north of Salt Lake. On May 10, 1869, as the cow-catchers of the respective locomotives touched, Stanford and Durant took turns hammering the final iron spike into a cross-

tie made out of stout California laurel. Telegraph operator Shilling Watson immediately transmitted word to the rest of the country: the "Empire Express" was finished. In Washington, Walt Whitman contemplated the modern wonders that were uniting the world: the Suez Canal, the trans-Atlantic telegraph cable, and now the North American transcontinental railroad.

As amazing as the organization and management of the great railroad project were, the work itself was even more so. Hard-driving men toiled in Nebraska's broiling summer heat and California's mountain snows for thirty to forty-five dollars a month. The Union Pacific hired 10,000 mostly Irish immigrants and Civil War veterans while the Central Pacific employed equal numbers of Chinese workers. Both companies hired freed slaves through the Freedmen Bureau. The men laid track faster than anyone thought they could. A newspaper reporter caught the spirit of the whole enterprise. "They labored with the regularity of machinery, dropping each rail in its place, spiking it down, and hen seizing another. Behind them, the locomotive; before, the tie-layers; beyond these the graders; and still further, in mountain recesses, the engineers. It was civilization pressing westward—the Conquest of Nature moving toward the Pacific. The men rested in fly-by-night railroad towns—North Platte,

Courtesy of Library of Congress

Central Pacific and Union Pacific rail lines meet at Promontory, Utah, to complete the first transcontinental railroad, May 10, 1869.

Nebraska; Cheyenne, Wyoming; and Reno, Nevada. With their saloons, brothels, and dingy boarding houses, early railroad towns were "Hell on Wheels."

Government support aided not only the Union Pacific/Central Pacific but also other transcontinental railroad projects, including the Northern Pacific, Southern Pacific, and the Atchison, Topeka, and Santa Fe. In all, 20 million acres of public land—once called "Indian Territory"—were handed out in 100-square-mile pieces alternating on either side of 400-foot rights-of-way. States chipped in additional amounts of land for sidings, stations, and supply yards. Congress authorized $60 million in loans to the railroad companies to help defray the cost of construction. The loans were graduated according to the difficulty of the terrain (up to $96,000 per mile over the mountains). The amounts were to be repaid when the railroads were completed and freight and passenger traffic began to generate revenue; however, in its eagerness to promote the enormously difficult projects, Congress left the terms vague.

By the end of the 1870s, only the Union Pacific/Central Pacific had been completed. The Panic of 1873 and subsequent depression had set back railroad construction and put several of the companies into bankruptcy. But with the completed transcontinental railroad and its branch lines, the stage was set for a transportation system that would allow the profitable shipment of cheap, bulk resources from the West to distant markets. The transcontinental railroads also signaled important environmental changes. The need for 2,500 wooden cross-ties per mile of track (15 to 20 percent of which had to be replaced every year due to decay) as well as for fuel, trestles, and telegraph poles virtually eliminated the sparse Nebraska forests and noticeably dented those of the Far West. And as people, capital, and machines began pouring into the West, changes in the West and its ecology became more dramatic.

Migration Into the West

> **What types of people were among the new waves of immigrants moving into the Far West after the Civil War?**

During the 1860s and 1870s, streams of immigrants flowed into the West. Gold-seekers opened the Bozeman Trail to the latest mineral bonanza in Montana. Texas cattlemen drove their herds to railheads in Kansas. And farmers staked homesteads on public land or farms purchased from the transcontinental railroads. In 1873, Congress followed up the Homestead Act with the **Timber Culture Act** that allotted homesteaders an additional 160 acres

on the Great Plains if they planted trees on one-quarter of it. The result was an enterprising population that filled up and transformed an environment previously sparsely populated by humans. Contrary to popular belief, their arrival established a trend that made the West the most urbanized section of the United States.

Beginning in the 1860s, Texas herders drove cattle northward into the central plains. Intersecting the Pacific railroads, cattle trails originated in the grasslands of Central and South Texas. The wiry Texas longhorns were hardly a butcher's dream (someone described them as "eight pounds of hamburger on 800 pounds of bone and horn"), but they were hardy and able to withstand the rigors of aridity, heat, and cold. Before the Civil War, Hispanic and Anglo ranchers had marketed the animals mostly for leather, but growing postwar markets in Midwestern and Eastern cities led producers to sell them for beef—tough and stringy as it was. Military forts, Indian reservations, railroad and mining towns, and growing Western cities like Denver, Salt Lake City, San Francisco, and Seattle heightened the commercial demand for beef.

An Illinois businessman named Joseph McCoy envisioned profits for himself, the cattlemen, and the railroads. Promising Texans ten times the longhorns' normal market price if they delivered their cattle to the Kansas and Pacific line in eastern Kansas, McCoy ushered in the heyday of the trail drive and the cowboy—Anglo, Hispanic, and African American. The **Chisholm Trail** ran from south Texas through Indian Territory (Oklahoma) to the dusty cow town of Abilene, one of many settlements that sprang up where the cattle trails crossed the railroads—Wichita and Dodge City were others. By the 1870s, stock raisers like Charles Goodnight, a successful trail driver, were locating their cattle herds permanently on the open pastures of Colorado, Wyoming, and Nebraska. In 1876, the innovative Goodnight used the steep cuts of Palo Duro Canyon in the Texas panhandle to establish the first enclosed ranch on the plains.

Environmental Impact

Most of the newcomers to the West after the Civil War believed that God had placed the vast resources of the area there for their use. The new arrivals pushed forward a series of environmental changes that radically altered the appearance and the ecology

> **Why was it probably inevitable that immigration into the Far West would eventually produce profound environmental changes?**

of the West. The newcomers came with the intention of taking natural resources from the West and, as a farmer in the Washington Territory put it, "to get the land subdued and the wilde nature out of it." Cutting timber for the railroads began the widespread deforestation of the Far West. Mining scraped away mountainsides and polluted streams. Cattle drives foreshadowed later overgrazing of the vast Great Plains. And the presence of growing numbers of people also had unintended consequences simply by altering social and biological relationships.

It is easy to blame immigrants from the East for all the transformations that took place in the landscape and the animal populations of the West during the second half of the nineteenth century. But the fact is that even the subsistence-based Hispanic and Native American societies changed their surroundings, and natural forces like droughts, flood, and windstorms reshaped the environment without any human involvement whatever.

THINKING BACK

1. What role(s) did government play in the rapid economic development of the Far West during and after the Civil War?
2. To what extent did individual initiative and resourcefulness promote economic expansion in the West?

THE LOCAL PERSPECTIVE: FOCUS ON WYOMING

| What led to the formation of the territory of Wyoming? |

In the 1860s, two of America's most renowned humorists, Artemus Ward and Samuel Clemens, traveled through Wyoming on the Western Trail. Neither could find anything funny to say about the Wyoming badlands. Ward, who had entertained Abraham Lincoln, described Wyoming as "the most wretched [country] I ever saw." Clemens, known as Mark Twain, was equally critical in commenting on the country, although he did admire the mountain vistas. So had the old mountain men, including David Jackson who lent his name to the stunning valley on the edge of Yellowstone Park known as Jackson Hole.

But it was not the great beauty of the Teton, Wind River, or Bighorn mountains that stretch across its northwestern corner that led to the formation of

Wyoming; nor did gold draw hordes of prospectors like neighboring Colorado. Transportation did the trick. President Andrew Johnson signed the **territorial organization bill** in 1868 to facilitate the construction of the transcontinental railroad. In 1862, Congress had passed legislation chartering the Central Pacific and Union Pacific railroad companies and providing both with subsidies to construct the country's first transcontinental railroad.

Several possible routes had been considered, including one across the Colorado Rockies. Denver businessmen vigorously lobbied the Union Pacific, which was building from east to west, for such a path since it would make the rapidly growing Western metropolis a transportation hub. Railroad engineers, however, selected **Sherman Pass** (named for the famous Civil War general) in southeastern Wyoming. Its 8,236-foot summit was 3,000 feet lower than the Colorado passes. Thus, the railroad lay some 100 miles north of Denver and gave birth to a new boomtown, Cheyenne. Cheyenne served as a construction center and connecting point for destinations north and south. Other towns sprang up as the line pushed westward—Laramie, Rawlins, and Rock Springs—across the southern breadth of the territory.

In 1870, the Cheyenne boom ended when the **Denver Pacific** railroad connected Denver with the Union Pacific. Just the year before, the Central Pacific and Union Pacific had met at Promontory Point in Utah. Denver now had rail access to both coasts. Cheyenne did too, but southeastern Wyoming showed less potential for economic development. Still, some cattle-raising facilities for forwarding freight and nearby Fort Russell provided economic stability of Cheyenne, but it never supplanted Denver as the metropolis of the central Rockies.

Although gold fever struck Colorado in the late 1850s and early 1860s and Montana in the 1860s and 1870s, mining was mostly a bust in Wyoming. In 1867, a minor gold rush gave rise to a ramshackle mining camp that took the name South Pass City, for its location on the continental divide, but it never amounted to much. Nor did other promising gold discoveries scattered here and there. The biggest and briefest excitement came in 1872, when a couple of prospectors claimed they found diamonds southeast of Rock Springs, just across the Colorado line. The area was abuzz for a while, until an investigation showed that the diamond mine had been "salted"—that is, implanted with diamonds. During the Reconstruction era, fraud was everywhere. Wyoming did in fact have a valuable mine deposit in the form of coal that could be used for fuel by the Union Pacific, but coal mining was not exciting, and not profitable enough yet for serious mining. In 1880, only ten mines were operating in Wyoming, and the territory's annual gold production was only $6,000—a day's work for successful miners in Colorado. The Union Pacific continued to dominate the economy, although ranching slowly but steadily expanded.

The progression from territory to statehood depended on population. During Reconstruction, people came to Wyoming for the same reason they moved to Colorado, Nevada, Utah, and other Rocky Mountain areas—to get a fresh start after the trials of the Civil War. It was basically the same motivation that drew Carpetbaggers into the South. When the bonanzas fizzled, the people moved on. Territorial government was no more stable than the local population or the Reconstruction era. Johnson's appointment of a territorial governor was blocked by Republicans in the United States Senate; Grant's appointees were easily confirmed but not always effective. Grant was no more reliable in his territorial appointments than he was in naming members of his cabinet.

Wyoming was a rough territory that was not particularly agreeable to women, except in one important matter. It was the first territory to grant women the right to vote. Perhaps this was a deliberate strategy to attract more women. Or it may have been the result of keen competition between Democrats and Republicans, like Southern Republicans used African Americans to create an electoral majority. Then again, Wyoming may have established **women's suffrage** out of principle. In any event, when Wyoming became the forty-fourth state in 1890, it was the only one in which women participated in choosing public officials.

Wyoming's history during Reconstruction reveals many of the elements of economic expansion, political reform, and corruption that characterized the rest of the country. Astride the first transcontinental railway, Wyoming also symbolizes the continental unification of the nation as it moved beyond the destruction and turmoil of the Civil War.

THINKING BACK

1. Why was it important to organize the Wyoming territory, and what factors combined to make that happen?
2. For such a rough territory that was fairly disagreeable to women, why does it stand out in the history of feminism?

CONCLUSION

Reconstruction was the most ambitious experiment in social reform Americans have undertaken. Coming in the wake of Civil War, however, it did not enjoy grassroots support. Indeed, it seemed to most white Southerners like a series of vengeful acts against a defeated and vulnerable people whose values and beliefs remained mostly intact. "Redemption" represented the ultimate triumph of the "**Southern way**" against intrusive federal power and the mercenary culture of industrial capitalism, an interpretation that permeated fictional and historical literature for almost a century. Radical Republicans held just as passionately to their belief in a different kind of freedom: the freedom of racial justice and equality. The idealism of Charles Sumner and Thaddeus Stevens never took deep root, however. Reconstruction's defenders blamed racial hatred and the brutality of the Ku Klux Klan for its failure. But African Americans probably sensed that the reality of Reconstruction lay somewhere in between these two views. The Republican party, steeped in Whig tradition, could not bring itself to support land distribution. They refused to ensure African-American autonomy by taking property from Southern whites. Despite its limited goals and failed efforts, though, Reconstruction set down another milestone in the growth of a democratic nation. And as economic growth and transformation of the South waned, attention shifted to the Far West. Reconstruction of the West replaced Reconstruction of the South.

SUGGESTED SOURCES FOR STUDENTS

Justin Berend, *Reconstructing Democracy: Grass Roots Black Politics in the Deep South after the Civil War* (2015), defines Reconstruction as an all-out attempt by blacks to continue the ongoing struggle to build a democratic nation.

Gregory P. Downs, *After Appomattox: Military Occupation and the Ends of War* (2015), shows that Reconstruction was not merely a follow-up to the Civil War but more of an extension of the war itself.

On the inclusion and exclusion of women in Reconstruction see Laura F. Edwards, *Gendered Strife and Confusion: The Political Culture of Reconstruction* (1997).

Carol Faulkner, *Women's Radical Reconstruction: The Freedmen's Aid Movement* (2004), examines the roles of Northern feminist women, black and white, in shaping Reconstruction policy and bringing relief to those liberated from enslavement.

The best overview of Reconstruction and an impressive synthesis of pertinent historical literature is Eric Foner, *Reconstruction: America's Unfinished Revolution, 1863-1877* (1988).

Thomas Holt, *White Over Black: Negro Political Leadership in South Carolina During Reconstruction* (1977), concentrates on the politics of race in the South.

Gerald David Jaynes, *Branches Without Roots: Genesis of the Black Working Class in the American South, 1862-1882* (1986) sees blacks in a reactive situation.

Leon F. Litwack, *Been in the Storm So Long: The Aftermath of Slavery* (1979), contains moving descriptions of how African Americans responded to emancipation as well as a brilliant analysis of how ex-slaves adjusted to their new lives as free people.

William E. Montgomery, *Under Their Own Vine and Fig Tree: The African-American Church in the South, 1865-1900* (1993) presents black churches as the most vital institutions in the formation of African-American communities in the postwar South.

Heather Cox Richardson, *The Death of Reconstruction: Race, Labor, and Politics in the Post-Civil War North, 1865-1901* (2001), explains that white people in the North turned from supporting freed African Americans and free labor at the outset of Reconstruction to believing that labor, whether white or black, was at war with capital in the modern political economy of the United States.

Julie Saville, *The Work of Reconstruction: Free Slave to Wage Laborer in South Carolina, 1860-1870* (1995), presents a more assertive and creative freed population.

Mark. W. Summers, *The Era of Good Stealings* (1993), finds that widespread public corruption in railroading and elsewhere undermined support for an active role for the government in the nation's economic expansion.

Joel Williamson, *The Crucible of Race: Black-White Relations in the American South Since Emancipation* (1984), includes an analysis of the white reaction to the gains of African Americans.

BEFORE WE GO ON

1. At the end of the Civil War, President Johnson sent Carl Schurz on an inspection tour of the conquered South. Schurz observed there "a revolution but half-accomplished." Did Reconstruction complete that revolution or did it fail? Explain.

2. Reconstruction reattached the rebellious states of the South to the federal Union. But did Reconstruction push the United States further toward becoming a unified nation or create even deeper divisions? Explain.

Building a Democratic Nation

3. As a result of Reconstruction, did the United States become a more or less democratic nation? Explain.

4. The West is often imagined as an area where economic development came through private enterprise. But, to what extent was the transformation of the West the result of cooperation between capitalism and government?

Connections

5. Since the founding of the United States, Americans had debated the value of centralized government over state autonomy. What did the Reconstruction experience add to that debate?

6. Reconstruction began amid widespread hope that the ideals of freedom and equality as laid down in the Declaration of Independence could be realized. How could you show that Reconstruction either validated that hope or invalidated it? How would America early in the twenty-first century affirm or contradict your conclusion?

Index

A

Abenaki people, 22
Abert, John, 400
Abolitionists
  Amistad case, 376
  burns arrest and, 437
  dissensions among, 356
  feminist revolt and, 357–358
  hostility to, 357
  literature, 438–439
  in Nevada, 482
  radical, 355–356
  southern, 354
  Underground Railroad and,
    430–431
Acadians, 156
Act Concerning Religion, 70
"Act in Restraint of Appeals, An," 54
Adams, Abigail, 152
  economic views of, 210
  Quasi-War, 224
  slavery opposition, 179
  women's rights advocacy, 177–178
Adams, Charles Francis, 472

Adams, John, 156, 167, 176, 243
  Abigail's admonishment of, 178
  administration of, 222–227
  body politic views, 185
  Boston Massacre, 148–149
  death of, 275
  egalitarians tendencies of, 176–177
  election of 1800, 226–227
  Harvard commencement, 187–188
  Maclay exchange with, 202–203
  marginalization of, 206
  political identity of, 144
  purification views, 185
  resignation of, 222
  vice presidential election of, 196
Adams, John Quincy, 236, 258–259,
    276, 404
  Amistad case, 376
  borderlands view, 296
  Mexican War view, 410
  Missouri Compromise and,
    311–312
  political party of, 314
  presidency of, 313–314
Adams, Louisa, 313

Adams-Onís Transcontinental
  Treaty, 278
Adams, Samuel, 148
  Constitutional Convention and,
    191, 194
  republican agenda of, 176–177
  Shays' Rebellion views, 190
Adobe, 17
Adventurers, 66
*Adventures of Col. Daniel Boon,
  The*, 174
Africa, 5
African Americans. *See also* Free
  blacks; Slaves
  citizenship for, 505–506
  Civil War volunteers, 467–468,
    479, 481
  Confederate fortifications by, 474
  in Continental Army, 159
  cultures of, 73
  democratic impulses of, 145
  early cultural contributions of, 124
  economic independence of, 503
  education of, 513–514
  election of 1868, 511

C

English colonies. *See also* British rule; *specific regions*
ascendancy of, 104–106
Asian, 393
convicts sent to, 105–106
democratic impulses in, 145
elites in, 149
Elizabeth's role, 54–55
families in, 64–65
governing of, 139–143
Jamestown, 66–67
Middle East, 393
origins, 53
personal perspective of, 64–65
population growth in, 104–105
profit motive in, 66
proprietary, 81–90
reshaping of, 176–177
Roanoke, 55
English Constitution, 140
English Reformation, 54
Enlightenment, 120–121
Entail, 177
Enumerated products, 142–143
Environment
European degradation of, 41–42
industrialization and, 372
North American, 9–10
respect for, 20–21
Western migration and, 521–522
Environmentalism, 349–350
Era of good feelings, 275–276
Ericsson, Leif, 38
Erie Canal, 288
Española, 40, 41
Essay on Human Understanding, 120
Essex Junto, 251
Estates General, 135
Europe
age of exploration in, 38–39
commercial empires in, 124
Commercial Revolution, 28
feudalism in, 26–27
idealism in, 134–135
imperial wars in, 134
maritime exploration by, 2–5
Middle Ages in, 26
nation-states in, 27
slave trade and, 5
socialism in, 392–393
technological advances in, 28–29
Evangelists
democratic thrust of, 338–340
emergence of, 121–123
oratory of, 338–339
promise of, 344

redemption philosophy of, 341
rise of, 338
Eveleigh, Samuel, 90
Everett, Edward, 451
Ex parte Merryman, 474

F

Factory system, 367–368
Fallen Timbers, Battle of, 216
Families
English colonial, 64–65
matrilineal, 22
middle class, 372
Native American, 19–20
nuclear, 64
Puritan, 80–81
slave, 384
Farewell Address, 221
Farmer's Almanack, 282
Farragut, David, 470, 477
Federalist Papers, 194
Federalists
agrarians opposition to, 204–205
defined, 194
election of 1796, 221–222
election of 1800, 226–227
judicial control by, 244
republicans *vs.*, 212–214
Rhode Island and, 195
three-fifths rule opposition, 259
Felipe II, King, 47
Female Association for the Relief of
Women and Children in Reduced
Circumstances, 337, 354
Female Hebrew Benevolent Society,
337
Feminism, 178, 357–358
Femme couvert, 178
Fenimore, Richard, 183–184
Fenno, John, 214
Ferguson, Patrick, 166
Fernando of Aragon, king, 27, 53
Fernando VII of Spain, 277
Fertile Crescent, 13
Feudalism, 26–27
Fifteenth Amendment, 507–508
"Fifty-four forty or fight," 406–409
Fifty-fourth Massachusetts
Regiment, 481
Filibusters, 432
Fillmore, Millard, 423, 433, 445
Filson, John, 174
Finley, Robert, 278
Finney, Charles Grandison, 338–339,
341, 347, 355

Fire-eaters, 423, 440, 461
First Society, 64
Fishing industry, 80
Fisk University, 514
Fitch, Caroline, 369
Fitzhugh, George, 438
Fitzpatrick, Thomas "Broken
Hand," 441
Fletcher v. Peck, 245
Florida
fortification of, 47
Indian revolts in, 50
seizing of, 276–277
Spanish control of, 164
Spanish exploration of, 47
Folk tales, 382
Food, 381–382
Foote, Andrew, 470, 477
Foote, Julia, 339
Force Bill, 322
Forced labor. *See* Slavery
Forester, Frank, 373
Forrest, Edwin, 310
Forrest, Nathan Bedford, 511
Fort Armstrong, 446
Fort Duquesne, 125
Fort Laramie Treaty, 441
Fort McHenry, 258
Fort Necessity, 125
Fort Orange, 84–85
Fort Snelling, 446
Fort Stanwix, Treaty of, 163
Fort Sumter attack, 464–465
Fort Vancouver, 385
Fountain of youth, 44
Fourier, Charles, 347
Fourierist, 347
Fourteenth Amendment,
505–506
Fox, George, 86
Fox, Kate, 343
Fox, Margaret, 343
Frame of Government, 86
France
American Revolution support,
161–162, 164
destabilization of, 135
industrialization in, 392–393
Napoleonic Wars, 253–254
North American exploration
by, 52
peace with, 225–226
privateers in, 51
Quasi-War with, 223–224
Second Republic, 392
U.S. Civil War and, 472

Franciscan friars
    California missions, 217–218
    Indian treatment by, 48
    missions founded by, 99–100
    proselytizing by, 48
    work of, 48–49
Francis I of France, 52
Francis Joseph, 393
Franco-Prussian War, 393
Franklin, Benjamin, 104, 156, 161, 167
    Constitutional Convention and,
        191, 193
    contributions of, 122
    French alliance efforts, 163
    French and Indian War role, 125
    market capitalism advocacy, 208
    reconciliation efforts, 150
    religious revivals and, 122
    on slavery, 145
    Stamp Act alternative, 146
    state sovereignty view, 186
    Townshend Act and, 148
    transportation views, 369
Franklin, Deborah, 104
Franks, Phila, 106
Frederick II of Prussia, 125
Fredericksburg, Battle of, 479
Free agency, 283–284
Free American Society, 181
Free blacks
    activities of, 181
    banning of, 319
    laws curtailing, 107–108
    ostracizing of, 278
    population of, 180
    slaves owned by, 378–379
Freedmen's Bureau, 503
Freedmen's Savings Bank, 503
Freedom Bureau, 512, 514
Free Enquirer, 347
Freeman, Comfort, 371–372
Freeman, Lucy, 371–372
Free Soil party, 421, 434
Free trade, 392
Free trappers, 272
Frelinghuysen, Theodore, 121
Fremont, John C., 400, 445, 474
French colonies. *See* New France
French-Indian War, 98–99, 125–127
French Quarter, 157
French Revolution, 134–136, 219–220
Freneau, Philip, 184, 214
Friendship and commerce,
    treaty of, 163
Fries, John, 226
Frobisher, Martin, 55

Fruitlands, 346
Ft. Stanwix, Treaty of, 182
Fugitive Slave Act, 436
    Lincoln's commitment to, 463
    passage of, 423
    personal perspective of, 430–431
    reaction to, 432
Fuller, Margaret, 346
Fulton, Robert, 287, 290
Fundamental Constitutions of
    Carolina, 87
Fundamental Orders
    of Connecticut, 78
Funding, 211
Fur trade, 75, 292–293, 297

G

Gadsden Purchase, 415–416
Gage, Thomas, 127, 152, 163
Gaines, Archibald, 430–431, 441
Gallatin, Albert, 241, 242, 258–259
Galloway, Joseph, 151
Gamble, James, 282
Ganz, Joachim, 56
Garden, Alexander, 120
Gardening, 14
Garfield, James A., 502
Garner, Margaret, 430–431, 438, 441
Garner, Robert, 430–431, 438
Garrison, William Lloyd, 355–356, 480
Gaspée, 150
Gates, Horatio, 163, 165, 188
Gazette of the United States, 214, 219
Geary, John W., 447–448
General Court of Massachusetts, 76
*General Shipping and Commercial
    List*, 369
Genêt, Edmond Charles, 219
Geography (Ptolemy), 39
George I of England, 140
George II of England, 140
George III of England, 157
    Boston Tea Party reaction, 150
    colonies loss and, 218
    mercenaries hired by, 154
    North's ministry and, 149
    Proclamation of 1763, 146
Georgia, 491–492
Georgia colony, 89–90
Georgian style, 109
Germans
    colonial immigration of, 105
    in labor force, 369
    nativists *vs.*, 436
    in South, 440

Gerry, Elbridge, 193
Ghana, 25
Ghent, Treaty of, 259
Gibbons, Thomas, 290
Gibbons v. Ogden, 324
Gilbert, Humphrey, 55, 57
Globalization, 2
Glorieta Pass, 485
Glorious Revolution, 115–116
Godey's Lady's Book, 309, 381
Gold Coast, 25
Gold Rush, 418, 422–423
Gold, Spanish quest for, 45
"Good death," 468
Goodnight, Charles, 521
Gorsuch, Edward, 437
Government
    bonds, 210–212
    British colonial, 139–142
    Carolina colony, 87–88
    contrasting views of, 203–205
    essence of, 141
    legitimacy of, 205
    New England colonies, 81
    separation of powers, 193
Graham's Magazine, 309
Graham, Sylvester, 307
Grand Canyon, 10
Grant, Ulysses S., 413
    corruption of, 516
    education of, 473
    Fort Henry capture, 470
    leadership of, 478
    occupation of Paducah, Ky, 467
    Pemberton and, 490
    victories of, 489–490
    wilderness campaign, 491
Grattan, John, 444
Gratz, Rebecca, 336–337, 339, 354
Gray, Robert, 249
Great auk, 373
Great Awakening. *See also* Evangelists
    first, 121–123, 179
    second, 282–284, 339
Great Basin, 21, 401
Great Britain. *See also* Parliament
    aggravations of, 218–219
    in China, 393
    colonialist loyal to, 156
    impressment policy of, 220
    industrialization in, 392
    Napoleonic Wars, 253–254
    naval superiority of, 253
    passions for war against, 255
    political power in, 65–66
    privateers in, 51

Hull, Isaac, 257
Hull, William, 257
Humboldt sink, 481
Hume, David, 204
Hundred Years War, 27
Hunter, David, 474
"Hunters of Kentucky, The," 274–275
Huntington, Collis P., 520
Huron people, 22
Husband, Herman, 149
Hutchinson, Anne, 77–78, 81, 84, 147
Hutchinson, Thomas, 147, 150, 155
Hutchins, Thomas, 189

I

Ice Age, 12
Ideology, 134
Immigration
    Chinese, 393
    colonial, demographics, 105–106
    middle colonies, 112–113
    nativists *vs.*, 436
    work force based on, 369–371
Impartial Administration of Justice
    Act, 151
Impending Crisis of the South, The, 380
Impost, 187–188, 207
Impressment, 220
Indentured servants, 71–72, 180
Indian Intercourse Act of 1790, 245
Indian Removal Act, 318
Indian Trade and Intercourse Act, 216
Indies, 39
Indigo crops, 108
Individualism, 348–349
Industrialization
    environmental impact of,
      372–373
    factory system, 367–368
    global perspective of, 392–394
    impact of, 367
    Mexican War and, 413–414
    slave labor in, 376–377
    social effects of, 371–372
    wages, 371
Industrial Revolution, 367, 372
Infant mortality, 104
Inner Light, 85
Institutes of the Christian Religion, 53
Intellectual visionaries, 346–347
Interior lines, 468
Internal improvements, 286
Internal Provinces, 216, 260
Intolerable Act, 151
Ireland, 56–57, 369

Irish
    African Americans *vs.*, 369
    in labor force, 369–370
    Mexican War role, 411
    nativists *vs.*, 437
    politics of, 224
    railroad building by, 519–520
Iron Act, 143
Ironclad warships, 476–477
Iroquois League
    colonial wars and, 124
    culture of, 23
    formation of, 19, 23
    French and Indian War role, 126
    Ohio Valley dominance of, 125
Irving, Washington, 309, 336
Isabella of Castille, queen, 27, 40, 53
Islam, 3
Island Number 10, 477
Isthmus of Panama, 44

J

Jackson, Andrew, 316, 342, 404
    annexation view, 406
    anti-abolitionist actions, 357
    election of 1824, 312–313
    hero worship of, 274–275
    legacy of, 323–327
    nullification position, 322–323
    petticoat affair, 304–305
    popularity of, 314
    presidency of, 320–323
    removal policy of, 317–318, 327
    ruthlessness of, 448
    Seminole raids, 276
    Texas policy of, 329
    War of 1812 and, 257, 258
Jackson, Claiborn F., 467
Jackson, David, 522
Jackson, Thomas J. "Stonewall," 469,
    473, 490
Jacobins, 136
James, Frank, 484
James I of England, 65–66
James II of England, 115
    ascendancy of, 65
    Barbados charter, 90
    church purification by, 74
    Virginia charter, 67
James, Jesse, 484
James P. Flint, 417
Jamestown colony
    establishment of, 66–67
    failures of, 67
    government in, 68

    religions in, 67–68
    revival of, 67–68
    tobacco boom in, 67–68
Japan, 393
Jaramillo, Maria Ignacia, 396
Jayhawkers, 484–485
Jay, John, 167
    anti-democratic views, 185
    election of 1800, 226
    Federalist Papers, 194
    impressment controversy, 220
    Spanish diplomacy by, 183, 188
Jay's Treaty, 220
Jefferson, Thomas, 150, 151
    about, 206
    alien acts view, 224
    budget cuts by, 242
    Chesapeake Affair and, 253
    Constitutional Convention and, 191
    court issues, 243–245
    death of, 275
    Declaration of Independence, 156
    economic views of, 210–212
    election of, 236
    on elections, 142
    French Revolution views, 219
    Hamilton's view of, 235
    ideology of, 134–135, 211–214
    Indian policies, 245–246
    leadership of, 237–239
    Louisiana Purchase, 247–249
    political parties and, 323–324
    reelection of, 247
    religious beliefs of, 177
    rhetorical style of, 338, 419
    Shays' Rebellion view, 190
    slavery and, 179, 181, 239, 241
    Stamp Act resolutions and, 147
    on town meetings, 81
    trade diplomacy by, 188
    vice presidency of, 222–223
    War of 1812 and, 258
    Western expansion by,
      247–252
Jenkins, Robert, 124–125
"Jennison's Jayhawkers," 484
Jews. *See also* Anti-Semitism
    colonial immigration of, 105
    exclusion of, 337
    Spanish expulsion of, 39
    Viennese, 393
Joao II, 39
Johnson, Andrew, 466, 492, 500
    impeachment of, 507
    loyalty of, 504
    reconstruction plan, 503–504

Johnson, Andrew (*continued*)
  transcontinental railroad and, 522
  votes by, 506–507
Johnson, Anthony, 73
Johnson, Herschel V., 451
Johnson, Richard M., 325, 342
Johnson, William, 379
Johnston, Albert Sidney, 413, 470,
  473, 475
Johnston, Joseph E., 469, 478, 491
Joint-stock company, 66
Jolliet, Louis, 102
Jolliffe, John, 441, 447
Jones, Absalom, 279
Journalism, 310
Journeymen, 112
Judiciary. *See* Supreme Court
Judiciary Act of 1789, 207
Judiciary Act of 1801, 243
Judiciary Act of 1802, 243
Julius Sneezer, 310

K

Kamehameha II, 359
Kansas
  Civil War and, 484–485
  Lecompton swindle, 447–448
  political strife in, 443–444
Kansas-Nebraska Act, 431, 442–444
Kant, Immanuel, 308
Karamanli, Pasha Yusef, 252
Karankawa Indians, 36
Kearny, Stephen W., 397, 413, 419
Keitt, Lawrence, 451
Kelley, Abby, 356
Kelley, Hall Jackson, 416
Kelley, Richard, 371
Kendall, Amos, 315
Kennewick Man, 8
Kent, James, 324
Kentucky, 163–164, 467
Kentucky Resolution, 225
Key, Francis Scott, 258
Kieft, Willem, 84
King Cotton Diplomacy, 472
King George's War, 124–125
King Philip's War, 115
King, Rufus, 247
King William's War, 124
Kitchen cabinet, 321
Knights of the White Camelia, 517
Know-nothings, 436, 444–445
Knox, Henry, 206
Knox, John, 54
Ku Klux Klan, 511, 517–518

L

La Amistad, 375–376
Labor, 113, 371
Laissez-faire, 307–308
Lakota Sioux, 11
Lamar, Mirabeau B., 405
Lame-duck, 243
Lanape, 82
Land
  distribution of, 77, 503
  grants, 435
  ownership of, 141–142
  Reconstruction policy, 514–515
  tenancy, 515
  value of, 112
Land Ordinance of 1785,
  188–189, 280
Lane, Charles, 346
Lane, Joseph, 418, 451
La Paz Bay, 44
Lapwai, 418
Larcum, Lucy, 286
La Reconquista, 27
Larkin, Thomas O., 360
La Salle, de Sieur, 102
Latin America, 136, 434–435
Laud, William, 74
Laurens, Henry, 167
Lawrence, Amos, 437
Lawrence, Kansas, 485
Leather jackets, 260
Leatherstocking novels, 309
Leaves of Grass, 349
Lecompton swindle, 447–448
Lee, Charles, 153
Lee, Henry "Lighthouse Harry," 205
Lee, Richard Henry, 150, 155–156
Lee, Robert E., 413
  Army of Northern Virginia, 478
  Harpers Ferry raid, 450
  military talents of, 465
  strategy of, 479
  surrender of, 489
Leflore, Greenwood, 378
Leisler, Jacob, 116
Leisler's Rebellion, 116
LeMoyne, Pierre, 102
*Letters from a Farmer in
  Pennsylvania*, 148
Lewis and Clark Expedition, 250
Lewis, Meriwether, 249–251
Liberal party, 516
Liberal revolutionary ideology, 134
Liberator, The, 355
Liberty Bell, 113

Liberty Tree, 147
Libraries, 352
Library of Congress, 238
Life Among the Lowly, 438
*Life and Memorable Actions of George
  Washington, The*, 184
*Life of David Crockett of the State of
  Tennessee*, 309–310
Lincoln, Abraham, 438, 475, 492
  1860 presidential campaign,
    451–452
  birth place, 467
  Bull Run and, 468
  cabinet of, 463
  conscription by, 471
  criticism of, 474–475
  election of 1864, 492
  fire-eaters and, 440
  Fort Sumter and, 464–465
  generals and, 478
  Harper's Ferry view, 450
  Johnson's loyalty to, 504
  Maryland secession and, 466–467
  Nevada enabling bill, 483
  northern resolve and, 490–491
  pre-inaugural activity, 462–463
  reconstruction plan, 502
  respect for, 481
  senatorial campaign, 448
  slavery views, 448–449
  war diplomacy by, 472
  war politics, 473–475
  war strategy of, 469–470
Lincoln-Douglas debates, 448–449
Lincoln, Mary Todd, 492
Lippard, George, 411
Lisa, Manuel, 216, 251, 292
Litchfield Academy, 178–179
Literature
  abolitionists, 438
  pioneer, 316–317
  romantic, 309
  transcendentalist, 348–349
Little Raven, 486
Little Women, 346
Livingston, Henry Beekman, 178
Livingston, Nancy Shippen, 178
Livingston, Robert J., 113, 149,
  290–291
Livingston, Robert R., 156, 184, 205,
  248, 287
Locke, John, 64, 120, 140
Log cabins, 111
Log College, 121
London *Times*, 413
Lone Star Republic, 329, 407

immunity and, 15
incorporation European
    innovations by, 43
interracial marriage among,
    100–101
Jefferson's treatment of, 245–246
Jefferson's vision for, 239
Kentucky raids by, 163–164
King Philips War and, 115
Manifest Destiny and, 398–399
market exchanges, 399
mass slaughter of, 46, 47
in Mexico, 293–294
Mormons and, 404
mound towns built by, 18–19
national identities of, 127–128
in Nevada, 482
in North Dakota, 296–297
origins of, 10–12
in Pacific Northwest, 385–386
pan-Indian confederation, 254
plants developed by, 14
political exclusion of, 316
political system, 19
population decline, 279
post–Civil War life, 519
raids by, 402–403
regional cultures of, 21–23
removal of, 317–318
revolts by, 49–50
Revolutionary War and, 161
Roanoke colony and, 55–56
slave owners, 378, 385
small pox epidemic among, 102
Spanish abuse of, 42, 49
in Texas, 327–328
transit agreements with, 441–442
trappers and, 273–274
War of 1812 and, 257
world view of, 19–21
Nativists, 436
Nats, 383–384
Naturalization Act, 224
Natural rights, 116, 140
Nature, 308–309, 350
Navajo, 21
Navigation Acts, 84, 142
Navy, 223, 476–477
Neblett, Lizzie, 487
"Negro rule," 518
Nelson, Horatio, 253
Neolin, 127
Netherlands, The
    colonies of, 82–85
    privateers in, 51
    Puritan's stay in, 74

slave trade and, 83, 106
sugar trade and, 90–91
Nevada, 481–483
New Amsterdam, 82–84
New England colonies. *See also*
    Puritans
    Chesapeake colonies *vs.*, 77
    covenant of, 74
    fractures in, 77
    participatory democracy in, 81
    religion in, 111–112
    scurvy in, 75
    societal texture, 111–112
    trade in, 75
    witches trials in, 116–117
New England Emigrant Aid
    Society, 443
Newfoundland, 38
New France
    expansion of, 101–104
    failure of, 52
    fur trade in, 101–102
    immigration to, 105–106
    missionaries, 101
    Monroe Doctrine and, 277–278
    settlements of, 99–100
New Harmony, 347
New Jersey, 82–85
New Jersey Plan, 192
New Lights, 122–123, 177
New Mexico
    Anglos in, 396–398
    Civil War and, 485
    colonization of, 47–50
    compromise of 1850, 423
    life in, 260
    new Americans in, 418–419
    occupation of, 411–413
    slavery in, 49–50
    Spanish exploration of, 45–46
New Orleans, 287
New River, 10
New School Presbyterianism, 284
Newsom, John, 366
New Spain. *See also* Conquistadores
    borderlands of, 99–100
    California missions, 217–218
    capital of, 43
    encomienda system in, 44
    establishment of, 43–44
    expansion of, 44–45
    forced labor in, 49
    frontier society of, 100–101
    immigration policy, 183
    immigration to, 105–106
    Indian revolts in, 49–50, 260

Louisiana in, 156–157, 247–248
missionaries in, 48–49
Monroe Doctrine and, 277–278
political turbulence in,
    293–294
rise of, 27–28
U.S. defeat of, 276
Newspapers. *See also specific
    publications*
    Industrial Revolution and, 369
    Mexican War coverage by, 414
Newton, Isaac, 120
New York colony, 82–85
New York Female Moral Reform
    Society, 342
New York Herald, 310
New York Sun, 310
Nicaragua, 434
Nicholas I of Russia, 393
Nicholls, Richard, 85
Nicholson, Joseph, 244
Nightingale, Florence, 487
Niles' Weekly, 369
Nina, 39–40
95 Theses, 53
Niwot, 486
Noblesse oblige, 367
Non-Intercourse Act, 254
North America
    ancient civilizations in, 15–16
    coastlines, reconnoitering of,
        44–45
    colonial wars in, 124–128
    French exploration of, 52
    landscapes, 9–10
    national identities in, 127
    post-Independence boundaries,
        166, 167
    products from, 42
    religious immigration, 5
North Dakota, 296–297
Northern colonies. *See also* New
    England colonies; Proprietary
    colonies
    African Americans in, 113–114
    Connecticut example, 117–118
    Enlightenment impact of,
        120–121
    expansion of, 111–117
    Great Awakening in, 121–123
    King Philip's War, 115
    rebellions in, 115–116
    reorganization of, 115–116
    trade network, 114–115
    urban centers, 118–120
Northern Confederacy, 251

Plutocracy, 378
Political culture, 144–145
Political parties, 203. *See also specific parties*
  ambivalence towards, 222
  democratization of, 310–311
  labor, 371
  philosophical differences, 213
  realignment of, 311–316
  rebuilding of, 314
  regionalism and, 221–222, 226–227
  second system of, 324
  sectional, 442–443
  southern, 405–406
Polk, James K., 421
  campaign of, 406–407
  Cuba and, 432–433
  intelligence of, 409
  Leonidas Polk, 467
  Mexican War and, 409–410, 414–415
  New Mexico occupation and, 411–413
  Oregon annexation and, 409
  Trist and, 414–415
Ponce de León, Juan, 44
Pontiac, Indian chief, 127
Pontiac's Rebellion, 127
Poor Richard's Almanac, 121
Pope, John, 478
Popular sovereignty, 215, 448
Porter, Lavinia, 401
Port Folio, 337
Port Hudson, Battle of, 490
Portland, Oregon, 417–418
Portugal
  colonalization by, 3–4
  commerce monopoly of, 51
  maritime exploration by, 4
  nation-state, 27
  slave trade and, 83
  Spain's dispute with, 40
  trading colonies, 134
Potlatch, 22
Potomac Company, 288
"Pottawatomie Massacre," 444
Potter, David M., 450
Powell, Henry, 90
Powell, John, 90
Powhatan
  English settlers and, 68–69
  political system, 20, 47
  tobacco grown by, 70
Prairie schooner, 401
Preble, Edward, 252
Predestination, doctrine of, 53

Pre-industrial America
  commerce in, 279–280
  courts in, 290–291
  fur trade in, 292–293, 297
  Great Awakening in, 282–284
  life in, 282
  Mexico, 293–296
  migrations in, 280–282
  panic of 1819, 291
  transportation in, 286–289
Presidents. *See also specific presidents*
  cabinet of, 206
  constitutional powers of, 194
  direct election of, 510
  election of, 196
Presidios, 99, 260
Preston, Thomas, 148
Price, Richard, 144
Price, Sterling, 467
Prigg v. Pennsylvania, 437
Primogeniture, 26, 177
Princeton, Battle of, 160
Principia Mathematica, 120
Prison, Elizabeth, 64–65
Prison, Nicholas, 64–65
Privateers, 51, 158
Privy Council, 140
Proclamation of 1763, 127, 146
Procter, William, 282
Promontory Point, Utah, 520
Property ownership, 141–142
Proprietary colonies, 69
  Carolinas, 87–89
  Dutch control, 82–85
  Georgia, 89–90
  overview of, 81–82
  Pennsylvania, 85–87
  socioeconomic development, 112–113
Prosser, Gabriel, 239–241, 383
Prosser, Thomas, 240
Prostitution, 342
Protective tariffs, 207
Protector of Indians, 49
Protestant Reformation, 53
Protestants, 70, 338
Providence Plantations, 78
Prussia, 393
Ptolemy, Claudius, 38–39
Public executions, 352
Public libraries, 352
Public lyceums, 352
Public school movement, 350–351
Pueblo Indians, 11
  environmental management by, 20–21

Pueblo Revolt, 50
Purgatory, 53
Puritans. *See also* Pilgrims
  antagonism of, 65
  communities of, 80–81
  economy of, 79–80
  emergence of, 54
  Enlightenment and, 120
  families of, 80–81
  fractures among, 77
  land distribution by, 77
  migrations of, 74–76
  romantic love among, 80
  separatist, 74
  settlements of, 74
  theology of, 76
  visionaries of, 76
Puritan Way, 76–77
Put-in-Bay, 257
"Put out" home, 286
Pybourn, Elias, 183
Pyramid Lake, 481, 483

Q

Qing Dynasty, 393
Quakers
  beliefs of, 85, 87
  colony of, 86
  founder, 86
  Indian treatment by, 87
  political power of, 112
  slavery opposition by, 180
Quantrill, William, 484–485
Quartering Act, 148, 151
Quasi-War, 223–224, 225, 226
Quebec Act, 151
Queen Anne's War, 124
Quitrents, 85

R

Radical Reconstruction
  abandonment of, 515–519
  congressional dominance, 506–507
  corruption in, 516
  economic impact of, 512
  record of, 509–510
  Southern states reaction to, 508–511
  strife from, 511
Radical Republicans, 501
  ascendancy of, 506–507
  election of 1866 and, 506
  embarrassment of, 518

West Indies
    commerce monopoly in, 51
    Dutch colonies in, 82
    economic transformation of,
        41–42
    native populations of, 41
    Spain's interest in, 40
    Spanish conquests of, 41
    trade acts, 143
West Virginia, 466
Wheatley, Phillis, 181
Whigs (American)
    abolitionist among, 356
    annexation views of, 405
    anti-slavery, 406
    division of, 433–434, 442–443
    election of 1840, 326–327
    election of 1848, 421
    election of 1852, 433–434
    evangelism and, 338, 342
    extinction of, 444
    nativists views, 436
    origins of, 144
    Wilmot's amendment and, 420
Whigs (British), 115, 140
Whiskey Rebellion, 214–215
Whiskey Rings, 516
Whitefield, George, 118, 121–122
White, Hugh Lawson, 325
White, John, 55
White supremacy, 517–519
Whitman, Marcus, 418
Whitman, Narcissa, 418
Whitman, Walt, 349
Whitney, Eli, 368
Whittier, John Greenleaf, 438
"Wide Awakes," 451
Wilberforce University, 514

"Wildcat" banks, 325
Wilderness campaign, 491
Wilkinson, Eliza, 159
Wilkinson, James, 188, 249, 251–252
Willamette River Valley, 416–418
William and Mary, 116
William III of England, 124, 143
William of Orange, 115–116
Williams, Eunice, 98–99, 123
Williams, John, 98
Williams, Roger, 77–78, 195
Williams, Samuel, 350
Wilmot, David, 420
Wilmot Proviso, 420
Wilson, James, 191
Winthrop, John, 75–76, 78, 112
Winthrop, John Jr., 120
Witch trials, 116–117
Wolfe, James, 125–127
Wollstonecraft, Mary, 135, 357
Women. *See also* Feminism
    anti-slavery efforts of, 356
    Civil War role, 468, 487
    Continental Army role, 159
    economic exclusion of, 316–317
    education and, 351–352
    factory workers, 368, 370
    fallen, 342
    fur processing by, 292
    literature, 309
    pioneers, 401, 416–417
    plantation, 110
    political exclusion of, 316
    post-Revolutionary status of,
        177–178
    reform efforts of, 341–342
    Second Great Awakening and, 283
    slaves owners, 378

    societies led by, 337
    suffrage for, 523
    wages, 371
Women's Indian Relief Society, 404
Women's suffrage, 508
Woodlands culture, 18–19
Woodmason, Charles, 145
Woolman, John, 180
Worcester v. Georgia, 318
Working class, 371
Working parties, 371
Wright, Frances, 347–348, 352
Writs of assistance, 145
Wyeth, Nathaniel, 282
Wyoming, 522–523

X

Ximénez, Fortún, 44
XYZ Affair, 222–223

Y

Yakima people, 22
Yancey, William Loundes, 462
Yankee merchants, 114
Yellow Stone, 292
Yeomen, 379–380
Yorktown, Battle of, 167
Young Americans, 432–433
Young, Brigham, 403–404, 482
Younger, Cole, 484
Younger, Jim, 484
Young Ladies Academy, 336

Z

Zuñi, 45

Physical Map of the World, November 2011

November 2011